REASON AND THE UN[RE]LIGIONS

Philoso... WIN... Religious Beliefs

REASON AND RELIGIONS

Philosophy Looks at the World's Religious Beliefs

STEVEN M. CAHN
The Graduate Center
The City University of New York

Australia • Brazil • Japan • Korea • Mexico • Singapore • Spain • United Kingdom • United States

WADSWORTH
CENGAGE Learning™

Reason and Religions: Philosophy Looks at the World's Religious Beliefs
Steven M. Cahn

Publisher: *Clark Baxter*
Senior Sponsoring Editor: *Joann Kozyrev*
Assistant Editor: *Joshua Duncan*
Editorial Assistant: *Marri Stratton*
Content Project Manager: *Jill Quinn*
Art Director: *Riezebos Holzbaur/
    Andrei Pasternak*
Production Technology Analyst: *Jeff Joubert*
Manufacturing Planner: *Sandee Milewski*
Rights Acquisition Specialist: *Mandy Groszko*
Production Service: *s4Carlisle*
Cover Designer: *Riezebos Holzbaur/
    Tim Heraldo*
Cover Image: *Astronomical Observations
(oil on canvas), Creti, Donato (1671-17490 /
Vatican Museums and Galleries, Vatican
City / The Bridgeman Art Library*
Compositor: *s4Carlisle*

For product information and technology assistance, contact us at **Cengage Learning Customer & Sales Support, 1-800-354-9706**

For permission to use material from this text or product, submit all request online at **www.cengage.com/permissions**. Further permissions questions can be emailed to **permissionrequest@cengage.com**.

Library of Congress Control Number: 2012939542
ISBN-13: 9781133594970
ISBN-10: 1133594972

Wadsworth
20 Channel Center Street
Boston, MA 02210
USA

Cengage Learning is a leading provider of customized learning solutions with office locations around the globe, including Singapore, the United Kingdom, Australia, Mexico, Brazil and Japan. Locate your local office at **international.cengage.com/region**

Cengage Learning products are represented in Canada by Nelson Education, Ltd.

For your course and learning solutions, visit **www.cengage.com**.

Purchase any of our products at your local college store or at our preferred online store **www.cengagebrain.com**. **Instructors:** Please visit **login.cengage.com** and log in to access instructor-specific resources.

Printed in the United States of America
1 2 3 4 5 6 7 16 15 14 13 12

To my wife,
Marilyn Ross, M.D.

CONTENTS

PART THREE
Arguments for God's Existence   52

A. The Ontological Argument   52

B. The Cosmological Argument   61

C. The Teleological Argument   76

D. The Moral Argument   98

PART FOUR
The Problem of Evil   102

A. God and Evil   102

PREFACE

The philosophical study of religions is an ancient branch of inquiry that attempts to clarify religious beliefs and subject them to critical scrutiny. Whereas some thinkers have employed the methods of philosophy to support a religion, others have used these same methods with quite different aims. All philosophy of religion, however, is concerned with questions that arise when religious doctrines are tested by the canons of reason.

The vast majority of introductory anthologies in this field are voluminous, filled with articles of daunting complexity, and weighted heavily toward issues concerning monotheism in general and Christianity in particular. That differing religious perspectives are prevalent around the globe is typically mentioned in passing, but readers are afforded little opportunity to learn the nature of these beliefs, why they are held, or how they might be assessed.

While this book offers full coverage of historical and contemporary reflections on the standard issues raised by Jewish, Christian, and Islamic versions of monotheism, approximately fifteen percent of the readings explore matters that arise in other religious traditions, including Zoroastrianism, Jainism, Hinduism, Buddhism, Confucianism, Taoism, and Zen Buddhism. The selections do not presume any knowledge of these religions, but combine exposition and evaluation. Surprisingly perhaps, the concerns raised in these articles often relate to possible solutions of traditional problems found in a standard philosophy of religion course, and throughout this book such connections are made apparent.

While this anthology is shorter than most others, the number of readings is larger, because many have been abbreviated to sharpen their focus and make them easier to grasp. I have also chosen writings that minimize arcane terminology, unexplained references, and convoluted arguments, thereby increasing the book's accessibility.

Those who want to learn more about a particular philosopher or a specific philosophical issue are urged to consult the *Encyclopedia of Philosophy* (Routledge, 1999), ed. Edward Craig. It contains detailed entries with bibliographies on every significant topic in the field.

My interest in finding a way to integrate materials concerning Asian religions into a standard analytic philosophy of religion course was intensified by a book titled *Meditation from Buddhist, Hindu, and Taoist Perspectives* (Peter Lang, 2009), written by a former doctoral advisee of mine, Robert Altobello, now a professor at SUNY Empire State College, where he teaches philosophy and religious studies. His interest in Asian thought and commitment to demystifying it encouraged me to undertake this work.

I wish to express my gratitude to Joann Kozyrev, senior sponsoring editor for philosophy and religion at Wadsworth/Cengage Learning, for her unwavering support. She offered valuable guidance while encouraging me to develop the project as I thought best. Working with her and assistant editor Joshua Duncan has been a delight. I also thank the staff at Wadsworth/Cengage for assistance throughout production.

Let me add that some selections were written when the custom was to use the noun "man" and the pronoun "he" to refer to all persons regardless of sex, and I have retained the authors' original wording. All notes in brackets are mine.

Now we turn to the readings.

P A R T   O N E

Introduction

---

1 WHAT IS RELIGION?

WILLIAM P. ALSTON

Religions differ in many ways, including their rituals, prayers, theistic systems, and moral beliefs. But what is religion? Can the term be defined? In our first reading, William P. Alston (1921–2009), who was a professor of philosophy at the University of Michigan, offers insightful answers.

A survey of various attempts to state the nature of religion reveals a confused picture. Consider the following examples.

1. Religion is the belief in an ever living God, that is, in a Divine Mind and Will ruling the Universe and holding moral relations with mankind.

    —JAMES MARTINEAU

2. By religion, then, I understand a propitiation or conciliation of powers superior to man which are believed to direct and control the course of Nature and of human life.

    —J. G. FRAZER

3. Religion is rather the attempt to express the complete reality of goodness through every aspect of our being.

    —F. H. BRADLEY

4. Religion is ethics heightened, enkindled, lit up by feeling.

    —MATTHEW ARNOLD

5. Religion is, in truth, that pure and reverential disposition or frame of mind which we call piety.

    —C. P. TIELE

6. The essence of religion consists in the feeling of an absolute dependence.

    —FRIEDRICH SCHLEIERMACHER

7. A man's religion is the expression of his ultimate attitude to the universe, the summed-up meaning and purport of his whole consciousness of things.

    —EDWARD CAIRD

These examples give us a fair idea of the range of attempts to define religion. Now it is not difficult to subject all these formulations to devastating

From William P. Alston, "Introduction" in *Religious Belief and Philosophical Thought*, ed. William P. Alston, Harcourt, Brace, & World, Inc., 1963. Reprinted by permission of Wadsworth Cengage Learning.

criticism. As for the first, there are, of course, many religions in which no such belief figures. No polytheism recognizes a single Divine Mind and Will ruling the Universe; and in some forms of Buddhism there is no recognition of a personal deity of any kind. With respect to the third and fourth examples, we can cite certain primitive communities in which there is no significant connection between the system of rites directed to the gods, which would normally be called the religion of the culture, and the moral code. The latter simply rests on tribal precedent and is not thought of as either originating with the gods or sanctioned by them. This is an unusual, but not impossible, state of affairs. And at the other end of the scale we have extreme mystical sects in which the aim for an immediate union with God crowds out any real concern for morality. As for the fifth and sixth, it seems impossible to find any particular feeling which is characteristic of religion and only of religion. If, for example, we take "absolute dependence" strictly it would seem to be present only in something like a strict monotheism. And if we do not insist on *absolute* dependence, we can find weaker forms of dependence in non-religious contexts. A man might feel considerable dependence on his boss, his wife, or the weather.

There are other difficulties. The formulations we have been considering can be viewed as stressing the doctrinal, the ethical, and the emotional aspects of religion, respectively. And it may well be doubted that any definition in terms of only one of these can give us an adequate idea of the nature of so complex a form of human activity and experience. This incompleteness is manifested in various ways. On the one hand, as the last paragraph indicated, it will be difficult to find any particular belief, feeling, or moral stance which is found in all religons. On the other hand, so long as we require only a certain kind of belief, moral attitude, or emotion, there is no guarantee that it exists within a religion rather than in some other sort of setting. A belief in a Divine Mind and Will ruling the universe might be held purely as a speculative hypothesis; it will not be a *religious* belief unless it makes contact with the believer's feeling, attitudes, and action in a characteristically religious way. And similarly it seems that the quest

for goodness might occur in a religious or in a nonreligious context. The seventh example is not subject to these criticisms; it escapes partiality by featuring a global term, *ultimate attitude*, which embraces belief, feeling, and moral endeavor. But one may still wonder whether all ultimate attitudes are necessarily religious, or whether there is not some further feature which makes religious attitudes religious. As James suggests in *The Varieties of Religious Experience*, it is doubtful whether a frivolous attitude toward life deserves to be called religious, even if it is the basic attitude of the person in question.

At this point the reader may well feel quite puzzled. None of these definitions is fully satisfactory. And yet surely after going through such a list we have a deeper understanding of the nature of religion than we did before. How can this be? How can the consideration of several inadequate definitions help us to realize what religion is like?

Perhaps our trouble arises from being dominated by an oversimple model of definition. In each case the objection was that one could find cases of religion to which the definition did not apply, or that the definition would apply to things that were not religions. Each formulation was seen to be either too narrow or too broad, or both. Now this is an objection only if one expects a definition of religion to provide a characteristic, or set of characteristics, which something has whenever it is a religion and only when it is a religion. That is, we expect the definition to provide both a necessary condition of religion (satisfied by every religion) and a sufficient condition (satisfied only by religion). We get this ideal from mathematics, a very atypical sphere of thought which, unfortunately, provides the logician with most of his examples. In geometry, for example, we can define a circle as a closed curve, each point on the circumference of which is equidistant from a fixed point called the center. Anything which satisfies these conditions is a circle, and anything which does not satisfy them is not a circle.

This sort of definition is possible not only in mathematics, though the neatest and most unmistakable examples of it occur there; we define, for example, a thermometer as an instrument for measuring temperature, or an oculist as a doctor specializing in the treatment of the eye. But there are other places where difficulties are encountered, most noticeably when we try to define terms which have to do with important segments or products of human culture. Consider for a moment the term *poem*.[1] What is the defining characteristic of a poem? Rhyme? What about blank verse? Meter? What about free verse? Other possible defining features which suggest themselves are an emphasis on the sound of words as such, the use of metaphors and other figures of speech, a preoccupation with imaginative and emotional material—all are often found in prose, for example, the novels of Thomas Wolfe. Many poems (particularly those called didactic) deal with quite prosaic and unimaginative themes. Wordsworth's poetry makes little use of figures of speech.

And yet the presence of these features certainly has something to do with making a literary composition a poem. None of them is irrelevant to the question of whether or not a piece of writing is a poem. We could call them "poem-making characteristics." The problem is to conceive the precise relation they have to being a poem. They cannot go to make up a definition in the mathematical sense, because neither individually nor collectively do they constitute a necessary condition for being a poem. As we have just seen no one of these features has to be present to make something a poem, nor is it necessary that a poem include them all. It may be that the presence of all these features would be a sufficient condition for "poemhood," but the fact that this congeries of characteristics is not also a necessary condition prevents it from forming a definition in the usual sense. Perhaps to get a necessary condition we need something in between some one feature and all the features. Let us say we cannot have a poem unless we have a sufficient number of these features realized, and to a sufficient extent. But how many does it take to make a "sufficient" number? There is no definite answer to that question. First, the features are weighted unequally. Meter goes a longer way toward making something a poem than do imaginative themes or figures of speech. Yet it is not possible to say how much more weight it has. Second, how many features are required will depend on the extent to

which each is realized—how definite is the meter, how vividly the content stimulates the imagination, how frequent are the figures of speech. And these gradations are likewise insusceptible to any exact measure. It seems that the best we can do by way of a definition is to say that a poem is a literary composition which contains a substantial number of these features to a substantial degree, and then rely on a series of examples to give our pupil a sense of what constitutes a substantial amount.

Something like this is true for religion. The definitions we have been considering, or most of them, have real value, just because they present characteristic features of religion—"religion-making characteristics." Perhaps the most that can be done by way of a definition of religion is to list such characteristic features. Here is such a list, which embodies the features stressed by one or another of the definitions we have been considering.

1. Beliefs in supernatural beings (gods).
2. A distinction between sacred and profane objects.
3. Ritual acts focused around sacred objects.
4. A moral code believed to be sanctioned by the gods.
5. Characteristically religious feelings (awe, sense of mystery, sense of guilt, adoration, etc.), which tend to be aroused in the presence of sacred objects and during the practice of ritual, and which are associated with the gods.
6. Prayer and other forms of communication with gods.
7. A world view. (By a world view I mean a general picture of the world as a whole and the place of the individual therein, this picture containing some specification of an over-all purpose or point, and an indication of how the individual fits into this whole.)
8. A more or less total organization of one's life based on the world view.
9. A social group bound together by the first eight factors.

It is important to realize that these various factors do not just happen to be thrown together in religion; they are intimately interfused in a variety of ways. Some of these connections have already been indicated in the way the items were specified, but there are many others as well. For example, the distinction between sacred and profane objects is primarily based on other items in this list. It is not some intrinsic feature of a thing that gives it the role of a sacred object in a religion, for things of every conceivable sort have occupied this position—animals, plants, topographical features like mountains, rivers, and springs, persons, heavenly bodies, articles of furniture, and so on. What leads the adherents of a religion to mark out certain objects as sacred is that those objects fill them with awe, dread, and a sense of mystery, and they tend to respond to them with ritual acts. This is a quasi-operational definition of "sacred." Again, the emotional reaction to sacred objects is typically rationalized by conceiving the object to be the dwelling place or manifestation of a supernatural personal being. That is, the beliefs about gods serve to explain the emotional reactions. The awe aroused by the wild bull leads to its identification with the god of wine and intoxication, Dionysus. And the awe aroused by a volcanic mountain may be translated into conceptual terms by speaking of the mountain as the habitation of a fierce god. The unique impression which Jesus of Nazareth made on certain of his contemporaries was expressed by their calling him the Son of God. This sounds as if the emotional reaction to objects comes first and is then explained by positing gods as its cause. But we cannot take the priority of any one of these items as a general rule. The acceptance of beliefs about the gods and about their earthly habitations can arouse, or help arouse, awe and other religious feelings in the presence of certain objects. Indeed the members of a religious community are taught to hold certain objects in awe, feel various emotions at certain times and places, by being taught various doctrines about the gods. Thus Christians are taught to regard the Cross and the consecrated bread and wine with reverence by being told of the Crucifixion and the Last Supper. Jews are taught to feel a certain way about unleavened bread by being told of the Exodus.

A similar reciprocal relationship holds between ritual and doctrine. On the one hand, a doctrine can supervene on an already established ritual, as its justification. Thus the story of Proserpine being carried off to the underworld and remaining there half the year seems to have been introduced as an explanation of a pre-existing magical fertility cult, in which an ear of grain, perhaps called the corn-maiden, is buried in the fall, and raised sprouting in the spring. Apparently there was first a wild ceremony in which a live bull was torn to pieces, and the raw flesh eaten, perhaps in order to incorporate the mysterious potency believed to reside therein; and then this rite was interpreted as a re-enactment of the occasion on which Dionysus (who has been identified with the bull) was torn to pieces by Titans, and the aim of the rite is reinterpreted as the attainment of union with the god. Similarly the Christian doctrine of transubstantiation arose out of the great significance which Christians already attached to the common memorial meal.

On the other hand, changes in doctrine can engender, modify, or abolish rituals. It seems likely that a growing conviction of the benevolence of God has played a part in the cessation of human sacrifice; intellectual difficulties in the doctrine of transubstantiation have been a factor in the de-emphasis or discontinuance of the sacrament of Holy Communion in many Christian sects; and the Christmas festival originated, at least in part, from the belief in the divinity of Jesus Christ (only in part, because it is a continuation of pagan festivals held at the winter solstice).

The only way we can adequately reflect our actual use of *religion* is to say that the word is applied whenever enough of these conditions are satisfied. But how much is enough? Let us not oversimplify by pretending that the application of the term requires any five out of seven, or a certain three plus any two of the others, or anything else of the sort. In fact we will never obtain an adequate idea of the working of the term *religion* until we abandon the clear-cut dichotomy between a term applying or not applying to something in favor of the more complex concept of the *extent* to which a term applies. We shall have to think of religion applying in some cases clearly, unequivocally (Christianity, Islam, Hinduism), but in other cases more or less questionably, tentatively (Communism, complete devotion to science).

At one end of the scale we have the ideally clear cases, the sort that one would cite if asked to give examples of religion: Roman Catholicism, Orthodox Judaism, Orphism. Here we have all the religion-making characteristics present in a clear way, and to a marked degree. In Roman Catholicism, for example, there is an elaborate cultus centering around sacred objects (priest, cross, altar, consecrated bread and wine); there are beliefs about God, to Whom these cultic acts are directed, Whose nature and doings form the rationale of the cultus; when the individual is participating in the rites, when he is in the presence of sacred objects, or when he is thinking of God, characteristically religious feelings are aroused in him, not always or invariably, but often enough to give a strong emotional coloration to the whole. There is a moral code believed to have been ordained and enforced by God. And all this provides the individual with a general picture of the cosmos and human history, and with an indication of his place therein.

Note that in singling out this type of religion as a paradigm case I am not suggesting that it is the best or truest kind of religion. The only sense in which it is best is a logical or semantic one. It is an ideally clear and unquestionable example of the application of the term *religion*. We should beware of supposing that in defining the term *religion*, we are trying to delineate the religious ideal or to determine what the most perfect sort of religion would be. In defining religion we are trying to make explicit the criteria we use for applying the term to anything, be it good or bad. The evaluative question, "What is the best religion?" in its very wording presupposes that the term *religion* applies to cases other than the best. Hence the elucidation of the nonevaluative use of the term must precede the evaluative job of determining the religious ideal.

Since the paradigm case is defined by a number of different features, there can be cases which deviate from it in a number of different ways, that is, by one or the other of these features becoming less prominent or dropping out altogether.

Ritual can be sharply de-emphasized, and with it the demarcation of certain objects as sacred. This de-emphasis has occurred in Protestantism and in Islam. It can even drop out altogether, as with the Quakers and other groups, who are mainly concerned with the cultivation of mystical experience.

Morality can have no connection with the other elements. (Cf. our discussion of the third and fourth definitions.)

Beliefs in supernatural beings can be whittled away to nothing. We have seen a development of this sort in Western culture over the last few hundred years. The deity has been successively relieved of his spatial habitation in heaven and of his temporal priority to the world. With the extension of natural knowledge, one range of phenomena after another has been removed from his direct and immediate control—the motions of heavenly bodies, the ebb and flow of disease, earthquake, tempest, and flood, the adaptation of living organisms to their environment, the course of history, even the stream of human conscious experience. When this tendency to kick God upstairs is given full reign, what is left is a remote and bodiless abstraction, which some religious groups have proceeded to ignore altogether. Thus in some Unitarian groups, and in Humanism, we have a religiously toned orientation around certain ideals, like social equality, and a moral code based thereon, but without the ardor being directed in any way toward a supernatural being, and without any cultus in which this ardor is expressed. One branch of Buddhism, the Hinayana, practiced in southeastern Asia also ignores supernatural beings, at least officially. Here the emphasis is on the cultivation of a moral and meditative discipline which will enable one to attain a state in which all craving has ceased (craving being considered the root of all evil in human life).

The social group which has the religion can be reduced to one member; that is, a person can develop his own private religious scheme. Spinoza, for example, worked out his own religion, which was based on a calm and joyful acceptance of everything that happened as necessarily flowing from the nature of the universe. The whole of nature, conceived as a unity, was the object of worship; and the worship consisted of, in Spinoza's phrase, an "intellectual love," that is, a joyful recognition that everything necessarily is as it is.

Finally, the typically religious emotions may be attenuated. It is doubtful that any group continues to realize the other religious elements unless a large proportion of its members entertain strong feelings. But it is possible for a particular individual to carry on with religious rituals, observe moral codes, even assent to the creed in a perfunctory way, without all this making any real and vital contact with his emotional life.

The important point is that as we come to examples which leave out more of the religion-making characteristics and/or in which the characteristics are exemplified less strongly, we feel less secure about applying the term. It seems more doubtful that they really are religions, and we will find less unanimity in the language community with respect to the application of the word. No one would doubt that Roman Catholicism, or Orthodox Judaism, or Orphism is a religion. If someone did doubt it, we should take that to indicate he did not know how to use the word *religion*. But one can doubt that Hinayana Buddhism, or Humanism, or Communism, or Spinoza's intellectual love of the universe, is a religion, without thereby giving grounds for doubt that he knows how to use the term.

Not all deviations from the paradigm equally give rise to doubt. We live in a nonritualistic society. Rites and symbols have very little meaning for us. Graduation exercises and initiation ceremonies are likely to make us uncomfortable or just bored. Therefore we do not tend to think of ritual as essential to religion; it is, we think, merely an outward trapping which can be sloughed off, leaving the inner reality undiminished. Hence we do not feel uncomfortable in calling the Quakers a religious group, although they have completely abjured ritual. But we do tend to put great store by belief in a god or gods. When there is a deviation from the paradigm in this respect, as in Communism or Hinayana Buddhism, we feel more reluctance in classing it as a religion.

This differential weighting of elements will vary from group to group, and even from person to person, which is equivalent to saying that not everyone has exactly the same concept of religion. And it is easy to understand why. According to the present analysis, a concept of religion consists of a paradigm case (or class of paradigm cases) analyzed into significant features, with different weights attached to these features. It seems that this is just the way in which the meaning of a term like *religion* is learned. Normally one starts by becoming familiar with some one religion, the one in which he is raised. This will become his paradigm case. But not yet. He does not acquire a concept of religion until he learns of other religions and compares them with his own. (It is noteworthy that there is no word corresponding to our word *religion* in the languages of cultures which have not made contact with a wide variety of other cultures.) As he becomes aware of more and more cultural phenomena, he will apply the word *religion* to those which do not differ too widely in fundamental respects from the paradigm. Thus the concepts of religion held by two persons will vary with variations in the paradigm case, in the weighting of various factors in the paradigm case, and in the tolerance of deviations (logical, not religious, tolerance). A Presbyterian will feel less compunction in applying *religion* to a nonritual group like the Quakers than will a Catholic. And one Catholic will feel less compunction than another if the first places less weight on ritual relative to other features of their common paradigm than does the other. And a Quaker will be more ready to call a highly mystical set of beliefs like Theosophy a religion than a Calvinist will, with his emphasis on creed and morality....

Thus once we see that we apply the term *religion* not in accordance with any rigid set of necessary and sufficient conditions, but on the basis of some vaguely specified permissible degree of deviation from a paradigm case, we can understand why we fall into perplexities and disputes over the application of the term, and also how these perplexities and disputes can be cleared up.

NOTE

1. This discussion of "poem" is mostly taken from C. L. Stevenson, "On 'What is a Poem?'" *Philosophical Review*, LXVI (1957), 329–62.

PART TWO

The Divine Attributes

A. OMNIPOTENCE

2 SOME PUZZLES CONCERNING OMNIPOTENCE

GEORGE MAVRODES

Judaism, Christianity, and Islam are often grouped as "Abrahamic" religions, because they all recognize Abraham as a founding figure. Their adherents are monotheists, affirming the existence of one God, typically described as an all-powerful, all-knowing, all-good eternal creator of the world. Before proceeding to consider whether God exists, however, we need to examine how the divine attributes themselves give rise to philosophical perplexities.

Let us begin with God's omnipotence and consider this conundrum: Can God create a stone so heavy that God cannot lift it? If God can create such a stone, then God apparently is not omnipotent, because the task of lifting the stone is beyond God's power. But if God cannot create such a stone, then likewise God is apparently not omnipotent, because a task has been described that God cannot perform. So in either case God is not omnipotent.

In our next selection, George Mavrodes, who is Professor Emeritus of Philosophy at the University of Michigan, maintains that the puzzle, properly framed, does not demonstrate any defect in the doctrine of God's omnipotence.

From *The Philosophical Review* 73 (1964).

The doctrine of God's omnipotence appears to claim that God can do anything. Consequently, there have been attempts to refute the doctrine by giving examples of things which God cannot do; for example, He cannot draw a square circle.

Responding to objections of this type, St. Thomas pointed out that "anything" should be here construed to refer only to objects, actions, or states of affairs whose descriptions are not self-contradictory.[1] For it is only such things whose nonexistence might plausibly be attributed to a lack of power in some agent. My failure to draw a circle on the exam may indicate my lack of geometrical skill, but my failure to draw a square circle does not indicate any such lack. Therefore, the fact that it is false (or perhaps meaningless) to say that God could draw one does no damage to the doctrine of His omnipotence.

A more involved problem, however, is posed by this type of question: can God create a stone too heavy for Him to lift? This appears to be stronger than the first problem, for it poses a dilemma. If we say that God can create a stone, then it seems that there might be such a stone. And if there might be a stone too heavy for Him to lift, then He is evidently not omnipotent. But if we deny that God can create such a stone, we seem to have given up His omnipotence already. Both answers lead us to the same conclusion.

Further, this problem does not seem obviously open to St. Thomas' solution. The form "x is able to draw a square circle" seems plainly to involve a contradiction, while "x is able to make a thing too heavy for x to lift" does not. For it may easily be true that I am able to make a boat too heavy for me to lift. So why should it not be possible for God to make a stone too heavy for Him to lift?

Despite this apparent difference, this second puzzle *is* open to essentially the same answer as the first. The dilemma fails because it consists of asking whether God can do a self-contradictory thing. And the reply that He cannot does no damage to the doctrine of omnipotence.

The specious nature of the problem may be seen in this way. God is either omnipotent or not.[2] Let us assume first that He is not. In that case the phrase "a stone too heavy for God to lift" may not be self-contradictory. And then, of course, if we assert either that God is able or that He is not able to create such a stone, we may conclude that He is not omnipotent. But this is no more than the assumption with which we began, meeting us again after our roundabout journey. If this were all that the dilemma could establish it would be trivial. To be significant it must derive this same conclusion *from the assumption that God is omnipotent*; that is, it must show that the assumption of the omnipotence of God leads to a *reductio*. But does it?

On the assumption that God is omnipotent, the phrase "a stone too heavy for God to lift" becomes self-contradictory. For it becomes "a stone which cannot be lifted by Him whose power is sufficient for lifting anything." But the "thing" described by a self-contradictory phrase is absolutely impossible and hence has nothing to do with the doctrine of omnipotence. Not being an object of power at all, its failure to exist cannot be the result of some lack in the power of God. And, interestingly, it is the very omnipotence of God which makes the existence of such a stone absolutely impossible, while it is the fact that I am finite in power which makes it possible for me to make a boat too heavy for me to lift.

But suppose that some die-hard objector takes the bit in his teeth and denies that the phrase "a stone too heavy for God to lift" is self-contradictory, even on the assumption that God is omnipotent. In other words, he contends that the description "a stone too heavy for an omnipotent God to lift" is self-coherent and therefore describes an absolutely possible object. Must I then attempt to prove the contradiction which I assume above as intuitively obvious? Not necessarily. Let me reply simply that if the objector is right in this contention, then the answer to the original question is "Yes, God can create such a stone." It may seem that this reply will force us into the original dilemma. But it does not. For now the objector can draw no damaging conclusion from this answer. And the reason is that he has just now contended that such a stone is compatible with the omnipotence of God. Therefore, from the possibility of God's creating such a stone it cannot be concluded that God is not omnipotent. The objector cannot have it both ways. The conclusion which he himself wishes to draw from an affirmative answer to the original question is itself the required proof that the descriptive phrase which appears there is self-contradictory. And "it is more appropriate to say that such things cannot he done, than that God cannot do them."[3]

The specious nature of this problem may also be seen in a somewhat different way.[4] Suppose that some theologian is convinced by this dilemma that he must give up the doctrine of omnipotence. But he resolves to give up as little as possible, just enough to meet the argument. One way he can do so is by retaining the infinite power of God with regard to lifting, while placing a restriction on the sort of stone He is able to create. The only restriction required here, however, is that God must not be able to create a stone too heavy for Him to lift. Beyond that the dilemma has not even suggested any necessary restriction. Our theologian has, in effect, answered the original question in the negative; and he now regretfully supposes that this has required him to give up the full doctrine of omnipotence. He is now retaining what he supposes to be the more modest remnants which he has salvaged from that doctrine.

We must ask, however, what it is which he has in fact given up. Is it the unlimited power of God to create stones? No doubt. But what stone is it which God is now precluded from creating? The stone too heavy for Him to lift, of course. But we must remember that nothing in the argument required the theologian to admit any limit on God's power with regard to the lifting of stones. He still holds that to be unlimited. And if God's power to lift is infinite, then His power to create may run to infinity also without outstripping that first power. The supposed limitation turns out to be no limitation at all, since it is specified only by reference to another power which is itself infinite. Our theologian need have no regrets, for he has given up nothing. The doctrine of the power of God remains just what it was before.

Nothing I have said above, of course, goes to prove that God is, in fact, omnipotent. All I have intended to show is that certain arguments intended to prove that He is not omnipotent fail. They fail because they propose, as tests of God's power, putative tasks whose descriptions are self-contradictory. Such pseudo-tasks, not falling within the realm of possibility, are not objects of power at all. Hence the fact that they cannot be performed implies no limit on the power of God, and hence no defect in the doctrine of omnipotence.

NOTES

1. St. Thomas Aquinas, *Summa Theologiae*, Ia, q. 25, a. 3.
2. I assume, of course, the existence of God, since that is not being brought in question here.
3. St. Thomas, *loc. cit.*
4. But this method rests finally on the same logical relations as the preceding one.

3   THE LOGIC OF OMNIPOTENCE

HARRY G. FRANKFURT

Faced with the quandary of whether an omnipotent being could create a stone too heavy for that being to lift, George Mavrodes argues in the previous selection that for an omnipotent being the description of the task is self-contradictory and, therefore, points to no defect in the being's omnipotence.

From *The Philosophical Review* 73 (1964).

Some might respond that an omnipotent being should not be bound by logic, and, therefore, should be able to create such a stone even if doing so is self-contradictory. In that case wouldn't the omnipotent being face the impossible task of lifting a stone that cannot be lifted? According to Harry G. Frankfurt, Professor Emeritus of Philosophy at Princeton University, the appropriate reply to that case is simple.

See if you can provide a persuasive answer. Then read on and see how Frankfurt handles the matter.

George Mavrodes has recently presented an analysis designed to show that, despite some appearances to the contrary, a certain well-known puzzle actually raises no serious difficulties in the notion of divine omnipotence.[1] The puzzle suggests a test of God's power—can He create a stone too heavy for Him to lift?—which, it seems, cannot fail to reveal that His power is limited. For He must, it would appear, either show His limitations by being unable to create such a stone or by being unable to lift it once He had created it.

In dealing with this puzzle, Mavrodes points out that it involves the setting of a task whose description is self-contradictory—the task of creating a stone too heavy for an omnipotent being to lift. He calls such tasks "pseudo-tasks" and he says of them: "Such pseudo-tasks, not falling within the realm of possibility, are not objects of power at all. Hence the fact that they cannot be performed implies no limit on the power of God, and hence no defect in the doctrine of omnipotence."[2] Thus his way of dealing with the puzzle relies upon the principle that an omnipotent being need not be supposed capable of performing tasks whose descriptions are self-contradictory.

Now this principle is one which Mavrodes apparently regards as self-evident, since he offers no support for it whatever except some references which indicate that it was also accepted by Saint Thomas Aquinas. I do not wish to suggest that the principle is false. Indeed, for all I know it may even be self-evident. But it happens to be a principle which has been rejected by some important philosophers.[3] Accordingly, it might be preferable to have an analysis of the puzzle in question which does not require the use of this principle. And in fact, such an analysis is easy to provide.

Suppose, then, that God's omnipotence enables Him to do even what is logically impossible and that He actually creates a stone too heavy for Him to lift. The critic of the notion of divine omnipotence is quite mistaken if he thinks that this supposition plays into his hands. What the critic wishes to claim, of course, is that when God has created a stone which He cannot lift He is then faced with a task beyond His ability and is therefore seen to be limited in power. But this claim is not justified.

For why should God not be able to perform the task in question? To be sure, it is a task—the task of lifting a stone which He cannot lift—whose description is self-contradictory. But if God is supposed capable of performing one task whose description is self-contradictory—that of creating the problematic stone in the first place—why should He not be supposed capable of performing another—that of lifting the stone? After all, is there any greater trick in performing two logically impossible tasks than there is in performing one?

If an omnipotent being can do what is logically impossible, then He can not only create situations which He cannot handle but also, since He is not bound by the limits of consistency, He can handle situations which He cannot handle.

NOTES

1. George Mavrodes, "Some Puzzles Concerning Omnipotence," *The Philosophical Review* 72 (1963), 221–23.
2. Ibid., p. 223.
3. Descartes, for instance, who in fact thought it blasphemous to maintain that God can do only what can be described in a logically coherent way: "The truths of mathematics ... were established by God and entirely depend on Him, as much as do all the rest of His creatures. Actually, it would be to speak of God as a Jupiter or Saturn and to subject Him to the Styx and to the Fates, to say that these

truths are independent of Him.... You will be told that if God established these truths He would be able to change them, as a king does his laws; to which it is necessary to reply that this is correct.... In general we can be quite certain that God can do whatever we are able to understand, but not that He cannot do what we are unable to understand. For it would be presumptuous to think that our imagination extends as far as His power" (letter to Mersenne, 15 April 1630). "God was as free to make it false that all the radii of a circle are equal as to refrain from creating the world" (letter to Mersenne, 27 May 1630). "I would not even dare to say that God cannot arrange that a mountain should exist without a valley, or that one and two should not make three; but I only say that He has given me a mind of such a nature that I cannot conceive a mountain without a valley or a sum of one and two which would not be three, and so on, and that such things imply contradictions in my conception" (letter to Arnauld, 29 July 1648). "As for the difficulty in conceiving how it was a matter of freedom and indifference to God to make it true that the three angles of a triangle should equal two right angles, or generally that contradictions should not be able to be together, one can easily remove it by considering that the power of God can have no limit.... God cannot have been determined to make it true that contradictions cannot be together, and consequently He could have been determined to make it true that contradictions cannot be together, and consequently he could have done the contrary" (letter to Mesland, 2 May 1644).

B. TIMELESSNESS

4 GOD ETERNAL

PAUL HELM

Adherents to the Abrahamic religions typically affirm that God has always existed and always will exist. But does this claim mean that God is everlasting, existing at all times, or eternal, existing outside time?

Paul Helm is a Teaching Fellow at Regent College, Vancouver, Canada. He maintains that God is timeless and changeless, yet enters into relations with things in time and has some concept of time.

The rationale for introducing the possibility that God exists in a timeless eternity lies in the fact that this supposition will enable more sense to be made of what would otherwise be difficult, and so to vindicate an unattenuated Christian theism. It is agreed that the idea of timeless eternity is obscure and not fully graspable, but there is nothing novel in the introduction of a concept such as *electron* or *virus* to make sense of data otherwise unaccountable. Yet it would not be appropriate to introduce the idea of timeless eternity, or more precisely of God's timeless eternity, if that idea is not so much obscure as downright incoherent. For if it is incoherent then although numbers and propositions may be timelessly eternal, God could not be....

There is no better place to begin than the celebrated account by Boethius:

That God is eternal, then, is the common judgment of all who live by reason. Let us therefore consider what eternity is, for this makes plain to us both the divine nature and knowledge. Eternity, then, is the complete possession all at once of illimitable life.... Therefore, whatever includes and possesses the whole fullness of illimitable life at once and is such that nothing future is absent from it and nothing past has flowed away, this is rightly judged to be eternal, and of this it is necessary

both that being in full possession of itself it be always present to itself and that it have the infinity of mobile time present to it.[1]

To say that God is eternal is thus to say that he is not in time. There is for him no past and no future. It makes no sense to ask how long God has existed, or to divide up his life into periods of time. He possesses the whole of his life at once: it is not lived successively.

Prima facie, a timelessly eternal God, an individual, has some relations with individuals who are in time. It is the fact of these positive relations which generates the charge that the idea of divine timeless eternity is immediately incoherent. This problem does not arise for other entities that philosophers have sometimes regarded as timeless, such as propositions and numbers, because they are incapable of entering into relations with individuals such as you and me. Propositions can be thought about ... and so they can 'change' only by now being thought about, and now ignored.

But things are different with an allegedly timeless being such as God, who has intelligence and will. He can not only be thought about, he can think, and the relations into which he enters with his creation appear to be real relations, even

From Paul Helm *Eternal God*, Second Edition, Oxford University Press, 2010. Reprinted by permission of the publisherOxford University Press.

though they cannot issue in any changes in God, since (by definition) God is timeless and changeless....

More than this, not only does God enter into relations with things in time but we must also suppose that he has some concept of time. For instance, he knows what it means for A to exist in time, or for it to occur before B and C. This much seems to be implicit in the idea of creation. To suppose otherwise would lead to insuperable difficulties. It would be to suppose that God created the universe having features which are likewise timeless, and this would mean that God was incapable of creating anything which changes.

It is more debatable whether having this concept of time, the idea of objects existing in a temporal sequence, God also has the concept of temporal indexicals such as 'yesterday', 'ago', 'now', and 'then'. If he is not in time himself these expressions cannot apply to him; *a fortiori* he cannot apply them to himself. But may not God have the idea of a person who understands that, say, his birthday was so many days ago? Does it follow that if God knows what it is like to have had a birthday ten days ago he must be in time? This does not seem plausible. A bachelor may know what it is like to be married. Is this only because bachelors could be married?...

We may say, then, that God knows (timelessly) the whole temporal series in rather the way in which for us certain things are known at a glance or in a flash of insight or intuition in which the active recalling of memories or the anticipation of the future plays no part. We may say, then, that God knows *at a glance* the whole of his temporally ordered creation in rather the way in which a crossword clue may be solved in a flash.

Where, then, is the conceptual problem? It may be stated as follows. 'But, on St. Thomas' view, my typing of this paper is simultaneous with the whole of eternity. Again, on this view, the great fire of Rome is simultaneous with the whole of eternity. Therefore, while I type these very words, Nero fiddles heartlessly on.'[2] and further:

The inner incoherence can be seen as follows. God's timelessness is said to consist in his existing at all moments of human time—simultaneously. Thus he is said to be simultaneously present at (and a witness of) what I did yesterday, what I am doing today, and what I will do tomorrow. But if t_1 is simultaneous with t_2 and t_2 with t_3, then t_1 is simultaneous with t_3. So if the instant at which God knows these things were simultaneous with both yesterday, today and tomorrow, then these days would be simultaneous with each other. So yesterday would be the same day as today and as tomorrow—which is clearly nonsense.[3]

As indeed it is.

How can this 'inner incoherence' as Swinburne calls it, be met? The obvious way to avoid it is by placing restrictions upon the idea of simultaneity so that it is not transitive in certain contexts. But there may be another way of meeting the difficulty. Why cannot the use of simultaneity in expressing the relation between the timeless God and individuals in time be abandoned altogether? For the concept of simultaneity is obviously one which implies time. If A and B are simultaneous they exist or occur at the same time. But God is time*less*. Suppose that there exists (timelessly) a set of propositions expressing the history of some event which is of the form 'A at t_1 and then B at t_2'. The occurrence of A is at a different time from the occurrence of B. Why should the question of what the temporal relation is between such a set of propositions and what they say about A and B ever be raised? It could be raised about the inscribing of the sentences, which is an event, but surely not about the inscription with a fixed meaning? Call the inscription a record; why does it make any sense to ask whether the record is *simultaneous* with the occurrence of A or B, and if so whether A and B must be simultaneous, thus reducing the idea of a timeless record of the events to absurdity? Swinburne objects to timeless eternity because he takes God's timelessness to 'consist in his existing at all moments of human time—simultaneously'.[4] But it is far from clear that this follows from Boethius' account, or from any account of timelessness that is attractive. Why cannot divine timelessness consist in a manner of existence which sustains no temporal relations with human time? If God timelessly exists he is neither earlier nor later nor simultaneous with any event of time. He exists time*less*ly.

5   GOD EVERLASTING

NICHOLAS WOLTERSTORFF

Nicholas Wolterstorff, who is Professor Emeritus of Philosophical Theology at Yale University, opposes Paul Helm's claim that God is eternal. Wolterstorff agrees that God is without beginning or end, but claims that God is not eternal but everlasting, existing in time.

Who is correct? As in the case of all philosophical problems, after considering all the relevant arguments, the responsibility for reaching conclusions is your own.

All Christian theologians agree that God is without beginning and without end. The vast majority have held, in addition, that God is *eternal*, existing outside of time. Only a small minority have contended that God is *everlasting*, existing within time.[1] In what follows I shall take up the cudgels for that minority, arguing that God as conceived and presented by the biblical writers is a being whose own life and existence is temporal.

The biblical writers do not present God as some passive factor within reality but as an agent in it. Further, they present him as acting within *human* history. The god they present is neither the impassive god of the Oriental nor the nonhistorical god of the Deist. Indeed, so basic to the biblical writings is their speaking of God as agent within history that if one viewed God as only an impassive factor in reality, or as one whose agency does not occur within human history, one would have to regard the biblical speech about God as at best one long sequence of metaphors pointing to a reality for which they are singularly inept, and as at worst one long sequence of falsehoods.

More specifically, the biblical writers present God as a redeeming God. From times most ancient, man has departed from the pattern of responsibilities awarded him at his creation by God. A multitude of evils has followed. But God was not content to leave man in the mire of his misery. Aware of what is going on, he has resolved, in response to man's sin and its resultant evils, to bring about renewal. He has, indeed, already been acting in accord with that resolve, centrally and decisively in the life, death, and resurrection of Jesus Christ.

What I shall argue is that if we are to accept this picture of God as acting for the renewal of human life, we must conceive of him as everlasting rather than eternal. God the Redeemer cannot be a God eternal. This is so because God the Redeemer is a God who *changes*. And any being which changes is a being among whose states there is temporal succession. Of course, there is an important sense in which God as presented in the Scriptures is changeless: he is steadfast in his redeeming intent and ever faithful to his children. Yet, *ontologically*, God cannot be a redeeming God without there being changeful variation among his states.

If this argument proves correct the importance of the issue here confronting us for Christian theology can scarcely be exaggerated. A theology which opts for God as eternal cannot avoid being in conflict with the confession of God as redeemer. And given the obvious fact that God is presented in the Bible as a God who redeems, a theology which opts for God as eternal cannot be a theology faithful to the biblical witness....

It might seem obvious that God, as described by the biblical writers, is a being who changes, and

From Nicholas Wolterstorff, "Everlasting God," in *God and the Good: Essays in Honor of Henry Stob*, eds. Clifton J. Orlebeke and Lewis B. Smedes, William B. Eerdmans Publishing Company, 1975. Reprinted by permission of the publisher.

who accordingly is fundamentally noneternal. For God is described as a being who *acts*—in creation, in providence, and for the renewal of mankind. He is an agent, not an impassive factor in reality. And from the manner in which his acts are described, it seems obvious that many of them have beginnings and endings, that accordingly they stand in succession relations to each other, and that these successive acts are of such a sort that their presence and absence on God's time-strand constitutes changes thereon. Thus it seems obvious that God is fundamentally noneternal.

God is spoken of as calling Abraham to leave Chaldea and later instructing Moses to return to Egypt. So does not the event of *God's instructing Moses* succeed that of *God's calling Abraham?* And does not this sort of succession constitute a change on God's time-strand—not a change in his "essence," but nonetheless a change on his time-strand? Again, God is spoken of as leading Israel through the Red Sea and later sending his Son into the world. So does not his doing the latter succeed his doing the former? And does not the fact of this sort of succession constitute a change along God's time-strand?

In short, it seems evident that the biblical writers regard God as having a time-strand of his own on which actions on his part are to be found, and that some at least of these actions vary in such a way that there are changes along the strand. It seems evident that they do not regard changes on time-strands as confined to entities in God's creation. The God who acts, in the way in which the biblical writers speak of God as acting, seems clearly to change.

Furthermore, is it not clear from how they speak that the biblical writers regarded many of God's acts as bearing temporal order-relations to events which are not aspects of him but rather aspects of the earth, of ancient human beings, and so forth? The four cited above, for example, seem all to be described thus. It seems obvious that God's actions as described by the biblical writers stand in temporal order-relations to all the other events in our own time-array.

However, I think it is not at all so obvious as on first glance it might appear that the biblical writers do in fact describe God as changing.

Granted that the language they use suggests this. It is not at once clear that this is what they wished to say with this language. It is not clear that this is how they were describing God. Let us begin to see why this is so by reflecting on the following passage from St. Thomas Aquinas:

Nor, if the action of the first agent is eternal, does it follow that His effect is eternal, ... God acts voluntarily in the production of things, ... God's act of understanding and willing is, necessarily, His act of making. Now, an effect follows from the intellect and the will according to the determination of the intellect and the command of the will. Moreover, just as the intellect determines every other condition of the thing made, so does it prescribe the time of its making; for art determines not only that this thing is to be such and such, but that it is to be at this particular time, even as a physician determines that a dose of medicine is to be drunk at such and such a particular time, so that, if his act of will were of itself sufficient to produce the effect, the effect would follow anew from his previous decision, without any new action on his part. Nothing, therefore, prevents our saying that God's action existed from all eternity, whereas its effect was not present from eternity, but existed at that time when, from all eternity, He ordained it (Summa Contra Gentiles II.35; cf. II.36, 4).

Let us henceforth call an event which neither begins nor ends an *everlasting* event. And let us call an event which either begins or ends, a *temporal* event. In the passage above, St. Thomas is considering God's acts of bringing about temporal events. So consider some such act; say, that of God's bringing about Israel's deliverance from Egypt. The temporal event in question, Israel's deliverance from Egypt, occurred (let us say) in 1225 B.C. But from the fact that what God brought about occurred in 1225 it does not follow, says Aquinas, that God's act of bringing it about occurred in 1225. In fact, it does not follow that this act had any beginning or ending whatsoever. And in general, suppose that God brings about some temporal event *e*. From the fact that *e* is temporal it does not follow, says Aquinas, that God's act of bringing about *e*'s occurrence is temporal. The temporality of the event which God brings about does not infect God's act of bringing it about. God's act of bringing it about may well be everlasting. This can perhaps more easily be seen, he says, if we remember that God, unlike us, does not have to "take steps" so as to bring about the occurrence of some event. He need only will that it occur. If God just wants it to be the case that *e* occur at *t, e* occurs at *t.*

Thus God can bring about changes in our history without himself changing. The occurrence of the event of Israel's deliverance from Egypt constitutes a change in our history. But there is no counterpart change among God's aspects by virtue of his bringing this event about.

Now let us suppose that the four acts of God cited above—instructing Moses, calling Abraham, leading Israel through the Red Sea, and sending his Son into the world—regardless of the impression we might gain from the biblical language used to describe them, also have the structure of God's bringing about the occurrence of some temporal event. Suppose, for example, that God's leading Israel through the Red Sea has the structure of God's bringing it about that Israel's passage through the Red Sea occurs. And suppose Aquinas is right that the temporality of Israel's passage does not infect with temporality God's act of bringing about this passage. Then what is strictly speaking the case is not that God's leading Israel through the Red Sea occurs during 1225. What is rather the case is that Israel's passage through the Red Sea occurs during 1225, and that God brings this passage about. And the temporality of the passage does not entail the temporality of God's bringing it about. This latter may be everlasting. So, likewise, the fact that the occurrence of this passage marks a change in our history does not entail that God's bringing it about marks a change among God's aspects. God may unchangingly bring about historical changes.

It is natural, at this point, to wonder whether we do not have in hand here a general strategy for interpreting the biblical language about God acting. Is it not perhaps the case that all those acts of God which the biblical writers speak of as beginning or as ending really consist in God performing the everlasting event of bringing about the occurrence of some temporal event?

Well, God does other things with respect to temporal events than bringing about their occurrence. For example, he also *knows* them. Why then should it be thought that the best way to interpret all the temporalevent language used to describe God's actions is by reference to God's action of bringing about the occurrence of some event? May it not be that the best way to interpret what is said with some of such language is by reference to one of those other acts which God performs with respect to temporal events? But then if God is not to change, it is not only necessary that the temporality of *e* not infect God's act of *bringing about* the occurrence of *e*, but also that *every* act of God such that he performs it with respect to *e* not be infected by the temporality of *e*. For example, if God *knows* some temporal event *e*, his knowledge of *e* must not be infected by the temporality of *e*.

So the best way of extrapolating from Aquinas's hint would probably be along the lines of the following theory concerning God's actions and the biblical speech about them. All God's actions are everlasting. None has either beginning or ending. Of these everlasting acts, the structure of some consists in God's performing some action with respect to some event. And at least some of the events that God acts with respect to are temporal events. However, in no case does the temporality of the event that God acts with respect to infect the event of his acting. On the contrary, his acting with respect to some temporal event is itself invariably an everlasting event. So whenever the biblical writers use temporal-event language to describe God's actions, they are to be interpreted as thereby claiming that God acts with respect to some temporal event. They are not to be interpreted as claiming that God's acting is itself a temporal event. God as described by the biblical writers is to be interpreted as acting, and as acting with respect to temporal events. But he is not to be interpreted as changing. All his acts are everlasting.

This, I think is a fascinating theory. If true, it provides a way of harmonizing the fundamental biblical teaching that God is a being who acts in our history, with the conviction that God does not change. How far the proposed line of biblical interpretation can be carried out, I do not know. I am not aware of any theologian who has ever tried to carry it out, though there are a great many theologians who might have relieved the tension in their thought by developing and espousing it. But what concerns us here is not so much what the theory can adequately deal with as what it cannot adequately deal with. Does the theory in fact provide us with a wholly satisfactory way of harmonizing the biblical presentation of God as acting in history with the conviction that God is fundamentally eternal?…

To refute the … Thomistic theory we would have to do one or the other of two things. We would have to show that some of the temporal-event language the biblical writers use in speaking of God's actions cannot properly be construed in the suggested way—that is, cannot be construed as used to put forth the claim that God acts in some way with respect to some temporal events. Or, alternatively, we would have to show that some of the actions that God performs with respect to temporal events are themselves temporal, either because they are infected by the temporality of the events or for some other reason.

One way of developing this latter alternative would be to show that some of God's actions must be understood as a response to the free actions of human beings—that what God does he sometimes does in response to what some human being does. I think this is in fact the case. And I think it follows, given that all human actions are temporal, that those actions of God which are "response" actions are temporal as well. But to develop this line of thought would be to plunge us deep into questions of divine omniscience and human freedom. So I shall make a simpler, though I think equally effective objection to the theory, arguing that in the case of certain of God's actions the temporality of the event that God acts on infects his own action with temporality.

Three such acts are the diverse though similar acts of knowing about some temporal event that it is occurring (that it is *present*), of knowing about some temporal event that it was occurring (that it is *past*), and of knowing about some temporal event that it will be occurring (that it is *future*). Consider the first of these. No one can know about some temporal event *e* that it is occurring except when it is occurring. Before *e* has begun to occur one cannot know that it is occurring, for it is not. Not after *e* has ceased to occur can one know that it is occurring, for it is not. So suppose that *e* has a beginning. Then P's knowing about *e* that it is occurring cannot occur until *e* begins. And suppose that *e* has an ending. Then P's knowing about *e* that it is occurring cannot occur beyond *e*'s cessation. But every temporal event has (by definition) either a beginning or an ending. So every case of knowing about some temporal event that it is occurring itself either begins or ends (or both). Hence the act of knowing about *e* that it is occurring is infected by the temporality of *e*. So also, the act of knowing about *e* that it was occurring, and the act of knowing about *e* that it *will be* occurring, are infected by the temporality of *e*.

But, God, as the biblical writers describe him, performs all three of these acts, and performs them on temporal events. He knows what is happening in our history, what has happened, and what will happen. Hence, some of God's actions are themselves temporal events. But surely the nonoccurrence followed by the occurrence followed by the nonoccurrence of such knowings constitutes a change on God's time-strand. Accordingly, God is fundamentally noneternal.

C. OMNISCIENCE

6 DIVINE OMNISCIENCE AND VOLUNTARY ACTION

NELSON PIKE

Another divine attribute typically affirmed by adherents of the Abrahamic religions is omniscience, knowledge without limit. In other words, nothing is supposed to escape God's purview. But if already among the items of God's knowledge are the outcomes of all the choices I shall make during my lifetime, are any of my actions free?

Nelson Pike (1930–2010), who was a Professor of Philosophy at the University of California, Irvine, argues that divine omniscience is incompatible with voluntary action. Note that he is not asserting that God exists or that God, if existing, is omniscient. Pike's claim is that on the supposition that God exists and is omniscient, no action is voluntary.

In Book V, sec. 3, of his *Consolatio Philosophiae*, Boethius entertained (though he later rejected) the claim that if God is omniscient, no human action is voluntary. This claim seems intuitively false. Surely, given only a doctrine describing God's *knowledge*, nothing about the voluntary status of human actions will follow. Perhaps such a conclusion would follow from a doctrine of divine omnipotence or divine providence, but what connection could there be between the claim that God is *omniscient* and the claim that human actions are determined? Yet Boethius thought he saw a problem here. He thought that if one collected together just the right assumptions and principles regarding God's knowledge, one could derive the conclusion that if God exists, no human action is voluntary. Of course, Boethius did not think that all the assumptions and principles required to reach this conclusion are true (quite the contrary), but he thought it important to draw attention to them nonetheless. If a theologian is to construct a doctrine of God's knowledge

which does not commit him to determinism, he must first understand that there is a way of thinking about God's knowledge which would so commit him.

In this paper, I shall argue that although his claim has a sharp counterintuitive ring, Boethius was right in thinking that there is a selection from among the various doctrines and principles clustering about the notions of knowledge, omniscience, and God which, when brought together, demand the conclusion that if God exists, no human action is voluntary. Boethius, I think, did not succeed in making explicit all of the ingredients in the problem. His suspicions were sound, but his discussion was incomplete. His argument needs to be developed. This is the task I shall undertake in the pages to follow. I should like to make clear at the outset that my purpose in rearguing this thesis is not to show that determinism is true, nor to show that God does not exist, nor to show that either determinism is true or God does not exist. Following Boethius, I shall not claim that the

From *The Philosophical Review* 74 (1965).

items needed to generate the problem are either philosophically or theologically adequate. I want to concentrate attention on the implications of a certain set of assumptions. Whether the assumptions are themselves acceptable is a question I shall not consider....

Last Saturday afternoon, Jones mowed his lawn. Assuming that God exists and is (essentially) omniscient in the sense outlined above, it follows that (let us say) eighty years prior to last Saturday afternoon, God knew (and thus believed) that Jones would mow his lawn at that time. But from this it follows, I think, that at the time of action (last Saturday afternoon) Jones was not *able*—that is, it was not *within Jones's power*—to refrain from mowing his lawn.[1] If at the time of action, Jones had been able to refrain from mowing his lawn, then (the most obvious conclusion would seem to be) at the time of action, Jones was able to do something which would have brought it about that God held a false belief eighty years earlier. But God cannot in anything be mistaken. It is not possible that some belief of His was false. Thus, last Saturday afternoon, Jones was not able to do something which would have brought it about that God held a false belief eighty years ago. To suppose that it was would be to suppose that, at the time of the action, Jones was able to do something that would have brought it about that one of God's beliefs was false. Hence, given that God believed eighty years ago that Jones would mow his lawn on Saturday, if we are to assign Jones the power on Saturday to refrain from mowing his lawn, this power must not be described as the power to do something that would have rendered one of God's beliefs false. How then should we describe it vis-a-vis God and His belief? So far as I can see, there are only two other alternatives. First, we might try describing it as the power to do something that would have brought it about that God believed otherwise than He did eighty years ago; or, secondly, we might try describing it as the power to do something that would have brought it about that God (Who, by hypothesis, existed eighty years earlier) did not exist eighty years earlier—that is, as the power to do something that would

have brought it about that any person who believed eighty years ago that Jones would mow his lawn on Saturday (one of whom was, by hypothesis, God) held a false belief, and thus was not God. But again, neither of these latter can be accepted. Last Saturday afternoon, Jones was not able to do something that would have brought it about that God believed otherwise than He did eighty years ago. Even if we suppose (as was suggested by Calvin) that eighty years ago God knew Jones would mow his lawn on Saturday in the sense that He "saw" Jones mowing his lawn as if this action were occurring before Him, the fact remains that God knew (and thus believed) eighty years prior to Saturday that Jones would mow his lawn. And if God held such a belief eighty years prior to Saturday, Jones did not have the power on Saturday to do something that would have made it the case that God did not hold this belief eighty years earlier. No action performed at a given time can alter the fact that a given person held a certain belief at a time prior to the time in question. This last seems to be an a priori truth. For similar reasons, the last of the above alternatives must also be rejected. On the assumption that God existed eighty years prior to Saturday, Jones on Saturday was not able to do something that would have brought it about that God did not exist eighty years prior to that time. No action performed at a given time can alter the fact that a certain person existed at a time prior to the time in question. This, too, seems to me to be an a priori truth. But if these observations are correct, then, given that Jones mowed his lawn on Saturday, and given that God exists and is (essentially) omniscient, it seems to follow that at the time of action, Jones did not have the power to refrain from mowing his lawn. The upshot of these reflections would appear to be that Jones's mowing his lawn last Saturday cannot be counted as a voluntary action. Although I do not have an analysis of what it is for an action to be *voluntary*, it seems to me that a situation in which it would be wrong to assign Jones the *ability* or *power* to do *other* than he did would be a situation in which it would also be wrong to speak of his action as voluntary. As a general remark, if God exists and is (essentially) omniscient in the sense specified above, no human action is voluntary.[2]

As the argument just presented is somewhat complex, perhaps the following schematic representation of it will be of some use.

1. "God existed at t_1" entails "If Jones did X at t_2, God believed at t_1 that Jones would do X at t_2."
2. "God believes X" entails "X is true."
3. It is not within one's power at a given time to do something having a description that is logically contradictory.
4. It is not within one's power at a given time to do something that would bring it about that someone who held a certain belief at the time prior to the time in question did not hold that belief at the time prior to the time in question.
5. It is not within one's power at a given time to do something that would bring it about that a person who existed at an earlier time did not exist at that earlier time.
6. If God existed at t_1 and if God believed at t_1 that Jones would do X at t_2 then if it was within Jones's power at t_2 to refrain from doing X, then (1) it was within Jones's power at t_2 to do something that would have brought it about that God held a false belief at t_1, or (2) it was within Jones's power at t_2 to do something which would have brought it about that God did not hold the belief He held at t_1, or (3) it was within Jones's power at t_2 to do something that would have brought it about that any person who believed at t_1, that Jones would do X at t_2 (one of whom was, by hypothesis, God) held a false belief and thus was not God—that is, that God (who by hypothesis existed at t_1) did not exist at t_1.
7. Alternative 1 in the consequent of item 6 is false. (from 2 and 3)
8. Alternative 2 in the consequent of item 6 is false. (from 4)
9. Alternative 3 in the consequent of item 6 is false. (from 5)
10. Therefore, if God existed at t_1 and if God believed at t_1, that Jones would do X at t_2, then it was not within Jones's power at t_2 to refrain from doing X. (from 6 through 9)
11. Therefore, if God existed at t_1, and if Jones did X at t_2, it was not within Jones's power at t_2 to refrain from doing X. (from 1 and 10)

In this argument, items 1 and 2 make explicit the doctrine of God's (essential) omniscience with which I am working. Items 3, 4, and 5 express what I take to be part of the logic of the concept of ability or power as it applies to human beings. Item 6 is offered as an analytic truth. If one assigns Jones the power to refrain from doing X at t_2 (given that God believed at t_1 that he would do X at t_2), so far as I can see, one would have to describe this power in one of the three ways listed in the consequent of item 6. I do not know how to argue that these are the only alternatives, but I have been unable to find another. Item 11, when generalized for all agents and actions, and when taken together with what seems to me to be a minimal condition for the application of "voluntary action," yields the conclusion that if God exists (and is essentially omniscient in the way I have described) no human action is voluntary.

It is important to notice that the argument given in the preceding paragraphs avoids use of two concepts that are often prominent in discussions of determinism.

In the first place, the argument makes no mention of the causes of Jones's action. Say (for example, with St. Thomas)[3] that God's foreknowledge of Jones's action was, itself, the cause of the action (though I am really not sure what this means). Say, instead, that natural events or circumstances caused Jones to act. Even say that Jones's action had no cause at all. The argument outlined above remains unaffected. If eighty years prior to Saturday, God believed that Jones would mow his lawn at that time, it was not within Jones's power at the time of action to refrain from mowing his lawn. The reasoning that justifies this assertion makes no mention of a causal series preceding Jones's action.

Secondly, consider the following line of thinking. Suppose Jones mowed his lawn last Saturday. It was then *true* eighty years ago that Jones would mow his lawn at that time. Hence, on Saturday, Jones was not able to refrain from mowing his lawn. To suppose that he was would be to suppose that he was able on Saturday to do something that would have made false a proposition that was *already true* eighty years earlier. This general kind of argument for determinism is usually associated with Leibniz, although it was anticipated in chapter ix of Aristotle's *De Interpretatione*. It has been used since, with some modification, in Richard Taylor's article, "Fatalism."[4] This argument, like the one I have offered above, makes no use of the notion of causation. It turns, instead, on the notion of its being *true eighty years ago* that Jones would mow his lawn on Saturday.

I must confess that I share the misgivings of those contemporary philosophers who have wondered what (if any) sense can be attached to a statement of the form "It was true at t_1 that E would occur at t_2."[5] Does this statement mean that had someone believed, guessed, or asserted at t_2 that E would occur at t_2, he would have been right?[6] (I shall have something to say about this form of determinism later in this paper.) Perhaps it means that at t_1 there was sufficient evidence upon which to predict that E would occur at t_2.[7] Maybe it means neither of these. Maybe it means nothing at all.[8] The argument presented above presupposes that it makes a straightforward sense to suppose that God (or just anyone) held a true belief eighty years prior to Saturday. But this is not to suppose that *what* God believed *was true eighty years prior to Saturday.* Whether (or in what sense) it was true eighty years ago that Jones would mow his lawn on Saturday is a question I shall not discuss. As far as I can see, the argument in which I am interested requires nothing in the way of a decision on this issue....

To conclude: I have assumed that any statement of the form "A knows X" entails a statement of the form "A believes X" as well as a statement of the form "X is true." I have then supposed (as an analytic truth) that if a given person is omniscient, that person (1) holds no false beliefs, and (2) holds beliefs about the outcome of human actions in advance of their performance. In addition, I have assumed that the statement "If a given person is God that person is omniscient" is an a priori statement. (This last I have labeled the doctrine of God's essential omniscience.) Given these items (plus some premises concerning what is and what is not within one's power), I have argued that if God exists it is not within one's power to do other than [He] does. I have inferred from this that if God exists, no human action is voluntary.

As emphasized earlier, I do not want to claim that the assumptions underpinning the argument are acceptable. In fact, it seems to me that a theologian interested in claiming both that God is omniscient and that men have free will could deny any one (or more) of them. For example, a theologian might deny that a statement of the form "A knows X" entails a statement of the form "A believes X" (some contemporary philosophers have denied this) or, alternatively, he might claim that this entailment holds in the case of human knowledge but fails in the case of God's knowledge. This latter would be to claim that when knowledge is attributed to God, the term "knowledge" bears a sense other than the one it has when knowledge is attributed to human beings. Then again, a theologian might object to the analysis of "omniscience" with which I have been working. Although I doubt if any Christian theologian would allow that an omniscient being could believe something false, he might claim that a given person could be omniscient although he did not hold beliefs about the outcome of human actions *in advance* of their performance. (This latter is the way Boethius escaped the problem.) Still again, a theologian might deny the doctrine of God's essential omniscience. He might admit that if a given person is God that person is omniscient, but he might deny that this statement formulates an a priori truth. This would be to say that although God is omniscient, He is not *essentially* omniscient. So far as I can see, within the conceptual framework of theology employing any one of these adjustments, the problem of divine foreknowledge outlined in this paper could not be formulated. There thus appears to be a rather wide range of alternatives open to the theologian at this point. It would be a mistake to think that commitment to determinism is an unavoidable implication of the Christian concept of divine omniscience.

But having arrived at this understanding, the importance of the preceding deliberations ought not to be overlooked. There is a pitfall in the doctrine of divine omniscience. That knowing involves believing (truly) is surely a tempting philosophical view (witness the many contemporary philosophers who have affirmed it). And the idea that God's attributes (including omniscience) are essentially connected to His nature, together with the idea that an omniscient being would hold no false beliefs and would hold beliefs about the outcome of human actions in advance of their performance, might be taken by some theologians as obvious candidates for inclusion in a finished Christian theology. Yet the theologian must approach these items critically. If they are embraced together, then if one affirms the existence of God, one is committed to the view that no human action is voluntary.

NOTES

1. The notion of someone being *able* to do something and the notion of something being *within one's power* are essentially the same. Traditional formulations of the problem of divine foreknowledge (e.g., those of Boethius and Augustine) made use of the notion of what is (and what is not) *within one's power*. But the problem is the same when framed in terms of what one is (and one is not) able to do. Thus, I shall treat the statements "Jones was able to do X," "Jones had the ability to do X," and "It was within Jones's power to do X" as equivalent. Richard Taylor, in "I Can," *Philosophical Review*, 69 (1960): 78–89, has argued that the notion of ability or power involved in these last three statements is incapable of philosophical analysis. Be this as it may, I shall not here attempt such an analysis. In what follows

I shall, however, be careful to affirm only those statements about what is (or is not) within one's power that would have to be preserved on any analysis of this notion having even the most distant claim to adequacy.

2. In Bk. II, ch. xxi, secs. 8–11 of *An Essay*, Locke says that an agent is not free with respect to a given action (e.g., that an action is done "under necessity") when it is not within the agent's power to do otherwise. Locke allows a special kind of case, however, in which an action may be *voluntary* though done under necessity. If a man chooses to do something without knowing that it is not within his power to do otherwise (e.g., if a man chooses to stay in a room without knowing that the room is locked), his action may be voluntary though he is not free to forbear it. If Locke is right in this (and I shall not argue the point one way or the other), replace "voluntary" with (let us say) "free" in the above paragraph and throughout the remainder of this paper.

3. Aquinas, *Summa Theologicae*, Pt. I, q. 14, a. 8.

4. Richard Taylor, "Fatalism," *Philosophical Review*, 71 (1962): 56–66. Taylor argues that if an event *E* fails to occur at *t*, then at *t*, it was true *E* would fail to occur at *t*. Thus, at *t*, no one could have the power to perform an action that would be sufficient for the occurrence of *E* at *t*. Hence, no one has the power at *t* to do something sufficient for an event that is not going to happen. The parallel between this argument and the one recited above can be seen very clearly if one reformulates Taylor's argument, pushing back the time at which it was true that *E* would not occur at *t*.

5. For a helpful discussion of difficulties involved here, see Rogers Albritton's "Present Truth and Future Contingency," a reply to Richard Taylor's "The Problem of Future Contingency," both in *Philosophical Review*, 66 (1957): 1–28.

6. Gilbert Ryle interprets it this way. See "It Was to Be," in *Dilemmas* (Cambridge, England, 1954).

7. Richard Gale suggests this interpretation in "Endorsing Predictions," *Philosophical Review*, 70 (1961): 376–85.

8. This view is held by John Turk Saunders in "Sea Fight Tomorrow?" *Philosophical Review*, 67 (1958): 367–78.

7 POWER OVER THE PAST

WILLIAM L. ROWE

One proposed solution to the problem Pike poses is explained in our next selection by William L. Rowe, who is Professor Emeritus of Philosophy at Purdue University. He argues that some facts about the past are not simply about the past and so may be within our power to affect.

   Rowe does not commit himself to the solution he explains but considers it a promising approach to demonstrating that divine omniscience and human freedom do not conflict.

We've had a look at perhaps the strongest argument for the view that the doctrine of divine foreknowledge ... is in fundamental conflict with the belief in human freedom, an argument that has troubled philosophers and theologians for centuries....

[One] solution challenges the claim that it is never in our power to determine the past, arguing that we do have the power to determine certain facts about the past, including certain facts about what God knew before we were even born. This solution was suggested by the most influential philosopher of the fourteenth century, William of Ockham (1285–1349).

The basic point on which the ... solution rests involves a distinction between two types of facts about the past: facts which are *simply* about the past, and facts which are *not simply* about the past. To illustrate this distinction, let's consider two facts about the past, facts about the year 1941.

> f_1: In 1941 Japan attacks Pearl Harbor.
>
> f_2: In 1941 a war begins between Japan and the United States that lasts four years.

Relative to the twenty-first century, f_1 and f_2 are both *simply* about the past. But suppose we consider the year 1943. Relative to 1943, f_1 is a fact that is simply about the past, but f_2 is not simply about the past. It is a fact about the past relative to 1943, for f_2 is, in part, a fact about

1941, and 1941 lies in 1943's past. But f_2, unlike f_1, implies a certain fact about 1944—namely,

> f_3: In 1944 Japan and the United States are at war.

Since f_2 implies f_3, a fact about the future relative to 1943, we can say that relative to 1943 f_2 is a fact about the past, but not simply a fact about the past. We have then three facts, f_1, f_2, and f_3, about which we can say that relative to the twenty-first century each is a fact simply about the past. Relative to 1943, however, only f_1 is simply about the past; f_2 is about the past but not simply about the past, and f_3 is not about the past at all.

Having illustrated the distinction between a fact which, relative to a certain time t, is simply about the past and a fact which, relative to t, is not simply about the past, we are now in a position to appreciate its importance. Think of 1943 and the groups of persons then in power in both Japan and the United States. Neither group had it in its power to do anything about f_1. Both groups may have regretted the actions which brought it about that f_1 is a fact about the past. But it is abundantly clear that among all the things which, in 1943, it was in their power to do, none is such that, had they done it, f_1 would not have been a fact about the past. It makes no sense to look back upon 1943 and say that if only one of these groups had *then* done such-and-such, f_1 would never have been a fact about the past. It makes no sense precisely because, relative to 1943, f_1 is

From William L. Rowe, *Philosophy of Religion*, Fourth Edition, Thomson/Wadsworth, 2007. Reprinted by permission of the publisher..

a fact *simply* about the past. Nothing that could have been done by anyone in 1943 would have in any way affected the fact that in 1941 Japan attacked Pearl Harbor.

But what about f_2, the fact that in 1941 a war begins between Japan and the United States that lasts four years. We know that in 1943 neither group did anything that affected this fact about 1941. The question, however, is whether there were things that were not done in 1943, things which, nevertheless, were in the power of one or both of the groups to do, such that, had they been done, a certain fact about 1941, f_2, would not have been a fact at all. Perhaps there were not. Perhaps the momentum of the war was such that neither group had the power to bring it to an end in 1943. Most of us, I suppose, think otherwise. We think that there probably were certain actions that were not, but could have been, taken by one or both of the groups in 1943, actions which, had they been taken, would have brought the war to an end in 1943. If what we think to be so is so, then it was in the power of one or both of the groups in 1943 to determine a fact about the past; it was in their power in 1943 to do something such that, had they done it, a certain fact about 1941, f_2, would not have been a fact about 1941. The basic reason why in 1943 f_2 may have been in their power, whereas f_1 certainly was not, is that, unlike f_1, f_2 is not simply about the past relative to 1943, for f_2 implies a certain fact about 1944—that in 1944, Japan and the United States are at war (f_3).

What the above reasoning suggests is that our conviction that the past is beyond our power to affect is certainly true, so far as facts which are simply about the past are concerned. Facts which are about the past, but *not simply* about the past, may not, however, be beyond our power to affect. And what Ockham saw is that the facts about divine foreknowledge which are used as the basis for denying human freedom are facts about the past, but *not simply* about the past. Consider again the fact that before you were born, God knew that you would be in class at 2:30 this Tuesday. We want to believe that at 2:00 it was in your power to do otherwise, to refrain from coming to class at 2:30. To ascribe this power to you implies that it was in your power at 2:00 to affect a fact about the past,

the fact that before you were born God knew that you would be in class at 2:30. This fact about the past, however, is not, relative to 2:00, a fact simply about the past. For it implies a fact about the future relative to 2:00—namely, that at 2:30 you are in class. And the solution we are exploring holds that such a fact about the past was in your power to affect if it was in your power at 2:00, as we believe it was, to have gone to a movie instead of coming to class. For it was then in your power to have done something such that, had you done it, what *is* a fact about a time before you were born *would not have been* a fact at all; instead, it would have been a fact that before you were born God knew that you would not be in class at 2:30. Of course, there will still be many facts about God's foreknowledge that are not in your power: all those facts, for example, that relative to the time you are at, are facts simply about the past. The very fact which may have been in your power at 2:00—the fact that before you were born God knew you would be in class at 2:30—is, at 2:45 when you are sitting in class regretting that you did not go to a movie, a fact that cannot *then* (at 2:45) be in your power, because at 2:45 it is a fact simply about the past. And there are many facts involving divine foreknowledge that are not simply about the past, which, nevertheless, are not in your power to affect, for the facts that they imply about the future do not fall within the scope of your power. For example, God knew before you were born that the sun would rise tomorrow. This fact about the past is not simply about the past because it implies a fact about tomorrow, that the sun will rise. It is nevertheless, a fact which is not in your power to affect.

The solution we have been considering ... denies ... that the past is never in our power. The solution argues that some facts about the past are not simply about the past, that some such facts may be within our power.... So, according to the ... solution, we have no good reasons for accepting the ... argument leading from divine foreknowledge to the denial of human freedom. And without such reasons, it has yet to be shown that there is any real difficulty in holding both that God knows before we are born everything we will do and that we sometimes have the power to do otherwise.

8 DOES GOD KNOW THE FUTURE?

STEVEN M. CAHN

In our next selection Steven M. Cahn, the editor of this volume and Professor of Philosophy at The Graduate Center of The City University of New York, maintains that if we have free will, God does not know the outcome of our future choices. After defending this claim against a series of objections, Cahn goes on to argue that despite God's not knowing the decisions we shall make, God might still be described appropriately as omniscient.

In the Book of Deuteronomy, God says to the people of Israel, "I have put before you life and death, blessing and curse. Choose life—if you and your offspring would live...."[1] Did God know which option the people would choose? If so, how could their choice have been free? For if God knew they would choose life, then to have chosen death would have confuted God's knowledge—which is impossible. If God knew they would choose death, then to have chosen life would also have confuted God's knowledge. But God gave the people a genuine choice. So even God did not know how they would choose.

I find this line of argument persuasive, but many notable thinkers have believed it unsound. In what follows I shall present briefly a sampling of their objections and my replies.

Objection 1. "Just as your memory does not force the past to have happened, God's fore-knowledge does not force the future to happen." So argued St. Augustine.[2]

Reply. Admittedly, my remembering that an event occurred does not cause the event's occurrence. And God's foreknowledge that an event will occur does not cause its occurrence. But if I know that an event occurred, then it is not within my power to alter its occurrence. Not only won't I alter it, I can't. Similarly, if God knows that an event will occur, then it is not within God's power

to alter its occurrence. Even assuming God is all-powerful, God can only do what is logically possible, for what is logically impossible is incoherent, and an incoherent task is no task at all. Thus if an event will occur, even if God does not cause its occurrence, God is bound by logic to allow its occurrence. In short, knowledge does not cause events, but, given definitive knowledge of events, they are unavoidable.

Objection 2. "[W]e estimate the intimacy of relationship between two persons by the fore-knowledge one has of the action of the other, without supposing that in either case the one or the other's freedom has thereby been endangered. So even divine foreknowledge cannot endanger freedom." So said the German theologian Friedrich Schleiermacher.[3]

Reply. We rarely claim more than strong belief about what others will do, for we realize that however likely our prediction, we may be proved wrong. But when we do possess knowledge, it is incompatible with free choice. For example, we know we all shall die. It follows that it is not within anyone's power to remain alive forever. If we knew not only *that* we would die but also when, where, and how we would die, then we could not avoid death in the known time, place, and manner. Strong beliefs can be confuted, but not knowledge.

Objection 3. "It is not true, then, that because God foreknew what would be within the power of

From Steven M. Cahn and David Shatz, *Questions About God: Today's Philosophers Ponder the Divine,* Oxford University Press, 2002. Reprinted by permission of the author.

our wills, nothing therefore lies within the power of our wills. For when He foreknew this, He did not foreknow nothing. Therefore, if He who foreknew what would lie within the power of our wills did not foreknow nothing, but something, then clearly something lies within in the power of our wills even though God has foreknowledge of it." Again, St. Augustine.[4]

Reply. This line of reasoning begs the question, assuming what is supposed to be proved. If God foreknew our free choices, then they would be free. But can God foreknow our free choices? The argument I presented originally concludes that God cannot foreknow our free choices. Simply assuming the possibility of such foreknowledge carries no weight against the argument and identifies no mistake in it.

Objection 4. "[S]ince God lives in the eternal present, His knowledge transcends all movement of time and abides in the simplicity of its immediate present. It encompasses the infinite sweep of past and future, and regards all things in its simple comprehension as if they were now taking place. Thus if you will think about the foreknowledge by which God distinguishes all things, you will rightly consider it to be not a foreknowledge of future events, but knowledge of a never changing present." So argued the Roman philosopher Boethius.[5]

Reply. We make certain choices before others. Indeed, certain choices presuppose others. For example, the choice to seek a divorce requires a prior choice to marry. Whatever is meant by the assertion that God transcends time (a murky claim), God presumably knows that we make certain choices before others. So God takes account of time. Admittedly, God is supposed to view the future as clearly as we view the present. But appeals to the clarity of God's knowledge only underscore why that knowledge is incompatible with the freedom of choices we are yet to make.

Objection 5. "[T]hough we do not know the true nature of God's knowledge ... yet we know that ... nothing of all existing things is hidden from Him and that His knowledge of them does not change their nature, but the possible retains its nature as a possibility. Anything in this enumeration that appears contradictory is so only owing to the structure of our knowledge, which has nothing in common with His knowledge except the name." So wrote the medieval Jewish sage Maimonides.[6]

Reply. If God's knowledge has nothing in common with human knowledge, then God's knowledge, unlike human knowledge, would not imply the truth of what is known. So God's knowledge, whatever its nature, may be compatible with free choice but only in some sense not relevant to the original argument. If we do not understand the meaning of the words we use, we cannot use them to make claims we understand.

Supposing that the argument with which I began can be sustained in the face of all criticisms (and much more can be said on both sides), does it follow that God lacks omniscience? Not if one adopts the view, which some commentators have attributed to Aristotle,[7] that statements about future choices are neither true nor false, but, at present, indeterminate. According to this view, it is not now true you will finish reading this entire book and not true you won't. Until you decide, the matter is indeterminate.

As the medieval Jewish philosopher Gersonides argued, to be omniscient is to know every true statement. Because it is not true you will finish reading the entire book and not true you won't, but true that the matter is indeterminate, an omniscient being does not know you will finish reading and does not know you won't, but does know the whole truth, namely, that the matter is indeterminate and depends on your free choice.

Thus assuming God is omniscient, God knows the entire physical structure of the universe but not the outcome of free choices. As Gersonides wrote, "[T]he fact that God does not have the knowledge of which possible outcome will be realized does not imply any defect in God (may He be blessed). For perfect knowledge of something is the knowledge of what that thing is in reality; when the thing is not apprehended as it is, this is error, not knowledge. Hence, God knows these things in the best manner possible...."[8]

In other words, when God offered the people of Israel both life and death, God, although omniscient, did not know which choice they would make. God knew all that was knowable, the whole truth. But the whole truth was that the choice of life or death rested with the people of Israel. They were responsible for their decision. God awaited, but could not foresee, the outcome of their exercise of freedom.

Some may find this view unsettling, because it implies that God's knowledge, while in a sense complete, does not include within its purview definitive answers to all questions about the future. But, like Gersonides, I find this conclusion consistent with the Holy Scriptures. As Gersonides wrote,

God (may He be blessed), by means of the Prophets, commands men who are about to suffer evil fortune that they mend their ways so that they will avert this punishment.... Now this indicates that what God knows of future events is known by Him as not necessarily occurring.[9]

In short, divine warnings imply uncertain outcomes.

I conclude with an admission. Certain Biblical passages may suggest, contrary to what I have argued, that God knows the future in all its details, including the outcome of future free choices. If such textual evidence were presented, how would I respond? I could echo Gersonides: "If the literal sense of the Torah differs from reason, it is necessary to interpret these passages in accordance with the demands of reason."[10] The task of developing such interpretations, if required, I would leave to others.

NOTES

1. *Tanakh: The Holy Scriptures* (Philadelphia: Jewish Publication Society, 1988), Deuteronomy 30:19.
2. *On Free Choice of the Will*, trans. Thomas Williams (Indianapolis: Hackett Publishing Company, 1993), Book III, sec. 4, p. 78.
3. *The Christian Faith*, eds. H.R. Mackintosh and J.S. Stewart (Edinburgh: T. and T. Clark, 1928), p. 228.
4. *The City of God Against the Pagans*, trans. R.W. Dysen (Cambridge: Cambridge University Press, 1998), Book V, sec. 10, p. 205.
5. *The Consolation of Philosophy*, trans. Richard Green (New York: Library of Liberal Arts, 1962), Book 5, prose 6, p. 116.
6. *The Guide of the Perplexed*, trans. Chaim Rabin (Indianapolis: Hackett Publishing Company, 1995), p. 163.
7. See, for example, Richard Taylor, "The Problem of Future Contingencies," *The Philosophical Review* 66 (1957), pp. 1–28.
8. *The Wars of the Lord*, trans. Seymour Feldman (Philadelphia: Jewish Publication Society, 1987), vol. 2, p. 118.
9. Ibid., p. 118.
10. Ibid., p. 98.

D. SUPREME GOODNESS

9 GOD AND MORALITY

STEVEN M. CAHN

Adherents to the Abrahamic religions typically affirm the supreme goodness of God. But is God supremely good because God always acts in accord with a standard of rightness, or because God creates the standard of rightness? In other words, does God choose the standard of rightness, or is God subject to the standard? Either answer raises difficulties, as I seek to explain in the following essay.

According to many religions, although not all, the world was created by God, an all-powerful, all-knowing, all-good being. Although God's existence has been doubted, let us for the moment assume its truth. What implications of this supposition would be relevant to our lives?

Some people would feel more secure in the knowledge that the world had been planned by an all-good being. Others would feel insecure, realizing the extent to which their existence depended on a decision of this being. In any case, most people, out of either fear or respect, would wish to act in accord with God's will.

Belief in God by itself, however, provides no hint whatsoever which actions God wishes us to perform or what we ought to do to please or obey God. We may affirm that God is all-good, yet have no way of knowing the highest moral standards. All we may presume is that, whatever these standards, God always acts in accordance with them. We might expect God to have implanted the correct moral standards in our minds, but this supposition is doubtful in view of the conflicts among people's intuitions. Furthermore, even if consensus prevailed, it might only be a means by which God tests us to see whether we have the courage to dissent from popular opinion.

According to many religions, although not all, the world was created by God, an all-powerful, all-knowing, all-good being. Although God's existence has been doubted, let us for the moment assume its truth. What implications of this supposition would be relevant to our lives?

Some people would feel more secure in the knowledge that the world had been planned by an all-good being. Others would feel insecure, realizing the extent to which their existence depended on a decision of this being. In any case, most people, out of either fear or respect, would wish to act in accord with God's will.

Belief in God by itself, however, provides no hint whatsoever which actions God wishes us to perform or what we ought to do to please or obey God. We may affirm that God is all-good, yet have no way of knowing the highest moral standards. All we may presume is that, whatever these standards, God always acts in accordance with them. We might expect God to have implanted the correct moral standards in our minds, but this supposition is doubtful in view of the conflicts among people's intuitions. Furthermore, even if consensus prevailed, it might only be a means by which God tests us to see whether we have the courage to dissent from popular opinion.

Some would argue that if God exists, then murder is immoral, because it destroys what God with infinite wisdom created. This argument, however, fails on several grounds. First, God also created germs, viruses, and disease-carrying rats. Because God created these things, ought they not be eliminated? Second, if God arranged for us to live, God also arranged for us to die. By killing, are we assisting the work of God? Third, God provided us with the mental and physical potential to commit murder. Does God wish us to fulfill this potential?

Thus God's existence alone does not imply any particular moral precepts.

We may hope our actions are in accord with God's standards, but no test is available to check whether what we do is best in God's eyes. Some seemingly good people suffer great ills, whereas some seemingly evil people achieve happiness. Perhaps in a future life these outcomes will be reversed, but we have no way of ascertaining who, if anyone, is ultimately punished and who ultimately rewarded.

Over the course of history, those who believed in God's existence typically were eager to learn God's will and tended to rely on those individuals who claimed to possess such insight. Diviners, seers, and priests were given positions of great influence. Competition among them was severe, however, for no one could be sure which oracle to believe.

In any case prophets died, and their supposedly revelatory powers disappeared with them. For practical purposes what was needed was a permanent record of God's will. This requirement was met by the writing of holy books in which God's will was revealed to all.

But even though many such books were supposed to embody the will of God, they conflicted with one another. Which was to be accepted? Belief in the existence of God by itself yields no answer.

Let us suppose, however, that an individual becomes persuaded that a reliable guide to God's will is contained in the Ten Commandments. This person, therefore, believes it wrong to commit adultery, steal, or murder.

But why is it wrong? Is it wrong because God says it is wrong, or does God say it is wrong because it is wrong?

This crucial issue was raised more than two thousand years ago in

Plato's remarkable dialogue, the Euthyphro. Plato's teacher, Socrates, who in most of Plato's works is given the leading role, asks the overconfident

Euthyphro whether actions are right because God says they are right, or whether God says actions are right because they are right.

In other words, Socrates was inquiring whether actions are right because of God's fiat or whether God is subject to moral standards. If actions are right because of God's command, then anything God commands would be right. Had God commanded adultery, stealing, and murder, then adultery, stealing, and murder would be right—surely an unsettling and to many an unacceptable conclusion.

Granted, some may be willing to adopt this discomforting view, but then they face another difficulty. If the good is whatever God commands, to say that God's commands are good amounts to saying that God's commands are

God's commands, a mere tautology or repetition of words. In that case, the possibility of meaningfully praising the goodness of God would be lost.

The lesson here is that might does not make right, even if the might is the infinite might of God. To act morally is not to act out of fear of punishment; it is not to act as one is commanded to act. Rather, it is to act as one ought to act, and how one ought to act is not dependent on anyone's power, even if the power be divine.

Thus actions are not right because God commands them; on the contrary, God commands them because they are right. What is right is independent of what God commands, for what God commands must conform to an independent standard in order to be right.

We could act intentionally in accord with this independent standard without believing in the existence of God; therefore morality does not rest on that belief. Consequently, those who do not believe in God can be highly moral (as well as immoral people), and those who do believe in the existence of God can be highly immoral (as well as moral) people. This conclusion should come as no surprise to anyone who has contrasted the benevolent life of the inspiring teacher the Buddha, an atheist, with the malevolent life of the monk Torquemada, who devised and enforced the boundless cruelties of the Spanish Inquisition.

In short, believing in the existence of God does not by itself imply any specific moral principles, and knowing God's will does not provide any justification for morality.

10 A MODIFIED DIVINE COMMAND THEORY

ROBERT M. ADAMS

Robert M. Adams, who is Research Professor of Philosophy at the University of North Carolina at Chapel Hill, considers the possibility that God might command us to act immorally. Should we obey such a command? If so, we act immorally. If not, we act against the will of God, whose commands are not then supreme. Adams seeks a way out of the impasse by defining a moral act as one that is in accord with the commands of a loving God. Whether some form of that strategy can succeed is a matter for readers to assess.

It will be helpful to begin with the statement of a simple, *unmodified* divine command theory of ethical wrongness. This is the theory that ethical wrongness *consists in* being contrary to God's commands, or that the word 'wrong' in ethical contexts *means* 'contrary to God's commands'. It implies that the following two statement forms are logically equivalent.

1. It is wrong (for A) to do X.
2. It is contrary to God's commands (for A) to do X.

Of course that is not all that the theory implies. It also implies that (2) is conceptually prior to (1), so that the meaning of (1) is to be explained in terms of (2), and not the other way around. It might prove fairly difficult to state or explain in what that conceptual priority consists, but I shall not go into that here. I do not wish ultimately to defend the theory in its unmodified form, and I think I have stated it fully enough for my present purposes....

The following seems to me to be the gravest objection to the divine command theory of ethical wrongness, in the form in which I have stated it. Suppose God should command me to make it my chief end in life to inflict suffering on other human beings, for no other reason than that he commanded it. (For convenience I shall abbreviate this hypothesis to 'Suppose God should command cruelty for its own sake'.) Will it seriously be claimed that in that case it would be wrong for me not to practice cruelty for its own sake? I see three possible answers to this question.

From Robert M. Adams, "A Modified Divine Command Theory of Ethical Wrongness," in *Religion and Morality: A Collection of Essays*, eds. Gene Outka and John P. Reeder, Jr., Doubleday & Company, Inc., 1973. Reprinted by permission of the publisher.

(1) It might be claimed that it is logically impossible for God to command cruelty for its own sake. In that case, of course, we need not worry about whether it would be wrong to disobey if he did command it. It is senseless to agonize about what one should do in a logically impossible situation. This solution to the problem seems unlikely to be available to the divine command theorist, however. For why would he hold that it is logically impossible for God to command cruelty for its own sake? Some theologians (for instance, Thomas Aquinas) have believed (a) that what is right and wrong is independent of God's will, *and* (b) that God always does right by the necessity of his nature. Such theologians, if they believe that it would be wrong for God to command cruelty for its own sake, have reason to believe that it is logically impossible for him to do so. But the divine command theorist, who does not agree that what is right and wrong is independent of God's will, does not seem to have such a reason to deny that it is logically possible for God to command cruelty for its own sake.

(2) Let us assume that it is logically possible for God to command cruelty for its own sake. In that case the divine command theory seems to imply that it would be wrong not to practice cruelty for its own sake. There have been at least a few adherents of divine command ethics who have been prepared to accept this consequence. William Ockham held that those acts which we call "theft," "adultery," and "hatred of God" would be meritorious if God had commanded them.[1] He would surely have said the same about what I have been calling the practice of "cruelty for its own sake."

This position is one which I suspect most of us are likely to find somewhat shocking, even repulsive. We should therefore be particularly careful not to misunderstand it. We need not imagine that Ockham disciplined himself to be ready to practice cruelty for its own sake if God should command it. It was doubtless an article of faith for him that God is unalterably opposed to any such practice. The mere logical possibility that theft, adultery, and cruelty might have been commanded by God (and therefore meritorious) doubtless did not represent in Ockham's view any real possibility.

(3) Nonetheless, the view that if God commanded cruelty for its own sake it would be wrong not to practice it seems unacceptable to me; and I think many, perhaps most, other Jewish and Christian believers would find it unacceptable too. I must make clear the sense in which I find it unsatisfactory. It is not that I find an internal inconsistency in it. And I would not deny that it may reflect, accurately enough, the way in which some believers use the word 'wrong'. I might as well frankly avow that I am looking for a divine command theory which at least might possibly be a correct account of how *I* use the word 'wrong'. I do not use the word 'wrong' in such a way that I would say that it would be wrong not to practice cruelty if God commanded it, and I am sure that many other believers agree with me on this point.

But now have I not rejected the divine command theory? I have assumed that it would be logically possible for God to command cruelty for its own sake. And I have rejected the view that if God commanded cruelty for its own sake, it would be wrong not to obey. It seems to follow that I am committed to the view that in certain logically possible circumstances it would not be wrong to disobey God. This position seems to be inconsistent with the theory that 'wrong' means 'contrary to God's commands'.

I want to argue, however, that it is still open to me to accept a modified form of the divine command theory of ethical wrongness. According to the modified divine command theory, when I say, 'It is wrong to do X', (at least part of) what I *mean* is that it is contrary to God's commands to do X. 'It is wrong to do X' *implies* 'It is contrary to God's commands to do X'. But 'It is contrary to God's commands to do X' implies 'It is wrong to do X' only if certain conditions are assumed—namely, only if it is assumed that God has the character which I believe him to have, of loving his human creatures. If God were really to command us to make cruelty our goal, then he would not have that character of loving us, and I would not say it would be wrong to disobey him.

But do I say that it would be wrong to obey him in such a case? This is the point at which I am in danger of abandoning the divine command theory completely. I do abandon it completely if I say both of the following things.

(A) It would be wrong to obey God if he commanded cruelty for its own sake.

(B) In (A), 'wrong' is used in what is for me its normal ethical sense.

If I assert both (A) and (B), it is clear that I cannot consistently maintain that 'wrong' in its normal ethical sense for me means or implies 'contrary to God's commands'.

But from the fact that I deny that it would be wrong to disobey God if He commanded cruelty for its own sake, it does not follow that I must accept (A) and (B). Of course someone might claim that obedience and disobedience would both be ethically permitted in such a case; but that is not the view that I am suggesting. If I adopt the modified divine command theory as an analysis of my present concept of ethical wrongness (and if I adopt a similar analysis of my concept of ethical permittedness), I will not hold either that it would be wrong to disobey, or that it would be ethically permitted to disobey, or that it would be wrong to obey, or that it would be ethically permitted to obey, if God commanded cruelty for its own sake. For I will say that my concept of ethical wrongness (and my concept of ethical permittedness) would "break down" if I really believed that God commanded cruelty for its own sake. Or to put the matter somewhat more prosaically, I will say that my concepts of ethical wrongness and permittedness could not serve the functions they now serve, because using those concepts I could not call any action ethically wrong or ethically permitted, if I believed that God's will was so unloving.

NOTE

1. Guillelmus de Occam, *Super 4 libros sententiarum*, bk. II, qu. 19, O, in vol. IV of his *Opera plurima* (Lyon, 1494–6; réimpression en fac-similé, Farnborough, Hants., England: Gregg Press, 1962). I am not claiming that Ockham held a divine command theory of exactly the same sort that I have been discussing.

11 GOD'S VIRTUES

LINDA TRINKOUS ZAGZEBSKI

Linda Trinkous Zagzebski, who is Professor of Philosophy at the University of Oklahoma, urges that we think of God not as a lawgiver, issuing commands, but as a moral exemplar, exhibiting mercy, compassion, and justice. Thus God could not command us to brutalize the innocent, as Adams hypothesized in the previous selection, because loving is one of God's essential motives.

Zagzebski does not view morality as a deontological system, such as Kant's, based on acting in accord with duties, or as a consequentialist system, such as John Stuart Mill's, based on maximizing preferred outcomes, but rather as a system of virtue ethics, such as Aristotle's, that focuses on developing character rather than following rules. So we should derive the goodness of human motives from the example provided by the supreme goodness of divine motives.

From Linda Trinkous Zagzebski, *Philosophy of Religion: An Historical Introduction*, Blackwell Publishing, 2007. Reprinted by permission of the publisher.

In a famous question in Plato's *Euthyphro*, Socrates asks, "Is the pious being loved by the gods because it is pious, or is it pious because it is being loved by the gods?" (10a). This question has subsequently been used as a dilemma for Divine Command (DC) theory, although Plato was using it to make a point about definition, not to refute a theory nobody held at the time. As applied to DC theory, the dilemma is this: If God wills the good (right) because it is good (right), then goodness (rightness) is independent of God's will, and the latter does not explain the former. On the other hand, if something is good (right) because God wills it, then it looks as if the divine will is arbitrary. God is not constrained by any moral reason from willing anything whatever, and it is hard to see how any non-moral reason could be the right sort of reason to determine God's choice of what to make good or right. The apparent consequence is that good/bad (right/wrong) are determined by an arbitrary divine will; God could have commanded cruelty or hatred, and if he had done so, cruel and hateful acts would have been right, even duties. This is an unacceptable consequence. It is contrary to our sense of the essential nature of the moral properties of certain acts, and the goodness of a God who could make cruelty good is not at all what we normally mean by good. It is therefore hard to see how it can be true that God himself is good in any important, substantive sense of good on this approach.

To solve this problem Robert Adams modifies DC theory to say that the property of rightness is the property of being commanded by a *loving* God. This permits Adams to allow that God could command cruelty for its own sake, but if God did so he would not love us, and if that were the case, Adams argues, morality would break down. Morality *is* dependent upon divine commands, but they are dependent upon the commands of a deity with a certain nature and with a certain relationship to us. Divine commands are not arbitrary, since they are constrained by God's nature, but neither do they affirm an independent realm of obligation. They are akin to the requirements persons make of those whom they love. Lovers impose demands on those they love, but a demand only constitutes a requirement under the assumption that the lover is good and the relationship itself is good.

Many other philosophers have proposed versions of DC theory, but my own preference is to look in a different direction for a way God is related to morality. My reason is not that I think that DC theory has insurmountable difficulties, but that DC theory is a kind of theory that makes morals fundamentally a matter of law, of obligation. I think that a virtue ethics is a preferable form of ethical theory, and that a virtue theory grounded in God's virtues is a better candidate to provide the metaphysical grounding of ethics than a theory grounded in God's will. In any case, I have proposed a theory in which God has a foundational role in ethics as an exemplar rather than as a lawgiver. This approach has advantages for the ethics of religions that identify particular persons as paradigmatically good, as in Christian ethics, and since it permits distinct but overlapping versions for different cultures, it has advantages for the task of constructing a common morality. I call the theory Divine Motivation theory.[1]

In Divine Motivation (DM) theory, all moral properties are grounded in the motives of God. Motives are emotions, but I call an emotion a motive when it is initiating action. Motive-dispositions are components of virtues. The divine motives can be considered divine emotions although I do not insist that they are literally emotions.[2] They are states like love and compassion. Whether or not these states are properly classified as emotions, they are motivating. God acts *out of* love, joy, compassion, and perhaps also anger and disgust. These are the states that I propose constitute the metaphysical basis for moral value. They are components of God's virtues. Given that we do not experience God directly, we identify virtues by the paradigmatic but imperfect instances of virtuous persons in our experience, and we acquire them by imitation.

The structure of the theory is exemplarist. The moral properties of persons, acts, and outcomes are defined via direct reference to an exemplar of a good person. God is the ultimate exemplar, but there are many finitely good human exemplars. Although we imitate finite exemplars, the metaphysical basis of value is God. Value in all forms derives from God, in particular, from God's motives. God's motives are perfectly good, and human motives are good in so far as they are like the divine motives as those motives would be expressed in finite and embodied beings. Motive-dispositions are constituents of virtues. A virtue is an enduring trait consisting of a good motive-disposition and reliable success in bringing about the aim, if any, of the good motive. God's virtues are paradigmatically good personal traits. Human virtues are those traits that imitate God's virtues as they would be expressed by human beings in human circumstances. The goodness of a state of affairs is derivative from the goodness of the divine motive. Outcomes get their moral value by their relation to good and bad motivations. For example, a state of affairs is a merciful one or a compassionate one or a just one because the divine motives that are constituents of mercy, compassion, and justice respectively aim at bringing them about. Acts get their moral value from the acts that would, would not, or might be done by God in the relevant circumstances.

The exemplarist structure of DM theory allows versions for different religions as well as cultural traditions that are non-religious but recognize common exemplars of goodness within the tradition. In Plato and the Stoics we become like God by becoming virtuous, which means to imitate Socrates or the Stoic Sage. In Christianity Jesus Christ is both God and man, the exemplar of God in human nature. For Aristotle, the exemplar is the person with practical wisdom. Other religions have exemplars as well–the Buddhist *arahant*, the Jewish *tzaddik*, and so on.[3] If there is a God of all peoples, it would not be surprising that there is as much commonality among the exemplars of different cultures and religious traditions as is compatible with the differences in their experiences and the degree to which they have reached an understanding of the divine. In contrast, DC theory has the problem of explaining how morality can be grounded in divine commands promulgated only to a certain group of people.

Let us return to the *Euthyphro* problem for DC theory. If morality is grounded in God's commands and if God can command anything, then it looks as if God could command brutalizing the innocent, in which case brutalizing the innocent

would have been an obligation. But that is unacceptable. As we saw above, Adams proposes that moral obligation is grounded in the commands of a loving God, but even though his proposal may succeed in answering the objection it is designed to address, it appears to be *ad hoc*. There is no intrinsic connection between a command and the property of being loving, so to tie morality to the commands of a loving God is to tie it to two distinct properties of God, only one of which involves commands. In DM theory there is no need to solve the problem of whether God could make it right that we brutalize the innocent by making any such modification to the theory, since being loving is one of God's essential motives. The right thing for humans to do is to act on motives that imitate the divine motives. Brutalizing the innocent is not an act that expresses a motive that imitates the divine motives. Hence, it is impossible for brutalizing the innocent to be right as long as (i) it is impossible for such an act to be an expression of a motive that is like the motives of God, and (ii) it is impossible for God to have different motives. Assumption (ii) follows from the plausible assumption that God's motives are part of his nature.[4]

The arbitrariness problem also does not arise in DM theory. That is because a will needs a reason, but a motive *is* a reason. The will, according to Aquinas, always chooses "under the aspect of good," which means that reasons are not inherent in the will itself.[5] In contrast, motives provide not only the impetus to action, but the reason *for* the action. If we know that God acts from a motive of love, there is no need to look for a further reason for the act. On the other hand, a divine command requires a reason, and if the reason is or includes fundamental divine motivational states such as love, it follows that even DC theory needs to refer to God's motives to avoid the consequence that moral properties are arbitrary and God himself is not good. This move makes divine motives more basic than the divine will even in DC theory.

DM theory also has the theoretical advantage of providing a unitary theory of all evaluative properties, divine as well as human. DC theory is most naturally interpreted as an ethics of law, a divine deontological theory, wherein the content of the law is promulgated by divine commands. God's own goodness and the rightness of God's own acts, however, are not connected to divine commands, since God does not give commands to himself. In contrast, DM theory makes the features of the divine nature in virtue of which God is morally good the foundation for the moral goodness of those same features in creatures. Both divine and human goodness are explained in terms of good motives, and the goodness of human motives is derived from the goodness of the divine motives.

NOTES

1. See my book by the same name. [*Divine Motivation Theory* (New York: Cambridge University Press, 2004.]

2. In philosophies influenced by Aristotelian psychology, such as that of Aquinas, emotions are thought to be essentially connected to the body and therefore do not apply to God. Personally, I see no reason to deny that emotions are components of the divine nature, but my theory requires only that there are states in God that are analogous to what we call emotions in humans in the same way that there are states in God analogous to what we call beliefs in humans.

3. See the prologue to Flanagan [*Varieties of Moral Personality* (Cambridge, MA: Harvard University Press, 1991] for a nice discussion of the many ways of sainthood and moral exemplariness.

4. This is assuming, of course, that the motives of which we are speaking are suitably general. Love is essential to God, but love of Adam and Eve is not, since Adam and Eve might not have existed.

5. Aquinas (1981 [1273]) *Summa Theologica* I-II, q. 1, art. 6, corpus.

E. PERFECTION

12 DIVINE PERFECTION AND FREEDOM

WILLIAM L. ROWE

In the Abrahamic religions, God is typically described as perfect in all respects, including perfect goodness and unlimited freedom. But might these attributes be in conflict? Might one have to be sacrificed to achieve the other? William L. Rowe, whose work we read previously, explores the problem and suggests that either God's goodness or God's freedom needs to be significantly qualified in order to avoid conflict between the two.

> Though God is a most perfectly free agent, he cannot but do always what is best and wisest in the whole.
>
> Samuel Clarke

Many thinkers in the theistic tradition have held that in addition to omnipotence and omniscience God's attributes must include perfect goodness and freedom. For the theistic God deserves unconditional gratitude, praise, and worship. But if a being were to fall short of perfect goodness, it would not be worthy of unreserved praise and worship. So, too, for divine freedom. If God were not free in some of his significant actions, if he always lacked the freedom not to do what he in fact does, we could hardly thank him or praise him for anything that he does. He would not be deserving of our gratitude and praise for the simple reason that he would act of necessity and not freely. So, along with omnipotence and omniscience, perfect goodness and significant freedom are fundamental attributes of the theistic God.

Some attributes are essential to an object. That object could not exist were it not to possess those attributes. Other attributes are such that the object could still exist were it to lack them. If the theistic God does exist, to which class do his attributes of omnipotence, omniscience, perfect goodness, and freedom belong? Are they essential to that being? Does that being possess those attributes in every possible world in which he exists? Or are they not essential? Most thinkers in the theistic tradition have held the view that these attributes are constitutive of God's nature; they are essential attributes of the being that has them. With this view in mind, my aim in this essay is to consider the question of whether God's perfect goodness, specifically his moral perfection, is consistent with his being free in many significant actions. Throughout, we will suppose that if God exists he is *essentially* omnipotent, omniscient, perfectly good, and free in many of his actions. What I want to determine is whether there is a serious difficulty in the endeavor to reconcile God's essential goodness and moral perfection with any significant degree of divine freedom.[1]

From William L. Rowe, "The Problem of Divine Perfection and Freedom," In *Reasoned Faith: Essays in Philosophical Theology in Honor of Norman Kretzmann*, Cornell University Press, 1993. Reprinted by permission of the publisher.

I begin the investigation with the question of whether God is ever free to do an evil (morally wrong) act. The answer, I believe, is no. Of course, being morally perfect, omnipotent, and omniscient, God will never in fact do an evil act. No being who knowingly and willingly performs an evil act is morally perfect. Since being free to do an evil act is consistent with never in fact doing an evil act, it may seem initially plausible to think that God could be free to perform such an act. But if God is free to perform an evil act, then he has it in his power to perform that act. And, if God has it in his power to perform an evil act, then he has it in his power to deprive himself of one of his essential attributes (moral perfection). But no being has the power to deprive itself of one of its essential attributes.[2] Therefore, God does not have it in his power to perform an evil act.

The reasoning in this argument proceeds as follows.

1. God has it in his power to bring it about that he performs an evil act. (Assumption to be refuted)
2. From God's performing an evil act it follows that God is not morally perfect.
3. If X has it in its power to bring about p, q follows from p, and q does not obtain, then X has it in its power to bring about q.
4. God has it in his power to bring it about that he is not morally perfect. (From 1 to 3.)
5. Being morally perfect is an essential attribute of God.
   Therefore,
6. God has it in his power to bring it about that he lacks one of his essential attributes.

Because (6) is clearly false, we must deny the initial assumption that God has power to bring it about that he performs an evil act. But if God does not have it in his power to perform an evil act, then performing an evil act is not something God is free to do.

It may seem that my argument to show that God is not free to do an evil act has already produced a serious difficulty in the theistic concept of God. For if God cannot do evil, what becomes of his omnipotence? After all, even we humans, with our quite limited power, are able to perform evil

deeds. If God does not have the power to do what even we can do, how can we reasonably hold that he is essentially omnipotent?

So long as we hold that omnipotence does not imply power to do what is not possible to be done, we need not conclude that God's lacking power to bring it about that he do something morally wrong renders him less than omnipotent.[3] For, as we've seen, it is strictly impossible for a being who logically cannot be other than morally perfect to do something evil.

If God is not free to do a morally wrong action, might he be free to do a morally right act? 'Morally right act' may mean either what is morally obligatory or what is morally permissible. If we are willing to countenance refraining from performing a certain action as an "action", then it is clear that God is not free with respect to performing any action that is morally obligatory for him to perform. For refraining from that action would be morally wrong, and, as we've seen, God is not free to do anything that is morally wrong for him to do. For God to be free in performing any action, it must be both in his power to perform it and in his power to refrain from performing it. But since refraining from doing what is morally obligatory is morally wrong, and being morally perfect is essential to God, he does not have the power to refrain from doing what is morally obligatory. In short, God does what is morally obligatory of necessity, not freely.

The way I've just put the point about God doing what is morally obligatory for him to do is not quite right. For it suggests that even though God does not freely do what he is morally obligated to do, he nevertheless does (of necessity) what he has a moral obligation to do. But the truth is that no action is such that God can have a moral obligation to perform it. For one cannot have a moral obligation to do what one cannot do freely. If a person freely does some act, then it was in the person's power not to do it.[4] Since it would be morally wrong for God not to do what he is morally obligated to do, it follows from my previous argument that God cannot do freely what he is morally obligated to do. But, since one cannot be morally obligated to do what one is not free to do, there are no actions God has a moral obligation to perform. At best we can say that God does of necessity those acts he would be morally obligated to do were he free to do them.

We've seen that because he is essentially a morally perfect being, God is neither free to do a morally wrong action nor free in doing a morally obligatory action. We've also seen that no action can be such that God has a moral obligation to do it (or not to do it). It looks, then, as though my initial efforts have yielded the result that God's absolute moral perfection places significant restraints on the scope of divine freedom. However, the fact that God is neither free to do what is wrong nor free in doing what is morally obligatory (what would be morally obligatory were God free with respect to doing or not doing it) may still leave considerable scope for God's freedom to be exercised.[5] For, so long as some of his important actions are morally permissible but not morally obligatory, we thus far have no reason to deny that God is free with respect to all such actions, that he has it in his power to do them and in his power not to do them. For example, it has long been held that God's action in creating the world was a free action, that God was free to create a world and free not to create a world.[6] Creating the world is certainly a very significant act, involving, as it does, a vast number of divine acts in actualizing the contingent states of affairs that constitute our world. If God enjoys freedom with respect to the world he creates, then, although his freedom is constrained in ways that ours is not, there would not appear to be any insurmountable problem to reconciling perfection and freedom.[7] To pursue the investigation of a possible conflict between God's moral perfection and his freedom, therefore, it will be helpful to turn our attention to God's action in creating the world. Specifically, we need to consider whether God's moral perfection leaves God free with respect to his creation of the world.

It is important to distinguish two questions concerning God's freedom in creating a world. There is the question of whether God is free to select among creatable worlds the one he will create.[8] There is also the question of whether God is free not to create a world at all. That these are quite different questions can be seen as follows. Suppose that among worlds creatable by an omnipotent being there is one that is morally better than all other worlds. On this supposition, one can imagine arguments for any of four positions. Someone might argue that although God is free not to create a world at all, if he chooses to create, he must create the best world he can. Hence, although he is free not to create the morally best world, he is not free to create any world other than it. Alternatively, someone might argue that God's perfect goodness absolutely necessitates that he create a good world. God is not free not to create a world. But God's perfection does not necessitate that he create the best world he can. He is free to create among the class of creatable good worlds. Third, someone might argue that God enjoys both sorts of freedom. He is free not to create at all. He is also free to create some good world other than the best that he can create. Finally, one might argue that God's being essentially perfect necessitates his creating that world which is superior to all others. God is not free to create some world other than the best, and he is not free not to create any world at all. In what follows, I focus primarily on my first question (whether God is free to select among creatable worlds).

In an important article, Robert Adams has argued that it need not be wrong for God to create a world that is *not as good as* some other world he could create.[9] Adams supposes that the world God creates contains creatures each of whom is as happy as it is in any possible world in which it exists. Moreover, no creature in this world is so miserable that it would be better had it not existed. Let's suppose there is some other possible world, with different creatures, that exceeds this world in its degree of happiness, a world that God could have created. So, God has created a world with a lesser degree of happiness than he could have. Has God wronged anyone in creating this world? Adams argues that God cannot have wronged the creatures in the other possible world, for merely possible beings don't have rights. Nor can he have wronged the creatures in the world he has created, for their lives could not be made more happy. Adams notes that God would have done something wrong in creating this world were the following principle true: "It is wrong to bring into existence, knowingly, a being less excellent than one could have brought into existence."[10] But this principle, Adams argues, is subject to counterexamples. Parents do no wrong when they refrain from taking drugs that would result in an abnormal gene structure in their children, even though taking the drugs would result in children who are superhuman both in intelligence and in prospects for happiness.

Suppose we agree with Adams on these points. Suppose, that is, that we agree that God is not morally obligated to create the best world that he can, that it would be morally permissible for God to create the best world he can, but also morally permissible for God to create any of a number of other good worlds of the sort Adams describes. If so, can't we conclude that there is no unresolvable conflict between God's being essentially morally perfect and his enjoying a significant degree of genuine freedom? For it now appears that God's moral perfection does not require him to create the best world. In short, he is free to create (or not create) any of a number of good worlds.

As forceful and persuasive as Adams's arguments are, I don't think they yield the conclusion that God's perfect goodness imposes no requirement on God to create the best world that he can create. What Adams's arguments show, at best, is that God's moral perfection imposes no *moral obligation* on God to create the best world he can. His arguments establish, at best, that God need not be doing anything *morally wrong* in creating some world other than the best world. But this isn't quite the same thing as showing that God's perfect goodness does not render it necessary that he create the best world he can. For, even conceding the points Adams tries to make, there still may be an inconsistency in a morally perfect being creating some world other than the best world he can create. My point here is this. One being may be morally better than another even though it is not better by virtue of the performance of some obligation that the other failed to perform. It may be morally better by virtue of performing some supererogatory act that the other being could have but did not perform. Analogously, a being who creates a better world than another being may be morally better, even though the being who creates the morally inferior world does not

thereby do anything wrong. Following Philip Quinn, I'm inclined to think that if an omnipotent being creates some world other than the best world it can create, then it is possible there should exist a being morally better than it is.[11] For it would be possible for there to be an omnipotent being who creates the best world that the first being could create but did not. I conclude then that if an essentially omnipotent, perfectly good being creates any world at all, it must create the best world it can. For although a being may do no wrong in creating less than the best it can create, a being whose nature is to be *perfectly good* is not such that it is possible for there to be a being morally better than it. If, however, a being were to create a world when there is a morally better world it could create, then it would be possible for there to be a being morally better than it.

What we have seen is that a being who is morally perfect and creates a world must create the very best world it can create. But what if there is no best world among those it can create? This would be so in either of two cases. First, it might be that for any world it creates there is a morally better world it can create. Second, it might be that there is no *unique* best world. Perhaps, instead, there are many morally unsurpassable worlds among the worlds God can create. Let's consider these two cases in turn.

On the assumption that for any world God creates there is a morally better world he can create, it is clear that it is impossible for God to do the best that he can. Whatever he does, it will be the case that he could have done better. This being so, it would seem only reasonable that God's perfect goodness is fully satisfied should he create a very good world. And we may safely assume that there are a large number of such worlds that he can create. So long as he creates one of these worlds, he will have satisfied the demands of his morally perfect nature. For the idea that he should create the best world he can is an idea that logically cannot be implemented. Hence, on the assumption of there being no morally unsurpassable world among the worlds God can create, it would seem that God's absolute moral perfection is fully compatible with his freely creating any one of a number of good worlds that lie in his power to create. To complain that God cannot then be perfect because he could have created a better world is to raise a complaint that no creative action God took would have enabled him to avoid. As William Wainwright notes:

> The critic complains that God could have created a better order. But even if God had created a better order, He would be exposed to the possibility of a similar complaint. Indeed, no created order better than our own is such that God would not be exposed to the possibility of a complaint of this sort. The complaint is thus inappropriate. Even though there are an infinite number of created orders better than our own, God can't be faulted simply because He created an order inferior to other orders that He might have created in their place.[12]

There is something forceful and right about this reasoning. If, no matter what world an omnipotent being creates, there is a morally better world that being can create, then, provided that the omnipotent being creates a significantly good world, it cannot be morally at fault for not having created a morally better world. But our question is whether a being in such a situation can be an *absolutely perfect being*. And for reasons I have already uncovered, I think the answer is no. A being is necessarily an absolutely perfect moral being only if it is not possible for there to be a being morally better than it. If a being creates a world when there is some morally better world that it could have created, then it is possible that there be a being morally better than it. Since our assumption implies that for any world an omnipotent being creates there is a morally better world it can create, it follows that any such being who creates even a very good world cannot be an absolutely perfect moral being. Although the omnipotent being in question could be a very good moral agent and enjoy a significant degree of freedom in creating among a number of very good worlds, it could not be an absolutely perfect moral being. The existence of the theistic God who creates a world is inconsistent with the supposition that among the worlds he can create there is no morally unsurpassable world.

Let's now consider the second way in which it could be true that no creatable world is better than all others. Suppose that among the worlds God can create there are a number of worlds that are morally unsurpassable. For reasons we've already considered, if God creates a world, he cannot create some world that is morally inferior to some other that he can create. Therefore, if there are a number of morally unsurpassable worlds among the worlds he can create, then if he creates at all he must create one of these worlds. But unlike the case when there is exactly one morally unsurpassable world among the worlds he can create, here we do seem to have found a wedge to open up space for some degree of divine freedom to exist in harmony with God's absolute moral perfection. For God would seem to be free to create any one of the morally unsurpassable worlds. In any case, God's absolute moral perfection imposes no requirement on his creation among the set of morally unsurpassable worlds.

Among the worlds creatable by an omnipotent being, either (1) there is exactly one morally unsurpassable world or (2) there is not. If there is not, then either (2a) there is no morally unsurpassable world or (2b) there are a number of morally unsurpassable worlds. If (1) is the case, then God is not free to select among creatable worlds. If (2a) is the case, God's being essentially morally perfect is inconsistent with his act of creating a world. If (2b) is the case, God's moral perfection leaves him free to select among morally unsurpassable worlds the one he will create.

Earlier, I distinguished two questions concerning God's freedom in creating a world. We have been discussing the question of God's freedom to select among creatable worlds the one he will create. It is now time to consider the other question of whether God is free not to create a world at all. Here we may limit our inquiry to the possibility that there is exactly one morally unsurpassable world among the worlds creatable by an omnipotent being. As we've seen, in this case God is not free to select any other world to create. If God creates, he must create the one world that is morally best. Our present question is whether in this situation God is free not to create at all.

Some possible world must be actual. What possible world would be actual if God exists but does not create at all? Presumably, it would be a world in which no positive, contingent state of affairs obtains. By 'a positive, contingent state of affairs' I mean any state of affairs such that from the fact that it obtains it follows that some contingent being (other than God, if he should be contingent) exists. Apart from God and whatever necessarily existing entities there are, in a world God inhabits but does not create no other being would exist. To answer our question of whether God is free not to create a world at all, we must compare the best world God can create with a world whose inhabitants are simply God and whatever necessarily existing entities there are. Assuming such a world would not be morally incommensurate with the morally unsurpassable world among worlds God can create, it is plausible to think that God is not free with respect to whether he will not create at all. For either the world he inhabits but does not create is better than the best world he can create or it is not. If it is better, then he is not free not to create a world at all; he necessarily refrains from creating. If it is worse, then he is not free not to create a world at all; he necessarily creates a world.[13] Might the world he inhabits but does not create be on a moral par with the best world among those an omnipotent being can create? If so, then, as in the case where there are a number of morally unsurpassable worlds omnipotence can create, we again have a wedge for creating space for some degree of divine freedom. But, in this scarcely possible situation, God's freedom would be restricted to creating the morally unsurpassable world or not creating at all.

I now can draw together the results of my study of the problem of divine perfection and freedom. The conclusions may be presented as follows.

1. God is not free to perform any evil act, nor is he free in doing what is morally obligatory.
2. If there is a world creatable by God that is morally better than any world he inhabits but does not create, God is *not* free not to create a world at all. If he exists, he is a creator of necessity.
3. If for any world creatable by an omnipotent being there is another creatable world that is morally better, the theistic God cannot exist and be a creator of anything.

4. If there is a single, morally best creatable world, God enjoys neither sort of freedom: he is not free not to create and he is not free to select among creatable worlds.[14]
5. If there are a number of morally unsurpassable, creatable worlds, then although God necessarily creates one or the other of them, he is free (so far as his moral perfection is concerned) to select among the morally unsurpassable worlds the one he will create.[15]

Traditional theists who hold that God is essentially perfect and yet possesses libertarian freedom of will and action have neglected, I believe, some of the implications that appear to follow from God's perfect goodness. For all we know about possible worlds, it may well be that God's perfect goodness is inconsistent with any degree of divine freedom in whether he creates or what world he creates. In any case, it would seem that his perfection places rather severe limitations on the scope of his freedom in creating a world.

The problem we have been considering is rooted in two basic points: God's perfect goodness is such as to preclude the *possibility* of a morally better being; God's freedom is such that he acts and wills freely only if it is in his power not to so act and will. If either point is significantly qualified or given up, the conclusions I've drawn may no longer obtain. If, for example, we give up the libertarian idea of freedom, then, following Jonathan Edwards, we might hold that God's actions are free even though necessitated by his perfect goodness.[16] On the other hand, we might endeavor to qualify God's perfect goodness so that it permits the possibility for God to have been better than he is.[17] Neither of these alternatives has been addressed in this essay.

NOTES

1. I take God's moral perfection to be logically implied by his perfect goodness.
2. It is understood here that a being has the power to deprive itself of a property only if it is possible for that being to lose that property and *continue to exist*.

3. For a discussion of this point see Joshua Hoffman, "Can God Do Evil?" *Southern Journal of Philosophy* 17 (1979): 213–20.

4. To avoid Frankfurt-type counterexamples, we should say that when an agent freely performs some action she caused her action and had the power not to cause that action. The power not to cause one's action is *not* the same as the power to prevent one's action. I ignore this complication in the text.

5. If we take *significant freedom*, as Alvin Plantinga does, to be the freedom to do or refrain from doing what is morally obligatory, it can be shown that God cannot be significantly free. See Wes Morriston, "Is God 'Significantly Free'?" *Faith and Philosophy* 2 (1983): 257–63.

6. For an excellent discussion and critical evaluation of the classical Judeo-Christian views on God's freedom with respect to creation see Norman Kretzmann, "A General Problem of Creation", and "A Particular Problem of Creation", in *Being and Goodness*, ed. Scott MacDonald (Ithaca and London: Cornell University Press, 1990).

7. There is a problem of understanding what God's moral perfection comes to, given that he can have no moral obligations. But this problem may not be unresolvable. See Thomas Morris, *Anselmian Explorations* (Notre Dame: University of Notre Dame Press, 1987), pp. 31–41.

8. Since there may be possible worlds that an omnipotent being cannot create, we need to restrict our discussion to the class of worlds creatable by God.

9. Robert Adams, "Must God Create the Best?" *Philosophical Review* 81 (1972): 317–32.

10. Ibid., p. 329.

11. Philip L. Quinn, "God, Moral Perfection, and Possible Worlds", in *God: The Contemporary Discussion*, ed. Frederick Sontag and M. Darrol Bryant (New York: The Rose of Sharon Press, Inc., 1982), pp. 197–213. Quinn remarks: "An omnipotent moral agent can actualize any actualizable world. If he actualizes one than which there is a morally better, he does not do the best he can, morally speaking, and so it is possible that there is an agent morally better than he is, namely an omnipotent moral agent who actualizes one of those morally better worlds" (p. 213).

12. William Wainwright, *Philosophy of Religion* (Belmont, Calif.: Wadsworth Publishing Company, 1988), p. 90.

13. This point is a plausible extension of our earlier principle: If X creates a morally inferior world to one X can create, then it is possible that there be a being morally better than X. Extending this principle, it is plausible to hold that if X can but does not create a world that is morally better than the one X inhabits, then it is possible that there be a being morally better than X.

14. The plausible assumption here is that if there is a single, morally best creatable world, then that world is morally better than any world God inhabits but does not create.

15. See n. 13.

16. Jonathan Edwards, *Freedom of the Will*, ed. Paul Ramsey (New Haven, Yale University Press, 1957).

17. See, for example, the suggestion by William Wainwright (drawn from Charles Hartshorne) that God's perfection might require only that he be unsurpassable by some *other* being (*Philosophy of Religion*, p. 9).

13   GOD AND FORGIVENESS

ANNE C. MINAS

According to the Hebrew Scriptures, God is compassionate, "forgiving iniquity, transgression, and sin" (Ex 34:7). According to the New Testament, we ought to forgive one another, "as God

From Anne C. Minas, "God and Forgiveness," *The Philosophical Quarterly* 25 (1975). Reprinted by permission of Blackwell Publishing Ltd.

in Christ has forgiven you" (Eph 4:32). According to the Qur'an, God is "most forgiving, most merciful" (73). Indeed, God's forgiveness is a central doctrine of all three Abrahamic religions, offering hope to all who err.

But Anne Minas, who was a professor of philosophy at the University of Waterloo in Ontario, Canada, argues that a divine being, possessing a perfect moral sense, a perfect moral will, perfect knowledge, and perfect benevolence, is logically precluded from forgiving. Indeed, she maintains that human frailty, not divine perfection, makes forgiveness possible. This article demonstrates that the perfections typically attributed to God may lead to unexpected complications.

To err is human, to forgive, divine. Most of us tend to believe this whether or not we also believe in the actual existence of a divine being. The non-believer reasons that if there were such a being he would forgive the wrong-doings of mortals, and insofar as he himself exercises forgiveness his nature approaches that which believers attribute to a deity. There is supposed to be something about being divine that makes a deity especially capable of exercising forgiveness; and, conversely, it is human frailty which prevents us from this exercise on occasions when we ought to forgive.

This belief in a connection between forgiving and being divine I want to show is mistaken, in a radical way. Far from its being the case that divine nature makes its possessor especially prone to forgive, such a nature makes forgiveness impossible. Such a being logically cannot forgive, since possession of divine attributes logically precludes conditions which are necessary for forgiveness. So, far from its being the case that human frailty makes forgiveness difficult or impossible, it is the possession of distinctly human, non-divine characteristics, that makes forgiveness appropriate for human beings. Only a human being can forgive—a divine being cannot.

In my discussion, I shall be assuming mainly that a divine being (if there is one) is perfect. He has a perfect moral sense, a perfect moral will, perfect knowledge, and perfect benevolence. I shall try not to make too many assumptions about the nature of forgiveness. The definitions given in the *Oxford English Dictionary* and the uses made of the word "forgiveness" are varied enough to rule out any assumption that forgiveness amounts to one kind of thing in all circumstances. So I shall instead take up various kinds of actions forgiveness

is, or might be, and show that not one of them is an action that could be performed by a perfect being.

I

The *OED* in some of its definitions of "forgive" directs forgiveness upon actions that are wrong. Part of definition 3 of "forgive" is "to give up resentment or claim to requital for, pardon (an offence)." In this connection it mentions Hobbes' writing on "An Authority to Forgive, or Retain Sins," in *Leviathan* (III xlii 274); and *Isaiah* XXXIII 24, about forgiving iniquities. So let us suppose that forgiveness of one kind involves the forgiver's believing that the person forgiven has done something wrong and that it is this wrong action that the forgiveness is being directed upon.

Forgiveness of this sort may simply be retraction or modification of a previous adverse moral judgment about the act in question. The eloping couple might be forgiven in this way by their parents. The parents, in their shock and dismay when first hearing the news, censure the action harshly. Later, however, they realize that their judgment about the elopement was too severe and so they modify or abandon it, and so forgive the couple.

Now with human beings this reversal or modification of moral judgment is sometimes laudable, sometimes not. It depends on whether the original judgment was correct, or whether the person who made the judgment had good reason to believe it correct. If the parents changed their minds about the elopement, that would probably be laudable, since presumably elopement is not wrong (or not *very* wrong) and the parents had no good reason to think it was. But suppose a son had asked his parents to reverse their censure of his having murdered his sister. There would be no cause to praise them if they somehow deluded themselves into believing that the son had not done anything really wrong. They would then apparently have lost all sense of right and wrong, at least as regards their son, not to mention any special feelings they might have had about this particular victim, their daughter. Forgiveness, in the sense of reversal of moral judgment, is not always in order for human beings.

But when it is a deity considering an action, reversal of moral judgment is never in order. When contradictory judgments are made about the same action, one of them is wrong, and a being with a perfect moral sense cannot (logically cannot) make wrong moral judgments. If he was right in his second appraisal of the situation, he was wrong in his first and vice versa. And this is quite aside from the difficulty of how a being who is not in time can reverse his judgments, having no time in which to do so.

The situation is not appreciably changed if forgiveness, in the sense of reversal of judgment, is granted because new facts have come to light which should affect an assessment of the situation. One human being may be forgiven by another for this reason. "I didn't understand the situation fully," the forgiver says. "At first I could see no reason for your firing Smith. But since then I have learned he has had his hand in the till, and has been malicious towards his subordinates, etc. I now see you were quite right in letting him go." It is fine for a human being to make a new assessment of an action when new facts come to light. It is impossible for an omniscient deity, however, because, being omniscient, he always knows all the facts. For him, there can be no such thing as learning something new. And, of course, for such a being there can be no such thing as a temporary lapse of consciousness where he overlooks, or temporarily fails to remember, a relevant fact. So such things cannot be reasons for reversal of judgment in a deity, although they certainly can be for us. For this reason it is a little hard to see how some one can argue with a deity that he or someone else ought to be forgiven, by trying to bring certain facts to his attention. One of the last things

Jesus said was "Father, forgive them, for they know not what they do." But how could Jesus have been trying to draw a certain fact to God's attention when God, being (as we sometimes say) omnipercipient, must have all facts in his attention all the time? He is also supposed to show perfect moral judgment in weighing facts, so it is equally insulting or, more accurately, blasphemous, to try to argue with God that a fact should have a particular moral weight in his consideration.

Sometimes it is thought that people ought to be forgiven for doing wrong for special considerations pertaining to their case. Such considerations include the motives of the agent (he stole the loaf of bread to feed his starving children), or special difficulties in which he found himself (he shot the burglar in self-defence), or any other special characteristics of the action (he went through the red light at 4 a.m. when the streets were virtually deserted). According to the rule (moral, legal, or whatever) he did something wrong, but the wrongness seems to be mitigated by special circumstances. But in cases like these, the fact of the matter is that the rule is too crude, or too general, to take the special circumstances into account. What someone who appeals to mitigating circumstances is arguing is that while the action is wrong according to the rule, it is not wrong (or not as wrong) in a more general, all things considered, sort of way. Forgiveness in this sense is really a kind of moral judgment; a recognition that the rule has only limited application to the assessment and that other factors must also be taken into account.

It is very difficult to see how God could make this kind of judgment, for what would the defective rule be for him? It could hardly be one of his own, one of the rules which he makes to define right and wrong (if this is indeed what he does) for why should he make a defective one? His only motivation, as far as I can see, would be considerations of simplicity and ease of understanding for human beings. This, however, would only function as a reason for giving human beings defective rules, and not for using them himself. Complexities being no problem for a perfectly omniscient being, he would, if he used rules at all to make moral assessments, use ones which had the degree of complexity necessary to take into account *all* morally relevant factors in a situation to be judged. Our rules would only be crude approximations to these perfectly accurate divine rules, and thus while it might appear to us as if God is making an exception to his own rules (not judging an action wrong which is wrong by our crude rules) this appearance would be delusory.

Finally, a human being may *condone* offences by others, meaning, according to *OED*, "to forgive or overlook (an offence) so as to treat it as nonexistent." This is especially appropriate with minor wrongdoings. For I take it that the idea of condoning is that of refusing to form an adverse moral judgment of an action, even though there may be some reason to do so. One overlooks, refuses to take account of, the immoral aspects of an action. Essentially, it is making an exception for a particular case for no reason. If this is a kind of forgiveness, as the definition suggests, it is again difficult to see how it is something a divine being can do. Being omniscient, he knows everything there is to be known, and is not able to overlook it, in the sense of refusing to know it. So in particular, he cannot do this with moral aspects of an action. In addition, condoning may show a certain lack of moral sense and so there is a second reason why a deity cannot do it. This is most clear when the immoral aspects are fairly substantial. Someone who condones mass murders shows a significant moral blindness, to say the least.

II

Reversing moral judgments, exhibiting moral blindness, and making exceptions to moral rules being impossible for perfect beings, it is time to consider other types of actions which might merit the name "forgiveness." In the passage quoted earlier, the *OED* mentioned giving up a claim to requital for an offence. When requital or punishment is remitted or reduced because of a new, more favourable judgment about the moral aspects of the case, then such cases become instances of the kinds discussed in the first part of this paper. This includes cases where special circumstances merit a special kind of judgment about the action. These are simply ways of forming judgments where all relevant circumstances are considered.[1]

But there are also cases where punishment is remitted without reversing or modifying a judgment about the wrongdoing the punishment was supposed to be punishment for. This kind of forgiveness is akin to clemency exercised by a judge in the courts, or pardon by a high official. Someone who is in a position to mete out punishment for a wrongdoing decides to give less punishment than what is called for by the nature of the wrongdoing, or no punishment at all.

It is easy to envisage the deity in the role of a judge who makes decisions about punishments and rewards. For it is he who decides the lots of humans in life after death and these lots are often conceived of as rewards or punishments. People who are good or bad in this life get good or bad lots, respectively, in the afterlife. In addition, it is often thought that virtue is rewarded and vice punished by the deity in this life. Misfortunes, for instance, are sometimes thought of as being sent by God as a punishment for wrongdoing.

What is not so easy to envisage, however, is how a perfectly just God can remit punishment. In the first place, what would be the mechanism by which the punishment was originally assigned which was then remitted by God? With human beings the assignment and remission typically is done by two separate agencies, the remitting agency taking precedence over the assigning one. A judge (the remitter) gives a lighter punishment than that prescribed by law (the assigner). Or a high political official, a governor, say, remits a punishment assigned by the courts. But who or what assigns punishments which God then remits? God himself? He then appears to be something of a practical joker, assigning punishments which he, with perfect foreknowledge, knows he is going to remit, perhaps doing this to scare some virtue into sinners. If not he but his laws assign the original punishment, essentially the same problem arises, namely why God makes laws that he knows he is going to override.

Other problems would appear here as well. One concerns the question of whether the punishment over which the sinner is being forgiven by God was what the sinner justly deserved. If it was, then in remitting him this punishment God is not giving the sinner what he deserves, and thus not behaving in a way consistent with his being a perfectly just being. If, on the other hand, the sinner did not deserve the punishment, then it was an unjust mechanism which assigned such punishment. If this mechanism were God's laws or decrees, then once again he would not be a perfectly just being, although he certainly would be more just in remitting one of his own unjust sentences than in letting it stand. If the mechanism assigning the punishment were, on the other hand, a human one, it is difficult to see why God should pay any attention to it. Ignoring this punishment would be a much more appropriate attitude than remitting it.

Another problem has to do with God's absolving only some sinners from their punishments. For either God forgives everyone or he does not. If he only forgives some people, and not others, then he might be behaving unjustly towards those whose punishment he allows to stand. If he picks out people to forgive for no special reason, then he is acting arbitrarily and immorally. A just God does not play favourites with rewards and punishments.

So is there a reason God might have for remitting punishment in some cases but not in others? We have been assuming that these are all cases where God does not reverse his moral condemnation of the actions, so this cannot be a reason. But one reason that is often cited is repentance on the part of the sinner. This repentance would be an overt expression of the agent's realization of having done wrong, his having the appropriate feelings about his actions, and his resolve not to repeat them. So in asking for forgiveness with this attitude, the penitent is not asking God for a new judgment on his actions—as noted earlier, this smacks of blasphemy—but rather a new and more favourable judgment on *him*, as an agent. He is not the wrongdoer he once was, but has a new, reformed, character.

We, as human beings, revise our judgments about people's characters in the light of evidence that they are repentant about their past misdeeds. But for an omniscient being, such revision would not be possible. In his omniscience, God would be able to foreknow the repentance of the agent; therefore he need not make, and could not have made, a judgment about the agent's character which did not take this act of repentance into account. It is difficult to see, moreover, why God should count the end of the agent's life, the post-repentance period, more heavily than the beginning in his final assessment of the agent's character. Because God is omniscient and outside time, all parts of a human life are known to him in exactly the same way, known to him much as a number series is known to us. We do not attach any special significance to the later numbers in the series just because they are later, nor do we believe they are better representatives of the series. Similarly God should not regard an agent's later character as the best representative of his total character.

We, on the other hand, do attach special significance to an agent's later character, for at least two reasons. One is that it is the man's most recent character with which we are (presently) confronted, and with which we have to deal. And the other is that insofar as we need, or want to make, predictions about his future character, the most recent evidence will tend to be the most reliable. These two reasons have importance in a utilitarian justification of infliction or withholding of punishment. The utilitarian treats punishment as a method for obtaining good results, one of the foremost being improvement of the agent's character, behaviour and motivation. Punishment is only justified to the extent it is effective in these areas. So a utilitarian would not be able to derive this kind of justification when he is considering punishing an already reformed character. The effect already having been gained, the punishment is superfluous as a method, and hence unjustified.

A utilitarian can thus consider withholding or remitting punishment for repentant, reformed agents. Now the question is, can God be such a utilitarian, consistently with his perfection, and thus exercise forgiveness in this particular way? He would be a God who uses threats and bribes to get people to behave themselves, threatening them with punishment if they misbehave, bribing them with forgiveness, remission of punishment, if they decide to behave.

It seems to me that this portrayal of God the manipulator is inconsistent with the image of divine perfection. There must be better, fairer, and more effective ways to instil into human beings a sense of right and wrong and a will to do the right. Moreover, the whole exercise of threats and bribes would presumably become inoperative at the end of an individual's life. Since he has no more opportunities to choose the wrong, there is no longer a utilitarian reason for punishing him as a threat. To condemn him to the eternal flames just as an example to mortals still on earth is not, I think, something that a just God could contemplate, particularly since these mortals seem to have no good way of knowing who has been condemned and who has not. So everyone would have to have his punishment remitted at the end of this life, i.e., everyone would have to be forgiven, a possibility that was mentioned, but not discussed, a little earlier. But then the whole activity of threats and bribes during an individual's life becomes meaningless, a little game God plays with us where everything comes all right in the end anyway. The juiciest rewards and the most terrible punishments he can mete out would be those in the after-life, and it is just these that he can have no utilitarian reasons for conferring.

Nor, I believe, can God remit punishment for a repentant sinner for non-utilitarian reasons, as has already been noted, although he must take reformed periods of the agent's life into account in making his judgment. But to weigh (in some non-utilitarian way) the amount of punishment, if any, due to a repentant character and give him just that much would be to disregard the pre-repentance period of the agent's life and this, I have argued, a just omniscient god could not do. Far from having the special significance which they are sometimes thought to have, death-bed confessions and pleas for forgiveness would be pretty useless. If the agent spent ten minutes of his life reformed, and seventy years of his life unreformed, the seventy years should count much more heavily when God is considering what kinds of punishment to mete out.

III

The kinds of forgiveness so far considered have been essentially ones involving either a reversal of moral judgment on the actions forgiven or a reversal of judgment about punishing the agent.

It may be felt that the discussion so far has missed the most central kinds of forgiveness, those, for instance, fitting this definition in the *OED:* "4. To give up resentment against, pardon (an offender)." Although pardoning an offender may mean remission of punishment, which I have already discussed, giving up resentment seems to be something different. Resentment being a kind of feeling or attitude, to give it up would be to change a feeling or attitude. This would not necessarily involve reversing a judgment. The change may be partly, or even wholly, non-cognitive.

Joseph Butler devotes two sermons to a discussion of resentment and forgiveness, viewing forgiveness as an avoidance of the abuses of resentment. He defines resentment thus: "the natural object or occasion of settled resentment then being injury as distinct from pain or loss … but from this [sudden anger], deliberate anger or resentment is essentially distinguished, as the latter is not naturally excited by, or intended to prevent mere harm without the appearance of wrong or injustice."[2] Resentment is a moral feeling or attitude whose object must be an action believed wrong or unjust, and not just any harm. Giving up of resentment might then mean giving up or reversing the belief that the action was wrong, as discussed in Part I of this paper; or it might mean merely giving up part or all of an accompanying feeling or attitude toward the action, while retaining the belief that it was wrong. It is forgiveness of this second sort that I want now to discuss.

Such seems to be the case of the forgiving father of the Prodigal Son. Presumably the father did not reverse his judgment of the son's prodigality, deciding that the son's actions were not so bad after all. Rather, it was in spite of this judgment that he was able to forgive him.

Something of this sort seems to be the kind of forgiveness Butler urges. He does not think we ought to reverse our moral judgments about those who have wronged us (except in instances where the evidence warrants it). Nor does he recommend giving up what he calls "a due, natural sense of the injury." Some moral attitudes and feelings toward a wrongdoing may be appropriate to retain in forgiveness. What has to be given up, according to Butler, seems to be what we might call taking the wrongdoing personally. For to forgive, according to him, is just "to be affected towards the injurious person in the same way any good men, uninterested in the case, would be, if they had the same just sense, which we have supposed the injured person to have, of the fault, after which there will yet remain real goodwill towards the offender."[3] To forgive is just to cease to have any personal interest in the injury. It is to regard it as if it had happened to someone else in whom we have no special interest, other than the general interest we have in all human beings. So the father might forgive his prodigal son by ceasing to take the son's prodigality personally. He regards it no longer as a wasting of *his* money, as something *his* son has done to *him*, but instead as a mere wasting of someone's good money.

How and why can this change in feeling happen? One suggestion is that the personal feelings are gradually forgotten, or wear off in some natural manner. "Forgive and forget" is what is sometimes said, and one possibility is that forgiving is forgetting. It could be argued that personal feelings only last naturally for so long and then wear off, unless the person makes a determined effort to retain or renew them, or as Butler puts it, "resentment has taken possession of the temper and will not quit its hold," suggesting that the mechanism by which this happens is "bare obstinacy."[4]

This may be true of human beings, but it cannot be true of God, and thus this kind of forgiveness is not open to him to exercise. An omniscient being cannot (logically) forget anything, so cannot in particular forget his feelings. And all his feelings are equally alive to him at all times, this being, I think, part of what is meant in calling him omnipercipient. In perceiving situations, he knows them in a way in which they are fully real to him, meaning that he reacts not just by forming judgments, but also with all appropriate feelings. Then, to be omnipercipient is to have all reactions to all situations equally vivid, regardless of when they happened. So the reactions of omnipercipient beings cannot change over time. So even if God were subject to change, and this change could take place in time (even though he is supposed to exist outside time) he would not be able to

change in this particular way, since this change involves a dimming of feeling.

Let us then consider a different kind of situation where resentment, in the sense of taking an injury personally, is dispelled, not through forgetting or some other kind of natural erosion, but as a result of conscious effort on the part of the forgiver. What reasons would he have for making this kind of effort?

When an injury is taken personally, the result is a certain breach between the injured person and the person who has injured him. This breach is not wholly due to the nature of the injury, nor to the injured person's reactions by way of judgment or sense of wrongness of the action. Other people could have these same reactions without such a breach occurring. Friends of the father of the Prodigal Son could agree with him in his judgments of the son's behaviour and could react with moral indignation at the son's waste without such reactions causing estrangement from the son. They have not themselves been injured, so there is no reason to take the prodigality personally. And also their relations with the boy are not such as to be affected by resentment in the way the father's are, since he is much more involved with the boy. This involvement, I think, also makes it more important for the father that the breach should be healed.

The father's motivation for forgiveness is thus to heal the breach, and this breach presumably is virtually intolerable because of his relationship with the boy. His involvement in and regard for the relationship require that he should not spoil it by feelings of personal injury.[5] Abandoning his feelings of personal injury is also required by a regard for the injuring party as a human being. Presumably more things should be taken into account in forming an attitude toward him than the injury he has caused. The trouble with a sense of personal injury is that it tends to swamp other considerations in the formation of attitudes. The person tends to be seen just as the agent of the injury and nothing else.

A final reason for trying to get rid of feelings of personal injury as soon as possible is that harbouring such feelings tends to be bad for the person who refuses to forgive. At least, this is what the psychologists tell us—that it is unhealthy to harbour and brood over personal resentments.

A change in attitude becomes particularly appropriate when the offender repents, shows remorse for his wrong-doing.[6] If the remorse is genuine he has dissociated himself from the wrong-doing in the sense that if he had it to do over again he would refrain, and he censures himself for having done it in the same way as if the agent had been someone else. So, since he is no longer the kind of person who would commit such an injury, an attitude that presupposes that he is such a person is inappropriate. And a sense of personal injury is, I think, just such an attitude since it is an attitude toward a person as the agent of a certain deed. Repentance as an overt sign of remorse makes such a difference in forgiveness (as an abandonment of a sense of personal injury) that it is sometimes difficult to see how forgiveness can take place without it. The parent who is willing to forgive a child anything, despite the fact that the child shows absolutely no signs of remorse, can be regarded as indulgent at best, and, at worst, as lacking a certain sense of appropriateness in his/her relations with the child. Too much of a readiness to forgive without repentance indicates a certain lack of awareness of personal injury, which in turn indicates a general lack of awareness in personal relations. Or sometimes the injuries are so great that the person really has no redeeming features which will outbalance them. Take the operators of the furnaces at Buchenwald, for example: if they are unrepentant what possible reasons could we have for forgiving them? In the absence of remorse there may not be any basis for realigning one's attitude toward the offender. The best one can do is just forget about him, taking the method of forgiveness I previously suggested.

Now, how could God figure in this kind of forgiveness? Since it presupposes a sense of taking an injury personally (it is this attitude that is remitted in forgiveness) it is very difficult to see how God could forgive in this way. For I think it is fairly clear that taking an injury personally, as opposed to having a general sense of its wrongness, is a distinctly human failing, an imperfection. Try to imagine a god sulking or brooding, perhaps plotting revenge because someone has, say, made off with the treasure in one of his churches, and you have imagined a less than perfect being. The Olympian gods and goddesses were noted for their pettiness in their relations with each other, with regard to injuries, real or imagined, and this is one good reason why they were not and are not regarded as perfect. A god whose perspective of another god or a person is distorted by a sense of personal injury—I argued earlier that this was an accompaniment of, if not part of, resentment and so was one reason for human forgiveness, getting rid of this attitude—is at the very least not omnipercipient, and probably also not just in his assessment of the human being who committed the injury. Relations with the injuring party are also severed, I maintained, by this attitude, and surely a perfect being could not allow this to happen. And the third reason for our getting rid of feelings of personal injury also serves as a reason for God's not having them at all. They are detrimental to one's psychological wellbeing, and in extreme cases make a person a candidate for the psychiatrist's couch. This sort of thing obviously cannot (logically) happen to a perfect being.

God, then, cannot forgive personal injuries where what is given up is personal resentment (OED—for "forgive"—"1. To give up, cease to harbour (resentment, wrath)") since he cannot have such feelings. But, it is sometimes said, God forgives us before we ask for forgiveness, sometimes even before we do wrong. Such a line of thinking perhaps would mean that God forgives before he resents, gives up the resentment before he has it, thus skipping the resentment phase of the process. More simply, he decides, wills not to harbour resentment. But the problem here is whether it makes any sense to make decisions where there is only one logically possible alternative. It is a little peculiar for me to make a decision about whether I am going to be the number 2, since I have only one alternative which is logically possible, and that is not to be the number 2. God presumably is in the same position with regard to harbouring resentment. Only the alternative of not harbouring it is logically open to him.

It is, however, sometimes maintained that God has all his perfections because he wills to have them, and so has made a meaningful decision in choosing them. If this is true, it would apply to a decision not (ever) to harbour resentment. But I think there are nonetheless good reasons not to count this as real forgiveness, since forgiveness has to be a giving up of something, and no one can give up something he never had. It would be as if I decided as a New Year's resolution to give up gambling, when I had never gambled. Also, repentance and remorse would lose their connection with God's foreness. Since he harbours no resentment anyway, there would be no point in setting matters straight by repenting. The only likely function repentance could have, in restoring a relationship with God which had been severed by isdeed, would be if the injury made some change in the *sinner's* attitude toward God which had severed the relationship, and if this attitude could be changed back by repentance. This may well happen (although I cannot understand just how the mechanism would work), but it is clearly not a case of God's forgiving, since it is not a case of God's doing anything. Everything that is done is done by the sinner, and it is in him that the changes take place.

IV

It's, moreover, only harm, or supposed harm, to himself that a person can take personally. Even if others are harmed as well, it is only the concomitant, or resultant, harm to oneself that causes feelings of personal resentment. If a son takes insults about his parents personally, for instance, this is because he believes that, when they are insulted, he is as well. Thus, forgiveness as a ceasing to hold personal resentment can only be directed toward actions which have wronged the forgiver (or which he believes have wronged him). And I think this is true of any kind of forgiveness—it is appropriately directed only toward actions which have wronged the forgiver. It would be a bit high-handed of me, for instance, to forgive someone else's husband's excessive drinking and womanizings when his wife felt not the least inclined in that direction—high-handed because I would have to construe his behaviour as wronging me rather than her. Only in certain restricted cases can one person forgive wrongs to another by proxy, as it

were. Typically this happens only when the forgiver bears a special relationship to the wronged person and the wronged person is dead. I could, for instance, conceivably forgive a wrong done to one of my dead ancestors if my relationship to him/her were such that if I were not to forgive the action, it would never be forgiven.

The implications here for God are that he can only forgive wrongs, sins, that are injuries to him. If he has universal powers of forgiveness, for all sins, sins must all have this characteristic.

Several problems arise immediately. One is how it is possible to wrong, to injure, a perfect being. His very perfection should make him immune from the kind of injury which makes forgiveness appropriate. The other problem is how even an imperfect being could construe as primarily wrongs to himself actions which seem mainly to harm someone else. On such a construction the person stolen from, raped, injured, killed, enslaved, is not really wronged at all, or at least the injury done him is rather minimal compared to that done to God by breaking his laws, contravening his wishes, or whatever. But this would have to be true if God is to forgive these actions, and especially if he is to forgive them independently of whether they have been forgiven by the ostensible injured party. To give God the first or primary right to forgive is to view him as the primary injured party.

Finally, I want to mention a kind of forgiveness which God alone is supposed to be able to exercise, which is associated with the washing away of one's sins. The idea, as nearly as I have been able to make out, is that before God forgives there are a certain number of wrongs which the person committed. Afterwards there are none. He did the actions all right, but after God's forgiveness, they are no longer wrong.

This is a little like a child's plea that a parent make things all right. The child imagines that rightness and wrongness depend wholly on the parent's say-so. So an action, or anything, might be changed from wrong to right, while remaining otherwise unchanged, because the parent first said it was wrong and then later says it is right. I think we sometimes expect God to set things right in the same way and we call this "forgiveness."

But much as we would like sometimes to retreat into these childhood fancies where God as parent makes things all right by some kind of magic, I think they embody too many confusions to make them worth considering. The first is the idea that the rightness or wrongness of an action can change without anything else about it changing. And another is the dependence of right or wrong on God's say-so. For in a situation like the ones being described it is not as if God gave us general precepts by which to live and they were right because they were expressions of the will of God. Many people have objections to the view that God's will has anything to do with right or wrong. But quite aside from these general objections, there is the problem that a god like the one being described does not impart to his decrees any generality. He literally changes wrong to right from one day to the next. This absence of generality, I think, disqualifies these changeable decrees from being *ethical* precepts. It also gives human beings considerable motivation for disobedience to God's will. If there is no telling how God is going to regard an action from one day to the next, then someone might want to take his chances on disobedience, figuring that what contravenes God's will one day will be favourably regarded the next.

With some actions, a necessary condition for their being wrong is an unfavourable reaction by someone affected by the action. So if the person ceases to show the reaction, the action is no longer wrong. The person to whom a promise is made can make a broken promise cease to be wrong by welcoming the fact that it was broken. The masochist, by welcoming injuries to himself, makes them cease to be injuries. Thus, if (1) all wrongs are injuries to God only and (2) they are the kind of wrongs which God eventually shows a favourable reaction to, God might be able to set all wrongs right.

I have already commented on (1) above, maintaining that it is very difficult to take the point of view that God is always the only one injured in a wrong-doing. (2), I think, is even more absurd. How could a morally sensitive and just God welcome human beings torturing, maiming, killing and causing suffering to one another?

So we cannot without logical and/or moral absurdity say of a fully divine being that it forgives in any sense I have been able to give to "forgive." Whether this is because divine forgiveness is beyond the scope of human understanding is another question, not the concern of this paper. I have only tried to show that divine forgiveness does appear absurd to the human understanding, or at least to mine.

NOTES

1. Alwynne Smart makes essentially this point in connection with mercy ("Mercy," in *The Philosophical Quarterly*, 17 (1967), 345–59). She argues that remission or modification of punishment in the light of special circumstances surrounding the crime is not a genuine exercise of mercy, but making a judgment about the appropriate punishment taking *all* relevant considerations into account.
2. Joseph Butler, *Fifteen Sermons Preached at the Rolls Chapel* (London, 1967), pp. 125 ff.
3. Butler, op. cit., p. 143.
4. Butler, op. cit., p. 129 ff.
5. Thus R. S. Downie argues ("Forgiveness," in *The Philosophical Quarterly*, 15 (1965), 128–34) that an injury severs the relationship of *agape* with the person injured, forgiveness restores it.
6. In fact, Strawson makes repentance, in the sense of repudiation of the injury, a necessary condition for forgiveness (P. F. Strawson, "Freedom and Resentment," in *Studies in the Philosophy of Thought and Action*, ed. Strawson [Oxford, 1968]) since he defines forgiveness thus: "and to forgive is to accept the repudiation and to forswear the resentment." In this paper Strawson makes a number of interesting comments about resentment, too many for me to discuss here.

PART THREE

Arguments for God's Existence

A. THE ONTOLOGICAL ARGUMENT

14 THE ONTOLOGICAL ARGUMENT

ANSELM AND GAUNILO

At this point, we temporarily put aside questions about the attributes of God and turn to the issue of whether God, as conceived in the Abrahamic religions, exists. Throughout the history of philosophy, various arguments have been offered to prove God's existence, but only one, the ontological argument, is a priori, making no appeal to empirical evidence and relying solely on an analysis of the concept of God.

Its classic formulation was provided by Saint Anselm (1033–1109), who was born in a village that is now part of Italy, was educated in a Benedictine monastery, and became Archbishop of Canterbury. He understood God to be the Being greater than which none can be conceived. Anselm reasoned that if God did not exist, then a greater being could be conceived, namely, a being that exists. In that case, the Being greater than which none can be conceived would not be the Being greater than which none can be conceived, which is a contradiction. So the Being greater than which none can be conceived must exist—that is,

From Saint Anselm and Gaunilo, "The Ontological Argument," trans. William E. Mann, in *Reason at Work: Introductory Readings in Philosophy*, Third Edition, eds. Steven M. Cahn, Patricia Kitcher, George Sher, and Peter Markie, Harcourt Brace College Publishers, 1996. Reprinted by permission of Thomson/Wadsworth.

God must exist. Indeed, Anselm goes on to claim that God cannot even be thought not to exist, because a being that cannot be thought not to exist is greater than one that can be thought not to exist.

The first known response to Anselm's argument was offered by his contemporary, Gaunilo, a monk of Marmoutier, France, about whom little is known. Gaunilo maintained that Anselm's line of reasoning could be used to prove the existence of an island greater than which none can be conceived, an absurd conclusion. In reply, Anselm maintained that the argument did not apply to an island because, unlike God, an island has a beginning and end and so can be thought not to exist.

ANSELM

Chapter II: That God Truly Exists

Therefore, Lord, You Who give understanding to faith, give to me: insofar as You know it to be advantageous, let me understand that You exist, as we believe, and also that You are that which we believe You to be. And indeed, we believe You to be something than which nothing greater could be conceived. Or is there thus not something of such a nature, since the fool has said in his heart—there is no God [Psalm 14:1, 53:1]. But surely this same fool, when he hears this very thing that I speak—"something than which nothing greater can be conceived"—understands that which he hears, and that which he understands is in his understanding, even if he does not understand it to exist. For it is one thing for a thing to be in the understanding, and another to understand a thing to exist. For when a painter conceives before hand that which he is to make, he certainly has it in the understanding, but he does not yet understand to exist that which he has not yet made. However, when he has painted it, he both has it in the understanding and understands that that which he has now made exists. Therefore, even the fool is convinced that something than which nothing greater can be conceived is at least in the understanding, since when he hears this, he understands it, and whatever is understood is in the understanding. And surely that than which a greater cannot be conceived cannot be in the understanding alone. For if it is even in the understanding alone, it can be conceived to exist in reality also, which is greater. Thus if that than which a greater cannot be conceived is in the understanding alone, then that than which a greater cannot be conceived itself is that than which a greater can be conceived. But surely this cannot be. Therefore without doubt something than which a greater cannot be conceived exists, both in the understanding and in reality.

Chapter III: That God Cannot Be Conceived Not to Exist

And surely it exists so truly that it could not be conceived not to exist. For something can be conceived to exist which could not be conceived not to exist, which is greater than that which can be conceived not to exist. Thus if that than which a greater cannot be conceived can be conceived not to exist, then that than which a greater cannot be conceived itself is not that than which a greater cannot be conceived, which cannot be made consistent. Thus something than which a greater cannot be conceived exists so truly that it could not be conceived not to exist.

And this You are, Lord our God. Thus so truly do You exist, Lord my God, that You could not be conceived not to exist. And justly so. For if some mind could conceive of something better than You, the creature would rise above the creator and would judge the creator, which is exceedingly absurd. And indeed, whatever is distinct from You alone can be conceived not to exist. Therefore You alone are the truest of all things and thus You have existence as the greatest of all things, since anything else does not exist so truly, and for that reason has less existence. And so why has the fool said in his heart that there is no God, when to a rational mind it would be so obvious that You exist as the greatest of all things? Why, unless because he is stupid and a fool?

Chapter IV: How the Fool Has Said in His Heart What Cannot Be Conceived

Indeed how has he said in his heart what he has not been able to conceive, or how has he not been able to conceive what he has said in his heart, when to say in the heart and to conceive are the same? If he truly—rather, *since* he truly—both has conceived (since he has spoken in his heart) and has not spoken in his heart (since he has not been able to conceive), then there is not only one way in which something is said in the heart or is conceived. For in one way a thing is conceived when a word signifying it is conceived; in another when that thing itself is understood. In the former way, thus, God can be conceived not to exist; in the latter, not at all. No one, in fact, understanding what God is, can conceive that God does not exist, although he may say these words in his heart, either without significance or with some extraneous significance. For God is that than which a greater cannot be conceived. He who understands this well certainly understands this very being to exist in such a way that it is not able not to exist in conception. Thus he who understands that God so exists, cannot conceive Him not to exist.

I give thanks to You, good Lord, I give thanks to You, because that which before I believed through Your giving to me, I now so understand through Your illuminating me that if I were unwilling to believe that You exist, I would not be able to understand that You exist.

A REPLY ON BEHALF OF THE FOOL (GAUNILO)

[1] To one doubting whether there is, or to one denying that there is, something of such a nature that nothing greater [than it] can be conceived, it is said here [in the *Proslogion*] that being is proved to exist: first because the one who denies or doubts it himself already has it in the understanding, since

one who hears what is said understands what is said; next because that which he understands is necessarily such that it is not only in the understanding but also in reality. And this is proved in the following way: because it is greater to be also in reality than only in the understanding, and if that being is only in the understanding, whatever would have been also in reality will be greater than it. And so that which is greater than all things will be less than something, and it will not be greater than all things, which is of course inconsistent. And therefore it is necessarily the case that that which is greater than all things, which has already been proved to be in the understanding, is not only in the understanding but also in reality, because otherwise it cannot be greater than all things. Perhaps he [the fool] can respond:

[2] This being is already said to be in my understanding for no other reason than that I understand what is said. Could it not be said that whatever things are fictitious and which in themselves are absolutely in no way existent things are similarly in the understanding, since if someone speaks of them, I understand whatever he says?

[6] For example: some say that somewhere in the ocean there is an island, which through the difficulty—or rather, the impossibility—of discovering that which does not exist, some have named "The Lost Island." And it is fabled that it abounds with riches and delights of all sorts of inestimable fruitfulness, much more than the Isles of the Blessed, and having no owner or inhabitant, it is in every way superior in its abundance of goods to all other lands that men inhabit taken together. If someone says all this to me, I shall easily understand what is said, in which nothing is difficult. But if now he goes on to say, as if it followed logically: "You can no more doubt that this island which is superior to all lands truly exists somewhere in reality, than that it is even clearly in your understanding; and since it is more superior to be not only in the understanding but also in reality, therefore it is necessary that it is existent, since if it did not exist, any other land in reality whatsoever would be superior to it, so that this very thing, already conceived by you to be superior, will not be superior"; if, I say, he should wish

to prove to me by means of the above that this island truly exists beyond doubt, either I should think that he was joking, or I should not know which of us I ought to consider the bigger fool—I, if I acceded to him, or he, if he thought he had proved with any certainty the existence of this island, unless he had first shown that its very superiority exists—just as a true and certain thing, and not as a false or uncertain thing—in my understanding.

A REPLY BY THE AUTHOR (ANSELM)

[III] But it is as though, you say, someone said that some island in the ocean, which surpasses all lands in its fertility, and which, because of the difficulty—or rather, impossibility—of discovering that which does not exist, is called "The Lost Island," cannot for that reason be doubted to exist truly in reality, since one easily understands the words describing it. I say with confidence that if anyone discovers for me something existing either in reality itself or only in conception—except that than which a greater cannot be conceived—to

which the logical pattern of my argument applies, I shall discover that lost island and give it to him, never more to be lost.

But clearly now it is seen that that than which a greater cannot be conceived cannot be conceived not to exist, because it exists as a matter of such certain truth. For otherwise it would not exist at all. In fact, if anyone says that he conceives that this being does not exist, I say that when he conceives of this either he conceives of something than which a greater cannot be conceived, or he does not. If he does not conceive of it, then he does not conceive not to exist that which he does not conceive. If he truly does conceive of it, he certainly conceives of something which cannot be conceived not to exist. For if it could be conceived not to exist, it could be conceived to have a beginning and an end. But this cannot be. Thus he who conceives of this being conceives of something which cannot be conceived not to exist. He who truly conceives this does not conceive this very thing not to exist—otherwise he conceives what cannot be conceived. Therefore that than which nothing greater can be conceived cannot be conceived not to exist.

15   THE ONTOLOGICAL ARGUMENT: A CRITIQUE

IMMANUEL KANT

Immanuel Kant (1724–1804), who lived his entire life in the Prussian town of Königsberg, is a preeminent figure in the history of philosophy. In his monumental *Critique of Pure Reason*, written in German, he argued that any version of the ontological argument fails because it treats existence as though it were a predicate or part of the description of something instead of an indication that the thing is found in the world. To use Kant's example, the concept of a hundred thalers (silver coins) remains the same regardless of whether any thalers exist. Of course, I can spend real thalers and not imaginary ones, but what I believe a thaler to be

From *Critique of Pure Reason*, trans. Norman Kemp Smith, St. Martin's Press and Macmillan, 1929. Reprinted by permission of Palgrave Macmillan.

does not change because I happen to possess one. If existence does not belong to the concept of anything, then it does not belong to the concept of God. Thus a being is no greater or more perfect because it exists, and so the ontological argument does not succeed.

In all ages men have spoken of an *absolutely necessary* being, and in so doing have endeavoured, not so much to understand whether and how a thing of this kind allows even of being thought, but rather to prove its existence. There is, of course, no difficulty in giving a verbal definition of the concept, namely, that it is something the non-existence of which is impossible. But this yields no insight into the conditions which make it necessary to regard the non-existence of a thing as absolutely unthinkable. It is precisely these conditions that we desire to know, in order that we may determine whether or not, in resorting to this concept, we are thinking anything at all....

[T]his concept ... has been supposed to have its meaning exhibited in a number of examples; and on this account all further enquiry into its intelligibility has seemed to be quite needless. Thus the fact that every geometrical proposition, as, for instance, that a triangle has three angles, is absolutely necessary, has been taken as justifying us in speaking of an object which lies entirely outside the sphere of our understanding as if we understood perfectly what it is that we intend to convey by the concept of that object....

To posit a triangle, and yet to rejecting its three angles, is self-contradictory; but there is no contradiction in rejecting the triangle together with its three angles. The same holds true of the concept of an absolutely necessary being. If its existence is rejected, we reject the thing itself with all its predicates; and no question of contradiction can then arise. There is nothing outside it that would then be contradicted, since the necessity of the thing is not supposed to be derived from anything external; nor is there anything internal that would be contradicted, since in rejecting the thing itself we have at the same time rejected all its internal properties. "God is omnipotent" is a necessary judgment. The omnipotence cannot be rejected if we posit a Deity, that is, an infinite being; for the two concepts are identical. But if we say, "There is no God," neither the omnipotence nor any other of its predicates is given; they are one and all rejected together with the subject, and there is therefore not the least contradiction in such a judgment....

"Being" is obviously not a real predicate; that is, it is not a concept of something which could be added to the concept of a thing. It is merely the positing of a thing, or of certain determinations, as existing in themselves....

A hundred real thalers do not contain the least coin more than a hundred possible thalers. For as the latter signify the concept, and the former the object and the positing of the object, should the former contain more than the latter, my concept would not, in that case, express the whole object, and would not therefore be an adequate concept of it. My financial position is, however, affected very differently by a hundred real thalers than it is by the mere concept of them (that is, of their possibility)....

By whatever and by however many predicates we may think a thing—even if we completely determine it—we do not make the least addition to the thing when we further declare that this thing *is*. Otherwise, it would not be exactly the same thing that exists, but something more than we had thought in the concept; and we could not, therefore, say that the exact object of my concept exists. If we think in a thing every feature of reality except one, the missing reality is not added by my saying that this defective thing exists. On the contrary, it exists with the same defect with which I have thought it, since otherwise what exists would be something different from what I thought. When, therefore, I think a being as the supreme reality, without any defect, the question still remains whether it exists or not....

The attempt to establish the existence of a supreme being by means of the famous ontological argument ... is therefore merely so much labour and effort lost; we can no more extend our stock of [theoretical] insight by mere ideas, than a merchant can better his position by adding a few noughts to his cash account.

16 THE ONTOLOGICAL ARGUMENT: AN ASSESSMENT

WILLIAM L. ROWE

In our next selection, William Rowe, whose work we read previously, explores further intricacies of the ontological argument. Although he does not find that the argument is sound, he reaches the surprising conclusion that what Anselm has demonstrated is that if the existence of God is possible, then God exists.

The ontological argument has intrigued thinkers throughout the centuries. While its abstractness may not win many converts to any religion, the argument retains the power to fascinate philosophers.

Suppose someone comes to us and says:

> I propose to define the term *God as an existing, wholly perfect being*. Now since it can't be true that an existing, wholly perfect being does not exist, it can't be true that God, as I've defined him, does not exist. Therefore, God must exist.

This argument appears to be a very simple Ontological Argument. It begins with a particular idea or concept of God and ends by concluding that God, so conceived, must exist. What can we say in response? We might start by objecting to this definition of *God*, claiming (1) that only predicates can be used to define a term, and (2) that existence is not a predicate. But suppose our friend is not impressed by this response—either because he thinks no one has fully explained what a predicate is or proved that existence isn't one, or because he thinks that anyone can define a word in whatever way he pleases. Can we allow our friend to define the word *God* in any way he pleases and still hope to show that it will not follow from that definition that there actually exists something to which this concept of God applies? I think we can. Let's first invite him, however, to consider some concepts other than this peculiar concept of God....

[T]he term *magician* may be applied both to Houdini and Merlin, even though the former existed whereas the latter did not. Noting that our friend has used *existing* as part of this definition of *God*, suppose we agree with him that we can define a word in any way we please, and, accordingly, introduce the following words with the following definitions:

> A *magican* is defined as an *existing magician*.
>
> A *magico* is defined as a *nonexisting magician*.

Here we have introduced two words and used *existing* or *nonexisting* in their definitions. Now something of interest follows from the fact that *existing* is part of our definition of a magican. For while it's true that Merlin was a *magician* it isn't true that Merlin was a *magican*. And something of interest follows from our including *nonexisting* in the definition of a magico. For while it's true that Houdini was a *magician* it isn't true that Houdini was a *magico*. Houdini was a *magician* and a *magican*, but not a *magico*, whereas Merlin was a *magician* and a *magico*, but not a *magican*.

What we have just seen is that introducing *existing* or *nonexisting* into the definition of a concept has a very important implication. If we introduce *existing* into the definition of a concept, it follows that no nonexisting thing can exemplify that concept. And if we introduce *nonexisting*

From William L. Rowe, *Philosophy of Religion: An Introduction*, Fourth Edition, Wadsworth Publishing Company, 2007. Reprinted by permission of Thomson/Wadsworth.

into the definition of a concept, it follows that no existing thing can exemplify that concept. No nonexisting thing can be a *magican* and no existing thing can be a *magico*.

But must some existing thing exemplify the concept *magican*? No! From the fact that *existing* is included in the definition of *magican* it does not follow that some existing thing is a *magican*—all that follows is that no nonexisting thing is a *magican*. If there were no magicians in existence there would be nothing to which the term *magican* would apply. This being so, it clearly does not follow merely from our definition of *magican* that some existing thing is a *magican*. Only if magicians exist will it be true that some existing thing is a *magican*.

We are now in a position to help our friend see that, from the mere fact that *God* is defined as an existing, wholly perfect being, it will not follow that some existing being is God. Something of interest does follow from his definition: namely, that no nonexisting being can be God. But whether some existing thing is God will depend entirely on whether some existing thing is a wholly perfect being. If no wholly perfect being exists there will be nothing to which this concept of God can apply. This being so, it clearly does not follow merely from this definition of *God* that some existing thing is God. Only if a wholly perfect being exists will it be true that God, as our friend conceives of him, exists.

The implications of these considerations for Anselm's ingenious argument can now be traced. Anselm conceives of God as a being than which none greater is possible. He then claims that existence is a great-making quality, something that has it is greater than it would have been had it lacked existence. Clearly then, no nonexisting thing can exemplify Anselm's concept of God. For if we suppose that some nonexisting thing exemplifies Anselm's concept of God and also suppose that that nonexisting thing might have existed in reality (is a possible thing), then we are supposing that that nonexisting thing (1) might have been a greater thing, and (2) is, nevertheless, a thing than which a greater is not possible. Thus far Anselm's reasoning is, I believe, impeccable. But what follows from it? All that

follows from it is that no nonexisting thing can be God (as Anselm conceives of God). All that follows is that given Anselm's concept of God, the proposition "Some nonexisting thing is God" cannot be true. But, as we saw earlier, this is also the case with the proposition "Some nonexisting thing is a magican." What remains to be shown is that some existing thing exemplifies Anselm's concept of God. What really does follow from his reasoning is that the only thing that logically could exemplify his concept of God is something which actually exists. And this conclusion is not without interest. But from the mere fact that nothing but an existing thing could exemplify Anselm's concept of God, it does not follow that some existing thing actually does exemplify his concept of God—no more than it follows from the mere fact that no nonexisting thing can be a magican that some existing thing is a magican.[1]

There is, however, one major difficulty in this critique of Anselm's argument. This difficulty arises when we take into account Anselm's implicit claim that God is a possible thing.... Possible things ... [are] all those things that, unlike the round square, are not impossible things. Suppose we concede to Anselm that God, as he conceives of him, is a possible thing. Now, of course, the mere knowledge that something is a possible thing doesn't enable us to conclude that that thing is an existing thing. For many possible things, like the Fountain of Youth, do not exist. But if something is a possible thing, then it is either an existing thing or a nonexisting thing. The set of possible things can be exhaustively divided into those possible things which actually exist and those possible things which do not exist. Therefore, if Anselm's God is a possible thing, it is either an existing thing or a nonexisting thing. We have concluded, however, that no nonexisting thing can be Anselm's God; therefore, it seems we must conclude with Anselm that some actually existing thing does exemplify his concept of God.

To see the solution to this major difficulty we need to return to an earlier example. Let's consider again the idea of a magican, an existing magician. It so happens that some magicians have existed—Houdini, The Great Blackstone, and others. But, of course, it might have been otherwise. Suppose, for the moment, that no magicians have ever existed. The concept "magician" would still have application, for it would still be true that Merlin was a magician. But what about the concept of a "magican?" Would any possible object be picked out by that concept? No! For no nonexisting thing could exemplify the concept "magican." And on the supposition that no magicians ever existed, no existing thing would exemplify the concept "magican."[2] We then would have a coherent concept "magican" which would not be exemplified by any possible object at all. For if all the possible objects which are magicians are nonexisting things, none of them would be a magican and, since no possible objects which exist are magicians, none of them would be a magican. We then would have a coherent, consistent concept "magican", which in fact is not exemplified by any possible object at all. Put in this way, our result seems paradoxical. For we are inclined to think that only contradictory concepts like "the round square" are not exemplified by any possible things. The truth is, however, that when *existing* is included in or implied by a certain concept, it may be the case that no possible object does in fact exemplify that concept. For no possible object that doesn't exist will exemplify a concept like "magican" in which *existing* is included; and if there are no existing things which exemplify the other features included in the concept—for example, "being a magician" in the case of the concept "magican"—then no possible object that exists will exemplify the concept. Put in its simplest terms, if we ask whether any possible thing is a magican, the answer will depend entirely on whether any existing thing is a magician. If no existing things are magicians, then no possible things are magicians. Some possible object is a magican just in case some actually existing thing is a magician.

Applying these considerations to Anselm's argument we can find the solution to our major difficulty. Given Anselm's concept of God and his principle that existence is a great-making quality, it really does follow that the only thing that logically could exemplify his concept of God is something which actually exists. But, we argued, it doesn't follow from these considerations alone that God actually exists, that some existing thing exemplifies Anselm's concept of God. The difficulty we fell into, however, is that when we add the premise that God is a possible thing, that some possible object exemplifies his concept of God, it really does follow that God actually exists, that some actually existing thing exemplifies Anselm's concept of God. For if some possible object exemplifies his concept of God, that object is either an existing thing or a nonexisting thing. But since no nonexisting thing could exemplify Anselm's concept of God, it follows that the possible object which exemplifies his concept of God must be a possible object that actually exists. Therefore, given (1) Anselm's concept of God, (2) his principle that existence is a great-making quality, and (3) the premise that God, as conceived by Anselm, is a possible thing, it really does follow that Anselm's God actually exists.

I think we now can see that in granting Anselm the premise that God is a possible thing we have granted far more than we intended to grant. All we thought we were granting is that Anselm's concept of God, unlike the concept of a round square, is not contradictory or incoherent. But without realizing it we were in fact granting much more than this, as became apparent when we considered the idea of a "magican." There is nothing contradictory in the idea of a magican, an existing magician. But in asserting that a magican is a possible thing, we are, as we saw, directly implying that some existing thing is a magician. For if no existing thing is a magician, the concept of a magican will apply to no possible object whatever. The same point holds with respect to Anselm's God. Since Anselm's concept of God logically cannot apply to some nonexisting thing, the only possible objects to which it could apply are possible objects which actually exist. Therefore, in granting that Anselm's God is a possible thing, we are granting far more than that his idea of God isn't incoherent or contradictory. Suppose, for example, that every existing being has some defect which it might not have had. Without realizing it, we were denying this when we granted that Anselm's God is a possible being. For if every existing being has a defect it might not have had, then every existing being might have been greater.

But if every existing being might have been greater, then Anselm's concept of God will apply to no possible object whatever. Therefore, if we allow Anselm his concept of God and his principle that existence is a great-making quality, then in granting that God, as Anselm conceives of him, is a possible being, we will be granting much more than that his concept of God is not contradictory. We will be granting, for example, that some existing thing is as perfect as it can be. For the plain fact is that Anselm's God is a possible thing only if some *existing* thing is as perfect as it can be.

Our final critique of Anselm's argument is simply this. In granting that Anselm's God is a possible thing, we are in fact granting that Anselm's God actually exists. But since the purpose of the argument is to prove to us that Anselm's God exists, we cannot be asked to grant as a premise a statement which is virtually equivalent to the conclusion that is to be proved. Anselm's concept of God may be coherent and his principle that existence is a great-making quality may be true. But all that follows from this is that no nonexisting thing can be Anselm's God. If we add to all of this the premise that God is a possible thing it will follow that God actually exists. But the additional premise claims more than that Anselm's concept of God isn't incoherent or contradictory. It amounts to the assertion that some existing being is supremely great. And since this is, in part, the point the argument endeavors to prove, the argument begs the question: it assumes the point it is supposed to prove.

If the above critique is correct, Anselm's argument fails as a proof of the existence of God. This is not to say, however, that the argument isn't a work of genius. Perhaps no other argument in the history of thought has raised so many basic philosophical questions and stimulated so much hard thought. Even if it fails as a proof of the existence of God, it will remain as one of the high achievements of the human intellect.

NOTES

1. An argument along the lines just presented may be found in J. Shaffer's illuminating essay, "Existence, Predication and the Ontological Argument," *Mind* LXXI (1962), pp. 307–25.
2. I am indebted to Professor William Wainwright for bringing this point to my attention.

B. THE COSMOLOGICAL ARGUMENT

17 THE FIVE WAYS

THOMAS AQUINAS

St. Thomas Aquinas (1225–1274), born near Naples, was the most influential philosopher of the medieval period. He joined the Dominican order and taught at the University of Paris. In his vast writings, composed in Latin, he sought to demonstrate that all Christian doctrines were consistent with reason, even if some transcended reason and were believed on faith, for example, that the world did not always exist but was created at a particular time.

Aquinas's greatest work was the *Summa Theologiae*, and its most famous passage, reprinted here, is the five ways to prove the existence of God. These arguments are a posteriori, relying on empirical evidence.

The first way depends on observing that in the world some things are in motion, leading to the conclusion that God, the first mover, exists. The second way depends on observing that in the world each thing that exists is caused to exist by something other than itself, leading to the conclusion that God, the first cause, exists. The third way depends on observing that some things that exist in the world might possibly not exist, leading to the conclusion that God, whose nonexistence is not possible, exists. The fourth way depends on observing that in the world some things are more or less good, leading to the conclusion that God, the greatest good and the cause of all other goodness, exists. The fifth way depends on observing that things in the world act together to achieve a good end, leading to the conclusion that God, who directs all things to their end, exists.

The existence of God can be proved in five ways.

The first and more manifest way is the argument from motion. It is certain, and evident to our senses, that in the world some things are in motion. Now whatever is moved is moved by another, for nothing can be moved except it is in potentiality to that towards which it is moved; whereas a thing moves inasmuch as it is in act. For motion is nothing else than the reduction of something from potentiality to actuality. But nothing can be reduced from potentiality to actuality, except by something in a state of actuality. Thus that which is actually hot, as fire, makes wood, which is potentially hot, to be actually hot, and thereby moves and changes it. Now it is not possible that the same thing should be at once in actuality and potentiality in the same respect, but only in different respects. For what is actually hot cannot simultaneously be potentially hot; but it is simultaneously potentially cold. It is therefore impossible that in the same respect and in the same way a thing should be both mover and moved, i.e., that it should move itself. Therefore, whatever is moved must be moved by another. If that by which it is moved be itself moved, then this also must needs be moved by another, and that by another again. But this cannot go on to infinity, because then there would be no first mover, and, consequently, no other mover, seeing that subsequent movers move only inasmuch as

From Anton C. Pegis, ed., *Basic Writings of Saint Thomas Aquinas*, Hackett Publishing Company, 1993. Reprinted by permission of the publisher.

they are moved by the first mover; as the staff moves only because it is moved by the hand. Therefore it is necessary to arrive at a first mover, moved by no other; and this everyone understands to be God.

The second way is from the nature of efficient cause. In the world of sensible things we find there is an order of efficient causes. There is no case known (neither is it, indeed, possible) in which a thing is found to be the efficient cause of itself; for so it would be prior to itself, which is impossible. Now in efficient causes it is not possible to go on to infinity, because in all efficient causes following in order, the first is the cause of the intermediate cause, and the intermediate is the cause of the ultimate cause, whether the intermediate cause be several, or one only. Now to take away the cause is to take away the effect. Therefore, if there be no first cause among efficient causes, there will be no ultimate, nor any intermediate, cause. But if in efficient causes it is possible to go on to infinity, there will be no first efficient cause, neither will there be an ultimate effect, nor any intermediate efficient causes; all of which is plainly false. Therefore it is necessary to admit a first efficient cause, to which everyone gives the name of God.

The third way is taken from possibility and necessity, and runs thus. We find in nature things that are possible to be and not to be, since they are found to be generated, and to be corrupted, and consequently, it is possible for them to be and not to be. But it is impossible for these always to exist, for that which can not-be at some time is not. Therefore, if everything can not-be, then at one time there was nothing in existence. Now if this were true, even now there would be nothing in existence, because that which does not exist begins to exist only through something already existing. Therefore, if at one time nothing was in existence, it would have been impossible for anything to have begun to exist; and thus even now nothing would be in existence—which is absurd. Therefore, not all beings are merely possible, but there must exist something the existence of which is necessary. But every necessary thing either has its necessity caused by another, or not. Now it is impossible to go on to infinity in necessary things

which have their necessity caused by another, as has been already proved in regard to efficient causes. Therefore we cannot but admit the existence of some being having of itself its own necessity, and not receiving it from another, but rather causing in others their necessity. This all men speak of as God.

The fourth way is taken from the gradation to be found in things. Among beings there are some more and some less good, true, noble, and the like. But *more* and *less* are predicated of different things according as they resemble in their different ways something which is the maximum, as a thing is said to be hotter according as it more nearly resembles that which is hottest; so that there is something which is truest, something best, something noblest, and, consequently, something which is most being, for those things that are greatest in truth are greatest in being, as it is written in *Metaph.* ii.[1] Now the maximum in any genus is the cause of all in that genus, as fire, which is the maximum of heat, is the cause of all hot things, as is said in the same book. Therefore there must also be something which is to all beings the cause of their being, goodness, and every other perfection; and this we call God.

The fifth way is taken from the governance of the world. We see that things which lack knowledge, such as natural bodies, act for an end, and this is evident from their acting always, or nearly always, in the same way, so as to obtain the best result. Hence it is plain that they achieve their end, not fortuitously, but designedly. Now whatever lacks knowledge cannot move towards an end, unless it be directed by some being endowed with knowledge and intelligence; as the arrow is directed by the archer. Therefore some intelligent being exists by whom all natural things are directed to their end; and this being we call God.

Reply Obj. 1. As Augustine says: *Since God is the highest good, He would not allow any evil to exist in His works, unless His omnipotence and goodness were such as to bring good even out of evil.* This is part of the infinite goodness of God, that He should allow evil to exist, and out of it produce good.

Reply Obj. 2. Since nature works for a determinate end under the direction of a higher agent, whatever is done by nature must be traced back to God as to its first cause. So likewise whatever is done voluntarily must be traced back to some higher cause other than human reason and will, since these can change and fail; for all things that are changeable and capable of defect must be traced back to an immovable and self-necessary first principle, as has been shown.

NOTE

1. [The reference is to Aristotle's *Metaphysics*.]

18   THE COSMOLOGICAL ARGUMENT: A CRITIQUE

MICHAEL MARTIN

Michael Martin is Professor Emeritus of Philosophy at Boston University. In our next selection, he explains why in general he does not accept cosmological arguments and in particular believes Aquinas's second and third ways to be unsound.

THE SIMPLE VERSION

In its simplest form the cosmological argument is this: Everything we know has a cause. But there cannot be an infinite regress of causes, so there must be a first cause. This first cause is God.

It is well to state the problems with this simple version of the argument, since, as we shall see, they are found in some of the more sophisticated versions as well. Perhaps the major problem with this version of the argument is that even if it is successful in demonstrating a first cause, this first cause is not necessarily God. A first cause need not have the properties usually associated with God. For example, a first cause need not have great, let alone infinite, knowledge or goodness. A first cause could be an evil being or the universe itself. In itself this problem makes the argument quite useless as support for the view that God exists. However, it has at least one other equally serious problem.

The argument assumes that there cannot be an infinite sequence of causes, but it is unclear why this should be so. Experience does not reveal causal sequences that have a first cause, a cause that is not caused. So the idea that there can be no infinite sequences and that there must be a first cause, a cause without a cause, finds no support in experience. This is not to say that experience indicates an infinite sequence of causes. Rather, the presumption of the existence of a first cause seems to be a nonempirical assumption that some people see as obvious or self-evident. From a historical point of view, however, any appeal to obviousness or self-evidence must be regarded with suspicion, for many things that have been claimed to be self-evidently true—for example, the divine right of kings and the earth as the center of the universe—have turned out not to be true at all.

Further, we have no experience of infinite causal sequences, but we do know that there are infinite series, such as natural numbers. One wonders why, if there can be infinite sequences in mathematics, there could not be one in causality.

From Michael Martin, *Atheism: A Philosophical Justification*, Temple University Press, 1990. Reprinted by permission of the publisher.

No doubt there are crucial differences between causal and mathematical series; but without further arguments showing precisely what these are, there is no reason to think that there could not be an infinite regression of causes. Some recent defenders of the cosmological argument have offered just such arguments, and I examine these arguments later. But even if they are successful, in themselves they do not show that the first cause is God.

MORE COMPLEX VERSIONS

As I have said, major problems facing the simple version of the cosmological argument reemerge in more sophisticated versions as well. Consider, for example, Aquinas's belief that God's existence could be demonstrated by rational arguments. In the *Summa Theologiae* he presents five arguments—what he calls ways—that he believes demonstrate the existence of God. The first three of his five ways are sophisticated versions of the simple cosmological argument presented alone. I consider ways two and three....

[In] the second way ... Aquinas attempts to show that there could not be an infinite series of efficient causes and consequently there must be a first cause. Although this notion of efficient cause is perhaps closer to our modern view of causality than the other Aristotelian concepts of cause he used, there are some important differences. An efficient cause of something, for Aristotle and Aquinas, is not a prior event but a substantial agent that brings about change. The paradigm cases of causation for an Aristotelian are heating and wetting. For example, if A heats B, then A produces heat in B; if A wets B, then A produces wetness in B. In general, if A Φs B, then A produces Φness in B. The priority of a cause need not be temporal; a cause is prior to its effects in the sense that the cause can exist without the effect but not conversely.

It is important to realize that Aquinas's argument purports to establish a first cause that maintains the universe here and now. His second way is not concerned with establishing a first cause of the universe in the distant past. Indeed, he believed that one could not demonstrate by philosophical argument that the universe had a beginning in time, although he believed that it did. This belief was a matter of faith, something that was part of

Christian dogma, not something that one could certify by reason. Thus he was not opposed on *philosophical* grounds to the universe's having no temporal beginning. As the above quotation makes clear, he believed that the here-and-now maintenance of the universe could not be understood in terms of an infinite causal series.

Two analogies can perhaps make the distinction between temporal and nontemporal causal sequences clear. Consider a series of falling dominos. It is analogous to a temporal causal sequence. Aquinas does not deny on philosophical grounds that infinite sequences of this sort can exist. But now consider a chain in which one link supports the next. There is no temporal sequence here. The sort of causal sequence that Aquinas says cannot go on forever but must end in a first cause is analogous to this.

The same problems that plagued the simple version of the argument plague this more sophisticated version. The first cause, even if established, need not be God; and Aquinas gives no non-question-begging reason why there could not be a nontemporal infinite regress of causes. This latter is an especially acute problem. Unless some relevant difference is shown between a temporal and a nontemporal infinite series, Aquinas's claim that an infinite temporal sequence cannot be shown to be impossible by philosophical argument seems indirectly to cast doubt on his claim that philosophical argument can show the impossibility of a nontemporal causal series....

To critically evaluate Aquinas's [third way], it is useful to reformulate it in the following steps.

1. Each existing thing is capable of not existing.
2. What is true of each thing is true of everything (the totality).
3. Therefore, everything could cease to exist.
4. If everything could cease to exist, then it has already occurred.
5. Therefore, everything has ceased to exist.
6. If everything has already ceased to exist and there could not be something brought into existence by nothing, then nothing exists now.
7. There could not be something brought into existence by nothing.
8. Therefore, nothing exists now.
9. But something does exist now.
10. Therefore, premise (1) is false.

11. Therefore, there must be some being that is not capable of not existing—that is, a necessary being.

12. Every necessary being must have the cause of its necessity either outside itself or not.

13. There cannot be an infinite series of necessary beings that have a cause of their necessity outside themselves.

14. Therefore, there is a necessary being that does not have the cause of its own necessity outside itself and that is the cause of the necessity of other beings.

15. Therefore, God exists.

Of the many problems with Aquinas's argument, the major one is similar to that facing the simple version of the cosmological argument considered above. Even if a necessary being is established, it need not be God, for the universe itself may be necessary. Thus the last step of the argument from (14) to (15) is unwarranted.

There are a number of particular problems with Aquinas's argument as well. In premise (2) the argument seems to commit the fallacy of composition. Just because each thing is capable of not existing, it is not obvious that the totality would be capable of not existing. Furthermore, premise (4) seems implausible in the extreme. There is no reason to suppose that just because something is capable of not existing, at some time this possibility has been realized.

In addition, the supposition in premise (7) that there could not be something brought into existence by nothing is by no means self-evident. At least, given the biblical authority of the book of Genesis, where God created the world out of nothing, it should not have seemed so to Aquinas. For if God could create the world out of nothing, one might suppose that something could be spontaneously generated out of nothing without God's help. Surely this is all step (7) is denying by the words "there could not be something brought into existence by nothing." Furthermore, recently proposed cosmological theories suggest that the universe may indeed have been generated from nothing. Although a critical evaluation of these recent theories is beyond the scope of this book, it is important to realize that such theories are being seriously discussed and debated by physicists, astronomers, and philosophers of science in respectable publications. Moreover, step (13) has all the problems inherited from Aquinas's arguments that there could not be an infinite series of efficient causes.

I must conclude, then, that these two deductive versions of the cosmological argument are unsound and therefore cannot be used to support a belief in God.

19 THE COSMOLOGICAL ARGUMENT

RICHARD TAYLOR

A contemporary version of the cosmological argument is presented by Richard Taylor (1919–2003), who was a professor of philosophy at the University of Rochester. He argues that the existence of the world requires an explanation, and that the most plausible one points to God, a being who exists necessarily—that is, who cannot fail to exist.

From Richard Taylor, *Metaphysics*, Fourth Edition, Prentice Hall, 1992. Reprinted by permission of Pearson Education, Inc.

THE PRINCIPLE OF SUFFICIENT REASON

Suppose you were strolling in the woods and, in addition to the sticks, stones, and other accustomed litter of the forest floor, you one day came upon some quite unaccustomed object, something not quite like what you had ever seen before and would never expect to find in such a place. Suppose, for example, that it is a large ball, about your own height, perfectly smooth and translucent. You would deem this puzzling and mysterious, certainly, but if one considers the matter, it is no more inherently mysterious that such a thing should exist than that anything else should exist. If you were quite accustomed to finding such objects of various sizes around you most of the time, but had never seen an ordinary rock, then upon finding a large rock in the woods one day you would be just as puzzled and mystified. This illustrates the fact that something that is mysterious ceases to seem so simply by its accustomed presence. It is strange indeed, for example, that a world such as ours should exist; yet few people are very often struck by this strangeness but simply take it for granted.

Suppose, then, that you have found this translucent ball and are mystified by it. Now whatever else you might wonder about it, there is one thing you would hardly question; namely, that it did not appear there all by itself, that it owes its existence to something. You might not have the remotest idea whence and how it came to be there, but you would hardly doubt that there was an explanation. The idea that it might have come from nothing at all, that it might exist without there being any explanation of its existence, is one that few people would consider worthy of entertaining.

This illustrates a metaphysical belief that seems to be almost a part of reason itself, even though few ever think upon it; the belief, namely, that there is some explanation for the existence of anything whatever, some reason why it should exist rather than not. The sheer nonexistence of anything, which is not to be confused with the passing out of existence of something, never requires a reason; but existence does. That there should never have been any such ball in the forest does not require any explanation or reason, but that there should ever be such a ball does. If one were to look upon a barren plain and ask why there is not and never has been any large translucent ball there, the natural response would be to ask why there should be; but if one finds such a ball, and wonders why it is there, it is not quite so natural to ask why it should *not* be—as though existence should simply be taken for granted. That anything should not exist, then, and that, for instance, no such ball should exist in the forest, or that there should be no forest for it to occupy, or no continent containing a forest, or no Earth, nor any world at all, do not seem to be things for which there needs to be any explanation or reason; but that such things should be *does* seem to require a reason.

The principle involved here has been called the principle of sufficient reason. Actually, it is a very general principle, and it is best expressed by saying that, in the case of any positive truth, there is some sufficient reason for it, something that, in this sense, makes it true—in short, that there is some sort of explanation, known or unknown, for everything.

Now, some truths depend on something else, and are accordingly called *contingent*, while others depend only upon themselves, that is, are true by their very natures and are accordingly called *necessary*. There is, for example, a reason why the stone on my window sill is warm; namely, that the sun is shining upon it. This happens to be true, but not by its very nature. Hence, it is contingent, and depends upon something other than itself. It is also true that all the points of a circle are equidistant from the center, but this truth depends upon nothing but itself. No matter what happens, nothing can make it false. Similarly, it is a truth, and a necessary one that if the stone on my window sill is a body, as it is, then it has a form, because this fact depends upon nothing but itself for its confirmation. Untruths are also, of course, either contingent or necessary, it being contingently false, for example, that the stone on my window sill is cold, and necessarily false that it is both a body and formless, because this is by its very nature impossible.

The principle of sufficient reason can be illustrated in various ways, as we have done, and if one thinks about it, he is apt to find that he presupposes it in his thinking about reality, but it cannot be proved. It does not appear to be itself a necessary truth, and at the same time it would be most odd to say it is contingent. If one were to try proving it, he would sooner or later have to appeal to considerations that are less plausible than the principle itself. Indeed, it is hard to see how one could even make an argument for it without already assuming it. For this reason it might properly be called a presupposition of reason itself. One can deny that it is true, without embarrassment or fear of refutation, but one is then apt to find that what he is denying is not really what the principle asserts. We shall, then, treat it here as a datum—not something that is provably true, but as something that people, whether they ever reflect upon it or not, seem more or less to presuppose.

THE EXISTENCE OF A WORLD

It happens to be true that something exists, that there is, for example, a world, and although no one ever seriously supposes that this might not be so, that there might exist nothing at all, there still seems to be nothing the least necessary in this, considering it just by itself. That no world should ever exist at all is perfectly comprehensible and seems to express not the slightest absurdity. Considering any particular item in the world it seems not at all necessary that the totality of these things, or any totality of things, should ever exist.

From the principle of sufficient reason it follows, of course, that there must be a reason not only for the existence of everything in the world but for the world itself, meaning by "the world" simply everything that ever does exist, except God, in case there is a god. This principle does not imply that there must be some purpose or goal for everything, or for the totality of all things; for explanations need not be, and in fact seldom are, teleological or purposeful. All the principle requires is that there be some sort of reason for everything. And it would certainly be odd to maintain that everything in the world owes its existence to something, that nothing in the world is either purely accidental, or such that it just bestows its own being upon itself, and then to deny this of the world itself. One can indeed *say* that the world is in some sense a pure accident, that there simply is no reason at all why this or any world should exist, and one can equally say that the world exists by its very nature, or is an inherently necessary being. But it is at least very odd and arbitrary to deny of this existing world the need for any sufficient reason, whether independent of itself or not, while presupposing that there is a reason for every other thing that ever exists.

Consider again the strange ball that we imagine has been found in the forest. Now, we can hardly doubt that there must be an explanation for the existence of such a thing, though we may have no notion what that explanation is. It is not, moreover, the fact of its having been found in the forest rather than elsewhere that renders an explanation necessary. It matters not in the least where it happens to be, for our question is not how it happens to be *there* but how it happens to be at all. If we in our imagination annihilate the forest, leaving only this ball in an open field, our conviction that it is a contingent thing and owes its existence to something other than itself is not reduced in the least. If we now imagine the field to be annihilated, and in fact everything else as well to vanish into nothingness, leaving only this ball to constitute the entire physical universe, then we cannot for a moment suppose that its existence has thereby been explained, or the need for any explanation eliminated, or that its existence is suddenly rendered self-explanatory. If we now carry this thought one step further and suppose that no other reality ever has existed or ever will exist, that this ball forever constitutes the entire physical universe, then we must still insist on there being some reason independent of itself why it should exist rather than not. If there must be a reason for the existence of any particular thing, then the necessity of such a reason is not eliminated by the mere supposition that certain other things do *not* exist. And again, it matters not at all what the thing in question is, whether it be large and complex, such as the world we actually find ourselves in, or whether it be something small, simple, and insignificant, such as a ball, a bacterium, or the merest grain of sand. We do not avoid the necessity of a reason for the existence of something merely by describing it in this way or that. And it would, in any event, seem quite plainly absurd to say that if the world were composed entirely of a single ball about six feet in diameter, or of a single grain of sand, then it would be contingent and there would have to be some explanation other than itself why such a thing exists, but that, since the actual world is vastly more complex than this, there is no need for an explanation of its existence, independent of itself.

BEGINNINGLESS EXISTENCE

It should now be noted that it is no answer to the question, why a thing exists, to state *how long* it has existed. A geologist does not suppose that she has explained why there should be rivers and mountains merely by pointing out that they are old. Similarly, if one were to ask, concerning the ball of which we have spoken, for some sufficient reason for its being, he would not receive any answer upon being told that it had been there since yesterday. Nor would it be any better answer to say that it had existed since before anyone could remember, or even that it had always existed; for the question was not one concerning its age but its existence. If, to be sure, one were to ask where a given thing came from, or how it came into being, then upon learning that it had always existed he would learn that it never really *came* into being at all; but he could still reasonably wonder why it should exist at all. If, accordingly, the world —that is, the totality of all things excepting God, in case there is a god—had really no beginning at all, but has always existed in some form or other, then there is clearly no answer to the question, where it came from and when; it did not, on this supposition, *come* from anything at all, at any time. But still, it can be asked why there is a world, why indeed there is a beginningless world, why there should have perhaps always been something rather than nothing. And, if the principle of

sufficient reason is a good principle, there must be an answer to that question, an answer that is by no means supplied by giving the world an age, or even an infinite age.

CREATION

This brings out an important point with respect to the concept of creation that is often misunderstood, particularly by those whose thinking has been influenced by Christian ideas. People tend to think that creation—for example, the creation of the world by God—*means* creation *in time*, from which it of course logically follows that if the world had no beginning in time, then it cannot be the creation of God. This, however, is erroneous, for creation means essentially *dependence*, even in Christian theology. If one thing is the creation of another, then it depends for its existence on that other, and this is perfectly consistent with saying that both are eternal, that neither ever came into being and hence, that neither was ever created at any point of time. Perhaps an analogy will help convey this point. Consider, then, a flame that is casting beams of light. Now, there seems to be a clear sense in which the beams of light are dependent for their existence upon the flame, which is their source, while the flame, on the other hand, is not similarly dependent for its existence upon them. The beams of light arise from the flame, but the flame does not arise from them. In this sense, they are the creation of the flame; they derive their existence from it. And none of this has any reference to time; the relationship of dependence in such a case would not be altered in the slightest if we supposed that the flame, and with it the beams of light, had always existed, that neither had ever *come* into being.

Now if the world is the creation of God, its relationship to God should be thought of in this fashion; namely, that the world depends for its existence upon God, and could not exist independently of God. If God is eternal, as those who believe in God generally assume, then the world may (though it need not) be eternal too, without that altering in the least its dependence upon God for its existence, and hence without altering its being the creation of God. The supposition of God's eternality, on the other hand, does not by itself imply that the world is eternal too; for there is not the least reason why something of finite duration might not depend for its existence upon something of infinite duration—though the reverse is, of course, impossible.

GOD

If we think of God as "the creator of heaven and earth," and if we consider heaven and earth to include everything that exists except God, then we appear to have, in the foregoing considerations, fairly strong reasons for asserting that God, as so conceived, exists. Now of course most people have much more in mind than this when they think of God, for religions have ascribed to God ever so many attributes that are not at all implied by describing him merely as the creator of the world; but that is not relevant here. Most religious persons do, in any case, think of God as being at least the creator, as that being upon which everything ultimately depends, no matter what else they may say about Him in addition. It is, in fact, the first item in the creeds of Christianity that God is the "creator of heaven and earth." And, it seems, there are good metaphysical reasons, as distinguished from the persuasions of faith, for thinking that such a creative being exists.

If, as seems clearly implied by the principle of sufficient reason, there must be a reason for the existence of heaven and earth—i.e., for the world—then that reason must be found either in the world itself, or outside it, in something that is literally supranatural, or outside heaven and earth. Now if we suppose that the world—i.e., the totality of all things except God—contains within itself the reason for its existence, we are supposing that it exists by its very nature, that is, that it is a necessary being. In that case there would, of course, be no reason for saying that it must depend upon God or anything else for its existence; for if it exists by its very nature, then it depends upon nothing but itself, much as the sun depends upon nothing but itself for its heat. This, however, is implausible, for we find nothing about the world or anything in it to suggest that it exists by its own

nature, and we do find, on the contrary, ever so many things to suggest that it does not. For in the first place, anything that exists by its very nature must necessarily be eternal and indestructible. It would be a self-contradiction to say of anything that it exists by its own nature, or is a necessarily existing thing, and at the same time to say that it comes into being or passes away, or that it ever could come into being or pass away. Nothing about the world seems at all like this, for concerning anything in the world, we can perfectly easily think of it as being annihilated, or as never having existed in the first place, without there being the slightest hint of any absurdity in such a supposition. Some of the things in the universe are, to be sure, very old; the moon, for example, or the stars and the planets. It is even possible to imagine that they have always existed. Yet it seems quite impossible to suppose that they owe their existence to nothing but themselves, that they bestow existence upon themselves by their very natures, or that they are in themselves things of such nature that it would be impossible for them not to exist. Even if we suppose that something, such as the sun, for instance, has existed forever, and will never cease, still we cannot conclude just from this that it exists by its own nature. If, as is of course very doubtful, the sun has existed forever and will never cease, then it is possible that its heat and light have also existed forever and will never cease; but that would not show that the heat and light of the sun exist by their own natures. They are obviously contingent and depend on the sun for their existence, whether they are beginningless and everlasting or not.

There seems to be nothing in the world, then, concerning which it is at all plausible to suppose that it exists by its own nature, or contains within itself the reason for its existence. In fact, everything in the world appears to be quite plainly the opposite, namely, something that not only need not exist, but at some time or other, past or future or both, does not in fact exist. Everything in the world seems to have a finite duration, whether long or short. Most things, such as ourselves, exist only for a short while; they come into being, then soon cease. Other things, like the heavenly bodies, last longer, but they are still corruptible, and from all that we can gather about them, they too seem destined eventually to perish. We arrive at the conclusion, then, that although the world may contain some things that have always existed and are destined never to perish, it is nevertheless doubtful that it contains any such thing, and, in any case, everything in the world is capable of perishing, and nothing in it, however long it may already have existed and however long it may yet remain, exists by its own nature but depends instead upon something else.

Although this might be true of everything in the world, is it necessarily true of the world itself? That is, if we grant, as we seem forced to, that nothing in the world exists by its own nature, that everything in the world is contingent and perishable, must we also say that the world itself, or the totality of all these perishable things, is also contingent and perishable? Logically, we are not forced to, for it is logically possible that the totality of all perishable things might itself be imperishable, and hence, that the world might exist by its own nature, even though it is composed exclusively of things that are contingent. It is not logically necessary that a totality should share the defects of its members. For example, even though every person is mortal, it does not follow from this that the human race, or the totality of all people, is also mortal; for it is possible that there will always be human beings, even though there are no human beings who will always exist. Similarly, it is possible that the world is in itself a necessary thing, even though it is composed entirely of things that are contingent.

This is logically possible, but it is not plausible. For we find nothing whatever about the world, any more than in its parts, to suggest that it exists by its own nature. Concerning anything in the world, we have not the slightest difficulty in supposing that it should perish, or even that it should never have existed in the first place. We have almost as little difficulty in supposing this of the world itself. It might be somewhat hard to think of everything as utterly perishing and leaving no trace whatever of its ever having been, but there seems to be not the slightest difficulty in imagining that the world should never have existed in the first place. We can, for instance, perfectly easily suppose that nothing in the world had ever existed except, let us suppose, a single grain of sand, and we can thus suppose that this grain of sand has forever constituted the whole universe. Now if we consider just this grain of sand, it is quite impossible for us to suppose that it exists by its very nature and could never have failed to exist. It clearly depends for its existence upon something other than itself, if it depends on anything at all. The same will be true if we consider the world to consist not of one grain of sand but of two, or of a million, or, as we in fact find, of a vast number of stars and planets and all their minuter parts.

It would seem, then, that the world, in case it happens to exist at all—and this is quite beyond doubt—is contingent and thus dependent upon something other than itself for its existence, if it depends upon anything at all. And it must depend upon something, for otherwise there could be no reason why it exists in the first place. Now, that upon which the world depends must be something that either exists by its own nature or does not. If it does not exist by its own nature, then it, in turn, depends for its existence upon something else, and so on. Now then, we can say either of two things; namely, (1) that the world depends for its existence upon something else, which in turn depends on still another thing, this depending upon still another, ad infinitum; or (2) that the world derives its existence from something that exists by its own nature and that is accordingly eternal and imperishable, and is the creator of heaven and earth. The first of these alternatives, however, is impossible, for it does not render a sufficient reason why anything should exist in the first place. Instead of supplying a reason why any world should exist, it repeatedly begs off giving a reason. It explains what is dependent and perishable in terms of what is itself dependent and perishable, leaving us still without a reason why perishable things should exist at all, which is what we are seeking. Ultimately, then, it would seem that the world, or the totality of contingent or perishable things, in case it exists at all, must depend upon something that is necessary and imperishable, and that accordingly exists, not in dependence upon something else, but by its own nature.

"SELF-CAUSED"

What has been said thus far gives some intimation of what meaning should be attached to the concept of a self-caused being; a concept that is quite generally misunderstood, sometimes even by scholars. To say that something—God, for example—is self-caused, or is the cause of its own existence, does not mean that this being brings itself into existence, which is a perfectly absurd idea. Nothing can *bring* itself into existence. To say that something is self-caused (*causa sui*) means only that it exists, not contingently or in dependence upon something else but by its own nature, which is only to say that it is a being which is such that it can neither come into being nor perish. Now, whether in fact such a being exists or not, there is in any case no absurdity in the idea. We have found, in fact, that the principle of sufficient reason seems to point to the existence of such a being, as that upon which the world, with everything in it, must ultimately depend for its existence.

"NECESSARY BEING"

A being that depends for its existence upon nothing but itself and is in this sense self-caused, can equally be described as a necessary being; that is to say, a being that is not contingent, and hence not perishable. For in the case of anything that exists by its own nature and is dependent upon nothing else, it is impossible that it should not exist, which is equivalent to saying that it is necessary. Many persons have professed to find the gravest difficulties in this concept, too, but that is partly because it has been confused with other notions. If it makes sense to speak of anything as an *impossible* being, or something that by its very nature does not exist, then it is hard to see why the idea of a necessary being, or something that in its very nature exists, should not be just as comprehensible. And of course, we have not the slightest difficulty in speaking of something, such as a square circle or a formless body, as an impossible being. And if it makes sense to speak of something as being perishable, contingent, and dependent upon something other than itself for its existence, as it surely does, then there seems to be no difficulty in thinking of

something as imperishable and dependent upon nothing other than itself for its existence.

"FIRST CAUSE"

From these considerations we can see also what is properly meant by a "first cause," an appellative that has often been applied to God by theologians and that many persons have deemed an absurdity. It is a common criticism of this notion to say that there need not be any first cause, because the series of causes and effects that constitute the history of the universe might be infinite or beginningless and must, in fact, be infinite in case the universe itself had no beginning in time. This criticism, however, reflects a total misconception of what is meant by a first cause. *First* here does not mean first in time, and when God is spoken of as a first cause He is not being described as a being that, at some time in the remote past, *started* everything. To describe God as a first cause is only to say that He is literally a *primary* rather than a secondary cause, an *ultimate* rather than a derived cause, or a being upon which all other things, heaven and earth, ultimately depend for their existence. It is, in short, only to say that God is the creator, in the sense of creation previously explained. Now this, of course, is perfectly consistent with saying that the world is eternal or beginningless. As we have seen, one gives no reason for the existence of a world merely by giving it an age, even if it is supposed to have an infinite age. To use a helpful analogy, we can say that the sun is the first cause of daylight and, for that matter, of the moonlight of the night as well, which means only that daylight and moonlight ultimately depend upon the sun for their existence. The moon, on the other hand, is only a secondary or derivative cause of its light. This light would be no less dependent upon the sun if we affirmed that it had no beginning, for an ageless and beginningless light requires a source no less than an ephemeral one. If we supposed that the sun has always existed, and with it its light, then we would have to say that the sun has always been the first—i.e., the primary or ultimate—cause of its light. Such is precisely the manner in which God should be thought of, and is by theologians often thought of, as the first cause of heaven and earth.

20   A NECESSARY BEING?

C. B. MARTIN

C. B. Martin (1924–2008) was a professor of philosophy at the University of Calgary, Canada. He considers the concept of a necessary being and concludes that while a being may be necessary in the sense that it does not depend on anything else for its existence, it cannot be logically necessary, because a possible state of affairs is that nothing at all exists. So logic cannot require the existence of God, a conclusion that brings to mind the concerns regarding the ontological argument.

It is my task to give all the meaning I can to the notion of a necessary being.

Let us suppose a being of the following sort:

1. A being for whose existence nothing else need exist.
2. A being that has always existed.
3. A being upon whom everything else depends for its existence.

One can even have a kind of verification procedure for such qualities. For (1) take away all other things and the being would remain in existence. For (3) take away the being and everything else would pass out of existence. For (2) at *any* time in the past this being could be observed to exist.

If there was such a being, its existence would be necessary in two ways.

a. It would not be contingent (*this* sense of "contingent" has to do with things and not propositions); that is, it would not be causally dependent upon anything else for its existence. Necessity here comes to cosmic self-sufficiency.
b. Its existence would be necessary for the existence of anything else. We may ask, "Why is there such a being?" and we can answer, "Since there was no time at which this being came into existence and since it in no way depends upon anything else for its existence, the question has no point." This being would

provide us with an excellent cosmological stopping place. Personally, I should be satisfied with less.

So far, this being could be a star—a very important star, of course—and it would be a matter of investigation to find out what it was about its composition and its relation to other things that allowed it to have the wonderful qualities listed above. If we wanted this being to be God, then among other things we should have to say that it was conscious and created everything else according to its purpose. We should have to say that it was all-wise, all-good, and all-powerful. Yet, even with all of these qualities, the necessity of this being would be such that:

a. This being exists, but it is conceivable that it should not have existed.
b. This being exists and it is conceivable that it will cease to exist.

The question "Why is there anything at all?" may be asked in such a way that the answer is to be in terms of something that is not merely a matter of how the world in fact is but rather of something that *must* be and *could* not be different. Even our self-sufficient being did not *have* to exist, and if it had not existed there might have been a world similar to this that was dependent upon another or upon no self-sufficient entity, or perhaps there might have been nothing at all. Of course, if there is such a self-sufficient,

From C. B. Martin, *Religious Belief*, Cornell University Press, 1959. Reprinted by permission of the publisher.

all-sustaining being, you cannot subtract it from the world without subtracting all other things as well. Thus the old theological slogan:

God — the world = God.

The world — God = Nothing.

But it does not follow from this that if this self-sufficient being had not existed there would have been no other sort of world or that the non-existence of such a being is inconceivable or that its existence is anything more than a fact about how things happen to be.

For many, God's existence must be logically necessary, though perhaps self-evident only to the infinite intellect. That is, the truth of the proposition "God exists" should be logically necessary. This, indeed, would put God outside of the world of fact and indeed of the world of possibility.

One of the basic ways in which one comes to acquire the concept of a necessary proposition is to learn that a necessary proposition is true in all conceivable states of affairs. No matter what were the case or not the case, the truth of a necessary proposition would be secure. Now, it seems to me that a possible state of affairs is that there should be nothing. But if this state of affairs was obtained, the proposition "God exists" would be false. Therefore "God exists" cannot be a necessary proposition. Opposition to this argument must take the form of showing the statement "There was and will be nothing" to be either meaningless or self-contradictory. But this would result in showing the statement "There was and will be something" to be either meaningless or tautological. In fact, *just* so far as I can understand what it is for a thing, *any* thing, to exist, just so far do I understand what it is for it not to exist.

If God's existence, then, cannot be logically necessary, let it be necessary in the ways that I have made clear. Such a necessary being would explain much. Once the notion of such a being is made clear, our philosophical work is at an end.

21   THE KALAM COSMOLOGICAL ARGUMENT

WILLIAM L. ROWE

William L. Rowe, whose work we read previously, here assesses a version of the cosmological argument that has its origin in medieval Arabic philosophy but has recently been the subject of much discussion. The argument has been dubbed "the Kalam argument," a term derived from an Arabic word referring to the interpretation of Islamic doctrine. The argument rests on the claim that the world necessarily had a beginning, and because time began with the beginning of the world, we can conclude that the cause of the world must be a timeless being, who is God.

A version of the Cosmological Argument that has its origin in Arabic philosophy is also receiving attention in the contemporary philosophy of religion.... [A]ccording to the Kalam argument it is *impossible* for an *actual infinite* to exist. If the Kalam argument is correct on this point,

From William L. Rowe, *Philosophy of Religion*, Fourth Edition, Thomson/Wadsworth, 2007. Reprinted by permission of the publisher.

then, since an actual series of events stretching endlessly into the past would be an actual infinite, it is impossible that such a series should exist. This does not mean that there could not be a series that is *potentially infinite*, a series that at any moment it is considered is finite, but that can be successively added to ad infinitum. For such a series would never be *actually* infinite. But why is an *actual infinite* series of past events leading up to the present claimed to be impossible? Consider such an unending series of events into the past. Suppose each of these events takes a certain amount of time, however small, to occur. No matter how little time it takes each event to occur, the claim is that since there is no *first event* in the series of past events, one could never reach the point where we now are, the present.

If we grant the impossibility of an actual infinite, we can be confident that our universe *had a beginning*. For if our universe never had a beginning, then the series of events of which its past temporal existence consists would constitute an actual infinite. But our confidence that our universe had a beginning need not rely on this philosophical argument; for according to the best estimates of current science our universe did have a beginning. It came into existence about 14.5 billion years ago, with the planet Earth coming into existence about 4.5 billion years ago, and living things on earth coming into existence about 3.5 billion years ago.

We can now state the first step in the Kalam Cosmological Argument as follows:

1. If our universe never had a beginning, an actual infinite series of past events has occurred.
2. An actual infinite series of events in time is impossible.

Therefore,

3. Our universe had a beginning.

The second step of the Kalam argument raises the question of whether the beginning of our universe had a cause. It is important to note that according to current science the beginning of our universe also marks that beginning of time.[1] So, there simply is no temporal moment *before* the beginning of our universe, no prior moment at which something or someone might act so as to cause our universe to begin. This means that if our universe were to have a cause, the cause (whatever it may be) could not have caused our universe by existing at some temporal moment *before* our universe existed and then acting so as to bring about the existence of our universe. How then could our universe have been caused to exist? A prominent advocate of the Kalam Cosmological Argument, William Lane Craig, has noted that a number of philosophers have countenanced *simultaneous causation*. He cites an example provided by Immanuel Kant: a heavy ball's resting on a cushion being the cause of a depression in that cushion. Craig concludes:

> There seems to be no conceptual difficulty in saying that the cause of the origin of the universe acted simultaneously (or coincidentally) with the origination of the universe. We should therefore say that the cause of the origin of the universe is causally prior to the Big Bang, though not temporally prior to the Big Bang.[2]

The idea, then, is that time begins with the beginning of the universe. The cause of the universe, whatever it may be, is itself not temporal, since its existence is required in order for the universe (and time) to come into existence. What properties must some timeless entity possess in order for it to nontemporally cause a temporal universe to exist, assuming that reason requires us to suppose that there must be a cause of the Big Bang? Craig reasons that such an entity would have the properties constituting the God of traditional theism: perfect goodness, omniscience, and omnipotence. The question that remains is whether a being must have these three properties in order for it to be the nontemporal cause of the temporal universe. Presumably, a being with these properties would be able to cause the existence of the temporal universe. But in inferring from what appears to us to have been caused (our universe) to the nature of the being that caused it, we cannot simply assume the being to have properties that aren't in any way required for it to be successful in being the cause of our universe. A being with sufficient power and knowledge to cause a temporal universe need not possess knowledge of absolutely everything that is knowable (omniscience). Nor need it possess perfect goodness. Moreover, if we look at the quality of a part of the product that has been produced, the one planet in the universe with which we are acquainted, we will be hard pressed to think that the cause of our universe would have to be a morally perfect being. It is rather difficult to argue that a being with sufficient power and knowledge, although lacking perfect goodness, would be unable to cause the existence of our universe. This objection, however, does not show that the Kalam Cosmological Argument can play no significant role in support of traditional theism. For the Cosmological argument, in either its traditional form ... or as represented in the Kalam version, is only one of several important arguments for the existence of the theistic God. If the Kalam argument supports the existence of a creator of the universe, some other argument may support the conclusion that a creator would possess moral perfection. And just as one branch may be insufficient to support a heavy object, but several tied together will be sufficient, so too the several arguments taken together may be sufficient to support the existence of a being that is omniscient, omnipotent, perfectly good, and the creator of the world.

NOTES

1. See Stephen Hawking's famous lecture "The Beginning of Time" at www://hawking.org.uk/lectures/index.html.
2. "Creation and Big-Bang Cosmology," www://leaderu.com/offices/billcraig/creation.html.

C. THE TELEOLOGICAL ARGUMENT

22   THE EVIDENCE OF DESIGN

WILLIAM PALEY

William Paley (1743–1805) was an English theologian and moral philosopher. He gave a classic presentation of another argument for the existence of God, the so-called teleological argument or argument to design. This argument proceeds from the premise of the world's magnificent order to the conclusion that the world must be the work of a Supreme Mind responsible for this order.

CHAPTER I: THE STATE OF THE ARGUMENT

In crossing a heath, suppose I pitched my foot against a stone and were asked how the stone came to be there. I might possibly answer that for anything I knew to the contrary it had lain there forever; nor would it, perhaps, be very easy to show the absurdity of this answer. But suppose I had found a watch upon the ground, and it should be inquired how the watch happened to be in that place. I should hardly think of the answer which I had before given, that for anything I knew the watch might have always been there. Yet why should not this answer serve for the watch as well as for the stone? Why is it not as admissible in the second case as in the first? For this reason, and for no other, namely, that when we come to inspect the watch, we perceive—what we could not discover in the stone—that its several parts are framed and put together for a purpose, e.g., that they are so formed and adjusted as to produce motion, and that motion so regulated as to point out the hour of the day; that if the different parts had been differently shaped from what they are, of a different size from what they are, or placed after any other manner or in any other order than that in which they are placed, either no motion at all would have been carried

on in the machine, or none which would have answered the use that is now served by it. To reckon up a few of the plainest of these parts and of their offices, all tending to one result; we see a cylindrical box containing a coiled elastic spring, which, by its endeavor to relax itself, turns round the box. We next observe a flexible chain—artificially wrought for the sake of flexure—communicating the action of the spring from the box to the fusee. We then find a series of wheels, the teeth of which catch in and apply to each other, conducting the motion from the fusee to the balance and from the balance to the pointer, and at the same time, by the size and shape of those wheels, so regulating that motion as to terminate in causing an index, by an equable and measured progression, to pass over a given space in a given time. We take notice that the wheels are made of brass, in order to keep them from rust; the springs of steel, no other metal being so elastic; that over the face of the watch there is placed a glass, a material employed in no other part of the work, but in the room of which, if there had been any other than a transparent substance, the hour could not be seen without opening the case. This mechanism being observed—it requires indeed an examination of the instrument, and perhaps some previous knowledge of the subject, to perceive and understand it; but being once, as we have

From William Paley, *Natural Theology* (1802).

said, observed and understood—the inference we think is inevitable, that the watch must have had a maker—that there must have existed, at some time and at some place or other, an artificer or artificers who formed it for the purpose which we find it actually to answer, who comprehended its construction and designed its use.

I. Nor would it, I apprehend, weaken the conclusion, that we had never seen a watch made—that we had never known an artist capable of making one—that we were altogether incapable of executing such a piece of workmanship ourselves, or of understanding in what manner it was performed; all this being no more than what is true of some exquisite remains of ancient art, of some lost arts, and, to the generality of mankind, of the more curious productions of modern manufacture. Does one man in a million know how oval frames are turned? Ignorance of this kind exalts our opinion of the unseen and unknown artist's skill, if he be unseen and unknown, but raises no doubt in our minds of the existence and agency of such an artist, at some former time and in some place or other. Nor can I perceive that it varies at all the inference, whether the question arises concerning a human agent or concerning an agent of a different species, or an agent possessing in some respects a different nature.

II. Neither, secondly, would it invalidate our conclusion, that the watch sometimes went wrong or that it seldom went exactly right. The purpose of the machinery, the design, and the designer might be evident, and in the case supposed, would be evident, in whatever way we accounted for the irregularity of the movement, or whether we could account for it or not. It is not necessary that a machine be perfect in order to show with what design it was made: still less necessary, where the only question is whether it were made with any design at all.

III. Nor, thirdly, would it bring any uncertainty into the argument, if there were a few parts of the watch, concerning which we could not discover or had not yet discovered in what manner they conduced to the general effect; or even some parts, concerning which we could not ascertain whether they conduced to that effect in any manner whatever. For, as to the first branch of the case, if by the loss, or disorder, or decay of the parts in question, the movement of the watch were found in fact to be stopped, or disturbed, or retarded, no doubt would remain in our minds as to the utility or intention of these parts, although we should be unable to investigate the manner according to which, or the connection by which, the ultimate effect depended upon their action or assistance; and the more complex is the machine, the more likely is this obscurity to arise. Then, as to the second thing supposed, namely, that there were parts which might be spared without prejudice to the movement of the watch, and that we had proved this by experiment, these superfluous parts, even if we were completely assured that they were such, would not vacate the reasoning which we had instituted concerning other parts. The indication of contrivance remained, with respect to them, nearly as it was before.

IV. Nor, fourthly, would any man in his senses think the existence of the watch with its various machinery accounted for, by being told that it was one out of possible combinations of material forms; that whatever he had found in the place where he found the watch, must have contained some internal configuration or other; and that this configuration might be the structure now exhibited, namely, of the works of a watch, as well as a different structure.

V. Nor, fifthly, would it yield his inquiry more satisfaction, to be answered that there existed in things a principle of order, which had disposed the parts of the watch into their present form and situation. He never knew a watch made by the principle of order; nor can he even form to himself an idea of what is meant by a principle of order distinct from the intelligence of the watchmaker.

VI. Sixthly, he would be surprised to hear that the mechanism of the watch was no proof of contrivance, only a motive to induce the mind to think so:

VII. And not less surprised to be informed that the watch in his hand was nothing more than the result of the laws of *metallic* nature. It is a perversion of language to assign any law as the efficient, operative cause of any thing. A law presupposes an agent, for it is only the mode according to which an agent proceeds; it implies a power, for it is the order according to which that power acts. Without this agent, without this power, which are both distinct from itself, the *law* does nothing, is nothing. The expression, "the law of metallic nature," may sound strange and harsh to a philosophic ear; but it seems quite as justifiable as some others which are more familiar to him, such as "the law of vegetable nature," "the law of animal nature," or, indeed, as "the law of nature" in general, when assigned as the cause of phenomena, in exclusion of agency and power, or when it is substituted into the place of these.

VIII. Neither, lastly, would our observer be driven out of his conclusion or from his confidence in its truth by being told that he knew nothing at all about the matter. He knows enough for his argument; he knows the utility of the end; he knows the subserviency and adaptation of the means to the end. These points being known, his ignorance of other points, his doubts concerning other points affect not the certainty of his reasoning. The consciousness of knowing little need not beget a distrust of that which he does know....

CHAPTER III: APPLICATION OF THE ARGUMENT

... Every indication of contrivance, every manifestation of design, which existed in the watch, exists in the works of nature; with the difference, on the side of nature, of being greater and more, and that in a degree which exceeds all computation. I mean that the contrivances of nature surpass the contrivances of art in the complexity, subtility, and curiosity of the mechanism; and still more, if possible, do they go beyond them in number and variety; yet, in a multitude of cases, are not less evidently mechanical, not less evidently contrivances, not less evidently accommodated to their end, or suited to their office, than are the most perfect productions of human ingenuity....

I know no better method of introducing so large a subject, than that of comparing a single thing with a single thing; an eye, for example, with a telescope. As far as the examination of the instrument goes, there is precisely the same proof that the eye was made for vision, as there is that the telescope was made for assisting it. They are made upon the same principles; both being adjusted to the laws by which the transmission and reflection of rays of light are regulated. I speak not of the origin of the laws themselves; but such laws being fixed, the construction, in both cases, is adapted to them. For instance, these laws require, in order to produce the same effect, that the rays of light, in passing from water into the eye, should be refracted by a more convex surface than when it passes out of air into the eye. Accordingly we find, that the eye of a fish, in that part of it called the crystalline lens, is much rounder than the eye of terrestrial animals. What plainer manifestation of design can there be than this difference? What could a mathematical instrument-maker have done more, to show his knowledge of his principle, his application of that knowledge, his suiting of his means to his end; I will not say to display the compass or excellence of his skill and art, for in these all comparison is indecorous, but to testify counsel, choice, consideration, purpose?

23   DIALOGUES CONCERNING NATURAL RELIGION (II, V–VII)

DAVID HUME

The Scotsman David Hume (1711–1776) was a widely read essayist, distinguished historian, and one of the most influential of all philosophers. His extraordinarily powerful *Dialogues Concerning Natural Religion* is one of the most important books in the philosophy of religion. During his lifetime, his friends, fearful of public disapproval, had dissuaded him from publishing the manuscript, but he took great pains to ensure that the work would not be lost, and it appeared in print three years after his death, although without any publisher's name attached.

"Natural religion" was the term used by eighteenth-century writers to refer to theological tenets that are provable by reason without appeal to revelation. The three participants in the *Dialogues* are distinguished by their views concerning the scope and limits of reason. Cleanthes claims that he can present arguments that demonstrate the truth of traditional Christian theology. Demea is committed to that theology but does not believe empirical evidence can provide any defense for his faith. Philo doubts that reason yields conclusive results in any field of inquiry and is especially critical of theological dogmatism.

In the sections of the book reprinted here, the argument to design is subjected to trenchant criticism.

PART II

… Not to lose any time in circumlocutions, said Cleanthes, … I shall briefly explain how I conceive this matter. Look round the world, contemplate the whole and every part of it: you will find it to be nothing but one great machine, subdivided into an infinite number of lesser machines, which again admit of subdivisions to a degree beyond what human senses and faculties can trace and explain. All these various machines, and even their most minute parts, are adjusted to each other with an accuracy which ravishes into admiration all men who have ever contemplated them. The curious adapting of means to ends, throughout all nature, resembles exactly, though it much exceeds, the productions of human contrivance—of human design, thought, wisdom, and intelligence. Since therefore the effects resemble each other, we are led to infer, by all the rules of analogy, that the causes also resemble, and that the Author of nature is somewhat similar to the mind of man, though possessed of much larger faculties, proportioned to the grandeur of the work which he has executed. By this argument a posteriori, and by this argument alone, do we prove at once the existence of a Deity and his similarity to human mind and intelligence.

I shall be so free, Cleanthes, said Demea, as to tell you that from the beginning I could not approve of your conclusion concerning the similarity of the Deity to men, still less can I approve of the mediums by which you endeavour to establish it. What! No demonstration of the Being of God! No abstract arguments! No proofs a priori! Are these which have hitherto been so much insisted on by philosophers all fallacy, all sophism? Can we reach no farther in this subject than experience and probability? I will not say that this is betraying the cause of a Deity; but surely, by this affected

From David Hume, *Dialogues Concerning Natural Religion* (1779).

candour, you give advantages to atheists which they never could obtain by the mere dint of argument and reasoning.

What I chiefly scruple in this subject, said Philo, is not so much that all religious arguments are by Cleanthes reduced to experience, as that they appear not to be even the most certain and irrefragable of that inferior kind. That a stone will fall, that fire will burn, that the earth has solidity, we have observed a thousand and a thousand times; and when any new instance of this nature is presented, we draw without hesitation the accustomed inference. The exact similarity of the cases gives us a perfect assurance of a similar event, and a stronger evidence is never desired nor sought after. But wherever you depart, in the least, from the similarity of the cases, you diminish proportionably the evidence, and may at last bring it to a very weak *analogy*, which is confessedly liable to error and uncertainty. After having experienced the circulation of the blood in human creatures, we make no doubt that it takes place in Titius and Maevius,[1] but from its circulation in frogs and fishes it is only a presumption, though a strong one, from analogy that it takes place in men and other animals. The analogical reasoning is much weaker when we infer the circulation of the sap in vegetables from our experience that the blood circulates in animals; and those who hastily followed that imperfect analogy are found, by more accurate experiments, to have been mistaken.

If we see a house, Cleanthes, we conclude, with the greatest certainty, that it had an architect or builder because this is precisely that species of effect which we have experienced to proceed from that species of cause. But surely you will not affirm that the universe bears such a resemblance to a house that we can with the same certainty infer a similar cause, or that the analogy is here entire and perfect. The dissimilitude is so striking that the utmost you can here pretend to is a guess, conjecture, a presumption concerning a similar cause; and how that pretension will be received in the world, I leave you to consider.

It would surely be very ill received, replied Cleanthes; and I should be deservedly blamed and detested did I allow that the proofs of Deity amounted to no more than a guess or conjecture. But is the whole adjustment of means to ends in a house and in the universe so slight a resemblance? the economy of final causes? the order, proportion; and arrangement of every part? Steps of a stair are plainly contrived that human legs may use them in mounting; and this inference is certain and infallible. Human legs are also contrived for walking and mounting; and this inference, I allow, is not altogether so certain because of the dissimilarity which you remark; but does it, therefore, deserve the name only of presumption or conjecture?

Good God! cried Demea, interrupting him, where are we? Zealous defenders of religion allow that the proofs of a Deity fall short of perfect evidence! And you, Philo, on whose assistance I depended in proving the adorable mysteriousness of the Divine Nature, do you assent to all these extravagant opinions of Cleanthes? For what other name can I give them? or, why spare my censure when such principles are advanced, supported by such an authority, before so young a man as Pamphilus?

You seem not to apprehend, replied Philo, that I argue with Cleanthes in his own way, and, by showing him the dangerous consequences of his tenets, hope at last to reduce him to our opinion. But what sticks most with you, I observe, is the representation which Cleanthes has made of the argument a posteriori; and, finding that the argument is likely to escape your hold and vanish into air, you think it so disguised that you can scarcely believe it to be set in its true light. Now, however much I may dissent, in other respects, from the dangerous principle of Cleanthes, I must allow that he has fairly represented that argument, and I shall endeavour so to state the matter to you that you will entertain no further scruples with regard to it.

Were a man to abstract from everything which he knows or has seen, he would be altogether incapable, merely from his own ideas, to determine what kind of scene the universe must be, or to give the preference to one state or situation of things above another. For as nothing which he clearly conceives could be esteemed impossible or implying a contradiction, every chimera of his fancy would be upon an equal footing; nor could he assign any just reason why he adheres to one idea or system, and rejects the others which are equally possible.

Again, after he opens his eyes and contemplates the world as it really is, it would be impossible for him at first to assign the cause of any one event, much less of the whole of things, or of the universe. He might set his fancy a rambling, and she might bring him in an infinite variety of reports and representations. These would all be possible, but, being all equally possible, he would never of himself give a satisfactory account for his preferring one of them to the rest. Experience alone can point out to him the true cause of any phenomenon.

Now, according to this method of reasoning, Demea, it follows (and is, indeed, tacitly allowed by Cleanthes himself) that order, arrangement, or the adjustment of final causes, is not of itself any proof of design, but only so far as it has been experienced to proceed from that principle. For aught we can know a priori, matter may contain the source or spring of order originally within itself, as well as mind does; and there is no more difficulty in conceiving that the several elements, from an internal unknown cause, may fall into the most exquisite arrangement, than to conceive that their ideas, in the great universal mind, from a like internal unknown cause, fall into that arrangement. The equal possibility of both these suppositions is allowed. But, by experience, we find (according to Cleanthes) that there is a difference between them. Throw several pieces of steel together, without shape or form, they will never arrange themselves so as to compose a watch. Stone and mortar and wood, without an architect, never erect a house. But the ideas in a human mind, we see, by an unknown, inexplicable economy, arrange themselves so as to form the plan of a watch or house. Experience, therefore, proves that there is an original principle of order in mind, not in matter. From similar effects we infer similar causes. The adjustment of means to ends is alike in the universe, as in a machine of human contrivance. The causes, therefore, must be resembling.

I was from the beginning scandalized, I must own, with this resemblance which is asserted between the Deity and human creatures, and must conceive it to imply such a degradation of the Supreme Being as no sound theist could endure. With your assistance, therefore, Demea, I shall endeavour to defend what you justly call the adorable mysteriousness of the Divine Nature, and shall refute this reasoning of Cleanthes, provided he allows that I have made a fair representation of it.

When Cleanthes had assented, Philo, after a short pause, proceeded in the following manner.

That all inferences, Cleanthes, concerning fact are founded on experience, and that all experimental reasonings are founded on the supposition that similar causes prove similar effects, and similar effects similar causes, I shall not at present much dispute with you. But observe, I entreat you, with what extreme caution all just reasoners proceed in the transferring of experiments to similar cases. Unless the cases be exactly similar, they repose no perfect confidence in applying their past observation to any particular phenomenon. Every alteration of circumstances occasions a doubt concerning the event; and it requires new experiments to prove certainly that the new circumstances are of no moment or importance. A change in bulk, situation, arrangement, age, disposition of the air, or surrounding bodies—any of these particulars may be attended with the most unexpected consequences. And unless the objects be quite familiar to us, it is the highest temerity to expect with assurance, after any of these changes, an event similar to that which before fell under our observation. The slow and deliberate steps of philosophers here, if anywhere, are distinguished from the precipitate march of the vulgar, who, hurried on by the smallest similitude, are incapable of all discernment or consideration.

But can you think, Cleanthes, that your usual phlegm and philosophy have been preserved in so wide a step as you have taken when you compared to the universe houses, ships, furniture, machines, and, from their similarity in some circumstances, inferred a similarity in their causes? Thought, design, intelligence, such as we discover in men and other animals, is no more than one of the springs and principles of the universe, as well as heat or cold, attraction or repulsion, and a hundred others which fall under daily observation. It is an active cause by which some particular parts of nature, we find, produce alterations on other parts. But can a conclusion, with any propriety, be transferred from parts to the whole? Does not the great disproportion bar all comparison and inference? From observing the growth of a hair, can we learn anything concerning the generation of a man? Would the manner of a leaf's blowing, even though perfectly known, afford us any instruction concerning the vegetation of a tree?

But allowing that we were to take the *operations* of one part of nature upon another for the foundation of our judgment concerning the *origin* of the whole (which never can be admitted), yet why select so minute, so weak, so bounded a principle as the reason and design of animals is found to be upon this planet? What peculiar privilege has this little agitation of the brain which we call *thought*, that we must thus make it the model of the whole universe? Our partiality in our own favour does indeed present it on all occasions, but sound philosophy ought carefully to guard against so natural an illusion.

So far from admitting, continued Philo, that the operations of a part can afford us any just conclusion concerning the origin of the whole, I will not allow any one part to form a rule for another part if the latter be very remote from the former. Is there any reasonable ground to conclude that the inhabitants of other planets possess thought, intelligence, reason, or anything similar to these faculties in men? When nature has so extremely diversified her manner of operation in this small globe, can we imagine that she incessantly copies herself throughout so immense a universe? And if thought, as we may well suppose, be confined merely to this narrow corner and has even there so limited a sphere of action, with what propriety can we assign it for the original cause of all things? The narrow views of a peasant who makes his domestic economy the rule for the government of kingdoms is in comparison a pardonable sophism.

But were we ever so much assured that a thought and reason resembling the human were to be found throughout the whole universe, and were its activity elsewhere vastly greater and more commanding than it appears in this globe, yet I cannot see why the operations of a world constituted, arranged, adjusted, can with any propriety be extended to a world which is in its embryo state, and is advancing towards that constitution and arrangement. By observation we know somewhat of the economy, action, and nourishment of a finished animal, but we must transfer with great caution that observation to the growth of a fetus in the womb, and still more to the formation of an animalcule in the loins of its male parent. Nature, we find, even from our limited experience, possesses an infinite number of springs and principles which incessantly discover themselves on every change of her position and situation. And what new and unknown principles would actuate her in so new and unknown a situation as that of the formation of a universe, we cannot, without the utmost temerity, pretend to determine.

A very small part of this great system, during a very short time, is very imperfectly discovered to us; and do we thence pronounce decisively concerning the origin of the whole?

Admirable conclusion! Stone, wood, brick, iron, brass, have not, at this time, in this minute globe of earth, an order or arrangement without human art and contrivance; therefore, the universe could not originally attain its order and arrangement without something similar to human art. But is a part of nature a rule for another part very wide of the former? Is it a rule for the whole? Is a very small part a rule for the universe? Is nature in one situation a certain rule for nature in another situation vastly different from the former?

And can you blame me, Cleanthes, if I here imitate the prudent reserve of Simonides, who, according to the noted story, being asked by Hiero, *What God was?* desired a day to think of it, and then two days more; and after that manner continually prolonged the term, without ever bringing in his definition or description? Could you even blame me if I had answered, at first, *that I did not know*, and was sensible that this subject lay vastly beyond the reach of my faculties? You might cry out sceptic and raillier, as much as you pleased; but, having found in so many other subjects much more familiar the imperfections and even contradictions of human reason, I never should expect any success from its feeble conjectures in a subject so sublime and so remote from the sphere of our observation. When two *species* of objects have always been observed to be conjoined together, I can *infer*, by custom, the existence of one wherever I *see* the existence of the other; and this I call an argument from experience. But how this argument can have place where the objects, as in the present case, are single, individual, without parallel or specific resemblance, may be difficult to explain. And will any man tell me with a serious countenance that an orderly universe must arise from some thought and art like the human because we have experience of it? To ascertain this reasoning it were requisite that we had experience of the origin of worlds; and it is not sufficient, surely, that we have seen ships and cities arise from human art and contrivance....

PART V

But to show you still more inconveniences, continued Philo, in your anthropomorphism, please to take a new survey of your principles. *Like effects prove like causes.* This is the experimental argument, and this, you say too, is the sole theological argument. Now it is certain that the liker the effects are which are seen and the liker the causes which are inferred, the stronger is the argument. Every departure on either side diminishes the probability and renders the experiment less conclusive. You cannot doubt of the principle; neither ought you to reject its consequences.

All the new discoveries in astronomy which prove the immense grandeur and magnificence of the works of nature are so many additional arguments for a Deity, according to the true system of theism; but, according to your hypothesis of experimental theism, they become so many objections, by removing the effect still farther from all resemblance to the effects of human art and contrivance....

If this argument, I say, had any force in former ages, how much greater must it have at present when the bounds of Nature are so infinitely enlarged and such a magnificent scene is opened to us? It is still more unreasonable to form our idea of so unlimited a cause from our experience of the narrow productions of human design and invention.

The discoveries by microscopes, as they open a new universe in miniature, are still objections, according to you, arguments, according to me. The further we push our researches of this kind, we are still led to infer the universal cause of all to be vastly different from mankind, or from any object of human experience and observation.

And what say you to the discoveries in anatomy, chemistry, botany?... These surely are no objections, replied Cleanthes; they only discover new instances of art and contrivance, it is still the image of mind reflected on us from innumerable objects. Add a mind *like the human*, said Philo. I know of no other, replied Cleanthes. And the liker, the better, insisted Philo. To be sure, said Cleanthes.

Now, Cleanthes, said Philo, with an air of alacrity and triumph, mark the consequences. *First*, by this method of reasoning you renounce all claim to infinity in any of the attributes of the Deity. For, as the cause ought only to be proportioned to the effect, and the effect, so far as it falls under our cognizance, is not infinite, what pretensions have we, upon your suppositions, to ascribe that attribute to the Divine Being? You will still insist that, by removing him so much from all similarity to human creatures, we give in to the most arbitrary hypothesis, and at the same time weaken all proofs of his existence.

Secondly, you have no reason, on your theory, for ascribing perfection to the Deity, even in his finite capacity, or for supposing him free from every error, mistake, or incoherence, in his undertakings. There are many inexplicable difficulties in the works of nature which, if we allow a perfect author to be proved a priori, are easily solved, and become only seeming difficulties requisite very much exceeds anything which we have ever seen conjoined in any single body, the former supposition becomes still more probable and natural. An intelligent being of such vast power and capacity as is necessary to produce the universe, or, to speak in the language of ancient philosophy, so prodigious an animal exceeds all analogy and even comprehension.

But further, Cleanthes: Men are mortal, and renew their species by generation; and this is common to all living creatures. The two great sexes of male and female, says Milton, animate the world. Why must this circumstance, so universal, so essential, be excluded from those numerous and limited deities? Behold, then, the theogeny of ancient times brought back upon us.

And why not become a perfect anthropomorphite? Why not assert the deity or deities to be corporeal, and to have eyes, a nose, mouth, ears, etc.? Epicurus maintained that no man had ever seen reason but in a human figure; therefore, the gods must have a human figure. And this argument, which is deservedly so much ridiculed by Cicero, becomes, according to you, solid and philosophical.

In a word, Cleanthes, a man who follows your hypothesis is able, perhaps, to assert or conjecture that the universe sometime arose from something like design; but beyond that position he cannot ascertain one single circumstance, and is left afterwards to fix every point of his theology by the utmost license of fancy and hypothesis. This world, for aught he knows, is very faulty and imperfect, compared to a superior standard, and was only the first rude essay of some infant deity who afterwards abandoned it, ashamed of his lame performance; it is the work only of some dependent, inferior deity, and is the object of derision to his superiors; it is the production of old age and dotage in some superannuated deity, and ever since his death has run on at adventures, from the first impulse and active force which it received from him. You justly give signs of horror, Demea, at these strange suppositions; but these, and a thousand more of the same kind, are Cleanthes' suppositions, not mine. From the moment the attributes of the Deity are supposed finite, all these have place. And I cannot, for my part, think that so wild and unsettled a system of theology is, in any respect, preferable to none at all.

These suppositions I absolutely disown, cried Cleanthes: they strike me, however, with no horror, especially when proposed in that rambling way in which they drop from you. On the contrary, they give me pleasure when I see that, by the utmost indulgence of your imagination, you never get rid of the hypothesis of design in the universe, but are obliged at every turn to have recourse to it. To this concession I adhere steadily; and this I regard as a sufficient foundation for religion.

PART VI

It must be a slight fabric, indeed, said Demea, which can be erected on so tottering a foundation. While we are uncertain whether there is one deity from the narrow capacity of man, who cannot trace infinite relations. But according to your method of reasoning, these difficulties become all real, and, perhaps, will be insisted on as new instances of likeness to human art and contrivance. At least, you must acknowledge that it is impossible for us to tell, from our limited views, whether this system contains any great faults or deserves any considerable praise if compared to other possible and even real systems. Could a peasant, if the *Aeneid* were read to him, pronounce that poem to be absolutely faultless, or even assign to it its proper rank among the productions of human wit, he who had never seen any other production?

But were this world ever so perfect a production, it must still remain uncertain whether all the excellences of the work can justly be ascribed to the workman. If we survey a ship, what an exalted idea must we form of the ingenuity of the carpenter who framed so complicated, useful, and beautiful a machine? And what surprise must we feel when we find him a stupid mechanic who imitated others, and copied an art which, through a long succession of ages, after multiplied trials, mistakes, corrections, deliberations, and controversies, had been gradually improving? Many worlds might have been botched and bungled, throughout an eternity, ere this system was struck out; much labour lost, many fruitless trials made, and a slow but continued improvement carried on during infinite ages in the art of world-making. In such subjects, who can determine where the truth, nay, who can conjecture where the probability lies, amidst a great number of hypotheses which may be proposed, and a still greater which may be imagined?

And what shadow of an argument, continued Philo, can you produce from your hypothesis to prove the unity of the Deity? A great number of men join in building a house or ship, in rearing a city, in framing a commonwealth; why may not several deities combine in contriving and framing a world? This is only so much greater similarity to human affairs. By sharing the work among several, we may so much further limit the attributes of each, and get rid of that extensive power and knowledge which must be supposed in one deity, and which, according to you, can only serve to weaken the proof of his existence. And if such foolish, such vicious creatures as man can yet often unite in framing and executing one plan, how much more those deities or demons, whom we may suppose several degrees more perfect!

To multiply causes without necessity is indeed contrary to true philosophy, but this principle applies not to the present case. Were one deity antecedently proved by your theory who were possessed of every attribute requisite to the production of the universe, it would be needless, I own (though not absurd) to suppose any other deity existent. But while it is still a question whether all these attributes are united in one subject or dispersed among several independent beings, by what phenomena in nature can we pretend to decide the controversy? Where we see a body raised in a scale, we are sure that there is in the opposite scale, however concealed from sight, some counterpoising weight equal to it; but it is still allowed to doubt whether that weight be an aggregate of several distinct bodies or one uniform united mass. And if the weight or many, whether the deity or deities, to whom we owe our existence, be perfect or imperfect, subordinate or supreme, dead or alive, what trust or confidence can we repose in them? What devotion or worship address to them? What veneration or obedience pay them? To all the purposes of life the theory of religion becomes altogether useless; and even with regard to speculative consequences its uncertainty, according to you, must render it totally precarious and unsatisfactory.

To render it still more unsatisfactory, said Philo, there occurs to me another hypothesis which must acquire an air of probability from the method of reasoning so much insisted on by Cleanthes. That like effects arise from like causes—this principle he supposes the foundation of all religion. But there is another principle of the same kind, no less certain and derived from the same source of experience, that, where several known circumstances are observed to be similar, the unknown will also be found similar. Thus, if we see the limbs of a human body, we conclude that it is also attended with a human head, though hid from us. Thus, if we see, through a chink in a wall, a small part of the sun, we conclude that were the wall removed we should see the whole body. In short, this method of reasoning is so obvious and familiar that no scruple can ever be made with regard to its solidity.

Now, if we survey the universe, so far as it falls under our knowledge, it bears a great resemblance to an animal or organized body, and seems actuated with a like principle of life and motion. A continual circulation of matter in it produces no disorder; a continual waste in every part is incessantly repaired; the closest sympathy is perceived throughout the entire system; and each part or member, in performing its proper offices, operates both to its own preservation and to that of the whole. The world, therefore, I infer, is an animal; and the Deity is the *soul* of the world, actuating it, and actuated by it....

This theory, I own, replied Cleanthes, has never before occurred to me, though a pretty natural one; and I cannot readily, upon so short an examination and reflection, deliver any opinion with regard to it. You are very scrupulous, indeed, said Philo; were I to examine any system of yours, I should not have acted with half that caution and reserve, in starting objections and difficulties to it.

However, if anything occur to you, you will oblige us by proposing it.

Why then, replied Cleanthes, it seems to me that, though the world does, in many circumstances, resemble an animal body, yet is the analogy also defective in many circumstances the most material: no organs of sense, no seat of thought or reason; no one precise origin of motion and action. In short, it seems to bear a stronger resemblance to a vegetable than to an animal, and your inference would be so far inconclusive in favor of the soul of the world....

PART VII

But here, continued Philo, in examining the ancient system of the soul of the world there strikes me, all of a sudden, a new idea which, if just, must go near to subvert all your reasoning, and destroy even your first inferences on which you repose such confidence. If the universe bears a greater likeness to animal bodies and to vegetables than to the works of human art, it is more probable that its cause resembles the cause of the former than that of the latter, and its origin ought rather to be abscribed to generation or vegetation than to reason or design. Your conclusion, even according to your own principles, is therefore lame and defective.

Pray open up this argument a little further, said Demea, for I do not rightly apprehend it in that concise manner in which you have expressed it.

Our friend Cleanthes, replied Philo, as you have heard, asserts that since no question of fact can be proved otherwise than by experience, the existence of a Deity admits not of proof from any other medium. The world, says he, resembles the works of human contrivance; therefore its cause must also resemble that of the other. Here we may remark that the operation of one very small part of nature, to wit, man, upon another very small part, to wit, that inanimate matter lying within his reach, is the rule by which Cleanthes judges of the origin of the whole; and he measures objects, so widely disproportioned, by the same individual standard. But to waive all objections drawn from this topic, I affirm that there are other parts of the universe (besides the machines of human invention) which bear still a greater resemblance to the fabric of the world, and which, therefore, afford a better conjecture concerning the universal origin of this system. These parts are animals and vegetables. The world plainly resembles more an animal or a vegetable than it does a watch or a knitting loom. Its cause, therefore, it is more probable, resembles the cause of the former. The cause of the former is generation or vegetation. The cause, therefore, of the world we may infer to be something similar or analogous to generation or vegetation.

But how is it conceivable, said Demea, that the world can arise from anything similar to vegetation or generation?

Very easily, replied Philo. In like manner as a tree sheds its seed into the neighboring fields and produces other trees; so the great vegetable, the world, or this planetary system, produces within itself certain seeds which, being scattered into the surrounding chaos, vegetate into new worlds. A comet, for instance, is the seed of a world; and after it has been fully ripened, by passing from sun to sun, and star to star, it is at last tossed into the unformed elements which everywhere surround this universe, and immediately sprouts up into a new system.

Or if, for the sake of variety (for I see no other advantage) we should suppose this world to be an animal; a comet is the egg of this animal; and in like manner as an ostrich lays its egg in the sand, which, without any further care, hatches the egg and produces a new animal, so ... I understand you, says Demea: But what wild, arbitrary suppositions are these? What *data* have you for such extraordinary conclusions? And is the slight, imaginary resemblance of the world to a vegetable or an animal sufficient to establish the same inference with regard to both? Objects which are in general so widely different; ought they to be a standard for each other?

Right, cries Philo: This is the topic on which I have all along insisted. I have still asserted that we have no *data* to establish any system of cosmogony. Our experience, so imperfect in itself and so limited both in extent and duration, can afford us no probable conjecture concerning the whole of things. But if we must needs fix on some hypothesis, by what rule, pray, ought we to determine our choice? Is there any other rule than the great similarity of the objects compared? And does not a plant or an animal, which springs from vegetation or generation, bear a stronger resemblance to the world than does any artificial machine, which arises from reason and design?

But what is this vegetation and generation of which you talk? said Demea. Can you explain their operations, and anatomize that fine internal structure on which they depend?

As much, at least, replied Philo, as Cleanthes can explain the operations of reason, or anatomize that internal structure on which *it* depends. But without any such elaborate disquisitions, when I see an animal, I infer that it sprang from generation; and that with as great certainty as you conclude a house to have been reared by design. These words *generation, reason* mark only certain powers and energies in nature whose effects are known, but whose essence is incomprehensible; and one of these principles, more than the other, has no privilege for being made a standard to the whole of nature.

In reality, Demea, it may reasonably be expected that the larger the views are which we take of things, the better will they conduct us in our conclusions concerning such extraordinary and such magnificent subjects. In this little corner of the world alone, there are four principles, *reason, instinct, generation, vegetation*, which are similar to each other, and are the causes of similar effects. What a number of other principles may we naturally suppose in the immense extent and variety of the universe could we travel from planet to planet, and from system to system, in order to examine each part of this mighty fabric? Any one of these four principles above mentioned (and a hundred others which lie open to our conjecture) may afford us a theory by which to judge of the origin of the world; and it is a palpable and egregious partiality to confine our view entirely to that

principle by which our own minds operate. Were this principle more intelligible on that account, such a partiality might be somewhat excusable; but reason, in its internal fabric and structure, is really as little known to us as instinct or vegetation; and, perhaps, even that vague, undeterminate word *nature* to which the vulgar refer everything is not at the bottom more inexplicable. The effects of these principles are all known to us from experience; but the principles themselves and their manner of operation are totally unknown; nor is it less intelligible or less conformable to experience to say that the world arose by vegetation, from a seed shed by another world, than to say that it arose from a divine reason or contrivance, according to the sense in which Cleanthes understands it.

But methinks, said Demea, if the world had a vegetative quality and could sow the seeds of new worlds into the infinite chaos, this power would be still an additional argument for design in its author. For whence could arise so wonderful a faculty but from design? Or how can order spring from anything which perceives not that order which it bestows?

You need only look around you, replied Philo, to satisfy yourself with regard to this question. A tree bestows order and organization on that tree which springs from it, without knowing the order, an animal in the same manner on its offspring; a bird on its nest; and instances of this kind are even more frequent in the world than those of order which arise from reason and contrivance. To say that all this order in animals and vegetables proceeds ultimately from design is begging the question; nor can that great point be ascertained otherwise than by proving, a priori, both that order is, from its nature, inseparably attached to thought, and that it can never of itself or from original unknown principles belong to matter.

NOTE

1. [Conventional names of ordinary persons, such as Smith and Jones.]

24 THE ARGUMENT FROM DESIGN

ROBERT HAMBOURGER

Robert Hambourger is Associate Professor of Philosophy at North Carolina Agricultural and Technical State University. He attempts to develop a version of the teleological argument that will withstand the sort of criticisms found in Hume's *Dialogues Concerning Natural Religion*. Whether Hambourger succeeds is, as usual, a judgment to be made by each reader.

Suppose that I happen by chance to be standing up at the moment you read this sentence. Can one then hope to explain why I stand as you read? I think it would be natural to answer in the negative. There is no reason why I was standing as you read; things just happened to work out that way. However, someone who takes seriously the principle of sufficient reason, that every truth has an explanation, will not accept this reply as the last word. Rather, I think, he will want to say that all one has to do to explain the occurrence in question in the sense *he* has in mind is to conjoin explanations of why, at a certain time, I was standing and why, at the same time, you were reading the sentence you were. Corresponding to these two possible answers, let me say that a conjunction of two or more states of affairs, or the co-occurrence of the states of affairs, has a *basic explanation* when and only when each state in the conjunction has an explanation, and I shall say that a basic explanation of a conjunction is a conjunction of explanations of its conjuncts. Further, let me say that the states in a conjunction of two or more states of affairs have an *explanation in common* when and only when explanations of any two states in the conjunction contain a significant part in common....

Now there are two points I would like to make using these distinctions. First, there would seem to be no logical guarantee that two logically independent states of affairs will have an

explanation in common. Things often happen by chance, and a supporter of the principle of sufficient reason can hope for no more than that every conjunction will have a basic explanation. Secondly, however, there are cases in which, as an epistemological matter of fact, we simply would not believe that certain states of affairs had occurred together by chance. And it is on this second point that the argument I shall present is based. For I believe there are natural phenomena which it would be extremely hard to believe occurred together by chance but which, it would seem, could only have an explanation in common if at least some of them were created by design. And thus, I think, by a two-step argument we might be able to prove that some natural phenomena are created intentionally.

I shall not offer an example of the sort of phenomena I have in mind until later. First let me illustrate the reasoning I hope to use with a fictitious example which, if my memory has not deceived me, is adapted from one I was given a number of years ago by [Elizabeth] Anscombe.

Suppose that one day a perfect picture, say, of a nativity scene were formed by the frost on someone's window. I think we almost certainly would believe that this occurrence was brought about by design,[1] though not necessarily by the design of a divine being. And if we were asked why, I think we would probably respond that if this were not so, there would be no way to explain why ice

From *Intention and Intentionality: Essays for G. E. M. Anscombe*, eds. Jenny Teichman and Cora Diamond, Cornell University Press, 1979. Reprinted by permission of the publisher.

formed on the window in the pattern it did. However, if by an explanation, we have in mind a basic explanation, this might well not be true.

Supposedly, in normal cases, various facts about weather conditions, the make-up of a pane of glass, the temperature and humidity in the room in which the pane is installed and the like, cause ice to form in the way it does on a window pane. And also, supposedly, there are possible conditions which, if they were to obtain, might cause ice to form a nativity scene on a given pane. Of course, these conditions might be very strange, but we do not know this. Suppose, in fact, that the nativity scene in our example arose by natural means from conditions that appeared quite normal, that those conditions themselves arose from normal-seeming conditions, etc. Then we can imagine that scientists could give a perfectly good basic explanation of why the pattern formed by the ice in our example was one that constituted a nativity scene.

First, one would explain why ice formed in the pattern it did on the relevant window in the way that one might hope to do so in normal cases, that is, by explaining why ice crystals of various sorts formed on various spots of the window. Then one would explain why the pattern that was formed made up a nativity scene, using facts about geometry, about basic human perceptual mechanisms, perhaps, and the like. The result would be a basic explanation of why the pattern that formed was a nativity scene.

What I think is interesting here, though, is this. If we were given such an explanation of the nativity scene in our example, we would still, I think, be no less inclined than before to believe that it resulted from design. If anything, by showing that the scene arose from processes that were, so to speak, part of the course of nature, such an explanation would make us more inclined to believe that it was designed by a being deserving of our worship and not merely by someone who had made a technological break through over ice.[2]

The question, then, I think, is: what reasoning do we use when we conclude that the nativity scene in our example was produced by design? And the answer, I believe, is the following. First, I think, we believe that ice could not form a nativity scene on a window merely by chance. That is, in our example, there must be an explanation in common of the fact that ice formed the pattern it did on a certain window and the fact that that pattern constitutes a nativity scene. Why we believe this is not completely clear. Ice very often forms beautiful patterns on window panes, and yet we are content to accept that it is by chance that the patterns that are formed are ones that strike us as beautiful. However, that we would not be content to hold similarly that a nativity scene resulted from chance I think is clear.

But if this is true, then the fact that the ice formed a certain pattern on the pane in our example and the fact that that pattern constitutes a nativity scene must share a significant part of their causes in common. And, therefore, either one of the facts is a significant part of the cause of the other, or a third state of affairs is a significant part of the cause of both. However, the fact that a certain pattern forms a nativity scene is a very general one. It results from facts about geometry, about what counts as a nativity scene, and, perhaps, about what patterns we see when we encounter various sorts of objects. And many of these facts are not caused at all, while the remainder, it would seem, as an empirical matter of fact, could be caused neither by the fact that ice formed in a certain pattern on a particular pane of glass nor by the sort of facts, for example, about local weather conditions and the make-up of a pane, that would cause ice to form in such a pattern. And, therefore, it seems that neither the fact that ice formed in a certain pattern nor causes of that fact could be significant parts of what caused the pattern to be a nativity scene.

However, in this case it must be that the fact that a certain pattern constitutes a nativity scene was an important part of what brought it about that the pattern appeared on the window in our example. And this, again as an empirical matter, seems to be something that could not happen unless the pattern was produced by design. For the fact that a pattern forms a nativity scene could give a designer reason to bring it about that it appeared on a window and, thus, play a significant role in an explanation of such a fact. However, if the pattern in our example was not brought about by design, then it seems out of the question to think that the fact that it constitutes a nativity scene might have been an important part of the cause of the very specific conditions holding in and around a particular piece of glass on a particular night that caused it to be formed in ice. And, thus, it seems that the nativity scene in our example must have been produced by design.

The case of the nativity scene, of course, is fictitious, but I believe that similar reasoning might well be able to show that in many actual cases natural phenomena have been produced by design. For in many cases complex states of affairs have come together in ways that have produced noteworthy features of the universe, and one might argue that it could not simply be by chance that they came together in ways that had such impressive results. That is, one might think that there must be an explanation in common of the facts that certain states of affairs have occurred and that, by having done so, they have produced the impressive results they have. However, the fact that various states of affairs would produce impressive results, if they occurred together, cannot, it would seem, be explained by the fact that the states actually did occur, nor by the sort of facts that would cause them to occur. And, therefore, the only alternative is that the fact that the states would produce impressive results helps to explain their occurrence. But, again, it would seem that this could not happen unless the states were caused to occur by a designer acting to produce their impressive results....

I think many people today are taken by a certain picture of the origin of life in which the theory of evolution plays a large part. As things are represented by this picture, it was simply a matter of good fortune that the earth came to provide an environment suitable for living creatures, though the good fortune here was not particularly surprising. For in a universe as vast as ours there are many stars like the sun, and—often enough—such stars should have planets whose size, composition, and orbit are similar to those of the earth. Then, once the earth afforded the proper environment, the first primitive organisms came into existence as results of what, it is hoped, were not too improbable series of chemical reactions, Again,

here, it was simply by chance that the chemical processes that occurred were ones that produced living creatures. Finally, once the first organisms were in existence, it is thought that the theory of evolution can account for the rest and that the mechanisms of chance mutation and natural selection embodied in the theory led to the development of more and more highly developed creatures until, finally, beings evolved that were capable of reason.

This picture of the origin of life seems to be widely held today. Indeed, I believe its popularity is an important feature of the intellectual history of the present age. Nonetheless, I think the picture is flawed. For one thing, we might believe that various chemical processes could produce very simple living creatures, even if the fact that they produced such creatures had nothing to do with the fact the processes came about. But we would not accept that very complex creatures could come about in this way. However, as Geach has noted,[3] the process of natural selection itself seems to presuppose the existence of creatures with highly developed genetic mechanisms and, so, cannot be used to explain their origin, And, therefore, we must find another plausible account of the origin of these mechanisms.

Natural selection can only take place among creatures that bear offspring that closely resemble their parents without resembling them too closely. For if offspring are exactly like their parents, then natural selection can occur only among characteristics already in existence and, thus, will not lead to the development of new characteristics. On the other hand, if offspring do not closely resemble their parents, then even if certain parents have highly adaptive characteristics and bear many more children than others, their children will not be very likely to inherit the characteristics, and the process will stop.

Of course, in fact creatures do have genetic mechanisms that facilitate natural selection, but the mechanisms are very complicated, and though they might themselves have evolved to some extent by natural selection, it would seem that any mechanism that led to offspring that resembled their parents closely enough but not too closely would have to be very complicated. And so, one would have to ask how they could come about, if not by design. As Geach writes:

> There can be no origin of species, as opposed to an Empedoclean chaos of varied monstrosities, unless creatures reproduce pretty much after their kind; the elaborate and ostensibly teleological mechanism of this reproduction logically cannot be explained as a product of evolution by natural selection from among chance variations, for unless the mechanism is presupposed there cannot be any evolution.[4]

Thus, there is much that is noteworthy about the development of living beings that cannot be explained by the theory of evolution. But even if this problem can be surmounted without recourse to a designer, there is a second difficulty.

Simplified accounts of the theory of evolution might make it appear inevitable that creatures evolved with the sorts of impressive and obviously adaptive features that might otherwise be thought to have been designed. For over a sufficient period, one might think, a few individuals would develop such features by chance mutation, and once some creatures had them, the obvious desirability of the features would be enough to explain their proliferation. However, this impression of inevitability, I think, is quite misleading.

Evolutionary change generally proceeds very slowly. We can be confident, for example, that no ancestors of birds suddenly came by wings in a single step and, likewise, that no ancestor of man came to have a brain capable of reason because of one chance mutation. Instead, these sorts of noteworthy and obviously adaptive features come about only as results of long series of evolutionary changes, each of which has to be adaptive and has to become dominant among members of a species, and the noteworthy features themselves cannot come about unless all the others do. Further, these smaller evolutionary changes cannot be counted on to be obviously adaptive, nor always to be adaptive for the same reasons that the larger, more noteworthy changes are. And most importantly, as the term 'adaptive' itself suggests, very often these small changes will be adaptive only because of fine details of, and changes in, the relationship between members of a species and their environment.

Consider the following passage from a recent biology textbook, for example:

> There is … good evidence that during the period in which Australopithecus lived there existed considerable expanses of lush savannah with scattered shrubs, trees, and grasses. There were berries and roots in abundance, and because such areas were suitable for grazing, these savannahs were well stocked with game. These areas provided new habitats, abundant in food, and so we surmise the australopithecines came down from the trees in which their own apelike ancestors lived in order to avail themselves of these new sources of food... Although descent from the trees does not always result in evolution of upright posture in primates…, through a lucky combination of anatomy and habits, these apemen became bipedal. Being bipedal meant that the hands were freed from locomotor function and could be employed in manipulative skills such as carrying and dragging objects, fashioning tools and weapons, and so on.[5]

This, in turn, led to improvements in the primitive tool-making ability that had preceded upright posture. And finally, 'with the advent of toolmaking, hunting for big game became a possibility, and the brain and the hand were now subject to the molding force of natural selection.'[6]

Now whether the precise details of the picture presented in this passage turn out to be true is not important here. What is important is that something of this sort almost certainly was true. Had not the grass in a certain area grown to the proper height, had not a certain food source become available or unavailable, had not various predators been present or absent, had not climatic conditions been what they were, etc. as ancestors of man developed, human beings would not have come into existence. And if they had not, there seems to be no reason to think other beings capable of reason would have evolved instead. After all, useful as intelligence is, no other species has come into existence with such a high level of it.

Furthermore, seemingly chance occurrences like these did not play a role only in the final stages of the evolution of human beings. It is likely that, at nearly every step in the evolutionary chain that led from the most primitive of creatures to people, similar sorts of occurrences played a role. In fact, without specific evidence one cannot assume even that it was inevitable that mammals, vertebrates, or even multi-celled creatures would evolve.

But then, one might ask, again, whether it could have been simply by chance that so many seemingly unconnected occurrences came together in just the way that would lead to the evolution of creatures capable of reason, and I think that one might well conclude that it could not have been.[7]

At least, it would be very strange, if the myriad occurrences needed to produce human beings came about in just the right way simply by chance and equally strange if the occurrences had an explanation in common, but the fact that they would produce intelligent beings had nothing to do with the fact that they came about. However, one might wonder how so many different sorts of occurrences could have an explanation in common and, indeed, have an explanation in common with the fact that they would lead to the evolution of beings capable of reason, unless they were produced by design?

Of course, I must admit that I cannot prove that the occurrences that led to the development of beings capable of reason could not have taken place by chance. To do so in a fully satisfactory manner, I think, would require a method for distinguishing those conjunctions of states of affairs which require explanations in common from those which do not, and this I do not know how to provide.[8] However, I find it hard to believe that so much could have happened simply by chance, and yet I think this is exactly what one must believe, if one believes that the universe was not created by design. I think, then, that it is safe to conclude that those who fear that the secular view of things, common today among so many intellectuals, robs the world of its mystery are quite mistaken.

NOTES

1. Anyone who believes a nativity scene could appear on a window without having been designed may substitute a more elaborate example for the one I am presenting. For example, it might be supposed that numerous perfect nativity scenes appear one Christmas morning on the windows of many practising Christians living in cold climates. Remarks similar to those I make below could then be made in connection with this example.

2. It should be noted that an analogous point could be made about the argument from design. Someone holding that certain natural phenomena were designed need not deny that the phenomena resulted from a chain of purely natural causes extending indefinitely far in the past. And, again, if a natural phenomenon one believes to have been produced by design turns out to have resulted from such a chain of causes, that fact may count as evidence for the eminence of its designer.

3. P. T.Geach, "An irrelevance of omnipotence", Philosophy vol. 48, No. 186 (1973), 327–33.

4. Ibid., p. 330.

5. I. W.Sherman and V. G.Sherman, Biology: A Human Approach (OUP, New York, 1975), p. 456.

6. Ibid.

7. Of course, one might conclude that such occurrences could have come together by chance. In particular one might argue that, unlikely as it may be that all the conditions needed to produce beings capable of reason should have arisen on earth, still in a universe as vast as ours we can expect that it should have happened somewhere, and earth just happens to be a place where it did happen. However, I think this argument is little more than an appeal to scepticism. One could as well argue that we do not know that the speed of light is constant in a vacuum, because if the speed of light were random one still would expect it to appear constant in some region or other of a large enough universe. The point in both cases is the same. Random processes can be imagined and—in a large enough universe—expected to mimic controlled processes, but when phenomena of the right sort would be sufficiently improbable if they occurred by chance, we have a right to conclude that they did not occur by chance.

8. The problem here, I think, is closely connected with *one* of the problems of induction. If a coin is tossed 1,000 times, and the results form certain patterns of heads and tails (for example, if the coin lands heads on all and only the prime numbered tosses), then we will believe that the pattern that was formed did not occur by chance, and we will expect future tosses to result in a similar pattern. On the other hand, other patterns of heads and tails would strike us as "random", and one would not expect them to be repeated by future tosses. But how do we distinguish the random patterns from the others?

25   DARWIN AND DESIGN

NICHOLAS EVERITT

Nicholas Everitt is Honorary Senior Fellow in Philosophy at the University of East Anglia, United Kingdom. He provides an overview of Darwin's discoveries and explains how in some respects that scientific work is relevant to assessing the teleological argument for the existence of God.

THE RELEVANCE OF DARWIN

Some authors have argued that Darwin's discoveries have no bearing on the strength of the argument to design (AD). Others see them as dealing the AD a fatal blow. Darwin's discoveries are indeed centrally relevant to the AD, as we shall see. But to see exactly why and how this is so, it is necessary to sketch a little background information.

For some centuries, Christian thinkers had taken the creation story of the Bible literally. One part of this story has it that God created the different species of animals and plants separately: from the beginning, the Garden of Eden was stocked with plants and with animals which belonged to different species. It followed that God must have created them separately. This separateness was thought of as fixed and eternal: each species had its own defining essence, given to it by God when he first created it, and which it then passed on to succeeding generations. That thought was then extended, in an entirely reasonable manner, to cover the whole of the living world: wherever there were different species, God must have created them different. No species, in other words, had developed from any other species.

The central aim of *The Origin of Species* was to challenge this belief. Darwin was not primarily seeking to explain why the world of nature displays seeming purpose and design; nor was he seeking to explain the origin of life. It is significant that his work is called *The Origin of Species*, and not, for example, *The Explanation of Seeming Design in Nature*, nor *The Origin of Life*. His main thesis was that some species had developed from others. What we think of today as two distinct species may in fact be linked historically by a chain of intervening life forms which are neither clearly of one species nor clearly of the other. Most famously, and especially in his later work *The Descent of Man*, he argued that humans and other currently existing species such as chimpanzees both developed from a single earlier species of primate. How widely did he think that this mutability of species extended? The main text of *The Origin* has nothing to say about this issue. The thesis it is defending could be put by saying that *a great many species that are now distinct have developed from a common ancestor*. It was not part of his main thesis to show that *all* life forms derive from a single source. However, in his concluding chapter, he addresses the question, and says the following:

> I cannot doubt that the theory of descent with modification embraces all the members of the same great class. I believe that animals have descended from at most only four or five progenitors, and plants from an equal or lesser number.
>
> Analogy would lead me one step further, namely, to the belief that all animals and plants have descended from some one prototype. But analogy may be a deceitful guide ... [however, all things considered] I should infer from analogy that probably all the organic beings which have ever lived on this earth have descended from some one primordial form.[1]

From Nicholas Everitt, *The Non-Existence of God*, Routledge, 2004. Reprinted by permission of the publisher.

That, then, is a thumbnail sketch of the theory of evolution – the claim that species evolved one from one another, rather than being separately created. But there is another essential component to Darwin's overall theory. For he not only maintained that species evolved one from another, he also suggested a mechanism by which this evolution could occur. Various mechanisms are possible in theory. Suppose we wonder how long-necked giraffes could evolve from short-necked herbivores. One possible explanation would be that God intervened in each succeeding generation of short-necked herbivores, making the neck of animals of each generation slightly longer, until the fully fledged giraffe form was reached. (Think of a factory operative who changes the settings on the production machines after each production run.) A second possible mechanism is the so-called theory of acquired characteristics favoured by Lamarck: each generation of originally short-necked herbivores kept stretching their necks, thereby giving themselves slightly longer necks; and this acquired characteristic they then passed on to their progeny who in turn repeated the process.

A third possibility, and the one which Darwin favoured, is the so-called theory of natural selection. This in turn has two components: first, there is the claim that although offspring are substantially similar to their parents, there is some degree of variation between generations; and second, the claim that the environment favours some of these variations more than others. The first of these ideas tells us that offspring are not exactly similar to their parents in all respects. They may, for example, have slightly more acute hearing or larger teeth, or be of slightly heavier or lighter build, and so on. The second idea then says that some of these variations will make the individual better adapted to the environment than individuals who lack the variation. 'Better adapted' here means ultimately 'being more likely to reproduce successfully' – but of course that is a trait that will have many components. Part of being able to reproduce successfully will be having the ability to obtain enough food; another part will be being able to escape from predators; another will be being able to withstand disease; another will be

being able to attract fertile mates. And so on. So for example, a cat which belongs to a night-hunting species, but which is born with slightly defective night vision, will have a lower chance of being a successful hunter, a lower chance of surviving in times of food shortages, a lower chance of being in good physical condition for mating, and a lower chance of producing offspring like itself, than the normal cat with good night vision. So the characteristic of poor night vision is ill-adapted to the cat's environment, and other things being equal is more likely not to be passed on to the succeeding generations. Correlatively, cats with good night vision will be better fitted to a night-hunting environment, and over time will reproduce more successfully than other cats, so that ultimately good night vision will be a near universal trait among nocturnal cats.

These better-adapted traits thus gradually spread through the whole population. Over a period of perhaps thousands of generations, and many different traits, there thus emerges by a process of natural selection a set of individuals who are sufficiently different from their ancestors to count as a different species.

The theory of natural selection, which was designed to explain how there have come to be a great many different species, thus has as a by-product an explanation of the appearance of design and purpose in the world of nature. The theory explains why, for example, nocturnal cats have all the appearance of having been *designed* (i.e. by a conscious designer), without needing to postulate the existence of a conscious designer.

Separating the theory of evolution from the theory of natural selection enables us to see that evolution *per se* is no threat at all to an argument to design. What is ruled out by the theory of evolution (i.e. the theory that the different species evolved from other species) is the theory of special creation (i.e. the theory that the different species were created separately from each other). These are two theories about *the origin of species difference*. They do not provide rival accounts of *why each member of a species seems designed for its own environment*. What *does* put pressure on the traditional AD is the theory of natural selection. AD and the theory of natural selection offer rival accounts of the mechanism which produces seeming design in the living world. The first requires a supernatural designer, the second requires only that in their reproduction, species produce new members who are substantially similar to their parents, but who can differ from the parents in small ways which give their offspring a reproductive advantage over their fellows. So, evidence in favour of the theory of natural selection must tell against the AD.

It would be beyond the scope of this text to provide a thorough assessment of the theory of natural selection. That is a task for detailed empirical scientific work, and is something which is anyway admirably performed by a number of other texts. Here we can simply note that there is huge (but not universal) agreement among competent practising biologists (a) that the theory of evolution is correct, and (b) that the theory of natural selection, even if not the whole story, is at least a major part of the story. Further, the majority of those who think that natural selection is only part of the story do not suggest that the rest of the story lies in interventions by a supernatural designer—that natural selection needs to be supplemented (as it were) with some *super*natural selection. Rather, they argue that some other purely physical mechanisms need to be invoked.

We will therefore take as read the biological case in favour of natural selection. There are, however, some broadly philosophical points which seek to limit or undermine the theory; and these we will consider in the next section.

CRITICISMS OF DARWIN

There are three points in particular which we will examine: that the theory of natural selection makes the appearance of seeming design a matter of 'blind chance'; that the theory does not disprove the existence of God; and that the theory offers no explanation for the origin of life.

First, hostile critics have sometimes complained that natural selection attributes the development of seeming design in nature to what they call 'blind chance', the implication usually being that this makes a Darwinian explanation for seeming design an absurdly improbable one. How justified is this reaction?

We can note first that the term *blind* chance seems to involve redundancy. Is the critic suggesting that there is an alternative kind of chance called 'sighted chance'? If not, let us speak simply of chance. The question then becomes whether a Darwinian explanation attributes seeming design to the operation of chance. The answer to this will depend on what we understand by 'chance'. Sometimes, we certainly use the term to contrast what happens by prior planning and design with what happens without such design. If two people independently decide to go to a conference, at which they subsequently meet, we could well say that they met by chance, meaning that their meeting was not pre-planned. To say that they met by chance is not itself an *explanation* of why they met—rather it *rules out* an explanation in terms of their prior planning. Nor does their meeting 'by chance' imply that there is no good explanation for the meeting (e.g. in terms of the fact that the conference was on a topic which interested them both, that the conference was fairly small, so that all those attending it would meet each other sooner or later, etc.). In this non-planned sense of 'chance', it is of course true that natural selection says that seeming design occurs 'by chance', for that says no more than that seeming design occurs without being the product of prior planning. In this sense of chance, it is just a matter of chance that every time the temperature rises above 0°C, ice melts; and every time an avalanche occurs on a mountain, the snow slides down rather than up. In other words, even events which are inevitable in the light of the laws of nature can be described as occurring 'by chance' in this 'unplanned' sense of 'chance'.

But the term 'chance' is sometimes used to describe events for which there is no explanation. Heisenberg's Uncertainty Principle, at least as it is often popularly presented, tells us that for some subatomic events, there are no causes: there is no explanation for the occurrence of such events, and in this sense, the occurrence of such events is a matter of chance. But in this sense, natural selection is certainly not saying that seeming design is a matter of chance. Indeed, the theory actually asserts the opposite, since it says there is a good causal explanation for the seeming design.

So, to the charge that natural selection makes seeming design a matter of chance, we can reply 'That is true in one sense of "chance", just as most things that happen are a matter of chance. But it is false in the other sense of "chance", since natural selection says that there is a perfectly good explanation of how and why the seeming design in nature appears and is maintained.'

A second common criticism of a Darwinian approach is to say that it does not prove that there is no God. Kenny, for example, has claimed that 'If the argument from design ever had any value, it has not been substantially affected by the scientific investigation of living organisms from Descartes through to the present day.[2] Kenny's thought is that it is possible to combine an acceptance of evolutionary theory and natural selection with a belief that the *ultimate* explanation of the phenomena must be in terms of the purposes of a designer. A divine designer would, as it were, design the *system* within which species would evolve in accordance with Darwinian natural selection.

But this is a disingenuous criticism. The original form of the AD focused specifically on the features of living things, and said explicitly that those features were very strong evidence for the existence of a divine designer. To the extent that natural selection offers a better explanation of those features than the God hypothesis, it *has* undermined the God hypothesis. The fact that the modern theist can pick on something quite different and say that *that* is evidence for the existence of a divine designer does nothing to show that Darwin's discoveries have not discredited the traditional form of the argument.

Further, the original arguers to design did not merely say that what they could observe in nature was *compatible with* the existence of a divine designer. They claimed that what they could observe was *overwhelming evidence in favour of* the existence of a designer. So even if all Darwin's discoveries could be rendered *compatible with* the AD (and we have implicitly argued above that they cannot be, since they are rival explanations), it would not follow that post-Darwin, the AD could claim the same support from our observations of the natural world. Post-Darwin, the AD no longer provides the best explanation for seeming design, and to that extent its credibility has, *contra* Kenny, been undermined by 'the scientific investigation of living organisms from Descartes through to the present day'.

One final comment is sometimes made to try to limit the power of natural selection. What the theory can do (so the objection goes) is provide a good explanation of how, given one type of organism, or one set of biological features, a further better adapted organism or set of features can develop. Given a creature with a light-sensitive patch on its skin able to detect the difference between light and dark, the theory can provide an explanation of how the creature's distant descendants could come to have a fully functioning eye. But this means that every explanation provided by the theory has to start with some already existing example of seeming design. So the theory can explain one seeming design in terms of another, but what it cannot do is explain seeming design as such.... The point is sometimes put by saying that the theory of natural selection cannot explain the origin of *life*. All that it can explain is how, once life exists, it develops in one way rather than another.

The short answer to this comment is that it is true, but that it represents a change of subject. The original AD did not say that the existence of *life per se* (e.g. in bacteria) was good evidence for the existence of a designer. It focused specifically on *certain complicated forms of life* for which it was difficult at the time to find any naturalistic explanation. When the explanation was found (i.e. by Darwin), it remained true that a further question could be raised about, life forms which the original proponents of the AD knew nothing about, and which displayed in much less striking form the seeming design on which they focused. But, once that is conceded, there does remain the entirely legitimate question of where and how life itself arises, and whether a good explanation (or even the best available explanation) might be one which called upon a divine designer.

As with the biological evidence in favour of natural selection, so with the state of current biological theorising about the origin of life—detailed assessment is a task beyond the scope of this text. There *is* a real puzzle here, and there is no consensus among biologists. Several radically different theories each have a number of distinguished supporters, and the lay outsider would be unwise to form even a secondhand judgement about which theory was the most credible. All that can be said is that none of the theories which is seriously canvassed by significant numbers of practising biologists invokes any kind of designer. To that extent, although the critic of the AD is right to say that the original theory of natural selection did not provide an explanation of the origin of life per se, he would be wrong to infer from this that by default a designer hypothesis was thereby shown to be more likely.

D. THE MORAL ARGUMENT

26 CONSCIENCE

JOHN HENRY NEWMAN

The moral argument for the existence of God finds proof of God's existence in our capacity for moral thought. Our next selection offers an example of such a proof, and was developed by John Henry Newman (1801–1890), an Anglican churchman who converted to Catholicism and became a cardinal. A master of English prose, he wrote *Apologia pro vita sua*, a religious autobiography, *Idea of a University Defined*, a defense of education as a moral enterprise, and *An Essay in Aid of a Grammar of Assent*, offering a justification of religious belief. In this excerpt from the latter work, he explains how each person's conscience points to the existence of an omnipotent, omniscient, and just Supreme Being.

... [W]hat I am directly aiming at, is to explain how we gain an image of God and give a real assent to the proposition that He exists. And next, in order to do this, of course I must start from some first principle;—and that first principle, which I assume and shall not attempt to prove, is ... that we have by nature a conscience.

I assume, then, that Conscience has a legitimate place among our mental acts; as really so, as the action of memory, of reasoning, of imagination, or as the sense of the beautiful; that, as there are objects which, when presented to the mind, cause it to feel grief, regret, joy, or desire, so there are things which excite in us approbation or blame, and which we in consequence call right or wrong; and which, experienced in ourselves, kindle in us that specific sense of pleasure or pain, which goes by the name of a good or bad conscience. This being taken for granted, I shall attempt to show that in this special feeling, which follows on the commission of what we call right or wrong, lie the materials for the real apprehension of a Divine Sovereign and Judge.

The feeling of conscience (being, I repeat, a certain keen sensibility, pleasant or painful,—self-approval and hope, or compunction and fear,—attendant on certain of our actions, which in consequence we call right or wrong) is twofold:—it is a moral sense, and a sense of duty; a judgment of the reason and a magisterial dictate. Of course its act is indivisible; still it has these two aspects, distinct from each other, and admitting of a separate consideration. Though I lost my sense of the obligation which I lie under to abstain from acts of dishonesty, I should not in consequence lose my sense that such actions were an outrage offered to my moral nature. Again; though I lost my sense of their moral deformity, I should not therefore lose my sense that they were forbidden to me. Thus conscience has both a critical and a judicial office, and though its promptings, in the breasts of the millions of human beings to whom it is given, are not in all cases correct, that does not necessarily interfere with the force of its testimony and of its sanction: its testimony that there is a right and a wrong, and its sanction to that testimony conveyed in the feelings which attend on right or wrong conduct. Here I have to speak of conscience in the latter point of view, not as supplying us, by means of its various acts, with the elements of morals, such as may be developed by the intellect into an ethical code, but simply as the dictate of an

From John Henry Newman, *An Essay in Aid of a Grammar of Assent* (1870).

authoritative monitor bearing upon the details of conduct as they come before us, and complete in its several acts, one by one.

Let us then thus consider conscience, not as a rule of right conduct, but as a sanction of right conduct. This is its primary and most authoritative aspect; it is the ordinary sense of the word. Half the world would be puzzled to know what was meant by the moral sense; but every one knows what is meant by a good or bad conscience. Conscience is ever forcing on us by threats and by promises that we must follow the right and avoid the wrong; so far it is one and the same in the mind of every one, whatever be its particular errors in particular minds as to the acts which it orders to be done or to be avoided; and in this respect it corresponds to our perception of the beautiful and deformed. As we have naturally a sense of the beautiful and graceful in nature and art, though tastes proverbially differ, so we have a sense of duty and obligation, whether we all associate it with the same certain actions in particular or not. Here, however, Taste and Conscience part company: for the sense of beautifulness, as indeed the Moral Sense, has no special relations to persons, but contemplates objects in themselves; conscience, on the other hand, is concerned with persons primarily, and with actions mainly as viewed in their doers, or rather with self alone and one's own actions, and with others only indirectly and as if in association with self. And further, taste is its own evidence, appealing to nothing beyond its own sense of the beautiful or the ugly, and enjoying the specimens of the beautiful simply for their own sake; but conscience does not repose on itself, but vaguely reaches forward to something beyond self, and dimly discerns a sanction higher than self for its decisions, as is evidenced in that keen sense of obligation and responsibility which informs them. And hence it is that we are accustomed to speak of conscience as a voice, a term which we should never think of applying to the sense of the beautiful; and moreover a voice, or the echo of a voice, imperative and constraining, like no other dictate in the whole of our experience.

And again, in consequence of this prerogative of dictating and commanding, which is of its essence, Conscience has an intimate bearing on our affections and emotions, leading us to reverence and awe, hope and fear, especially fear, a feeling which is foreign for the most part, not only to Taste, but even to the Moral Sense, except in consequence of accidental associations. No fear is felt by any one who recognizes that his conduct has not been beautiful, though he may be mortified at himself, if perhaps he has thereby forfeited some advantage; but, if he has been betrayed into any kind of immorality, he has a lively sense of responsibility and guilt, though the act be no offence against society,—of distress and apprehension, even though it may be of present service to him,—of compunction and regret, though in itself it be most pleasurable,—of confusion of face, though it may have no witnesses. These various perturbations of mind which are characteristic of a bad conscience, and may be very considerable,—self-reproach, poignant shame, haunting remorse, chill dismay at the prospect of the future,—and their contraries, when the conscience is good, as real though less forcible, self-approval, inward peace, lightness of heart, and the like,—these emotions constitute a specific difference between conscience and our other intellectual senses,—common sense, good sense, sense of expedience, taste, sense of honour, and the like,—as indeed they would also constitute between conscience and the moral sense, supposing these two were not aspects of one and the same feeling, exercised upon one and the same subject-matter.

So much for the characteristic phenomena, which conscience presents, nor is it difficult to determine what they imply. I refer once more to our sense of the beautiful. This sense is attended by an intellectual enjoyment, and is free from whatever is of the nature of emotion, except in one case, viz. when it is excited by personal objects; then it is that the tranquil feeling of admiration is exchanged for the excitement of affection and passion. Conscience too, considered as a moral sense, an intellectual sentiment, is a sense of admiration and disgust, of approbation and blame: but it is something more than a moral sense; it is always, what the sense of the beautiful is only in certain cases; it is always emotional. No wonder then that it always implies what that sense only sometimes implies; that it always involves the recognition of a living object, towards which it is directed. Inanimate things cannot stir our affections; these are correlative with persons. If, as is the case, we feel responsibility, are ashamed, are frightened, at transgressing the voice of conscience, this implies that there is One to whom we are responsible, before whom we are ashamed, whose claims upon us we fear. If, on doing wrong, we feel the same tearful, broken-hearted sorrow which overwhelms us on hurting a mother; if, on doing right, we enjoy the same sunny serenity of mind, the same soothing, satisfactory delight which follows on our receiving praise from a father, we certainly have within us the image of some person, to whom our love and veneration look, in whose smile we find our happiness, for whom we yearn, towards whom we direct our pleadings, in whose anger we are troubled and waste away. These feelings in us are such as require for their exciting cause an intelligent being: we are not affectionate towards a stone, nor do we feel shame before a horse or a dog; we have no remorse or compunction on breaking mere human law: yet, so it is, conscience excites all these painful emotions, confusion, foreboding, self-condemnation; and on the other hand it sheds upon us a deep peace, a sense of security, a resignation, and a hope, which there is no sensible, no earthly object to elicit. 'The wicked flees, when no one pursueth;' then why does he flee? whence his terror? Who is it that he sees in solitude, in darkness, in the hidden chambers of his heart? If the cause of these emotions does not belong to this visible world, the Object to which his perception is directed must be Supernatural and Divine; and thus the phenomena of Conscience, as a dictate, avail to impress the imagination with the picture of a Supreme Governor, a Judge, holy, just, powerful, all-seeing, retributive, and is the creative principle of religion, as the Moral Sense is the principle of ethics....

Thus conscience is a connecting principle between the creature and his Creator; and the firmest hold of theological truths is gained by habits of personal religion. When men begin all their works with the thought of God, acting for His sake, and to fulfil His will, when they ask His blessing on themselves and their life, pray to Him for the objects they desire, and see Him in the event, whether it be according to their prayers or not, they will find everything that happens tend to confirm them in the truths about Him which live in their imagination, varied and unearthly as those truths may be. Then they are brought into His presence as that of a Living Person, and are able to hold converse with Him, and that with a directness and simplicity, with a confidence and intimacy, mutatis mutandis, which we use towards an earthly superior; so that it is doubtful whether we realize the company of our fellow-men with greater keenness than these favoured minds are able to contemplate and adore the Unseen, Incomprehensible Creator.

27   NEWMAN ON CONSCIENCE: A CRITIQUE

J. L. MACKIE

J. L. Mackie (1917–1981) was an Australian philosopher who taught at the University of Oxford. In our next selection, he offers a critique of Newman's version of the moral argument for the existence of God.

From J. L. Mackie, *The Miracle of Theism*, Oxford University Press, 1982. Reprinted by permission of the publisher.

... [Newman's] argument rests on three premisses: that conscience is legitimate or authoritative; that it looks beyond the agent himself to a further imperative and a higher sanction; and that these must stem from a person, an intelligent being, if they are to arouse powerful emotions with exactly the tone of those that moral awareness involves. If we grant all three premisses, we must admit that the argument is cogent, though the god that it introduces need not have the infinite attributes of Descartes's god, or Anselm's. But must we grant all three premisses? In fact this argument faces a dilemma. If we take conscience at its face value and accept as really valid what it asserts, we must say that there is a rational prescriptivity about certain kinds of action in their own right: that they are of this or that kind is in itself a reason for doing them or for refraining from them. There is a to-be-done-ness or a not-to-be-done-ness involved *in that kind of action in itself.* If so, there is no need to look beyond this to any supernatural person who commands or forbids such action. Equally the regret, guilt, shame, and fear associated with the consciousness of having done wrong, although normally such feelings arise only in relations with persons, are in this special case natural and appropriate: what conscience, taken at its face value, tells us is that this is how one should feel about a wrong action simply in itself. That is, if we whole-heartedly accept Newman's first premiss, we must reject the second and the third. But if we do not take conscience at its face value, if we seek critically to understand how conscience has come into existence and has come to work as it does, then we do indeed find persons in the background, but human persons, not a divine one. If we stand back from the experience of conscience and try to understand it, it is overwhelmingly plausible to see it as an introjection into each individual of demands that come from other people; in the first place, perhaps, from his parents and immediate associates, but ultimately from the traditions and institutions of the society in which he has grown up, or of some special part of that society which has had the greatest influence upon him. In thus understanding conscience we do, admittedly, look beyond conscience itself and beyond the agent himself, but we look to natural, human, sources, not to a god. We are now in a way accepting Newman's second and third premisses, but modifying the first. It is not easy to accept all three. Newman's argument walks, as it were, a tight-rope, allowing to conscience, as it claims, an authority and an origin independent of all human feelings and demands, and yet not endorsing its claim to complete autonomy. But it is arbitrary to choose just this degree of critical reinterpretation, no more and no less.

Perhaps Newman will rely not on conscience in general, as a mode of thinking almost universal among human beings, but on the particular form of conscience which already ties its moral ideas to belief in a god. If he takes this special form of conscience at its face value, he can indeed assert all three premisses; but then his argument will carry conviction only with those who already accept his conclusion. Addressed to a wider public or to an initially open-minded audience, it becomes the hopelessly weak argument that there must be a god because some people believe that there is a god and have incorporated this belief into their moral thought. Something more would be needed to show that this special form of moral thinking is distinctively valid, and this would have to include an independent argument precisely for the existence of a god of the appropriate sort.

PART FOUR

The Problem of Evil

A. GOD AND EVIL

28 DIALOGUES CONCERNING NATURAL RELIGION (X–XI)

DAVID HUME

The lack of proof that God exists is not by itself a proof that God does not exist. To reach that conclusion requires a separate argument, and a much-discussed one is the problem of evil.

Why should evil be found in a world created by an all-good, all-powerful being? A being who is all-good would do everything possible to abolish evil. A being who is all-powerful would be able to abolish evil. Therefore, if an all-good, all-powerful being existed, evil would not. But evil is a reality. So an all-good, all-powerful being is not.

We now resume reading David Hume's *Dialogues Concerning Natural Religion* at the point where the discussion turns to the problem of evil.

PART X

It is my opinion, I own, replied Demea, that each man feels, in a manner, the truth of religion within his own breast, and, from a consciousness of his imbecility and misery rather than from any reasoning, is led to seek protection from that Being on whom he and all nature is dependent. So anxious or so

From David Hume, *Dialogues Concerning Natural Religion* (1779).

tedious are even the best scenes of life that futurity is still the object of all our hopes and fears. We incessantly look forward and endeavour, by prayers, adoration, and sacrifice, to appease those unknown powers whom we find, by experience, so able to afflict and oppress us. Wretched creatures that we are! What resource for us amidst the innumerable ills of life did not religion suggest some methods of atonement, and appease those terrors with which we are incessantly agitated and tormented?

I am indeed persuaded, said Philo, that the best and indeed the only method of bringing everyone to a due sense of religion is by just representations of the misery and wickedness of men. And for that purpose a talent of eloquence and strong imagery is more requisite than that of reasoning and argument. For is it necessary to prove what everyone feels within himself? It is only necessary to make us feel it, if possible, more intimately and sensibly.

The people, indeed, replied Demea, are sufficiently convinced of this great and melancholy truth. The miseries of life, the unhappiness of man, the general corruptions of our nature, the unsatisfactory enjoyment of pleasures, riches, honours—these phrases have become almost proverbial in all languages. And who can doubt of what all men declare from their own immediate feeling and experience?

In this point, said Philo, the learned are perfectly agreed with the vulgar; and in all letters, *sacred* and *profane*, the topic of human misery has been insisted on with the most pathetic eloquence that sorrow and melancholy could inspire. The poets, who speak from sentiment, without a system, and whose testimony has therefore the more authority, abound in images of this nature. From Homer down to Dr. Young, the whole inspired tribe have ever been sensible that no other representation of things would suit the feeling and observation of each individual.

As to authorities, replied Demea, you need not seek them. Look round this library of Cleanthes. I shall venture to affirm that, except authors of particular sciences, such as chemistry or botany, who have no occasion to treat of human life, there is scarce one of those innumerable writers from whom the sense of human misery has

not, in some passage or other, extorted a complaint and confession of it. At least, the chance is entirely on that side; and no one author has ever, so far as I can recollect, been so extravagant as to deny it.

There you must excuse me, said Philo: Leibniz has denied it, and is perhaps the first who ventured upon so bold and paradoxical an opinion; at least, the first who made it essential to his philosophical system.

And by being the first, replied Demea, might he not have been sensible of his error? For is this a subject in which philosophers can propose to make discoveries especially in so late an age? And can any man hope by a simple denial (for the subject scarcely admits of reasoning) to bear down the united testimony of mankind, founded on sense and consciousness?

And why should man, added he, pretend to an exemption from the lot of all other animals? The whole earth, believe me, Philo, is cursed and polluted. A perpetual war is kindled amongst all living creatures. Necessity, hunger, want stimulate the strong and courageous; fear, anxiety, terror agitate the weak and infirm. The first entrance into life gives anguish to the new-born infant and to its wretched parent; weakness, impotence, distress attend each stage of that life, and it is, at last, finished in agony and horror.

Observe, too, says Philo, the curious artifices of nature in order to embitter the life of every living being. The stronger prey upon the weaker and keep them in perpetual terror and anxiety. The weaker, too, in their turn, often prey upon the stronger, and vex and molest them without relaxation. Consider that innumerable race of insects, which either are bred on the body of each animal or, flying about, infix their stings in him. These insects have others still less than themselves which torment them. And thus on each hand, before and behind, above and below, every animal is surrounded with enemies which incessantly seek his misery and destruction.

Man alone, said Demea, seems to be, in part, an exception to this rule. For by combination in society he can easily master lions, tigers, and bears, whose greater strength and agility naturally enable them to prey upon him.

On the contrary, it is here chiefly, cried Philo, that the uniform and equal maxims of nature are most apparent. Man, it is true, can, by combination, surmount all his *real* enemies and become master of the whole animal creation; but does he not immediately raise up to himself *imaginary* enemies, the demons of his fancy, who haunt him with superstitious terrors and blast every enjoyment of life? His pleasure, as he imagines, becomes in their eyes a crime; his food and repose give them umbrage and offence; his very sleep and dreams furnish new materials to anxious fear; and even death, his refuge from every other ill, presents only the dread of endless and innumerable woes. Nor does the wolf molest more the timid flock than superstition does the anxious breast of wretched mortals.

Besides, consider, Demea: This very society by which we surmount those wild beasts, our natural enemies, what new enemies does it not raise to us? What woe and misery does it not occasion? Man is the greatest enemy of man. Oppression, injustice, contempt, contumely, violence, sedition, war, calumny, treachery, fraud—by these they mutually torment each other, and they would soon dissolve that society which they had formed were it not for the dread of still greater ills which must attend their separation.

But though these external insults, said Demea, from animals, from men, from all the elements, which assault us from a frightful catalogue of woes, they are nothing in comparison of those which arise within ourselves, from the distempered condition of our mind and body. How many lie under the lingering torment of diseases?…

The disorders of the mind, continued Demea, though more secret, are not perhaps less dismal and vexatious. Remorse, shame, anguish, rage, disappointment, anxiety, fear, dejection, despair—who has ever passed through life without cruel inroads from these tormentors? How many have scarcely ever felt any better sensations? Labour and poverty, so abhorred by everyone, are the certain lot of the far greater number; and those few privileged persons who enjoy ease and opulence never reach contentment or true felicity. All the goods of life united would not make a very happy man, but all the ills united would make a wretch indeed, and any one of them almost (and who can be free from every one?), nay, often the absence of one good (and who can possess all?) is sufficient to render life ineligible.

Were a stranger to drop on a sudden into this world, I would show him, as a specimen of its ills, an hospital full of diseases, a prison crowded with malefactors and debtors, a field of battle strewed with carcases, a fleet floundering in the ocean, a nation languishing under tyranny, famine, or pestilence. To turn the gay side of life to him and give him a notion of its pleasures—whither should I conduct him? To a ball, to an opera, to court? He might justly think that I was only showing him a diversity of distress and sorrow.

There is no evading such striking instances, said Philo, but by apologies which still further aggravate the charge. Why have all men, I ask, in all ages, complained incessantly of the miseries of life? … They have no just reason, says one: these complaints proceed only from their discontented repining, anxious disposition…. And can there possibly, I reply, be a more certain foundation of misery than such a wretched temper?

But if they were really as unhappy as they pretend, says my antagonist why do they remain in life? …

Not satisfied with life, afraid of death—

This is the secret chain, say I, that holds us. We are terrified, not bribed to the continuance of our existence.

It is only a false delicacy, he may insist, which a few refined spirits indulge, and which has spread these complaints among the whole race of mankind…. And what is this delicacy, I ask, which you blame? Is it anything but a greater sensibility to all the pleasures and pains of life? And if the man of a delicate, refined temper, by being so much more alive than the rest of the world, is only so much more unhappy, what judgment must we form in general of human life?

Let men remain at rest, says our adversary, and they will be easy. They are willing artificers of their own misery…. No! reply I: an anxious languor follows their repose: disappointment, vexation, trouble, their activity and ambition.

I can observe something like what you mention in some others, replied Cleanthes, but I confess I feel little or nothing of it in myself, and hope that it is not so common as you represent it.

If you feel not human misery yourself, cried Demea, I congratulate you on so happy a singularity. Others, seemingly the most prosperous, have not been ashamed to vent their complaints in the most melancholy strains. Let us attend to the great, the fortunate emperor, Charles V, when tired with human grandeur, he resigned all his extensive dominions into the hands of his son. In the last harangue which he made on that memorable occasion, he publicly avowed *that the greatest prosperities which he had ever enjoyed had been mixed with so many adversities that he might truly say he had never enjoyed any satisfaction or contentment.* But did the retired life in which he sought for shelter afford him any greater happiness? If we may credit his son's account, his repentance commenced the very day of his resignation.

Cicero's fortune, from small beginnings, rose to the greatest luster and renown; yet what pathetic complaints of the ills of life do his familiar letters, as well as philosophical discourses, contain? And suitably to his own experience, he introduces Cato, the great, the fortunate Cato protesting in his old age that had he a new life in his offer he would reject the present.

Ask yourself, ask any of your acquaintance, whether they would live over again the last ten or twenty years of their life. No! but the next twenty, they say, will be better....

Thus, at last, they find (such is the greatness of human misery, it reconciles even contradictions) that they complain at once of the shortness of life and of its vanity and sorrow.

And is it possible, Cleanthes, said Philo, that after all these reflections, and infinitely more which might be suggested, you can still persevere in your anthropomorphism, and assert the moral attributes of the Deity, his justice, benevolence, mercy, and rectitude, to be of the same nature with these virtues in human creatures? His power, we allow, is infinite; whatever he wills is executed; but neither man nor any other animal is happy; therefore, he does not will their happiness. His wisdom is infinite; he is never mistaken in choosing the means to

any end; but the course of nature tends not to human or animal felicity; therefore, it is not established for that purpose. Through the whole compass of human knowledge there are no inferences more certain and infallible than these. In what respect, then, do his benevolence and mercy resemble the benevolence and mercy of men?

Epicurus' old questions are yet unanswered.

Is he willing to prevent evil, but not able? then is he impotent. Is he able, but not willing? then is he malevolent. Is he both able and willing? whence then is evil?

You ascribe, Cleanthes (and I believe justly), a purpose and intention to nature. But what, I beseech you, is the object of that curious artifice and machinery which she has displayed in all animals— the preservation alone of individuals, and propagation of the species? It seems enough for her purpose, if such a rank be barely upheld in the universe, without any care or concern for the happiness of the members that compose it. No resource for this purpose: no machinery in order merely to give pleasure or ease; no fund of pure joy and contentment; no indulgence without some want or necessity accompanying it. At least, the few phenomena of this nature are over-balanced by opposite phenomena of still greater importance.

Our sense of music, harmony, and indeed beauty of all kinds, gives satisfaction, without being absolutely necessary to the preservation and propagation of the species. But what racking pains, on the other hand, arise from gouts, gravels, megrims, toothaches, rheumatisms, where the injury to the animal machinery is either small or incurable? Mirth, laughter, play, frolic seem gratuitous satisfactions which have no further tendency; spleen, melancholy, discontent, superstition are pains of the same nature. How then does the Divine benevolence display itself, in the sense of you anthropomorphites? None but we mystics, as you were pleased to call us, can account for this strange mixture of phenomena, by deriving it from attributes infinitely perfect but incomprehensible.

And have you, at last, said Cleanthes smiling, betrayed your intentions, Philo? Your long agreement with Demea did indeed a little surprise me, but I find you were all the while erecting a concealed battery against me. And I must confess that you have now fallen upon a subject worthy of your noble spirit of opposition and controversy. If you can make out the present point, and prove mankind to be unhappy or corrupted, there is an end at once of all religion. For to what purpose establish the natural attributes of the Deity, while the moral are still doubtful and uncertain?

You take umbrage very easily, replied Demea, at opinions the most innocent and the most generally received, even amongst the religious and devout themselves; and nothing can be more surprising than to find a topic like this—concerning the wickedness and misery of man—charged with no less than atheism and profaneness. Have not all pious divines and preachers who have indulged their rhetoric on so fertile a subject, have they not easily, I say, given a solution of any difficulties which may attend it? This world is but a point in comparison of the universe, this life but a moment in comparison of eternity. The present evil phenomena, therefore, are rectified in other regions, and in some future period of existence. And the eyes of men, being then opened to larger views of things, see the whole connection of general laws, and trace, with adoration, the benevolence and rectitude of the Deity through all the mazes and intricacies of his providence.

No! replied Cleanthes, no! These arbitrary suppositions can never be admitted, contrary to matter of fact, visible and uncontroverted. Whence can any cause be known but from its known effects? Whence can any hypothesis be proved but from the apparent phenomena? To establish one hypothesis upon another is building entirely in the air; and the utmost we ever attain by these conjectures and fictions is to ascertain the bare possibility of our opinion, but never can we, upon such terms, establish its reality.

The only method of supporting Divine benevolence—and it is what I willingly embrace—is to deny absolutely the misery and wickedness of man. Your representations are exaggerated; your melancholy views mostly fictitious; your inferences contrary to fact and experience. Health is more common than sickness; pleasure than pain; happiness than misery. And for one vexation which we meet with, we attain, upon computation, a hundred enjoyments.

Admitting your position, replied Philo, which yet is extremely doubtful, you must at the same time allow that, if pain be less frequent than pleasure, it is infinitely more violent and durable. One hour of it is often able to outweigh a day, a week, a month of our common insipid enjoyments; and how many days, weeks, and months are passed by several in the most acute torments? Pleasure, scarcely in one instance, is ever able to reach ecstasy and rapture; and in no one instance can it continue for any time at its highest pitch and altitude. The spirits evaporate, the nerves relax, the fabric is disordered, and the enjoyment quickly degenerates into fatigue and uneasiness. But pain often, good God, how often! rises to torture and agony; and the longer it continues, it becomes still more genuine agony and torture. Patience is exhausted, courage languishes, melancholy seizes us, and nothing terminates our misery but the removal of its cause or another event which is the sole cure of all evil, but which, from our natural folly, we regard with still greater horror and consternation.

But not to insist upon these topics, continued Philo, though most obvious, certain, and important, I must use the freedom to admonish you, Cleanthes, that you have put the controversy upon a most dangerous issue, and are unawares introducing a total scepticism into the most essential articles of natural and revealed theology. What! no method of fixing a just foundation for religion unless we allow the happiness of human life, and maintain a continued existence even in this world, with all our present pains, infirmities, vexations, and follies, to be eligible and desirable! But this is contrary to everyone's feeling and experience; it is contrary to an authority so established as nothing can subvert. No decisive proofs can ever be produced against this authority; nor is it possible for you to compute, estimate, and compare all the pains and all the pleasures in the lives of all men and of all animals; and thus, by your resting the whole system of religion on a point which, from its very nature, must for ever be uncertain, you tacitly confess that that system is equally uncertain.

But allowing you what never will be believed, at least, what you never possibly can prove, that animal or, at least, human happiness in this life exceeds its misery, you have yet done nothing;

for this is not, by any means, what we expect from infinite power, infinite wisdom, and infinite goodness. Why is there any misery at all in the world? Not by chance, surely. From some cause then. Is it from the intention of the Deity? But he is perfectly benevolent. Is it contrary to his intention? But he is almighty. Nothing can shake the solidity of this reasoning, so short, so clear, so decisive, except we assert that these subjects exceed all human capacity, and that our common measures of truth and falsehood are not applicable to them—a topic which I have all along insisted on, but which you have, from the beginning, rejected with scorn and indignation.

But I will be contented to retire still from this entrenchment, for I deny that you can ever force me in it. I will allow that pain or misery in man is *compatible* with infinite power and goodness in the Deity, even in your sense of these attributes: what are you advanced by all these concessions? A mere possible compatibility is not sufficient. You must *prove* these pure, unmixed, and uncontrollable attributes from the present mixed and confused phenomena, and from these alone. A hopeful undertaking! Were the phenomena ever so pure and unmixed, yet, being finite, they would be insufficient for that purpose. How much more, where they are also so jarring and discordant!

Here, Cleanthes, I find myself at ease in my argument. Here I triumph. Formerly, when we argued concerning the natural attributes of intelligence and design, I needed all my sceptical and metaphysical subtlety to elude your grasp. In many views of the universe and of its parts, particularly the latter, the beauty and fitness of final causes strike us with such irresistible force that all objections appear (what I believe they really are) mere cavils and sophisms; nor can we then imagine how it was ever possible for us to repose any weight on them. But there is no view of human life or of the condition of mankind from which, without the greatest violence, we can infer the moral attributes or learn that infinite benevolence, conjoined with infinite power and infinite wisdom, which we must discover by the eyes of faith alone. It is your turn now to tug the labouring oar, and to support your philosophical subtleties against the dictates of plain reason and experience.

PART XI

I scruple not to allow, said Cleanthes, that I have been apt to suspect the frequent repetition of the word *infinite*, which we meet with in all theological writers, to savor more of panegyric than of philosophy, and that any purposes of reasoning, and even of religion, would be better served were we to rest contented with more accurate and more moderate expressions. The terms *admirable, excellent, superlatively great, wise*, and *holy*—these sufficiently fill the imaginations of men, and anything beyond, besides that it leads into absurdities, has no influence on the affections or sentiments. Thus, in the present subject, if we abandon all human analogy, as seems your intention, Demea, I am afraid we abandon all religion and retain no conception of the great object of our adoration. If we preserve human analogy, we must forever find it impossible to reconcile any mixture of evil in the universe with infinite attributes; much less can we ever prove the latter from the former. But supposing the Author of Nature to be finitely perfect, though far exceeding mankind, a satisfactory account may then be given of natural and moral evil, and every untoward phenomenon be explained and adjusted. A less evil may then be chosen in order to avoid a greater; inconveniences be submitted to in order to reach a desirable end; and, in a word, benevolence, regulated by wisdom and limited by necessity, may produce just such a world as the present. You, Philo, who are so prompt at starting views and reflections and analogies, I would gladly hear, at length, without interruption, your opinion of this new theory; and if it deserve our attention, we may afterwards, at more leisure, reduce it into form.

My sentiments, replied Philo, are not worth being made a mystery of; and, therefore, without any ceremony, I shall deliver what occurs to me with regard to the present subject. It must, I think, be allowed that, if a very limited intelligence whom we shall suppose utterly unacquainted with the universe were assured that it were the production of a very good, wise, and powerful being, however finite, he would, from his conjectures, form *beforehand* a different notion of it from what we find it to be by experience; nor would he ever imagine, merely form these attributes of the cause of which he is informed, that the effect could be so full of vice and misery and disorder, as it appears in this life. Supposing now that this person were brought into the world, still assured that it was the workmanship of such a sublime and benevolent being, he might, perhaps, be surprised at the disappointment, but would never retract his former belief if founded on any very solid argument, since such a limited intelligence must be sensible of his own blindness and ignorance, and must allow that there may be many solutions of those phenomena which will forever escape his comprehension. But supposing, which is the real case with regard to man, that this creature is not antecedently convinced of a supreme intelligence, benevolent, and powerful, but is left to gather such a belief from the appearances of things— this entirely alters the case, nor will he ever find any reason for such a conclusion. He may be fully convinced of the narrow limits of his understanding, but this will not help him in forming an inference concerning the goodness of superior powers, since he must form that inference from what he knows, not from what he is ignorant of. The more you exaggerate his weakness and ignorance, the more diffident you render him, and give him the greater suspicion that such subjects are beyond the reach of his faculties. You are obliged, therefore, to reason with him merely from the known phenomena, and to drop every arbitrary supposition or conjecture.

Did I show you a house or palace where there was not one apartment convenient or agreeable; where the windows, door, fires, passages, stairs, and the whole economy of the building were the source of noise, confusion, fatigue, darkness, and the extremes of heat and cold, you would certainly blame the contrivance, without any further examination. The architect would in vain display his subtilty, and prove to you that, if this door or that window were altered, greater ills would ensue. What he says may be strictly true: The alteration of one particular, while the other parts of the building remain, may only augment the inconveniences. But still you would assert in general that, if the architect had had skill and good intentions,

he might have formed such a plan of the whole, and might have adjusted the parts in such a manner as would have remedied all or most of these inconveniences. His ignorance, or even your own ignorance of such a plan, will never convince you of the impossibility of it. If you find any inconveniences and deformities in the building, you will always, without entering into any detail, condemn the architect.

In short, I repeat the question: Is the world, considered in general and as it appears to us in this life, different from what a man or such a limited being would, *beforehand*, expect from a very powerful, wise, and benevolent Deity? It must be strange prejudice to assert the contrary. And from thence I conclude that, however consistent the world may be, allowing certain suppositions and conjectures with the ideal of such a Deity, it can never afford us an inference concerning his existence. The consistency is not absolutely denied, only the inference. Conjectures, especially where infinity is excluded from the divine attributes, may perhaps be sufficient to prove a consistency, but can never be foundations for any inference.

There seem to be *four* circumstances on which depend all or the greatest part of the ills that molest sensible creatures; and it is not impossible but all these circumstances may be necessary and unavoidable. We know so little beyond common life, or even of common life, that, with regard to the economy of a universe, there is no conjecture, however wild, which may not be just; nor any one, however plausible, which may not be erroneous. All that belongs to human understanding, in this deep ignorance and obscurity, is to be sceptical or at least cautious, and not to admit of any hypothesis whatever, much less of any which is supported by no appearance of probability. Now this I assert to be the case with regard to all the causes of evil and the circumstances on which it depends. None of them appear to human reason in the least degree necessary or unavoidable, nor can we suppose them such, without the utmost license of imagination.

The *first* circumstance which introduces evil is that contrivance or economy of the animal creation by which pains, as well as pleasures, are employed to excite all creatures to action, and make them vigilant in the great work of self-preservation. Now pleasure alone, in its various degrees, seems to human understanding sufficient for this purpose. All animals might be constantly in a state of enjoyment; but when urged by any of the necessities of nature, such as thirst, hunger, weariness; instead of pain, they might feel a diminution of pleasure by which they might be prompted to seek that object which is necessary to their subsistence. Men pursue pleasure as eagerly as they avoid pain; at least, they might have been so constituted. It seems, therefore, plainly possible to carry on the business of life without any pain. Why then is any animal ever rendered susceptible of such a sensation? If animals can be free from it an hour, they might enjoy a perpetual exemption from it, and it required as particular a contrivance of their organs to produce that feeling as to endow them with sight, hearing, or any of the senses. Shall we conjecture that such a contrivance was necessary, without any appearance of reason; and shall we build on that conjecture as on the most certain truth?

But a capacity of pain would not alone produce pain were it not for the *second* circumstance, viz., the conducting of the world by general laws; and this seems nowise necessary to a very perfect being. It is true, if everything were conducted by particular volitions, the course of nature would be perpetually broken, and no man could employ his reason in the conduct of life. But might not other particular volitions remedy this inconvenience? In short, might not the Deity exterminate all ill, wherever it were to be found, and produce all good, without any preparation or long progress of cause and effects?

Besides, we must consider that, according to the present economy of the world, the course of nature, though supposed exactly regular, yet to us appears not so, and many events are uncertain, and many disappoint our expectations. Health and sickness, calm and tempest, with an infinite number of other accidents whose causes are unknown and variable, have a great influence both on the fortunes of particular persons and on the prosperity of public societies; and indeed all human life, in a manner, depends on such accidents.

A being, therefore, who knows the secret springs of the universe might easily, by particular volitions, turn all these accidents to the good of mankind and render the whole world happy, without discovering himself in any operation. A fleet whose purposes were salutary to society might always meet with a fair wind; good princes enjoy sound health and long life; persons born to power and authority be framed with good tempers and virtuous dispositions. A few such events as these, regularly and wisely conducted, would change the face of the world; and yet would no more seem to disturb the course of nature or confound human conduct than the present economy of things where the causes are secret and variable and compounded. Some small touches given to Caligula's brain in his infancy might have converted him into a Trajan. One wave, a little higher than the rest, by burying Caesar and his fortune in the bottom of the ocean, might have restored liberty to a considerable part of mankind. There may, for aught we know, be good reasons why Providence interposes not in this manner, but they are unknown to us; and, though the mere supposition that such reasons exist may be sufficient to *save* the conclusion concerning the divine attributes, yet surely it can never be sufficient to *establish* that conclusion.

If everything in the universe be conducted by general laws, and if animals be rendered susceptible of pain, it scarcely seems possible but some ill must arise in the various shocks of matter and the various concurrence and opposition of general laws; but this ill would be very rare were it not for the *third* circumstance which I proposed to mention, viz., the great frugality with which all powers and faculties are distributed to every particular being. So well adjusted are the organs and capacities of all animals, and so well fitted to their preservation, that, as far as history or tradition reaches, there appears not to be any singly species which has yet been extinguished in the universe. Every animal has the requisite endowments, but these endowments are bestowed with so scrupulous an economy that any considerable diminution must entirely destroy the creature. Wherever one power is increased, there is a proportional abatement in the others. Animals which excel in swiftness are commonly defective in force. Those which possess both are either imperfect in some of their senses or are oppressed with the most craving wants. The human species, whose chief excellence is reason and sagacity, is of all others the most necessitous, and the most deficient in bodily advantages, without clothes, without arms, without food, without lodging, without any convenience of life, except what they owe to their own skill and industry. In short, nature seems to have formed an exact calculation of the necessities of her creatures; and, like a *rigid master*, has afforded them little more powers of endowments than what are strictly sufficient to supply those necessities. An *indulgent parent* would have bestowed a large stock in order to guard against accidents, and secure the happiness and welfare of the creature in the most unfortunate concurrence of circumstances. Every course of life would not have been so surrounded with precipices that the least departure from the true path, by mistake or necessity, must involve us in misery and ruin. Some reserve, some fund, would have been provided to ensure happiness, nor would the powers and the necessities have been adjusted with so rigid an economy. The Author of Nature is inconceivably powerful; his force is supposed great, if not altogether inexhaustible; nor is there any reason, as far as we can judge, to make him observe this strict frugality in his dealings with his creatures. It would have been better, were his power extremely limited, to have created fewer animals, and to have endowed these with more faculties for their happiness and preservation. A builder is never esteemed prudent who undertakes a plan beyond what his stock will enable him to finish.

In order to cure most of the ills of human life, I require not that man should have the wings of the eagle, the swiftness of the stag, the force of the ox, the arms of the lion, the scales of the crocodile or rhinoceros; much less do. I demand the sagacity of an angel or cherubim. I am contented to take an increase in one single power or faculty of his soul. Let him be endowed with a greater propensity to industry and labor, a more vigorous spring and activity of mind, a more constant bent to business and application. Let the whole species possess naturally an equal diligence with that which many individuals are able to attain by habit and reflection, and the most beneficial consequences, without any allay of ill, is the immediate and necessary result of this endowment. Almost all the moral as well as natural evils of human life arise from idleness; and were our species, by the original constitution of their frame, exempt from this vice or infirmity, the perfect cultivation of land, the improvement of arts and manufactures, the exact execution of every office and duty, immediately follow; and men at once may fully reach that state of society which is so imperfectly attained by the best regulated government. But as industry is a power, and the most valuable of any, nature seems determined, suitably to her usual maxims, to bestow it on men with a very sparing hand; and rather to punish him severely for his deficiency in it than to reward him for his attainments. She has so contrived his frame that nothing but the most violent necessity can oblige him to labor; and she employs all his other wants to overcome, at least in part, the want of diligence, and to endow him with some share of a faculty of which she has thought fit naturally to bereave him. Here our demands may be allowed very humble, and therefore the more reasonable. If we required the endowments of superior penetration and judgment, of a more delicate taste of beauty, of a nicer sensibility to benevolence and friendship, we might be told that we impiously pretend to break the order of nature, that we want to exalt ourselves into a higher rank of being, that the presents which we require, not being suitable to our state and condition, would only be pernicious to us. But it is hard, I dare to repeat it, it is hard that, being placed in a world so full of wants and necessities, where almost every being and element is either our foe or refuses its assistance... we should also have our temper to struggle with, and should be deprived of that faculty which can alone fence against these multiplied evils.

The *fourth* circumstance whence arises the misery and ill of the universe is the inaccurate workmanship of all the springs and principles of the great machine of nature. It must be acknowledged that there are few parts of the universe which seem not to serve some purpose, and whose removal would not produce a visible defect and disorder in the whole. The parts hang all together, nor can one be touched without affecting the rest, in a greater or less degree. But at the same time, it must be observed that none of these parts or principles, however useful, are so accurately adjusted as to keep precisely within those bounds in which their utility consists; but they are, all of them, apt, on every occasion, to run into the extreme or the other. One would imagine that this grand production had not received the last hand of the maker— so little finished is every part, and so coarse are the strokes with which it is expected. Thus the winds are requisite to convey the vapors along the surface of the globe, and to assist men in navigation; but how often, rising up to tempests and hurricanes, do they become pernicious? Rains are necessary to nourish all the plants and animals of the earth; but how often are they defective? how often excessive? Heat is requisite to all life and vegetation, but is not always found in the due proportion. On the mixture and secretion of the humors and juices of the body depend the health and prosperity of the animal; but the parts perform not regularly their proper function. What more useful than all the passions of the mind, ambition, vanity, love, anger? But how often do they break their bounds and cause the greatest convulsions in society? There is nothing so advantageous in the universe but what frequently becomes pernicious, by its excess or defect; nor has nature guarded, with the requisite accuracy, against all disorder or confusion. The irregularity is never perhaps so great as to destroy any species, but is often sufficient to involve the individuals in ruin and misery.

On the concurrence, then, of these *four* circumstances does all or the greatest part of natural evil depend. Were all living creatures incapable of pain, or were the world administered by particular volitions, evil never could have found access into the universe; and were animals endowed with a large stock of powers and faculties, beyond what strict necessity requires, or were the several springs and principles of the universe so accurately framed as to preserve always the just temperament and medium, there must have been very little ill in comparison of what we feel at present. What then shall we pronounce on this occasion? Shall we say that these circumstances are not necessary,

and that they might easily have been altered in the contrivance of the universe? This decision seems too presumptuous for creatures so blind and ignorant. Let us be more modest in our conclusions. Let us allow that, if the goodness of the Deity (I mean a goodness like the human) could be established on any tolerable reasons *a priori*, these phenomena, however untoward, would not be sufficient to subvert that principle, but might easily, in some unknown manner, be reconcilable to it. But let us still assert that, as this goodness is not antecedently established but must be inferred from the phenomena, there can be no grounds for such an inference while there are so many ills in the universe, and while these ills might so easily have been remedied, as far as human understanding can be allowed to judge on such a subject. I am sceptic enough to allow that the bad appearances, notwithstanding all my reasonings, may be compatible with such attributes as you suppose, but surely they can never prove these attributes. Such a conclusion cannot result from scepticism, but must arise from the phenomena, and from our confidence in the reasonings which we deduce from these phenomena.

Look round this universe. What an immense profusion of beings, animated and organized, sensible and active! You admire this prodigious variety and fecundity. But inspect a little more narrowly these living existences, the only beings worth regarding. How hostile and destructive to each other! How insufficient all of them for their own happiness! How contemptible or odious to the spectator! The whole presents nothing but the idea of a blind nature, impregnated by a great vivifying principle, and pouring forth from her lap, without discernment or parental care, her maimed and abortive children!

Here the Manichaean system occurs as a proper hypothesis to solve the difficulty; and, no doubt, in some respects it is very specious and has more probability than the common hypothesis, by giving a plausible account of the strange mixture of good and ill which appears in life. But if we consider, on the other hand, the perfect uniformity and agreement of the parts of the universe, we shall not discover in it any marks of the combat of a malevolent with a benevolent being. There is indeed an opposition of pains and pleasures in the feelings of sensible creatures; but are not all the operations of nature carried on by an opposition of principles, of hot and cold, moist and dry, light and heavy? The true conclusion is that the original source of all things is entirely indifferent to all these principles, and has no more regard to good above ill than to heat above cold, or to drought above moisture, or to light above heavy.

There may *four* hypothesis be framed concerning the first causes of the universe: that they are endowed with perfect goodness; that they have perfect malice; that they are opposite and have both goodness and malice; that they have neither goodness nor malice. Mixed phenomena can never prove the two former unmixed principles; and the uniformity and steadiness of general laws seem to oppose the third. The fourth, therefore, seems by far the most probable.

What I have said concerning natural evil will apply to moral with little or no variation; and we have no more reason to infer that the rectitude of the Supreme Being resembles human rectitude than that his benevolence resembles the human. Nay, it will be thought that we have still greater cause to exclude from him moral sentiments, such as we feel them, since moral evil, in the opinion of many, is much more predominant above moral good than natural evil above natural good.

But even though this should not be allowed, and though the virtue which is in mankind should be acknowledged much superior to the vice; yet, so long as there is any vice at all in the universe, it will very much puzzle you anthropomorphites how to account for it. You must assign a cause for it, without having recourse to the first cause. But as every effect must have a cause, and that cause another, you must either carry on the progression *in infinitum* or rest on that original principle, who is the ultimate cause of all things....

Hold! hold! cried Demea: Whither does your imagination hurry you? I joined in alliance with you in order to prove the incomprehensible nature of the Divine Being, and refute the principles of Cleanthes, who would measure everything by human rule and standard. But I now find you running into all the topics of the greatest libertines

and infidels, and betraying that holy cause which you seemingly espoused. Are you secretly, then, a more dangerous enemy than Cleanthes himself?

And are you so late in perceiving it? replied Cleanthes. Believe me, Demea, your friend Philo, from the beginning, has been amusing himself at both our expense; and it must be confessed that the injudicious reasoning of our vulgar theology has given him but too just a handle of ridicule. The total infirmity of human reason, the absolute incomprehensibility of the Divine Nature, the great and universal misery, and still greater wickedness of men—these are strange topics, surely, to be so fondly cherished by orthodox divines and doctors. In ages of stupidity and ignorance, indeed, these principles may safely be espoused; and perhaps no views of things are more proper to promote superstition than such as encourage the blind amazement, the difference, and melancholy of mankind. But at present...

Blame not so much, interposed Philo, the ignorance of these reverend gentlemen. They know how to change their style with the times. Formerly, it was a most popular theological topic to maintain that human life was vanity and misery, and to exaggerate all the ills and pains which are incident to men. But of late years, divines, we find, begin to retract this position and maintain, though still with some hesitation, that there are more goods than evils, more pleasures than pains, even in this life. When religion stood entirely upon temper and education, it was thought proper to encourage melancholy; as indeed, mankind never have recourse to superior powers so readily as in that disposition. But as men have now learned to form principles and to draw consequences, it is necessary to change the batteries, and to make use of such arguments as will endure at least some scrutiny and examination. This variation is the same (and from the same causes) with that which I formerly remarked with regard to scepticism.

Thus Philo continued to the last his spirit of opposition, and his censure of established opinions. But I could observe that Demea did not at all relish the latter part of the discourse; and he took occasion soon after, on some pretence or other, to leave the company.

29 THE LOGICAL PROBLEM OF EVIL

WILLIAM L. ROWE

Is a contradiction involved in the claim that a world containing evil was created by an all-good, all-powerful being? William L. Rowe, whose work we read previously, considers this question and finds that believing in both God and evil is not logically inconsistent. In other words, the presence of evil may render the existence of God improbable but not impossible.

The logical form of the problem of evil is the view that the existence of evil in our world is *logically inconsistent* with the existence of the theistic God....

The ... problem implies that theism is internally inconsistent, for the theist accepts each of two statements which are logically inconsistent. The two statements in question are:

1. God exists and is omnipotent, omniscient, and wholly good.
2. Evil exists.

These two statements, so the logical form of the problem insists, are logically inconsistent in the same way as

3. This object is red.

is inconsistent with

4. This object is not colored.

Suppose, for the moment, that the proponent of the logical form of the problem of evil were to succeed in proving to us that statements 1 and 2 are logically inconsistent. We would then be in the position of having to reject either 1 or 2, for if two statements are logically inconsistent, it is impossible for both of them to be true. If one of them is true, then the other *must* be false. Moreover, since we could hardly deny the reality of evil in our world, it seems we would have to reject belief in the theistic God; we would be driven to the conclusion that atheism is true. Indeed, even if we should be tempted to reject 2, leaving us the option of believing 1, this temptation is not one to which most theists could easily yield. For most theists adhere to religious traditions which emphasize the reality of evil in our world. In the Judeo-Christian tradition, for example, murder is held to be an evil, sinful act, and it can hardly be denied that murder occurs in our world. So, since theists generally accept and emphasize the reality of evil in our world, it would be something of a disaster for theism if the central claim in the logical form of the problem of evil were established: that 1 is logically inconsistent with 2.

ESTABLISHING INCONSISTENCY

How can we establish that two statements are inconsistent? Sometimes nothing needs to be established because the two statements are *explicitly contradictory*, as, for example, the statements "Elizabeth is over five feet tall" and "Elizabeth is not over five feet tall." Often, however, two inconsistent statements are not explicitly contradictory. In such cases we can establish that they are inconsistent by deriving from them two statements that are explicitly contradictory. Consider statements 3 and 4, for example. It's clear that these two statements are logically inconsistent; they cannot both be true. But they are not explicitly contradictory. If asked to prove that 3 and 4 are

From William L. Rowe, *Philosophy of Religion: An Introduction,* Fourth Edition, Wadsworth Publishing Company, 2007. Reprinted by permission of Thomson/Wadsworth.

inconsistent, we can do this by deriving explicitly contradictory statements from them. To derive the explicitly contradictory statements we need to add another statement to 3 and 4.

5. Whatever is red is colored.

From 3, 4, and 5 we can then easily derive the explicitly contradictory pair of statements, "This object is colored" (from 3 and 5) and "This object is not colored" (repetition of 4). This, then, is the procedure we may follow if we are asked to establish our claim that two statements are logically inconsistent.

Before we consider whether the proponent of the logical form of the problem of evil can *establish* the claim that statements 1 and 2 are logically inconsistent, one very important point about the procedure for establishing that two statements are logically inconsistent needs to be clearly understood. When we have two statements which are not explicitly contradictory, and we want to establish that they are logically inconsistent, we do this by adding some further statement or statements to them and then deriving from the entire group (the original pair and the additional statement or statements) a pair of statements that are explicitly contradictory. Now the point that needs very careful attention is this: in order for this procedure to work, the statement or statements we add must be not just true but *necessarily true*. Notice, for example, that the statement we added to 3 and 4 in order to establish that they are inconsistent is a necessary truth—it is logically impossible for something to be red but not colored. If, however, the additional statement or statements used in order to deduce the explicitly contradictory statements are true, but not necessarily true, then although we may succeed in deducing explicitly contradictory statements, we will *not* have succeeded in showing that the original pair of statements are logically inconsistent.

To see that this is so let's consider the following pair of statements:

6. The object in my right hand is a coin.
7. The object in my right hand is not a dime.

Clearly, 6 and 7 are *not* logically inconsistent, for both of them might be, or might have been, true. They aren't logically inconsistent because there is nothing logically impossible in the idea

that the coin in my right hand should be a quarter or a nickel. (Contrast 6 and 7 with 3 and 4. Clearly there is something logically impossible in the idea that this object be red and yet not colored.) But notice that we can add a statement to 6 and 7 such that from the three of them explicitly contradictory statements can be derived.

8. Every coin in my right hand is a dime.

From 6, 7, and 8 we can derive the explicitly contradictory pair of statements, "The object in my right hand is a dime" (from 6 and 8) and "The object in my right hand is not a dime" (repetition of 7). Now suppose 8 is true, that in fact every coin in my right hand is a dime. We will have succeeded, then, in deducing explicitly contradictory statements from our original pair, 6 and 7, with the help of the *true* statement 8. But, of course, by this procedure we won't have established that 6 and 7 are logically inconsistent. Why not? Because 8—the additional statement—although true, is not necessarily true. Statement 8 is not a necessary truth because I might (logically) have had a quarter or a nickel in my right hand. Statement 8 is in fact true, but since it logically could have been false, it is not a necessary truth. We must, then, keep clearly in mind that to *establish* two statements to be logically inconsistent by adding a statement and then deriving explicitly contradictory statements, the additional statement must be not just true, but necessarily true.

APPLICATION TO THE LOGICAL PROBLEM OF EVIL

Since (1) "God exists and is omnipotent, omniscient, and wholly good" and (2) "Evil exists" are not explicitly contradictory, those who hold that 1 and 2 are logically inconsistent need to make good this claim by adding a necessarily true statement to 1 and 2 and deducing explicitly contradictory statements. But what statement might we add? Suppose we begin with

9. An omnipotent, omniscient, good being will prevent the occurrence of any evil whatever.

From 1, 2, and 9 we can derive the explicitly contradictory statements, "No evil exists" (from 1 and 9) and "Evil exists" (repetition of 2). So if we can show that statement 9 is necessarily true, we will have succeeded in establishing the thesis of the logical form of the problem of evil: that 1 and 2 are logically inconsistent. But is 9 necessarily true? Well, recalling our discussion of omnipotence, it would seem that God would have the power to prevent any evil whatever, for "preventing the occurrence of an evil" does not appear to be a logically contradictory task like "making a round square." But it is no easy matter to establish that 9 is necessarily true. For in our own experience we know that evil is sometimes connected with good in such a way that we are powerless to achieve the good without permitting the evil. Moreover, in such instances, the good sometimes outweighs the evil, so that a good being might intentionally permit the evil to occur in order to realize the good which outweighs it.

Gottfried Leibniz gives the example of a general who knows that in order to achieve the good of saving the town from being destroyed by an attacking army he must order his men to defend the town, with the result that some of his men will suffer and die. The good of saving the women and children of the town outweighs the evil of the suffering and death of a few of the town's defenders. Although he could have prevented their suffering and death by ordering a hasty retreat of his forces, the general cannot do so without losing the good of saving the town and its inhabitants. It certainly does not count against the general's goodness that he permits the evil to occur in order to achieve the good which outweighs it. Perhaps, then, some evils in our world are connected to goods which outweigh them in such a way that even God cannot achieve the goods in question without permitting the evils to occur that are connected to those goods. If this is so, statement 9 is not necessarily true.

Of course, unlike the general's, God's power is unlimited, and it might be thought that no matter how closely evil and good may be connected, God could always achieve the good and prevent the evil. But this overlooks the possibility that the occurrence of some evils in our world is *logically necessary* for the achievement of goods which outweigh them, so that the task of bringing about those goods without permitting the evils that are connected to them is as impossible a task as making a round square. If so, then, again, while being omnipotent God could prevent the evils in question from occurring, he could not, even though omnipotent, achieve the outweighing goods while preventing the evils from occurring.[1] Therefore, since (i) omnipotence is not the power to do what is logically impossible and (ii) it may be logically impossible to prevent the occurrence of certain evils in our world and yet achieve some very great goods that outweigh those evils, we cannot be sure that statement 9 is necessarily true; we can't be sure that an omnipotent, wholly good being will prevent the occurrence of any evil whatever.

What we have just seen is that the attempt to establish that 1 and 2 are inconsistent by deducing explicitly contradictory statements from 1, 2, and 9 is a failure. For although 1, 2, and 9 do yield explicitly contradictory statements, we are not in a position to know that 9 is necessarily true.

The suggestion that emerges from the preceding discussion is that we replace 9 with

10. A good, omnipotent, omniscient being prevents the occurrence of any evil that is not logically necessary for the occurrence of a good which outweighs it.

Statement 10, unlike 9, takes into account the possibility that certain evils might be so connected to goods which outweigh them that even God cannot realize those goods without permitting the evils to occur. Statement 10, then, appears to be not only true but necessarily true. The problem now, however, is that from 1, 2, and 10, explicitly contradictory statements cannot be derived. All that we can conclude from 1, 2, and 10 is that the evils which do exist in our world are logically necessary for the occurrence of goods which outweigh them, and that statement is not an explicit contradiction.

The general difficulty affecting attempts to establish that 1 and 2 are logically inconsistent is now apparent. When we add a statement, such as 9, which allows us to derive explicitly contradictory statements, we cannot be sure that the additional statement is necessarily true. On the other hand, when we add a statement, such as 10, which does seem to be necessarily true, it turns out that explicitly contradictory statements cannot be derived. No one has succeeded in producing a statement which is known to be necessarily true *and* which, when added to 1 and 2, enables us to derive explicitly contradictory statements. In view of this, it is reasonable to conclude that the logical form of the problem of evil is not much of a problem for theism. Its central thesis, that 1 and 2 are logically inconsistent, is a thesis that no one has been able to establish by a convincing argument.

NOTE

1. Suppose, for example, that there are occasions when the act of *forgiving someone for an evil deed* is a good that outweighs the evil deed that is forgiven. Clearly, even an omnipotent being could not bring about this good without permitting the evil deed it outweighs. Again, *courageously bearing pain* might be a good that on occasion outweighs the evil of the pain that is courageously borne. But it is logically impossible for someone to bear courageously an evil pain, without the occurrence of an evil pain.

30 THE PROBLEM OF EVIL

JOHN H. HICK

John H. Hick (1922-2012) was Danforth Professor Emeritus of the Philosophy of Religion at Claremont Graduate University and H. G. Wood Professor Emeritus of Theology at the University of Birmingham. In the next selection, he develops from a Christian perspective one of the best-known answers to the problem of evil. He views moral evils, those for which people are responsible, as tied inextricably to the exercise of our free will, so that one is not possible without the other. He views physical evils, those for which people are not responsible, as providing the opportunity for "soul making," the development of the best qualities of the human personality. He admits, however, that his theodicy, his defense of God's goodness and omnipotence in the face of evil, requires life after death to justify all the world's pains and sorrows.

To many, the most powerful positive objection to belief in God is the fact of evil. Probably for most agnostics it is the appalling depth and extent of human suffering, more than anything else, that makes the idea of a loving Creator seem so implausible and disposes them toward one or another of the various naturalistic theories of religion.

As a challenge to theism, the problem of evil has traditionally been posed in the form of a dilemma: if God is perfectly loving, he must wish to abolish evil; and if he is all-powerful, he must be able to abolish evil. But evil exists; therefore God cannot be both omnipotent and perfectly loving.

Certain solutions, which at once suggest themselves, have to be ruled out so far as the Judaic Christian faith is concerned.

To say, for example (with contemporary Christian Science), that evil is an illusion of the human mind, is impossible within a religion based upon the stark realism of the Bible. Its pages faithfully reflect the characteristic mixture of good and evil in human experience. They record every kind of sorrow and suffering, every mode of man's

From John H. Hick, *Philosophy of Religion*, Fourth Edition, Prentice Hall, 1990. Reprinted by permission of the publisher.

inhumanity to man and of his painfully insecure existence in the world. There is no attempt to regard evil as anything but dark, menacingly ugly, heart-rending, and crushing. In the Christian scriptures, the climax of this history of evil is the crucifixion of Jesus, which is presented not only as a case of utterly unjust suffering, but as the violent and murderous rejection of God's Messiah. There can be no doubt, then, that for biblical faith evil is unambiguously evil and stands in direct opposition to God's will.

Again, to solve the problem of evil by means of the theory (sponsored, for example, by the Boston "Personalist" School)[1] of a finite deity who does the best he can with a material, intractable and coeternal with himself, is to have abandoned the basic premise of Hebrew-Christian monotheism; for the theory amounts to rejecting belief in the infinity and sovereignty of God.

Indeed, any theory that would avoid the problem of the origin of evil by depicting it as an ultimate constituent of the universe, co-ordinate with good, has been repudiated in advance by the classic Christian teaching, first developed by Augustine, that evil represents the going wrong of something that in itself is good.[2] Augustine holds firmly to the Hebrew-Christian conviction that the universe is *good*—that is to say, it is the creation of a good God for a good purpose. He completely rejects the ancient prejudice that matter is evil. There are, according to Augustine, higher and lower, greater and lesser goods in immense abundance and variety; but everything that has being is good in its own way and degree, except in so far as it may have become spoiled or corrupted. Evil—whether it be an evil will, an instance of pain, or some disorder or decay in nature—has not been set there by God, but represents the distortion of something that is inherently valuable. Whatever exists is, as such, and in its proper place, good; evil is essentially parasitic upon good, being disorder and perversion in a fundamentally good creation. This understanding of evil as something negative means that it is not willed and created by God; but it does not mean (as some have supposed) that evil is unreal and can be disregarded. On the contrary, the first effect of

this doctrine is to accentuate even more the question of the origin of evil.

Theodicy,[3] as many modern Christian thinkers see it, is a modest enterprise, negative rather than positive in its conclusions. It does not claim to explain, nor to explain away, every instance of evil in human experience, but only to point to certain considerations that prevent the fact of evil (largely incomprehensible though it remains) from constituting a final and insuperable bar to rational belief in God.

In indicating these considerations it will be useful to follow the traditional division of the subject. There is the problem of *moral evil* or wickedness: why does an all-good and all-powerful God permit this? And there is the problem of the *nonmoral evil* of suffering or pain, both physical and mental: why has an all-good and all-powerful God created a world in which this occurs?

Christian thought has always considered moral evil in its relation to human freedom and responsibility. To be a person is to be a finite center of freedom, a (relatively) free and self-directing agent responsible for one's own decisions. This involves being free to act wrongly as well as to act rightly. The idea of a person who can be infallibly guaranteed always to act rightly is self-contradictory. There can be no certainty in advance that a genuinely free moral agent will never choose amiss. Consequently, the possibility of wrongdoing or sin is logically inseparable from the creation of finite persons, and to say that God should not have created beings who might sin amounts to saying that he should not have created people.

This thesis has been challenged in some recent philosophical discussions of the problem of evil, in which it is claimed that no contradiction is involved in saying that God might have made people who would be genuinely free but who could at the same time be guaranteed always to act rightly. A quote from one of these discussions follows:

> If there is no logical impossibility in a man's freely choosing the good on one, or on several occasions, there cannot be a logical impossibility in his freely

choosing the good on every occasion. God was not, then, faced with a choice between making innocent automata and making beings who, in acting freely, would sometimes go wrong: there was open to him the obviously better possibility of making beings who would act freely but always go right. Clearly, his failure to avail himself of this possibility is inconsistent with his being both omnipotent and wholly good.[4]

A reply to this argument is indirectly suggested in another recent contribution to the discussion.[5] If by a free action we mean an action that is not externally compelled but that flows from the nature of the agent as he reacts to the circumstances in which he finds himself, there is indeed no contradiction between our being free and our actions being "caused" (by our own nature) and therefore being in principle predictable. There is a contradiction, however, in saying that God is the cause of our acting as we do but that we are free beings *in relation to God*. There is, in other words, a contradiction in saying that God has made us so that we shall of necessity act in a certain way, and that we are genuinely independent persons in relation to him. If all our thoughts and actions are divinely predestined, however free and morally responsible we may seem to be to ourselves, we cannot be free and morally responsible in the sight of God but must instead be his helpless puppets. Such "freedom" is like that of a patient acting out a series of posthypnotic suggestions: he appears, even to himself, to be free, but his volitions have actually been predetermined by another will, that of the hypnotist, in relation to whom the patient is not a free agent.

A different objector might raise the question of whether or not we deny God's omnipotence if we admit that he is unable to create persons who are free from the risks inherent in personal freedom. The answer that has always been given is that to create such beings is logically impossible. It is no limitation upon God's power that he cannot accomplish the logically impossible, since there is nothing here to accomplish, but only a meaningless conjunction of words[6]—in this case "person who is not a person." God is able to create beings of any and every conceivable kind; but creatures who lack moral freedom, however superior they might be to human beings in other respects, would not be what we mean by persons. They would constitute a different form of life that God might have brought into existence instead of persons. When we ask why God did not create such beings in place of persons the traditional answer is that only persons could, in any meaningful sense, become "children of God," capable of entering into a personal relationship with their Creator by a free and uncompelled response to his love.

When we turn from the possibility of moral evil as a correlate of man's personal freedom to its actuality, we face something that must remain inexplicable even when it can be seen to be possible. For we can never provide a complete causal explanation of a free act; if we could, it would not be a free act. The origin of moral evil lies forever concealed within the mystery of human freedom.

The necessary connection between moral freedom and the possibility, now actualized, of sin throws light upon a great deal of the suffering that afflicts mankind. For an enormous amount of human pain arises either from the inhumanity or the culpable incompetence of mankind. This includes such major scourges as poverty, oppression and persecution, war, and all the injustice, indignity, and inequity that occur even in the most advanced societies. These evils are manifestations of human sin. Even disease is fostered to an extent, the limits of which have not yet been determined by psychosomatic medicine, by emotional and moral factors seated both in the individual and in his social environment. To the extent that all of these evils stem from human failures and wrong decisions, their possibility is inherent in the creation of free persons inhabiting a world that presents them with real choices followed by real consequences.

We may now turn more directly to the problem of suffering. Even though the major bulk of actual human pain is traceable to man's misused freedom as a sole or part cause, there remain other sources of pain that are entirely independent of the human will, for example, earthquake, hurricane, storm, flood, drought, and blight. In practice, it is often impossible to trace a boundary between the suffering that results from human wickedness and folly and that which falls upon mankind from without; both kinds of suffering are inextricably mingled together in human experience. For our present purpose, however, it is important to note that the latter category does exist and that it seems to be built into the very structure of our world. In response to it, theodicy, if it is wisely conducted, follows a negative path. It is not possible to show positively that each item of human pain serves a divine purpose of good; but, on the other hand, it does seem possible to show that the divine purpose as it is understood in Judaism and Christianity could not be forwarded in a world that was designed as a permanent hedonistic paradise.[7]

An essential premise of this argument concerns the nature of the divine purpose in creating the world. The skeptic's assumption is that man is to be viewed as a completed creation and that God's purpose in making the world was to provide a suitable dwelling-place for this fully formed creature. Since God is good and loving, the environment that he has created for human life to inhabit will naturally be as pleasant and comfortable as possible. The problem is essentially similar to that of a man who builds a cage for some pet animal. Since our world, in fact, contains sources of hardship, inconvenience and danger of innumerable kinds, the conclusion follows that this world cannot have been created by a perfectly benevolent and all-powerful deity.[8]

Christianity, however, has never supposed that God's purpose in the creation of the world was to construct a paradise whose inhabitants would experience a maximum of pleasure and a minimum of pain. The world is seen, instead, as a place of "soul making" or person making in which free beings, grappling with the tasks and challenges of their existence in a common environment, may become "children of God" and "heirs of eternal life." A way of thinking theologically of God's continuing creative purpose for man was suggested by some of the early Hellenistic Fathers of the Christian Church, especially Irenaeus. Following hints from Saint Paul, Irenaeus taught that man has been made as a person in the image of God but has not yet been brought as a free and responsible agent into the finite likeness of God, which is revealed in Christ.[9] Our world, with all its rough edges, is the sphere in which this second and harder stage of the creative process is taking place.

This conception of the world (whether or not set in Irenaeus's theological framework) can be supported by the method of negative theodicy. Suppose, contrary to fact, that this world were a paradise from which all possibility of pain and suffering where excluded. The consequences would be very far-reaching. For example, no one could ever injure anyone else: the murderer's knife would turn to paper or his bullets to thin air; the bank safe, robbed of a million dollars, would miraculously become filled with another million dollars (without this device, on however large a scale, proving inflationary); fraud, deceit, conspiracy, and treason would somehow always leave the fabric of society undamaged. Again, no one would ever be injured by accident: the mountain climber, steeplejack, or playing child falling from a height would float unharmed to the ground; the reckless driver would never meet with disaster. There would be no need to work, since no harm could result from avoiding work; there would be no call to be concerned for others in time of need or danger, for in such a world there could be no real needs or dangers.

To make possible this continual series of individual adjustments, nature would have to work by "special providences" instead of running according to general laws that men must learn to respect on penalty of pain or death. The laws of nature would have to be extremely flexible: sometimes gravity would operate, sometimes not; sometimes an object would be hard and solid, sometimes soft. There could be no science, for there would be no enduring world structure to investigate. In eliminating the problems and hardships of an objective environment, with its own laws, life would become like a dream in which, delightfully but aimlessly, we would float and drift at ease.[10]

One can at least begin to imagine such a world. It is evident that our present ethical concepts would have no meaning in it. If, for example, the notion of harming someone is an essential element in the concept of a wrong action, in our hedonistic paradise there could be no wrong actions—nor any right actions in distinction from wrong. Courage and fortitude would have no point in an environment in which there is, by definition, no danger or difficulty. Generosity, kindness, the *agape* aspect of love, prudence, unselfishness, and all other ethical notions which presuppose life in an objective environment could not even be formed. Consequently, such a world, however well it might promote pleasure, would be very ill adapted for the development of the moral qualities of human personality. In relation to this purpose, it might be the worst of all possible worlds!

It would seem, then, that an environment intended to make possible the growth in free beings of the finest characteristics of personal life must have a good deal in common with our present world. It must operate according to general and dependable laws; and it must involve real dangers, difficulties, problems, obstacles, and possibilities of pain, failure, sorrow, frustration, and defeat. If it did not contain the particular trials and perils that—subtracting man's own very considerable contribution—our world contains, it would have to contain others instead.

To realize this is not, by any means, to be in possession of a detailed theodicy. It is to understand that this world, with all its "heartaches and the thousand natural shocks that flesh is heir to," an environment so manifestly not designed for the maximization of human pleasure and the minimization of human pain, may nevertheless be rather well adapted to the quite different purpose of "soul making."[11]

These considerations are related to theism as such. Specifically Christian theism goes further in the light of the death of Christ, which is seen paradoxically both (as the murder of the divine Son) as the worst thing that has ever happened and (as the occasion of man's salvation) as the best thing that has ever happened. As the supreme evil turned to supreme good, it provides the paradigm for the distinctively Christian reaction to evil. Viewed from the standpoint of Christian faith, evils do not cease to be evils; and certainly, in view of Christ's healing work, they cannot be said to have been sent by God. Yet, it has been the persistent claim of those seriously and wholeheartedly committed to Christian discipleship that tragedy, though truly tragic, may nevertheless be turned, through a man's reaction to it, from a cause of despair and alienation from God to a stage in the fulfillment of God's loving purpose for that individual. As the greatest of all evils, the crucifixion of Christ, was made the occasion of man's redemption, so good can be won from other evils. As Jesus saw his execution by the Romans as an experience which God desired him to accept, an experience which was to be brought within the sphere of the divine purpose and made to serve the divine ends, so the Christian response to calamity is to accept the adversities, pains, and afflictions which life brings, in order that they can be turned to a positive spiritual use.[12]

At this point, theodicy points forward in two ways to the subject of life after death, which is to be discussed in later chapters.

First, although there are many striking instances of good being triumphantly brought out of evil through a man's or a woman's reaction to it, there are many other cases in which the opposite has happened. Sometimes obstacles breed strength of character, dangers evoke courage and unselfishness, and calamities produce patience and moral steadfastness. But sometimes they lead, instead, to resentment, fear, grasping selfishness, and disintegration of character. Therefore, it would seem that any divine purpose of soul making that is at work in earthly history must continue beyond this life if it is ever to achieve more than a very partial and fragmentary success.[13]

Second, if we ask whether the business of soul making is worth all the toil and sorrow of human life, the Christian answer must be in terms of a future good great enough to justify all that has happened on the way to it.

NOTES

1. Edgar Brightman's *A Philosophy of Religion* (Englewood Cliffs, N.J.: Prentice-Hall, Inc., 1940), Chaps. 8–10, is a classic exposition of one form of this view.

2. See Augustine's *Confessions*, Book VII, Chap. 12; *City of God*, Book XII, Chap. 3; *Enchiridion*, Chap. 4.

3. The word "theodicy," from the Greek *theos* (God) and *dike* (righteous), means the justification of God's goodness in the face of the fact of evil.

4. J. L. Mackie, "Evil and Omnipotence," *Mind* (April, 1955), p. 209. A similar point is made by Antony Flew in "Divine Omnipotence and Human Freedom," *New Essays in Philosophical*

Theology. An important critical comment on these arguments is offered by Ninian Smart in "Omnipotence, Evil, and Supermen," *Philosophy* (April, 1961), with replies by Flew (January, 1962) and Mackie (April, 1962).

5. Flew, in *New Essays in Philosophical Theology.*
6. As Aquinas said, "… nothing that implies a contradiction falls under the scope of God's omnipotence." *Summa Theologica*, Part 1, Question 25, Art. 4.
7. From the Greek *hedone*, pleasure.
8. This is essentially David Hume's argument in his discussion of the problem of evil in his *Dialogues.*
9. See Irenaeus's *Against Heresies*, Book IV, Chaps. 37 and 38.
10. Tennyson's poem, *The Lotus-Eaters*, well expresses the desire (analyzed by Freud as a wish to return to the peace of the womb) for such "dreamful ease."
11. This brief discussion has been confined to the problem of human suffering. The large and intractable problem of animal pain is not taken up here.

For a discussion of it see, for example, Austin Farrer, *Love Almighty and Ills Unlimited* (Garden City, N.Y.: Doubleday & Company, Inc., 1961), Chap. 5, and John Hick, *Evil and the God of Love* (London: Collins, The Fontana Library, 1968), pp. 345–53.

12. This conception of providence is stated more fully in John Hick, *Faith and Knowledge*, 2nd ed. (Ithaca, N.Y.: Cornell University Press, 1966), Chap. 10, some sentences from which are incorporated in this paragraph.
13. The position presented above is developed more fully in the author's *Evil and the God of Love*, 1966 (London: Fontana paperback ed., 1968). For an important philosophical critique of theodicies see Edward H. Madden and Peter H. Hare, *Evil and the Concept of God* (Springfield, Ill.: Charles C. Thomas, Publishers, 1968). Some of the most important recent articles on the subject are collected in Nelson Pike, ed., *God and Evil* (Englewood Cliffs, N.J.: Prentice-Hall, Inc., 1964).

31   THE PROBLEM OF GOODNESS

STEVEN M. CAHN

Instead of considering the world as the creation of an all-good, all-powerful God, we could view it as the work of an all-evil, all-powerful Demon. But, in that case, how could we explain the existence of good? We could argue that every good is part of a greater evil. That supposition, admittedly, would be unconvincing, but for similar reasons so is any theodicy that depends on the claim that every evil is part of a greater good. Thus argues Steven M. Cahn, editor of this book and Professor of Philosophy at The Graduate Center of The City University of New York.

For many centuries philosophers have grappled with what has come to be known as *the problem of evil.* Succinctly stated, the problem is: Could a world containing evil have been created by an omnipotent, omniscient, omnibenevolent being?

Considering the vast literature devoted to this issue, perhaps surprisingly little attention has been given to an analogous issue that might appropriately be referred to as *the problem of goodness.* Succinctly stated, the problem is: Could a world containing goodness have been created by an omnipotent, omniscient, omnimalevolent being?

This essay has two aims. The first is to provide a reasonable solution to the problem of goodness. Traditional theists find the hypothesis of creation by a benevolent deity far more plausible than the

From Steven M. Cahn, *Puzzles & Perplexities: Collected Essays*, Second Edition, Lexington Books, 2009. Reprinted with minor revisions by permission of the author.

hypothesis of creation by a malevolent demon, and they may, therefore, believe the problem of goodness to be irrelevant to their commitments. My second aim is to demonstrate that this belief is mistaken.

Before proceeding, let us restate the problem of goodness in more formal fashion.

1. Assume that an omnipotent, omniscient, omnimalevolent Demon created the world.
2. If the Demon exists, the world would contain no goodness.
3. But the world contains goodness.
4. Therefore, the Demon does not exist.

Since the conclusion of the argument follows from the premises, those who wish to deny the conclusion must deny one of the premises. No demonist (the analogue to a theist) would question premise (1), so in order to avoid the conclusion of the argument, an attack would have to be launched against either premise (2) or premise (3).

What if a demonist attempted to deny premise (3)? Suppose goodness were regarded as an illusion. Would this move solve the problem?

I think not, for such a claim is either patently false or else involves a distortion of the usual meaning of the term "good." If the word is being used in its ordinary sense, then acts of kindness, expressions of love, and creations of beauty are good. Because obviously such things do occur, goodness exists.

If one insists that such things are not good, then the expression "good" is being used eccentrically, and the claim loses its import. One might as well defend the view that all persons are pigs by defining "persons" as "omnivorous hoofed mammals of the family Suidae." Such "persons" are not persons at all. Similarly, a supposedly omnimalevolent Demon who cherishes personal affection and great works of art is certainly not omnimalevolent and is probably no demon.

Premise (3) can thus be adequately defended, and if demonists are to find an answer to the problem of goodness, they must attack premise (2). How can the world contain goodness if the creator is omnimalevolent and possesses the power and the knowledge to carry out evil intentions? To paraphrase Epicurus, is the Demon willing to prevent good, but not able? Then He[1] is impotent. Is He able, but not willing? Then He is benevolent. Is He both able and willing? From where, then, comes goodness?

Some might believe hopeless the attempt to justify the Demon's malevolence in the face of goodness. But sophisticated demonists would realize that much play is left in their position. They would not agree that just because goodness exists in the world, it could not have been created by an omnimalevolent Demon. After all, isn't it possible that whatever goodness exists is logically necessary for this world to be the most evil one the Demon could have created? Not even an omnipotent being can contravene the laws of logic, for such a task is senseless, and so if each and every good in the world were logically tied to the achievement of the greatest evil, the omnimalevolent Demon, in order to bring about the greatest possible evil, would have been forced to allow the existence of these goods.

The demonist thus rejects premise (2) of the argument and argues instead for premise (2'):

(2') If the Demon exists, then every good in the world is logically necessary in order for this world to be the most evil the Demon could have created.

Now if we substitute premise (2') for premise (2) in the original argument, that argument falls apart, for the conclusion no longer follows from the premises. One can affirm without contradiction both the existence of an omnipotent, omniscient, omnimalevolent Demon who created the world and the existence of goodness in the world, so long as one also affirms that every good is logically necessary in order for this world to be the most evil one the Demon could have created. Demonists thus appear to have escaped the force of the problem of goodness.

Things are not so simple, however, for now demonists are faced by yet another argument that challenges their belief.

1. Assume that an omnipotent, omniscient, omnimalevolent Demon created the world.
2. If the Demon exists, then every good in the world is logically necessary in order for this world to be the most evil one the Demon could have created.

3. But strong reasons suggest that not every good in the world is logically necessary in order for this world to be the most evil one the Demon could have created.

4. Therefore, strong reasons suggest that the Demon does not exist.

This second argument, unlike the first, claims that belief in the Demon is not illogical but unreasonable. Beautiful mountain ranges, spectacular sunsets, the plays of Shakespeare, and the quartets of Beethoven do not enhance the evils of the world. Acts of altruism, generosity, and kindheartedness do not increase the world's sinister aspects. In other words, this argument challenges demonists to suggest plausible reasons for their view that every good makes possible a world containing even greater evils than would be possible without these goods.

The reader will have observed that thus far the discussion of the problem of goodness exactly parallels traditional discussions of the problem of evil; all the arguments and counterarguments presented are equally applicable *mutatis mutandis* to either problem. What may be surprising, however, is that we can develop a reply to the problem of goodness along the same lines suggested by John Hick's reply to the problem of evil.[2]

We begin by distinguishing two types of goodness: moral and physical. *Moral goods* are those for which human beings are responsible, such as acts of altruism, generosity, and kindheartedness. *Physical goods* are those for which human beings are not responsible, such as sunshine, breathable air, and drinkable water.

The justification of moral goods proceeds by tying their existence to our free will. Surely, performing a bad act freely is more evil than performing it involuntarily. The Demon could have ensured that human beings would always perform bad actions, but then those actions would not have been free, because the Demon would have ensured their occurrence.[3] Simply performing them, therefore, would not have produced the greatest possible evil, because greater evil can be produced by free persons than by unfree ones. The Demon had to provide human beings with freedom so that they might perform their bad actions voluntarily, thus maximizing evil.

As for the justification of physical goods, we should not suppose that the Demon's purpose in creating the world was to construct a chamber of tortures in which the inhabitants would be forced to endure a succession of unrelieved pains. The world can be viewed, instead, as a place of "soul breaking," in which free human beings, by grappling with the exhausting tasks and challenges in their environment, can thereby have their spirits broken and their wills-to-live destroyed.[4]

This conception of the world can be supported by what, following Hick, we may call "the method of negative justification."[5] Suppose, contrary to fact, the world were arranged so that nothing could ever go well. No one could help anyone else, no one could perform a courageous act, no one could complete any worthwhile project. Presumably, such a world could be created through innumerable acts of the Demon, who would alter the laws of nature as necessary.

Our present ethical concepts would thereby become useless. What would frustration mean in an environment without hope? What would selfishness be if no one could make use of help? Such a world, however efficiently it promoted pain, would be ill adapted for the development of the worst qualities of the human personality.

This line of argument, just as Hick's, points forward in two ways to life after death. First, although we can find many striking instances of evil's being produced from good, such as the pollution of beautiful lakes or the slashing of great paintings, still in many other cases good leads to altruism or strengthening of character. Therefore any demonic purpose of soul breaking at work in earthly history must continue beyond this life to achieve more than a fragmentary success.[6]

Second, if we ask whether the business of soul breaking is so evil that it nullifies all the goodness we find, the demonist's answer must be in terms of a future evil great enough to justify all that has happened.[7]

Have we now provided an adequate response to the problem of goodness? It is as strong as Hick's reply to the problem of evil, but in my view neither is successful. Nor do I see any plausible ways of strengthening either one. What is the evidence that, as Hick proposes, the horrors of bubonic plague somehow contribute to a better world? What is the evidence, as the believer in the Demon suggests, that the beauty of a sunset somehow contributes to a worse world? What is the evidence that, as Hick proposes, the free will of a Hitler achieved greater good than would have been achieved by his performing right actions involuntarily? What is the evidence that, as the believer in the Demon suggests, the free will of a Socrates achieved greater evil than would have been achieved by his performing wrong actions involuntarily?

If this world is neither the worst possible nor the best possible, then it could not have been created by either an all-powerful, all-evil Demon or an all-powerful, all-good God. Thus although the problem of goodness and the problem of evil do not show either demonism or theism to be impossible, the problems show both doctrines to be highly improbable. If demonists or theists can produce any other evidence in favor of their positions, then they can increase the plausibility of their views, but otherwise the reasonable conclusion is that neither the Demon nor God exists.

NOTES

1. My use of "He" is not intended to imply that the Demon is masculine.
2. See previous selection.
3. I here assume without argument that freedom and determinism are incompatible. Those who believe otherwise face more difficulty in resolving the problem of goodness and the problem of evil.
4. Hick sees the world as a place of "soul making," in which free beings grapple with challenges of their existence and may thereby become "children of God."
5. Hick refers to "the method of negative theodicy," which supposes that the world is arranged without pain or suffering.
6. Hick says the same for "any divine purpose of soul making."
7. Hick appeals to "a future good great enough" to serve as such a justification.

32   THE PROBLEM OF EVIL AND SOME VARIETIES OF ATHEISM

WILLIAM L. ROWE

In our next selection, William L. Rowe, whose work we read previously, argues that the existence of evil can serve as a rational justification for atheism, the denial of the existence of God. Rowe, however, maintains that theism, belief in the existence of God, might for some be a rationally justified position. Thus Rowe considers himself a defender of what he dubs "friendly atheism."

This paper is concerned with three interrelated questions. The first is: Is there an argument for atheism based on the existence of evil that may rationally justify someone in being an atheist? To this first question I give an affirmative answer and try to support that answer by setting forth a strong argument for atheism based on the existence of evil.[1] The second question is: How can the theist

From William L. Rowe, "The Problem of Evil and Some Varieties of Atheism," *American Philosophical Quarterly*, vol. 16, no. 4, 1979. Reprinted by permission of the journal.

best defend his position against the argument for atheism based on the existence of evil? In response to this question I try to describe what may be an adequate rational defense for theism against any argument for atheism based on the existence of evil. The final question is: What position should the informed atheist take concerning the rationality of theistic belief? Three different answers an atheist may give to this question serve to distinguish three varieties of atheism: unfriendly atheism, indifferent atheism, and friendly atheism. In the final part of the paper I discuss and defend the position of friendly atheism.

Before we consider the argument from evil, we need to distinguish a narrow and a broad sense of the terms "theist," "atheist," and "agnostic." By a "theist" in the narrow sense I mean someone who believes in the existence of an omnipotent, omniscient, eternal, supremely good being who created the world. By a "theist" in the broad sense I mean someone who believes in the existence of some sort of divine being or divine reality. To be a theist in the narrow sense is also to be a theist in the broad sense, but one may be a theist in the broad sense—as was Paul Tillich—without believing that there is a supremely good, omnipotent, omniscient, eternal being who created the world. Similar distinctions must be made between a narrow and a broad sense of the terms "atheist" and "agnostic." To be an atheist in the broad sense is to deny the existence of any sort of divine being or divine reality. Tillich was not an atheist in the broad sense. But he was an atheist in the narrow sense, for he denied that there exists a divine being that is all-knowing, all-powerful and perfectly good. In this paper I will be using the terms "theism," "theist," "atheism," "atheist," "agnosticism," and "agnostic" in the narrow sense, not in the broad sense.*

I

In developing the argument for atheism based on the existence of evil, it will be useful to focus on some particular evil that our world contains in considerable abundance. Intense human and animal suffering, for example, occurs daily and in great plentitude in our world. Such intense suffering is a clear case of evil. Of course, if the intense suffering leads to some greater good, a good we could not have obtained without undergoing the suffering in question, we might conclude that the suffering is justified, but it remains an evil nevertheless. For we must not confuse the intense suffering in and of itself with the good things to which it sometimes leads or of which it may be a necessary part. Intense human or animal suffering is in itself bad, an evil, even though it may sometimes be justified by virtue of being a part of, or leading to, some good which is unobtainable without it. What is evil in itself may sometimes be good as a means because it leads to something that is good in itself. In such a case, while remaining an evil in itself, the intense human or animal suffering is, nevertheless, an evil which someone might be morally justified in permitting.

Taking human and animal suffering as a clear instance of evil which occurs with great frequency in our world, the argument for atheism based on evil can be stated as follows:

1. There exist instances of intense suffering which an omnipotent, omniscient being could have prevented without thereby losing some greater good or permitting some evil equally bad or worse.[2]
2. An omniscient, wholly good being would prevent the occurrence of any intense suffering it could, unless it could not do so without thereby losing some greater good or permitting some evil equally bad or worse.
3. There does not exist an omnipotent, omniscient, wholly good being.

What are we to say about this argument for atheism, an argument based on the profusion of one sort of evil in our world? The argument is valid; therefore, if we have rational grounds for accepting its premises, to that extent we have rational grounds for accepting atheism. Do we, however, have rational grounds for accepting the premises of this argument?

Let's begin with the second premise. Let s_1 be an instance of intense human or animal suffering

*From *American Philosophical Quarterly*, 16 (1979), by permission of the journal.

which an omniscient, wholly good being could prevent. We will also suppose that things are such that s_1 will occur unless prevented by the omniscient, wholly good (OG) being. We might be interested in determining what would be a *sufficient* condition of OG failing to prevent s_1. But, for our purpose here, we need only try to state a *necessary* condition for OG failing to prevent s_1. That condition, so it seems to me, is this:

> *Either* (i) there is some greater good, G, such that G is obtainable by OG only if OG permits s_1,[3]
>
> *or* (ii) there is some greater good, G, such that G is obtainable by OG only if OG permits either s_1 or some evil equally bad or worse,
>
> *or* (iii) s_1 is such that it is preventable by OG only if OG permits some evil equally bad or worse.

It is important to recognize that (iii) is not included in (i). For losing a good greater than s_1 is not the same as permitting an evil greater than s_1. And this because the *absence* of a good state of affairs need not itself be an evil state of affairs. It is also important to recognize that s_1 might be such that it is preventable by OG *without* losing G (so condition (i) is not satisfied) but also such that if OG did prevent it, G would be lost *unless* OG permitted some evil equal to or worse than s_1. If this were so, it does not seem correct to require that OG prevent s_1. Thus, condition (ii) takes into account an important possibility not encompassed in condition (i).

Is it true that if an omniscient, wholly good being permits the occurrence of some intense suffering it could have prevented, then either (i) or (ii) or (iii) obtains? It seems to me that it is true. But if it is true then so is premise (2) of the argument for atheism. For that premise merely states in more compact form what we have suggested must be true if an omniscient, wholly good being fails to prevent some intense suffering it could prevent. Premise (2) says that an omniscient, wholly good being would prevent the occurrence of any intense suffering it could, unless it could not do so without thereby losing some greater good or permitting some evil equally bad or worse. This

premise (or something not too distant from it) is, I think, held in common by many atheists and nontheists. Of course, there may be disagreement about whether something is good, and whether, if it is good, one would be morally justified in permitting some intense suffering to occur in order to obtain it. Someone might hold, for example, that no good is great enough to justify permitting an innocent child to suffer terribly.[4] Again, someone might hold that the mere fact that a given good outweighs some suffering and would be lost if the suffering were prevented, is not a morally sufficient reason for permitting the suffering. But to hold either of these views is not to deny (2). For (2) claims only that *if* an omniscient, wholly good being permits intense suffering *then* either there is some greater good that would have been lost, or some equally bad or worse evil that would have occurred, had the intense suffering been prevented. (2) does not purport to describe what might be a *sufficient* condition for an omniscient, wholly good being to permit intense suffering, only what is a *necessary* condition. So stated, (2) seems to express a belief that accords with our basic moral principles, principles shared by both theists and nontheists. If we are to fault the argument for atheism, therefore, it seems we must find some fault with its first premise.

Suppose in some distant forest lightning strikes a dead tree, resulting in a forest fire. In the fire a fawn is trapped, horribly burned, and lies in terrible agony for several days before death relieves its suffering. So far as we can see, the fawn's intense suffering is pointless. For there does not appear to be any greater good such that the prevention of the fawn's suffering would require either the loss of that good or the occurrence of an evil equally bad or worse. Nor does there seem to be any equally bad or worse evil so connected to the fawn's suffering that it would have had to occur had the fawn's suffering been prevented. Could an omnipotent, omniscient being have prevented the fawn's apparently pointless suffering? The answer is obvious, as even the theist will insist. An omnipotent, omniscient being could have easily prevented the fawn from being horribly burned, or, given the burning, could have spared the fawn the intense suffering by quickly ending its life, rather than allowing the fawn to lie in terrible agony for several days. Since the fawn's intense suffering was preventable and, so far as we can see, pointless, doesn't it appear that premise (1) of the argument is true, that there do exist instances of intense suffering which an omnipotent, omniscient being could have prevented without thereby losing some greater good or permitting some evil equally bad or worse?

It must be acknowledged that the case of the fawn's apparently pointless suffering does not *prove* that (1) is true. For even though we cannot see how the fawn's suffering is required to obtain some greater good (or to prevent some equally bad or worse evil), it hardly follows that it is not so required. After all, we are often surprised by how things we thought to be unconnected turn out to be intimately connected. Perhaps, for all we know, there is some familiar good outweighing the fawn's suffering to which that suffering is connected in a way we do not see. Furthermore, there may well be unfamiliar goods, goods we haven't dreamed of, to which the fawn's suffering is inextricably connected. Indeed, it would seem to require something like omniscience on our part before we could lay claim to *knowing* that there is no greater good connected to the fawn's suffering in such a manner that an omnipotent, omniscient being could not have achieved that good without permitting that suffering or some evil equally bad or worse. So the case of the fawn's suffering surely does not enable us to *establish* the truth of (1).

The truth is that we are not in a position to prove that (1) is true. We cannot know with certainty that instances of suffering of the sort described in (1) do occur in our world. But it is one thing to *know* or *prove* that (1) is true and quite another thing to have *rational grounds* for believing (1) to be true. We are often in the position where in the light of our experience and knowledge it is rational to believe that a certain statement is true, even though we are not in a position to prove or to know with certainty that the statement is true. In the light of our past experience and knowledge it is, for example, very reasonable to believe that neither Goldwater nor McGovern will ever be elected President, but we are scarcely in the position of knowing with certainty that neither will ever be elected President. So, too, with (1), although we cannot know with certainty that it is true, it perhaps can be rationally supported, shown to be a rational belief.

Consider again the case of the fawn's suffering. Is it reasonable to believe that there is some greater good so intimately connected to that suffering that even an omnipotent, omniscient being could not have obtained that good without permitting that suffering or some evil at least as bad? It certainly does not appear reasonable to believe this. Nor does it seem reasonable to believe that there is some evil at least as bad as the fawn's suffering such that an omnipotent being simply could not have prevented it without permitting the fawn's suffering. But even if it should somehow be reasonable to believe either of these things of the fawn's suffering, we must then ask whether it is reasonable to believe either of these things of *all* the instances of seemingly pointless human and animal suffering that occur daily in our world. And surely the answer to this more general question must be no. It seems quite unlikely that *all* the instances of intense suffering occurring daily in our world are intimately related to the occurrence of greater goods or the prevention of evils at least as bad; and even more unlikely, should they somehow all be so related, that an omnipotent, omniscient being could not have achieved at least some of those goods (or prevented some of those evils) without permitting the instances of intense suffering that are supposedly related to them. In the light of our experience and knowledge of the variety and scale of human and animal suffering in our world, the idea that none of this suffering could have been prevented by an omnipotent being without thereby losing a greater good or permitting an evil at least as bad seems an extraordinary absurd idea, quite beyond our belief. It seems then that although we cannot *prove* that (1) is true, it is, nevertheless, altogether *reasonable* to believe that (1) is true, that (1) is a *rational* belief.[5]

Returning now to our argument for atheism, we've seen that the second premise expresses a basic belief common to many theists and nontheists. We've also seen that our experience and knowledge of the variety and profusion of suffering in our world provides *rational support* for the first premise. Seeing that the conclusion, "There does not exist an omnipotent, omniscient, wholly good being" follows from these two premises, it does seem that we have *rational support* for atheism, that it is reasonable for us to believe that the theistic God does not exist.

II

Can theism be rationally defended against the argument for atheism we have just examined? If it can, how might the theist best respond to that argument? Since the argument from (1) and (2) to (3) is valid, and since the theist, no less than the nontheist, is more than likely committed to (2), it's clear that the theist can reject this atheistic argument only by rejecting its first premise, the premise that states that there are instances of intense suffering which an omnipotent, omniscient being could have prevented without thereby losing some greater good or permitting some evil equally bad or worse. How, then, can the theist best respond to this premise and the considerations advanced in its support?

There are basically three responses a theist can make. First, he might argue not that (1) is false or probably false, but only that the reasoning given in support of it is in some way *defective*. He may do this either by arguing that the reasons given in support of (1) are *in themselves* insufficient to justify accepting (1), or by arguing that there are other things we know which, when taken in conjunction with these reasons, do not justify us in accepting (1). I suppose some theists would be content with this rather modest response to the basic argument for atheism. But given the validity of the basic argument and the theist's likely acceptance of (2), he is thereby committed to the view that (1) is false, not just that we have no good reasons for accepting (1) as true. The second two responses are aimed at showing that it is reasonable to believe that (1) is false. Since the theist is committed to this view, I shall focus the discussion on these two attempts, attempts which we can distinguish as "the direct attack" and "the indirect attack."

By a direct attack, I mean an attempt to reject (1) by pointing out goods, for example, to which suffering may well be connected, goods which an omnipotent, omniscient being could not achieve without permitting suffering. It is doubtful, however, that the direct attack can succeed. The theist may point out that some suffering leads to moral and spiritual development impossible without suffering. But it's reasonably clear that suffering often occurs in a degree far beyond what is required for character development. The theist may say that some suffering results from free choices of human beings and might be preventable only by preventing some measure of human freedom. But, again, it's clear that much intense suffering occurs not as a result of human free choices. The general difficulty with this direct attack on premise (1) is twofold. First, it cannot succeed, for the theist does not know what greater goods might be served, or evils prevented, by each instance of intense human or animal suffering. Second, the theist's own religious tradition usually maintains that in this life it is not given to us to know God's purpose in allowing particular instances of suffering. Hence, the direct attack against premise (1) cannot succeed and violates basic beliefs associated with theism.

The best procedure for the theist to follow in rejecting premise (1) is the indirect procedure. This procedure I shall call "the G. E. Moore shift," so-called in honor of the twentieth century philosopher, G. E. Moore, who used it to great effect in dealing with the arguments of the skeptics. Skeptical philosophers such as David Hume have advanced ingenious arguments to prove that no one can know of the existence of any material object. The premises of their arguments employ plausible principles, principles which many philosophers have tried to reject directly, but only with questionable success. Moore's procedure was altogether different. Instead of arguing directly against the premises of the skeptic's arguments, he simply noted that the premises implied, for example, that he (Moore) did not know of the existence of a pencil. Moore then proceeded indirectly against the skeptic's premises by arguing:

I do know that this pencil exists.

If the skeptic's principles are correct I cannot know of the existence of this pencil.

∴ The skeptic's principles (at least one) must be incorrect.

Moore then noted that his argument is just as valid as the skeptic's, that both of their arguments contain the premise "If the skeptic's principles are correct Moore cannot know of the existence of this pencil," and concluded that the only way to choose between the two arguments (Moore's and the skeptic's) is by deciding which of the first premises it is more rational to believe—Moore's premise "I do know that this pencil exists" or the skeptic's premise asserting that his skeptical principles are correct. Moore concluded that his own first premise was the more rational of the two.[6]

Before we see how the theist may apply the G. E. Moore shift to the basic argument of atheism, we should note the general strategy of the shift. We're given an argument: p, q, therefore, r. Instead of arguing directly against p, another argument is constructed—not-r, q, therefore, not-p—which begins with the denial of the conclusion of the first argument, keeps its second premise, and ends with the denial of the first premise as its conclusion. Compare, for example, these two:

I. p II. not–r

$$\frac{q}{r} \qquad \frac{q}{\text{not–}p}$$

It is a truth of logic that if I is valid II must be valid as well. Since the arguments are the same so far as the second premise is concerned, any choice between them must concern their respective first premises. To argue against the first premise (p) by constructing the counter argument II is to employ the G. E. Moore shift.

Applying the G. E. Moore shift against the first premise of the basic argument for atheism, the theist can argue as follows:

not-3. There exists an omnipotent, omniscient, wholly good being.

2. An omniscient, wholly good being would prevent the occurrence of any intense suffering it could, unless it could not do so without thereby losing some greater good or permitting some evil equally bad or worse.

therefore,

not-1. It is not the case that there exist instances of intense suffering which an omnipotent, omniscient being could have prevented without thereby losing some greater good or permitting some evil equally bad or worse.

We now have two arguments: the basic argument for atheism from (1) and (2) to (3), and the theist's best response, the argument from (not-3) and (2) to (not-1). What the theist then says about (1) is that he has rational grounds for believing in the existence of the theistic God (not-3), accepts (2) as true, and sees that (not-1) follows from (not-3) and (2). He concludes, therefore, that he has rational grounds for rejecting (1). Having rational grounds for rejecting (1), the theist concludes that the basic argument for atheism is mistaken.

III

We've had a look at a forceful argument for atheism and what seems to be the theist's best response to that argument. If one is persuaded by the argument for atheism, as I find myself to be, how might one best view the position of the theist? Of course, he will view the theist as having a false belief, just as the theist will view the atheist as having a false belief. But what position should the atheist take concerning the *rationality* of the theist's belief? There are three major positions an atheist might take, positions which we may think of as some varieties of atheism. First, the atheist may believe that no one is rationally justified in believing that the theistic God exists. Let us call this position "unfriendly atheism." Second, the atheist may hold no belief concerning whether any theist is or isn't rationally justified in believing that the theistic God exists. Let us call this view "indifferent atheism." Finally, the atheist may believe that some theists are rationally justified in believing that the theistic God exists. This view we shall call "friendly atheism." In this final part of the paper I propose to discuss and defend the position of friendly atheism.

If no one can be rationally justified in believing a false proposition then friendly atheism is a paradoxical, if not incoherent position. But surely the truth of a belief is not a necessary condition of someone's being rationally justified in having that belief. So in holding that someone is rationally justified in believing that the theistic God exists, the friendly atheist is not committed to thinking that the theist has a true belief. What he is committed to is that the theist has rational grounds for his belief, a belief the atheist rejects and is convinced he is rationally justified in rejecting. But is this possible? Can someone, like our friendly atheist, hold a belief, be convinced that he is rationally justified in holding that belief, and yet believe that someone else is equally justified in believing the opposite? Surely this is possible. Suppose your friends see you off on a flight to Hawaii. Hours after take-off they learn that your plane has gone down at sea. After a twenty-four hour search, no survivors have been found. Under these circumstances they are rationally justified in believing that you have perished. But it is hardly rational for you to believe this, as you bob up and down in your life vest, wondering why the search planes have failed to spot you. Indeed, to amuse yourself while awaiting your fate, you might very well reflect on the fact that your friends are rationally justified in believing that you are now dead, a proposition you disbelieve and are rationally justified in disbelieving. So, too, perhaps an atheist may be rationally justified in his atheistic belief and yet hold that some theists are rationally justified in believing just the opposite of what he believes.

What sort of grounds might a theist have for believing that God exists? Well, he might endeavor to justify his belief by appealing to one or more of the traditional arguments: Ontological, Cosmological, Teleological, Moral, etc. Second, he might appeal to certain aspects of religious experience, perhaps even his own religious experience. Third, he might try to justify theism as a plausible theory in terms of which we can account for a variety of phenomena. Although an atheist must hold that the theistic God does not exist, can he not also believe, and be justified in so believing, that some of these "justifications of theism" do actually rationally justify some theists in their belief that there exists a supremely good, omnipotent, omniscient being? It seems to me that he can.

If we think of the long history of theistic belief and the special situations in which people are sometimes placed, it is perhaps as absurd to think that no one was ever rationally justified in believing that the theistic God exists as it is to think that no one was ever justified in believing that human beings would never walk on the moon. But in suggesting that friendly atheism is preferable to unfriendly atheism, I don't mean to rest the case on what some human beings might reasonably have believed in the eleventh or thirteenth century. The more interesting question is whether some people in modern society, people who are aware of the usual grounds for belief and disbelief and are acquainted to some degree with modern science, are yet rationally justified in accepting theism. Friendly atheism is a significant position only if it answers this question in the affirmative.

It is not difficult for an atheist to be friendly when he has reason to believe that the theist could not reasonably be expected to be acquainted with the grounds for disbelief that he (the atheist) possesses. For then the atheist may take the view that some theists are rationally justified in holding to theism, but would not be so were they to be acquainted with the grounds for disbelief—those grounds being sufficient to tip the scale in favor of atheism when balanced against the reasons the theist has in support of his belief.

Friendly atheism becomes paradoxical, however, when the atheist contemplates believing that the theist has all the grounds for atheism that he, the atheist, has, and yet is rationally justified in maintaining his theistic belief. But even so excessively friendly a view as this perhaps can be held by the atheist if he also has some reason to think that the grounds for theism are not as telling as the theist is justified in taking them to be.[7]

In this paper I've presented what I take to be a strong argument for atheism, pointed out what I think is the theist's best response to that argument, distinguished three positions an atheist might take concerning the rationality of theistic belief, and made some remarks in defense of the position called "friendly atheism." I'm aware that the central points of the paper are not likely to be warmly received by many philosophers. Philosophers who are atheists tend to be tough minded—holding that there are no good reasons for supposing that theism is true. And theists tend either to reject the view that the existence of evil provides rational grounds for atheism or to hold that religious belief has nothing to do with reason and evidence at all. But such is the way of philosophy.

NOTES

1. Some philosophers have contended that the existence of evil is *logically inconsistent* with the existence of the theistic God. No one, I think, has succeeded in establishing such an extravagant claim. Indeed, granted incompatibilism, there is a fairly compelling argument for the view that the existence of evil is logically consistent with the existence of the theistic God. [For a lucid statement of this argument see Alvin Plantinga, *God, Freedom, and Evil* (New York 1974), 29–59.] There remains, however, what we may call the *evidential* form—as opposed to the *logical* form—of the problem of evil: the view that the variety and profusion of evil in our world, although perhaps not logically inconsistent with the existence of the theistic God, provides, nevertheless, *rational support* for atheism. In this paper I shall be concerned solely with the evidential form of the problem, the form of the problem which, I think, presents a rather severe difficulty for theism.

2. If there is some good, G, greater than any evil, (1) will be false for the trivial reason that no matter what evil, E, we pick the conjunctive good state of affairs consisting of G and E that will outweigh E and be such that an omnipotent being could not obtain it without permitting E. [See Alvin Plantinga, *God and Other Minds* (Ithaca, 1967), 167.] To avoid this objection we may insert "unreplaceable" into our premises (1) and (2) between "some" and "greater." If E isn't required for G, and G is better than G plus E, then the good conjunctive state of affairs composed of G and E would be *replaceable* by the greater good of G alone. For the sake of simplicity, however, I will ignore this complication both in the formulation and discussion of premises (1) and (2).

3. Three clarifying points need to be made in connection with (1). First, by "good" I don't mean to exclude the fulfilment of certain moral principles. Perhaps preventing s_1 would preclude certain actions prescribed by the principles of justice. I shall allow that the satisfaction of certain principles of justice may be a good that outweighs the evil of

s_1. Second, even though (1) may suggest it, I don't mean to limit the good in question to something that would follow in *time* the occurrence of s_1. And, finally, we should perhaps not fault OG if the good, G, that would be lost were s_1 prevented is not actually greater than s_1, but merely such that allowing s_1, and G, as opposed to preventing s_1 and thereby losing G, would not alter the balance between good and evil. For reasons of simplicity, I have left this point out in stating (i), with the result that (i) is perhaps a bit stronger than it should be.

4. See Ivan's speech in bk. v, ch. iv, of *The Brothers Karamazov.*

5. One might object that the conclusion of this paragraph is stronger than the reasons given warrant. For it is one thing to argue that it is unreasonable to think that (1) is false and another thing to conclude that we are therefore justified in accepting (1) as true. There are propositions such that believing them is much more reasonable than disbelieving them, and yet are such that *withholding judgment* about them is more reasonable than believing them. To take an example of Chisholm's: It is more reasonable to believe that the Pope will be in Rome (on some arbitrarily picked future date) than to believe that he won't: but it is perhaps more reasonable to suspend judgment on the question of the Pope's whereabouts on that particular date, than to believe that he will be in Rome. Thus it might be objected, that while we've shown that believing (1) is more reasonable than disbelieving (1), we haven't shown that believing (1) is more reasonable than withholding belief. My answer to this objection is that there are things we know which render (1) probable to the degree that it is more reasonable to believe (1) than to suspend judgment on (1). What are these things we know? First, I think, is the fact that there is an enormous variety and profusion of intense human and animal suffering in our world. Second, is the fact that much of this suffering seems quite unrelated to any greater goods (or the absence of equal or greater evils) that might justify it. And, finally, there is the fact that such suffering as is related to greater goods (or the absence of equal or greater evils) does not, in many cases, seem so intimately related as to require its permission by an omnipotent being bent on securing those goods (the absence of those evils). These facts, I am claiming, make it more reasonable to accept (1) than to withhold judgment on (1).

6. See, for example, the two chapters on Hume in G. E. Moore, *Some Main Problems of Philosophy* (London, 1953).

7. Suppose that I add a long sum of numbers three times and get result *x*. I inform you of this so that you have pretty much the same evidence I have for the claim that the sum of the numbers is *x*. You then use your calculator twice over and arrive at result *y*. You, then, are justified in believing that the sum of the numbers is not *x*. However, knowing that your calculator has been damaged and is therefore unreliable, and that you have no reason to think that it is damaged, I may reasonably believe not only that the sum of the numbers is *x*, but also that you are justified in believing that the sum is not *x*. Here is a case, then, where you have all of my evidence for *p*, and yet I can reasonably believe that you are justified in believing not-*p*—for I have reason to believe that your grounds for not-*p* are not as telling as you are justified in taking them to be.

33   CHRISTIANITY AND HORRENDOUS EVILS

MARILYN MCCORD ADAMS

Marilyn McCord Adams is Research Professor of Philosophy at the University of North Carolina at Chapel Hill. She is also an ordained priest in the Episcopal Church. She argues that in the face of the most horrendous evils, the reasonableness of Christianity can be maintained only by affirming the incommensurate good of intimacy with God.

For present purposes, I define "horrendous evils" as "evils the participation in (the doing or suffering of) which gives one reason prima facie to doubt whether one's life could (given their inclusion in it) be a great good to one on the whole." Such reasonable doubt arises because it is so difficult humanly to conceive how such evils could be overcome. Borrowing Chisholm's contrast between *balancing off* (which occurs when the opposing values of *mutually exclusive* parts of a whole partially *or* totally cancel each other out) and *defeat* (which cannot *occur* by the mere addition to the whole of a new part of opposing value, but involves some "organic unity" among the values of parts and wholes, as when the positive aesthetic value of a whole painting defeats the ugliness of a small colour patch),[1] horrendous evils seem prima facie, not only to balance off but to engulf the positive value of a participant's life. Nevertheless, that very horrendous proportion, by which they threaten to rob a person's life of positive meaning, cries out not only to be engulfed, but to be made meaningful through positive and decisive defeat....

In my opinion, the reasonableness of Christianity can be maintained in the face of horrendous evils only by drawing on resources of religious value theory, for one way for God to be *good to* created persons is by relating them appropriately to relevant and great goods. But philosophical and religious theories differ importantly on what valuables they admit into their ontology. Some maintain that "what you see is what you get," but nevertheless admit a wide range of

From Marilyn McCord Adams, "Horrendous Evils and the Goodness of God," *Proceedings of the Aristotelian Society*, Supplementary Vol. 63 (1989). Reprinted by permission of The Aristotelian Society.

valuables, from sensory pleasures, the beauty of nature and cultural artifacts, the joys of creativity, to loving personal intimacy. Others posit a transcendent good (e.g., the Form of the Good in Platonism, or God, the Supremely Valuable Object, in Christianity). In the spirit of Ivan Karamazov, I am convinced that the depth of horrific evil cannot be accurately estimated without recognizing it to be incommensurate with any package of merely non-transcendent goods and so unable to be balanced off, much less defeated, thereby.

Where the *internal* coherence of Christianity is the issue, however, it is fair to appeal to its own store of valuables. From a Christian point of view, God is a being greater than which cannot be conceived, a good incommensurate with both created goods and temporal evils. Likewise, the good of beatific, face-to-face intimacy with God is simply incommensurate with any merely non-transcendent goods or ills a person might experience. Thus, the good of beatific face-to-face intimacy with God would *engulf* (in a sense analogous to Chisholmian balancing off) even the horrendous evils humans experience in this present life here below, and overcome any prima-facie reasons the individual had to doubt whether his/her life would or could be worth living.

Engulfing personal horrors within the context of the participant's life would vouchsafe to that individual a life that was a great good to him/her on the whole. I am still inclined to think it would guarantee that immeasurable divine goodness to any person thus benefited. But there is good theological reason for Christians to believe that God would go further, beyond engulfment to defeat. For it is the nature of persons to look for meaning, both in their lives and in the world. Divine respect for and commitment to created personhood would drive God to make all those sufferings which threaten to destroy the positive meaning of a person's life meaningful through positive defeat.

How could God do it? So far as I can see, only by integrating participation in horrendous evils into a person's relationship with God. Possible dimensions of integration are charted by Christian soteriology. I pause here to sketch three:[2] (i) First,

because God in Christ participated in horrendous evil through His passion and death, human experience of horrors can be a means of *identifying* with Christ, either through *sympathetic* identification (in which each person suffers his/her own pains, but their similarity enables each to know what it is like for the other) or through *mystical* identification (in which the created person is supposed literally to experience a share of Christ's pain[3]). (ii) Julian of Norwich's description of heavenly welcome suggests the possible defeat of horrendous evil through divine gratitude. According to Julian, before the elect have a chance to thank God for all He has done for them, God will say, "Thank you for all your suffering, the suffering of your youth." She says that the creature's experience of divine gratitude will bring such full and unending joy as could not be merited by the whole sea of human pain and suffering throughout the ages.[4] (iii) A third idea identifies temporal suffering itself with a vision into the inner life of God, and can be developed several ways. Perhaps, contrary to medieval theology, God is not impassible, but rather has matched capacities for joy and for suffering. Perhaps, as the Heidelberg catechism suggests, God responds to human sin and the sufferings of Christ with an agony beyond human conception.[5] Alternatively, the inner life of God may be, strictly speaking and in and of itself, beyond both joy and sorrow. But, just as (according to Rudolf Otto) humans experience divine presence now as *tremendum* (with deep dread and anxiety), now as *fascinans* (with ineffable attraction), so perhaps our deepest suffering as much as our highest joys may themselves be direct visions into the inner life of God, imperfect but somehow less obscure in proportion to their intensity. And if a face-to-face vision of God is a good for humans incommensurate with any nontranscendent goods or ills, so any vision of God (including horrendous suffering) would have a good aspect in so far as it is a vision of God (even if it has an evil aspect in so far as it is horrendous suffering). For the most part, horrors are not recognized as experiences of God (any more than the city slicker recognizes his visual image of a brown patch as a vision of Beulah the cow in the distance). But, Christian mysticism might claim, at least from the post-mortem perspective of the beatific vision, such sufferings will be seen for what they were, and retrospectively no one will wish away any intimate encounters with God from his/her life-history in this world. The created person's experience of the beatific vision together with his/her knowledge that intimate divine presence stretched back over his/her ante-mortem life and reached down into the depths of his/her worst suffering, would provide retrospective comfort independent of comprehension of the reasons-why akin to the two-year-old's assurance of its mother's love. Taking this third approach, Christians would not need to commit themselves about what in any event we do not know: namely, whether we will (like the two-year-old) ever grow up enough to understand the reasons why God permits our participation in horrendous evils. For by contrast with the best of earthly mothers, such divine intimacy is an incommensurate good and would cancel out for the creature any need to know why.

NOTES

1. Roderick Chisholm, "The Defeat of Good and Evil", in Marilyn McCord Adams and Robert Merrihew Adams (eds), *The Problem of Evil* (New York: Oxford University Press, 1990), ch. 3.

2. In my paper "Redemptive Suffering: A Christian Solution to the Problem of Evil", in Robert Audi and William J. Wainwright (eds), *Rationality, Religious Belief, and Moral Commitment: New Essays in Philosophy of Religion* (Cornell University Press, 1986), pp. 248–67, I sketch how horrendous suffering can be meaningful by being made a vehicle of divine redemption for victim, perpetrator, and onlooker, and thus an occasion of the victim's collaboration with God. In "Separation and Reversal in Luke–Acts", in Thomas Morris (ed.), *Philosophy and the Christian Faith* (Notre Dame, Ind.: Notre Dame University Press, 1988), pp. 92–117, I attempted to chart the redemptive plot-line whereby horrendous sufferings are made meaningful by being woven into the divine redemptive plot. My considered opinion is that such collaboration would be too strenuous for the human condition were it not to be supplemented by a more explicit and beatific divine intimacy.

3. For example, Julian of Norwich tells us that she prayed for and received the latter (*Revelations of Divine Love*, ch. 17). Mother Theresa of Calcutta seems to construe Matthew 25: 31–46 to mean that the poorest and the least *are* Christ, and that their sufferings *are* Christ's (Malcolm Muggeridge, *Something Beautiful for God* (New York: Harper & Row, 1960). pp. 72–5).

4. *Revelations of Divine Love*, ch. 14.

5. Cf. Alvin Plantinga, "Self-Profile", in James E. Tomberlin and Peter van Inwagen (eds), *Profiles: Alvin Plantinga* (Dordrecht, Boston, Mass., and Lancaster, Pa.: Reidel, 1985), p. 36.

34 THE PROBLEM OF EVIL AND THE DESIRES OF THE HEART

ELEONORE STUMP

Eleonore Stump is Professor of Philosophy at St. Louis University. She argues that the suffering of innocents cannot be justified only by the good of human flourishing, because the loss of the desires of one's heart also needs to be addressed. Considering this claim in light of the

From Eleonore Stump, "The Problem of Evil and the Desires of the Heart," in Jonathan Kvanvig, ed., *Oxford Studies in the Philosophy of Religion*, vol. I, 2008. Reprinted by permission of the publisher.

previous essay by Marilyn McCord Adams, one might ask why, if all people can attain intimacy with God, some do so while attaining the desires of their heart while others do so without attaining such desires. Does fulfillment of these desires matter in the long run? Stump maintains they do.

I. INTRODUCTION

The problem of evil is raised by the existence of suffering in the world. Can one hold consistently both that the world has such suffering in it and that it is governed by an omniscient, omnipotent, perfectly good God, as the major monotheisms claim? An affirmative answer to this question has often enough taken the form of a theodicy. A theodicy is an attempt to show that these claims are consistent by providing a morally sufficient reason for God to allow suffering. In the history of the discussions of the problem of evil, a great deal of effort has been expended on proposing and defending, or criticizing and attacking, theodicies and the putative morally sufficient reasons which theodicies propose.

Generally, a putative morally sufficient reason for God to allow suffering is centred on a supposed benefit which could not be gotten without the suffering and which outweighs it. And the benefit is most commonly thought of as some intrinsically valuable thing supposed to be essential to general human flourishing, such as the significant use of free will or virtuous character, either for human beings in general or for the sufferer in particular.[1]

So, for example, in his insightful reflections on the sort of sufferings represented by the afflictions of Job, the impressive tenth-century Jewish thinker Saadiah Gaon says,

> Now He that subjects the soul to its trials is none other than the Master of the universe, who is, of course, acquainted with all its doings. This testing of the soul [that is, the suffering of Job] has been compared to the assaying by means of fire of [lumps of metal] that have been referred to as gold or silver. It is thereby that the true nature of their composition is clearly established. For the original gold and silver remain, while the alloys that have been mingled with them are partly burned and partly take flight... The pure, clear souls that have been refined are thereupon exalted and ennobled.[2]

The same approach is common in contemporary times. So, for example, John Hick has proposed a soul-making theodicy, which justifies suffering as building the character of the sufferer and thereby contributing to the flourishing of the sufferer.[3] Or, to take a very different example which nonetheless makes the same point, Richard Swinburne has argued that suffering contributes to the flourishing of sufferers because, among other things, a person's suffering makes him useful to others, and being useful to others is an important constituent of human well-being in general.[4]

Those who have attacked theodicies such as these have tended to focus on the theodicist's claims about the connections between the putative benefit and the suffering. Opponents of theodicy have argued that the proposed benefit could have been obtained without the suffering, for example, or that the suffering is not a morally acceptable means to that (or any other) benefit. But these attacks on theodicy share an assumption with the attempted theodicies themselves. Both the attacks and the attempted theodicies suppose that a person's generic human flourishing would be sufficient to justify God in allowing that a person's suffering if only the suffering and the flourishing were connected in the right way. In this paper, I want to call this assumption into question.

I will argue that the sufferings of unwilling innocents cannot be justified only in terms of the intrinsically valuable things which make for general human flourishing (however that flourishing is understood). I will argue that even if such flourishing is connected in the appropriate ways to the suffering in a person's life, intrinsically valuable things essential to flourishing are not by themselves sufficient to constitute a morally sufficient reason for God to allow human suffering. That is because human beings can set their hearts on things which are not necessary for such flourishing, and they suffer when they lose or fail to get what they set their hearts on.[5] That suffering also needs to be addressed in consideration of the problem of evil.

II. THE DESIRES OF THE HEART

The suffering to which I want to call attention can be thought of in terms of what the Psalmist calls "the desires of the heart."[6] When the Psalmist says, "Delight yourself in the Lord, and he will give you the desires of your heart,"[7] we all have some idea what the Psalmist is promising. We are clear, for example, that some abstract theological good which a person does not care much about does not count as one of the desires of that person's heart. Suffering also arises when a human being fails to get a desire of her heart or has and then loses a desire of her heart.

I do not know how to make the notion of a desire of the heart precise; but, clearly, we do have some intuitive grasp of it, and we commonly use the expression or others related to it in ordinary discourse. We say, for example, that a person is heartsick because he has lost his heart's desire. He is filled with heartache because his heart's desire is kept from him. He loses heart, because something he had put his heart into is taken from him. It would have been different for him if he had wanted it only half-heartedly; but since it was what he had at heart, he is likely to be heartsore a long time over the loss of it, unless, of course, he has a change of heart about it—and so on, and on.

Perhaps we could say that a person's heart's desire is a particular kind of commitment on her part to something—a person or a project—which matters greatly to her but which need not be essential to her flourishing, in the sense that human flourishing for her may be possible without it. So, for example, Coretta Scott King's life arguably exemplifies flourishing, on any ordinary measure of human flourishing and yet her husband's assassination was undoubtedly heartbreaking for her. If there is such a thing as a web of belief, with some beliefs peripheral and others central to a person's set of beliefs, maybe there is also a web of desire.

A desire of a person's heart is a desire which is at or near the centre of the web of desire for her. If she loses what she wants when her desire is at or near the centre of the web, then other things which she had wanted begin to lose their ability to attract her because what she had most centrally wanted is gone. The web of desire starts to fall apart when the centre does not hold, we might say. That is why the ordinary good things of life, like food and work, fail to draw a person who has lost the desires of her heart. She is heartbroken, we say, and that is why she has no heart for anything else now.

If things essential to general human flourishing are intrinsically valuable for all human beings, then those things which are the desires of the heart can be thought of as the things which have the value they do for a particular person primarily because she has set her heart on them, like the value a child has for its parents, the value they have *for her* is derivative from her love of them, not the other way around. A loving father, trying to deal gently with his small daughter's childish tantrums, finally said to her with exasperated adult feeling, "It isn't reasonable to cry about these things!" Presumably, the father means that the things for which his little daughter was weeping did not have much value on the scale which measures the intrinsic value of good things essential to human flourishing; and, no doubt, he was right in that assessment. But there is another scale by which to measure, too, and that is the scale which measures the value a thing has for a particular person because of the love she has for it. The second scale cannot be reduced to the first. Clearly, we care not just about general human flourishing and the intrinsically valuable things essential to it. We also care about those things which are the desires of our hearts, and we suffer when we are denied our heart's desires. I would say that it is not reasonable to say to a weeping child that it is not reasonable for her to weep about the loss of something she had her heart set on.

Suffering which stems from a loss of the heart's desires is often enough compatible with flourishing.[8] As far as that goes, for any particular historical person picked as an exemplar of a flourishing life, it is certainly arguable that, at some time in her life, that person will have lost or failed to get something on which she had fixed her heart. Think, for example, not only of Coretta Scott King but also of Sojourner Truth, who was sold away from her parents at the age of nine, or Harriet Tubman, who suffered permanent neurological damage from the beatings she sustained in adolescence. If any human lives manifest flourishing, the lives of these women certainly do. Each of them is an exemplar of a highly admirable, meaningful life. Yet each of these women undoubtedly experienced heartbreak.

In fact, stern-minded thinkers in varying cultures, including some Stoics, Buddhists, and many in the Christian tradition, have been fiercely committed to the position that human flourishing is independent of the vicissitudes of fortune. On their view, human flourishing ought to be understood in a way which makes it compatible even with such things as poverty, disease and disabilities, the death of loved ones, betrayal by intimate friends, estrangements from friends or family, and imprisonment. But it certainly seems as if each of these is sufficient to break the heart of a person who suffers them if the person is not antecedently in the grip of such a stem-minded attitude.

So, for example, in the history of the medieval Christian tradition, human flourishing was commonly taken as a matter of a certain relationship with God, mediated by the indwelling of the Holy Spirit. On this view of flourishing, most of the evils human beings suffer are compatible with flourishing. That is because, as Christian confessional literature makes clear, a human person can feel that she is in such a relationship with God, even when she is afflicted with serious suffering of body or mind....

And yet something more needs to be said. The problem is that suffering is not confined to things which undermine a person's flourishing and keep him from being *fine*, in this deep sense of "fine." What is bad about the evils human beings suffer is not just that they can undermine a person's flourishing, but also that they can keep her from having the desires of her heart, when the desires of her heart are for something which is not essential for general human flourishing. Suffering arises also from the loss of the desires of one's heart; and, in considerations of the problem of evil and proposed theodicies, this suffering needs to be addressed as well. This suffering also needs to be justified.

NOTES

1. There is a large, contentious philosophical literature on the nature of human flourishing or well-being, and it is not part of my purpose to try to engage that literature here. For my purposes in this paper, I will understand flourishing to consist in just those things necessary in a person's life for that person's life to be admirable and meaningful.
2. Saadiah Gaon 1948: 246–7.
3. Hick 1966. For Hick's defence of his solutions against objections, see, for example, Hick 1968a: 539–46, and Hick 1968b: 591–602.
4. See Swinburne 1998.
5. In Adams 1999, Marilyn Adams makes a distinction which is at least related to the distinction I am after here. She says, "the value of a person's life may be assessed from the inside (in relation to that person's own goals, ideals, and choices) and from the outside (in relation to the aims, tastes, values, and preferences of others)... My notion is that for a person's life to be a great good to him/her on the whole, the external point of view (even if it is God's) is not sufficient" (p. 145).
6. The expression "the desire of the heart" is also ambiguous. It can mean either a particular kind of desire or else the thing which is desired in that way. When we say, "the desire of his heart was to be a great musician," the expression refers to a desire; when we say, "In losing her, he lost the desire of his heart," the expression refers to the thing desired. I will not try to sort out this ambiguity here; I will simply trust to the context to disambiguate the expression.
7. Ps. 37: 4–5.
8. Except for conceptions of flourishing which make flourishing identical to the satisfaction of desires, but equating flourishing just with desire satisfaction is problematic enough that it can be left to one side here.

REFERENCES

Adams, Marilyn, *Horrendous Evils and the Goodness of God* (Ithaca, NY: Cornell University Press, 1999).

Hick, John, *Evil and the God of Love* (New York: Harper and Row, 1966).

— "God, Evil and Mystery," *Religious Studies* 3 (1968a): 539–46.

— "The Problem of Evil in the First and Last Things," *Journal of Theological Studies* 19 (1968b): 591–602.

Saadiah Gaon, *The Book of Beliefs and Opinions*, tr. Samuel Rosenblatt (New Haven, CT: Yale University Press, 1948).

Swinburne, Richard, *Providence and the Problem of Evil* (Oxford: Oxford University Press, 1998).

B. EVIL FORCES

35 SATAN

ALVIN PLANTINGA

The world contains goods and evils. If an all-good, all-powerful deity created the world, an obvious challenge would be to explain why evils exist. If an all-evil, all-powerful deity created the world, an equally obvious challenge would be to explain why goods exist. Both questions could be answered by supposing that two forces are at work in the world: a force for good and a force for evil. The goods are the work of the good force; the evils are the work of the evil force.

Alvin Plantinga, who is Professor Emeritus of Philosophy at the University of Notre Dame, attributes much evil to Satan and his cohorts. Why does God permit the activity of these forces for evil? Plantinga suggests that Satan is valuable because a being that has more freedom and much power, even to do evil, has greater worth than one that has less freedom and limited power.

Even if, unlike Plantinga, you find implausible the claim that Satan and his cohorts exist, you might agree that if evils could be attributed to Satanic forces, then explaining why evils exist would no longer present a problem for those who believe in the existence of an all-good, all-powerful deity. The remaining question, however, would be why such a deity would allow evil forces to operate.

[O]ne goodmaking feature of a world is the existence, in it, of free and rational creatures. But free creatures come in a variety of versions, and not all free creatures are equal with respect to value, i.e., to the value of the worlds in which they exist. In general, the more free creatures resemble God, the more valuable they are and the more valuable are the worlds in which they exist. In particular, creatures that have a great deal of power, including power to do both good and evil, are more valuable than creatures who are free, but whose power is limited or meager. God therefore created a world in which there are creatures with at least two features: (a) a great deal of power, including the power to work against God, and (b) the freedom to turn their backs upon God, to rebel against him, fight against what he values. Thus

Milton's Satan declares "Evil, be Thou my Good!"; in so doing he announces his intention to take up arms against God, to resist him, to try to destroy what God values, to do his best to wreck God's world, to promote what God hates. Suffering is intrinsically a bad thing; accordingly God hates it; Satan therefore aims to promote suffering, to cause as much of it as he can. Much of the suffering in the world results in this way from the free actions of creatures who actively oppose God and what he values. But free creatures also cause suffering, sometimes, not because they intend in this way actively to oppose God, but just because they don't have any objection to inflicting suffering on others in order to achieve their own selfish or foolish ends. Here one thinks of the enormous suffering inflicted, in the twentieth

From Supralapsarianism, or 'O Felix Culpa,' in Peter van Inwagen, ed., *Christian Faith and the Problem of Evil*, William B. Eerdmans Publishing Company, 2004. Reprinted by permission of the publisher.

century, on the population of the former Soviet Union in order to attain that Marxist paradise; Stalin and his henchmen recklessly ran roughshod over the rights and goods of others in order to achieve something they saw as valuable. At least some of the suffering the world displays results from the free actions of significantly free creatures.

But what about so-called natural evil, evil that cannot be attributed to the free actions of human beings? What about the suffering due to disease, earthquake, flood, famine, pestilence, and the like? What about animal suffering and the savagery displayed in the natural world? What about the Ichneumonid wasp Darwin found so upsetting, a wasp that lays its eggs in a live caterpillar, so that when the eggs hatch, the pupae eat the caterpillar alive from the inside? Well, perhaps, as Peter van Inwagen suggests, this is the price God had to pay for a regular world. But there is another and more traditional suggestion here. Perhaps the term 'natural evil' is something of a misnomer, or perhaps, at any rate, the contrast between natural evil and moral evil is misleading in that the former is really an instance of the latter. It is plausible to think that there are deeper layers to the sin and evil the world displays, than that exhibited by human beings and embodied in their actions. According to the apostle Paul, the whole creation is groaning, and groaning because of sin.[1] Here a traditional suggestion is that suffering and evil of this sort is to be attributed to the actions of Satan and his cohorts; Satan is a mighty non-human free creature who rebelled against the Lord long before human beings were on the scene; and much of the natural evil the world displays is due to the actions of Satan and his cohorts.[2]

This suggestion is not at present widely popular in Western academia, and not widely endorsed by the contemporary intellectual elite. But it is less than clear that Western academia has much to say by way of evidence against the idea. That beings of these sorts should be involved in the history of our world seems to me (as to, e.g., C. S. Lewis and many others) not at all unlikely, in particular not unlikely with respect to

Christian theism. The thought that much evil is due to Satan and his cohorts is of course entirely consistent with God's being omnipotent, omniscient, and perfectly good; furthermore it isn't nearly as improbable with respect to "what we now know" as most philosophers seem to assume. Objections to it consist much more in amused contempt or instinctive revulsion than in reasoned refutation.

NOTES

1. "For the creation was subjected to frustration, not by its own choice, but by the will of the one who subjected it, in hope that the creation itself will be liberated from its bondage to decay and brought into the glorious freedom of the children of God. We know that the whole creation has been groaning as in the pains of childbirth right up to the present time" (Romans 1:18-22).

2. Thus, for example, Dom Bruno Well:

So the fallen angels which have power over the universe and over this planet in particular, being motivated by an intense angelic hatred of God and of all creatures, have acted upon the forces of matter, actuating them in false proportions so far as lay in their power, and this from the very outset of evolution, thus producing a deep-set disorder in the very heart of the universe which manifests itself today in the various physical evils which we find in nature, and among them the violence, the savagery, and the suffering of animal life. This does not mean that, for instance, an earthquake or a thunderstorm is due directly to satanic action. It is due to purely natural causes, but these causes are what they now are owing to the deep-set disorder in the heart of nature resulting from this action of fallen spirits, most subtly mingled with the action of good spirits, throughout the long ages of the world's formation — 'an enemy came and sowed tares also amid the wheat'.

Why Does God Permit Evil? (London: Burns, Oates & Washbourne Ltd., 1941), pp. 49-50. Aquinas approvingly quotes Damascene to the same effect: "The devil was one of the angelic powers who presided over the terrestrial order" (ST I, Q. 110, a. 1, ad 3).

36   THE COSMIC DUALISM OF ZOROASTRIANISM

JENNY ROSE

Alvin Plantinga's resorting to Satan and his cohorts to provide a solution to the problem of evil is, as Plantinga demonstrates, consistent with Christian thought. But many centuries before the development of Christianity, the picture of the world as a battleground between the forces of good and the forces of evil was a key element in Zoroastrianism, which became the official state religion of the Persian empire in the 6th century B. C. E. and was strongly supported by Darius the Great (522-486 B. C. E.), whose forces were defeated by the Greeks at the battle of Marathon and under whose auspices the Jews completed the rebuilding of the Temple in Jerusalem in 515 B. C. E. The Zoroastrian scriptures are known as the *Avesta* (the word for "law" in Pahlavi, a Persian dialect). Today Zoroastrianism is practiced by the Parsees in India and small communities in Iran.

Zoroastrians believe in a supreme God, Ahura Mazda, and the foe of that God, Ahriman. Ahura Mazda is responsible for goodness, Ahriman for evil. The struggle between them is incessant, although Ahriman is doomed to defeat. Thus for Zoroastrians the problem of evil never arises.

Some basics of Zoroastrianism are explained in our next reading, authored by Jenny Rose, Associate Professor of Religion at Claremont Graduate University.

AHURA MAZDA

The name of the supreme God of the Zoroastrian faith is Ahura Mazda (or Ohrmazd). He is self-created, omniscient, omnipresent, holy, invisible, and beyond human conceptualization. He is neither begotten, nor is there anyone who is his equal. He is, as his name implies, the Wise Lord, the Most Knowing One, and the Most Far-Seeing One. In fact, in a passage recorded in the Avesta, Ahura Mazda says of himself: "My sixth name is Understanding; my seventh is Intelligent One; my eighth name is Knowledge; my ninth is Endowed With Knowledge; my twentieth is Mazda (Wisdom). I am the Wise One; my name is the Wisest of the Wise".

This infinite wisdom, or omniscience, is absolute, so that he knows everything before it happens. Consequently, he is all-pervading, and there is no conceivable place where he is not. He is also changeless, first and foremost, the most perfect being, the greatest, the most powerful, the one who was, is, and will be forever.

Ahura Mazda is the creator of the universe, the author of the celestial and terrestrial worlds. He has brought forth rivers, trees, forests, wind, clouds, sun, moon, stars, and the seasons. He guards heaven and earth from falling, and everything follows the sequence he has ordained from the beginning. He created the human body and endowed it with life, mind, and conscience. He is the dispenser of every material good and spiritual blessing, because it is in his nature to be beneficent to all his creation.

As the sovereign lord of all existence and as the creator and sustainer of the entire universe, he rules according to his own will. He is a friend and helper of human beings, deeply interested in their welfare. Hence, the righteous praise him with one

From Jenny Rose, *Zoroastrianism: An Introduction*, I. B. Tauris, 2011. Reprinted by permission of the publisher.

accord as their father and lord, while the entire creation sings to his glory....

Ahura Mazda is the eternal source of all blessings and benefactions. To those who turn to him in joy and sorrow, and who trust in his infinite goodness, he is all merciful. His goodness extends to the good and evil alike, for his nature can never contemplate evil of any kind. He knows the infirmities of human nature ... and therefore forgives the transgressions of the penitent. He is the divine law-giver and sovereign judge; naturally, his justice demands that each person receive his or her just dues. Rebels, therefore, have little hope of receiving reward from Ahura Mazda. Nevertheless, the wicked are not lost forever. For the all-merciful Ahura Mazda will ultimately, at the end of time, redeem them from their sinful past.

Thus, to know Ahura Mazda is to live in accordance with his divine will; to offer to him praise, worship, and devotion; to please him in purity of thought, word, and deed; to serve him not out of fear but out of love; and to further his cause by joining his forces to combat evil. Ahura Mazda has no beginning or end. His absolute nature, particularly his character of wisdom and goodness, remain unchanged forever.

AHRIMAN

... Evil, in the Zoroastrian faith, is considered to have as independent and complete an existence as good. Both exist entirely separate from each other and are primeval. Neither good originates from evil, nor evil from good. The fundamental purpose of all human beings is to maintain the well-being of the created order of Ahura Mazda. He is absolutely good and, therefore, cannot be considered the creator of any kind of evil, natural or moral. All the evil in the world is the creative work of Ahriman.

Ahriman, then, is considered to be the inveterate foe of the supreme God, Ahura Mazda, and the origin of all suffering, affliction, bodily deformities, evil, and death. His place was originally in the pit of endless darkness, but in the beginning of Ahura Mazda's creation he rushed upon the entire world to bring harm and destruction. For every one of Ahura Mazda's benevolent spiritual powers, Ahriman conjured up an opposing malevolent creature of equivalent rank and power as aides to counterbalance every good creation of Ahura Mazda with an evil one of his own. Thus, the phenomenal world consists of pairs of conflicting opposites: light/dark, truth/falsehood, health/sickness, rain/drought, pure/impure, good creatures/noxious creatures, life/death, heaven/hell.

Because Ahriman is not omniscient, he cannot foresee his own final defeat. And since he is an after-thinker, he knows nothing of events to come. He is stupid, ill-informed, totally ignorant, and blind. He was not even aware of the existence of Ahura Mazda until he arose from his eternal place in the abyss.

Ahriman prompts all human beings to perform evil deeds and instigates discord, violence, and licentiousness. He deceives human beings and obstructs them from hearing and accepting the message of Ahura Mazda. He is a father of lies, a murderer from the beginning, and the source of death. He is an oppressor of mankind's happiness as well as the inveterate enemy of Ahura Mazda. He rules over a large host of evil spirits that will all be defeated eventually in a decisive combat.

One of Ahriman's many malicious acts was to infest the earth with noxious creatures, such as snakes, scorpions, lizards, frogs, and many others. Hence, killing these noxious creatures is considered by Zoroastrians a meritorious deed. Again, Ahriman introduced evil into vegetation by producing weeds, thorns, poison ivy, and many other harmful elements of nature. But little does he realize that his evil existence will cease at the hands of Ahura Mazda when the end of his allotted time arrives.

COSMIC DUALISM

The Zoroastrian concept of dualism, as noted above, is not the metaphysical dualism of spirit and matter that the Pythagorean and Orphic religions taught, and Plato and other philosophers believed. It is the dualism of two opposing, personified forces in the universe, a good God and an evil adversary. This type of thinking may be described as cosmic dualism, since the entire cosmos, heaven, earth, and the underworld, along with their inhabitants, are involved in the opposition between the powers of good and evil.

Ahura Mazda personifies the principle and source of all good: success, glory, honour, physical health, and immortality. Ahriman embodies the principle and source of all evil: misfortune, disaster, war, sickness, and death. Ahura Mazda created heaven, earth, and mankind. Moreover, he represents light, truth, justice, and life. Ahriman is the originator and initiator of all evil. He represents darkness, falsehood, injustice, and the absence of life.

The struggle of Ahura Mazda and Ahriman in Zoroastrian teaching extends over the entire seen and unseen world. This world is a great battlefield in which the beneficent powers of Ahura Mazda ceaselessly contend with the baleful forces of Ahriman. Light struggles with darkness, the vivifying waters with drought and barrenness, warmth with icy conditions, useful animals with beasts of prey, industrious peasants and herdsmen with marauding nomads, civilized people with barbarians; the destructive forces both in nature and in society are not guided by chance or blind laws, but by the warring of benevolent and malevolent powers.

To Zoroastrians, therefore, the universe is an eternal battleground where a pair of coexistent, divine, and warring principles combat. In every sphere and in every situation demanding a decision between two opposites, human beings have to make a choice between these two principles. The consequences alone imply that the principle of good is more powerful than the principle of evil, and that therefore Ahura Mazda eventually triumphs.

Thus, Zoroastrian teaching depicts Ahura Mazda and Ahriman as two adversaries having contrary and incompatible natures. They seem to have existed in this state from the beginning, since the question of their origin is not raised. What is emphatically stated, however, is that good is good and evil is evil, and it is impossible for the one to proceed from the other. To deny the existence of a separate principle of evil is unthinkable in Zoroastrian belief, because it is tantamount to imputing evil to Ahura Mazda.

If Ahura Mazda is good, then he cannot produce evil; if he is perfect, then nothing can be added to him. All the evil and injury in this universe is caused by Ahriman. How can one conceive of Ahura Mazda as an omnipotent and wholly perfect god if Ahriman is responsible for evil and can invade and hold sway over the creation of Ahura Mazda? The answer lies in the limitation of the power of Ahriman and the triumph of Ahura Mazda in the end. Ahriman is never equal to Ahura Mazda. He is handicapped by possessing "backward knowledge." He cannot foresee what Ahura Mazda invents; all he can do is to set up an opposed power, a means of attack. Hence, Ahriman is limited in power, knowledge, and time, and ultimately doomed to defeat.

C. KARMA, REBIRTH, AND EVIL

37 KARMA AND REBIRTH

RAYNOR JOHNSON

If we understand the problem of evil as the challenge of explaining how an all-good, all-powerful God can create a world containing evil, then that issue presents no difficulty for anyone who does not affirm the existence of such a deity. But the problem of evil can be reformulated as the challenge of explaining how a good world can contain evil. In other words, if the world has a moral structure, why do bad things happen to good people, and good things happen to bad people?

The major religions of South Asia, including Jainism, Hinduism, and Buddhism, about each of which we shall read more later, explain the existence of evil by invoking two related doctrines: karma and rebirth. Karma is the English form of the Sanskrit word "karman," meaning "action." The term refers to impersonal causal laws that describe how the world works, ensuring that an individual's good acts lead to pleasant results, while bad acts lead to unpleasant results. Admittedly, such consequences may not occur in the course of a single life. They take effect, however, when we are reborn. If our actions have been morally good, our next life will occur in more favorable circumstances; if our actions have been morally bad, our next life will occur in less favorable circumstances.

In our next selection Raynor Johnson (1901–1987), an English physicist who developed an interest in psychical research, presents a case for karma and rebirth.

I. THE CASE FOR PRE-EXISTENCE

We start from indisputable ground. Here we are on earth, going through a set of experiences in physical form along with millions of others. We were born into these conditions, into a particular nation and a particular family, without, so far as we are aware, having had any opportunity of choice in these matters. Let us look particularly at the tragic side of life, because this presents the thoughtful person with doubts and problems far more than does the attractive and happy side of life. We see children born into the world under the greatest variety of conditions. Some have sound, healthy bodies with good brains, keen, alert and capable, when fully matured, of sustaining great thoughts. Others are handicapped from the beginning with unhealthy bodies, blindness, deafness, disease and defective intelligence. For some the environment is one of security and affection, encouragement, culture and aesthetic interest; for others it is depravity, squalor and ugliness, and one of indifference or gross cruelty by the parents. For some, opportunity stands knocking at the door waiting to welcome and assist; for others it passes by, or knocks too late. Are these things just chance, or are they "planned by God"? If neither of these alternatives is acceptable, what explanation have we to offer which carries with it the reasonable assurance that we live in a just

From Raynor Johnson, *The Imprisoned Splendor*, Hodder and Stoughton, 1953. Reprinted by permission of the publisher.

world? If God is just, and good and all-loving, the person who supposes each soul born into the world to be a new creation of God is faced with a real dilemma. There is no doubt that the conditions into which some souls are born preclude their proper development in this life. In some cases the physical body is a wretched tenement … In other cases the environment of fear, cruelty and brutality is calculated to crush and brutalise before the child's personality can possibly resist it. Is it conceivable that God is capable of doing something which any ordinary decent person would do all in his power to prevent or mitigate? The Christian, at least, should remember the words of Jesus, "If ye then, being evil, know how to give good gifts unto your children, *how much more* shall your Father which is in heaven give good things to them that ask Him?" The commonplace orthodox answer to this dilemma is quite frankly an evasion. It runs something like this. "Certainly there is inequality, but in the light of a future state there is justice too. Life, we must remember, is a handicap race. To whom much was given, from him much will be required. Shakespeares and Newtons must make good use of their talents. The … suffering and crushed must do their best, realising that God is just and merciful, that He only expects achievement commensurate with their talents, and that in the end all will have been found to be worth while." However true these affirmations may be, they do not face the problem, which is concerned not with compensations in a future state, but with an explanation of the present state. There is an obvious way out of the difficulty—namely, to abandon the idea that each soul born into this world is in some mysterious way a fresh creation of God. If we do so we need not assume that chance or accident is an alternative "explanation" of the gross inequalities at birth. We can take our stand on the Law of Cause and Effect, and say that all these grossly unequal conditions of birth and childhood are the results of prior causes. Since these causes are not by any means apparent in the present lives, this involves as a logical necessity the pre-existence of souls. It is then possible to affirm

that we are the product of our past, that present circumstances arise as the result of self-generated forces in states of prior existence.

It is curious that in the West we have come to accept the Law of Cause and Effect without question in the scientific domain, but seem reluctant to recognise its sway on other levels of significance. Yet every great religion teaches this as part of its ethical code. "Whatsoever a man sows that shall he also reap." In [Asian] philosophy this is the great Law of Karma. Whatsoever a man sows, whether in the field of action or thought, sometime and somewhere the fruits of it will be reaped by him. As a boomerang thrown by a skilled person will move rapidly away to a great distance on a circular path, but finally returns to the hand of the thrower, so there is an inexorable law of justice which runs through the world on all these levels. There is no question of rewards and punishments at all: it is simply a question of inevitable consequence, and applies equally to good things and evil things….

Such a viewpoint is logical, and avoids the incredible supposition that God places one newly created soul in a position of advantage and another in a position of extreme disadvantage, and in effect tells them both to make the best of it. If we suppose that a man is born [disabled] because of his activity in previous lives it may seem brutal, but let us be clear that it is not the explanation which is brutal, but the facts. Heredity, of course, is operative: no one denies this. It must, however, be seen as an effect as well as a cause. Looking behind the heredity, we infer, on this view, that the Law of Karma operates so as to direct or draw a person to be born to certain parents under certain conditions.

The pre-existence of the human soul is also supported by the widely different degrees of spiritual achievement we find around us. There is a vast gulf between the spiritual quality of the best person we know and the worst, between the saint or sage on the one hand and a degenerate wretch on the other. It is so great a gulf that many consider it cannot be accounted for in terms of failure or achievement in one life-span of seventy years. It seems to me to represent a gulf quite as enormous as that which on the physical evolutionary level separates primitive and advanced forms of life. It suggests the probability that the two spiritual states are the culmination of very varying moral and spiritual struggle through a long past....

The commonplace matter of family differences is one which must frequently create speculation. Physical differences and likenesses are doubtless covered by genetical laws, but differences of a profound kind in mental, moral and artistic characteristics sometimes occur, and remain quite inexplicable on biological grounds. This would not be unreasonable if we assume that each soul has a long past behind it, and was drawn to incarnate according to karmic laws in a family whose parents could provide him with the physical vehicle and environment most suited to his further development. It has been remarked that Johann Sebastian Bach was born into a family with a long musical tradition, but we need not infer from this that his genius could be accounted for by his heredity. Rather the view would be that his musical genius needed a special quality of physical vehicle and a certain environment for its satisfactory expression and further progress, and his soul chose, or was directed towards, parents capable of providing that opportunity. The soul determines the heredity, not the heredity the soul....

2. THE IDEA OF REINCARNATION

If the case for pre-existence is considered a strong one, then the idea of re-incarnation presents no logical difficulties, whatever be the emotional reaction to it. What the soul has done once by the process of incarnation in a physical body, it can presumably do again.... We should of course bear in mind that what is meant by the phrase "have lived before" is not that the physical form Raynor Johnson has lived on earth previously, but rather that Raynor Johnson is only a particular and temporary expression of an underlying immortal soul which has adopted previous and quite possibly different appearances....

3. SOME OBJECTIONS TO REINCARNATION

There is a number of questions which inevitably arise in the mind of anyone who seriously considers this subject.

Why do persons not remember their past lives? It is, I think, a reasonable reply to say that when we know how memory works we may hope to have an answer. The memory of events in our present life gets more and more sparse and uncertain as we go back to early years. Few people can recall much of the third year of their life, and almost certainly nothing of the second year of life. This datum of observation suggests that we ought not *normally* to expect to recover memories of pre-existent life, and their absence should not be taken as evidence against pre-existence. It may be remarked that under hypnosis extremely early memories have been recovered from the deeper mind, which must clearly store them somehow. All that we may deduce from this is that if the memories of pre-existent lives are in fact recoverable, we should only expect it to be possible in unusual circumstances or with a special technique....

There are some persons who feel antipathetic to the conception of Karma on the ground that it leads to fatalism. By fatalism we understand a philosophy of life which assumes that all that we experience arises from a destiny or powers outside ourselves which we can in no way influence or control. It makes human life the sport of destiny, and necessarily leads to resigned indifference or cynicism. Such a philosophy is not a legitimate deduction from the idea of Karma, which says, rather, that there is no fate or destiny which we have not made and do not make for ourselves. We are today the product of our long past, and we shall be tomorrow what we make of ourselves today.

38 KARMA, REBIRTH, AND THE PROBLEM OF EVIL

WHITLEY R. P. KAUFMAN

In our next selection, Whitley R. P. Kaufman, Associate Professor of Philosophy at the University of Massachusetts Lowell, argues that the doctrines of karma and rebirth do not provide a satisfactory explanation of how a moral world can contain evil.

According to the seed that's sown
So is the fruit ye reap therefrom.
Doer of good will gather good,
Doer of evil, evil reaps.
Sown is the seed, and thou shalt taste
The fruit thereof.
Samyutta Nikaya[1]

The doctrine of karma and rebirth represents perhaps the most striking difference between Western (Judeo-Christian and Islamic) religious thought and the great Indian religious traditions (Hindu, Buddhist, Jain). To be sure, Western theology also makes use of a retributive explanation of evil in which an individual's suffering is accounted for by his previous wrongdoing. But given the obviously imperfect correlation between sin and suffering in an individual's lifetime, Western religions have resorted to other explanations of suffering (including, notoriously, that of Original Sin). However, Indian thought boldly combines this retributionism with the idea of multiple human incarnations, so that all suffering in this life can be explained by each individual's prior wrongdoing, whether in this or in a prior life, and all wrongdoing in the present life will be punished in either this or a future life. In this way, Indian thought is able to endorse a complete and consistent retributive explanation of evil: all suffering can be explained by the wrongdoing of the sufferer himself. As Ananda Coomaraswamy de-

clares, in answer to the question "Who did sin, this man or his parents, that he was born blind?": "The Indian theory replies without hesitation, *this man.*"[2]

It is frequently claimed that the doctrine of karma and rebirth provides Indian religion with a more emotionally and intellectually satisfying account of evil and suffering than do typical Western solutions to the problem of evil. Thus, for Max Weber, karma

stands out by virtue of its consistency as well as by its extraordinary metaphysical achievement: It unites virtuoso-like self-redemption by man's own effort with universal accessibility of salvation, the strictest rejection of the world with organic social ethics, and contemplation as the paramount path to salvation with an inner-worldly vocational ethic.[3]

Arthur Herman, in his classic *The Problem of Evil and Indian Thought*, similarly asserts the superiority of karma to all Western theodicies: "Unlike the Western theories, … the doctrine of rebirth is capable of meeting the major objections against which those Western attempts all failed" (Herman 1976, p. 287).[4] Michael Stoeber also claims that the Indian idea of rebirth is "more plausible" than traditional Christian ideas such as purgatory (Stoeber 1992, p. 167). And the karma doctrine appears to be increasing in popularity in the West as well, perhaps because of these perceived advantages.

However, despite these and similar enthusiastic endorsements, karma as a theodicy has still

From Whitley R. P. Kaufman, "Karma, Rebirth, and the Problem of Evil," *Philosophy East & West* 59:1, 2005. Reprinted by permission of the University of Hawaii Press.

received comparatively little critical analysis in comparison with the scrutiny to which dominant Western ideas such as Original Sin or free will have been subjected.... In this essay ... I will limit my discussion to the specific question of whether a karma-and-rebirth theory, even if true, could solve the problem of evil. That is, can it provide a satisfactory explanation of the (apparent) unfairness, injustice, and innocent suffering in the world? I will argue here that the doctrine, in whatever form it is proposed, suffers from serious limitations that render it unlikely to provide a satisfactory solution to the problem of evil....

KARMA AS SYSTEMATIC THEODICY: FIVE MORAL OBJECTIONS

The advantages of the karma theory are obvious and I will not dwell on them here. It is repeatedly pointed out, for example, that it can explain the suffering of innocent children, or congenital illnesses, with which Western thought has great difficulty. It is further argued that it is a more profoundly just doctrine, in that the fact of multiple existences gives the possibility of multiple possibilities for salvation – indeed, that in the end there can be universal salvation. This is again in contrast to the Western tradition, in which there is only one bite at the apple; those who fail in this life are doomed to eternal perdition. However, the doctrine as a whole is subject to a number of serious objections. Here I will present five distinct objections to the rebirth doctrine, all of which raise serious obstacles to the claim that rebirth can provide a convincing solution to the Problem of Evil. I do not claim this to be an exhaustive list, nor do I claim that everyone will agree with each of them. However, I think that they are serious enough as to require at the very least a fuller and more detailed defense of karma as theodicy than has so far been given.

The Memory Problem

An oft-raised objection to the claim of prior existences is the utter lack of any memory traces of previous lives. Both Paul Edwards and Bruce Reichenbach point out the oddity that all of us have had long, complex past lives, yet none of us have any recollection of them at all. More often, this objection is raised to cast doubt on whether we did in fact have any past lives at all. But my concern here is the *moral* issue raised by this deficiency: justice demands that one who is being made to suffer for a past crime be made aware of his crime and understand why he is being punished for it. Thus, even Christmas Humphreys in his vigorous defense of karma concedes the "injustice of our suffering for the deeds of someone about whom we remember nothing" (Humphreys 1983, p. 84). A conscientious parent explains to his child just why he is being punished; our legal system treats criminal defendants in just the same way. Would not a compassionate deity or a just system make sure the guilty party knows what he has done wrong? It is true that one's belief that all crime is eventually punished might serve a disciplinary function even where one is not aware just what one is being punished for at the time. However, the fact that the sufferer can never know just what crime he is being punished for at a given time, that the system of meting out punishments is so random and unpredictable, constitutes a violation of a basic principle of justice.

Moreover, the memory problem renders the karmic process essentially useless as a means of moral education. Yet, strikingly, it is regularly claimed by adherents that one of the great virtues of karma and rebirth is precisely that "the doctrine presupposes the possibility of moral growth" and that rewards and punishments "constitute a discipline of natural consequences to educate man morally."[5] For example, suppose I am diagnosed with cancer: this must be a punishment for something I have done wrong – but I have no idea what I did to deserve this, or whether it occurred yesterday, last week, or infinitely many past lives ago. For that matter, I might be committing a sin right now – only I will not know it is a sin, because the punishment might occur next week, next year, or in the next life. Radakrishnan suggests that retaining memory could be a hindrance to our moral development, since it would bring in memories of lower existences in the past (see Minor 1986, p. 32). But even if this is occasionally true, it is hardly plausible to say it is better *never* or even rarely to remember past deeds or lives; acknowledging past mistakes is in general an important (even essential) educating force in our lives. Yet none of us does remember such past events, nor is there definitive evidence that anyone has *ever* recalled a past life.

The memory problem is particularly serious for the karmic doctrine, since most wrongs will be punished in a later life, and most suffering is the result of wrongdoing in prior existences. (Recall that the theory is forced into this position in order to explain the obvious fact that most misdeeds do *not* get automatically punished in this world, and most suffering is not obviously correlated with wickedness.) How, then, can it be said that the doctrine promotes moral education? It is not an answer to say that our knowledge of moral duties can come from elsewhere, from religious scripture, for example. For the point is that the mechanism of karma itself is poorly designed for the purposes of moral education or progress, given the apparently random and arbitrary pattern of rewards and punishments. If moral education were truly the goal of karma and rebirth, then either punishment would be immediately consequent on sin, or at least one would have some way of knowing what one was being punished (or rewarded) for.

In fact, the difficulty is not merely one of moral education. It has been pointed out that the total lack of memory renders the theory more of a *revenge* theory than a retributive one – and hence morally unacceptable.[6] That is, it suggests that justice is satisfied merely because satisfaction has been taken on the perpetrator of the crime, ignoring completely a central moral element of punishment: that the offender where possible be made aware of his crime, that he acknowledge what he has done wrong and repent for it, that he attempt to atone for his crime, and so forth. As such the rebirth theory fails to respect the moral agency of the sinner in that it is apparently indifferent to whether or not he understands that what he has done is wrong. As Reichenbach rightly points out, the lack of memory prevents one from undergoing the moral process involved in repentance for one's crimes and even attempted

rectification for them (p. 95). Further, as Francis Clooney recognizes, the lack of memory of prior lives undermines the pastoral effectiveness of karma as providing comfort to the sufferer: "little comfort is given to the suffering person who is usually thought not to remember anything of the culprit past deeds" (p. 535). A vague assurance that one must have done unremembered terrible deeds in the past is hardly satisfactory.

The Proportionality Problem

The rebirth solution to the Problem of Evil purports to explain every ill and benefit of this life by prior good or bad conduct. To be a morally adequate solution it must presuppose as well (although this is rarely stated explicitly) a proportionality principle – that the severity of suffering be appropriately proportioned to the severity of the wrong. But herein lies a problem: given the kinds and degrees of suffering we see in this life, it is hard to see what sort of sins the sufferers could have committed to deserve such horrible punishment. Think of those who slowly starve to death along with their family in a famine; those with severe depression or other mental illness; those who are tortured to death; young children who are rendered crippled for life in a car accident; those who die of incurable brain cancer; those burned to death in a house fire. It is difficult to believe that every bit of this kind of suffering was genuinely earned. One may grant that we as finite humans are not always in a position to judge what is just or unjust from God's perspective; nevertheless, the point of the rebirth theory is precisely to make suffering comprehensible to us as a form of justice. Indeed, belief in karma might make us tend to enact even more brutal and cruel penalties (e.g., torturing to death) if we try to model human justice on this conception of what apparently counts as divine justice.

The evidence from our own practices is that in fact we do not consider such punishments morally justified. For example, capital punishment is considered excessive and inappropriate as punishment even for a crime as serious as rape. Yet according to the karma theory every one of us without exception is condemned to "capital punishment," that is, inevitable physical death, even apart from the various other sufferings we have to endure. An eye-for-an-eye version of the rebirth theory holds that if one is raped in this life it is because one must have been a rapist in a past life, and what could be fairer than that whatever harm one caused to others will be caused to you later? But it is hard to believe that we are all subject to death because we have all been murderers in a past life. Moreover, this answer simply will not work for most diseases (one cannot "cause" another to have Parkinson's or brain cancer). (It also leads to an infinite regress problem, on which see below). It is certainly hard to stomach the notion that the inmates of Auschwitz and Buchenwald did something so evil in the past that they merely got what was coming to them – but the rebirth theory is committed to just this position.

Nor does the idea of the "pool of karmic residues" solve this problem: it is equally hard to believe that even an enormous accumulation of past bad acts could justify the horrible suffering of this world, or indeed that fairness would allow all one's lesser wrongs to accumulate and generate a single, horrible punishment rather than smaller punishments over a longer period. Indeed, it raises the question of fairness of the mechanism: why would some people be punished separately for each individual wrong, while others are punished only all at once and horribly (further undermining the possibility of moral education, one might note)?

The Infinite Regress Problem

In order to explain an individual's circumstances in the present life, karma refers to the events of his prior life. But in order to explain the circumstances of that prior life, we need to invoke the events of his previous life – and so on, ad infinitum. The problem is quite general: how did the karmic process begin? What was the first wrong? Who was the original sufferer? This familiar objection points out that rebirth provides no solution at all, but simply pushes the problem back.[7] And the response typically given by defenders of rebirth is quite inadequate: they claim that the process is simply beginningless (*anādi*), that the karmic pro-

cess extends back infinitely in time.[8] But this is no answer at all; indeed, it violates a basic canon of rationality, that the "explanation" not be equally as problematic as the problem being explained. Thus, explains Wendy O'Flaherty: "Karma 'solves' the problem of the origin of evil by saying that there *is* no origin.... But this ignores rather than solves the problem" (p. 17).

Roy Perrett has responded to this criticism by arguing that the doctrine of karma satisfactorily explains each individual instance of suffering, and it is unreasonable to demand that it give an "ultimate explanation" of the origin of suffering. After all, he says, "explanation has to come to an end somewhere" (Perrett 1985, p. 7). However, the fallacy in this argument can be illustrated by analogy. Consider the "theory" that the world is supported on the back of an elephant, which in turn rests on the back of a tortoise. Now if this is to be an explanatory account of what supports the world, it only begs the question: what supports the tortoise? A famous (probably apocryphal) exchange between Bertrand Russell and an anonymous woman goes as follows:

Woman: The world rests on the back of a giant turtle.
Russell: What does the turtle rest on?
Woman: Another turtle.
Russell: What does *it* rest on?
Woman: Another turtle.
Russell: What does *it* rest on?

The discussion goes on this way for quite some time, until the woman becomes exasperated and blurts out: "Don't you see, Professor Russell, it's turtles *all the way down*!" It will hardly do for the woman to claim that, as her solution explains how the world is supported in each individual instance, she need not worry about the infinite regress. This solution is the equivalent of borrowing money in order to pay off a debt: a solution that merely postpones the problem is no solution at all.

It is also noteworthy that the denial of a beginning to the process sidesteps the question of divine responsibility for the beginning of evil in the world. If there is a creator, then why is he not responsible for the misdeeds of his creations?

There is no easy answer to this question, but neither can it be avoided altogether. Christianity has long been criticized for its doctrine of the Fall of Man and Original Sin for these same reasons. I do not claim here that the Christian solution succeeds, but only that the Indian solution does not evade these difficulties, either.

The Problem of Explaining Death

If rebirth is to account for all human suffering, it must, of course, explain the paradigmatic case of innocent suffering: death itself. But the problem here is that in the typical rebirth theory death seems not to be presented as punishment for wrong, but rather is *presupposed* as the mechanism by which karma operates. That is, it is through rebirth that one is rewarded or punished for one's past wrongs (by being born in high or low station, healthy or sickly, etc.). But there can be no rebirth unless there is death. So even if one is moving up in the scale of karma to a very high birth for one's great virtue, one must still undergo death. This would appear to undermine the moral justification for (arguably) the greatest of evils, death itself. For in most versions of the theory death is not even taken as something that needs explaining, but is rather assumed as simply the causal process by which karma operates. Indeed, one might well ask why *everyone* is mortal; why are there not at least some who have been virtuous enough to live indefinitely? Did we all commit such terrible wrongs right away that we have always been subject to death? Typically, though, death and rebirth are not themselves morally justified but simply taken as the neutral mechanism of karma (see, e.g., Humphreys, p. 22).

There are several ways one might try to get around this problem. Max Weber suggests that the finiteness of good deeds in our life accounts for the finiteness of our life span.[9] But this entails a quite different karmic system, one in which one is punished not for positive misdeeds, but for the lack of infinitely many good deeds. It also seems to suggest that we are morally required to be infinitely good to avoid death – a rather implausible moral demand on us and one that undermines the moral justification of karma to be a fair system of

rewards and punishments (one might ask why we are not rewarded with infinitely long life for not committing "infinite evil"). Moreover, there is a troublesome hint of circularity in Weber's solution: it seems odd to say that the finiteness of our life span derives from the finiteness of our goodness; to do infinitely much good one apparently needs an infinitely long life.

Another possible solution is simply to deny that death is indeed an evil, since it is the means by which one reaches greater rewards in life. But this is hardly satisfying, for there is no reason at all that death needs to be the mechanism by which one attains one's rewards: why not simply reward the person with health, wealth, and long life, without having to undergo rebirth in the first place? Karma certainly does not need death and rebirth: as soon as one accumulates sufficient merit, one could be instantly transformed into a higher state of existence. Further, this solution simply resorts to denial of the commonsense fact that death usually involves a terrible and often physically painful disruption of one's existence, including the separation from all one's loved ones and from all that one holds dear.

A different strategy might be to say that the ultimate reward is indeed escape from death, the release from the cycle of *saṃsāra* or rebirth, as many Indians believe. The trouble with this solution is, to put it colloquially, that it throws out the baby with the bathwater. The problem of evil arises not because life itself is an unmitigated evil, but because it contains such a strange mixture of good and evil. Karma implies that all of the good in life – health, wealth, happiness – is due to our good deeds. Why, then, is not perfect goodness rewarded with a perfectly good earthly life (one without death, pain, sickness, poverty, etc.)? If the idea that the ultimate goal is escape from life itself, it simply goes too far.[10] The idea of Nirvāna in Indian thought is often identified with release from not only the evil in life, but from all aspects of life, the good and the bad.[11] But to say that life itself (not just the bad aspects of it) is the problem cannot be a solution to the problem of evil, but rather an admission of failure to solve it. For why is life bad, full of suffering and misery, rather than good? It is also an implausible claim, since experience shows that life can be very good indeed, so why is it not good all the time?

The Free Will Problem

The karma solution is often presented as the ideal solution that respects free moral agency: one determines one's own future by one's present deeds. In fact, as is often pointed out, karma is paradoxically both a fatalist and a freewill theory. For Keyes, karma "manages to affirm and deny human responsibility at the same time" (p. 175); Walli tries to account for this peculiarity by interpreting karma in two stages: in the early stages of existence it is fatalistic, but later it becomes a "moral force" (Walli 1977, p. 328). It is often noted that, despite the promise of control over one's destiny, in practice the doctrine of karma can often result instead in an attitude of fatalistic pessimism in the believer. Thus, Berger argues that by legitimating the conditions of all social classes, karma "constitutes the most thoroughly conservative religious system devised in history" (p. 65).

Karma is also praised as a freewill theory on the grounds that it gives the individual multiple (infinitely many?) chances to reach salvation in future lives. However, it is not clear whether the multiple-life theory in fact constitutes an advantage over Christian doctrine. Since in Christianity the individual has but one life in which to earn salvation, this entails a high degree of moral importance to one's life (especially given that death could come at any time). In contrast, for karma there is no such urgency, for all mistakes and misdeeds can be rectified in the fullness of future lives. The significance of a particular lifetime, let alone a particular action, is radically diminished if the "life of the individual is only an ephemeral link in a causal chain that extends infinitely into both past and future" (Berger, p. 65). Again, this could encourage fatalism, a sense that one's choice here and now does not matter much in the greater scheme of things.

But a deeper problem is whether the doctrine of karma can in fact be squared at all with the existence of free moral agency. The difficulty can be illustrated with the following example. Consider the potential terrorist, who is deciding whether to draw attention to his political cause by detonating a bomb in a civilian area. How are we to reconcile the automatic functioning of karma with the man's choice? The karma solution must face a dilemma here. There is either of the following possibilities:

(1) Karma functions in a determinate and mechanical fashion. Then, whomever the terrorist kills will not be innocent but deserving of their fate. From the terrorist's perspective, if he is the agent of karma his action is no more blameworthy than that of the executioner who delivers the lethal injection. Indeed, no matter what evils he does in the world, he can always justify them to himself by saying he is merely an agent for karma, carrying out the necessary punishments for these "wicked" people. Alternatively, it may be that his potential victims do not deserve to die this way, in which case the man must be determined not to kill them. In either case, freedom of the will (supposedly a virtue of the karma theory) is absent.

(2) The other possibility might be countenanced as a way to preserve freedom of the will. Perhaps it really is up to the terrorist to choose whether to kill his victims. Indeed, let us say that he has the potential to create genuine evil: to kill innocent, undeserving civilians. But now the problem is that a central, indeed crucial, tenet of the karma theory has been abandoned: that *all suffering* is deserved and is justified by one's prior wrongful acts. For now we have admitted the genuine possibility of gratuitous evil, innocent suffering—just what the theory was designed to deny. One could, of course, suggest that such gratuitous suffering will eventually be fully compensated for in a future life. But this, as Arthur Herman recognizes, would be a theory very different from that of karma. It would be a doctrine that asserts that all suffering will be *compensated* for (eventually) rather than holding that all suffering is *justified* (i.e., by one's misdeeds). Herman rightly rejects this alternative version of the theory as a recompense, not a karma, theory (p. 213).[12]

This dilemma also undermines the idea of karma as a predictive, causal law (a status often asserted for it). Further, either horn of the dilemma undermines the moral-education function of karma as well (see Herman, p. 215). In (1) one cannot learn because one apparently cannot do wrong. In (2) if one suffers, one can never know if it is because one has done wrong or because of the gratuitous harm caused by the wrongdoing of others. Similarly, if one enjoys success one can never know if it is because of one's merits or because it is payback for the gratuitous evil one suffered earlier.

Reichenbach (p. 94) suggests a way in which some defenders of the doctrine of karma have tried to evade this difficulty and preserve the reality of free will: by asserting that karma explains only evil that is not caused by wrongful human choices (i.e., karma is a theory of "moral evil" rather than of "natural evil"). But this strategy is troublesome. First, there are innumerable cases where the categories of moral-versus-natural evil seem to break down: harm caused or contributed to by human negligence (negligent driving of a car, failing to make buildings earthquake proof); harm that was not directly caused but that was anticipated and could have been prevented (starvation in Africa); harm caused in cases of insanity or diminished mental capacity; harm caused while in a state of intoxication (drunk driving); and so forth. In such cases it is doubtful that we could draw a clear distinction between moral and natural evil, but the strategy fails if one cannot draw such a line. Moreover, the great comforting and consoling function of the karma doctrine is gone: one cannot be sure whether or not one's suffering is retribution for past wrong, and one cannot even know which of one's sufferings are punishments for one's prior wrongs and which are not. Even more importantly, this strategy represents not so much a solution to the difficulty as a whole-hearted concession to the radical limitations of the theory, an admission that enormous amounts of suffering cannot be explained or justified in terms of just punishment for past wrongs. One can no longer be sure whether the circumstances one is born into (e.g., poverty) are the result of one's previous sins or of someone else's wrongdoing. This revised explanation of moral evil presumes that suffering can be random, inexplicable, meaningless, freely chosen without regard to the victim's deserts, while the explanation of natural evil presumes that all suffering is explicable and

justified. One might wonder whether the explanations of moral and natural evil are now so much at such cross-purposes that the rebirth theory as a whole loses its coherence.

Thus, the dilemma seems to show that karma is simply not consistent with the genuine possibility of free moral choice. The basic problem here is the deep tension (even incompatibility) between the causal determinism implicit in the karma doctrine and the ideal of free moral responsibility, which makes one fully responsible for one's actions. Most commentators never successfully reconcile the two, if indeed they can be reconciled. An example is Hiriyanna, who insists that "everything that happens in the moral realm is preordained;" but that this is fully consistent with human freedom, by which he means "being determined by oneself" (pp. 46–7 and n. 23). It is not clear how one can escape this contradiction. The more one insists on human freedom, the less are events in the world subject to karmic determination.

The difficulty is even worse for the interpretation of karma that extends the idea of causal determinism to one's character or disposition in future lives. Thus, someone who does evil will inherit in the next life not only lowly circumstances but also a wicked, malevolent disposition; those who have a good disposition owe it to their good deeds in previous lives. Now even one's character and moral choice are influenced, even determined by, one's past lives; this threatens to do away with free moral choice altogether. And once one has a wicked disposition, it is a puzzle how one can escape spiraling down into further wrongdoing, or at best being permanently stuck at a given moral level, if karma has already determined one's moral character. (The problem is exaggerated even further if one accepts the view that particularly bad people become animals; how could one ever escape one's animal state, since animals do not appear to be capable of moral choice at all?)

There is in the end a fatalistic dilemma for the theory. Either the karma theory is a complete and closed causal account of evil and suffering or it is not. That is, either the present state of affairs is fully explained causally by reference to prior events (including human actions) or it is not. If it is fully explained, then there can be no progress or indeed no change at all in the world. Past evil will generate present evil, and present evil will in turn cause equivalent future evil. There is no escape from the process. Alternatively, if there is the possibility of change, then karma must no longer be a complete causal account. That is, it fails as a systematic theory and therefore cannot in fact solve the problem of evil, since there must be evil in the world for which it cannot account.

KARMA AND THE VERIFIABILITY PROBLEM

There is one final matter that I think has significant moral relevance in this debate: the charge that the rebirth (or preexistence) doctrine is objectionable because it is *unveritiable* (or unfalsifiable).[13] Whatever happens is consistent with the theory; no fact could apparently falsify it. Whatever the terrorist does is (as Humphreys insists) simply the determination of karma. Further, one has no capacity effectively to predict the future by this theory. Even if one has done wrong (assuming that there are precise guidelines for what counts as wrongdoing, a difficult assumption in a world of moral dilemmas), one has no way of knowing just what the punishment will be, or when it will occur, in this life or the next. A remarkable example of the willing endorsement of the advantages of unfalsifiability is made by Arthur Herman in defending karma:

> Thus no matter how terrible and awe-inspiring the suffering may be, the rebirth theorist can simply attribute the suffering to previous misdeeds done in previous lives, and the puzzle is over. Extraordinary evil is solved with no harm done to the majesty and holiness of deity.[14]

Another defender of karma and transmigration also unwittingly demonstrates the problem with such theories. He claims that the evidence for transmigration is provided by the law of karma itself (i.e., the law of moral cause and effect), since without the transmigration of souls, karma would be an inadequate solution to the Problem of Evil.[15] Such a justification is transparently circular: it presupposes that the karma solution is true in order to defend it.

Now, one might fairly doubt whether, in general, religious claims can meaningfully be held to the same standards of empirical verification as scientific claims. Nonetheless, the virtue of testability and falsifiability is that it provides a check against all of the familiar human biases: dogmatism, ethnocentrism, and so on. This is a particular problem for the karma theory, since the very unfalsifiability of the doctrine can be used to rationalize the status quo or justify oppression or unfairness on the grounds that their suffering is punishment for their prior wrongs (for they would simply have to pay their debt later). It is widely acknowledged that the repressive caste system in India lasted so long in large part because the doctrine of karma encouraged Indians to accept social oppression as the mechanical workings of karma. Hiriyanna remarkably presents it as an *advantage* of the karma theory that in India sufferers cannot blame God or their neighbors for their troubles, but only themselves (even if their neighbors are indeed unjustly oppressing them).[16] Human fallibility being what it is, the idea that all suffering is due to a previous wrongful action provides a great temptation to rationalize the status quo with reference to unverifiable claims about one's past wrongs. This is surely too great a price to pay for whatever pastoral comfort such fatalistic reassurance provides.

CONCLUSION

I conclude that the doctrine of karma and rebirth, taken as a systematic rational account of human suffering by which all individual suffering is explained as a result of that individual's wrongdoing, is unsuccessful as a theodicy.

NOTES

1. Cited in Keys, p. 262.
2. Coomaraswamy 1964, p. 108. The reference, of course, is to John 9:2, in which Jesus rejects the retributive explanation of a man's blindness.
3. Weber 1947, p. 359.
4. In the second edition, Herman backs off this claim, and says that he now thinks that the traditional problem of evil is "insolvable" (p. viii).
5. Hiriyanna, p. 49; see also Stoeber, p. 178.

6. See, for example, Nayak, quoted in Stoeber, p. 178.
7. See, for example, Watts 1964, p. 38; Hick 1976, pp. 309, 314; Hick 1990, p. 139; and O'Flaherty, p. 17.
8. See Herman, p. 263, and Hiriyanna, pp. 47, 198....
9. Weber 1964, p. 145.
10. See Hick 1976, pp. 321, 437.
11. Hiriyanna, p. 69.
12. See also Reichenbach, p. 17.
13. A problem raised both by Paul Edwards (1996) and Bruce Reichenbach (1990).
14. Herman, p. 287.
15. Hiriyanna, p. 47.
16. Ibid., p. 48 (although he does not specifically mention caste). See Humphreys, p. 55 (the condition of cripples and dwarfs can be justified by their sins).

REFERENCES

Berger Peter, 1967. *The Sacred Canopy*. Garden City, NY: Doubleday.

Clooney, Francis. 1989. "Evil, Divine Omnipotence, and Human Freedom: Vedanta's Theology of Karma." *Journal of Religion* 69: 530–48.

Coomaraswamy, Ananda. 1964. *Buddha and the Gospel of Buddhism*. New York: Harper and Row.

Edwards, Paul. 1996. *Reincarnation: A Critical Examination*. New York: Prometheus Books.

Herman, Arthur. 1976. *The Problem of Evil in Indian Thought*. Delhi: Motilal Banarsidass.

Hick, John. 1976. *Death and Eternal Life*. New York: Harper and Row.

———. 1990. *Philosophy of Religion*. Englewood Cliffs, NJ: Prentice-Hall.

Hiriyanna, M. 1995. *The Essentials of Indian Philosophy*. Delhi: Motilal Banarsidass.

Humphreys, Christmas. 1983. *Karma and Rebirth*. London: Curzon Press.

Keyes, Charles. 1983. "Merit-Transference in the Kammic Theory of Popular Theravada Buddhism." In *Karma*, edited by Charles Keyes and Valentine Daniel. Berkeley: University of California Press.

Minor, Robert. 1986. "In Defense of Karma and Rebirth: Evolutionary Karma." In Ronald Neufeldt, ed., *Karma and Rebirth*. Albany: State University of New York Press.

O'Flaherty, Wendy Doniger. 1976. *The Origins of Evil in Hindu Mythology*. Berkeley: University of California Press.

Perrett, Roy. 1985. "Karma and the Problem of Suffering." *Sophia* 24: 4–10.

Reichenbach, Bruce. 1990. *The Law of Karma*. Honolulu: University of Hawai'i Press.

Stoeber, Michael. 1992. *Evil and the Mystics' Cod*. Toronto: University of Toronto Press.

Walli, Koshelya. 1977. *Theory of Karman in Indian Thought*. Bharata Mahisha.

Watts, Alan. 1964. *Beyond Theology*. New York: Vintage Books.

Weber, Max. 1947. *Essays in Sociology*. Translated by H. H. Certh and C. Wright Mills. London: K. Paul, Trench, Trubner.

———. 1964. *The Sociology of Religion*. Translated by Ephraim Fischoff. Boston: Beacon Press. (Original publication date in German: 1922).

PART FIVE

Avenues to the Divine

A. PRAYER

39 PETITIONARY PRAYER

ELEONORE STUMP

Returning to the Abrahamic religions, we find that their adherents are most interested not in proofs for or against the existence of God but rather in exploring avenues to experiencing God. After all, attempted proofs or disproofs of God's existence are of little concern to those who find themselves in God's presence.

One way to seek to experience God is through prayer, and a common form of prayer is petitionary prayer, in which the believer asks God to grant a specific request. But if God is omnipotent, omniscient, and all-good, wouldn't God do what is best regardless of whether anyone prays for a specific outcome? What is the use of petitionary prayer? These and related issues are explored by Eleonore Stump, whose work we read previously.

Ordinary Christian believers of every period have in general taken prayer to be fundamentally a request made of God for something specific believed to be good by the one praying. The technical name for such prayer is "impetration"; I am going to refer to it by the more familiar designation "petitionary prayer." There are, of course, many important kinds of prayer which are not requests; for example, most of what is sometimes called "the higher sort of prayer"—praise, adoration,

From Eleonore Stump, "Petitionary Prayer," *American Philosophical Quarterly* 16, 1979. Reprinted by permission of the journal.

thanksgiving—does not consist in requests and is not included under petitionary prayer. But basic, common petitionary prayer poses problems that do not arise in connection with the more contemplative varieties of prayer, and it is petitionary prayer with its special problems that I want to examine.... The cases which concern me in this paper are those in which someone praying a petitionary prayer makes a specific request freely (at least in his own view) of an omniscient, omnipotent, perfectly good God, conceived of in the traditional orthodox way. I am specifying that the prayers are made freely because I want to discuss this problem on the assumption that man has free will and that not everything is predetermined. I am making this assumption, first because I want to examine the problem of petitionary prayer as it arises for ordinary Christian believers, and I think their understanding of the problem typically includes the assumption that man has free will, and secondly because adopting the opposite view enormously complicates the attempt to understand and justify petitionary prayer. If all things are predetermined—and worse, if they are all predetermined by the omnipotent and omniscient God to whom one is praying—it is much harder to conceive of a satisfactory justification for petitionary prayer. One consequence of my making this assumption is that I will not be drawing on important traditional Protestant accounts of prayer such as those given by Calvin and Luther, for instance, since while they may be thoughtful, interesting accounts, they assume God's complete determination of everything.

I think that I can most effectively and plausibly show the problem which interests me by presenting a sketchy analysis of the Lord's Prayer. It is a prayer attributed to Christ himself, who is supposed to have produced it just for the purpose of teaching his disciples how they ought to pray. So it is an example of prayer which orthodox Christians accept as a paradigm, and it is furthermore, a clear instance of petitionary prayer. Consequently, it is a particularly good example for my purposes. In what follows, I want to make clear, I am not concerned either to take account of contemporary Biblical exegesis or to contribute to it. I want simply to have a look at the prayer—in fact,

at only half the prayer—as it is heard and prayed by ordinary twentieth-century Christians.

As the prayer is given in Luke 11, it contains seven requests. The last four have to do with the personal needs of those praying, but the first three are requests of a broader sort.

The first, "Hallowed be thy name," is commonly taken as a request that God's name be regarded as holy.[1] I am not sure what it means to regard God's name as holy, and I want to avoid worries about the notion of having attitudes towards God's *name*. All the same, I think something of the following sort is a sensible interpretation of the request. The common Biblical notion of holiness has at its root a sense of strong separateness.[2] And it may be that to regard God's name as holy is only to react to it very differently from the way in which one reacts to any other name—and that could happen because it seems specially precious or also (for example) because it seems specially feared. On this understanding of the request, it would be fulfilled if everyone (or almost everyone) took a strongly emotional and respectful attitude towards God's name. But it may be that this is too complicated as an interpretation of the request, and that to regard God's name as holy is simply to love and revere it. In that case, the request is fulfilled if everyone or almost everyone regards God's name very reverentially. And there are New Testament passages which foretell states of affairs fulfilling both these interpretations of the request—prophesying a time at or near the end of the world when all men fear or love God's name, and a time when the inhabitants of earth are all dedicated followers of God.[3]

The second request in the Lord's Prayer is that God's kingdom come. Now according to orthodox Judaeo-Christian beliefs, God is and always has been ruler of the world. What then does it mean to ask for the advent of his kingdom? Plainly, there is at least some sense in which the kingdom of heaven has not yet been established on earth and can be waited and hoped for. And this request seems to be for those millennial times when everything on earth goes as it ought to go, when men beat their swords into plowshares (Is. 2:4) and the wolf dwells at peace with the lamb

(Is. 11:6, 65:25). This too, then, is a request for a certain state of affairs involving all or most men, the state of affairs at the end of the world prophesied under one or another description in Old and New Testament passages (cf., e.g., Rev. 21:1–4).

And it seems closely related to the object of the third request, "Thy will be done on earth as it is in heaven." There is, of course, a sense in which, according to Christian doctrine, God's will is always done on earth. But that is the sense in which God allows things to happen as they do (God's so-called "permissive will"). God permits certain people to have evil intentions, he permits certain people to commit crimes, and so on, so that he wills to let happen what does happen; and in this sense his will is always done. But in heaven, according to Christian doctrine, it is not that God permits what occurs to occur, and so wills in accordance with what happens, but rather that what happens happens in accordance with his will. So only the perfect good willed unconditionally by God is ever done in heaven. For God's will to be done on earth in such a way, everyone on earth would always have to do only good. This request, then, seems to be another way of asking for the establishment of God's kingdom on earth; and it also seems linked with certain New Testament prophecies—there will be a "new earth," and the righteous meek with inherit it (cf., e.g., Mt. 5:5 and Rev. 5:10 and 21:1–4).

What I think is most worth noticing in this context about all three of these first requests of the Lord's Prayer is that it seems absolutely pointless, futile, and absurd to make them. All three seem to be requests for the millennium or for God's full reign on earth. But it appears from New Testament prophecies that God has already determined to bring about such a state of affairs in the future. And if God has predetermined that there will be such a time, then what is asked for in those three requests is already sure to come. But, then, what is the point of making the prayer? Why ask for something that is certain to come whether you beg for it or flee from it? It is no answer to these questions to say, as some theologians have done,[4] that one prays in this way just because Jesus prescribed such a prayer. That attempt at an answer simply transfers responsibility

for the futile action from the one praying to the one being prayed to; it says nothing about what sense there is in the prayer itself. On the other hand, if, contrary to theological appearances, the things prayed for are not predetermined and their occurrence or nonoccurrence is still in doubt, *could* the issue possibly be resolved by someone's asking for one or another outcome? If Jimmy Carter, say (or some other Christian), does not ask for God's kingdom to come, will God therefore fail to establish it? Or will he establish it *just because* Jimmy Carter asked for it, though he would not have done so otherwise? Even Carter's staunchest supporters might well find it frightening to think so; and yet if we do not answer these questions in the affirmative, the prayer seems futile and pointless. So either an omniscient, omnipotent, perfectly good God has predetermined this state of affairs or he hasn't; and either way, asking for it seems to make no sense. This conclusion is applicable to other cases of petitionary prayer as well. To take just one example, suppose that Jimmy Carter prays the altruistic and Christian prayer that a particular atheistic friend of his be converted and so saved from everlasting damnation. If it is in God's power to save that man, won't he do so without Jimmy Carter's prayers? Won't a perfectly good God do all the good he can no matter what anyone prays for or does not pray for? Consequently, either God or his goodness will save the man in any case, so that the prayer is pointless, or there is some point in the prayer but God's goodness appears impugned....

Christian literature contains a number of discussions of the problem with petitionary prayer and various attempts to solve it. For the sake of brevity, I want to look just at the proposed solution Aquinas gives. It is the most philosophically sophisticated of the solutions I know.... The basic argument he relies on to rebut various objections against the usefulness of prayer is this. Divine Providence determines not only what effects there will be in the world, but also what causes will give rise to those effects and in what order they will do so. Now human action, too, are causes. "For," Thomas says, "we pray not in order to change the divine disposition but for the sake of acquiring by petitionary prayer what God has disposed to be achieved by prayer."[5]

Perhaps the first worry which this argument occasions stems from the appearance of theological determinism in it: God determines not only what effects there will be but also what the causes of those effects will be and in what order the effects will be produced. It is hard to see how such a belief is compatible with freedom of the will. In the preamble to this argument, however, Thomas says he is concerned *not* to deny free will but, on the contrary, to give an account of prayer which preserves free will. So I want simply to assume that he has in mind some distinction or some theory which shows that, despite appearances, his argument is not committed to a thorough-going determinism, and I am going to ignore any troubles in the argument having to do with the compatibility of predestination or foreknowledge and free will.

For present purposes, what is more troublesome about this argument is that it does not provide any real help with the problem it means to solve. According to Thomas, there is nothing absurd or futile about praying to God, given God's nature, because God has by his providence arranged things so that free human actions and human prayers will form part of the chain of cause and effect leading to the state of the world ordained in God's plan. And so, on Thomas's view, prayer should not be thought of as an attempt to get God to do something which he would not otherwise do but rather as an effort to produce an appropriate and preordained cause which will result in certain effects since God in his providence has determined things to be so. Now surely there can be no doubt that, according to Christian doctrine, God wants men to pray and answers prayers; and consequently it is plain that God's plan for the world includes human prayers as causes of certain effects. The difficulty lies in explaining how such a doctrine makes sense. Why should prayers be included in God's plan as causes of certain effects? And what sense is there in the notion that a perfect and unchangeable God, who disposes and plans everything, fulfills men's prayers asking him to do one thing or another? Thomas's argument, I think, gives no help with

these questions and so gives no help with this problem of petitionary prayer.

This argument of Thomas's is roughly similar in basic strategy to other traditional arguments for prayer[6] and is furthermore among the most fully developed and sophisticated arguments for prayer, but it seems to me inadequate to make sense of petitionary prayer. I think, then, that it is worthwhile exploring a sort of argument different from those that stress the connection between God's omniscience or providence and men's prayers. In what follows I want to offer a tentative and preliminary sketch of the way in which such an argument might go.

Judaeo-Christian concepts of God commonly represent God as loving mankind and wanting to be loved by men in return.... [T]o say that God loves men and wants to be loved in return is to say something that has a place in philosophical theology and is indispensable to Christian doctrine. Throughout the Old and New Testaments, the type of loving relationship wanted between man and God is represented by various images, for example, sometimes as the relationship between husband and wife, sometimes as that between father and child. And sometimes (in the Gospel of John, for instance) it is also represented as the relationship between true friends.[7] But if the relationship between God and human beings is to be one which at least sometimes can be accurately represented as the love of true friendship, then there is a problem for both parties to the relationship, because plainly it will not be easy for there to be friendship between an omniscient, omnipotent, perfectly good person and a fallible, finite, imperfect person. The troubles of generating and maintaining friendship in such a case are surely the perfect paradigms of which the troubles of friendship between a Rockefeller child and a slum child are just pale copies. Whatever other troubles there are for friendship in these cases, there are at least two dangers for the disadvantaged or inferior member of the pair. First, he can be so overcome by the advantages or superiority of his "friend" that he becomes simply a shadowy reflection of the other's personality, a slavish follower who slowly loses all sense of his own tastes and desires and will. Some people, of course, believe that just this sort of attitude towards God is what Christianity wants and gets from the best of its adherents; but I think that such a belief goes counter to the spirit of the Gospels, for example, and I don't think that it can be found even in such intense mystics as St. Teresa and St. John of the Cross. Secondly, in addition to the danger of becoming completely dominated, there is the danger of becoming spoiled in the way that members of a royal family in a ruling house are subject to. Because of the power at their disposal in virtue of their connections, they often become tyrannical, willful, indolent, self-indulgent, and the like. The greater the discrepancy in status and condition between the two friends, the greater the danger of even inadvertently overwhelming and oppressing or overwhelming and spoiling the lesser member of the pair; and if he is overwhelmed in either of these ways, the result will be replacement of whatever kind of friendship there might have been with one or another sort of using. Either the superior member of the pair will use the lesser as his lackey, or the lesser will use the superior as his personal power source. To put it succinctly, then, if God wants some kind of true friendship with men, he will have to find a way of guarding against both kinds of overwhelming.

It might occur to someone to think that even if we assume the view that God wants friendship between himself and human beings, it does not follow that he will have any of the problems just sketched, because he is omnipotent.[8] If he wants friendship of this sort with men, one might suppose, let him just will it and it will be his. I do not want to stop here to argue against this view in detail, but I do want just to suggest that there is reason for thinking it to be incoherent, at least on the assumption of free will adopted at the beginning of this paper, because it is hard to see how God could bring about such a friendship magically, by means of his omnipotence, and yet permit the people involved to have free will. If he could do so, he could make a person freely love him in the right sort of way, and it does not seem reasonable to think he could do so.[9] On the face of it, then, omnipotence alone does not do away with the two dangers for friendship that I sketched above. But the institution of petitionary

prayer, I think, can be understood as a safeguard against these dangers.

It is easiest to argue that petitionary prayer serves such a function in the case of a man who prays for himself. In praying for himself, he makes an explicit request for help, and he thereby acknowledges a need or a desire and his dependence on God for satisfying that need or desire. If he gets what he prayed for, he will be in a position to attribute his good fortune to God's doing and to be grateful to God for what God has given him. If we add the undeniable uncertainty of his getting what he prays for, then we will have safeguards against what I will call (for lack of a better phrase) overwhelming spoiling. These conditions make the act of asking a safeguard against tyrannical and self-indulgent pride, even if the one praying thinks of himself grandly as having God on his side.

We can see how the asking guards against the second danger, of oppressive overwhelming, if we look for a moment at the function of roughly similar asking for help when both the one asking and the one asked are human beings. Suppose a teacher sees that one of his students is avoiding writing a paper and is thereby storing up trouble for himself at the end of the term. And suppose that the student *asks* the teacher for extra help in organizing working time and scheduling the various parts of the work. In that case I think the teacher can without any problem give the student what he needs, provided, of course, that the teacher is willing to do as much for any other student, and so on. But suppose, on the other hand, that the student does not ask the teacher for help and that the teacher instead calls the student at home and simply presents him with the help he needs in scheduling and discipline. The teacher's proposals in that case are more than likely to strike the student as meddling interference, and he is likely to respond with more or less polite variations on "Who asked you?" and "Mind your own business." Those responses, I think, are healthy and just. If the student were having ordinary difficulties getting his work done and yet docilely and submissively accepted the teacher's unrequested scheduling of his time, he would have taken the first step in the direction of unhealthy passivity towards his teacher. And if he and his teacher developed that sort of relationship, he could end by becoming a lackey-like reflection of his teacher. Bestowing at least some benefits only in response to requests for them is a safeguard against such an outcome when the members of the relationship are not equally balanced.

It becomes much harder to argue for this defense of prayer as soon as the complexity of the case is increased even just a little. Take, for example, Monica's praying for her son Augustine. There is nothing in Monica's praying for Augustine which shows that *Augustine* recognizes that he has a need for God's help or that *he* will be grateful if God gives him what *Monica* prays for. Nor is it plain that *Monica's* asking shields Augustine from oppressive overwhelming by God. So it seems as if the previous arguments fail in this case. But consider again the case in which a teacher sees that a student of his could use help but does not feel that he can legitimately volunteer his help unasked. Suppose that John, a friend of that student, comes to see the teacher and says, "I don't know if you've noticed, but Jim is having trouble getting to his term paper. And unless he gets help, I think he won't do it at all and will be in danger of flunking the course." If the teacher now goes to help Jim and is rudely or politely asked "What right have you got to interfere?" he'll say, "Well, in fact, your friend came to me and *asked* me to help." And if John is asked the same question, he will probably reply, "But I'm your friend; I had to do *something*." I think, then, that because John asks the teacher, the teacher is in a position to help with less risk of oppressive meddling than before. Obviously, he cannot go very far without incurring that risk as fully as before; and perhaps the most he can do if he wants to avoid oppressive meddling is to try to elicit from *Jim* in genuinely uncoercive ways a request for help. And, of course, I chose Monica and Augustine to introduce this case because, as Augustine tells it in the *Confessions*, God responded to Monica's fervent and continued prayers for Augustine's salvation by arranging the circumstances of Augustine's life in such a way that finally Augustine himself freely asked God for salvation.

One might perhaps think that there is something superfluous and absurd in God's working through the intermediary of prayer in this way. If Jim's friend can justify his interference on the grounds that he is Jim's friend and has to do *something*, God can dispense with this sort of petitionary prayer, too. He can give aid unasked on the grounds that he is the *creator* and has to do something. But suppose that Jim and John are only acquaintances who have discussed nothing more than their schoolwork; and suppose that John, by overhearing Jim's phone conversations, has come to believe that all Jim's academic troubles are just symptoms of problems he is having with his parents. If John asks the teacher to help Jim with his personal problems, and if the teacher begins even a delicate attempt to do so by saying that John asked him to do so, he and John could both properly be told to mind their own business. It is not the *status* of his relationship or even the depth of his care and compassion for Jim which puts John in a position to defend himself by saying "But I'm your friend." What protects John against the charge of oppressive meddling is rather the degree to which Jim has freely, willingly, shared his life and thoughts and feelings with John. So John's line of defense against the charge of oppressive meddling can be attributed to God only if the person God is to aid has willingly shared his thoughts and feelings and the like with God. But it is hard to imagine anyone putting himself in such a relation to a person he believes to be omnipotent and good without his also *asking* for whatever help he needs.

Even if the argument can be made out so far, one might be inclined to think that it will not be sufficient to show the compatibility of God's goodness with the practice of petitionary prayer. If one supposes that God brought Augustine to Christianity in response to Monica's prayers, what is one to say about Augustine's fate if Monica had not prayed for him? And what does this view commit one to maintain about people who neither pray for themselves nor are prayed for? It looks as if an orthodox Christian who accepts the argument about petitionary prayer so far will be committed to a picture of this sort. God is analogous to a human father with two very different children. Both Old and New Testaments depict God as doing many good things for men without being asked to do so, and this human father, too, does unrequested good things for both his children. But one child, who is healthy and normal, with healthy, normal relations to his father, makes frequent requests of the father which the father responds to and in virtue of which he bestows benefits on the child. The other child is selectively blind, deaf, dumb, and suffering from whatever other maladies are necessary to make it plausible that he does not even know he has a father. Now either there are some benefits that the father will never bestow unless and until he is asked; and in that case he will do less for his defective child, who surely has more need of his help than does the healthy child. Or, on the other hand, he will bestow all his benefits unasked on the defective child, and then he seems to make a mockery of his practice with the normal child of bestowing some benefits only in response to requests—he is, after all, willing to bestow the same benefits without being asked. So it seems that we are still left with the problem we started with: either God is not perfectly good or the practice of petitionary prayer is pointless. But suppose the father always meets the defective child's needs and desires even though the child never comes to know of the existence of his father. The child knows only that he is always taken care of, and when he needs something, he gets what he needs. It seems to me intuitively clear that such a practice runs a great risk, at least, of making the defective child willful and tyrannical. But even if the defective child is not in danger of being made worse in some respects in this situation, still it seems plain that he would be better off if the father could manage to put the child in a position to know his father and to frame a request for what he wants. So I think a good father will fulfill the child's needs unasked; but I think that he can do so without making a mockery of his practice of bestowing benefits in response to requests only if putting the child in a position to make requests is among his first concerns.

And as for the question whether God would have saved Augustine without Monica's prayers, I think that there is intermediate ground between the assertion that Monica's prayers are necessary to Augustine's salvation, which seems to impugn God's goodness, and the claim that they are altogether without effect, which undercuts petitionary prayer. It is possible, for example, to argue that God would have saved Augustine without Monica's prayers but not in the same amount of time or not by the same process or not with the same effect. Augustine, for instance, might have been converted to Christianity but not in such a way as to become one of its most powerful authorities for centuries.[10]

With all this, I have still looked only at cases that are easy for my position; when we turn to something like a prayer for Guatemala after the earthquake—which begins to come closer to the sort of petitions in the first half of the Lord's Prayer—it is much harder to know what to say. And perhaps it is simply too hard to come up with a reasonable solution here because we need more work on the problem of evil. Why would a good God permit the occurrence of earthquakes in the first place? Do the reasons for his permitting the earthquake affect his afterwards helping the country involved? Our inclination is surely to say that a good God must *in any case* help the earthquake victims, so that in this instance at any rate it is pointless to pray. But plainly we also have strong inclinations to say that a good God must in any case prevent earthquakes in populated areas. And since orthodox Christianity is committed to distrusting these latter inclinations, it is at least at sea about the former ones. Without more work on the problem of evil, it is hard to know what to say about the difference prayer might make in this sort of case.

I think it is worth noticing, though, that the first three requests of the Lord's Prayer do not run into the same difficulties. Those requests seem generally equivalent to a request for the kingdom of God on earth, that state of affairs in which, of their own free will, all men on earth are dedicated, righteous lovers of God. Now suppose it is true that God would bring about his kingdom on earth even if an individual Christian such as Jimmy Carter did not pray for it. It does not follow in this case, however, that the prayer in question is pointless and makes no difference. Suppose no one prayed for the advent of God's kingdom on earth or felt a need or desire for those millennial times strongly enough to pray for them. It seems unreasonable to think that God could bring about his earthly kingdom under those conditions, or if he could, that it would be the state of affairs just described, in which earth is populated by people who *freely* love God. And if so, then making the requests in the first half of the Lord's Prayer resembles other, more ordinary activities in which only the effort of a whole group is sufficient to achieve the desired result. One man can't put out a forest fire, but if everyone in the vicinity of a forest fire realized that fact and on that basis decided not to try, the fire would rage out of control. So in the case of the opening petitions of the Lord's Prayer, too, it seems possible to justify petitionary prayer without impugning God's goodness.

Obviously, the account I have given is just a preliminary sketch for the full development of this solution, and a good deal more work needs to be done on the problem. Nonetheless, I think that this account is on the right track and that there is a workable solution to the problem of petitionary prayer which can be summarized in this way. God must work through the intermediary of prayer, rather than doing everything on his own initiative, for man's sake. Prayer acts as a kind of buffer between man and God. By safeguarding the weaker member of the relation from the dangers of overwhelming domination and overwhelming spoiling, it helps to promote and preserve a close relationship between an omniscient, omnipotent, perfectly good person and a fallible, finite, imperfect person. There is, of course, something counter-intuitive in this notion that prayer acts as a buffer; prayer of all sorts is commonly and I think correctly said to have as one of its main functions the production of closeness between man and God. But not just any sort of closeness will result in friendship, and promoting the appropriate sort of closeness will require inhibiting or preventing inappropriate sorts of closeness, so that a relationship of friendship depends on the maintenance of both closeness and distance between the two friends. And while I do not mean to denigrate the im-

portance of prayer in producing and preserving the appropriate sort of closeness, I think the problem of petitionary prayer at issue here is best solved by focusing on the distance necessary for friendship and the function of petitionary prayer in maintaining that distance....

It should be plain that there is nothing in this analysis of prayer which *requires* that God fulfil every prayer; asking God for something is not in itself a sufficient condition for God's doing what he is asked. Christian writings are full of examples of prayers which are not answered, and there are painful cases of unanswered prayer in which the one praying must be tempted more to the belief that God is his implacable enemy than to the sentimental-seeming belief that God is his friend. This paper proposes no answer for these difficulties. They require a long, hard, careful look at the problem of evil, and that falls just outside the scope of this paper.

And, finally, it may occur to someone to wonder whether the picture of God presented in this analysis is at all faithful to the God of the Old or New Testaments. Is this understanding of God and prayer anything that Christianity ought to accept or even find congenial? It seems to me that one could point to many stories in either the Old or New Testament in support of an affirmative answer—for example, Elijah's performance on Mt. Carmel (I Kings 18), or the apostles' prayer for a successor to Judas (Acts 1:24–26). But for a small and particularly nice piece of evidence, we can turn to the story in the Gospel of Luke which describes Jesus making the Lord's Prayer and giving a lecture on how one is to pray. According to the Gospel, Jesus is praying and in such a way that his disciples see him and know that he is praying. One of them makes a request of him which has just a touch of rebuke in it: teach us to pray, as *John* taught *his* disciples to pray (Lk. 11:1). If there is a note of rebuke there, it seems just. A religious master should teach his disciples to pray, and a good teacher does not wait until he is asked to teach his students important lessons. But Jesus is portrayed as a good teacher of just this sort in the Gospel of Luke.[11] Does the Gospel, then, mean its readers to understand that Jesus would not have taught his disciples how to pray if they had not requested it? And if it does not, why is Jesus portrayed as waiting until he is asked? Perhaps the Gospel means us to understand[12] that Jesus does so just in order to teach by experience as well as by sermon what is implicit throughout the Lord's Prayer: that asking makes a difference.

NOTES

1. *Cf.*, for example, the similar understanding of this petition in two very different theologians: Augustine, *Homilies on the Gospels*, Serm. 6; and Calvin, *Institutes of the Christian Religion*, III. xx. 41.

2. The most common Old Testament word for "holy" and its correlates is some form of "kādash," the basic, literal meaning of which is separation, withdrawal, or state of being set apart; *cf.* Gesenius, *A Hebrew and English Lexicon of the Old Testament*. In the New Testament, the most frequently used word is *"hagiazō"* and its correlates, the basic meaning of which also includes the notion of being separate and being set apart; *cf.* Thayer, *A Greek–English Lexicon of the New Testament*, and Arndt and Gringrich, *A Greek–English Lexicon of the New Testament and Other Early Christian Literature*.

3. *Cf.*, *e.g.*, Is. 2:2–21, 45:23, and 65:23; Matt. 24; Mk. 13; Lk. 21; and Rev. 6:15–17.

4. See, for example, Martin Luther, *Large Catechism* pt. III. 169. Luther's argument for prayer has more force in the context of the catechism than it does in the context of a philosophical discussion, because Luther's purpose there is the practical one of blocking what he understands as believers' *excuses* for not praying.

5. See reply, a. 2.

6. *Cf.*, *e.g.*, Origen, *op. cit.*, and Augustine, *City of God*, Bk. V, ix.

7. See especially Jn. 15:12–15.

8. I want to avoid detailed discussion of the various controversies over omnipotence. For present purposes, I will take this as a rough definition of omnipotence: a being is omnipotent if and only if he can do anything which it is not logically impossible for him to do and if he can avoid doing anything which it is not logically necessary for him to do.

9. Controversy over this point is related to the more general controversy over whether or not it is possible for an omnipotent, omniscient, perfectly good God to create men who would on every occasion freely do what is right. For a discussion of that general controversy and arguments that it is not possible for God to do so, see Alvin Plantinga's *God and Other Minds* (Ithaca, 1967), pp. 132–148; I am in agreement with the general tenor of Plantinga's remarks in that section of his book.

10. I have presented the case of Monica and Augustine in a simplified form in order to have an uncomplicated hard case for the view I am arguing. As far as the historical figures themselves are concerned, it is plain that Monica's overt, explicit, passionate concern for her son's conversion greatly influenced the course of his life and shaped his character from boyhood on. It is not clear whether Augustine would have been anything like the man he was if his mother had not been as zealous on behalf of his soul as she was, if she had not prayed continually and fervently for his salvation and let him know she was doing so. Augustine's character and personality were what they were in large part as a result of her fierce desire for his espousal of Christianity; and just his knowledge that his beloved mother prayed so earnestly for his conversion must have been a powerful natural force helping to effect that conversion. In this context the question whether God could have saved Augustine without Monica's prayers takes on different meaning, and an affirmative answer is much harder to give with reasoned confidence.

11. See, for example, the lessons taught in the two incidents described in Lk. 21:1–6.

12. I have used awkward circumlocutions in this paragraph in order to make plain that it is not my intention here to make any claims about the historical Jesus or the intentions of the Gospel writer. I am not concerned in this paper to do or to take account of contemporary theories of Biblical exegesis. My point is only that the story in the Gospel, as it has been part of ordinary Christian tradition, lends itself to the interpretation I suggest.

40   THE CONCEPT OF WORSHIP

JAMES RACHELS

Prayers need not be petitions but may, instead, be expressions of adoration. But to go beyond praising God and engage in worshipping God raises a philosophical problem. Is total subservience to the deity consistent with being a moral agent? In other words, if you are required to do whatever God tells you to do, can you at the same time retain your commitment to do what you think is right? Of course, you may believe that what God tells you do is right. That decision, however, is one you yourself make and not one God makes for you. In our next selection, James Rachels (1941-2003), who was a professor of philosophy at the University of Alabama at Birmingham, argues that no one, not even God, has an unqualified claim on our beliefs and actions.

The concept of worship has received surprisingly little attention from philosophers of religion. When it has been treated, the usual approach is by way of referring to God's awesomeness or mysteriousness: to worship is to "bow down in silent awe" when confronted with a being that is "terrifyingly mysterious."[1] But neither of these notions is of much help in understanding worship. Awe is certainly not the same thing as worship; one can be awed by a performance of *King Lear*, or by witnessing an eclipse of the sun or an earthquake, or by meeting one's favorite film star, without worshiping any of these things. And a great many things are both terrifying and mysterious that we have not the slightest inclination to worship—the Black Death probably fits that description for many people. So we need an account of worship that does not rely on such notions as awesomeness and mysteriousness.…

Worship is something that is done; but it is not clear just what is done when one worships. Other actions, such as throwing a ball or insulting one's neighbor, seem transparent enough; but not so with worship. When we celebrate Mass in the Roman Catholic Church, for example, what are we doing (apart from eating a wafer and drinking wine)? Or when we sing hymns in a Protestant church, what are we doing (other than merely singing songs)? What is it that makes these acts of *worship*? One obvious point is that these actions, and others like them, are ritualistic in character; so before we can make any progress in understanding worship, perhaps it will help to ask about the nature of ritual.

First we need to distinguish the ceremonial form of a ritual from what is supposed to be accomplished by it. Consider, for example, the ritual of investiture for an English prince. The prince kneels; the queen (or king) places a crown on his head; and he takes an oath: "I do become your liege man of life and limb and of earthly worship, and faith and trust I will bear unto thee to live and die against all manner of folks." By this ceremony the prince is elevated to his new station, and by this oath he acknowledges the commitments that, as prince, he will owe the queen. In one sense, the ceremonial form of the ritual is unimportant; it is possible that some other procedure might have been laid down, without the point of the ritual being affected in any way. Rather than placing a crown on his head, the queen might break an egg into his palm (that could symbolize all sorts of things). Once this was established as the procedure, it would do as well as the other. It would still be the ritual of investiture, so long as it was understood that by the ceremony a prince is created. The performance of a ritual, then, is in

From James Rachels, "God and Human Attitudes," *Religious Studies* 7 (1971). Reprinted by permission of Cambridge University Press.

certain respects like the use of language. In speaking, sounds are uttered, and, thanks to the conventions of the language, something is said, or affirmed, or done; and in a ritual performance, a ceremony is enacted, and, thanks to the conventions associated with the ceremony, something is done, or affirmed, or celebrated....

So, once we understand the social system in which there are queens, princes, and subjects, and therefore understand the role assigned to each within that system, we can sum up what is happening in the ritual of investiture in this way: someone is being made a prince, and he is accepting that role with all that it involves. Similar explanations could be given for other rituals, such as the marriage ceremony: two people are being made husband and wife, and they are accepting those roles with all that they involve.

The question to be asked about the ritual of worship is what analogous explanation can be given of it. The ceremonial form of the ritual may vary according to the customs of the religious community; it may involve singing, drinking wine, counting beads, sitting with a solemn expression on one's face, dancing, making a sacrifice, or what have you. But what is the point of it?

... [T]he worshiper thinks of himself as inhabiting a world created by an infinitely wise, infinitely powerful, perfectly good God; and it is a world in which he, along with other people, occupies a special place in virtue of God's intentions. This gives him a certain role to play: the role of a "child of God." In worshiping God, one is acknowledging and accepting this role, and that is the point of the ritual of worship. Just as the ritual of investiture derives its significance from its place within the social system of queens, princes, and subjects, the ritual of worship gets its significance from an assumed system of relationships between God and human beings. In the ceremony of investiture, the prince assumes a role with respect to the queen and the citizenry. In marriage, two people assume roles with respect to one another. And in worship, a person accepts and affirms his role with respect to God.

Worship presumes the superior status of the one worshiped. This is reflected in the logical point that there can be no such things as mutual or reciprocal worship, unless one or the other of the parties is mistaken as to his own status. We can very well comprehend people loving one another or respecting one another, but not (unless they are misguided) worshiping one another. This is because the worshiper necessarily assumes his own inferiority; and since inferiority is an asymmetrical relation, so is worship. (The nature of the "superiority" and "inferiority" involved here is of course problematic; but in the account I am presenting, it may be understood on the model of superior and inferior positions within a social system.) This is also why humility is necessary on the part of the worshiper. The role to which he commits himself is that of the humble servant, "not worthy to touch the hem of his garment." Compared to God's gloriousness, "all our righteousnesses are as filthy rags." So in committing oneself to this role, one is acknowledging God's greatness and one's own relative worthlessness. This humble attitude is not a mere embellishment of the ritual: on the contrary, worship, unlike love or respect, requires humility. Pride is a sin, and pride before God is incompatible with worshiping him.

The function of worship as "glorifying" or "praising" God, which is often taken to be primary, may be regarded as derivative from the more fundamental nature of worship as commitment to the role of God's child. "Praising" God is giving him the honor and respect due to one in his position of eminence, just as one shows respect and honor in giving fealty to a king.

In short, the worshiper is in this position: He believes that there is a being, God, who is the perfectly good, perfectly powerful, perfectly wise Creator of the universe; and he views himself as the child of God, made for God's purposes and responsible to God for his conduct. And the ritual of worship, which may have any number of ceremonial forms according to the customs of the religious community, has as its point the acceptance of, and commitment to, this role as God's child, with all that this involves. If this account is accepted, then there is no mystery as to the relation between the act of worship and the worshiper's other activity. Worship will be regarded not as an isolated act taking place on Sunday morning, with no necessary connection to one's behavior the rest of the week, but as a ritualistic expression of, and commitment to, a role that dominates one's whole way of life.[2]

An important feature of roles is that they can be violated: we can act and think consistently with a role, or we can act and think inconsistently with it. The prince can, for example, act inconsistently with his role as prince by giving greater importance to his own interests and welfare than to the queen's; in this case, he is no longer her liege man. And a father who does not attend to the welfare of his children is not acting consistently with his role as a father, and so on. What would count as violating the role to which one is pledged in virtue of worshiping God?

In Genesis two familiar stories, both concerning Abraham, are relevant. The first is the story of the near sacrifice of Isaac. We are told that Abraham was "tempted" by God, who commanded him to offer Isaac as a human sacrifice. Abraham obeyed—he prepared an altar, bound Isaac to it, and was about to kill him until God intervened at the last moment, saying, "Lay not thine hand upon the lad, neither do thou any thing unto him: for now I know that thou fearest God, seeing thou hast not withheld thy son, thine only son from me" (Gen. 22:12). So Abraham passed the test. But how could he have failed? What was his temptation? Obviously, his temptation was to disobey God; God had ordered him to do something contrary both to his wishes and to his sense of what would otherwise have been right. He could have defied God, but he did not—he subordinated himself, his own desires and judgments, to God's command, even when the temptation to do otherwise was strongest.

It is interesting that Abraham's record in this respect was not perfect. We also have the story of him bargaining with God over the conditions for saving Sodom and Gomorrah from destruction. God had said that he would destroy those cities because they were so wicked; but Abraham gets God to agree that if fifty righteous men can be found there, the cities will be spared. Then he persuades God to lower the number to forty-five, then forty, then thirty, then twenty, and finally ten. Here we have a different Abraham, not servile and obedient, but willing to challenge God and bargain with him. However, even as he bargains with God, Abraham realizes that there is

something radically inappropriate about it: he says, "Behold now, I have taken upon me to speak unto the Lord, which am but dust and ashes.... Oh let not the Lord be angry" (Gen. 18:27, 30).

The fact is that Abraham could not, consistent with his role as God's subject, set his own judgment and will against God's. The author of Genesis was certainly right about this. We cannot recognize any being *as God* and at the same time set ourselves against him. The point is not merely that it would be imprudent to defy God, since we certainly can't get away with it. Rather, there is a stronger, logical point involved—namely, that if we recognize any being as God, then we are committed, in virtue of that recognition, to obeying him.

To see why this is so, we must first notice that "God" is not a proper name like "Richard Nixon" but a title like "president of the United States" or "king."[3] Thus, "Jehovah is God" is a nontautological statement in which the title "God" is assigned to Jehovah, a particular being, just as "Richard Nixon is president of the United States" assigns the title "president of the United States" to a particular man. This permits us to understand how statements like "God is perfectly wise" can be logical truths, which is problematic if "God" is regarded as a proper name. Although it is not a logical truth that any particular being is perfectly wise, it nevertheless is a logical truth that if any being is God (that is, if any being properly holds that title), then that being is perfectly wise. This is exactly analogous to saying that although it is not a logical truth that Richard Nixon has the authority to veto congressional legislation, nevertheless it is a logical truth that if Richard Nixon is president of the United States, then he has that authority.

To bear the title "God," then, a being must have certain qualifications: he must be all-powerful and perfectly good in addition to being perfectly wise. And in the same vein, to apply the title "God" to a being is to recognize him as one to be obeyed. The same is true, to a lesser extent, of "king"; to recognize anyone as king is to acknowledge that he occupies a place of authority and has a claim on one's allegiance as his subject. And to recognize any being as God is to acknowledge that he has unlimited authority and an unlimited claim on one's allegiance. Thus, we might regard Abraham's reluctance to defy Jehovah as grounded not only in his fear of Jehovah's wrath but as a logical consequence of his acceptance of Jehovah as God. Albert Camus was right to think that "from the moment that man submits God to moral judgment, he kills Him his own heart."[4] What a man can "kill" by defying or even questioning God is not the being that (supposedly) *is* God but his own conception of that being as God. That God is not to be judged, challenged, defied, or disobeyed is at bottom a truth of logic. To do any of these things is incompatible with taking him as one to be worshiped....

So the idea that any being could be worthy of worship is much more problematic than we might have at first imagined. In saying that a being is worthy of worship, we would be recognizing him as having an unqualified claim on our obedience. The question, then, is whether there could be such an unqualified claim. It should be noted that the description of a being as all-powerful, all-wise, and so on would not automatically settle the issue; for even while admitting the existence of such an awesome being, we might still question whether we should recognize him as having an unlimited claim on our obedience.

There is a long tradition in moral philosophy, from Plato to Kant, according to which such a recognition could never be made by a moral agent. According to this tradition, to be a moral agent is to be autonomous, or self-directed. Unlike the precepts of law or social custom, moral precepts are imposed by the agent upon himself, and the penalty for their violation is, in Kant's words, "self-contempt and inner abhorrence."[5] The virtuous person is therefore identified with the person of integrity, the person who acts according to precepts that she can, on reflection, conscientiously approve in her own heart.

On this view, to deliver oneself over to a moral authority for directions about what to do is simply incompatible with being a moral agent. To say "I will follow so-and-so's directions no matter what they are and no matter what my own conscience would otherwise direct me to do" is to opt out of moral thinking altogether; it is to abandon one's role as a moral agent. And it does not matter whether "so-and-so" is the law, the customs of one's society, or Jehovah. This does not, of course, preclude one from seeking advice on moral matters and even on occasion following that advice blindly, trusting in the good judgment of the adviser. But this is justified by the details of the particular case— for example, that you cannot form any reasonable judgment of your own because of ignorance or inexperience or lack of time. What is precluded is that a person should, while in possession of his wits, adopt this style of decision making (or perhaps we should say this style of abdicating decision making) as a general strategy of living, or abandon his own best judgment when he can form a judgment of which he is reasonably confident.

We have, then, a conflict between the role of worshiper, which by its very nature commits one to total subservience to God, and the role of moral agent, which necessarily involves autonomous decision making. The role of worshiper takes precedence over every other role the worshiper has; when there is any conflict, the worshiper's commitment to God has priority over everything. But the first commitment of a moral agent is to do what in his own heart he thinks is right.

NOTES

1. These phrases are from John Hick, *Philosophy of Religion* (Englewood Cliffs, N.J.: Prentice-Hall, 1963), 13–14.
2. This account of worship, specified here in terms of what it means to worship God, may easily be adapted to the worship of other beings, such as Satan. The only changes required are (a) that we substitute for beliefs about God analogous beliefs about Satan, and (b) that we understand the ritual of worship as committing the Satan-worshiper to a role as Satan's servant in the same way that worshiping God commits theists to the role of his servant.
3. Cf. Nelson Pike, "Omnipotence and God's Ability to Sin," *American Philosophical Quarterly* 6 (1969): 208–9; and C.B. Martin, *Religious Belief* (Ithaca, N.Y.: Cornell University Press, 1964), chap. 4.
4. Albert Camus, *The Rebel*, trans. Anthony Bower (New York: Vintage, 1956), 62.
5. Immanuel Kant, *Foundations of the Metaphysics of Morals*, trans. Lewis White Beck (Indianapolis: Bobbs-Merrill, 1959), 44.

B. MIRACLES

41 OF MIRACLES

DAVID HUME

Can we come to some understanding of God through the study of God's works as revealed in miracles?

David Hume, whose writings we read previously, thought not. He argued that believing an event to be a miracle, that is, a deity's transgression of a law of nature, is almost surely unreasonable, for the human testimony on which such beliefs are based is highly improbable compared with the evidence in support of the regularity of the world's order. Furthermore, reports are invariably suspect because the witnesses are likely to exhibit foolishness or dishonesty.

In reading this essay, keep in mind that while Hume is best known today as a philosopher, in his own day he was celebrated as a historian, the author of a six-volume *History of England*. His expertise in both fields is evident in this discussion of miracles.

PART I

I flatter myself that I have discovered an argument ..., which, if just, will, with the wise and learned, be an everlasting check to all kinds of superstitious delusion, and consequently will be useful as long as the world endures. For so long, I presume, will the accounts of miracles and prodigies be found in all history, sacred and profane.

Though experience be our only guide in reasoning concerning matters of fact, it must be acknowledged that this guide is not altogether infallible, but in some cases is apt to lead us into errors. One who in our climate should expect better weather in any week of June than in one of December, would reason justly, and conformably to experience; but it is certain that he may happen, in the event, to find himself mistaken. However, we may observe that, in such a case, he would have no cause to complain of experience, because it commonly informs us beforehand of the uncertainty, by that contrariety of events, which we may learn from a diligent observation. All effects follow not with like certainty from their supposed causes. Some events are found, in all countries and all ages, to have been constantly conjoined together. Other are found to have been more variable, and sometimes to disappoint our expectations; so that, in our reasonings concerning matter of fact, there are all imaginable degrees of assurance, from the highest certainty to the lowest species of moral evidence....

A wise man, therefore, proportions his belief to the evidence. In such conclusions as are founded on an infallible experience, he expects the event with the last degree of assurance, and regards his past experience as a full *proof* of the future existence of that event. In other cases, he proceeds with more caution: He weighs the opposite experiments; he considers which side is supported by the greater number of experiments; to that side he inclines, with doubt and hesitation; and when at last he fixes his judgement, the evidence exceeds not what we properly call *probability*. All probability, then, supposes an opposition of experiments and observations, where the one

From *An Enquiry Concerning Human Understanding* (1748).

side is found to overbalance the other, and to produce a degree of evidence, proportioned to the superiority. A hundred instances or experiments on one side, and fifty on another, afford a doubtful expectation of any event; though a hundred uniform experiments, with only one that is contradictory, reasonably beget a pretty strong degree of assurance. In all cases, we must balance the opposite experiments, where they are opposite, and deduct the smaller number from the greater, in order to know the exact force of the superior evidence....

A miracle is a violation of the laws of nature; and as a firm and unalterable experience has established these laws, the proof against a miracle, from the very nature of the fact, is as entire as any argument from experience can possibly be imagined. Why is it more than probable that all men must die; that lead cannot, of itself, remain suspended in the air; that fire consumes wood, and is extinguished by water; unless it be that these events are found agreeable to the laws of nature, and there is required a violation of these laws, or in other words a miracle to prevent them? Nothing is esteemed a miracle if it ever happen in the common course of nature. It is no miracle that a man, seemingly in good health, should die on a sudden: because such a kind of death, though more unusual than any other, has yet been frequently observed to happen. But it is a miracle that a dead man should come to life, because that has never been observed, in any age or country. There must, therefore, be a uniform experience against every miraculous event, otherwise the event would not merit that appellation. And as a uniform experience amounts to a proof, there is here a direct and full *proof*, from the nature of the fact, against the existence of any miracle; nor can such a proof be destroyed, or the miracle rendered credible, but by an opposite proof, which is superior.[1]

The plain consequence is (and it is a general maxim worthy of our attention), "That no testimony is sufficient to establish a miracle, unless the testimony be of such a kind that its falsehood would be more miraculous than the fact which it endeavours to establish: and even in that case there is a mutual destruction of arguments, and the superior only gives us an assurance suitable to that degree of force, which remains, after deducting the inferior." When any one tells me that he saw a dead man restored to life, I immediately consider with myself, whether it be more probable that this person should either deceive or be deceived, or that the fact which he relates should really have happened. I weigh the one miracle against the other; and according to the superiority which I discover, I pronounce my decision, and always reject the greater miracle. If the falsehood of his testimony would be more miraculous than the event which he relates; then, and not till then, can he pretend to command my belief or opinion.

PART II

In the foregoing reasoning we have supposed that the testimony, upon which a miracle is founded, may possibly amount to an entire proof, and that the falsehood of that testimony would be a real prodigy: But it is easy to show, that we have been a great deal too liberal in our concession, and that there never was a miraculous event established on so full an evidence.

For *first*, there is not to be found, in all history, any miracle attested by a sufficient number of men, of such unquestioned good-sense, education, and learning as to secure us against all delusion in themselves; of such undoubted integrity as to place them beyond all suspicion of any design to deceive others; of such credit and reputation in the eyes of mankind as to have a great deal to lose in case of their being detected in any falsehood; and at the same time attesting facts, performed in such a public manner and in so celebrated a part of the world, as to render the detection unavoidable: All which circumstances are requisite to give us a full assurance in the testimony of men.

Secondly. We may observe in human nature a principle, which, if strictly examined, will be found to diminish extremely the assurance which we might, from human testimony, have in any kind of prodigy. The maxim, by which we commonly conduct ourselves in our reasonings, is that the objects of which we have no experience resemble those of which we have; that what we have found to be most usual is always most probable; and that where there is an opposition of arguments, we ought to give the preference to such as are founded on the greatest number of past observations. But though, in proceeding by this rule, we readily reject any fact which is unusual and incredible in an ordinary degree; yet in advancing farther, the mind observes not always the same rule; but when anything is affirmed utterly absurd and miraculous, it rather the more readily admits of such a fact, upon account of that very circumstance which ought to destroy all its authority. The passion of *surprise* and *wonder* arising from miracles, being an agreeable emotion, gives a sensible tendency towards the belief of those events from which it is derived. And this goes so far that even those who cannot enjoy this pleasure immediately, nor can believe those miraculous events of which they are informed, yet love to partake of the satisfaction at second-hand or by rebound, and place a pride and delight in exciting the admiration of others....

The many instances of forged miracles, and prophecies, and supernatural events, which in all ages have either been detected by contrary evidence, or which detect themselves by their absurdity, prove sufficiently the strong propensity of mankind to the extraordinary and the marvellous, and ought reasonably to beget a suspicion against all relations of this kind. This is our natural way of thinking, even with regard to the most common and most credible events. For instance: There is no kind of report which rises so easily, and spreads so quickly, especially in country places and provincial towns, as those concerning marriages; insomuch that two young persons of equal condition never see each other twice, but the whole neighbourhood immediately join them together. The pleasure of telling a piece of news so interesting, of propagating it, and of being the first reporters of it, spreads the intelligence. And this is so well known that no man of sense gives attention to these reports till he find them confirmed by some greater evidence. Do not the same passions, and others still stronger, incline the generality of mankind to believe and report, with the greatest vehemence and assurance, all religious miracles?

Thirdly. It forms a strong presumption against all supernatural and miraculous relations, that they are observed chiefly to abound among ignorant and barbarous nations; or if a civilized people has ever given admission to any of them, that people will be found to have received them from ignorant and barbarous ancestors, who transmitted them with that inviolable sanction and authority, which always attend received opinions. When we peruse the first histories of all nations, we are apt to imagine ourselves transported into some new world, where the whole frame of nature is disjointed, and every element performs its operations in a different manner from what it does at present. Battles, revolutions, pestilence, famine, and death are never the effect of those natural causes which we experience. Prodigies, omens, oracles, judgments quite obscure the few natural events that are intermingled with them. But as the former grow thinner every page, in proportion as we advance nearer the enlightened ages, we soon learn that there is nothing mysterious or supernatural in the case, but that all proceeds from the usual propensity of mankind towards the marvellous, and that, though this inclination may at intervals receive a check from sense and learning, it can never be thoroughly extirpated from human nature....

I may add as a *fourth* reason which diminishes the authority of prodigies, that there is no testimony for any, even those which have not been expressly detected, that is not opposed by an infinite number of witnesses; so that not only the miracle destroys the credit of testimony, but the testimony destroys itself. To make this the better understood, let us consider that, in matters of religion, whatever is different is contrary; and that it is impossible the religions of ancient Rome, of Turkey, of Siam, and of China should, all of them, be established on any solid foundation. Every miracle, therefore, pretended to have been wrought in any of these religions (and all of them abound in miracles), as its direct scope is to establish the particular system to which it is attributed, so has it the same force, though more indirectly, to overthrow every other system. In destroying a rival system, it likewise destroys the credit of those miracles on which that system was established; so that all the prodigies of different religions are to be regarded as contrary facts, and the evidences of these prodigies, whether weak or strong, as opposite to each other....

Upon the whole, then, it appears that no testimony for any kind of miracle has ever amounted to a probability, much less to a proof; and that, even supposing it amounted to a proof, it would be opposed by another proof, derived from the very nature of the fact which it would endeavour to establish. It is experience only which gives authority to human testimony; and it is the same experience which assures us of the laws of nature. When, therefore, these two kinds of experience are contrary, we have nothing to do but subtract the one from the other, and embrace an opinion, either on one side or the other, with that assurance which arises from the reminder. But according to the principle here explained, this subtraction, with regard to all popular religions, amounts to an entire annihilation; and therefore we may establish it as a maxim that no human testimony can have such force as to prove a miracle, and make it a just foundation for any such system of religion.

I beg the limitations here made may be remarked, when I say that a miracle can never be proved, so as to be the foundation of a system of religion. For I own that otherwise there may possibly be miracles, or violations of the usual course of nature, of such a kind as to admit of proof from human testimony; though perhaps it will be impossible to find any such in all the records of history. Thus, suppose, all authors, in all languages agree that from the first of January 1600 there was a total darkness over the whole earth for eight days: Suppose that the tradition of this extraordinary event is still strong and lively among the people: That all travellers, who return from foreign countries, bring us accounts of the same tradition, without the least variation or contradiction. It is evident that our present philosophers, instead of doubting the fact, ought to receive it as certain, and ought to search for the causes whence it might be derived. The decay, corruption, and dissolution of nature, is an event rendered probable by so many analogies, that any phenomenon which seems to have a tendency towards that catastrophe comes within the reach of human testimony, if that testimony be very extensive and uniform.

But suppose that all the historians who treat of England should agree that, on the first of January 1600, Queen Elizabeth died; that both before and after her death she was seen by her physicians and the whole court, as is usual with persons of her rank; that her successor was acknowledged and proclaimed by the parliament; and that, after being interred a month, she again appeared, resumed the throne, and governed England for three years. I must confess that I should be surprised at the concurrence of so many odd circumstances, but should not have the least inclination to believe so miraculous an event. I should not doubt of her pretended death, and of those other public circumstances that followed it: I should only assert it to have been pretended, and that it neither was, nor possibly could be real. You would in vain object to me the difficulty, and almost impossibility of deceiving the world in an affair of such consequence; the wisdom and solid judgement of that renowned queen; with the little or no advantage which she could reap from so poor an artifice: all this might astonish me; but I would still reply that the knavery and folly of men are such common phenomena, that I should rather believe the most extraordinary events to arise from their concurrence, than admit of so signal a violation of the laws of nature.

But should this miracle be ascribed to any new system of religion; men in all ages have been so much imposed on by ridiculous stories of that kind, that this very circumstance would be a full proof of a cheat, and sufficient, with all men of sense, not only to make them reject the fact, but even reject it without farther examination. Though the Being to whom the miracle is ascribed be, in this case, Almighty, it does not upon that account become a whit more probable; since it is impossible for us to know the attributes or actions of such a Being, otherwise than from the experience which we have of his productions in the usual course of nature. This still reduces us to past observation, and obliges us to compare the instances of the violation of truth in the testimony of men, with those of the violation of the laws of nature by miracles, in order to judge which of them is most likely and probable. As the violations of truth are more common in the testimony concerning religious miracles than in that concerning any other matter of fact, this must diminish very much the authority of the former testimony, and make us form a general resolution never to lend any attention to it, with whatever specious pretence it may be covered....

I am the better pleased with the method of reasoning here delivered, as I think it may serve to confound those dangerous friends or disguised enemies to the *Christian Religion*, who have undertaken to defend it by the principles of human reason. Our most holy religion is founded on *Faith*, not on reason; and it is a sure method of exposing it to put it to such a trial as it is by no means fitted to endure....

[T]he *Christian Religion* not only was at first attended with miracles, but even at this day cannot be believed by any reasonable person without one. Mere reason is insufficient to convince us of its veracity: and whoever is moved by *Faith* to assent to it is conscious of a continued miracle in his own person, which subverts all the principles of his understanding, and gives him a determination to believe what is most contrary to custom and experience.

NOTE

1. Sometimes an event may not, *in itself, seem* to be contrary to the laws of nature, and yet, if it were real, it might, by reason of some circumstances, be denominated a miracle; because, in *fact*, it is contrary to these laws. Thus if a person, claiming a divine authority, should command a sick person to be well, a healthful man to fall down dead, the clouds to pour rain, the winds to blow, in short, should order many natural events, which immediately follow upon his command; these might justly be esteemed miracles, because they are really, in this case, contrary to the laws of nature. For if any suspicion remain, that the event and command concurred by accident, there is no miracle, and a transgression of these laws; because nothing can be more contrary to nature than that the voice or command of a man should have such an influence. A miracle may be accurately defined, *a transgression of a law of nature by a particular volition of the Deity, or by the interposition of some invisible agent.* A miracle may either be discoverable by men or not. This alters not its nature and essence. The raising of a house or ship into the air is a visible miracle. The raising of a feather, when the wind wants ever so little of a force requisite for that purpose, is as real a miracle, though not so sensible with regard to us.

42 GOD AND MIRACLES

RICHARD SWINBURNE

Richard Swinburne, who was Nolloth Professor of the Philosophy of the Christian Religion at the University of Oxford, disagrees with Hume's view of miracles. Swinburne believes that the evidence that an event was a miracle can be strong enough to help establish the existence of God.

... [I]f there is a God, who, being perfectly good, will love his creatures, one would expect him to interact with us occasionally more directly on a personal basis, rather than merely through the natural order of the world which he constantly sustains—to answer our prayers and to meet our

From Richard Swinburne, *Is There a God?*, Oxford University Press, 1996. Reprinted by permission of the publisher.

needs. He will not, however, intervene in the natural order at all often, for, if he did, we would not be able to predict the consequences of our actions and so we would lose control over the world and ourselves. If God answered most prayers for a relative to recover from cancer, then cancer would no longer be a problem for humans to solve. Humans would no longer see cancer as a problem to be solved by scientific research—prayer would be the obvious method of curing cancer. God would then have deprived us of the serious choice of whether to put money and energy into finding a cure for cancer or not to bother; and of whether to take trouble to avoid cancer (e.g. by not smoking) or not to bother. Natural laws determining that certain events will cause good effects and other ones cause bad effects enable us to discover which produce which and to use them for ourselves. Natural laws are like rules, instituted by parents, schools, or governments, stating that these actions will be punished and those ones rewarded. Once we discover the rules, we acquire control over the consequences of our actions— we can then choose whether to be rewarded or to risk being punished. But loving parents will rightly occasionally break their own rules in answer to special pleading—it means that they are persons in interaction, not just systems of rules. And for a similar reason one might expect God occasionally to break his own rules, and intervene in history.

One might expect God occasionally to answer prayer when it is for a good cause—such as the relief of suffering and restoration to health of mind or body, and for awareness of himself and of important spiritual truths. And one might also expect him to intervene occasionally without waiting for our prayer—to help us to make the world better in various ways when we have misused our freedom. A divine intervention will consist either in God acting in areas where natural laws do not determine what happens (perhaps our mental life is not fully determined by natural laws), or in God temporarily suspending natural laws. Let us call interventions of the latter kind miracles and interventions of the former kind non-miraculous interventions. A miracle is a violation or suspension of natural laws, brought about by God. Does human

history contain events of a kind which God, if he exists, would be expected to bring about and yet which do not occur as a result of the operation of natural laws? It certainly contains large numbers of events of the kind which God would be expected to bring about, but about which we have no idea whether they occurred as a result of the operation of natural laws or not. I pray for my friend to get better from cancer and he does. Since we do not normally know in any detail the exact state of his body when he had cancer, nor do we know in any detail the natural laws which govern the development of cancer, we cannot say whether the recovery occurs as a result of natural laws or not. The pious believer believes that God intervened, and the hard-headed atheist believes that only natural laws were at work. Human history also contains *reports* of many events which, *if* they occurred as reported, clearly would not have occurred as a result of natural laws, and which are also events of a kind that God might be expected to bring about. The Second Book of Kings records that a sick and doubting King Hezekiah sought a sign of encouragement from God that he, Hezekiah, would recover and that God would save Jerusalem from the Assyrians. In response to the prayer of the prophet Isaiah that God would give Hezekiah a sign, the shadow cast by the sun reportedly went 'backwards ten steps' (2 Kgs. 20: 11). The latter can only have happened if the laws of mechanics (governing the rotation of the earth on its axis, and so the direction of the sun from Jerusalem), or the laws of light (governing how light from the sun forms shadows in the region of Hezekiah's palace), had been suspended.

I suggest that, in so far as we have other reason to believe that there is a God, we have reason to believe that God intervenes in history in some such cases (we may not know which) and so that some of the events happened as described, although not necessitated to do so by natural laws. It would be odd to suppose that God, concerned for our total well-being, confined his interventions to those areas (if any) where natural laws leave it undetermined what will happen—for example, confined his interventions to influencing the mental lives of human beings. If he has reason to interact with us, he has reason very occasionally to intervene to suspend those natural laws by which our life is controlled; and in particular, since the bodily processes which determine our health are fairly evidently subject to largely deterministic natural laws, he has reason very occasionally to intervene in those. Conversely, in so far as we have other reason to believe that there is no God, we have reason to believe that natural processes are the highest-level determinants of what happens and so that no events happen contrary to laws of nature. In other words, background knowledge (our other reasons for general belief about how the world works—e.g. reasons for believing that there is a God, or that there is no God) is rightly a very important factor in assessing what happened on particular occasions …

But, while background knowledge must be a powerful factor in determining what is reasonable to believe about what happened on particular occasions, it is not, of course, the only factor. We have the detailed historical evidence of what observers seem to recall having happened, what witnesses claim to have observed, and any physical traces of past events (documents, archaeological remains, and so on).

That background knowledge must weigh heavily in comparison with the detailed historical evidence in assessing particular claims about the past can be seen from innumerable non-religious examples. If a well-established scientific theory leads you to expect that stars will sometimes explode, then some debris in the sky of a kind which could have been caused by an exploding star but which (though improbably) just might have some other cause may be reasonably interpreted as debris left by an exploding star. But, if a well-established theory says that stars cannot explode, you will need very strong evidence that the debris could not have had another cause before interpreting it as debris of an exploding star. However, in the case of purported miraculous interventions, the background knowledge will be of two kinds. It will include the scientific knowledge of what are the relevant laws of nature—for example, the laws of light and the laws governing the rotation of the earth, which (since laws of nature operate almost all the time) lead us to expect that on that particular occasion Hezekiah's shadow did not move

backwards. But it will also include the other evidence that there is a God able and having reason sometimes (but not necessarily on any one particular occasion) to intervene to suspend the operation of natural laws. In view of these conflicting bodies of background knowledge, we would need quite a bit of particular historical evidence to show that, on any particular occasion, God intervened in a miraculous way. The historical evidence could be backed up by argument that that particular purported miracle was one which God had strong reason for bringing about.

To balance detailed historical evidence against background evidence of both kinds to establish what happened on any particular occasion is a difficult matter on which we are seldom going to be able to reach a clear verdict. But detailed historical evidence about what happened could in principle be substantial. To take a simple, imaginary, and not especially religiously significant example, we ourselves might have apparently seen someone levitate (that is, rise in the air, not as a result of strings or magnets or any other known force for which we have checked). Many witnesses, proved totally trustworthy on other occasions where they would have had no reason to lie, might report having observed such a thing. There might even be traces in the form of physical effects which such an event would have caused—for example, marks on the ceiling which would have been caused by a levitating body hitting it. But against all this there will still be the background knowledge of what are the laws of nature, in this case the laws of gravity; and all the evidence in favour of these being the laws of nature will be evidence that they operated at the time in question, and so that no levitation occurred.

Note that any detailed historical evidence that the levitation occurred will, as such, be evidence against the laws of gravity being the laws of nature —just as evidence that some piece of metal did not expand when heated would be evidence that it is not a law of nature that all metals expand when heated. But if, much though we may try, we fail to find further exceptions to our purported law—if, for example, we cannot produce another levitation by recreating the circumstances in which the former one purportedly occurred—that will be grounds for believing that, if the former occurred, it was not an event in accord with some hitherto undiscovered law of nature, but rather a violation or suspension of a law.

In such cases, we would, I think, be most unlikely to have enough detailed historical evidence that the event occurred to outweigh the scientific background knowledge that such events cannot occur, unless we also had substantial religious background knowledge showing not merely that there is a God but that he had very good reason on this particular occasion to work this particular miracle. In the case of a purported levitation. I doubt that we would ever have such evidence. That is not, of course, to say that levitations do not occur, only that we are most unlikely to have enough reason to believe that one did occur on any particular occasion. Note that in all such cases what we are doing is to seek the simplest theory of what happened in the past which leads us to account for the data (what I have here called the detailed historical evidence), and which fits in best with our background knowledge....

I am, however, inclined to think that we do have enough historical evidence of events occurring contrary to natural laws of a kind which God would have reason to bring out to show that probably some of them (we do not know which) are genuine miracles. There are many reports of purported miracles, ancient and modern, some of them quite well documented. (See for example, the cure of the Glasgow man from cancer described in D. Hickey and G. Smith, *Miracle* (1978), or some of the cases discussed in Rex Gardiner, *Healing Miracles* (1986). For a more sceptical account of some purported Lourdes miracles, see, for contrast, D. J. West, *Eleven Lourdes Miracles* (1957).) Or, rather, we have enough detailed historical evidence in some such cases given that we have a certain amount of background evidence to support the claim that there is a God, able and willing to intervene in history. But, of course, the reader must consider the evidence in such cases for himself or herself. The occurrence of such detailed historical evidence is itself further evidence of the existence of God ... because one would expect to have it if there is a God but not otherwise—for if natural laws are the highest-level de-

terminants of what happens, there is every reason to expect that they will not be suspended.

It is so often said in such cases that we 'may be mistaken'. New scientific evidence may show that the event as reported was not contrary to natural laws—we simply misunderstood what were the natural laws. Maybe we have just misunderstood how cancer develops; a patient sometimes 'spontaneously' recovers by purely natural processes. Or, if many people claim to have observed someone levitate, maybe they have all been subject to hallucination. Maybe. But the rational enquirer in these matters, as in all matters, must go on the evidence available. If that evidence shows that the laws of nature are such and such, that if the event happened as described it was contrary to them, that the new evidence had no tendency to show that the supposed laws are not the true laws (because in all other similar cases they are followed), that there is very strong historical evidence (witnesses, and so on) that the event occurred, then it is rational to believe that a miracle occurred. We are rational to believe, while allowing the possibility that evidence might turn up later to show that we are mistaken. 'We may be mistaken' is a knife which cuts both ways—we may be mistaken in believing that an event is not a divine intervention when really it is, as well as the other way round.

Historians often affirm that, when they are investigating particular claims about past events important to religious traditions—for example, about what Jesus did and what happened to him—they do so without making any religious or anti-religious assumptions. In practice most of them do not live up to such affirmations. Either they heavily discount such biblical claims as that Jesus cured the blind on the grounds that such things do not happen; or (more commonly in past centuries) they automatically accept the testimony of witnesses to what Jesus did, on the grounds that biblical witnesses are especially reliable. But what needs to be appreciated is that background evidence ought to influence the investigator—as it does in all other areas of enquiry. Not to allow it to do so is irrational.

The existence of detailed historical evidence for the occurrence of violations of natural laws of a kind which God, if there is a God, would have had reason to bring about is itself evidence for the existence of God. Though not nearly enough on its own, it makes its contribution; and with other evidence... it could be enough to establish the existence of God, if the other evidence is not enough on its own. Consider, by analogy, a detective investigating a crime and considering the hypothesis that Jones committed the crime. Some of his clues will be evidence for the occurrence of some event, an event which, if it occurred, would provide evidence in its turn for the hypothesis that Jones committed the crime. The former might, for example, be the evidence of witnesses who claim to have seen Jones near the scene of the crime. Even if Jones was near the scene of the crime, that is in its turn on its own fairly weak evidence that he committed the crime. Much more evidence is needed. But because the testimony of witnesses is evidence for Jones having been near the scene of the crime, and Jones having been near the scene is some evidence that he committed it, the testimony of the witnesses is nevertheless some (indirect) evidence for his having committed the crime. Likewise, evidence of witnesses who claim to observe a violation of natural laws is indirect evidence for the existence of God, because the occurrence of such violations would be itself more direct evidence for the existence of God. If the total evidence becomes strong enough, then it will justify asserting that God exists, and hence that the event in question was not merely a violation, but brought about by God and thus a miracle.

C. MYSTICISM

43   MYSTICISM

WILLIAM JAMES

Another possible avenue to God lies through mystical experiences in which people report direct contact with the divine.

The best-known treatment of mysticism is found in William James's book *The Varieties of Religious Experience*. James (1842–1910), who earned a medical degree but never practiced and was the older brother of the novelist Henry James, became professor of philosophy and psychology at Harvard University. He relied on his knowledge of both disciplines in his detailed survey and analysis of mystical experiences. He concluded that they were authoritative for the individuals who underwent them and believed them, but not for others. Nevertheless, he believed that these experiences offered valuable insights into the range of human consciousness.

LECTURES XVI AND XVII

Mysticism

Over and over again in these lectures I have raised points and left them open and unfinished until we should have come to the subject of Mysticism. Some of you, I fear, may have smiled as you noted my reiterated postponements. But now the hour has come when mysticism must be faced in good earnest, and those broken threads wound up together. One may say truly, I think, that personal religious experience has its root and centre in mystical states of consciousness; so for us, who in these lectures are treating personal experience as the exclusive subject of our study, such states of consciousness ought to form the vital chapter from which the other chapters get their light. Whether my treatment of mystical states will shed more light or darkness, I do not know, for my own constitution shuts me out from their enjoyment almost entirely, and I can speak of them only at second hand. But though forced to look upon the subject so externally, I will be as objective and receptive as I can; and I think I shall at

least succeed in convincing you of the reality of the states in question, and of the paramount importance of their function.

First of all, then, I ask, What does the expression "mystical states of consciousness" mean? How do we part off mystical states from other states?

The words "mysticism" and "mystical" are often used as terms of mere reproach, to throw at any opinion which we regard as vague and vast and sentimental, and without a base in either facts or logic. For some writers a "mystic" is any person who believes in thought-transference, or spirit-return. Employed in this way the word has little value: there are too many less ambiguous synonyms. So, to keep it useful by restricting it, I will… simply propose to you four marks which, when an experience has them, may justify us in calling it mystical for the purpose of the present lectures. In this way we shall save verbal disputation, and the recriminations that generally go therewith.

1. *Ineffability.*—The handiest of the marks by which I classify a state of mind as mystical is negative. The subject of it immediately says

---

From William James, *The Varieties of Religious Experience* (1902).

that it defies expression, that no adequate report of its contents can be given in words. It follows from this that its quality must be directly experienced; it cannot be imparted or transferred to others. In this peculiarity mystical states are more like states of feeling than like states of intellect. No one can make clear to another who has never had a certain feeling, in what the quality or worth of it consists. One must have musical ears to know the value of a symphony; one must have been in love one's self to understand a lover's state of mind. Lacking the heart or ear, we cannot interpret the musician or the lover justly, and are even likely to consider him weak-minded or absurd. The mystic finds that most of us accord to his experiences an equally incompetent treatment.

2. *Noetic quality.*—Although so similar to states of feeling, mystical states seem to those who experience them to be also states of knowledge. They are states of insight into depths of truth unplumbed by the discursive intellect. They are illuminations, revelations, full of significance and importance, all inarticulate though they remain; and as a rule they carry with them a curious sense of authority for after-time.

These two characters will entitle any state to be called mystical, in the sense in which I use the word. Two other qualities are less sharply marked, but are usually found. These are:

3. *Transiency.*—Mystical states cannot be sustained for long. Except in rare instances, half an hour, or at most an hour or two, seems to be the limit beyond which they fade into the light of common day. Often, when faded, their quality can but imperfectly be reproduced in memory; but when they recur it is recognized; and from one recurrence to another it is susceptible of continuous development in what is felt as inner richness and importance.

4. *Passivity.*—Although the oncoming of mystical states may be facilitated by preliminary voluntary operations, as by fixing the attention, or going through certain bodily performances, or in other ways which manuals of mysticism prescribe; yet when the characteristic sort of consciousness once has set in, the mystic feels as if his own will were in abeyance, and indeed sometimes as if he were grasped and held by a superior power. This latter peculiarity connects mystical states with certain definite phenomena of secondary or alternative personality, such as prophetic speech, automatic writing, or the mediumistic trance. When these latter conditions are well pronounced, however, there may be no recollection whatever of the phenomenon, and it may have no significance for the subject's usual inner life, to which, as it were, it makes a mere interruption. Mystical states, strictly so called, are never merely interruptive. Some memory of their content always remains, and a profound sense of their importance. They modify the inner life of the subject between the times of their recurrence. Sharp divisions in this region are, however, difficult to make, and we find all sorts of gradations and mixtures.

These four characteristics are sufficient to mark out a group of states of consciousness peculiar enough to deserve a special name and to call for careful study....

In the Christian church there have always been mystics. Although many of them have been viewed with suspicion, some have gained favor in the eyes of the authorities. The experiences of these have been treated as precedents, and a codified system of mystical theology has been based upon them, in which everything legitimate finds its place. The basis of the system is "orison" or meditation, the methodical elevation of the soul towards God....

The first thing to be aimed at in orison is the mind's detachment from outer sensations, for these interfere with its concentration upon ideal things. Such manuals as Saint Ignatius's *Spiritual Exercises* recommend the disciple to expel sensation by a graduated series of efforts to imagine holy scenes. The acme of this kind of discipline would be a semi-hallucinatory monoideism—an imaginary figure of Christ, for example, coming fully to occupy the mind. Sensorial images of this sort, whether literal or symbolic play an enormous part in mysticism. But in certain cases imagery may fall away entirely, and in the very highest raptures it tends to do so. The state of consciousness becomes then insusceptible of any verbal description. Mystical teachers are unanimous as to this. Saint John of the Cross, for instance, one of the best of them, thus describes the condition called the "union of love," which, he says, is reached by "dark contemplation." In this the Deity compenetrates the soul, but in such a hidden way that the soul

finds no terms, no means, no comparison whereby to render the sublimity of the wisdom and the delicacy of the spiritual feeling with which she is filled.... We receive this mystical knowledge of God clothed in none of the kinds of images, in none of the sensible representations, which our mind makes use of in other circumstances. Accordingly in this knowledge, since the senses and the imagination are not employed, we get neither form nor impression, nor can we give any account or furnish any likeness, although the mysterious and sweet-tasting wisdom comes home so clearly to the inmost parts of our soul. Fancy a man seeing a certain kind of thing for the first time in his life. He can understand it, use and enjoy it, but he cannot apply a name to it, nor communicate any idea of it, even though all the while it be a mere thing of sense. How much greater will be his powerlessness when it goes beyond the senses! This is the peculiarity of the divine language. The more infused, intimate, spiritual, and supersensible it is, the more does it exceed the senses, both inner and outer, and impose silence upon them.... The soul then feels as if placed in a vast and profound solitude, to which no created thing has access, in an immense and boundless desert, desert the more delicious the more solitary it is. There, in this abyss of wisdom, the soul grows by what it drinks in from the well-springs of the comprehension of love,... and recognizes, however sublime and learned may be the terms we employ, how utterly vile, insignificant, and improper they are, when we seek to discourse of divine things by their means.[1]

I cannot pretend to detail to you the sundry stages of the Christian mystical life. Our time would not suffice, for one thing; and moreover, I confess that the subdivisions and names which we find in the Catholic books seem to me to represent nothing objectively distinct. So many men, so many minds: I imagine that these experiences can be as infinitely varied as are the idiosyncrasies of individuals.

The cognitive aspects of them, their value in the way of revelation, is what we are directly concerned with, and it is easy to show by citation how strong an impression they leave of being revelations of new depths of truth. Saint Teresa is the expert of experts in describing such conditions, so I will turn immediately to what she says of one of the highest of them, the "orison of union."

"In the orison of union," says Saint Teresa, "the soul is fully awake as regards God, but wholly asleep as regards things of this world and in respect of herself. During the short time the union lasts, she is as it were deprived of every feeling, and even if she would, she could not think of any single thing. Thus she needs to employ no artifice in order to arrest the use of her understanding: it remains so stricken with inactivity that she neither knows what she loves, nor in what manner she loves, nor what she wills. In short, she is utterly dead to the things of the world and lives solely in God.... I do not even know whether in this state she has enough life left to breathe. It seems to me she has not; or at least that if she does breathe, she is unaware of it. Her intellect would fain understand something of what is going on within her, but it has so little force now that it can act in no way whatsoever. So a person who falls into a deep faint appears as if dead....

"Thus does God, when he raises a soul to union with himself, suspend the natural action of all her faculties. She neither sees, hears, nor understands, so long as she is united with God. But this time is always short, and it seems even shorter than it is. God establishes himself in the interior of this soul in such a way, that when she returns to herself, it is wholly impossible for her to doubt that she has been in God, and God in her. This truth remains so strongly impressed on her that, even though many years should pass without the condition returning, she can neither forget the favor she received, nor doubt of its reality. If you, nevertheless, ask how it is possible that the soul can see and understand that she has been in God, since during the union she has neither sight nor understanding, I reply that she does not see it then, but that she sees it clearly later, after she has returned to herself, not by any vision, but by a certitude which abides with her and which God alone can give her. I knew a person who was ignorant of the truth that God's mode of being in everything must be either by presence, by power, or by essence, but who, after having received the grace of which I am speaking, believed this truth in the most unshakable manner. So much so that, having consulted a half-learned man who was as ignorant on this point as she had been before she was enlightened, when he replied that God is in us only by 'grace,' she disbelieved his reply, so sure she was of the true answer; and when she came to ask wiser doctors, they confirmed her in her belief, which much consoled her....

"But how, you will repeat, *can* one have such certainty in respect to what one does not see? This question, I am powerless to answer. These are secrets of God's omnipotence which it does not appertain to me to penetrate. All that I know is that I tell the truth; and I shall never believe that any soul who does not possess this certainty has ever been really united to God."[2]

The kinds of truth communicable in mystical ways, whether these be sensible or supersensible, are various. Some of them relate to this world— visions of the future, the reading of hearts, the sudden understanding of texts, the knowledge of distant events, for example; but the most important revelations are theological or metaphysical.

Saint Ignatius confessed one day to Father Laynez that a single hour of meditation at Manresa had taught him more truths about heavenly things than all the teachings of all the doctors put together could have taught him.... One day in orison, on the steps of the choir of the Dominican church, he saw in a distinct manner the plan of divine wisdom in the creation of the world. On another occasion, during a procession, his spirit was ravished in God, and it was given him to contemplate, in a form and images fitted to the weak understanding of a dweller on the earth, the deep mystery of the holy Trinity. This last vision flooded his heart with such sweetness, that the mere memory of it in after times made him shed abundant tears.[3]

Similarly with Saint Teresa. "One day, being in orison," she writes," it was granted me to perceive in one instant how all things are seen and contained in God. I did not perceive them in their proper form, and nevertheless the view I had of them was of a sovereign clearness, and has remained vividly impressed upon my soul. It is one of the most signal of all the graces which the Lord has granted me.... The view was so subtle and delicate that the understanding cannot grasp it."[4]

She goes on to tell how it was as if the Deity were an enormous and sovereignly limpid diamond, in which all our actions were contained in such a way that their full sinfulness appeared evident as never before. On another day, she relates, while she was reciting the Athanasian Creed,

Our Lord made me comprehend in what way it is that one God can be in three Persons. He made me see it so clearly that I remained as extremely surprised as I was comforted,... and now, when I think of the holy Trinity, or hear It spoken of, I understand how the three adorable Persons form only one God and I experience an unspeakable happiness.

On still another occasion, it was given to Saint Teresa to see and understand in what wise the Mother of God had been assumed into her place in Heaven.[5]

The deliciousness of some of these states seems to be beyond anything known in ordinary consciousness. It evidently involves organic sensibilities, for it is spoken of as something too extreme to be borne, and as verging on bodily pain.[6] But it is too subtle and piercing a delight for ordinary words to denote. God's touches, the wounds of his spear, references to ebriety and to nuptial union have to figure in the phraseology by which it is shadowed forth. Intellect and senses both swoon away in these highest states of ecstasy. "If our understanding comprehends," says Saint Teresa, "it is in a mode which remains unknown to it, and it can understand nothing of what it comprehends. For my own part, I do not believe that it does comprehend, because, as I said, it does not understand itself to do so. I confess that it is all a mystery in which I am lost."[7] In the condition called *raptus* or ravishment by theologians, breathing and circulation are so depressed that it is a question among the doctors whether the soul be or be not temporarily dissevered from the body. One must read Saint Teresa's descriptions and the very exact distinctions which she makes, to persuade one's self that one is dealing, not with imaginary experiences, but with phenomena which, however rare, follow perfectly definite psychological types.

To the medical mind these ecstasies signify nothing but suggested and imitated hypnoid states, on an intellectual basis of superstition, and a corporeal one of degeneration and hysteria. Undoubtedly these pathological conditions have existed in many and possibly in all the cases, but that fact tells us nothing about the value for knowledge of the consciousness which they induce. To pass a spiritual judgment upon these states, we must not content ourselves with superficial medical talk, but inquire into their fruits for life.

Their fruits appear to have been various. Stupefaction, for one thing, seems not to have been altogether absent as a result. You may remember the helplessness in the kitchen and schoolroom of poor Margaret Mary Alacoque. Many other ecstatics would have perished but for the care taken of them by admiring followers. The "otherworldliness" encouraged by the mystical consciousness makes this over-abstraction from practical life peculiarly liable to befall mystics in whom the character is naturally passive and the intellect feeble; but in natively strong minds and characters we find quite opposite results. The great Spanish mystics, who carried the habit of ecstasy as far as it has often been carried, appear for the most part to have shown indomitable spirit and energy, and all the more so for the trances in which they indulged.

Saint Ignatius was a mystic, but his mysticism made him assuredly one of the most powerfully practical human engines that ever lived. Saint John of the Cross, writing of the intuitions and "touches" by which God reaches the substance of the soul, tells us that

> They enrich it marvelously. A single one of them may be sufficient to abolish at a stroke certain imperfections of which the soul during its whole life had vainly tried to rid itself, and to leave it adorned with virtues and loaded with supernatural gifts. A single one of these intoxicating consolations may reward it for all the labors undergone in its life—

even were they numberless. Invested with an invincible courage, filled with an impassioned desire to suffer for its God, the soul then is seized with a strange torment—that of not being allowed to suffer enough.[8]

Saint Teresa is as emphatic, and much more detailed.... Where in literature is a more evidently veracious account of the formation of a new centre of spiritual energy, than is given in her description of the effects of certain ecstasies which in departing leave the soul upon a higher level of emotional excitement?

> Often, infirm and wrought upon with dreadful pains before the ecstasy, the soul emerges from it full of health and admirably disposed for action ... as if God had willed that the body itself, already obedient to the soul's desires, should share in the soul's happiness.... The soul after such a favor is animated with a degree of courage so great that if at that moment its body should be torn to pieces for the cause of God, it would feel nothing but the liveliest comfort. Then it is that promises and heroic resolutions spring up in profusion in us, soaring desires, horror of the world, and the clear perception of our proper nothingness.... What empire is comparable to that of a soul who, from this sublime summit to which God has raised her, sees all the things of earth beneath her feet, and is captivated by no one of them? How ashamed she is of her former attachments! How amazed at her blindness! What lively pity she feels for those whom she recognizes still shrouded in the darkness!... She groans at having ever been sensitive to points of honor, at the illusion that made her ever see as honor what the world calls by that name. Now she sees in this name nothing more than an immense lie of which the world remains a victim. She discovers, in the new light from above, that in genuine honor there is nothing spurious, that to be faithful to this honor is to give our respect to what deserves to be respected really, and to consider as nothing, or as less than nothing, whatsoever perishes and is not agreeable to God.... She laughs when she sees grave persons, persons of orison, caring for points of honor for which she now feels profoundest contempt. It is suitable to the dignity of their rank to act thus, they pretend, and it makes them more useful to others. But she knows that in despising the dignity of their rank for the pure love of God they would do more good in

a single day than they would effect in ten years by preserving it.... She laughs at herself that there should ever have been a time in her life when she made any case of money, when she ever desired it... Oh! if human beings might only agree together to regard it as so much useless mud, what harmony would then reign in the world!... With what friendship we would all treat each other if our interest in honor and in money could but disappear from earth! For my own part, I feel as if it would be a remedy for all our ills.[9]

Mystical conditions may, therefore, render the soul more energetic in the lines which their inspiration favors. But this could be reckoned an advantage only in case the inspiration were a true one. If the inspiration were erroneous, the energy would be all the more mistaken and misbegotten.... Do mystical states establish the truth of those theological affections in which the saintly life has its root?

In spite of their repudiation of articulate self-description, mystical states in general assert a pretty distinct theoretic drift. It is possible to give the outcome of the majority of them in terms that point in definite philosophical directions. One of these directions is optimism, and the other is monism. We pass into mystical states from out of ordinary consciousness as from a less into a more, as from a smallness into a vastness, and at the same time as from an unrest to a rest. We feel them as reconciling, unifying states. They appeal to the yes-function more than to the no-function in us. In them the unlimited absorbs the limits and peacefully closes the account. Their very denial of every adjective you may propose as applicable to the ultimate truth—He, the Self, the Atman, is to be described by "No! no!" only, say the Upanishads—though it seems on the surface to be a no-function, is a denial made on behalf of a deeper yes. Whoso calls the Absolute anything in particular, or says that it is *this*, seems implicitly to shut it off from being *that*—it is as if he lessened it. So we deny the "this," negating the negation which it seems to us to imply, in the interests of the higher affirmative attitude by which we are possessed....

I have now sketched with extreme brevity and insufficiency, but as fairly as I am able in the time allowed, the general traits of the mystic range of consciousness. *It is on the whole pantheistic and optimistic, or at least the opposite of pessimistic. It is anti-naturalistic, and harmonizes best with twice-bornness and so-called other-worldly states of mind.*

My next task is to inquire whether we can invoke it as authoritative. Does it furnish any *warrant for the truth* of the twice-bornness and supernaturality and pantheism which it favors? I must give my answer to this question as concisely as I can.

In brief my answer is this—and I will divide it into three parts:

1. Mystical states, when well developed, usually are, and have the right to be, absolutely authoritative over the individuals to whom they come.

2. No authority emanates from them which should make it a duty for those who stand outside of them to accept their revelations uncritically.

3. They break down the authority of the non-mystical or rationalistic consciousness, based upon the understanding and the senses alone. They show it to be only one kind of consciousness. They open out the possibility of other orders of truth, in which, so far as anything in us vitally responds to them, we may freely continue to have faith.

I will take up these points one by one.

1

As a matter of psychological fact, mystical states of a well-pronounced and emphatic sort *are* usually authoritative over those who have them. They have been "there," and know. It is vain for rationalism to grumble about this. If the mystical truth that comes to a man proves to be a force that he can live by, what mandate have we of the majority to order him to live in another way? We can throw him into a prison or a madhouse, but we cannot change his mind—we commonly attach it only the more stubbornly to its beliefs. It mocks our utmost efforts, as a matter of fact, and in point of logic it absolutely escapes our jurisdiction. Our own more "rational" beliefs are based on evidence exactly similar in nature to that which mystics quote for theirs. Our senses, namely, have assured us of certain states of fact; but mystical experiences are as direct perceptions of fact for those who have them as any sensations ever were for us. The records show that even though the five senses be in abeyance in them, they are absolutely sensational in their epistemological quality, if I may be pardoned the barbarous expression—that is, they are face to face presentations of what seems immediately to exist.

The mystic is, in short, *invulnerable*, and must be left, whether we relish it or not, in undisturbed enjoyment of his creed. Faith, says Tolstoy, is that by which men live. And faith-state and mystic state are practically convertible terms.

2

But I now proceed to add that mystics have no right to claim that we ought to accept the deliverance of their peculiar experiences, if we are ourselves outsiders and feel no private call thereto. The utmost they can ever ask of us in this life is to admit that they establish a presumption. They form a consensus and have an unequivocal outcome; and it would be odd, mystics might say, if such a unanimous type of experience should prove to be altogether wrong. At bottom, however, this would only be an appeal to numbers, like the appeal of rationalism the other way; and the appeal to numbers has no logical force. If we acknowledge it, it is for "suggestive," not for logical reasons: we follow the majority because to do so suits our life.

But even this presumption from the unanimity of mystics is far from being strong. In characterizing mystic states as pantheistic, optimistic, etc., I am afraid I over-simplified the truth. I did so for expository reasons, and to keep the closer to the classic mystical tradition. The classic religious mysticism, it now must be confessed, is only a "privileged case." It is an *extract*, kept true to type by the selection of the fittest specimens and their preservation in "schools." It is carved out from a much larger mass; and if we take the larger mass as seriously as religious mysticism has historically taken itself, we find that the supposed unanimity largely disappears. To begin with, even religious mysticism itself, the kind that accumulates traditions and makes schools, is much less unanimous than I have allowed. It has been both ascetic and antinomianly self-indulgent within the Christian church. It is dualistic in Sankhya, and monistic in Vedanta philosophy. I called it pantheistic; but the great Spanish mystics are anything but pantheists. They are with few exceptions non-metaphysical minds, for whom "the category of personality" is absolute. The "union" of man with God is for them much more like an occasional miracle than like an original identity. How different again, apart from the happiness common to all, is the mysticism of Walt Whitman ... and other naturalistic pantheists, from the more distinctively Christian sort. The fact is that the mystical feeling of enlargement, union, and emancipation has no specific intellectual content whatever of its own. It is capable of forming matrimonial alliances with material furnished by the most diverse philosophies and theologies, provided only they can find a place in their framework for its peculiar emotional mood. We have no right, therefore, to invoke its prestige as distinctively in favor of any special belief, such as that in absolute idealism, or in the absolute monistic identity, or in the absolute goodness, of the world. It is only relatively in favor of all these things—it passes out of common human consciousness in the direction in which they lie.

So much for religious mysticism proper. But more remains to be told, for religious mysticism is only one half of mysticism. The other half has no accumulated traditions except those which the textbooks on insanity supply. Open any one of these, and you will find abundant cases in which "mystical ideas" are cited as characteristic symptoms of enfeebled or deluded states of mind. In delusional insanity, paranoia, as they sometimes call it, we may have a *diabolical* mysticism, a sort of religious mysticism turned upside down. The same sense of ineffable importance in the smallest events, the same texts and words coming with new meanings, the same voices and visions and leadings and missions, the same controlling by extraneous powers; only this time the emotion is pessimistic: instead of consolations we have desolations; the meanings are dreadful; and the powers are enemies to life. It is evident that from the point of view of their psychological mechanism, the classic mysticism and these lower mysticisms spring from the same mental level, from that great subliminal or transmarginal region of which science is beginning to admit the existence, but of which so little is really known. That region contains every kind of matter: "seraph and snake" abide there side by side. To come from thence is no infallible credential. What comes must be sifted and tested, and run the gauntlet of confrontation with the total context of experience, just like what comes from the outer world of sense. Its value must be ascertained by empirical methods, so long as we are not mystics ourselves.

Once more, then, I repeat that non-mystics are under no obligation to acknowledge in mystical states a superior authority conferred on them by their intrinsic nature.

3

Yet, I repeat once more, the existence of mystical states absolutely overthrows the pretension of non-mystical states to be the sole and ultimate dictators of what we may believe. As a rule, mystical states merely add a supersensuous meaning to the ordinary outward data of consciousness. They are excitements like the emotions of love or ambition, gifts to our spirit by means of which facts already objectively before us fall into a new expressiveness and make a new connexion with our active life. They do not contradict these facts as such, or deny anything that our senses have immediately seized. It is the rationalistic critic rather who plays the part of denier in the controversy, and his denials have no strength, for there never can be a state of facts to which new meaning may not truthfully be added, provided the mind ascend to a more enveloping point of view. It must always remain an open question whether mystical states may not possibly be such superior points of view windows through which the mind looks out upon a more extensive and inclusive world. The difference of the views seen from the different mystical windows need not prevent us from entertaining this supposition. The wider world would in that case prove to have a mixed constitution like that of this world, that is all. It would have its celestial and its infernal regions, its tempting and its saving moments, its valid experiences and its counterfeit ones, just as our world has them; but it would be a wider world all the same. We should have to use its experiences by selecting and subordinating and substituting just as is our custom in this ordinary naturalistic world; we should be liable to error just as we are now; yet the counting in of that wider world of meanings, and the serious dealing with it, might, in spite of all the perplexity, be indispensable stages in our approach to the final fullness of the truth.

In this shape, I think, we have to leave the subject. Mystical states indeed wield no authority due simply to their being mystical states. But the higher ones among them point in directions to which the religious sentiments even of non-mystical men incline. They tell of the supremacy of the ideal, of vastness, of union, of safety, and of rest. They offer us *hypotheses*, hypotheses which we may voluntarily ignore, but which as thinkers we cannot possibly upset. The supernaturalism and optimism to which they would persuade us may, interpreted in one way or another, be after all the truest of insights into the meaning of this life.

NOTES

1. Saint John of the Cross: *The Dark Night of the Soul*, book ii, ch. xvii, in *Vie et Oeuvres*, 3me édition, Paris, 1893, iii, 428–432. Chapter xi of book ii of Saint John's *Ascent of Carmel* is devoted to showing the harmfulness for the mystical life of the use of sensible imagery.
2. *The Interior Castle*, Fifth Abode, ch. i, in *Oeuvres*, translated by Bouix, iii, 421–424.
3. Bartoli-Michel: *Histoire de S. Ignace de Loyola*, i. 34–36....
4. *Vie*, pp. 581, 582.
5. Loc. cit., p. 574.
6. Saint Teresa discriminates between pain in which the body has a part and pure spiritual pain (*Interior Castle*, 6th Abode, ch. xi). As for the bodily part in these celestial joys, she speaks of it as "penetrating to the narrow of the bones, whilst earthly pleasures affect only the surface of the senses. I think," she adds, "that this is a just description, and I cannot make it better." Ibid., 5th Abode, ch. i.
7. *Vie*, p. 198.
8. *Oeuvres*, ii, 320.
9. *Vie*, pp. 229, 200, 232, 233–234, 243.

44   PERCEIVING GOD

WILLIAM P. ALSTON

William P. Alston, whose work we read previously, views mystical experience as a form of perception that, assuming God exists, enables us to interact with God. Does such experience offer knowledge of God? Alston concludes that, as in the case of perceptual claims, we should accept them unless we have sufficient reason to the contrary.

I

I pick out what I am calling "experience of God" by the fact that the subject takes the experience (or would take it if the question arose) to be a direct awareness of God. Here is a clear example cited in William James's *The Varieties of Religious Experience.*

> (1) ... all at once I ... felt the presence of God—I tell of the thing just as I was conscious of it—as if his goodness and his power were penetrating me altogether. Then, slowly, the ecstasy left my heart; that is, I felt that God had withdrawn the communion which he had granted.... I asked myself if it were possible that Moses on Sinai could have had a more intimate communication with God. I think it well to add that in this ecstasy of mine God had neither form, color, odor, nor taste; moreover, that the feeling of his presence was accompanied by no determinate localization.... But the more I seek words to express this intimate intercourse, the more I feel the impossibility of describing the thing by any of our usual images. At bottom the expression most apt to render what I felt is this: God was present, though invisible; he fell under no one of my senses, yet my consciousness perceived him.

Note that I do not restrict "experience of God" to cases in which it is really God of whom the subject is aware. The term, as I use it, ranges over all experiences that the subject *takes* to have this status. Thus the general category would be more exactly termed *"supposed* experience of God," where calling it "supposed" does not prejudice the question of whether it is genuine or not.

However, I will generally omit this qualification. Note too that my category of "experience of God" is much narrower than "religious experience," which covers a diverse and ill-defined multitude of experiences.

In restricting myself to *direct* awareness of God I exclude cases in which one takes oneself to be aware of God through the beauties of nature, the words of the Bible or of a sermon, or other natural phenomena. For example:

> (2) I feel him [God] in the sunshine or rain; and awe mingled with a delicious restfulness most nearly describes my feelings.

My reason for concentrating on direct experience of God, where there is no other object of experience in or through which God is experienced, is that these experiences are the ones that are most plausibly regarded as *presentations* of God to the individual, in somewhat the way in which physical objects are presented to sense perception, as I will shortly make explicit.

Within this territory I will range over both lay and professional examples, both ordinary people living in the world and monastics who more or less devote their lives to attaining union with God. The category also embraces both focal and background experiences; though in order to discern the structure of the phenomenon we are well advised to concentrate on its more intense forms.

There is also the distinction between experiences with and without sensory content. In (1) the subject explicitly denies that the experience

---

Originally titled "Religious Experience as Perception of God" and reprinted by permission of the estate of William P. Alston.

was sensory in character. Here is an example that does involve sensory content.

> (3) During the night ... I awoke and looking out of my window saw what I took to be a luminous star which gradually came nearer, and appeared as a soft slightly blurred white light. I was seized with violent trembling, but had no fear. I knew that what I felt was great awe. This was followed by a sense of overwhelming love coming to me, and going out from me, then of great compassion from this Outer Presence. (Cited in T. Beardsworth, *A Sense of Presence*.)

In this discussion I will concentrate on non-sensory experiences. The main reason for this choice is that since God is purely spiritual, a non-sensory experience has a greater chance of presenting Him as He is than any sensory experience. If God appears to us as bearing a certain shape or as speaking in a certain tone of voice, that is a long way from representing Him as He is in Himself. I shall refer to nonsensory experience of God as "mystical experience," and the form of perception of God that involves that experience as "mystical perception." I use these terms with trepidation, for I do not want them to carry connotations of the merging of the individual subject into the One, or any of the other salient features of what we may term "classical mystical experience." (See William James.) They are to be understood simply as shorthand for "supposed nonsensory experience (perception) of God."

Many people find it incredible, unintelligible, or incoherent to suppose that there could be something that counts as *presentation*, that contrasts with abstract thought in the way sense perception does, but is devoid of sensory content. However, so far as I see, this simply evinces lack of speculative imagination or perhaps a mindless parochialism. Why should we suppose that the possibilities of experiential givenness, for human beings or otherwise, are exhausted by the powers of *our* five senses? Surely it is possible, to start with the most obvious point, that other creatures should possess a sensitivity to other physical stimuli that play a role in their functioning analogous to that played by our five senses in our lives. And, to push the matter a bit further, why

can't we also envisage presentations that do not stem from the activity of any physical sense organs, as is apparently the case with mystical perception?

II

As the title indicates, I will be advocating a "perceptual model" of mystical experience. To explain what I mean by that, I must first say something about sense perception, since even if we suppose, as I do, that perception is not restricted to its sensory form, still that is the form with which we are far and away most familiar, and it is by generalizing from sense perception that we acquire a wider concept of perception.

As I see the matter, at the heart of perception (sensory or otherwise) is a phenomenon variously termed *presentation, appearance,* or *givenness*. Something is presented to one's experience (awareness) *as* so-and-so, as blue, as acrid, as a house, as Susie's house, or whatever. I take this phenomenon of *presentation*, to be essentially independent of conceptualization, belief, or judgment. It is possible, in principle, for this book to visually present itself to me as blue even if I do not *take* it to be blue, *think* of it as blue, *conceptualize* it as blue, *judge* it to be blue, or anything else of the sort. No doubt, in mature human perception presentation is intimately intertwined with conceptualization and belief, but presentation does not consist in anything like that. The best way to see this is to contrast actually seeing the book with thinking about the book, or making judgments about it, in its absence. What is involved in the former case but not in the latter that makes the difference? It can't be anything of a conceptual or judgmental order, for anything of that sort can be present in the latter case when the book is not seen. Reflection on this question leads me to conclude that what makes the difference is that when I see the book it is *presented* to my awareness; it occupies a place in my visual field. This crucial notion of presentation cannot be analyzed; it can be conveyed only by helping another to identify instances of it in experience, as I have just done.

On the view of perception I favor, the "Theory of Appearing," perceiving X simply consists in

X's appearing to one, or being presented to one, as so-and-so. That's all there is to it, as far as what perception is, in contrast to its causes and effects. Where X is an external physical object like a book, to perceive the book is just for the book to appear to one in a certain way.

In saying that a direct awareness that does not essentially involve conceptualization and judgment is at the heart of perception, I am *not* denying that a person's conceptual scheme, beliefs, cognitive readinesses, and so on, can affect the *way* an object presents itself to the subject, what it presents itself *as*. Things do look and sound differently to us after we are familiar with them, have the details sorted out, can smoothly put everything in its place without effort. My house presents a different appearance to me now after long habituation than it did the first time I walked in. Whereas Stravinsky's *The Rite of Spring* sounded like a formless cacophony the first time I heard it, it now presents itself to me as a complex interweaving of themes. In saying this I am not going back on my assertion that X's presenting itself to one's awareness as P is not the same as S's *taking* S to be P. The latter involves the application of the concept of P to X, but the former does not, even though the character of the presentation can be influenced by one's conceptual repertoire and one's beliefs. But though my conceptual capacities and tendencies can affect the *way* objects appear to me, they have no power over *what object it is* that looks (sounds …) that way. When I look at my living room, the same objects present themselves to my visual awareness as when I first saw it. It is essential not to confuse *what* appears with what it appears *as*.

Even if to perceive X is simply for X to appear to one in a certain way, there can be further necessary conditions for someone to perceive X, for there can be further conditions for X's appearing to one. First, and this is just spelling out one thing that is involved in X's appearing to one, X must exist. I can't (*really*) perceive a tree unless the tree is there to be perceived. Second, it seems to be necessary for X's appearing to me (for my perceiving X) that X make an important *causal* contribution to my current experience. If there is a thick concrete wall between me and a certain house,

thereby preventing light reflected from the house from striking my retina, then it couldn't be that that house is visually presented to me. I will assume such a causal condition in this discussion. Third, I will also assume a doxastic condition, that perceiving X at least tends to give rise to beliefs about X. This is much more questionable than the causal condition, but in any event we are concerned here with cases in which perception does give rise to beliefs about what is perceived.

III

Now we are ready to turn to the application of the perceptual model to mystical experience. In this essay I will not try to show that mystical experience (even sometimes) constitutes (genuine) perception of God. Remembering the necessary conditions of perception just mentioned, this would involve showing that God exists and that He makes the right kind of causal contribution to the experiences in question. What I will undertake here is the following. (1) I will argue that mystical experience is the right sort of experience to constitute a genuine perception of God if the other requirements are met. (2) I will argue that there is no bar in principle to these other requirements being satisfied if God does exist. This adds up to a defence of the thesis that it is quite possible that human beings do sometimes perceive God if God is "there" to be perceived. In other words, the thesis defended is that if God exists, then mystical experience is quite properly thought of as mystical perception.

If mystical experience is not construed perceptually, how can it be understood? The most common alternative is to think of it as made up of purely subjective feelings and sensations, to which is added an *explanation* according to which the experience is due to God. A recent example of this approach is the important book, *Religious Experience*, by Wayne Proudfoot. Proudfoot goes so far as to identify the "noetic" quality that James and many others have noted in mystical experience with the supposition by the subject that the experience must be given a theological rather than a naturalistic explanation.

It is not difficult to show that the people I have quoted and countless others take their mystical experiences to be perceptual, to involve what I have been calling a direct presentation of God to their awareness, though they do not typically use this terminology. They take their experience to contrast with thinking about God, calling up mental images, entertaining propositions, reasoning, or remembering something about God, just as seeing a tree contrasts with these other cognitive relations to it. They take it that God has been *presented* or *given* to their consciousness in generically the same way as that in which objects in the environment are *presented* to one's consciousness in sense perception. They emphasize the difference between presence to consciousness and absence. Saint Teresa says that God "presents Himself to the soul by a knowledge brighter than the sun." Again she contrasts a "consciousness of the presence of God" with "spiritual feelings and effects of great love and faith of which we become conscious," and with "the fresh resolutions which we make with such deep emotion." Although she takes it that the latter is a "great favour" that "comes from God," still it does not amount to God's actually being present. Another writer who clearly makes this distinction is Angela of Foligno.

> (4) At times God comes into the soul without being called; and He instills into her fire, love, and sometimes sweetness; and the soul believes this comes from God, and delights therein. But she does not yet know, or see, that He dwells in her; she perceives His grace, in which she delights.... And beyond this the soul receives the gift of seeing God. God says to her "Behold Me!" and the soul sees Him dwelling within her. She sees Him more clearly than one man sees another. For the eyes of the soul behold a plenitude of which I cannot speak: a plenitude which is not bodily but spiritual, of which I can say nothing. And the soul rejoices in that sight with an ineffable joy; and this is the manifest and certain sign that God indeed dwells in her.

Thus it is quite clear that the people cited, who are representative of a vast throng, take their experiences to be structured the way, on my view, perception generally is structured. In fact, it may be thought that it is too easy to show this, too much like shooting fish in a barrel. For haven't I chosen my cases on the basis of the subjects' taking themselves to be directly aware of God? They are tailor-made for my purpose. I must plead guilty to picking cases that conform to my construal. But the significant point is that it is so easy to find such cases and that they are so numerous, given the fact that most mystical experiences are not reported at all. As pointed out earlier, I do not wish to deny that there are other forms of "religious experience" and even other forms of experience of God, such as the indirect experiences of God mentioned earlier. My contention is that there is a large body of experiences of God that are perceptual in character, and that they have played a prominent role in Christianity and other religions.

I don't know what could be said against this position except to claim that people who report such experiences are all confused about the character of their experience. Let's consider the following charge.

> These people were all having strongly affective experiences that, because of their theological assumptions and preoccupations, they confused with a direct experience of God. Thus (1) was in an unusual state of exaltation that he interpreted as the power and goodness of God penetrating him. In (4) the "ineffable joy" that Angela says to be "the manifest and certain sign that God indeed dwells in her" is simply a state of feeling that her theological convictions lead her to *interpret* as an awareness of the presence of God. Another possibility is that the person is suddenly seized with an extremely strong conviction of the presence of God, together with sensations and feelings that seem to confirm it. Thus Teresa says that she "had a most distinct feeling that He was always on my right hand, a witness of all I did."

It is conceivable that one should suppose that a purely affective experience or a strongly held conviction should involve the experiential presentation of God when it doesn't, especially if there is a strong need or longing for the latter. But, even if an individual's account of the character of his/her own experience is not infallible, it must certainly be taken seriously. Who is in a better position to determine whether S is having an experience as of something's presenting itself to S as divine than S?

We would need strong reasons to override the subject's confident report of the character of her experience. And where could we find such reasons? I suspect that most people who put forward these alternative diagnoses do so because they have general philosophical reasons for supposing either that God does not exist or that no human being could perceive Him, and they fail to recognize the difference between a *phenomenological* account of object presentation, and the occurrence of veridical perception. In any event, once we get straight about all this, I cannot see any reason for doubting the subjects' account of the character of their experience, whatever reasons there may be for doubting that God Himself does in fact appear to them.

If these cases are to conform to our account of perceptual consciousness, they must seem to involve God's appearing to the person as being and/or doing so-and-so. And our subjects do tell us this. God is experienced as good, powerful, loving, compassionate, and as exhibiting "plenitude." He is experienced as speaking, forgiving, comforting, and strengthening. And yet how can these be ways in which God presents Himself to experience? Power and goodness are complex dispositional properties or bases thereof, dispositions to act in various ways in various situations. And to forgive or to strengthen someone is to carry out a certain intention. None of this can be read off the phenomenal surface of experience. This is quite different from something's presenting itself to one's sensory consciousness as red, round, sweet, loud, or pungent. Isn't it rather that the subject is *interpreting*, or *taking*, what she is aware of as being good or powerful, as forgiving or strengthening? But then what is God *experienced* as being or doing? We seem to still lack an answer.

But that charge misconstrues the situation. The basic point is that we have different sorts of concepts for specifying how something looks, sounds, tastes, or otherwise perceptually appears. There are *phenomenal* concepts that specify the felt qualities that objects present themselves as bearing—round, red, acrid, etc. But there are also *comparative* concepts that specify a mode of appearance in terms of the sort of objective thing that typically appears in that way. In reporting sensory appearances we typically use comparative concepts whenever the appearances involve something more complex than one or two basic sensory qualities. Thus we say, "She looks like Susie," "It tastes like a pineapple," "It sounds like Bach." In these cases there undoubtedly is some complex pattern of simple sensory qualities, but it is beyond our powers to analyze the appearance into its simple components. We are thrown back on the use of comparative concepts to report how something looks, sounds, or tastes. And so it is in our religious cases. Our subjects tell us that God presented Himself to their experience as a good, powerful, compassionate, forgiving being could be expected to appear. In reporting modes of divine appearance in this way, they are proceeding just as we typically do in reporting modes of sensory appearance.

IV

Now for the task of showing that if God exists there is no bar to the (not infrequent) satisfaction of the causal and doxastic conditions by the subject of mystical experience. First consider the doxastic condition. It is clear that mystical experience typically gives rise to beliefs about God. To be sure, those who perceive God as loving, powerful, and so on, usually believed that God is that way long before they had that experience. But the same is true of sense perception. My 50,000th look at my house doesn't generate any important new beliefs. I knew just what my house looks like long before that 50,000th look. That is why I put the doxastic condition in terms of a "tendency" to engender beliefs about what is perceived. However, in both sensory and mystical cases some kinds of new beliefs will almost always be produced. Even if I don't see anything new about my house on that umpteenth look, I at least learn that it is blue and tall *today*. When what we perceive is a person the new beliefs will be more interesting. On my 50,000th look at my wife I not only learn that she is still beautiful today, but I learn what she is doing right now. And similarly with God. One who perceives God will thereby come to learn that God is strengthening her or comforting her *then*, or telling her so-and-so *then*. There is, if anything, even less of a problem with the doxastic condition here.

The causal condition calls for a bit more discussion. First, there is no reason to think it impossible that God, if He exists, does causally contribute to the occurrence of mystical experiences. Quite the contrary. If God exists and things are as supposed by classical theism, God causally contributes to everything that occurs. That follows just from the fact that nothing would exist without the creative and sustaining activity of God. And with respect to many things, including mystical experiences, God's causality presumably extends farther than that, though the precise story will vary from one theology to another. To fix our thoughts let us say that it is possible (and remember that we are concerned here only with whether this causal condition *can* be satisfied) that at least some of these experiences occur only because God intentionally presents Himself to the subject's awareness as so-and-so.

It may well be pointed out that not every causal contributor to an experience is perceived via that experience. When I see a house, light waves and goings on in my nervous system form parts of the causal chain leading to the visual experience, but I don't see them. Thus it is not enough that God figures somehow or other in the causes of the experience; He would have to make the right kind of causal contribution. But what is the right kind? There is no one answer to this question for all perceptual modalities. The causal contribution a seen object makes to the production of visual experience (transmitting light to the retina) is different from the causal contribution a felt object makes to tactile experience, and different from the causal contribution a heard object makes to aural experience. And how do we tell, for each modality, what the crucial causal contribution is? We have no a priori insight into this. We cannot abstract from everything we have learned from perception and still ascertain how an object must be causally related to a visual experience in order to be what is seen in that experience. Quite the contrary. We learn this by first determining in many cases what is *seen*, felt, or heard in those cases, and then looking for some causal contribu-

tion that is distinctive of the object perceived. That is, we have first to be able to determine *what is seen;* then on the basis of that we determine how an entity has to be causally related to the visual experience to be seen therein. We have no resources for doing it the other way around, first determining the specific causal requirement and then picking out objects seen on the basis of what satisfies that requirement.

The application of this to divine perception is as follows. We will have a chance of determining how God has to be causally related to an experience in order to be perceived only if we can first determine in a number of cases that it is God who is being perceived. And since that is so, we can't rule out the possibility of perceiving God on the grounds that God can't be related to the relevant experience in the right way. For unless we do sometimes perceive God we are unable to determine what the right way is. Hence, so long as God does make some causal contribution to the relevant experiences, we can't rule out God's being perceived in those experiences on the grounds that He isn't causally related to them in the right way. To be sure, by the same token we cannot show that we do perceive God by showing that God is causally related to the experiences in the right way. But showing that is no part of our purpose here. It will be sufficient to show that, so far as we can see, there is no reason to doubt that it is possible that God should satisfy an appropriate causal requirement for being perceived in at least some of the cases in which people take themselves to be directly aware of Him.

V

If my arguments have been sound, we are justified in thinking of the experience of God as a mode of perception in the same generic sense of the term as sense perception. And if God exists, there is no reason to suppose that this perception is not sometimes veridical rather than delusory. I will conclude by mentioning a couple of respects in which this conclusion is of importance.

First, the main function of the experience of God in theistic religion is that it constitutes a mode, an avenue of communion between God and us. It makes it possible for us to enter into personal interaction with God. And if it involves our directly perceiving God in a sense generically the same as that in which we perceive each other, this can be personal intercourse in a literal sense, rather than some stripped down, analogical or symbolic reconception thereof. We can have the real thing, not a metaphorical substitute.

Second, there are bearings on the cognitive significance of this mode of experience. If it is perceptual in character, and if it is possible that the other requirements should be satisfied for it to be a genuine perception of God, then the question of whether it is genuine is just a question of whether it is what it seems to its subject to be. Thus the question of genuineness arises here in just the same way as for sense perception, making possible a uniform treatment of the epistemology of the two modes of experience. This is not to beg the question of the genuineness of mystical perception. It could still be true that sense perception is the real thing, whereas mystical perception is not. And it could still be true that sense perception provides knowledge about its objects, whereas mystical perception yields no such results.

The point is only that the *problems*, both as to the status of the perception and as to the epistemic status of perceptual beliefs, arise in the same form for both. This contrasts with the situation on the widespread view that "experience of God" is to be construed as purely subjective feelings and sensations to which supernaturalistic causal hypotheses are added. On that view the issues concerning the two modes of experience will look very different, unless one is misguided enough to treat sense perception in the same fashion. For on this subjectivist construal the subject is faced with the task of justifying a causal hypothesis before he can warrantedly claim to be perceiving God. Whereas if the experience is given a perceptual construal from the start, we will at least have to take seriously the view that a claim to be perceiving God is prima facie acceptable on its own merits, pending any sufficient reasons to the contrary.[1]

NOTE

1. See my *Perceiving God* (Cornell University Press, 1991) for a development of this last idea.

45   PERCEIVING GOD: A CRITIQUE

WILLIAM L. ROWE

William Alston contended that we should accept the reports of those who claim to perceive God unless we have sufficient reason to the contrary. William L. Rowe, whose work we read previously, disagrees. He argues that we do not know what would count as a sufficient reason for deciding that someone's religious experiences are delusive, because God's ways are not understandable. Furthermore, such experiences are embedded in a plurality of religious traditions. How can we accept all these conflicting reports of different divine presences?

From *Philosophy of Religion: An Introduction*, Fourth Edition, Wadsworth Publishing Company, 2007. Reprinted by permission of Thomson/Wadsworth.

Experiences in which one senses the immediate presence of a divine being may include some visual and auditory content.... But other experiences of the divine do not contain sensory content. Here is a report of one such experience.

> all at once I ... felt the presence of God—I tell of the thing just as I was conscious of it—as if his goodness and his power were penetrating me altogether.... Then, slowly, the ecstasy left my heart; that is, I felt that God had withdrawn the communion which he had granted, ... I think it well to add that in this ecstasy of mine God had neither form, color, odor, nor taste; moreover, that the feeling of his presence was accompanied with no determinate localization.... At bottom the expression most apt to render what I felt is this: God was present, though invisible; he fell under no one of my senses, yet my consciousness perceived him.[1]

The question before us is whether the existence of such experiences as these provide us (or at least those who have them) with a *good reason* to believe that God (or some sort of divine being) exists. Initially, one might be tempted to think that they do not on the grounds that reports of religious experiences may be nothing more than reports of certain *feelings* (joy, ecstasy, etc.) that now and then come over some people who already believe in God and are perhaps all too eager to feel themselves singled out for a special appearance by the divine. Against such an objection, however, we should note that a number of those who report having ordinary religious experiences are keenly aware of the difference between experiences of one's own feelings (joy, sadness, peacefulness, etc.) and experiences that involve a sense of the presence of some other being. They are also aware of the fact that wanting a certain experience may lead one to mistake some other experience for it. Unless we have some very strong reason not to, we should take their reports as sincere, careful efforts to express the contents of their experiences. And those reports are not primarily reports of subjective psychological states; they are reports of encounters with what is taken to be an independently existing divine being.

But still, even if we acknowledge that the experiences cannot fairly be described as reports of nothing more than one's feelings, why should we think they are veridical perceptions of what they seem to be? Macbeth's experience of a dagger isn't fairly described as Macbeth having a certain feeling; it is an experience which purports to be of some object apart from himself. But the experience was a hallucination. Why shouldn't we think that experiences in which one senses the immediate presence of God (or some divine figure) are all hallucinatory? The answer given by those who think religious experiences constitute a good reason to believe God exists is that we should dismiss them as delusory only if we have some special reason to think that they are delusory. And in the absence of such special reasons, the rational thing to do is to view them as probably veridical. It will help us to look at this line of argument in some detail.

If a person has an experience which he or she takes to be of some particular object, is the fact that he or she has that experience a *good reason* to think that particular object exists? Our first reaction is to say no. We are inclined to say no because we all can think of experiences which seem to be of some particular object, when in fact no such object exists. Consider two examples. You walk into a room and have a visual experience that you take to be a perception of a red wall. Unknown to you there are red lights shining on the white wall you are looking at, thus making it appear red. Here you are experiencing an actually existing wall that happens to be white, but there is no red wall for you to perceive. How then can the fact that you have an experience which clearly seems to be a perception of a red wall be a good reason for thinking that there actually is a red wall? Again, unknown to you someone puts a powerful hallucinogenic drug in your coffee resulting in your having an experience which you take to be a perception of a large, coiled snake in front of the chair in which you are sitting. Unlike our first example (there is a wall, it's just not red), there is no snake at all that you are seeing. Others in the room who have no reason to deceive you assure you that there is no snake in the room. Your experience of the snake is entirely delusory. So, how can the fact that you have an experience which clearly seems to be a perception of a coiled snake be a good reason for thinking that the coiled snake exists?

For an experience to be a good reason for believing a claim to be true is for that experience to rationally justify you in believing that claim *provided that you have no reasons for thinking otherwise*. Reasons for thinking otherwise are either (a) reasons for thinking that claim to be false or (b) reasons for thinking that, given the circumstances in which it occurs, the experience is not sufficiently indicative of the truth of the claim. Consider again our second example. Since we know that actually existing physical things (including snakes) would be seen by the other people in the room if they are really there, you come to have a Type A reason for thinking otherwise. That is, when others who are in a position to see it say there is no snake, you come to have some reason for thinking that the snake does not actually exist. In our first example, if we suppose that all you come to know is that red lights are shining on the wall and that such lights would make the wall appear red even if it is white, then our reason to think otherwise is not itself a reason to think that there is no red wall. It is a Type B reason. What it tells us is that, whether the wall is red or not, in the circumstances that exist (red lights are shining on the wall) your experience is not sufficiently indicative of its being true that the wall is red. For you now know that you could be having that experience even if the wall is white.

What we've seen is that we must distinguish an experience being a good reason for a claim from that experience justifying that claim *no matter what else we know*. Those who think that having an experience that one takes to be of some particular object is a *good reason* to think that particular object exists recognize that we may know or come to know Type A or Type B reasons to think otherwise. All they insist is that in the *absence* of such defeating reasons, one who has such an experience is rationally justified in believing that the particular object exists. One prominent philosopher has argued that what is at stake here is a basic principle of rationality, a principle he calls the Principle of Credulity.[2] According to this principle, if a person has an experience which seems to be of x, then, unless there is some reason to think

otherwise, it is rational to believe that x exists. If we grant this principle, it would seem arbitrary to refuse to apply it to religious experiences, experiences in which one senses the immediate presence of the divine. So, unless we have some reason to question these experiences, it would seem rational to believe that God or some divine being exists....

[W]e should note two difficulties in the view that the Principle of Credulity renders it rational for us to accept ordinary religious experiences as veridical. The first difficulty is that the Principle of Credulity presupposes that we have some understanding of what reasons there might be for questioning our experiences and some way of telling whether or not these reasons are present. Consider again our example of your experience which you take to be a perception of a large, coiled snake. Like other physical objects that make up the world we perceive by our five senses, snakes are public objects that are observable by others who satisfy certain conditions. That is, we can predict that people with good eyesight will see a snake (if one is there) provided there is good light and they look in the right direction. It is because physical objects are subject to such predictions that we can understand what reasons there might be for questioning an experience which seems to be a perception of a snake and can often tell whether such reasons are present. In the case of divine beings, however, matters are quite different. Presumably, it is entirely up to God whether to reveal his presence to some human being. If God does so, he may or may not disclose himself to others who are in a similar situation. What this means is that it is quite difficult to discover reasons for thinking that someone's ordinary religious experience is delusive. But since the Principle of Credulity supposes that we understand what reasons there might be to question an experience, some doubt exists as to whether the principle can be fairly applied to experiences whose subjects take them to be perceptions of the presence of a divine being. Of course, since God is a perfectly good being, we can from that fact alone discover some reason for thinking an experience that purports to be of God is delusive. For suppose someone reports an experience which he takes to be a perception of God commanding him to kill all those who sincerely seek to live a moral and holy life. We can be confident that God did not reveal that message and thus have a reason for thinking the experience to be delusive. Some doubt remains, however, whether there is an adequate range of reasons for questioning religious experiences to warrant much confidence in the application of the Principle of Credulity to them. Thus, once we come to learn that a presumption of the Principle of Credulity is not adequately satisfied by religious experiences, it is at least doubtful that the principle justifies us in holding religious experiences to be genuine perceptions of reality.

Suppose someone who has not had religious experiences examines various reports of those who have enjoyed them. One salient feature of these experiences is that most of them are embedded in one or another of a plurality of religious traditions, traditions that cannot all be true. For example, Saul's experience on the road to Damascus is embedded in Christianity as an experience of Jesus as a divine being. No such experience is a part of Judaism or Islam. Indeed, within these religious traditions Jesus is not a divine being at all. Experiences of Allah in Islam or God in Judaism are not experiences of a divine being who is a trinity of persons, as is the Christian God. In Hinduism one may have an experience of Krishna, but not Jesus, as a divine being. Moreover, Hinduism also includes a strain in which the divine presence,

Brahman, is experienced as something other than a person. It seems unlikely that all of these religious experiences can be veridical perceptions of a divine presence. These experiences are embedded in and support rival religious traditions that contradict one another. Realizing this, what view should be held by a person who has not had any religious experiences? If the Principle of Credulity works for any, it will work equally well for all. But they can hardly all be veridical perceptions of a divine presence. Faced with this situation, it would appear that the rational thing for this person to do is not to accept any one of these religious experiences as veridical. So, even if we agree to continue applying the Principle of Credulity to religious experiences, it may well be that the person who has not had a religious experience is rationally justified in not accepting such experiences as veridical perceptions of reality. For the fact that these experiences are embedded in and support conflicting religious traditions may provide that person with a reason for not accepting any particular religious experience as veridical.

NOTES

1. Quoted in William James, *The Varieties of Religious Experience* (New York: The Modern Library, 1936), pp. 67–68.
2. Richard Swinburne, *The Existence of God* (Oxford: The Clarendon Press, 1979), p. 254.

46   BUDDHIST MEDITATION

CHRISTOPHER W. GOWANS

Buddhism, with over 300 million adherents, is one of the world's leading religions. The older of its two main branches, Theravada Buddhism, or "The Doctrine of the Elders," is today found primarily in Sri Lanka and throughout Southeast Asia; the other branch, Mahayana Buddhism, or "The Greater Vehicle," is widespread in Vietnam, Tibet, China, Korea, and Japan. Relatively

From Christopher W. Gowans, *Philosophy of the Buddha*, Routledge, 2003. Reprinted by permission of Taylor & Francis. Section numberings are the editor's. The notes are based on other passages in the author's work.

few Buddhists remain in India, the country where the religion originated approximately 2,500 years ago.

Therevada Buddhism is atheistic, viewing the Buddha as a supreme teacher, and stressing individual effort to achieve understanding through intense concentration. In contrast, Mahayana Buddhism recognizes an ultimate reality, of which the Buddha is a manifestation, thus serving as a source of spiritual strength.

Buddhist meditation is in some respects akin to mysticism but in other ways quite different. In our next selection Christopher W. Gowans, who is Professor of Philosophy at Fordham University, presents essentials of Buddhist belief, explains the central role given to meditation, and assesses the reliability of the knowledge that the meditative experience is supposed to yield.

I

The person we know as the Buddha was born ... near the present-day border of India and Nepal, sometime between the seventh and the fifth centuries BCE. He was called Siddhattha Gotama (Siddhārtha Gautama in Sanskrit)....

Siddhattha's father, Suddhodana, was a relatively powerful and wealthy leader of a small tribe called the Sakka, structured more as a republic than a kingdom, and located in the Ganges river basin near the foothills of the Himalayan mountains (Kapilavatthu was its capital). His mother Mahāmāyā died a week after his birth, and he was raised by Mahāpajāpatī, an aunt who became his father's second wife. Little is known of Siddhattha's early life. Presumably he was raised in considerable prosperity and received a good education by the standards of the time. He was also reputed to have been extremely attractive physically. Aged sixteen, he married the beautiful Yasodharā. Several years later, when he was twenty-nine, she gave birth to their first (and, it would turn out, only) child, their son Rāhula. That Siddhattha was married, had a son, and was probably in line to acquire the power and wealth of his father no doubt made him a very fortunate and much envied young man in Sakka....

His father was determined that he should become a ruler, and to ensure this outcome he protected his son from everything unpleasant in life. An early omen should have warned Śuddhodana that his son had a different destiny. At the age of twelve, Siddhattha was found meditating under a tree during a festival. Eventually, he discovered what everyone comes to know – that there is suffering in human life. One day he left the palace and saw a decrepit, bent-over old man walking with a stick to support him. Thus Siddhattha realized that human beings are not forever young: we all age and grow old. On a second outing, he saw a man who was extremely ill. Thus Siddhattha realized that human beings are not forever healthy: we are all liable to sickness. On a third excursion, he saw a dead man in a funeral procession. Thus Siddhattha realized that human beings do not live forever: we all die eventually.

The threefold discovery that aging, illness and death are facts of every human life was a shock to Siddhattha. He was overcome with disgust and shame. He wondered: What is the meaning of human suffering? What is its cause? Can it be overcome? How can such questions be answered? On a fourth outing, Siddhattha saw a man who had left home, shaved his head, and donned yellow robes: he was seeking a life of wisdom, virtue and tranquillity outside the conventional life of society, and he became an initial role-model for Siddhattha. The Buddha said later:

> While still young, a black-haired young man endowed with the blessing of youth, in the prime of life, though my mother and father wished otherwise and wept with tearful faces, I shaved off my hair and beard, put on the yellow robe, and went forth from the home life into homelessness.

This was the beginning of Siddhattha's effort to understand human suffering. He was twenty-nine years old and would persist for six years before attaining enlightenment....

II

After a long and arduous struggle, the Buddha believed he discovered that true happiness is achieved precisely where we might think it least likely to be found – in freedom from craving, clinging, and attachment to what we desire. The state of non-attachment is the primary fruit of enlightenment. It is the promised culmination of a difficult and complex journey, an intellectual, moral, and meditative undertaking – the Eightfold Path – that, successfully completed, releases two powerful forces within us: compassion for other living beings and joyful appreciation of each moment of our lives irrespective of what happens to us. These forces have a latent presence in each of us, the Buddha taught, but for most of us, because of our attachments, they manifest themselves only weakly and sporadically. Still, by attaining the state of non-attachment, compassion and joy are made available to each of us, and with these comes tranquillity, the mark of genuine happiness. This is one meaning of the Buddha's life of homelessness: real happiness is to be found not in the fulfillment of our conventional pursuits, but in a fundamental reorientation of our attitudes towards those pursuits – that is, in freedom from the craving and attachment typically associated with our desires for success.

No doubt stream-observers[1] noticed that, in the end, the Buddha grew old, got sick, and died. He did not purport to have found a way to eliminate these sources of suffering in life as we know it. He did not announce the discovery of a fountain of youth. Rather, he proclaimed that full enlightenment would enable us to achieve happiness in this life despite aging, sickness, and death, and that it would release us from the cycle of rebirth into similar lives so as to attain another form of being free from all suffering. Though it is said to be beyond adequate description in our language, *Nibbāna*[2] is a state we can achieve while living this life as well as one beyond life as we ordinarily know it.

This is the central message the life of the Buddha is meant to convey: true happiness may be achieved not by gaining what we seek to possess, but by cultivating a state of non-attachment with regard to our desires. This is the message we are meant to apply to our own lives. It is at once powerful and perplexing, powerful because it offers a road to well-being immune to vicissitudes we all recognize, and perplexing – for many, I suspect – for a variety of psychological and philosophical reasons. The Buddha encouraged his followers to understand his teaching for themselves. Stream-observers can do this only by confronting what perplexes them and reflecting on the extent to which this teaching has resources to resolve their concerns....

III

The Buddha's teaching is primarily practical rather than theoretical in its orientation. The aim is to show persons how to overcome suffering and attain *Nibbāna*....

The Four Noble Truths are the centerpiece of the Buddha's message.... The Buddha's central teaching has the form of a medical diagnosis and plan of treatment: it describes a disease and its symptoms, identifies its cause, outlines what freedom from this disease would be like, and prescribes the course of treatment required to attain this healthy state....

Here is the description of the disease and its symptoms:

> *First Noble Truth.* Now this, *bhikkhus,*[3] is the noble truth of suffering: birth is suffering, aging is suffering, illness is suffering, death is suffering; union with what is displeasing is suffering; separation from what is pleasing is suffering; not to get what one wants is suffering; in brief, the five aggregates subject to clinging are suffering.

The key term here and throughout is *dukkha*. It is ordinarily translated into English as 'suffering'. This is correct in part, but it is misleading. The description above features aging, sickness and death (the observation of which first led Siddhattha to seek enlightenment) and we naturally associate these with suffering. But for the other items listed – union with what is displeasing, separation from what is pleasing, and not getting what one wants – 'suffering' sometimes is the right term and sometimes seems too strong. The Buddha clearly has in mind a broad range of ways in which our lives may be unsatisfactory. For the time being, we may summarize the first Noble Truth as the claim that human lives regularly lack contentment, fulfillment, perfection, security, and the like....

The next Noble Truth is a claim about the cause of discontentment in human life. Here is how the Buddha explained it:

> *Second Noble Truth.* Now this, *bhikkhus*, is the noble truth of the origin of suffering: it is this craving which leads to renewed existence, accompanied by delight and lust, seeking delight here and there; that is, craving for sensual pleasures, craving for existence, craving for extermination.

There is much in this passage that is likely to perplex us. For now, what is important is the contention that suffering and other forms of distress have a cause associated with various kinds of desire – craving, clinging, attachment, impulse, greed, lust, thirst, and so on are terms frequently employed in this connection. The Second Noble Truth states that the source of our discontentment is found not simply in our desires, but in the connection we forge between desires and happiness. In its simplest form, it asserts that we are typically unhappy because we do not get what we desire to have, or we do get what we desire not to have. We do not get the promotion we wanted, and we do get the disease we feared. Outcomes such as these are common in human life. These outcomes, and the anxieties their prospect produces, are causes of our discontentment....

4 NIBBĀNA

... Obtaining what we are hoping to gain and safety from what we are trying to avoid will not bring us real happiness. This can only be achieved by a radical transformation of our desires and aversions – and especially of our attitudes towards them. We have arrived at the next Truth:

> *Third Noble Truth.* Now this, *bhikkhus*, is the noble truth of the cessation of suffering: it is the remainderless fading away and cessation of that same craving, the giving up and relinquishing of it, freedom from it, nonreliance on it.

True happiness in life, the opposite of suffering, is brought about by reaching a state in which, on my reading, we eliminate many of our desires and stop clinging or attaching ourselves to all of them. The Buddha referred to this state with the term 'Nibbāna'....

On my interpretation, there are at least two aspects of this difficult idea. First, in the absence of the belief that I am a self distinct from other selves, I would no longer think of some desires as mine, as things with which I deeply identify and so need to satisfy to achieve my well-being. As a result, there would no longer be an unhealthy drive or obsession to fulfill these desires. Second, in the absence of the belief that I am a self with identity, a substance persisting through time in some respects unchanged, I would no longer be preoccupied with regrets about the past unfulfillment of my desires and worries about the prospects for their future fulfillment. Liberated in these ways from attachment to desires as mine, from pinning my happiness on their satisfaction, there would be freedom to focus attention on the present moment at all times. The implicit message of the Buddha is that, in this state of awareness, no matter what happened, there would always be something of value, something good, in what was experienced. Not clinging to the fulfillment of our desires would release a capacity for joy at each moment in our lives.

For a person who has attained *Nibbāna*, life is a process of living selflessly in which, unencumbered by the false belief that we are selves, we are enabled to live compassionate and joyful lives. To this it may be added that our lives would also possess great peace and tranquility. They would be lives of perfect contentment and true happiness.

In addition to *Nibbāna* in this life, the Buddha described *Nibbāna* as a state beyond this life and the entire cycle of rebirth (henceforth, when it is important to distinguish these, I will refer to them respectively as *Nibbāna*-in-life and *Nibbāna*-after-death). Though he thought it could not be described adequately in our concepts, we may say by way of a preliminary that he believed *Nibbāna*-after-death is neither a state in which one exists as a self nor a state of absolute nothingness. It is a form of selfless existence in which there is realization of some union with *Nibbāna* understood as ultimate reality beyond change and conditioning. This is a state in which suffering, and all that causes suffering, is entirely absent. *Nibbāna* both in this life and beyond is a state of perfect well-being and tranquility, one that all conscious beings have reason to seek.

5 WISDOM, VIRTUE, AND CONCENTRATION

Even if we were convinced that *Nibbāna* would be the ultimate happiness, we might well wonder whether it would be possible for us to attain it. The Buddha's practical orientation made this a primary concern. He believed it is possible to achieve *Nibbāna*, but very difficult to do so. We have come to the final Truth:

> *Fourth Noble Truth.* Now this, *bhikkhus*, is the noble truth of the way leading to the cessation of suffering. It is this Noble Eightfold Path; that is right view, right intention, right speech, right action, right livelihood, right effort, right mindfulness, right concentration.

* * *

The eight steps of the path are to be pursued not in sequence, but all together, with each step reinforcing the others (though the last two, right mindfulness and right concentration, are the culmination). The Buddha divided these steps into three parts: *wisdom* pertains primarily to intellectual development and conviction (right view and intention), *virtue* concerns moral or ethical training (right speech, action, and livelihood), and *concentration* – often rendered as 'meditation' – involves a set of mental disciplines (right effort, mindfulness, and concentration).

The first part, wisdom, instructs us to acquire a thorough comprehension of the Four Noble Truths and all that they involve....

Comprehension of the Four Noble Truths requires more than intellectual cultivation. We also need a fundamental commitment to understanding them, and our emotions and desires must be disciplined so that they do not distract us or lead us astray. Hence, the Buddha said we must renounce sensual desire, ill will, and cruelty. In this respect, he thought thinking and feeling, the mind and the heart, were closely connected.

The second part of the path concerns morality or ethics. Enlightenment requires moral as well as intellectual and emotional preparation. The Buddha spoke of morality at length, and he expected much more of members of the *Sangha*[4] than of lay followers. But there are basic precepts that apply to all persons. These fall into three categories. Right speech requires that we speak in ways that are truthful, friendly, useful, and productive of harmony. Right action dictates that we do not kill any living beings (human or animal), nor steal, nor have illegitimate sexual relations. Right livelihood says we should not earn our living by harming others (for example, by selling arms). Violation of these precepts, the Buddha thought, would only reinforce self-centered desires and would hinder attainment of *Nibbāna*.

The third part of the path – concentration, or meditation – is the least familiar to persons in the West, but the most significant for the Buddha.... Though the Buddha taught many forms of meditation, the general aim of these mental disciplines is twofold: first, to purify the mind of disturbances so as to bring about a peaceful, concentrated, attentive and mindful mental state; and second, to know reality as it actually is by observing that all things in our ordinary experience are impermanent, involve suffering, and are empty of any self. The ultimate aim is not to escape from the world nor to acquire special powers: it is to attain *Nibbāna*.

IV

A central contention of the Buddha is that the most important avenue to acquiring the knowledge he teaches is not reason but meditation, and Buddhist meditation has no significant correlate in Western epistemological discussions. Meditation is not rooted in subjective feelings or desires, nor is its aim a non-cognitive, dream-like condition. On the contrary, meditation is said to provide us with a form of objective knowledge of reality, the knowledge that enables us to overcome suffering. But the knowledge meditation gives us is not based on a rational grasp of self-evident truths, it is not the result of logical inferences, and it is not grounded in the ordinary experience of the five senses. Buddhist understanding as a whole may draw on all these epistemological sources. But meditation itself is *sui generis* and cannot be reduced to or understood in terms of any of them.

The Buddha taught two kinds of meditation: serenity meditation (*samatha-bhāvanā*) and insight meditation (*vipassanā-bhāvanā*). For both, to be effective, a good deal of intellectual, emotional, and moral preparation is required. The aim of serenity meditation is to purify the mind of various obstacles so that it may attain the highest degree of concentration. The Buddha thought our minds were typically in so much turmoil that, in the absence of radical modification, they had no hope of truly understanding reality. Serenity meditation involves extensive training in focusing our attention wholly and exclusively on a single object so as to end this turmoil and gain the ability to concentrate.

This provides a foundation for insight meditation. Here, the purpose is to directly know reality as it truly is. Insight meditation is a matter of heightened and attentive awareness rather than intellectual or theoretical thought. It involves detailed and mindful observation of all aspects of one's person through which one comes to realize the impermanence of things, the suffering associated with this, the absence of any self, and ultimately the Four Noble Truths. Insight meditation is a kind of experience, in a broad sense of the term, but experience that is quite different from, and beyond that ordinarily provided by, the five senses. The eventual outcome is the realization of *Nibbāna*, an immediate comprehension of the unconditioned realm beyond the ordinary world of sense experience, an understanding that cannot adequately be described in language, but that liberates us from attachment and enables us to live with compassion, joy, and tranquility....

V

Let us assume that both the Buddha and many of his followers, during his lifetime and since, have sincerely reported to have gained enlightenment on the basis of meditation and other aspects of the Eightfold Path. How should stream-observers assess the epistemic worth of these reports?...

We have an account of what the life of an *arahant*[5] is supposed to be like. Suppose it turned out that purported *arahants* did not generally live in this way. For example, suppose they lacked compassion or were rather attached to material goods. Since the knowledge they are said to have is supposed to bring it about that they do not live this way, this would be a reason to doubt that they have this knowledge. Of course, there can always be fraudulent cases. However, it may be said on behalf of the Buddha that *arahants* – and perhaps more generally persons who are especially accomplished in the teaching of the Buddha – do largely live the lives they are expected to live. If this were true, the objection would be answered. On the other hand, the fact that they live this way, though it might encourage our confidence, would not necessarily show that they have the knowledge claimed. There could be other explanations.

Similarly, if persons who report meditative knowledge were known to be unreliable in various ways (for example, by having a bad memory, being especially gullible, giving inconsistent reports, and so on), then this would be another ground for doubt. Once again, it may be said in support of the Buddha that this is not generally the case (not that no such person is unreliable, but that they are not typically so). If this were correct, we would have a response to the objection. Also, as before, reliability in these respects would not necessarily confirm meditative knowledge. In both this and the previous case, empirical research presumably could confirm or disconfirm the claims made on behalf of the Buddha.

Another source of doubt might be found in the apparent disanalogies between sense-experience and meditative experience. To a very great extent, sense-experience is a common possession of all human beings, but nothing close to this can be said of meditative experience. On account of this, reports based on sense-experience can be checked by numerous persons, but reports about *Nibbāna* as ultimate reality, or about the attainment of *Nibbāna*-after-death, for example, cannot similarly be checked. In response, it may be said in defense of the Buddha that there are forms of knowledge based on sense-experience that are possessed by only a few persons – for instance, knowledge of coffee or wine based on its taste, or knowledge of the medical significance of an X-ray. These are cases of genuine knowledge based on sense-experience, but they require special abilities and training to acquire. Something similar might be said about Buddhist meditation. Moreover, it may be said that to a large extent reports based on Buddhist meditation can be checked by others, but only those who have undertaken the Eightfold Path. Hence, there is a significant role for intersubjective verification of these reports. Finally, it may also be noted that there are some kinds of reports we accept as generally authoritative even though they cannot be verified by other persons – for example, introspective reports about whether a person has a headache. Perhaps intersubjective verification is not essential for knowledge.

Suspicion may also be raised by the claim that the knowledge meditators are said to acquire is so heavily influenced by their expectations, given their Buddhist beliefs, that it is not reliable. In effect, meditators experience in meditation what they expect to experience, not what is objectively there to be experienced. Of course, it is often the case that our expectations influence what we think we observe. But from this fact we ordinarily conclude not that all beliefs where this can happen are doubtful, but that particular ones are doubtful that we have reason to suspect are adversely influenced by expectations. By parity of reasoning, it may be said on the Buddha's behalf, this cannot be a basis for casting doubt on all reports based on meditation unless it can be shown that all or nearly all meditators are unduly influenced in this way. And it seems unlikely that this could be shown. Just as there are persons who are capable of an objective assessment of their own team's chances in the championship game, so there may be meditators who are capable of an objective assessment of what meditation reveals.

It might also be said that the beliefs of meditators can be explained in purely naturalistic terms on the basis of psychology or physiology. For example, it might be claimed that serenity meditation puts the brain in a highly unusual state, and that the supposed knowledge that meditators gain is nothing more than an effect of this state. One difficulty with this critique is that all beliefs have a naturalistic explanation. Whether a particular naturalistic explanation supplies a basis for skepticism about some class of beliefs depends on whether we have grounds for thinking the explanation undermines the reliability of the beliefs. For example, we might think that a particular kind of drug-induced state was unreliable if persons in that state made reports we could show on independent grounds to be false (say, if they always forgot their address). Conversely, we might believe that another kind of drug-induced state was especially reliable if persons in that state performed much better intellectually (say, if they could do more complex mathematical calculations). A Buddhist might respond that meditation may well alter the state of the brain. What must be shown, but cannot be, is that there are independent grounds for supposing the reports of Buddhist meditation are unreliable. In any case, it seems clear that the issue of reliability would have to be brought into this discussion.

Finally, it might be argued that reports based on Buddhist meditation are part of a larger class of reports based on religious experience in many different traditions (Hindu, Jewish, Christian, Muslim, and so on), and that the reports in this larger class often contradict one another. Therefore, there is reason to question all these reports, including the Buddhist ones. The Buddhist might respond that it is not evident why Buddhist meditation should be considered part of the larger class of religious experiences. Buddhist meditation is a highly specific set of techniques that are quite different from anything found in other religious traditions. Why should the fact that persons in those other traditions who rely on different approaches and give reports incompatible with Buddhism count against the authority of the reports based on Buddhist meditation? Since the reports from other traditions are not based on Buddhist techniques, there is no reason to expect that they would be consistent with the teachings of the Buddha.

In response, a modification of this objection may be given that does not depend on classifying Buddhist meditation as one form of religious experience. It contends that the conflicting experience-based reports of other religious traditions could be justified to the same extent as the reports based on Buddhist meditation. That is, analogous and equally plausible responses to the objections already given could be made on behalf of the reports in these different traditions, and since these reports cannot all be true, we have reason to question all of them, including the Buddhist ones. This is a more serious objection. However, in order to be established, it would have to be shown that equally plausible responses could be made in all the traditions, and this is a large agenda. There are several possibilities here. Perhaps a close look at reports that genuinely could be said to be equally plausible do not conflict to the extent supposed. Or perhaps the respects in which these religious traditions do conflict are not directly based on religious experiences. Or perhaps we do not know enough about these issues to adequately assess this objection. The defender of the Buddha would probably say that, insofar as there is real conflict, the reports based on Buddhist meditation are better justified. It would be difficult to prove this, but it may be just as difficult to refute it.

In short, there are a number of grounds for challenging the epistemic credentials of Buddhist meditation, but Buddhists are not without resources for answering these challenges. Stream-observers can determine for themselves whether these responses are adequate. However, even if they were adequate, this would only show that there are no grounds for doubt, not that Buddhist meditation actually provides the knowledge claimed. To establish that it does, the Buddha has much to say.... Beyond these, he has only one thing to say: follow the Eightfold Path, and in particular meditate, and you will find out for yourself.

NOTES

1. [Those who are culturally part of the contemporary Western world and have no Buddhist upbringing.]
2. [Sanskrit, *Nirvana.*]
3. [Monks.]
4. [Monastic order.]
5. [Fully enlightened ones; the Buddha's first followers.]

PART SIX

Describing the Divine

A. WHEN WORDS FAIL

47 BEYOND WORDS

ANGELA OF FOLIGNO

We pause now to consider an objection to much of the discussion thus far. As we have considered the divine attributes, arguments for God's existence, the problem of evil, and avenues to the divine, we have been presuming that we can use human words to grasp truths about God. But is this attempt doomed to failure? Are we seeking to describe what is indescribable?

In this section we shall consider various attempts to deal with this challenge. One approach is simply to deny that we can speak of the divine. William James maintained that the content of mystical experience is ineffable, defying communication. Perhaps all talk of God is similarly beyond any expression.

We shall consider this claim from the standpoint of four different religious traditions. First, we shall read an excerpt from the writing of Angela of Foligno (c. 1248–1309), a Christian mystic who, after leaving her husband and children, embarked on an intense spiritual quest that led her to give away all her possessions, spend long hours in prayer, and practice severe penance. She believed that this regimen was successful, and that on numerous occasions she, in fact, directly experienced God. Nevertheless, she found that God was "too great to be conceived or understood."

From *Angela of Foligno: Passionate Mystic of the Double Abyss*, ed. Paul Lachance, New City Press, 2006. Reprinted by permission of the publisher.

THE DAZZLING DARKNESS OF GOD

... I saw him in a darkness, and in a darkness precisely because the good that he is, is far too great to be conceived or understood. Indeed, anything conceivable or understandable does not attain this good or even come near it. My soul was then granted a most certain faith, a secure and most firm hope, a continual security about God which took away all my fear. In this good, which is seen in the darkness, I recollected myself totally. I was made so sure of God that in no way can I ever entertain any doubts about him or of my possession of him. Of this I have the utmost certitude. And in this most efficacious good seen in this darkness now resides my most firm hope, one in which I am totally recollected and secure.

STANDING OR LYING IN THE MIDST OF THE TRINITY

... On the other hand, God draws me to himself. But if I say that he draws me to himself with gentleness or love or anything which can be named, conceived, or imagined, that is completely false; for he does not draw me by anything which can be named or conceived by even the wisest in the world. Even if I say that it is the All Good which draws me, I destroy it. For in this state, it seems to me that I am standing or lying in the midst of the Trinity, and that is what I see with such darkness. This draws me more than anything else I have experienced so far, more than any good ever spoken of before. So much more so that there is nothing to compare to it. Everything I say now about it seems to say nothing or to be badly said.

* * *

NOTHING CAN EXPLAIN GOD

And immediately upon presenting himself to the soul, God likewise discloses himself and expands the soul and gives it gifts and consolations which the soul has never before experienced, and which are far more profound than earlier ones. In this state, the soul is drawn out of all darkness and granted a greater awareness of God than I would have thought possible. This awareness is of such clarity, certitude, and abysmal profundity that there is no heart in the world that can ever in any way understand it or even conceive it. Even my own heart cannot think about it by itself, or ever return to it to understand or even conceive anything about it. This state occurs only when God, as a gift, elevates the soul to himself, for no heart by itself can in any way expand itself to attain it. Therefore, there is absolutely nothing that can be said about this experience, for no words can be found or invented to express or explain it, no expansion of thought or mind can possibly reach to those things; they are so far beyond everything—for there is nothing which can explain God. I repeat there is absolutely nothing which can explain God. Christ's faithful one affirmed with utmost certitude and wanted it understood that there is absolutely nothing which can explain God.

THE SECRETS OF THE SCRIPTURES

Holy Scripture, she added, is so sublime that there is no one in the world wise enough, not even anyone with learning and spirit, who would not find it totally beyond their capacity to understand Scripture fully; still, they babble something about it. But of these ineffable workings which are produced in the soul when God discloses himself to it, nothing at all can be said or babbled. Because my soul is often elevated into the secret levels of God and sees the divine secrets, I am able to understand how the Scriptures were written; how they are made easy and difficult; how they seem to say something and contradict it; how some derive no profit from them; how those who do not observe them are damned and Scripture is fulfilled in them; and how others who observe them are saved by them. I see all this from above. Thus when I return to myself after perceiving these divine secrets, I can say some words with security about them, but then I speak entirely from outside the experience, and say words that come nowhere near describing the divine workings that are produced in my soul. My statements about them ruin the reality they represent. This is why I say that I blaspheme in speaking about them.

48   HINDUISM AND GOD

HUSTON SMITH

Over 4,000 years old and composed of numerous sects, Hinduism is the religion of the vast majority of the people of India. Hindus accept karma and seek liberation from suffering and rebirth by eliminating passions, acquiring knowledge of reality, and, finally, achieving union with the divine.

Hinduism also supports a caste system, according to which all people are born into one of four social groups: from lower to higher, they are servants and unskilled laborers, merchants and farmers, rulers and warriors, and spiritual and intellectual leaders, the *Brahmins*. Each has its characteristic rules and customs.

As to theology, different schools of Hinduism offer different doctrines. A common theme, however, is that words fail us as we attempt to describe the divine. In our next selection, Huston Smith, who is Professor Emeritus of Religion and Adjunct Professor of Philosophy at Syracuse University, offers an overview of Hinduism's varying approaches to God.

The first principle of Japanese *ikebana* flower arrangement is to learn what to leave out. This is also the first principle to be learned in speaking of God, the Hindus insist. People are forever trying to lay hold of Reality with words, only in the end to find mystery rebuking their speech and their syllables swallowed by silence. The problem is not that our minds are not bright enough. The problem lies deeper. Minds, taken in their ordinary, surface sense, are the wrong kind of instrument for the undertaking. The effect, as a result, is like trying to ladle the ocean with a net, or lasso the wind with a rope. The awe-inspiring prayer of Shankara, the Thomas Aquinas of Hinduism, begins with the invocation, "Oh Thou, before whom all words recoil."

The human mind has evolved to facilitate survival in the natural world. It is adapted to deal with finite objects. God, on the contrary, is infinite and of a completely different order of being from what our minds can grasp. To expect our minds to corner the infinite is like asking a dog to understand Einstein's equation with its nose. This analogy becomes misleading if, pressed in a different direction, it suggests that we can never know the Abysmal God. The *yogas*[1] ... are roads to precisely such realization. But the knowledge to which they lead transcends the knowledge of the rational mind; it rises to the deep yet dazzling darkness of the mystical consciousness.[2] The only literally accurate description of the Unsearchable of which the ordinary mind is capable is *neti ... neti*, not this ... not this. If you traverse the length and breadth of the universe saying of everything you can see and conceive, "not this ... not this," what remains will be God.[3]

And yet words and concepts cannot be avoided. Being the only equipment at our mind's disposal, any conscious progress toward God must be made with their aid. Though concepts can never carry the mind to its destination, they can point in the right direction.

We may begin simply with a name to hang our thoughts on. The name the Hindus give to the supreme reality is *Brahman*, which has a dual etymology, deriving as it does from both *br*, to breathe, and *brih*, to be great. The chief attributes to be linked with the name are *sat*, *chit*, and

From Huston Smith, *The World's Religions*, 50th Anniversary Edition, HarperOne, 1991. Reprinted by permission of HarperCollins Publishers.

ananda; God is being, awareness, and bliss. Utter reality, utter consciousness, and utterly beyond all possibility of frustration—this is the basic Hindu view of God. Even these words cannot claim to describe God literally, however, for the meanings they carry for us are radically unlike the senses in which they apply to God. What pure being would be like, being infinite with absolutely nothing excluded, of this we have scarcely an inkling. Similarly with awareness and joy. In Spinoza's formulation God's nature resembles our words about as much as the dog star resembles a dog. The most that can be said for these words is that they are pointers; our minds do better to move in their direction than in the opposite. God lies on the further side of being as we understand it, not nothingness; beyond minds as we know them, not mindless clay; beyond ecstasy, not agony.

This is as far as some minds need go in their vision of God: infinite being, infinite consciousness, infinite bliss—all else is at best commentary, at worst retraction. There are sages who can live in this austere, conceptually thin atmosphere of the spirit and find it invigorating; they can understand with Shankara that "the sun shines even without objects to shine upon." Most people, however, cannot be gripped by such high-order abstractions. That C. S. Lewis is among their number is proof that their minds are not inferior, only different. Professor Lewis tells us that while he was a child his parents kept admonishing him not to think of God in terms of any form, for these could only limit his infinity. He tried his best to heed their instructions, but the closest he could come to the idea of a formless God was an infinite sea of grey tapioca.

This anecdote, the Hindus would say, points up perfectly the circumstance of the man or woman whose mind must bite into something concrete and representational if it is to find life sustaining meaning. Most people find it impossible to conceive, much less be motivated by, anything that is removed very far from direct experience. Hinduism advises such people not to try to think of God as the supreme instance of abstractions like being or consciousness, and instead to think of God as the archetype of the noblest reality they encounter in the natural world.

This means thinking of God as the supreme person (*Ishvara* or *Bhagavan*), for people are nature's noblest crown.... This, in Pascal's Western idiom, is the God of Abraham, Isaac, and Jacob, not the God of the philosophers. It is God as parent, lovingly merciful, omniscient, almighty, our eternal contemporary, the companion who understands.

God so conceived is called *Saguna Brahman*, or God-with-attributes as distinct from the philosophers' more abstract *Nirguna Brahman*, or God-without-attributes. *Nirguna Brahman* is the ocean without a ripple; *Saguna Brahman* the same ocean alive with swells and waves. In the language of theology, the distinction is between personal and transpersonal conceptions of God. Hinduism has included superb champions of each view, notably Shankara for the transpersonal and Ramanuja for the personal; but the conclusion that does most justice to Hinduism as a whole and has its own explicit champions like Sri Ramakrishna is that both are equally correct. At first blush this may look like a glaring violation of the law of ... [non-contradiction]. God may be either personal or not, we are likely to insist, but not both. But is this so? What the disjunction forgets, India argues, is the distance our rational minds are from God in the first place. Intrinsically, God may not be capable of being two contradictory things—we say may not because logic itself may melt in the full blaze of the divine incandescence. But concepts of God contain so much alloy to begin with that two contradictory ones may be true, each from a different angle, as both wave and particles may be equally accurate heuristic devices for describing the nature of light.[4] On the whole India has been content to encourage the devotee to conceive of *Brahman* as either personal or transpersonal, depending on which carries the most exalted meaning for the mind in question.

God's relation to the world likewise varies according to the symbolism that is embraced. Conceived in personal terms, God will stand in relation to the world as an artist to his or her handiwork. God will be Creator (Brahma), Preserver (Vishnu), and Destroyer (Shiva), who in the end resolves all finite forms back into the primordial nature from which they sprang. On the other hand, conceived transpersonally, God stands above the struggle, aloof from the finite in every respect. "As the sun does not tremble, although its image trembles when you shake the cup filled with water in which the sun's light is reflected; thus the Lord also is not affected by pain, although pain be felt by that part of him which is called the individual soul."[5] The world will still be God-dependent. It will have emerged in some unfathomable way from the divine plenitude and be sustained by its power. "He shining, the sun, the moon and the stars shine after Him; by His light all is lighted. He is the Ear of the ear, the Mind of the mind, the Speech of the speech, the Life of life, the Eye of the eye."[6] But God will not have intentionally willed the world, nor be affected by its inherent ambiguity, imperfections, and finitude.

The personalist will see little religious availability in this idea of a God who is so far removed from our predicaments as to be unaware of our very existence. Is it not religion's death to despoil the human heart of its final treasure, the diamond of God's love? The answer is that God serves an entirely different function for the transpersonalist, one that is equally religious, but different all the same. If one is struggling against a current it is comforting to have a master swimmer by one's side. It is equally important that there be a shore, solid and serene, that lies beyond the struggle as the terminus of all one's splashings. The transpersonalist has become so possessed by the goal as to forget all else, even the encouragement of supporting companions.

NOTES

1. [Methods of training.]
2. Compare Thomas à Kempis: "There is a distance incomparable between the things men imagine by natural reason and those which illuminated men hold by contemplation."
3. Western parallels to this *via negativa*, the way to God through radical negation, are to be found in the writings of most of her great mystics and theologians. There is St. Bernard's "*nescio, nescio*," and Angela of Foligno's "Not this! Nor this! I blaspheme," as she struggles to put her overwhelming experience of God into words. "Then only is there truth in what we know concerning God," says St. Gregory, "when we are made sensible that we cannot know anything concerning Him." And Meister Eckhart insists that God must be loved "as not-God, not-spirit, no-person, not-image, just be loved as He is, a sheer pure absolute One, sundered from all twoness, and in whom we must eternally sink from nothingness to nothingness."
4. A Western parallel to the Hindu view on this point occurs in Simone Weil's *Waiting for God* (1951. Reprint. [New York: Harper & Row, 1973], 32): "A case of contradictories, both of them true. There is a God. There is no God. Where is the problem? I am quite sure that there is a God in the sense that I am sure my love is no illusion. I am quite sure there is no God, in the sense that I am sure there is nothing which resembles what I can conceive when I say the word."
5. Abbreviated from Shankara's Commentary on *The Brahma Sutra*, II.iii.46.
6. Composite, drawn from *Katha Upanishad*, II.ii.15; *Mundaka Upanishad*, II.ii.10; *Svetasvatara*, V.vi.14.

49   THE TAO

RAY BILLINGTON

Along with Confucianism and Zen Buddhism, about both of which we shall read subsequently, Taoism stands as one of the three major religious traditions in China. Its central focus is not God but "the Tao," the first principle of the universe, which is unknowable. But if words

From Ray Billington, *Religion Without God*, Routledge, 2002. Reprinted by permission of Taylor & Francis.

fail us, how can we follow the central precept of Taoism, to live in harmony with the Tao? In our next selection, Ray Billington, who headed the Philosophy department at the University of the West of England, Bristol, offers a brief exposition of the Taoist outlook.

What ... does 'Tao' mean? To be able to give a direct answer to this seemingly straightforward question would, paradoxically, be to fall into error, since, as the opening verse of the most famous of all Taoist classics states unambiguously,

> The tao that can be told is not the eternal Tao;
> The name that can be named is not the eternal Name.

This couplet is from the *Tao Te Ching*, the 'classic of the way and its power'. According to Chinese tradition, it was written by Lao Tzu, a famous teacher and mystic of the sixth century BCE, just before he removed himself from civilisation in order to become a recluse. It is now generally agreed by sinologists that the work is the product of many hands (Lao Tzu means 'great master', which is more a title than a name); that it was compiled over some centuries; and was finalised in its present form around the second century BCE.

According to the *Tao Te Ching*, the Tao is *the first principle of the universe, the all-embracing reality from which everything else arises.* Although the Tao remains eternally unknowable, its power (Te) can enter into every human being, so that the test of one's commitment to Taoism is viewed as the extent to which one's life is in harmony with the Tao. (The Chinese hieroglyphic for 'philosophy' depicts a hand and a mouth, symbolising a condition where words are consistent with deeds.)... Taoism does not proceed to make any case for God, or gods, as divine powers operating under the Tao's auspices, so to speak. Section 42 of the *Tao Te Ching* puts the matter rather differently:

> The Tao gives birth to One.
> One gives birth to Two.
> Two gives birth to Three.
> Three gives birth to all things.

The 'One' to which the Tao gives birth ... is Ch'i, or primordial breath (wind, spirit, energy, like the Hebrew word *Ruach* as used in Genesis 1: 2: 'The spirit of God moved upon the face of the waters'). It is the life-force that pervades and vitalises all things, the cosmic energy which brought the universe into being and continues to sustain it....

For Taoists even the Ch'i remains remote. It can be experienced, but only with time and dedication. If the Te, the power of the Tao in each individual life, is to be evinced, a force is needed which can be experienced more immediately. It is here that Taoists turn to the 'Two' to which the Ch'i gives birth. These are the twin forces of yin and yang, the polar opposites by which the universe functions, such as negative and positive, cold and heat, darkness and light, intuition and rationality, femininity and masculinity, earth and heaven. Neither of these can be without the other, and neither has any meaning without the other. We know the meaning of 'hot' only in relation to 'cold', of 'wet' to 'dry', of 'tall' to 'short', of 'dark' to 'light', of 'life' to 'death'. (We know that we are alive only because we know that we were once, and shall again be, dead. If we were eternal, there would be no word either for 'eternal' or for 'living'.)...

[N]either yin nor yang is ever motionless; each is continuously moving into the other, which means that one must learn to recognise when to apply yin, and when yang, energies. This again means allowing the intuition to exert itself: to know when to speak out and when to remain quiet; when to be gentle and when to be violent; when to be active and when to stand and stare. Both the workaholic and the playboy are, according to the yin-yang doctrine, living distorted and incomplete lives because only half of their natures is being allowed expression. Neither the ant nor the grasshopper in Aesop's fable would receive Taoism's stamp of approval.

The 'Three' to which the Two give birth are heaven, earth and humanity. [I]t is when there is harmony between these three — the yang of heaven, the yin of earth, and the human occupants of the arena which between them they bring into being – that the Te can be identified in people's lives. The final stage is the creation of 'all things' which we encounter and experience, for which 'the Three' are responsible.

The important consideration with Taoism, however, ... is not to speculate on the meaning of the idea of the Tao, but to find out how to respond to its power (Te) in one's own life. The aim, ... is to be natural, and the *Tao Te Ching* gives many hints about how this state may be achieved. One way is to practise *wu-wei*. This is often translated as living a life of 'non-action', but a more accurate translation would be not to take any *inappropriate* action. The most famous exponent of Taoism who was unquestionably a historical figure was the teacher of the third century BCE, Chuang-Tzu (Master Chuang). He argued that many of the things we do and the words we speak are simply a waste of time and breath, since the situation we are discussing or trying to affect cannot be changed by our efforts: all we're actually doing, he said, was 'flaying the air'. Or worse: our frenetic efforts may actually lead to the loss of what was wholesome and acceptable in itself. We destroy a lily by gilding it; a snake is no longer a snake if we paint legs on it; we shall not help young wheat to grow by tugging at it. We must practise patience ... acting only at the right time and with the minimum amount of effort. In fact, if we learn how to wait, we shall frequently find that no action is necessary in any case. The *Tao Te Ching* (15) states:

> Do you have the patience to wait
> till your mud settles and the water is clear?
> Can you remain unmoving
> till the right action arises by itself?

* * *

Wu-wei means striking only when the iron is hot, sowing one's seed — whether in deed or word — and leaving it time to burgeon. Where disagreement with another person occurs, its approach is to present one's viewpoint unambiguously, then leave it time to germinate — if there is any worth in the idea — in the mind of the other, rather than to overcome the other with decibels or, worse, to force him to accept a viewpoint or an activity against either his will or his personal assessment of the situation. Wu-wei is the way of the diplomat, not the dictator; of the philosopher, not the proselytiser.

Another concept in Taoism with which wu-wei is linked is *fu*, meaning 'returning'. This could be interpreted as aligning oneself with the yin and yang by understanding that seasons, whether in nature or in a nation's culture and values, arrive and pass, only to return again and pass away again, so that the wise person will accommodate his living to the eternal process of change. More basically Taoist is the concept of fu as returning, or, at any rate, remaining loyal, to one's roots:

> If you let yourself be blown to and fro,
> you lose touch with your root.
> If you let restlessness move you,
> you lose touch with who you are.
>
> (op. cit., 26)

* * *

[A]nother Taoist virtue ... is *p'u* literally an unhewn block, and is an image used to denote simplicity, even innocence: not arising from ignorance, but from a backcloth of full awareness of the human condition: childlikeness without being childish.... To live according to p'u is to speak as one feels, to behave according to the person one is, or has become; in other words, to act naturally. The *Tao Te Ching* (25) states:

> Man follows the earth.
> Earth follows the universe.
> The universe follows the Tao.
> The Tao follows only itself.

That final phrase has also been translated as 'suchness', the spontaneous and intuitive state of *tzu-yan*, meaning 'being such of itself', 'being natural'. In human beings, it includes everything which is free of human intention or external influences: that which is in harmony with itself. It may therefore be linked with wu-wei with its call for action only when it is appropriate — that is, when it is the natural action for those particular circumstances. When a person achieves this condition (which is not easy), he or she can be described as being at one with the Tao. It will not be achieved by academic research, or the study of sacred texts, or through a correct observance of ritual: ... Taoism relegates all these activities to a low ranking on the scale of spiritual aids. It will be gained by living one's life in accordance with the natural forces of the universe, expressed both in nature itself and in human nature.

50 TWELVE ZEN STORIES

Buddhism was introduced in China in the first century. After hundreds of years, Buddhist and Taoist ideas blended to yield Zen Buddhism, which more than a millennium later spread to Japan.

Zen places comparatively little emphasis on ritual, morality, or book learning. Rather, Zen finds enlightenment in spontaneous experience and challenges adherents with koans, puzzles that seek to force respondents to abandon reason. Such a query is this famous one: "Can you show me the sound of one hand clapping?"

Our next selection contains a dozen Zen stories that illustrate how paradox can provide a path to understanding, even when intellect appears to fail. The ultimate lesson is supposed to be the elimination of all dualities, including any separation between consciousness and the object of meditation.

A CUP OF TEA

NAN-IN, a Japanese master during the Meiji era (1868–1912), received a university professor who came to inquire about Zen.

Nan-in served tea. He poured his visitor's cup full, and then kept on pouring.

The professor watched the overflow until he no longer could restrain himself. "It is overfull. No more will go in!"

"Like this cup," Nan-in said, "you are full of your own opinions and speculations. How can I show you Zen unless you first empty your cup?"

IS THAT SO?

THE ZEN MASTER Hakuin was praised by his neighbors as one living a pure life.

A beautiful Japanese girl whose parents owned a food store lived near him. Suddenly, without any warning, her parents discovered she was with child.

This made her parents angry. She would not confess who the man was, but after much harassment at last named Hakuin.

In great anger the parents went to the master. "Is that so?" was all he would say.

After the child was born it was brought to Hakuin. By this time he had lost his reputation, which did not trouble him, but he took very good care of the child. He obtained milk from his neighbors and everything else the little one needed.

A year later the girl-mother could stand it no longer. She told her parents the truth—that the real father of the child was a young man who worked in the fishmarket.

From *Zen Flesh/Zen Bones*, compiled by Paul Reps and Nyogen Senzaki, Tuttle Publishing, 1957.

The mother and father of the girl at once went to Hakuin to ask his forgiveness, to apologize at length, and to get the child back again.

Hakuin was willing. In yielding the child, all he said was: "Is that so?"

THE MOON CANNOT BE STOLEN

RYOKAN, a Zen master, lived the simplest kind of life in a little hut at the foot of a mountain. One evening a thief visited the hut only to discover there was nothing in it to steal.

Ryokan returned and caught him. "You may have come a long way to visit me," he told the prowler, "and you should not return empty-handed. Please take my clothes as a gift."

The thief was bewildered. He took the clothes and slunk away.

Ryokan sat naked, watching the moon. "Poor fellow," he mused, "I wish I could give him this beautiful moon."

HAPPY CHINAMAN

ANYONE WALKING about Chinatowns in America will observe statues of a stout fellow carrying a linen sack. Chinese merchants call him Happy Chinaman or Laughing Buddha.

This Hotei [sage] lived in the T'ang dynasty. He had no desire to call himself a Zen master or to gather many disciples about him. Instead he walked the streets with a big sack into which he would put gifts of candy, fruit, or doughnuts. These he would give to children who gathered around him in play. He established a kindergarten of the streets.

Whenever he met a Zen devotee he would extend his hand and say: "Give me one penny." And if anyone asked him to return to a temple to teach others, again he would reply: "Give me one penny."

Once as he was about his play-work another Zen master happened along and inquired: "What is the significance of Zen?"

Hotei immediately plopped his sack down on the ground in silent answer.

"Then," asked the other, "what is the actualization of Zen?"

At once the Happy Chinaman swung the sack over his shoulder and continued on his way.

MUDDY ROAD

TANZAN AND EKIDO were once traveling together down a muddy road. A heavy rain was still falling.

Coming around a bend, they met a lovely girl in a silk kimono and sash, unable to cross the intersection.

"Come on, girl," said Tanzan at once. Lifting her in his arms, he carried her over the mud.

Ekido did not speak again until that night when they reached a lodging temple. Then he no longer could restrain himself. "We monks don't go near females," he told Tanzan, "especially not young and lovely ones. It is dangerous. Why did you do that?"

"I left the girl there," said Tanzan. "Are you still carrying her?"

THE SOUND OF ONE HAND

THE MASTER of Kennin temple was Mokurai, Silent Thunder. He had a little protégé named Toyo who was only twelve years old. Toyo saw the older disciples visit the master's room each morning and evening to receive instruction in sanzen or personal guidance in which they were given koans to stop mind-wandering.

Toyo wished to do sanzen also.

"Wait a while," said Mokurai. "You are too young."

But the child insisted, so the teacher finally consented.

In the evening little Toyo went at the proper time to the threshold of Mokurai's sanzen room. He struck the gong to announce his presence, bowed respectfully three times outside the door, and went to sit before the master in respectful silence.

"You can hear the sound of two hands when they clap together," said Mokurai. "Now show me the sound of one hand."

Toyo bowed and went to his room to consider this problem. From his window he could hear the music of the geishas. "Ah, I have it!" he proclaimed.

The next evening, when his teacher asked him to illustrate the sound of one hand, Toyo began to play the music of the geishas.

"No, no," said Mokurai. "That will never do. That is not the sound of one hand. You've not got it at all."

Thinking that such music might interrupt, Toyo moved his abode to a quiet place. He meditated again. "What can the sound of one hand be?" He happened to hear some water dripping. "I have it," imagined Toyo.

When he next appeared before his teacher, Toyo imitated dripping water.

"What is that?" asked Mokurai. "That is the sound of dripping water, but not the sound of one hand. Try again."

In vain Toyo meditated to hear the sound of one hand. He heard the sighing of the wind. But the sound was rejected.

He heard the cry of an owl. This also was refused.

The sound of one hand was not the locusts.

For more than ten times Toyo visited Mokurai with different sounds. All were wrong. For almost a year he pondered what the sound of one hand might be.

At last little Toyo entered true meditation and transcended all sounds. "I could collect no more," he explained later, "so I reached the soundless sound."

Toyo had realized the sound of one hand.

EVERY-MINUTE ZEN

Zen students are with their masters at least ten years before they presume to teach others. Nan-in was visited by Tenno, who, having passed his apprenticeship, had become a teacher. The day happened to be rainy, so Tenno wore wooden clogs and carried an umbrella. After greeting him Nan-in remarked: "I suppose you left your wooden clogs in the vestibule. I want to know if your umbrella is on the right or left side of the clogs."

Tenno, confused, had no instant answer. He realized that he was unable to carry his Zen every minute. He became Nan-in's pupil, and he studied six more years to accomplish his every-minute Zen.

IN THE HANDS OF DESTINY

A great Japanese warrior named Nobunaga decided to attack the enemy although he had only one-tenth the number of men the opposition commanded. He knew that he would win, but his soldiers were in doubt.

On the way he stopped at a Shinto shrine and told his men: "After I visit the shrine I will toss a coin. If heads comes, we will win; if tails, we will lose. Destiny holds us in her hand."

Nobunaga entered the shrine and offered a silent prayer. He came forth and tossed a coin. Heads appeared. His soldiers were so eager to fight that they won their battle easily.

"No one can change the hand of destiny," his attendant told him after the battle.

"Indeed not," said Nobunaga, showing a coin which had been doubled, with heads facing either way.

THE SUBJUGATION OF A GHOST

A young wife fell sick and was about to die. "I love you so much," she told her husband, "I do not want to leave you. Do not go from me to any other woman. If you do, I will return as a ghost and cause you endless trouble."

Soon the wife passed away. The husband respected her last wish for the first three months, but then he met another woman and fell in love with her. They became engaged to be married.

Immediately after the engagement a ghost appeared every night to the man, blaming him for not keeping his promise. The ghost was clever too. She told him exactly what had transpired between himself and his new sweetheart. Whenever he gave his fiancée a present, the ghost would describe it in detail. She would even repeat conversations, and it so annoyed the man that he could not sleep. Someone advised him to take his problem to a Zen master who lived close to the village. At length, in despair, the poor man went to him for help.

"Your former wife became a ghost and knows everything you do," commented the master. "Whatever you do or say, whatever you give your beloved, she knows. She must be a very wise ghost. Really you should admire such a ghost. The next time she appears, bargain with her. Tell her that she knows so much you can hide nothing from her, and that if she will answer you one question, you promise to break your engagement and remain single."

"What is the question I must ask her?" inquired the man.

The master replied: "Take a large handful of soy beans and ask her exactly how many beans you hold in your hand. If she cannot tell you, you will know she is only a figment of your imagination and will trouble you no longer."

The next night, when the ghost appeared the man flattered her and told her that she knew everything.

"Indeed," replied the ghost, "and I know you went to see that Zen master today."

"And since you know so much," demanded the man, "tell me how many beans I hold in this hand!"

There was no longer any ghost to answer the question.

ONE NOTE OF ZEN

AFTER KAKUA visited the emperor he disappeared and no one knew what became of him. He was the first Japanese to study Zen in China, but since he showed nothing of it, save one note, he is not remembered for having brought Zen into his country.

Kakua visited China and accepted the true teaching. He did not travel while he was there. Meditating constantly, he lived on a remote part of a mountain. Whenever people found him and asked him to preach he would say a few words and then move to another part of the mountain where he could be found less easily.

The emperor heard about Kakua when he returned to Japan and asked him to preach Zen for his edification and that of his subjects.

Kakua stood before the emperor in silence. He then produced a flute from the folds of his robe, and blew one short note. Bowing politely, he disappeared.

REAL PROSPERITY

A RICH MAN asked Sengai to write something for the continued prosperity of his family so that it might be treasured from generation to generation.

Sengai obtained a large sheet of paper and wrote: "Father dies, son dies, grandson dies."

The rich man became angry. "I asked you to write something for the happiness of my family! Why do you make such a joke as this?"

"No joke is intended," explained Sengai. "If before you yourself die your son should die, this would grieve you greatly. If your grandson should pass away before your son, both of you would be broken-hearted. If your family, generation after generation, passes away in the order I have named, it will be the natural course of life. I call this real prosperity."

A LETTER TO A DYING MAN

BASSUI WROTE the following letter to one of his disciples who was about to die:

"The essence of your mind is not born, so it will never die. It is not an existence, which is perishable. It is not an emptiness, which is a mere void. It has neither color nor form. It enjoys no pleasures and suffers no pains.

"I know you are very ill. Like a good Zen student, you are facing that sickness squarely. You may not know exactly who is suffering, but question yourself: What is the essence of this mind? Think only of this. You will need no more. Covet nothing. Your end which is endless is as a snowflake dissolving in the pure air."

51 ZEN BUDDHISM

HUSTON SMITH

For further explanation of Zen Buddhism, we turn to Huston Smith, whose work we read previously. Focusing on the Japanese version of Zen, which strongly influenced many aspects of Japanese culture, including its art, landscaping, poetry, and painting, Smith seeks to explain how Zen does not draw you away from the world but introduces you to the world seen differently.

Entering Zen is like stepping through Alice's looking glass. One finds oneself in a topsy-turvy wonderland where everything seems quite mad—charmingly mad for the most part, but mad all the same. It is a world of bewildering dialogues, obscure conundrums, stunning paradoxes, flagrant contradictions, and abrupt non sequiturs, all carried off in the most urbane, cheerful, and innocent style imaginable. Here are some examples:

A master, Gutei, whenever he was asked the meaning of Zen, lifted his index finger. That was all. Another kicked a ball. Still another slapped the inquirer.

A novice who makes a respectful allusion to the Buddha is ordered to rinse his mouth out and never utter that dirty word again....

A monk approaches a master saying, "I have just come to this monastery. Would you kindly give me some instruction?" The master asks, "Have you eaten your breakfast yet?" "I have." "Then go wash your bowls." The inquirer acquired the understanding he was seeking through this exchange.

A group of Zen masters, gathered for conversation, have a great time declaring that there is no such thing as Buddhism, or Enlightenment, or anything even remotely resembling *nirvana*. They set traps for one another, trying to trick someone into an assertion that might imply the contrary. Practiced as they are, they always artfully elude traps and pitfalls, whereupon the entire company bursts into glorious, room-shaking laughter.

What goes on here? Is it possible to make any sense out of what at first blush looks like Olympian horseplay, if not a direct put-on? Can they possibly be serious in this kind of spiritual doubletalk, or are they simply pulling our legs?

The answer is that they are completely serious, though it is true that they are rarely solemn. And though we cannot hope to convey their perspective completely, it being of Zen's essence that it cannot be impounded in words, we can give some hint as to what they are up to.

Let us admit at the outset that ... for we shall have to use words to talk about a position that is acutely aware of their limitations. Words occupy an ambiguous place in life. They are indispensable to our humanity, for without them we would be but howling yahoos. But they can also deceive, or at least mislead, fabricating a virtual reality that fronts for the one that actually exists. A parent can be fooled into thinking it loves its child because it addresses the child in endearing terms. A nation can assume that the phrase "under God" in its Pledge of Allegiance shows that its citizens believe in God when all it really shows is that they believe in *believing* in God. With all their admitted uses, words have three limitations. At worst they construct an artificial world wherein our actual feelings are camouflaged and people are reduced to stereotypes. Second, even when their descriptions are reasonably accurate, descriptions are not the things described—menus are not the meal. Finally, as

From Huston Smith, *The World's Religions*, 50th Anniversary Edition, HarperOne, 1991. Reprinted by permission of HarperCollins Publishers.

mystics emphasize, our highest experiences elude words almost entirely....

Mystics in every faith report contacts with a world that startles and transforms them with its dazzling darkness. Zen stands squarely in this camp, its only uniqueness being that it makes breaking the language barrier its central concern.

Only if we keep this fact in mind have we a chance of understanding this outlook, which in ways is the strangest expression of mature religion. It was the Buddha himself, according to Zen tradition, who first made the point by refusing (in the Flower Sermon we have already alluded to) to equate his experiential discovery with any verbal expression. Bodhidharma continued in this tradition by defining the treasure he was bringing to China as a special transmission outside the scriptures." Zen ... has its texts; they are intoned in tis monasteries morning and evening. But one glance at these distinctive texts will reveal how unlike other scriptures they are. Almost entirely they are given to pressing home the fact that Zen cannot be equated with any verbal formula whatsoever. Account after account will depict disciples interrogating their masters about Zen, only to receive a roared "Ho!" for answer. For the master sees that through such questions, seekers are trying to fill the lack in their lives with words and concepts instead of realizations. Indeed, students will be lucky if they get off with verbal rebuffs. Often a rain of blows will be the retort as the master, utterly uninterested in the disciples' physical comfort, resorts to the most forceful way he can think of to pry the questioner out of his mental rut.

As we might expect, this unique stance toward scripture is duplicated in Zen's attitude toward creeds. In contrast to most religions, which pivot around a creed of some sort, Zen refuses to lock itself into a verbal casing; it is "not founded on written words, and [is] *outside* the established teachings," to return to Bodhidharma's putting of the point. Signposts are not the destination, maps are not the terrain. Life is too rich and textured to be fitted into pigeonholes, let alone equated with them. No affirmation is more than a finger pointing to the moon. And, lest attention turn to the finger, Zen will point, only to withdraw its finger

at once. Other faiths regard blasphemy and disrespect for God's word as sins, but Zen masters may order their disciples to rip their scriptures to shreds and avoid words like Buddha or *nirvana* as if they were smut. They intend no disrespect. What they are doing is straining by every means they can think of to blast their novices out of solutions that are only verbal. "Not everyone who says to me, 'Lord, Lord,' will enter the kingdom of heaven" (Matthew 7:21). Zen is not interested in theories about enlightenment; it wants the real thing. So it shouts, and buffets, and reprimands, without ill will entering in the slightest. All it wants to do is force the student to crash the word-barrier. Minds must be sprung from their verbal bonds into a new mode of apprehending....

We in the West rely on reason so fully that we must remind ourselves that in Zen we are dealing with a perspective that is convinced that reason is limited and must be supplemented by another mode of knowing.

For Zen, if reason is not a ball and chain, anchoring mind to earth, it is at least a ladder too short to reach to truth's full heights. It must, therefore, be surpassed ... Zen is not trying to placate the mundane mind. It intends the opposite; to upset the mind—unbalance it and eventually provoke revolt against the canons that imprison it. But this puts the matter too mildly. By forcing reason to wrestle with what from its normal point of view is flat absurdity; by compelling it to conjoin things that are ordinarily incompatible, Zen tries to drive the mind to a state of agitation wherein it hurls itself against its logical cage with the desperation of a cornered rat. By paradox and non sequitur Zen provokes, excites, exasperates, and eventually exhausts the mind until it sees that thinking is never more than thinking *about*, or feeling more than feeling *for*. Then, having gotten the rational mind where it wants it— reduced to an impasse—it counts on a flash of sudden insight to bridge the gap between secondhand and firsthand life....

The first important breakthrough is an intuitive experience called *kensho* or *satori*. Though its preparation may take years, the experience itself comes in a flash, exploding like a silent rocket deep within the subject and throwing everything into a new perspective.

[S]atori is Zen's version of the mystical experience, which, wherever it appears, brings joy, at-one-ment, and a sense of reality that defies ordinary language. But whereas the tendency is to relate such experiences to the zenith of the religious quest, Zen places them close to the point of departure. In a very real sense Zen training begins with *satori*. For one thing, there must be further *satoris* as the trainee learns to move with greater freedom in this realm. But the important point is that Zen, drawing half its inspiration from the practical, common-sense, this-worldly orientation of the Chinese to balance the mystical other worldly half it derived from India, refuses to permit the human spirit to withdraw—shall we say retreat?—into the mystical state completely.

The genius of Zen lies in the fact that it neither leaves the world in the less-than-ideal state in which it finds it, nor withdraws from the world in aloofness or indifference. Zen's object is to infuse the temporal *with* the eternal—to widen the doors of perception so that the wonder of the *satori* experience can flood the everyday world.

With the possible exception of the Buddha himself, in no one is that business ever completely finished. Yet by extrapolating hints in the Zen corpus we can form some idea of what the condition of "the man who has nothing further to do" would be like.

First, it is a condition in which life seems distinctly good. Asked what Zen training leads to, a Western student who had been practicing for seven years in Kyoto answered, "No paranormal experiences that I can detect. But you wake up in the morning and the world seems so beautiful you can hardly stand it."

Along with this sense of life's goodness there comes, secondly, an objective outlook on one's relation to others; their welfare impresses one as being as important as one's own. Looking at a dollar bill, one's gaze may be possessive; looking at a sunset, it cannot be. Zen attainment is like looking at the sunset. Requiring (as it does) awareness to the full, issues like "whose awareness?" or "awareness of what?" do not arise. Dualisms dissolve. As they do there comes over one a feeling of gratitude to the past and responsibility to things present and future.

Third, the life of Zen (as we have sought to emphasize) does not draw one away from the world; it returns one to the world—the world robed in new light. We are not called to worldly indifference, as if life's object were to spring soul from body as piston from syringe. The call is to discover the satisfaction of full awareness even in its bodily setting. "What is the most miraculous of all miracles?" "That I sit quietly by myself." Simply to see things as they are, as they truly are in themselves, is life enough. It is true that Zen values unity, but it is a unity that is simultaneously empty (because it erases lines that divide) and full (because it replaces those lines with ones that connect). Stated in the form of a Zen algorithm, "All is one, one is none, none is all." Zen wears the air of divine ordinariness: "Have you eaten? Then wash your bowls." If you cannot find the meaning of life in an act as simple as that of doing the dishes, you will not find it anywhere…

With this perception of the infinite in the finite there comes, finally, an attitude of generalized agreeableness. "Yesterday was fair, today it is raining"; the experiencer has passed beyond the opposites of preference and rejection. As both pulls are needed to keep the relative world turning, each is welcomed in its proper turn.…

Fifth, as the dichotomies between self and other, finite and infinite, acceptance and rejection are transcended, even the dichotomy between life and death disappears.

B. NEGATION

52 NEGATIVE ATTRIBUTES

MOSES MAIMONIDES

Let us next consider a different approach to the difficulty of describing the divine. It was offered by Rabbi Moses ben Maimon (1135–1204), known as Maimonides, who was the most influential Jewish philosopher of the medieval period and has been called "the most significant Jewish philosopher of all time." He was born in Cordova, Spain, became a court physician in Cairo, Egypt, where he was the leader of the Jewish community, and wrote monumental works on Jewish law as well as his philosophical masterpiece, *The Guide of the Perplexed*. In his view God is beyond the power of human conceptualization.

According to Maimonides, the only way to describe God is to use negative attributes. Thus one speaks of God not as existing but as not nonexistent, not as powerful but as not non-powerful, not as knowing but as not not-knowing. In this way one seeks to avoid the pitfalls inherent in making any positive assertion about that which exceeds our understanding.

It is the negative attributes which we must employ to guide our mind … to the utmost limit of what man can apprehend of God. For instance, it has been proved to us that something must exist apart from those objects which our senses apprehend and which our reason can encompass with its knowledge. We say about this thing that it exists, meaning that it is absurd to say that He does not exist. Then we apprehend that its existence is not like the existence of, say, the elements, which are lifeless bodies, and consequently say that He lives, meaning that God is not subject to death. Then we apprehend that this being is also not like the existence of heaven, which is a living body, and consequently we say that He is not a body. Then we apprehend that this being is not like the existence of an Intelligence, which is neither a body nor subject to death, but is due to a cause, and consequently say that God is eternal, meaning that there is no cause which called Him into being. Then we apprehend that the existence of this Being, which is its essence, is not only sufficient

for that Being itself to exist, but many existences emanate from it. It is, however, not like the emanation of heat from the fire or the automatic connection between light and the sun, but it is an emanation which He perpetually keeps going, giving it a constant flow arranged according to a wise plan.… We shall say on account of these arrangements that He is omnipotent, omniscient, and possessed of will. By these attributes we mean to say that He is neither powerless nor ignorant nor distracted or disinterested. When we say He is not powerless, we mean that His existence is sufficient to bring into existence things other than Himself. When we say He is not ignorant, we mean that He apprehends, i.e., lives, for whatever apprehends lives. When we say He is not distracted or disinterested, we mean that all those existing things run along an ordered and planned course, not without supervision and coming into being just by chance, just like anything which a person possessed of will plans with purpose and will. Then we apprehend that there is no other being like this

From Moses Maimonides, *The Guide of the Perplexed*, trans. Chaim Rabin, Hackett Publishing Company, 1995. Reprinted by permission of the publisher.

one. When we, therefore, say He is One, we mean thereby to deny any plurality.

Thus it becomes clear that every attribute with which we describe Him ... has the purport of negating its own absence if our intention thereby is to apprehend His essence rather than His works. These negative terms are also not used absolutely of God, but only in the manner mentioned before, that one denies of a thing something that by the nature of things could not exist in it, as when we say of a wall that it does not see....

We can only apprehend that He is; that there exists a Being unlike any other being which He brought into existence, having nothing whatsoever in common with them, who has no plurality in Him, and is not powerless to bring into existence things other than He himself, and that His relation to the world is that of the captain to the ship. This also is not a true relation, and not even remotely resembles the real one, but it serves to guide the mind to the idea that God governs the universe, meaning that He supports it and keeps its order as it should be....

Praise be to Him who is such that when our minds try to visualize His essence, their power of apprehending becomes imbecility; when they study the connection between His works and His will, their knowledge becomes ignorance; and when our tongues desire to declare His greatness by descriptive terms, all eloquence becomes impotence and imbecility.

53   POSITIVE ATTRIBUTES

LEVI GERSONIDES

Rabbi Levi ben Gershom (1288–1344), known as Gersonides, lived in Province, France. He was renowned as an astronomer, mathematician, and Biblical commentator, and also as a remarkably acute philosopher, deeply committed to rational inquiry and prepared to interpret all religious beliefs in the light of scientific knowledge.

Maimonides thought we cannot refer to God using words in their ordinary sense. Gersonides disagreed, and in his typically bold fashion maintained that in describing God we can use words straightforwardly, although recognizing that they refer to God "primarily," describing God's essence, and to human beings "secondarily," describing characteristics that emanate from God. God's knowledge, for example, far exceeds our own, but "we say that God has knowledge because of the knowledge we find in us." As is his style, Gersonides offers one forceful argument after another, as he defends the view that using terms we understand we can reason about God.

[T]he first thing to do is to examine whether the term "knowledge" is equivocal with respect to divine and human knowledge, such that the difference between them is as Maimonides thought.... It seems to us that Maimonides' position on this question of divine cognition is not implied by any philosophical principles; indeed, reason denies this view, as I will show. It seems rather that theological considerations have forced him to this view.

From *The Wars of the Lord*, vol. 2, trans. Seymour Feldman, The Jewish Publication Society, 1999. Reprinted by permission of the publisher. The material in brackets was inserted by the translator.

That philosophical argument rules out Maimonides' position on this topic will be demonstrated as follows. It would seem that God's knowledge is equivocal with respect to our knowledge in the sense of prior and posterior predication, that is, the term "knowledge" is predicated of God (may He be blessed) *primarily* and of others *secondarily*. For in God knowledge is identical with His essence, whereas in anyone else knowledge is the effect of God's knowledge. In such a case the term is applied to God in a prior sense and to other things in a posterior sense. The same is true with respect to such terms as "exists," "one," "essence," and the like, i.e., they are predicated of God primarily and of other things secondarily. For His existence, unity, and essence belong to Him essentially, whereas the existence, unity, and essence of every [other] existent thing emanate from Him. Now when something is of this kind, the predicate applies to it in a prior sense, whereas the predicate applies in a posterior sense to the other things that are called by it insofar as they are given this property directly by the substance that has the property in the prior sense.... Hence, it seems that the difference between divine and human cognition is a difference in terms of greater perfection, for this is what is implied by prior and posterior predication. Now if what we have said is true, and since it is obvious that the most perfect knowledge is more true with respect to specificity and determinateness, it would follow that God's knowledge is more true with respect to specificity and determinateness. Hence, it cannot be that what is considered knowledge with respect to God can be called "belief," "error," or "confusion" with respect to man.

We can show in another way that the difference between divine and human cognition is not as Maimonides thought. It is evident that we proceed to affirm attributes of God from that with which we are familiar. That is, we say that God knows because of the knowledge found in us. For example, since we apprehend that the knowledge belonging to our intellect is a perfection of our intellect—without which it could not be an intellect in act [i.e., perfect]—we predicate of God that He knows by virtue of the fact, which we have demonstrated concerning Him, that God

(may He be blessed) is indubitably an intellect in act. It is self-evident that when a predicate is affirmed of some object because it is true of some other thing, it is not predicated of both things in an absolutely equivocal sense, for between things that are absolutely equivocal there is no analogy.... Hence, it is clear that the term "knowledge" is not completely equivocal when applied to God (may He be blessed) and man. Since this term cannot be applied univocally with respect to God and man, it must be predicated in the sense of priority and posteriority. The same holds for other attributes that are predicated of both God (may He be blessed) and man. Thus, the difference between divine and human knowledge is one of greater perfection, albeit exceedingly so, and this type of knowledge is more precise and clear....

The inadequacy of Maimonides' contention about the [absolute] difference between our knowledge and God's knowledge can be shown in another way. With respect to those attributes concerning which we want to know whether or not they can be predicated of God, it is evident that such predicates have one meaning regardless whether we affirm or deny them. For example, if we want to know whether God is corporeal or incorporeal, the term "corporeal" has the same meaning in some sense in either case. For if the term "body" has a completely different connotation in the negation from the meaning it has in the affirmation, these statements would not be considered genuine contradictions, as is obvious.... Hence, since it is clear when we deny attributes of God that are found in us that such attributes are not completely equivocal with respect to God (may He be blessed) and us, the same is true when we affirm of God predicates that are true of us. For example, we say that God is immovable, since if He were movable He would be a body, for all movable objects [are bodies]. Now it is evident that in this proposition the term "movable" is not completely equivocal with respect to the term "movable" when it is applied to nondivine things. For if it were, there would be no proof that God is not movable, since the movable object that must be a body is that which is movable in the domain of human phenomena, whereas the term "movable" (in the completely equivocal sense) would not imply that it is a body. Hence, since it is evident that the predicates we deny of God are not absolutely equivocal, neither are the terms that we affirm of Him. For at first we were uncertain whether to affirm or deny such predicates of God (may He be blessed). Then when the inquiry was completed, we were able to affirm or deny such predicates of Him. In general, if the terms used in affirming predicates of Him were absolutely equivocal, there would be no term applicable to things in our world that would be more appropriate to deny than to affirm of God or [more appropriate] to affirm than to deny to Him. For example, someone could say "God is a body" but not mean by the term "body," "a magnitude"; rather he would mean something that is completely equivocal with the term "body" as we usually use it. Similarly, someone could say "God does not have knowledge," since the term "knowledge" would not [on this view] have the same meaning for him in this statement as it does for us. It will not do to object that we indeed deny corporeality of God because it is an imperfection for us, whereas we affirm knowledge of Him because it is a perfection for us. For the *term* "corporeality" is not [itself] an imperfection, and it is the term that we deny of Him, but the content of the term is the imperfection. Similarly, the *term* "knowledge" is not [itself] a perfection; its content is. The proof of this is as follows. If by the term "corporeality" we were to connote what the term "knowledge" connotes, and conversely, corporeality would be a perfection for us and knowledge an imperfection. Moreover, we do not affirm or deny anything of God except by determining at the outset whether it is proper or improper for *Him;* we do not ask whether or not it is a perfection for *us.* Thus, it is clear that reason shows that the term "knowledge" is not completely equivocal with respect to God (may He be blessed) and man....

On the basis of this entire discussion, it is now evident that reason shows that the term "knowledge" is predicated of God (may He be blessed) primarily and of creatures secondarily, not absolutely equivocally, and that the principles [of religious language] adopted by Maimonides in order to remove the objections of the philosophers concerning the problem of divine knowledge are not acceptable.

C. ANALOGY

54 THE USE OF ANALOGY

THOMAS AQUINAS

Our next selection is another excerpt from the *Summa Theologiae* of Thomas Aquinas. Here he considers the view of Moses Maimonides, whom Aquinas refers to as "Rabbi Moses," that when we use words to describe God they do not have the same meaning as when we use them ordinarily. In Aquinas's terminology, the issue is whether when names are applied to God and to creatures the terms are "predicated univocally" (that is, with the same meaning) or "in a purely equivocal sense" (that is, with different meanings).

Aquinas's conclusion is that the terms are used neither univocally nor equivocally but analogously. For example, the term "healthy" can be applied to an animal and by analogy to a related medicine, such as one that causes health in the animal. Similarly, the term "wise" can be applied to a human being and by analogy to God.

[A]s regards names of God said absolutely and affirmatively, as *good, wise*, and the like, various and many opinions have been held. For some have said that all such names, although they are applied to God affirmatively, nevertheless have been brought into use more to remove something from God than to posit something in Him. Hence they assert that when we say that God lives, we mean that God is not like an inanimate thing; and the same in like manner applies to other names. This was taught by Rabbi Moses. Others say that these names applied to God signify His relationship towards creatures: thus in the words, *God is good*, we mean, God is the cause of goodness in things; and the same interpretation applies to other names.

Both of these opinions, however, seem to be untrue ... because in neither of them could a reason be assigned why some names more than others should be applied to God. For He is assuredly the cause of bodies in the same way as He is the cause of good things; therefore if the words *God is good* signified no more than, *God is the cause of good things*, it might in like manner be said that God is a body, inasmuch as He is the cause of bodies....

[W]hen any name expressing perfection is applied to a creature, it signifies that perfection as distinct from the others according to the nature of its definition; as, for instance, by this term *wise* applied to a man, we signify some perfection distinct from a man's essence, and distinct from his power and his being, and from all similar things. But when we apply *wise* to God, we do not mean to signify anything distinct from His essence or power or being. And thus when this term *wise* is applied to man, in some degree it circumscribes and comprehends the thing signified; whereas this is not the case when it is applied to God, but it leaves the thing signified as uncomprehended and as exceeding the signification of the name. Hence it is evident that this term *wise* is not applied in the same way to God and to man. The same applies to other terms. Hence, no name is predicated univocally of God and of creatures.

From Anton C. Pegis, ed., *Basic Writings of Saint Thomas Aquinas*, Hackett Publishing Company, 1997. Reprinted by permission of the publisher.

Neither, on the other hand, are names applied to God and creatures in a purely equivocal sense, as some have said. Because if that were so, it follows that from creatures nothing at all could be known or demonstrated about God; for the reasoning would always be exposed to the fallacy of equivocation.... Therefore it must be said that these names are said of God and creatures in an *analogous* sense, that is, according to proportion.

This can happen in two ways: either according as many things are proportioned to one (thus, for example *healthy* is predicated of medicine and urine in relation and in proportion to health of body, of which the latter is the sign and the former the cause), or according as one thing is proportioned to another (thus, *healthy* is said of medicine and an animal, since medicine is the cause of health in the animal body). And in this way some things are said of God and creatures analogically, and not in a purely equivocal nor in a purely univocal sense.... For in analogies, the idea is not, as it is in univocals, one and the same; yet it is not totally diverse as in equivocals; but the name which is thus used in a multiple sense signifies various proportions to some one thing, *e.g.*, *healthy*, applied to urine, signifies the sign of animal health; but applied to medicine, it signifies the cause of the same health....

The arguments adduced ... prove indeed that ... names are not predicated univocally of God and creatures; yet they do not prove that they are predicated equivocally.

55 THE INADEQUACY OF ANALOGY

F. C. COPLESTON

To help in assessing Thomas Aquinas's theory of how God can be described using language analogically, we turn to the work of Father F. C. Copleston (1907–1994), who was Professor of Metaphysics at the Gregorian University in Rome.

He admits, as he believes Aquinas would, that staying within the sphere of analogy does not make possible an adequate understanding of God. Copleston, however, maintains that Aquinas's approach does yield at least some knowledge of the divine nature. A key question to consider is whether an inadequate understanding of God differs significantly from no understanding at all.

Aquinas points out that when we predicate of God negative terms like "immutable" or "incorporeal" we remove, as it were, something from God, mutability or corporeity; that is, we deny the applicability to God of terms like "mutable" or "corporeal." We are concerned primarily with denying something of God rather than with affirming something positively of the divine substance. But there are other terms, like "wise" and "good" which are predicated of God positively and affirmatively; and it is in regard to the meaning of these terms that a special difficulty arises. Exclusive adherence to the negative way would lead to agnosticism about the divine nature; for a

From F. C. Copleston, *Aquinas: An Introduction to the Life and Work of the Great Medieval Thinker*, Penguin Books, 1955. Reprinted by permission of the publisher.

mere addition of negations would not result in positive knowledge. On the other hand, the use of the affirmative way, that is, affirming of God positive predicates, gives rise to a difficult problem. Some terms are predicated of God only metaphorically, as when God is called a "rock." But … [w]hen it is said that God is "wise" or "good" the terms are not used merely metaphorically: it is said that God is "really," and not merely metaphorically, wise and good. But at once we seem to be faced with a dilemma. If we mean that God is wise in precisely the same sense that a human being is or can be wise, we make God a kind of superman, and we are involved in anthropomorphism. If on the other hand the term is used purely equivocally, if, that is, its meaning when predicated of God is entirely different from its meaning when predicated of a human being, … its meaning is evacuated, without any other meaning being substituted….

Aquinas' answer to the problem is that when terms like "wise" or "good" are predicated of God they are predicated neither univocally nor equivocally but in an analogical sense…. To say that certain terms are predicated analogically of God does not mean, of course, that we have an adequate positive idea of what is objectively signified by the term when it is predicated of God. Our knowledge of perfections is derived from creatures, and this origin necessarily colours our concepts of those perfections. We necessarily think and speak of God in terms which, from the linguistic point of view, refer primarily to creatures, and we can only approximate towards, while never reaching, an adequate understanding of what is meant by saying that God is "wise" or "good" or "intelligent" or "living"….

In Aquinas' account of our natural knowledge of the divine nature there is, then, a certain agnosticism. When we say that God is wise we affirm of God a positive attribute; but we are not able to give any adequate description of what is objectively signified by the term when it is predicated of God. If we are asked what we mean when we say that God is wise, we may answer that we mean that God possesses wisdom in an infinitely higher degree than human beings. But we cannot provide any adequate description of the content, so

to speak, of this infinitely higher degree; we can only approximate towards it by employing the way of negation. What is affirmed is positive, but the positive content of the concept in our minds is determined by our experience of creaturely wisdom, and we can only attempt to purify it or correct its inadequacies by means of negations. Obviously enough, this process will never lead to an adequate positive understanding of the objective meaning of (that is, of what is objectively signified by) the terms predicated of God. But Aquinas never claimed that it would. On the contrary, he did not hesitate to draw the logical conclusion. "The first cause surpasses human understanding and speech. He knows God best who acknowledges that whatever he thinks and says falls short of what God really is." Aquinas would have been quite unmoved by the accusation that he could not give the exact significance of the terms predicated of God; for he never pretended to be able to give it.

Now, it is clear that predicating intelligence of God is not exactly like predicating intelligence of a dog. If I call a dog "intelligent," I use the word analogically; but if I am asked what I mean by it I can point to some of the dog's activities. Human beings and their intelligent activities, dogs and their activities, all the terms of the analogy fall within the range of experience. But we cannot observe God or point to God. The question therefore arises whether there is any objective justification for predicating certain terms of God rather than other terms. Or the question can be put in this way. Although no sensible man would demand an adequate account of the positive meaning of the word "intelligent" as used of God, how do we know that the word denotes a reality when it is predicated of God? …

It may be said, of course, that there is in fact some resemblance between the case of calling a dog "intelligent" and that of calling God "intelligent." For though I cannot point to God acting in the same way that I can point to the dog acting, I can draw attention to effects of God's activity which fall within the field of our experience. Does not Aquinas himself do this in his fifth proof of God's existence? … Can I not therefore by pointing to the perfections of creatures indicate the meaning of the terms which I predicate of God?

This is true. But the meaning which I indicate in this way is, as Aquinas was well aware, the meaning which the term has for me in my own mind, and it by no means follows that this is adequate to the objective reality connoted by the term when predicated of God. This can be shown by an example. Suppose that my one and only reason for calling God "intelligent" is that I consider that there is an intelligible world-system and that this is the creation of a transcendent being whom I name "God." In this case when I think of God as intelligent I think of Him as the sort of being capable of creating this world-system. And if I am asked to explain what I mean by calling God "intelligent," I mention the world-system. But it does not follow that I can give an adequate positive explanation of what the divine intelligence is in itself. The divine intelligence is identical with the divine being, and God transcends all His effects. There must, of course, be some control of analogical predication in the context. That is to say, if analogical predication about God is not to be wild talk, there must be some assignable reason for using one term rather than another. And these reasons will colour the meaning of the terms in my mind. But the explanation of the meaning of the terms which I can give is not adequate, and cannot be adequate, to the objective reality connoted by the terms. As Aquinas saw clearly, a certain measure of "agnosticism" is inevitable. It could be avoided only by relapsing into anthropomorphism on the one hand or on the other by holding that all statements about God are so many myths which may have some useful function, perhaps as a stimulus to moral conduct and certain affective attitudes, but which are not put forward as being true. And Aquinas was not prepared to accept either an anthropomorphic view of God or an interpretation of theological propositions as so many myths.

Aquinas' "agnosticism," then, is not agnosticism in the modern sense. He has no doubt about the existence of God, and he is far from saying that we can know nothing about the divine nature or that we can make only negative statements about it. At the same time he is acutely conscious of the empirical foundation of all human knowledge and of the consequences of this in natural theology. We cannot help thinking and speaking of God in terms which, linguistically speaking, refer primarily to the finite objects of our experience, and we move always within the sphere of analogy. This means that our knowledge of God is necessarily imperfect and inadequate.

D. METAPHOR

56   EXPERIENCE AND METAPHOR

JANET MARTIN SOSKICE

Janet Martin Soskice, who is a Fellow in Theology and Religious Studies at the University of Cambridge, offers a different way to understand descriptions of God. She focuses on the role of metaphor in language and believes the meaning of metaphors that apply to God can be found in religious experience and tradition. According to Soskice, to say that God's presence is like that of a wind is to draw on a series of "stumbling approximations" used by those who believe they experience God and understandable by means of Christian sacred texts and accepted modes of interpretation.

The descriptive vocabulary which any individual uses is ... dependent on the community of interest and investigation in which he finds himself, and the descriptive vocabulary which a community has at its disposal is embedded in particular traditions of investigation and conviction; for example, the geneticist will assume that it is a biochemical mechanism which is responsible for trait inheritance and not magical spells or curses. His descriptive language is forged in a particular context of investigation where there is agreement on matters such as what constitutes evidence, what are genuine arguments, what counts as a fact, and so on ...

Corresponding to the scientific communities of interest, there are religious communities of interest (Christians, for example) which are bound by shared assumptions, interests, and traditions of interpretation, and share a descriptive vocabulary.

The Christian, too, makes claims on the basis of experience which, although different from the kind on which scientific judgements are based, is experience nonetheless. It is important to clarify what we mean by "experience" in this context; it is a portmanteau term to cover two sorts, the first being the dramatic or pointed religious experiences of the kind which might prompt one to say, "whatever appeared to me on the mountain was God," or "whatever caused me to change my life was God." The second are the diffuse experiences which form the subject of subsequent metaphysical reflection, the kind on which Aquinas based his proofs for the existence of God; for example, the experience of contingency which prompts us to postulate the non-contingent, the experience of cause which prompts us to postulate the uncaused, the experience of order which prompts us to postulate an ordering agent, and so on. On this view, even the abstractions of natural theology are based, in the long run, on experience—although of a diffuse kind. When an individual, or the wider religious community, decides upon a particular model or image as a means of elucidating experience, pointed or diffuse, they do so as heirs to an established tradition of explanation and a common descriptive vocabulary.... The religious teacher is not always privileged with experiences denied to the common run; he

From Janet Martin Soskice, *Metaphor and Religious Language*, Oxford University Press, 1985. Reprinted by permission of the publisher.

may equally be someone with the gift of putting into words what others have sensed. He may have the ability to find metaphors and choose models which illuminate the experience of others, for example, be the first to say that God's presence is like that of a powerful wind. The great divine and the great poet have this in common: both use metaphor to say that which can be said in no other way but which, once said, can be recognized by many....

But it is not necessary to believe that, at one moment in the history of Israel, the model of God as spirit was given, by cosmic disclosure, in a fully elaborated state and immediately embraced by everyone. It is more likely that this was one of many stumbling approximations used to articulate experiences judged to be of God and that, over the years, this particular model was preferred to others by those attempting to describe similar experiences, that it was enriched by the association of wind with breath and gradually became so much a part of the community's descriptive vocabulary that to speak of God as "spirit" became an accustomed manner of speech. In this way, over time, there comes into being a rich assortment of models whose sources may be unknown but which have been gradually selected out by the faithful as being especially adequate to their experience. This accumulation of favoured models, embellished by the glosses of generations, gives the context for Christian reflection and provides the matrix for the descriptive vocabulary which Christians continue to employ in attempts to describe their experience....

So, to explain what it means to Christians to say that God is a fountain of living water, or a vine-keeper, or a rock, or fortress, or king requires an account not merely of fountains, rocks, vines, and kings but of a whole tradition of experiences and of the literary tradition which records and interprets them.

This, incidentally, is an answer to the frequently put question, "on what basis are some of the Christian's models given priority over others?" Choice is not unconditioned; we do not choose the model of God as shepherd over that of God as poultry keeper or cattleman at random. A favoured model continues to be so in virtue of its own applicability certainly, but also because the history of its application makes it already freighted with meaning. To say that God is "king" recalls a whole history of kingship and insubordination recorded in the biblical texts....

From the literary observation we return to the philosophical one, for the touchstone of these chronicles of faith is experience, experiences pointed or diffuse, the experience of individuals and of communities which are believed to be experiences of the activity of a transcendent God. The language used to account for them is metaphorical and qualified, it stands within a tradition of use and is theory-laden, yet in so far as it is grounded on experience it is referential, and it is the theological realist's conviction that that to which it refers, the source of these experiences, is God who is the source and cause of all that is....

It is a commonplace that in the twentieth century we have lost the living sense of the biblical metaphors which our forefathers had. Sometimes it is suggested that this is a consequence of urban life where few have any contact with shepherds and sheep, kings, and vines. This simple view fails to see that the distinctively Christian reading of the metaphors of God as shepherd, or king, or vine-keeper could never be had simply by knowing about sheep, kings, and vines, and forgets that the Scottish crofter of a previous generation who had no experience of grape vines or Temples had no trouble construing Jesus's claim to be the true vine or Temple. Other times, it is said that we have lost this living sense because we no longer read the Bible and there is much in this, yet it is not difficult to imagine that there are some Christians (extreme fundamentalists) who know the text word for word, yet for whom, precisely because they regard it as simply a book of historical fact, much of its allusive significance is lost. If it is true that biblical imagery is lifeless to modern man (and it is not obvious that this is so), this is more likely to be the legacy of historical criticism, of the search for the historical Jesus, and of attempts made by Christians both liberal and conservative to salvage his exact words and acts from the dross of allusion and interpretation with which the gospel writers surrounded them. It is the legacy of a literalism which equates religious truth with historical facts, whatever these might be. Christianity is indeed a religion of the book, but not of a book of this sort of fact. Its sacred texts are chronicles of experience, armouries of metaphor, and purveyors of an interpretive tradition. The sacred literature thus both records the experiences of the past and provides the descriptive language by which any new experience may be interpreted. If this is so, then experience, customarily regarded as the foundation of natural theology, is also the touchstone of the revealed. All the metaphors which we use to speak of God arise from experiences of that which cannot adequately be described, of that which Jews and Christians believe to be "He Who Is." ...

> Though thou with clouds of anger do disguise
> Thy face; yet through that maske I know those eyes,
> Which, though they turne away sometimes,
> They never will despise.

God, in Donne's poem, is beloved and dreaded, horribly absent and compellingly present. This is the beginning and end of theology.

57 METAPHOR WITHOUT MEANING

PAUL EDWARDS

To assert that a word is being used metaphorically neither explains its meaning nor ensures that it has any meaning at all. In our next selection, Paul Edwards (1923–2004), who was a professor of philosophy at Brooklyn College of The City University of New York, distinguishes what he terms "reducible metaphors" from those that are not. He describes a reducible metaphor as one whose meaning can be explained in literal terms.

According to Edwards, only reducible metaphors can be used to make genuine assertions. Thus, he believes that descriptions of God using irreducible metaphors lack meaning.

The concession by an author that he is using a certain word metaphorically is tantamount to admitting that, in a very important sense ... he does not mean what he says. It does not automatically tell us what he does mean or whether in fact he means anything at all....

Often indeed when words are used metaphorically, the context or certain special conventions make it clear what is asserted. Thus, when a certain historian wrote that "the Monroe Doctrine has always rested on the broad back of the British navy," it would have been pedantic and foolish to comment "what on earth does he mean—doesn't he know that navies don't have backs?" Or if a man, who has been involved in a scandal and is advised to flee his country, rejects the advice and says, "No, I think I'll stay and face the music," it would be absurd to object to his statement on the ground that it is not exactly music that he is going to hear. In these cases we know perfectly well what the authors mean although they are using certain words metaphorically. But we know this because we can eliminate the metaphorical expression, because we can specify the content of the

From Paul Edwards, "Professor Tillich's Confusions," *Mind* 74 (1965). Reprinted by permission of Oxford University Press.

assertion in non-metaphorical language, because we can supply the literal equivalent.

The examples just cited are what I shall call "reducible metaphors." ... [I]n calling a metaphor "reducible" all I mean is that the truth-claims made by the sentence in which it occurs can be reproduced by one or more sentences all of whose components are used in literal senses....

[M]any ... fail to notice the difference between metaphors which are reducible in the sense just explained and those which are not. When a sentence contains an irreducible metaphor, it follows at once that the sentence ... fails to make a genuine assertion. For what has happened is that the sentence has been deprived of the referent it would have had ... if the expression in question had been used in its literal sense. To say that the metaphor is irreducible is to say in effect that no new referent can be supplied....

It may be said that I have not been fair to ... [those] who defend themselves by insisting that they are using certain expressions metaphorically or analogously. It may be said that I have emphasized the negative implications of this admission—that the words in question are not used in their literal senses—without doing justice to its positive implications. For, it may be argued, when it is said that a certain word is used "analogously," it *is* implied that the term has a referent, namely a referent which is in some important respect similar to the referent it has when used literally....

But ... merely saying that a sentence, or any part of it, has meaning does not by itself give it meaning. Such a claim does not assure us that the sentence is intelligible. Similarly the claim that a sentence has an "analogous" referent is a claim and no more—it may be false. If I say, to use an example given by Sidney Hook,[1] that the sea is angry, the word "angry" really has a referent which is analogous to its referent when used literally. I can in this case specify the features of the sea to which I am referring when I call it angry and I can also specify the similarities between these features and the anger of human beings. If, however, I say that Being-itself is angry, I could not independently identify the features of Being-itself to which I am supposedly referring. Nor of course could I specify the similarities between the anger of human beings and the putative anger of Being-itself. My claim that "angry" is used analogously in this sentence in a sense in which this implies that it has a referent would be false or at any rate baseless.

NOTE

1. "The Quest for Being," *The Journal of Philosophy*, 1953, p. 715.

PART SEVEN

Belief Without Proof

A. BELIEF AS STRATEGY

58 THE WAGER

BLAISE PASCAL

If philosophical arguments are inadequate to prove the existence of God and the evidence from miracles and mystical experience is not convincing, might other reasons suffice to justify theism? Blaise Pascal (1623–1662), the French mathematician, physicist, and philosopher, offered an argument that belief in God is useful even if not supported by the available evidence.

According to Pascal's celebrated "wager," if we believe in God, and God exists, then we attain heavenly bliss; if we believe in God, and God doesn't exist, little is lost. On the other hand, if we don't believe in God, and God does exist, then we are doomed to the torments of damnation; if we don't believe in God, and God doesn't exist, little is gained. So belief is the safest strategy.

If there is a God, he is infinitely beyond our comprehension, since, having neither parts nor limits, he bears no relation to ourselves. We are therefore incapable of knowing either what he is, or if he is.

That being so, who will dare to undertake a resolution of this question? It cannot be us, who bear no relationship to him.

From Blaise Pascal, *Pensées*, trans. Honor Levi, Oxford University Press, 1995. Reprinted by permission of the publisher.

Who will then blame the Christians for being unable to provide a rational basis for their belief, they who profess a religion for which they cannot provide a rational basis? They declare that it is a folly (1 Cor. 1: 18) in laying it before the world: and then you complain that they do not prove it! If they did prove it, they would not be keeping their word. It is by the lack of proof that they do not lack sense. "Yes, but although that excuses those who offer their religion as it is, and that takes away the blame from them of producing it without a rational basis, it does not excuse those who accept it."

Let us therefore examine this point, and say: God is, or is not. But towards which side will we lean? Reason cannot decide anything. There is an infinite chaos separating us. At the far end of this infinite distance a game is being played and the coin will come down heads or tails. How will you wager? Reason cannot make you choose one way or the other, reason cannot make you defend either of the two choices.

So do not accuse those who have made a choice of being wrong, for you know nothing about it! "No, but I will blame them not for having made this choice, but for having made any choice. For, though the one who chooses heads and the other one are equally wrong, they are both wrong. The right thing is not to wager at all."

Yes, but you have to wager. It is not up to you, you are already committed. Which then will you choose? Let us see. Since you have to choose, let us see which interests you the least. You have two things to lose: the truth and the good, and two things to stake: your reason and will, your knowledge and beatitude; and your nature has two things to avoid: error and wretchedness. Your reason is not hurt more by choosing one rather than the other, since you do have to make the choice. That is one point disposed of. But your beatitude? Let us weigh up the gain and the loss by calling heads that God exists. Let us assess the two cases: if you win, you win everything; if you lose, you lose nothing. Wager that he exists then, without hesitating! "This is wonderful. Yes, I must wager. But perhaps I am betting too much." Let us see. Since there is an equal chance of gain and loss, if you won only two lives instead of one, you

could still put on a bet. But if there were three lives to win, you would have to play (since you must necessarily play), and you would be unwise, once forced to play, not to chance your life to win three in a game where there is an equal chance of losing and winning. But there is an eternity of life and happiness. And that being so, even though there were an infinite number of chances of which only one were in your favour, you would still be right to wager one in order to win two, and you would be acting wrongly, since you are obliged to play, by refusing to stake one life against three in a game where out of an infinite number of chances there is one in your favour, if there were an infinitely happy infinity of life to be won. But here there is an infinitely happy infinity of life to be won, one chance of winning against a finite number of chances of losing, and what you are staking is finite. That removes all choice: wherever there is infinity and where there is no infinity of chances of losing against one of winning, there is no scope for wavering, you have to chance everything. And thus, as you are forced to gamble, you have to have discarded reason if you cling on to your life, rather than risk it for the infinite prize which is just as likely to happen as the loss of nothingness.

For it is no good saying that it is uncertain if you will win, that it is certain you are taking a risk, and that the infinite distance between the *certainty* of what you are risking and the *uncertainty* of whether you win makes the finite good of what you are certainly risking equal to the uncertainty of the infinite. It does not work like that. Every gambler takes a certain risk for an uncertain gain; nevertheless he certainly risks the finite uncertainty in order to win a finite gain, without sinning against reason. There is no infinite distance between this certainty of what is being risked and the uncertainty of what might be gained: that is untrue. There is, indeed, an infinite distance between the certainty of winning and the certainty of losing. But the uncertainty of winning is proportional to the certainty of the risk, according to the chances of winning or losing. And hence, if there are as many chances on one side as on the other, the odds are even, and then the certainty of what you risk is equal to the uncertainty of winning. It is very far from being infinitely distant from it. So our argument is infinitely strong, when the finite is at stake in a game where there are equal chances of winning and losing, and the infinite is to be won.

That is conclusive, and, if human beings are capable of understanding any truth at all, this is the one.

"I confess it, I admit it, but even so … Is there no way of seeing underneath the cards?" "Yes, Scripture and the rest, etc." "Yes, but my hands are tied and I cannot speak a word. I am being forced to wager and I am not free, they will not let me go. And I am made in such a way that I cannot believe. So what do you want me to do?" "That is true. But at least realize that your inability to believe, since reason urges you to do so and yet you cannot, arises from your passions. So concentrate not on convincing yourself by increasing the number of proofs of God but on diminishing your passions. You want to find faith and you do not know the way? You want to cure yourself of unbelief and you ask for the remedies? Learn from those who have been bound like you, and who now wager all they have. They are people who know the road you want to follow and have been cured of the affliction of which you want to be cured. Follow the way by which they began: by behaving just as if they believed, taking holy water, having masses said, etc. That will make you believe quite naturally, and according to your animal reactions." "But that is what I am afraid of." "Why? What do you have to lose?"

59 PASCAL'S WAGER: A CRITIQUE

SIMON BLACKBURN

Simon Blackburn, Professor of Philosophy at the University of Cambridge, does not accept Pascal's reasoning. According to Blackburn, Pascal is assuming that the existence of no God is the only alternative to the existence of a Christian God who cares what people believe but is less concerned with why they believe it. Suppose, however, a God exists who punishes those who hold theistic beliefs without evidence, while rewarding those who in the absence of evidence refrain from believing. In that case, not believing would be the safer bet.

So the key question is: How do we decide on what basis rewards and punishments, if any, will be distributed? Regarding this crucial matter, the wager provides no guidance.

The standard way to present [Pascal's wager] … is in terms of a two-by-two box of the options:

	God exists	God does not
I believe in him	+infinity!	0
I do not believe in him	–infinity!	0

The zeros on the right correspond to the thought that not much goes better or worse in this life, whether or not we believe. This life is of vanishingly little account compared to what is promised to believers. The plus-infinity figure corresponds to infinite bliss. The minus-infinity figure in the bottom left corresponds to the traditional jealous God, who sends to Hell those who do not

From Simon Blackburn, *Think*, Oxford University Press, 1998, Reprinted by permission of the publisher.

believe in him, and of course encourages his followers to give them a hard time here, as well. But the minus-infinity figure can be soft-pedalled. Even if we put 0 in the bottom left-hand box, the wager looks good. It would be good even if God does not punish disbelief, because there is still that terrific payoff of "+infinity" cranking up the choice. In decision-theory terms, the option of belief "dominates," because it can win, and cannot lose. So—go for it!

Unfortunately the lethal problem with this argument is simple, once it is pointed out.

Pascal starts from a position of metaphysical ignorance. We just know nothing about the realm beyond experience. But the set-up of the wager presumes that we *do* know something. We are supposed to know the rewards and penalties attached to belief in a Christian God. This is a God who will be pleasured and reward us for our attendance at mass, and will either be indifferent or, in the minus-infinity option, seriously discombobulated by our nonattendance. But this is a case of false options. For consider that if we are really ignorant metaphysically, then it is at least as likely that the options pan out like this:

> There is indeed a very powerful, very benevolent deity. He (or she or they or it) has determined as follows. The good human beings are those who follow the natural light of reason, which is given to

them to control their beliefs. These good humans follow the arguments, and hence avoid religious convictions. These ones with the strength of mind not to believe in such things go to Heaven. The rest go to Hell.

This is not such a familiar deity as the traditional jealous God, who cares above all that people believe in him. (Why is God so jealous? Alas, might his jealousy be a projection of human sectarian ambitions and emotions? Either you are with us or against us! The French sceptic Voltaire said that God created mankind in his image, and mankind returned the compliment.) But the problem for Pascal is that if we really know nothing, then we do not know whether the scenario just described is any less likely than the Christian one he presented. In fact, for my money, a God that punishes belief is just as likely, and a lot more reasonable, than one that punishes disbelief.

And of course, we could add the Humean point that whilst for Pascal it was a simple two-way question of mass versus disbelief, in the wider world it is also a question of the Koran versus mass, or L. Ron Hubbard versus the Swami Maharishi, or the Aquarian Concepts Community Divine New Order Government versus the First Internet Church of All. The wager has to be silent about those choices.

60   PASCAL'S WAGER: AN ASSESSMENT

LINDA TRINKAUS ZAGZEBSKI

In our next selection, Linda Trinkaus Zagzebski, whose work we read previously, considers three objections to Pascal's wager. She finds that they point to problems in the wager but may not require that Pascal's line of reasoning be abandoned.

From Linda Trinkaus Zagzebski, *Philosophy of Religion: An Historical Introduction*, Blackwell Publishing, 2007. Reprinted by permission of the publisher.

Pascal's wager has a number of well-known objections, some of them coming from theists and some from non-theists. Let us consider three of them.

1. *The many gods objection.* Pascal assumes the wager is over belief in the Christian God. It is a God who promises eternal life for belief in him. But this means that the wager is between the existence of a God of a certain kind and no God. That is not a forced wager because there are other possibilities. To put the point another way, there are many wagers: Christian God or no Christian God, Muslim God or no Muslim God, Hindu God or no Hindu God, etc. And this is a problem because for some of these you could make the same kind of wager, yet you really can only bet on one, assuming that betting on one commits you to betting against the others. But which one should you bet on?

One answer to this objection is that Pascal is thinking of live options, something you could really believe. Presumably he thinks that the God of only one religion would be a possibility for you. Pascal's era was not one in which there were churches, temples, mosques, and synagogues within easy driving distance of the average person making the wager. So it means that Pascal's wager is not intended for everybody. It is for people who: (1) think both Christianity and atheism are intellectually unproven but also unrefuted, so from a rational viewpoint both are live options; (2) have a roughly Christian view of God as a being who rewards his worshipers with heaven; and (3) are in the emotional position of struggle, trying to choose. Presumably that would apply to many people, and many other people would be in the analogous position of betting on the God of a different religion. Clearly, though, the situation is much more complex for a person for whom more than one religion that promises an infinite payoff is a live option.

2. *The wager presupposes a low view of God and religious faith.* A second objection is that God does not want believers who believe on the basis of a wager motivated by self-interest. This is not what religious faith is all about. This objection is often expressed by religious people who find the wager repugnant. The reply to this objection is

that Pascal is formulating an appeal to a certain kind of person, one who is perched precariously between belief and unbelief. Given that he thought of the wager as the precursor to real faith, not faith itself, the person who makes the wager would sincerely try to believe in God. She would not remain indefinitely in the state of the gambler who is motivated only by potential gain. There is no guarantee that she will eventually acquire real faith, but she won't unless she tries, just as the entrepreneur has no guarantee of success in business, but he knows for sure that he won't succeed if he doesn't make the attempt. If the theistic bettor succeeds, her original motive will eventually be replaced by the attitude of religious faith….

3. *We can't believe by making a choice.* There are many things you can't just decide to believe. Suppose somebody tries to bribe you into believing there will be an earthquake in Antarctica on April 19, 2020. Could you do it? You can't just believe because it is in your interest to do so. No matter how much money you are offered, it is probably impossible to make yourself believe certain things if the evidence does not support it. If the choice is not forced, your reason tells you to withhold judgment. And it is hard to see how you could muster the motive to believe, given that earthquakes in Antarctica probably do not connect to anything you already care about at all.

But there are several disanalogies between the Antarctica example and Pascal's wager. As we have seen, Pascal does not think you can start believing in an instant. Second, Pascal thinks the choice is forced, and it is about something you already care about. If you take the time to cultivate the belief by acting as if you believe, you may eventually end up really believing. Here is an analogy given by James Cargile[1] defending Pascal's view that you could get yourself to believe in God given (a) the right motivation, (b) no firm belief to begin with, and (c) a bit of time. Suppose a billionaire jazz lover declares that in two years he will toss a coin. If it comes up heads he will give a million dollars to every devoted jazz fan. If it comes up tails he won't do anything. Every Sunday for the next two years a one-hour jazz concert is scheduled. If you attend these concerts religiously, listen to jazz at every other opportunity, and avoid listening to any other kind of music, it is quite likely that you will become a lover of jazz. Of course, it's not likely to work if you hated jazz from the beginning, but if you start out neutral, there is a good chance it will work. In any case, Pascal is addressing someone who is neutral about the existence of God.

But here is another analogy that is more problematic. It highlights both the issue of whether you can make yourself feel something, and whether it is morally reprehensible to do so even if you can. Suppose a wealthy man falls in love with a poor woman and wants to marry her, but she feels nothing for him, neither positive nor negative. If she can get herself to love him, she will get a lot of money. One problem is that she has to try to love the man, and while the chances that she will succeed vary with the case, there is rarely a very high probability that it will. But that is not an unsurmountable problem, since even a low probability of success may be enough to make the effort to love him worthwhile. The real problem is that the motive is suspect. No one objects when a woman tries to love a man in order to have a happy relationship with someone she does not want to hurt, but the situation is problematic when she is motivated by the prospect of a reward external to the relationship itself. Nonetheless, human motives are complex, and we often consider it acceptable, even commendable, when people consider the external rewards of a marriage to some extent. Parents routinely advise their children to pick a mate with a good income, and nobody considers that deplorable. But it would be a foolhardy parent who would advise her child to choose a mate with the best income and *then* try to love the person. Is Pascal's wager analogous to the foolhardy parent? If so, can it be altered to avoid the problematic features of the marriage analogy?

NOTE

1. James Cargile, "Pascal's Wager," in Steven M. Cahn and Savid Shatz, eds., *Contemporary Philosophy of Religion*. Oxford University Press, 1982, pp. 229-236.

61 THE ETHICS OF BELIEF

W. K. CLIFFORD

Is holding beliefs on the basis of insufficient evidence ever justifiable? W.K. Clifford (1845-1879), an English philosopher and mathematician, thought not. He argued that beliefs influence actions, that our actions may affect others for good or ill, and that believing on weak grounds leads to thoughtless actions that may harm those who rely on us to be conscientious about what we say and do. To stifle doubts and believe more firmly than the available evidence supports is a form of dishonesty that weakens our character by undermining concern for truth.

A shipowner was about to send to sea an emigrant-ship. He knew that she was old, and not over-well built at the first; that she had seen many seas and climes, and often had needed repairs. Doubts had been suggested to him that possibly she was not seaworthy. These doubts preyed upon his mind, and made him unhappy; he thought that perhaps he ought to have her thoroughly overhauled and refitted, even though this should put him to great expense. Before the ship sailed,

From W. K. Clifford, *Lectures and Essays* (1879).

however, he succeeded in overcoming these melancholy reflections. He said to himself that she had gone safely through so many voyages and weathered so many storms that it was idle to suppose she would not come safely home from this trip also. He would put his trust in Providence, which could hardly fail to protect all these unhappy families that were leaving their fatherland to seek for better times elsewhere. He would dismiss from his mind all ungenerous suspicions about the honesty of builders and contractors. In such ways he acquired a sincere and comfortable conviction that his vessel was thoroughly safe and seaworthy; he watched her departure with a light heart, and benevolent wishes for the success of the exiles in their strange new home that was to be; and he got his insurance-money when she went down in mid-ocean and told no tales.

What shall we say of him? Surely this, that he was verily guilty of the death of those men. It is admitted that he did sincerely believe in the soundness of his ship; but the sincerity of his conviction can in no wise help him, because *he had no right to believe on such evidence as was before him.* He had acquired his belief not by honestly earning it in patient investigation, but by stifling his doubts. And although in the end he may have felt so sure about it that he could not think otherwise, yet inasmuch as he had knowingly and willingly worked himself into that frame of mind, he must be held responsible for it.

Let us alter the case a little, and suppose that the ship was not unsound after all; that she made her voyage safely, and many others after it. Will that diminish the guilt of her owner? Not one jot. When an action is once done, it is right or wrong for ever; no accidental failure of its good or evil fruits can possibly alter that. The man would not have been innocent, he would only have been not found out. The question of right or wrong has to do with the origin of his belief, not the matter of it; not what it was, but how he got it; not whether it turned out to be true or false, but whether he had a right to believe on such evidence as was before him.

There was once an island in which some of the inhabitants professed a religion teaching neither the doctrine of original sin nor that of eternal punishment. A suspicion got abroad that the professors of this religion had made use of unfair means to get their doctrines taught to children. They were accused of wresting the laws of their country in such a way as to remove children from the care of their natural and legal guardians; and even of stealing them away and keeping them concealed from their friends and relations. A certain number of men formed themselves into a society for the purpose of agitating the public about this matter. They published grave accusations against individual citizens of the highest position and character, and did all in their power to injure these citizens in the exercise of their professions. So great was the noise they made, that a Commission was appointed to investigate the facts; but after the Commission had carefully inquired into all the evidence that could be got, it appeared that the accused were innocent. Not only had they been accused on insufficient evidence, but the evidence of their innocence was such as the agitators might easily have obtained, if they had attempted a fair inquiry. After these disclosures the inhabitants of that country looked upon the members of the agitating society, not only as persons whose judgment was to be distrusted, but also as no longer to be counted honourable men. For although they had sincerely and conscientiously believed in the charges they had made, yet *they had no right to believe on such evidence as was before them.* Their sincere convictions, instead of being honestly earned by patient inquiring, were stolen by listening to the voice of prejudice and passion.

Let us vary this case also, and suppose, other things remaining as before, that a still more accurate investigation proved the accused to have been really guilty. Would this make any difference in the guilt of the accusers? Clearly not; the question is not whether their belief was true or false, but whether they entertained it on wrong grounds. They would no doubt say, "Now you see that we were right after all; next time perhaps you will believe us." And they might be believed, but they would not thereby become honourable men. They would not be innocent, they would only be not found out. Every one of them, if he chose to examine himself *in foro conscientiae,*[1] would know that he had acquired and nourished a belief, when he had no right to believe on such evidence as was before him; and therein he would know that he had done a wrong thing.

It may be said, however, that in both of these supposed cases it is not the belief which is judged to be wrong, but the action following upon it. The ship-owner might say, "I am perfectly certain that my ship is sound, but still I feel it my duty to have her examined, before trusting the lives of so many people to her." And it might be said to the agitator, "However convinced you were of the justice of your cause and the truth of your convictions, you ought not to have made a public attack upon any man's character until you had examined the evidence on both sides with the utmost patience and care."

In the first place, let us admit that, so far as it goes, this view of the case is right and necessary; right, because even when a man's belief is so fixed that he cannot think otherwise, he still has a choice in regard to the action suggested by it, and so cannot escape the duty of investigating on the ground of the strength of his convictions; and necessary, because those who are not yet capable of controlling their feelings and thoughts must have a plain rule dealing with overt acts.

But this being premised as necessary, it becomes clear that it is not sufficient, and that our previous judgment is required to supplement it. For it is not possible so to sever the belief from the action it suggests as to condemn the one without condemning the other. No man holding a strong belief on one side of a question, or even wishing to hold a belief on one side can investigate it with such fairness and completeness as if he were really in doubt and unbiased; so that the existence of a belief not founded on fair inquiry unfits a man for the performance of this necessary duty.

Nor is that truly a belief at all which has not some influence upon the actions of him who holds it. He who truly believes that which prompts him to an action has looked upon the action to lust after it, he has committed it already in his heart. If a belief is not realized immediately in open deeds, it is stored up for the guidance of the future. It goes to make a part of that aggregate of beliefs which is the link between sensation and action at every moment of all our lives, and which is so organized and compacted together that no part of it can be isolated from the rest, but every new addition modifies the structure of the whole. No real belief, however trifling and fragmentary it may seem, is ever truly insignificant; it prepares us to receive more of its like, confirms those which resembled it before, and weakens others; and so gradually it lays a stealthy train in our inmost thoughts, which may someday explode into overt action, and leave its stamp upon our character for ever.

And no one man's belief is in any case a private matter which concerns himself alone. Our lives are guided by that general conception of the course of things which has been created by society for social purposes. Our words, our phrases, our forms and processes and modes of thought, are common property, fashioned and perfected from age to age; an heirloom which every succeeding generation inherits as a precious deposit and a sacred trust to be handed on to the next one, not unchanged but enlarged and purified, with some clear marks of its proper handiwork. Into this, for good or ill, is woven every belief of every man who has speech of his fellows. An awful privilege, and an awful responsibility, that we should help to create the world in which posterity will live.

In the two supposed cases which have been considered, it has been judged wrong to believe on insufficient evidence, or to nourish belief by suppressing doubts and avoiding investigation. The reason of this judgment is not far to seek; it is that in both these cases the belief held by one man was of great importance to other men. But forasmuch as no belief held by one man, however seemingly trivial the belief, and however obscure the believer, is ever actually insignificant or without its effect on the fate of mankind, we have no choice but to extend our judgment to all cases of belief whatever. Belief, that sacred faculty which prompts the decisions of our will, and knits into harmonious working all the compacted energies of our being, is ours not for ourselves, but for humanity. It is rightly used on truths which have been established by long experience and waiting toil, and which have stood in the fierce light of free and fearless questioning. Then it helps to bind men together, and to strengthen and direct their common action. It is desecrated when given to unproved and unquestioned statements, for the solace and private pleasure of the believer; to add a tinsel splendour to the plain straight road of our life and display a bright mirage beyond it; or even to drown the common sorrows of our kind by a self-deception which allows them not only to cast down, but also to degrade us. Whoso would deserve well of his fellows in this matter will guard the purity of his belief with a very fanaticism of jealous care, lest at any time it should rest on an unworthy object, and catch a stain which can never be wiped away.

It is not only the leader of men, statesman, philosopher, or poet, that owes this bounden duty to mankind. Every rustic who delivers in the village alehouse his slow, infrequent sentences, may help to kill or keep alive the fatal superstitions which clog his race. Every hard-worked wife of an artisan may transmit to her children beliefs which shall knit society together, or rend it in pieces. No simplicity of mind, no obscurity of station, can escape the universal duty of questioning all that we believe.

It is true that this duty is a hard one, and the doubt which comes out of it is often a very bitter thing. It leaves us bare and powerless where we thought that we were safe and strong. To know all about anything is to know how to deal with it under all circumstances. We feel much happier and more secure when we think we know precisely what to do, no matter what happens, than when we have lost our way and do not know where to turn. And if we have supposed ourselves to know all about anything, and to be capable of doing what is fit in regard to it, we naturally do not like to find that we are really ignorant and powerless, that we have to begin again at the beginning, and try to learn what the thing is and how it is to be dealt with—if indeed anything can be learnt about it. It is the sense of power attached to a sense of knowledge that makes men desirous of believing, and afraid of doubting.

This sense of power is the highest and best of pleasures when the belief on which it is founded is a true belief, and has been fairly earned by investigation. For then we may justly feel that it is common property, and hold good for others as well as for ourselves. Then we may be glad, not that I have learned secrets by which I am safer and stronger, but that *we men* have got mastery over more of the world; and we shall be strong, not for ourselves, but in the name of Man and in his strength. But if the belief has been accepted on insufficient evidence, the pleasure is a stolen one. Not only does it deceive ourselves by giving us a sense of power which we do not really possess, but it is sinful, because it is stolen in defiance of our duty to mankind. That duty is to guard ourselves from such beliefs as from a pestilence, which may shortly master our own body and then spread to the rest of the town. What would be thought of one who, for the sake of a sweet fruit, should deliberately run the risk of bringing a plague upon his family and his neighbours?

And, as in other such cases, it is not the risk only which has to be considered; for a bad action is always bad at the time when it is done, no matter what happens afterwards. Every time we let ourselves believe for unworthy reasons, we weaken our powers of self-control, of doubting, of judicially and fairly weighing evidence. We all suffer severely enough from the maintenance and support of false beliefs and the fatally wrong actions which they lead to, and the evil born when one such belief is entertained is great and wide. But a greater and wider evil arises when the credulous character is maintained and supported, when a habit of believing for unworthy reasons is fostered and made permanent. If I steal money from any person, there may be no harm done by the mere transfer of possession; he may not feel the loss, or it may prevent him from using the money badly. But I cannot help doing this great wrong towards Man, that I make myself dishonest. What hurts society is not that it should lose its property, but that it should become a den of thieves, for then it must cease to be society. This is why we ought not to do evil, that good may come; for at any rate this great evil has come, that we have done evil and are made wicked thereby. In like manner, if I let myself believe anything on insufficient evidence, there may be no great harm done by the mere belief; it may be true after all, or I may never have occasion to exhibit it in outward acts. But I cannot help doing this great wrong towards Man, that I make myself credulous. The danger to society is not merely that it should believe wrong things, though that is great enough; but that it should become credulous, and lose the habit of testing things and inquiring into them; for then it must sink back into savagery.

The harm which is done by credulity in a man is not confined to the fostering of a credulous character in others, and consequent support of false beliefs. Habitual want of care about what I believe leads to habitual want of care in others about the truth of what is told to me. Men speak the truth to one another when each reveres the truth in his own mind and in the other's mind; but how shall my friend revere the truth in my mind when I myself am careless about it, when I believe things because I want to believe them, and because they are comforting and pleasant? Will he not learn to cry, "Peace," to me, when there is no peace? By such a course I shall surround myself with a thick atmosphere of falsehood and fraud, and in that I must live. It may matter little to me, in my cloud-castle of sweet illusions and darling lies; but it matters much to Man that I have made my neighbours ready to deceive. The credulous man is father to the liar and the cheat; he lives in the bosom of this his family, and it is no marvel if he should become even as they are. So closely are our duties knit together, that whoso shall keep the whole law, and yet offend in one point, he is guilty of all.

To sum up: it is wrong always, everywhere, and for anyone, to believe anything upon insufficient evidence.

If a man, holding a belief which he was taught in childhood or persuaded of afterwards, keeps down and pushes away any doubts which arise about it in his mind, purposely avoids the reading of books and the company of men that call in question or discuss it, and regards as impious those questions which cannot easily be asked without disturbing it—the life of that man is one long sin against mankind.

If this judgment seems harsh when applied to those simple souls who have never known better, who have been brought up from the cradle with a horror of doubt, and taught that their eternal welfare depends on *what* they believe, then it leads to the very serious question. *Who hath made Israel to sin?*

It may be permitted me to fortify this judgment with the sentence of Milton[2]—

> A man may be a heretic in the truth; and if he believe things only because his pastor says so, or the assembly so determine, without knowing other reason, though his belief be true, yet the very truth he holds becomes his heresy.

And with this famous aphorism of Coleridge[3]—

> He who begins by loving Christianity better than Truth, will proceed by loving his own sect or Church better than Christianity, and end in loving himself better than all.

Inquiry into the evidence of a doctrine is not to be made once for all, and then taken as finally settled. It is never lawful to stifle a doubt; for either it can be honestly answered by means of the inquiry already made, or else it proves that the inquiry was not complete.

"But," says one, "I am a busy man; I have no time for the long course of study which would be necessary to make me in any degree a competent judge of certain questions, or even able to understand the nature of the arguments."

Then he should have no time to believe.

NOTES

1. [Conscientiously.]
2. *Areopagitica.*
3. *Aids to Reflections.*

62 THE WILL TO BELIEVE

WILLIAM JAMES

William James, whose work we read previously, disagreed with Clifford. James contended that when you face an important choice between two appealing options and cannot wait for further evidence, you are justified in believing and acting as your passion decides. According to James, we should not allow the fear of holding a false belief to prevent us from losing the benefits of believing what may be true.

James claims that the essence of religion is contained in two fundamental claims: (1) the best things are the more eternal things, and (2) we are better off if we believe (1). Note that in a footnote he says that "if the action required or inspired by the religious hypothesis is in no way different from that dictated by the naturalistic hypothesis, then religious faith is a pure superfluity, better pruned away, and controversy about its legitimacy is a piece of idle trifling, unworthy of serious minds." An intriguing question is whether believing in (1) and (2), which James considers the core of the religious attitude, requires a different action than rejecting (1) and (2).

I

Let us give the name of *hypothesis* to anything that may be proposed to our belief; and just as the electricians speak of live and dead wires, let us speak of any hypothesis as either *live* or *dead*. A live hypothesis is one which appeals as a real possibility to him to whom it is proposed. If I ask you to believe in the Mahdi,[1] the notion makes no electric connection with your nature—it refuses to scintillate with any credibility at all. As an hypothesis it is completely dead. To an Arab, however (even if he be not one of the Mahdi's followers), the hypothesis is among the mind's possibilities: it is alive. This shows that deadness and liveness in an hypothesis are not intrinsic properties, but relations to the individual thinker. They are measured by his willingness to act. The maximum of liveness in an hypothesis means willingness to act irrevocably. Practically, that means belief; but there is some believing tendency wherever there is willingness to act at all.

Next, let us call the decision between two hypotheses an *option*. Options may be of several kinds. They may be—1, *living* or *dead*; 2, *forced* or *avoidable*; 3, *momentous* or *trivial*; and for our purposes we may call an option a *genuine* option when it is of the forced, living and momentous kind.

1. A living option is one in which both hypotheses are live ones. If I say to you: "Be a theosophist or be a mahomedan," it is probably a dead option, because for you neither hypothesis is likely to be alive. But if I say "Be an agnostic or be a Christian," it is otherwise: trained as you are, each hypothesis makes some appeal, however small, to your belief.
2. Next, if I say to you: "Choose between going out with your umbrella or without it," I do not offer you a genuine option, for it is not forced. You can easily avoid it by not going out at all. Similarly, if I say "Either love me or hate me," "Either call my theory true or call it false," your option is avoidable. You may remain indifferent to me, neither loving nor hating, and you may decline to offer any judgment as to my theory. But if I say "Either accept this truth or go without it," I put on you a forced option, for there is no standing

From William James, *The Will to Believe and Other Essays in Popular Philosophy* (1898).

place outside of the alternative. Every dilemma based on a complete logical disjunction, with no possibility of not choosing, is an option of this forced kind.

3. Finally, if I were Dr. Nansen and proposed to you to join my North Pole expedition, your option would be momentous; for this would probably be your only similar opportunity, and your choice now would either exclude you from the North Pole sort of immortality altogether or put at least the chance of it into your hands. He who refuses to embrace a unique opportunity loses the prize as surely as if he tried and failed. *Per contra*,[2] the option is trivial when the opportunity is not unique, when the stake is insignificant, or when the decision is reversible if it later proves unwise. Such trivial options abound in the scientific life. A chemist finds an hypothesis live enough to spend a year in its verification: he believes in it to that extent. But if his experiments prove inconclusive either way, he is quit for his loss of time, no vital harm being done.

It will facilitate our discussion if we keep all these distinctions well in mind.

II

The next matter to consider is the actual psychology of human opinion. When we look at certain facts, it seems as if our passional and volitional nature lay at the root of all our convictions. When we look at others, it seems as if they could do nothing when the intellect had once said its say. Let us take the latter facts up first.

Does it not seem preposterous on the very face of it to talk of our opinions being modifiable at will? Can our will either help or hinder our intellect in its perceptions of truth? Can we, by just willing it, believe that Abraham Lincoln's existence is a myth, and that the portraits of him in *McClure's Magazine* are all of someone else? Can we, by any effort of our will, or by any strength of wish that it were true, believe ourselves well and about when we are roaring with rheumatism in bed, or feel certain that the sum of the two one-dollar bills in our pocket must be a hundred

dollars? We can *say* any of these things, but we are absolutely impotent to believe them; and of just such things is the whole fabric of the truths that we do believe in made up....

In Pascal's *Thoughts* there is a celebrated passage known in literature as Pascal's wager. In it he tries to force us into Christianity by reasoning as if our concern with truth resembled our concern with the stakes in a game of chance. Translated freely his words are these: You must either believe or not believe that God is—which will you do? Your human reason cannot say. A game is going on between you and the nature of things which at the day of judgment will bring out either heads or tails. Weigh what your gains and your losses would be if you should stake all you have on heads, or God's existence: If you win in such case, you gain eternal beatitude; if you lose, you lose nothing at all. If there were an infinity of chances, and only one for God in this wager, still you ought to stake your all on God; for though you surely risk a finite loss by this procedure, any finite loss is reasonable, even a certain one is reasonable, if there is but the possibility of infinite gain. Go, then, and take holy water, and have masses said; belief will come and stupefy your scruples—*Cela vous fera croire et vous abêtira.*[3] Why should you not? At bottom, what have you to lose?

You probably feel that when religious faith expresses itself thus, in the language of the gaming-table, it is put to its last trumps. Surely Pascal's own personal belief in masses and holy water had far other springs; and this celebrated page of his is but an argument for others, a last desperate snatch at a weapon against the hardness of the unbelieving heart. We feel that a faith in masses and holy water adopted willfully after such a mechanical calculation would lack the inner soul of faith's reality; and if we were ourselves in the place of the Deity, we should probably take particular pleasure in cutting off believers of this pattern from their infinite reward. It is evident that unless there be some pre-existing tendency to believe in masses and holy water, the option offered to the will by Pascal is not a living option. Certainly no Turk ever took to masses and holy water on its account; and even to us Protestants these means of salvation seem such foregone impossibilities that Pascal's logic, invoked for them specifically, leaves us unmoved. As well might the Mahdi write to us, saying "I am the Expected One whom God has created in his effulgence. You shall be infinitely happy if you confess me; otherwise you shall be cut off from the light of the sun. Weigh, then, your infinite gain if I am genuine against your finite sacrifice if I am not!" His logic would be that of Pascal; but he would vainly use it on us, for the hypothesis he offers us is dead. No tendency to act on it exists in us to any degree.

The talk of believing by our volition seems, then, from one point of view, simply silly. From another point of view it is worse than silly, it is vile. When one turns to the magnificent edifice of the physical sciences, and sees how it was reared; what thousands of disinterested moral lives of men lie buried in its mere foundations; what patience and postponement, what choking down of preference, what submission to the icy laws of outer fact are wrought into its very stones and mortar; how absolutely impersonal it stands in its vast augustness—then how besotted and contemptible seems every little sentimentalist who comes blowing his voluntary smoke-wreaths, and pretending to decide things from out of his private dream! Can we wonder if those bred in the rugged and manly school of science should feel like spewing such subjectivism out of their mouths? The whole system of loyalties which grow up in the schools of science go dead against its toleration; so that it is only natural that those who have caught the scientific fever should pass over to the opposite extreme, and write sometimes as if the incorruptibly truthful intellect ought positively to prefer bitterness and unacceptableness to the heart in its cup....

> "It fortifies my soul to know
> That, though I perish, Truth is so—"

sings Clough, whilst Huxley exclaims: "My only consolation lies in the reflection that, however bad our posterity may become, so long as they hold by the plain rule of not pretending to believe what they have no reason to believe because it may be to their advantage so to pretend [the word 'pretend' is surely here redundant],

they will not have reached the lowest depths of immorality." And that delicious *enfant terrible*[4] Clifford writes: "[Belief] is desecrated when given to unproved and unquestioned statements, for the solace and private pleasure of the believer.... Whoso would deserve well of his fellows in this matter will guard the purity of his belief with a very fanaticism of jealous care, lest at any time it should rest on an unworthy object, and catch a stain which can never be wiped away.... If [a] belief has been accepted on insufficient evidence [even though the belief be true, as Clifford on the same page explains], the pleasure is a stolen one.... It is sinful, because it is stolen in defiance of our duty to mankind. That duty is to guard ourselves from such beliefs as from a pestilence, which may shortly master our own body and then spread to the rest of the town.... It is wrong always, everywhere, and for anyone, to believe anything upon insufficient evidence."

III

All this strikes one as healthy, even when expressed, as by Clifford, with somewhat too much of robustious pathos in the voice. Free-will and simple wishing do seem, in the matter of our credences, to be only fifth wheels to the coach. Yet if anyone should thereupon assume that intellectual insight is what remains after wish and will and sentimental preference have taken wing, or that pure reason is what then settles our opinions, he would fly quite as directly in the teeth of the facts.

It is only our already dead hypotheses that our willing nature is unable to bring to life again. But what has made them dead for us is for the most part a previous action of our willing nature of an antagonistic kind. When I say "willing nature," I do not mean only such deliberate volitions as may have set up habits of belief that we cannot now escape from—I mean all such factors of belief as fear and hope, prejudice and passion, imitation and partisanship, the circumpressure of our caste and set. As a matter of fact we find ourselves believing, we hardly know how or why. Mr. Balfour gives the name of "authority" to all those influences, born of the intellectual climate, that make hypotheses possible or impossible for us, alive or dead. Here in this room, we all of us believe in molecules and the conservation of energy, in democracy and necessary progress, in Protestant Christianity and the duty of fighting for "the doctrine of the immortal Monroe," all for no reasons worthy of the name. We see into these matters with no more inner clearness, and probably with much less, than any disbeliever in them might possess. His unconventionality would probably have some grounds to show for its conclusions; but for us, not insight, but the *prestige* of the opinions, is what makes the spark shoot from them and light up our sleeping magazines of faith. Our reason is quite satisfied, in nine hundred and ninety-nine cases out of every thousand of us, if it can find a few arguments that will do to recite in case our credulity is criticized by someone else. Our faith is faith in someone else's faith, and in the greatest matters this is most the case. Our belief in truth itself, for instance, that there is a truth, and that our minds and it are made for each other—what is it but a passionate affirmation of desire, in which our social system backs us up? We want to have a truth; we want to believe that our experiments and studies and discussions must put us in a continually better and better position towards it; and on this line we agree to fight out our thinking lives. But if a pyrrhonistic sceptic asks us *how we know* all this, can our logic find a reply? No! Certainly it cannot. It is just one volition against another—we are willing to go in for life upon a trust or assumption which he, for his part, does not care to make.

As a rule we disbelieve all facts and theories for which we have no use. Clifford's cosmic emotions find no use for Christian feelings. Huxley belabors the bishops because there is no use for sacerdotalism in his scheme of life. Newman, on the contrary, goes over to Romanism, and finds all sorts of reasons good for staying there, because a priestly system is for him an organic need and delight. Why do so few "scientists" even look at the evidence for telepathy, so called? Because they think, as a leading biologist, now dead, once said to me, that even if such a thing were true, scientists ought to band together to keep it suppressed and concealed. It would undo the uniformity of Nature and all sorts of other things without which scientists cannot carry on their pursuits. But if this very man had been shown something which as a scientist he might *do* with telepathy, he might not only have examined the evidence, but even have found it good enough. This very law which the logicians would impose upon us—if I may give the name of logicians to those who would rule out our willing nature here—is based on nothing but their own natural wish to exclude all elements for which they, in their professional quality of logicians, can find no use.

Evidently, then, our non-intellectual nature does influence our convictions. There are passional tendencies and volitions which run before and others which come after belief, and it is only the latter that are too late for the fair; and they are not too late when the previous passional work has been already in their own direction. Pascal's argument, instead of being powerless, then seems a regular clincher, and is the last stroke needed to make our faith in masses and holy water complete. The state of things is evidently far from simple; and pure insight and logic, whatever they might do ideally, are not the only things that really do produce our creeds.

IV

Our next duty, having recognized this mixed-up state of affairs, is to ask whether it be simply reprehensible and pathological, or whether, on the contrary, we must treat it as a normal element in making up our minds. The thesis I defend is, briefly stated, this: *Our passional nature not only lawfully may, but must, decide an option between propositions, whenever it is a genuine option that cannot by its nature be decided on intellectual grounds; for to say, under such circumstances, "Do not decide, but leave the question open," is itself a passional decision—just like deciding yes or no—and is attended with the same risk of losing the truth....*

VII

One more point, small but important, and our preliminaries are done. There are two ways of looking at our duty in the matter of opinion—ways entirely different, and yet ways about whose difference the theory of knowledge seems hitherto to have shown very little concern. *We must know the truth;* and *we must avoid error*—these are our first and great commandments as would-be knowers; but they are not two ways of stating an identical commandment, they are two separable laws. Although it may indeed happen that when we believe the truth *A*, we escape as an incidental consequence from believing the falsehood *B*, it hardly ever happens that by merely disbelieving *B* we necessarily believe *A*. We may in escaping *B* fall into believing other falsehoods, *C* or *D*, just as bad as *B*; or we may escape *B* by not believing anything at all, not even *A*.

Believe truth! Shun error!—these, we see, are two materially different laws; and by choosing between them we may end by colouring differently our whole intellectual life. We may regard the chase for truth as paramount, and the avoidance of error as secondary; or we may, on the other hand, treat the avoidance of error as more imperative, and let truth take its chance. Clifford, in the instructive passage which I have quoted, exhorts us to the latter course. Believe nothing, he tells us, keep your mind in suspense forever, rather than by closing it on insufficient evidence incur the awful risk of believing lies. You, on the other hand, may think that the risk of being in error is a very small matter when compared with the blessings of real knowledge, and be ready to be duped many times in your investigation rather than postpone indefinitely the chance of guessing true. I myself find it impossible to go with Clifford. We must remember that these feelings of our duty about either truth or error are in any case only expressions of our passional life. Biologically considered, our minds are as ready to grind out falsehood as veracity, and he who says "Better go without belief forever than believe a lie!" merely shows his own preponderant private horror of becoming a dupe. He may be critical of many of his desires and fears, but this fear he slavishly obeys. He cannot imagine anyone questioning its binding force. For my own part, I have also a horror of being duped; but I can believe that worse things than being duped may happen to a man in this world: so Clifford's exhortation has to my ears a thoroughly fantastic sound. It is like a general informing his soldiers that it is better to keep out of battle forever than to risk a single wound. Not so are victories either over enemies or over nature gained. Our errors are surely not such awfully solemn things. In a world where we are so certain to incur them in spite of all our caution, a certain lightness of heart seems healthier than this excessive nervousness on their behalf. At any rate, it seems the fittest thing for the empiricist philosopher.

VIII

And now, after all this introduction, let us go straight at our question. I have said, and now repeat it, that not only as a matter of fact do we find our passional nature influencing us in our opinions, but that there are some options between opinions in which this influence must be regarded both as an inevitable and as a lawful determinant of our choice.

I fear here that some of you my hearers will begin to scent danger, and lend an inhospitable ear. Two first steps of passion you have indeed had to admit as necessary—we must think so as to avoid dupery, and we must think so as to gain truth; but the surest path to those ideal consummations, you will probably consider, is from now onwards to take no farther passional step.

Well, of course I agree as far as the facts will allow. Wherever the option between losing truth and gaining it is not momentous, we can throw the chance of *gaining truth* away, and at any rate save ourselves from any chance of *believing falsehood*, by not making up our minds at all till objective evidence has come. In scientific questions, this is almost always the case; and even in human affairs in general, the need of acting is seldom so urgent that a false belief to act on is better than no belief at all. Law courts, indeed, have to decide on the best evidence attainable for the moment, because a judge's duty is to make law as well as to ascertain it, and (as a learned judge once said to me) few cases are worth spending much time over: the great thing is to have them decided on *any* acceptable principle, and got out of the way. But in our dealings with objective nature we obviously are recorders, not makers, of the truth; and decisions for the mere sake of deciding promptly and getting on to the next business would be wholly out of place. Throughout the breadth of physical nature facts are what they are quite independently of us, and seldom is there any such hurry about them that the risks of being duped by believing a premature theory need be faced. The questions here are always trivial options, the hypotheses are hardly living (at any rate not living for us spectators), the choice between believing truth or falsehood is seldom forced. The attitude of sceptical balance is therefore the absolutely wise one if we would escape mistakes. What difference, indeed, does it make to most of us whether we have or have not a theory of the Röntgen rays, whether we believe or not in mind-stuff, or have a conviction about the causality of conscious states? It makes no difference. Such options are not forced on us. On every account it is better not to make them, but still keep weighing reasons *pro et contra*[5] with an indifferent hand.

I speak, of course, here of the purely judging mind. For purposes of discovery such indifference is to be less highly recommended, and science would be far less advanced than she is if the passionate desires of individuals to get their own faiths confirmed had been kept out of the game.... On the other hand, if you want an absolute duffer in an investigation, you must, after all, take the man who has no interest whatever in its results: he is the warranted incapable, the positive fool. The most useful investigator, because the most sensitive observer, is always he whose eager interest in one side of the question is balanced by an equally keen nervousness lest he become deceived. Science has organized this nervousness into a regular *technique*, her so-called method of verification; and she has fallen so deeply in love with the method that one may even say she has ceased to care for truth by itself at all. It is only truth as technically verified that interests her. The truth of truths might come in merely affirmative form, and she would decline to touch it. Such truth as that, she might repeat with Clifford, would be stolen in defiance of her duty to mankind. Human passions, however, are stronger than technical rules. "Le coeur a ses raisons," as Pascal says, "que la raison ne connaît point";[6] and however indifferent to all but the bare rules of the

game the umpire, the abstract intellect, may be, the concrete players who furnish him the materials to judge of are usually, each one of them, in love with some pet "live hypothesis" of his own. Let us agree, however, that wherever there is no forced option, the dispassionately judicial intellect with no pet hypothesis, saving us, as it does, from dupery at any rate, ought to be our ideal.

The question next arises: Are there not somewhere forced options in our speculative questions, and can we (as men who may be interested at least as much in positively gaining truth as in merely escaping dupery) always wait with impunity till the coercive evidence shall have arrived? It seems a priori improbable that the truth should be so nicely adjusted to our needs and powers as that. In the great boarding-house of nature, the cakes and the butter and the syrup seldom come out so even and leave the plates so clean. Indeed, we should view them with scientific suspicion if they did.

IX

Moral questions immediately present themselves as questions whose solution cannot wait for sensible proof. A moral question is a question not of what sensibly exists, but of what is good, or would be good if it did exist. Science can tell us what exists; but to compare the *worths*, both of what exists and of what does not exist, we must consult not science, but what Pascal calls our heart. Science herself consults her heart when she lays it down that the infinite ascertainment of fact and correction of false belief are the supreme goods for man. Challenge the statement and science can only repeat it oracularly, or else prove it by showing that such ascertainment and correction bring man all sorts of other goods which man's heart in turn declares. The question of having moral beliefs at all or not having them is decided by our will. Are our moral preferences true or false, or are they only odd biological phenomena, making things good or bad for *us*, but in themselves indifferent? How can your pure intellect decide? If your heart does not *want* a world of moral reality, your head will assuredly never make you believe in one. Mephistophelian scepticism, indeed, will satisfy the head's play-instincts much better than any rigorous idealism can. Some men (even at the student age) are so naturally cool-hearted that the moralistic hypothesis never has for them any pungent life, and in their supercilious presence the hot young moralist always feels strangely ill at ease. The appearance of knowingness is on their side, of naïveté and gullibility on his. Yet, in the inarticulate heart of him, he clings to it that he is not a dupe, and that there is a realm in which (as Emerson says) all their wit and intellectual superiority is no better than the cunning of a fox. Moral scepticism can no more be refuted or proved by logic than intellectual scepticism can. When we stick to it that there *is* truth (be it of either kind), we do so with our whole nature, and resolve to stand or fall by the results. The sceptic with his whole nature adopts the doubting attitude; but which of us is the wiser, Omniscience only knows.

Turn now from these wide questions of good to a certain class of questions of fact, questions concerning personal relations, states of mind between one man and another. *Do you like me or not?*—for example. Whether you do or not depends, in countless instances, on whether I meet you halfway, am willing to assume that you must like me, and show you trust and expectation. The previous faith on my part in your liking's existence is in such cases what makes your liking come. But if I stand aloof, and refuse to budge an inch until I have objective evidence, until you shall have done something apt, as the absolutists say, *ad extorquendum assensum meum,*[7] ten to one your liking never comes. How many women's hearts are vanquished by the mere sanguine insistence of some man that they *must* love him! he will not consent to the hypothesis that they cannot. The desire for a certain kind of truth here brings about that special truth's existence; and so it is in innumerable cases of other sorts. Who gains promotions, boons, appointments, but the man in whose life they are seen to play the part of live hypotheses, who discounts them, sacrifices other things for their sake before they have come, and takes risks for them in advance? His faith acts on the powers above him as a claim, and creates its own verification.

A social organism of any sort whatever, large or small, is what it is because each member proceeds to his own duty with a trust that the other members will simultaneously do theirs. Wherever a desired result is achieved by the co-operation of many independent persons, its existence as a fact is a pure consequence of the precursive faith in one another of those immediately concerned. A government, an army, a commercial system, a ship, a college, an athletic team, all exist on this condition, without which not only is nothing achieved, but nothing is even attempted. A whole train of passengers (individually brave enough) will be looted by a few highwaymen, simply because the latter can count on one another, while each passenger fears that if he makes a movement of resistance, he will be shot before anyone else backs him up. If we believed that the whole car-full would rise at once with us, we should each severally rise, and train-robbing would never even be attempted. There are, then, cases where a fact cannot come at all unless a preliminary faith exists in its coming. *And where faith in a fact can help create the fact,* that would be an insane logic which should say that faith running ahead of scientific evidence is the "lowest kind of immorality" into which a thinking being can fall. Yet such is the logic by which our scientific absolutists pretend to regulate our lives!

X

In truths dependent on our personal action, then, faith based on desire is certainly a lawful and possibly an indispensable thing.

But now, it will be said, these are all childish human cases, and have nothing to do with great cosmical matter, like the question of religious faith. Let us then pass on to that. Religions differ so much in their accidents that in discussing the religious question we must make it very generic and broad. What then do we now mean by the religious hypothesis? Science says things are; morality says some things are better than other things; and religion says essentially two things.

First, she says that the best things are the more eternal things, the overlapping things, the things in the universe that throw the last stone, so to speak, and say the final word. "Perfection is eternal"—this phrase of Charles Secrétan seems a good way of putting this first affirmation of religion, an affirmation which obviously cannot yet be verified scientifically at all.

The second affirmation of religion is that we are better off even now if we believe her first affirmation to be true.

Now let us consider what the logical elements of this situation are *in case the religious hypothesis in both its branches be really true.* (Of course, we must admit that possibility at the outset. If we are to discuss the question at all, it must involve a living option. If for any of you religion be a hypothesis that cannot, by any living possibility be true, then you need go no farther. I speak to the "saving remnant" alone.) So proceeding, we see, first, that religion offers itself as *a momentous* option. We are supposed to gain, even now, by our belief, and to lose by our non-belief, a certain vital good. Secondly, religion is a *forced* option, so far as that good goes. We cannot escape the issue by remaining sceptical and waiting for more light, because, although we do avoid error in that way *if religion be untrue,* we lose the good, *if it be true,* just as certainly as if we positively chose to disbelieve. It is as if a man should hesitate indefinitely to ask a certain woman to marry him because he was not perfectly sure that she would prove an angel after he brought her home. Would he not cut himself off from that particular angel-possibility as decisively as if he went and married someone else? Scepticism, then, is not avoidance of option; it is option of a certain particular kind of risk. *Better risk loss of truth than chance of error—*that is your faith-vetoer's exact position. He is actively playing his stake as much as the believer is; he is backing the field against the religious hypothesis, just as the believer is backing the religious hypothesis against the field. To preach scepticism to us as a duty until "sufficient evidence" for religion be found, is tantamount therefore to telling us, when in presence of the religious hypothesis, that to yield to our fear of its being error is wiser and better than to yield to our hope that it may be true. It is not intellect against all passions, then; it is only intellect with one passion laying down its law. And by what, forsooth, is

the supreme wisdom of this passion warranted? Dupery for dupery, what proof is there that dupery through hope is so much worse than dupery through fear? I, for one, can see no proof; and I simply refuse obedience to the scientist's command to imitate his kind of option, in a case where my own stake is important enough to give me the right to choose my own form of risk. If religion be true and the evidence for it be still insufficient, I do not wish, by putting your extinguisher upon my nature (which feels to me as if it had after all some business in this matter), to forfeit my sole chance in life of getting upon the winning side—that chance depending, of course, on my willingness to run the risk of acting as if my passional need of taking the world religiously might be prophetic and right.

All this is on the supposition that it really may be prophetic and right, and that, even to us who are discussing the matter, religion is a live hypothesis which may be true. Now to most of us religion comes in a still farther way that makes a veto on our active faith even more illogical. The more perfect and more eternal aspect of the universe is represented in our religions as having personal form. The universe is no longer a mere *It* to us, but a *Thou,* if we are religious; and any relation that may be possible from person to person might be possible here. For instance, although in one sense we are passive portions of the universe, in another we show a curious autonomy, as if we were small active centers on our own account. We feel, too, as if the appeal of religion to us were made to our own active goodwill, as if evidence might be forever withheld from us unless we met the hypothesis halfway. To take a trivial illustration: just as a man who in a company of gentlemen made no advances, asked a warrant for every concession, and believed no one's word without proof, would cut himself off by such churlishness from all the social rewards that a more trusting spirit would earn—so here, one who should shut himself up in snarling logicality and try to make the gods extort his recognition willy-nilly, or not get it at all, might cut himself off forever from his only opportunity of making the gods' acquaintance. This feeling, forced on us we know not whence, that by obstinately believing that there are gods (although not to do so would be so easy both for our logic and our life) we are doing the universe the deepest service we can, seems part of the living essence of the religious hypothesis. If the hypothesis *were* true in all its parts, including this one, then pure intellectualism, with its veto on our making willing advances, would be an absurdity; and some participation of our sympathetic nature would be logically required. I, therefore, for one, cannot see my way to accepting the agnostic rules for truth-seeking, or willfully agree to keep my willing nature out of the game. I cannot do so for this plain reason, that *a rule of thinking which would absolutely prevent me from acknowledging certain kinds of truth if those kinds of truth were really there, would be an irrational rule.* That for me is the long and short of the formal logic of the situation, no matter what the kinds of truth might materially be.

I confess I do not see how this logic can be escaped. But sad experience makes me fear that some of you may still shrink from radically saying with me, *in abstracto*,[8] that we have the right to believe at our own risk any hypothesis that is live enough to tempt our will. I suspect, however, that if this is so, it is because you have got away from the abstract logical point of view altogether, and are thinking (perhaps without realizing it) of some particular religious hypothesis which for you is dead. The freedom to "believe what we will" you apply to the case of some patent superstition; and the faith you think of is the faith defined by the schoolboy when he said, "Faith is when you believe something that you know ain't true." I can only repeat that this is misapprehension. *In concreto*,[9] the freedom to believe can only cover living options which the intellect of the individual cannot by itself resolve; and living options never seem absurdities to him who has them to consider. When I look at the religious question as it really puts itself to concrete men, and when I think of all the possibilities which both practically and theoretically it involves, then this command that we shall put a stopper on our heart, instincts and courage, and *wait*—acting of course meanwhile more or less as if religion were *not* true[10]—till doomsday, or till such time as our intellect and senses working together may have raked in evidence enough—this command, I say, seems to

me the queerest idol ever manufactured in the philosophic cave. Were we scholastic absolutists, there might be more excuse. If we had an infallible intellect with its objective certitudes, we might feel ourselves disloyal to such a perfect organ of knowledge in not trusting to it exclusively, in not waiting for its releasing word. But if we are empiricists, if we believe that no bell in us tolls to let us know for certain when truth is in our grasp, then it seems a piece of idle fantasticality to preach so solemnly our duty of waiting for the bell. Indeed we *may* wait if we will—I hope you do not think that I am denying that—but if we do so, we do so at our peril as much as if we believed. In either case we *act*, taking our life in our hands. No one of us ought to issue vetoes to the other, nor should we bandy words of abuse. We ought, on the contrary, delicately and profoundly to respect one another's mental freedom—then only shall we bring about the intellectual republic; then only shall we have that spirit of inner tolerance without which all our outer tolerance is soulless, and which is empiricism's glory; then only shall we live and let live, in speculative as well as in practical things.

NOTES

1. [The redeemer, according to Islam, who will come to bring justice on earth and establish universal Islam.]
2. [In contrast.]
3. [Even this will make you believe and deaden your acuity.]
4. [One who is strikingly unorthodox.]
5. [For and against.]
6. [The heart has its reasons, which reason does not know.]
7. [For compelling my assent.]
8. [In abstract.]
9. [In practice.]
10. Since belief is measured by action, he who forbids us to believe religion to be true, necessarily also forbids us to act as we should if we did believe it to be true. The whole defence of religious faith hangs upon action. If the action required or inspired by the religious hypothesis is in no way different from that dictated by the naturalistic hypothesis, then religious faith is a pure superfluity, better pruned away, and controversy about its legitimacy is a piece

of idle trifling, unworthy of serious minds. I myself believe, of course, that the religious hypothesis gives to the world an expression which specifically determines our reactions, and makes them in a large part unlike what they might be on a purely naturalistic scheme of belief.

63   THE WILL TO BELIEVE: A CRITIQUE

NICHOLAS EVERITT

How does James's defense of belief differ from Pascal's? Does James's approach avoid the problems that beset Pascal's Wager?

In our next selection, Nicholas Everitt, whose work we read previously, offers answers to these questions. He recognizes important differences between the views of Pascal and James but does not find James's approach any more successful than Pascal's.

James judges as irrational a rule that would forbid us from believing that God exists even if that belief is true. In response, Everitt finds equally irrational a rule that would forbid us from believing that God does not exist even if that belief is true. James allows that the theist may rely on passion to justify belief. Everitt in turn wonders why the atheist may not rely on an opposing passion to justify nonbelief. In short, Everitt finds that James's reasoning can be used to justify nonbelief as well as belief, and thus James's argument favors neither position.

We can note first of all how [James's argument] differs from the Pascalian argument.... First, the Wager at least in its extended versions can be applied to the belief in God's existence even if there is some good evidence that God does not exist. So, the Pascalian maintains that even if it is epistemically irrational to believe in God, it can simultaneously be consequentially rational to believe. James, by contrast, invokes the permissibility of accepting a belief which is consequentially rational *only if* the belief is unresolvable, i.e., undecidable in terms of evidence. This means that the potential target audience for the Jamesian argument is to that extent much smaller than for the Wager: the Wager applies equally to those who think that "God exists" is intellectually resolvable, and to those who deny this. But the Jamesian argument applies only to those who think that the belief is intellectually unresolvable, and who further think that the choice whether to accept the belief is living, forced and momentous.

Second, the Wager assumes that you will reap the benefits of believing (and the penalties of disbelieving) only if God exists; for it is only in the afterlife (if there is one) that the pay-offs of the Wager are forthcoming. James, by contrast, locates the benefits and losses in the here-and-now. Even if there is no God and so your belief is false, you will benefit now from holding the belief: it will help make your life go better. The atheist and the agnostic are losing out *now* through not believing. James makes no assumption about any benefits accruing in an afterlife to believers.

From Nicholas Everitt, *The Non-Existence of God*, Routledge, 2004. Reprinted by permission of Taylor & Francis.

Third, the Pascalian ... has to make some very implausible assumptions about the nature of God and his likely response to belief and disbelief among his creatures. James, on the other hand, makes no explicit assumptions about the nature of God, and all his argument requires are some commonplaces of traditional theism, such as that God cares for us, responds to our needs, helps us in times of difficulty, and so on. And his argument does not require that these commonplaces be true, but only that they be believed, for the benefits come from the belief, whether or not it is true.

There are, then, some important differences between the Pascalian and James. But does James mark an improvement on the Wager? It is difficult to think so, for every step in his argument is open to challenge. First, and perhaps least importantly, we can question whether the existence of God is really intellectually unresolvable. Many people have, of course, thought that it was—but they are generally those who are ignorant of the immensely detailed argumentation that surrounds the claim. It would be a reasonable empirical assumption that the great majority of people who have seriously considered the issue of God's existence have thought that the evidence did favour either belief or disbelief. In other words, they have thought that belief was epistemically rational or irrational, and hence would have denied that a belief in God was the kind of belief to which James's line of thought could apply. To say this is not by itself, of course, to say that they think that the evidence is *overwhelming*, or that it justifies *certainty*, but only that it justifies belief.

Suppose, however, that James is right in his assumption that the existence of God is intellectually unresolvable. A second objection then arises, about James's assumption that a person's passional nature is involved in deciding how to respond to open propositions. James is caught in a strange lack of consistency here. In respect of intellectually resolvable propositions, he accepts that our passional nature has no legitimate role to play: the requirement to believe propositions for which there is overall good evidence, and to disbelieve those for which the evidence is poor, he accepts is a requirement of reason. But if that is so, why is the requirement to suspend judgement in all

those cases where the evidence is lacking or evenly balanced not also a requirement of reason? Given that he rightly thinks that reason is the guide in the first two cases, why does it suddenly cease to be so in relation to the third? James provides no explanation or justification for this strange asymmetry.

The third problem focuses on James's negative rule concerning how our passional nature should guide us. He tells us that we should not accept a rule which would prevent us from accepting as true any propositions which in fact are true, i.e., even when we have no evidence that they are true. But on the face of it, the rule he rejects sounds an excellent negative rule to accept! If there are any propositions which are in principle unresolvable, they are propositions for or against which we cannot get good evidence; and in that case, it sounds eminently reasonable to withhold both assent and dissent.... [I]t has to be shown that there are beneficial consequences from believing propositions in relation to which one has no evidence. What James really needs is a much more restricted thesis than the one he advances. He rejects a rule which would prevent him from accepting propositions in relation to which he has no evidence. But the most that his argument requires him to reject is a rule which would prevent him from accepting propositions in relation to which he has no evidence, *where the acceptance of the propositions would bring him some benefits.*

More seriously for James's argument, his negative rule does not have the application to theism which he supposes. His actual words were:

(A) "a rule of thinking which would absolutely prevent me from acknowledging certain kinds of truth if those kinds of truth were really there, would be an irrational rule."

Differently expressed, this says:

(B) It would be irrational of me to adopt a rule about belief formation which would forbid me from believing any proposition that is in fact true.

Applied to theism in particular this says:

(C) It would be irrational of me to adopt a rule about belief formation which would forbid me from believing that God exists if in fact he does exist.

But if (C) is true, so presumably is (D):

(D) It would be irrational of me to adopt a rule about belief formation which would forbid me from believing that God does not exist, if in fact he does not exist.

If there were any grounds for accepting (C), they would surely equally be grounds for accepting (D). So if the theist can appeal to his passional nature to justify his acceptance of theism, it seems that the atheist can appeal to *his* passional nature to justify his acceptance of atheism. In other words, what principle (A) licenses is the acceptance of one *or other* in a pair of open propositions: it has no means of picking out which proposition the passionally moved believer should accept.

It might be thought that James does have good grounds for distinguishing between accepting the existence of God, and accepting the non-existence of God. For he tells us that "we are better off even now" if we believe in religion. Although he himself does not elaborate on this claim, a friendly reading of his position could take this to be an omission which can easily be remedied. All that has to be done is to point to the benefits which a belief in God brings to the believer.

However, this reply on James's behalf does mean that his argument is committed to giving further hostages to fortune. For he then needs to supply empirical evidence that belief rather than disbelief does have this beneficial consequence. For some people, no doubt it is belief which makes their life go better; but for other people, it may well be disbelief. And if this is so, the potential audience for James's argument is diminished yet again.

B. BELIEF AS CERTAINTY

64   BELIEF WITHOUT ARGUMENT

ALVIN PLANTINGA

If the existence of God cannot be proved by reason, might belief in God nevertheless be rational? Alvin Plantinga, who is Professor Emeritus of Philosophy at the University of Notre Dame, answers in the affirmative. He contends that the existence of God is not the conclusion of an argument but a premise, one that should be accepted as a basic belief not in need of support. In other words, belief in the existence of God is an innate tendency, equally as obvious as belief in the existence of one's spouse.

To the objection that this approach to belief in God is akin to a believer in the Great Pumpkin taking as a premise that the Great Pumpkin returns every Halloween, Plantinga replies that belief in the Great Pumpkin is not basic, because we have no tendency to accept beliefs about the Great Pumpkin, and furthermore, the Great Pumpkin does not exist. The adequacy of Plantinga's reply is a matter for the reader to ponder.

Suppose we think of natural theology as the attempt to prove or demonstrate the existence of God. This enterprise has a long and impressive history—a history stretching back to the dawn of Christendom and boasting among its adherents many of the truly great thinkers of the Western world. Chief among these is Thomas Aquinas, whose work, I think, is the natural starting point for Christian philosophical reflection, Protestant as well as Catholic. Here we Protestants must be, in Ralph McInerny's immortal phrase, Peeping Thomists. Recently—since the time of Kant, perhaps—the tradition of natural theology has not been as overwhelming as it once was: yet it continues to have able defenders both within and without officially Catholic philosophy.

Many Christians, however, have been less than totally impressed. In particular Reformed or Calvinist theologians have for the most part taken a dim view of this enterprise. A few Reformed thinkers ... endorse the theistic proofs; but for the most part the Reformed attitude has ranged from indifference, through suspicion and hostility, to outright accusations of blasphemy. And this stance is initially puzzling. It looks a little like the attitude some Christians adopt towards faith healing: it can't be done, but even if it could, it shouldn't be. What exactly, or even approximately, do these sons and daughters of the Reformation have against proving the existence of God? What *could* they have against it? What could be less objectionable to any but the most obdurate atheist?

PROOF AND BELIEF IN GOD

... According to John Calvin, who is as good a Calvinist as any, God has implanted in us all an

From Alvin Plantinga, "The Reformed Objection to Natural Theology," *Christian Scholar's Review* 11 (1982). Reprinted by permission of the publisher.

innate tendency, or nisus, or disposition to believe in him:

> "There is within the human mind, and indeed by natural instinct, an awareness of divinity." This we take to be beyond controversy. To prevent anyone from taking refuge in the pretense of ignorance, God himself has implanted in all men a certain understanding of his divine majesty. Ever renewing its memory, he repeatedly sheds fresh drops. Since, therefore, men one and all perceive that there is a God and that he is their Maker, they are condemned by their own testimony because they have failed to honor him and to consecrate their lives to his will. If ignorance of God is to be looked for anywhere, surely one is most likely to find an example of it among the more backward folk and those more remote from civilization. Yet there is, as the eminent pagan says, no nation so barbarous, no people so savage, that they have not a deep-seated conviction that there is a God. So deeply does the common conception occupy the minds of all, so tenaciously does it inhere in the hearts of all! Therefore, since from the beginning of the world there has been no region, no city, in short, no household, that could do without religion, there lies in this a tacit confession of a sense of deity inscribed in the hearts of all.[1]
>
> Indeed, the perversity of the impious, who though they struggle furiously are unable to extricate themselves from the fear of God, is abundant testimony that this conviction, namely, that there is some God, is naturally inborn in all, and is fixed deep within, as it were in the very marrow.... From this we conclude that it is not a doctrine that must first be learned in school, but one of which each of us is master from his mother's womb and which nature itself permits no one to forget.[2]

Calvin's claim, then, is that God has created us in such a way that we have a strong propensity or inclination towards belief in him. This tendency has been in part overlaid or suppressed by sin. Were it not for the existence of sin in the world, human beings would believe in God to the same degree and with the same natural spontaneity that we believe in the existence of other persons, an external world, or the past. This is the natural human condition; it is because of our presently unnatural sinful condition that many of us find belief in God difficult or absurd. The fact is, Calvin

thinks, one who doesn't believe in God is in an epistemically substandard position—rather like a man who doesn't believe that his wife exists, or thinks she is like a cleverly constructed robot and has no thoughts, feelings, or consciousness.

Although this disposition to believe in God is partially suppressed, it is nonetheless universally present. And it is triggered or actuated by widely realized conditions:

> Lest anyone, then, be excluded from access to happiness, he not only sowed in men's minds that seed of religion of which we have spoken, but revealed himself and daily discloses himself in the whole workmanship of the universe. As a consequence, men cannot open their eyes without being compelled to see him.[3]

Like Kant, Calvin is especially impressed in this connection, by the marvelous compages of the starry heavens above:

> Even the common folk and the most untutored, who have been taught only by the aid of the eyes, cannot be unaware of the excellence of divine art, for it reveals itself in this innumerable and yet distinct and well-ordered variety of the heavenly host.[4]

And Calvin's claim is that one who accedes to this tendency and in these circumstances accepts the belief that God has created the world—perhaps upon beholding the starry heavens, or the splendid majesty of the mountains, or the intricate, articulate beauty of a tiny flower—is entirely within his epistemic rights in so doing. It isn't that such a person is justified or rational in so believing by virtue of having an implicit argument—some version of the teleological argument, say. No; he doesn't need any argument for justification or rationality. His belief need not be based on any other propositions at all; under these conditions he is perfectly rational in accepting belief in God in the utter absence of any argument, deductive or inductive. Indeed, a person in these conditions, says Calvin, *knows* that God exists, has knowledge of God's existence, apart from any argument at all. Elsewhere Calvin speaks of "arguments from reason" or rational arguments:

> The prophets and apostles do not boast either of their keenness or of anything that obtains credit for

them as they speak; nor do they dwell upon rational proofs. Rather, they bring forward God's holy name, that by it the whole world may be brought into obedience to him. Now we ought to see how apparent it is not only by plausible opinion but by dear truth that they do not call upon God's name heedlessly or falsely. If we desire to provide in the best way for our consciences—that they may not be perpetually beset by the instability of doubt or vacillation, and that they may not also boggle at the smallest quibbles—we ought to seek our conviction, in a higher place than human reasons, judgments, or conjectures, that is, in the secret testimony of the Spirit.[5]

Here the subject for discussion is not belief in the existence of God, but belief that God is the author of the Scriptures; I think it is clear, however, that Calvin would say the same thing about belief in God's existence. The Christian doesn't need natural theology, either as the source of his confidence or to justify his belief. Furthermore, the Christian *ought* not to believe on the basis of argument; if he does, his faith is likely to be unstable and wavering. From Calvin's point of view, believing in the existence of God on the basis of rational argument is like believing in the existence of your spouse on the basis of the analogical argument for other minds—whimsical at best and not at all likely to delight the person concerned.

FOUNDATIONALISM

We could look further into the precise forms taken by the Reformed objection to Natural Theology; time is short, however; what I shall do instead is tell you what I think underlies these objections, inchoate and unfocused as they are. The reformers mean to say, fundamentally, that belief in God can properly be taken as basic. That is, a person is entirely within his epistemic rights, entirely rational, in believing in God, even if he has no argument for this belief and does not believe it on the basis of any other beliefs he holds. And in taking belief in God as properly basic, the reformers were implicitly rejecting a whole picture or way of looking at knowledge and rational belief; call it *classical foundationalism*. This picture has been enormously popular ever since the days of Plato

and Aristotle; it remains the dominant way of thinking about knowledge, justification, belief, faith, and allied topics. Although it has been thus dominant, Reformed theologians and thinkers have, I believe, meant to reject it. What they say here tends to be inchoate and not well-articulated; nevertheless the fact is they meant to reject classical foundationalism. But how shall we characterize the view rejected? The first thing to see is that foundationalism is a *normative* view. It aims to lay down conditions that must be met by anyone whose system of beliefs is *rational;* and here "rational" is to be understood normatively. According to the foundationalist, there is a right way and a wrong way with respect to belief. People have responsibilities, duties and obligations with respect to their believings just as with respect to their (other) actions. Perhaps this sort of obligation is really a special case of a more general moral obligation; or perhaps, on the other hand, it is sui generis. In any event there are such obligations: to conform to them is to be rational and to go against them is to be irrational. To be rational, then, is to exercise one's epistemic powers *properly*—to exercise them in such a way as to go contrary to none of the norms for such exercise.

Foundationalism, therefore, is in part a normative thesis. I think we can understand this thesis more fully if we introduce the idea of a *noetic structure*. A person's noetic structure is the set of propositions he believes together with certain epistemic relations that hold among him and these propositions. Thus some of his beliefs may be *based on* other things he believes; it may be that there are a pair of propositions A and B such that he believes *A on the basis of B*. Although this relation isn't easy to characterize in a revealing and nontrivial fashion, it is nonetheless familiar. I believe that the word "umbrageous" is spelled u-m-b-r-a-g-e-o-u-s: this belief is based on another belief of mine, the belief that that's how the dictionary says it's spelled. I believe that $72 \times 71 = 5112$. This belief is based upon several other beliefs I hold—such beliefs as that $1 \times 72 = 72$; $7 \times 2 = 14$; $7 \times 7 = 49$; $49 + 1 = 50$; and others. Some of my beliefs, however, I accept but don't accept on the basis of any other beliefs. I believe that $2 + 1 = 3$, for example, and don't believe it on the basis of other propositions. I also believe that I am seated at my desk, and that there is a mild pain in my right knee. These too are basic for me; I don't believe them on the basis of any other propositions.

An account of a person's noetic structure, then, would include a specification of which of his beliefs are basic and which are non-basic. Of course it is abstractly possible that *none* of his beliefs is basic; perhaps he holds just three beliefs, A, B, and C, and believes each of them on the basis of the other two. We might think this improper or irrational, but that is not to say it couldn't be done. And it is also possible that *all* of his beliefs are basic; perhaps he believes a lot of propositions, but doesn't believe any of them on the basis of any others. In the typical case, however, a noetic structure will include both basic and non-basic beliefs.

Secondly, an account of a noetic structure will include what we might call an index of degree of belief. I hold some of my beliefs much more firmly than others. I believe both that 2 + 1 = 3 and that London, England, is north of Saskatoon, Saskatchewan; but I believe the former more resolutely than the latter....

Thirdly, a somewhat vaguer notion; an account of S's noetic structure would include something like an index of *depth of ingression*. Some of my beliefs are, we might say, on the periphery of my noetic structure. I accept them, and may even accept them quite firmly; but if I were to give them up, not much else in my noetic structure would have to change. I believe there are some large boulders on the top of the Grand Teton. If I come to give up this belief, however (say by climbing it and not finding any), that change wouldn't have extensive reverberations throughout the rest of my noetic structure; it could be accommodated with minimal alteration elsewhere. So its depth of ingression into my noetic structure isn't great. On the other hand, if I were to come to believe that there simply is no such thing as the Grand Teton, or no mountains at all, or no such thing as the state of Wyoming, that would have much greater reverberations. And if, *per impossible*,[6] I were to come to think there hadn't been much of a past (that the world was created just

five minutes ago, complete with all its apparent memories and traces of the past), or that there weren't any other persons, that would have even greater reverberations; these beliefs of mine have great depth of ingression into my noetic structure.

Now classical foundationalism is best construed, I think, as a thesis about *rational* noetic structures. A noetic structure is rational if it could be the noetic structure of a person who was completely rational. To be completely rational, as I am here using the term, is not to believe only what is true, or to believe all the logical consequences of what one believes, or to believe all necessary truths with equal firmness, or to be uninfluenced by emotion; it is, instead, to do the right thing with respect to one's believings. As we have seen, the foundationalist holds that there are responsibilities and duties that pertain to believings as well as to actions, or other actions; these responsibilities accrue to us just by virtue of our having the sorts of noetic capabilities we do have. There are norms or standards for beliefs. To criticize a person as irrational, then, is to criticize her for failing to fulfill these duties or responsibilities, or for failing to conform to the relevant norms or standards. From this point of view, a rational person is one whose believings meet the appropriate standards. To draw the ethical analogy, the irrational is the impermissible; the rational is the permissible.

A rational noetic structure, then, is one that could be the noetic structure of a perfectly rational person. And classical foundationalism is, in part, a thesis about such noetic structures. The foundationalist notes, first of all, that some of our beliefs are based upon others. He immediately adds that a belief can't properly be accepted on the basis of just *any* other belief; in a rational noetic structure, A will be accepted on the basis of B only if B *supports* A, or is a member of a set of beliefs that together support A. It isn't clear just what this supports relation is; different foundationalists propose different candidates. One candidate, for example, is *entailment*; A supports B only if B is entailed by A, or perhaps is self-evidently entailed by A, or perhaps follows from A by an argument where each step is a self-evident entailment.

Another and more permissive candidate is probability; perhaps A supports B if B is likely or probable with respect to A. And of course there are other candidates.

More important for present purposes, however, is the following claim: in a rational noetic structure, there will be some beliefs that are not based upon others: call these its *foundations*. If every belief in a rational noetic structure were based upon other beliefs, the structure in question would contain infinitely many beliefs. However things may stand for more powerful intellects—angelic intellects, perhaps—human beings aren't capable of believing infinitely many propositions. Among other things, one presumably doesn't believe a proposition one has never heard of, and no one has had time, these busy days, to have heard of infinitely many propositions. So every rational noetic structure has a foundation.

Suppose we say that *weak* foundationalism is the view that (1) every rational noetic structure has a foundation, and (2) in a rational noetic structure, non-basic belief is proportional in strength to support from the foundations. When I say Reformed thinkers have meant to reject foundationalism, I do not mean to say that they intended to reject weak foundationalism. On the contrary; the thought of many of them tends to support or endorse weak foundationalism. What then do they mean to reject? Here we meet a further and fundamental feature of classic varieties of foundationalism: they all lay down certain conditions of proper or rational basicality. From the foundationalist point of view, not just any kind of belief can be found in the foundations of a rational noetic structure; a belief, to be properly basic (i.e., basic in a rational noetic structure) must meet certain conditions. It is plausible to see Thomas Aquinas, for example, as holding that a proposition is properly basic for a person only if it is self-evident to him (such that his understanding or grasping it is sufficient for his seeing it to be true) or "evident to the senses," as he puts it. By this latter term I think he means to refer to propositions whose truth or falsehood we can determine by looking or listening or employing some other sense—such propositions as

1. There is a tree before me
2. I am wearing shoes

   and

3. That tree's leaves are yellow.

   Many foundationalists have insisted that propositions basic in a rational noetic structure must be *certain* in some important sense. Thus it is plausible to see Descartes as holding that the foundations of a rational noetic structure don't include such propositions as (1)–(3) but more cautious claims—claims about one's own mental life, for example:

4. It seems to me that I see a tree
5. I seem to see something green

   or, as Professor Chisholm puts it,

6. I am appeared greenly to.

Propositions of this latter sort seem to enjoy a kind of immunity from error not enjoyed by those of the former. I could be mistaken in thinking I see a pink rat; perhaps I am hallucinating or the victim of an illusion. But it is at the least very much harder to see that I could be mistaken in believing that I *seem* to see a pink rat, in believing that I am appeared pinkly (or pink ratly) to. Suppose we say that a proposition with respect to which I enjoy this sort of immunity from error is *incorrigible* for me; then perhaps Descartes means to hold that a proposition is properly basic for S only if it is either self-evident or incorrigible for S.

Aquinas and Descartes, we might say, are *strong* foundationalists; they accept weak foundationalism and add some conditions for proper basicality. Ancient and medieval foundationalists tended to hold that a proposition is properly basic for a person only if it is either self-evident or evident to the senses; modern foundationalists—Descartes, Locke, Leibniz and the like—tended to hold that a proposition is properly basic for S only if either self-evident or incorrigible for S. Of course this is a historical generalization and is thus subject to contradiction by scholars, such being the penalty for historical generalization; but perhaps it is worth the risk. And now suppose we say that *classical foundationalism* is the disjunction of ancient and medieval with modern foundationalism.

THE REFORMED REJECTION OF CLASSICAL FOUNDATIONALISM

These Reformed thinkers, I believe, are best understood as rejecting classical foundationalism. They were inclined to accept weak foundationalism, I think; but they were completely at odds with the idea that the foundations of a rational noetic structure can at most include propositions that are self-evident or evident to the senses or incorrigible. In particular, they were prepared to insist that a rational noetic structure can include belief in God as basic....

In the passages I quoted earlier on, Calvin claims the believer doesn't need argument—doesn't need it, among other things, for epistemic respectability. We may understand him as holding, I think, that a rational noetic structure may perfectly well contain belief in God among its foundations. Indeed, he means to go further, and in two separate directions. In the first place, he thinks a Christian *ought* not believe in God on the basis of other propositions; a proper and well formed Christian noetic structure will *in fact* have belief in God among its foundations. And in the second place Calvin claims that one who takes belief in God as basic can nonetheless know that God exists. Calvin holds that one can *rationally accept* belief in God as basic; he also claims that one can *know* that God exists even if he has no argument, even if he does not believe on the basis of other propositions. A weak foundationalist is likely to hold that some properly basic beliefs are such that anyone who accepts them, *knows* them. More exactly, he is likely to hold that among the beliefs properly basic for a person S, some are such that if S accepts them S knows them. A weak foundationalist could go on to say that *other* properly basic beliefs can't be known, if taken as basic, but only rationally believed; and he might think of the existence of God as a case in point. Calvin will have none of this; as he sees it, one needs no arguments to know that God exists.

Among the central contentions of these Reformed thinkers, therefore, are the claims that belief in God is properly basic, and the view that one who takes belief in God as basic can also *know* that God exists.

THE GREAT PUMPKIN OBJECTION

Now I enthusiastically concur in these contentions of Reformed epistemology, and by way of conclusion I want to defend them against a popular objection. It is tempting to raise the following sort of question. If belief in God is properly basic, why can't just any belief be properly basic? Couldn't we say the same for any bizarre aberration we can think of? What about voodoo or astrology? What about the belief that the Great Pumpkin returns every Halloween? Could I properly take *that* as basic? And if I can't, why can I properly take belief in God as basic? Suppose I believe that if I flap my arms with sufficient vigor, I can take off and fly about the room; could I defend myself against the charge of irrationality by claiming this belief is basic? If we say that belief in God is properly basic, won't we be committed to holding that just anything, or nearly anything, can properly be taken as basic, thus throwing wide the gates to irrationalism and superstition?

Certainly not. What might lead one to think the Reformed epistemologist is in this kind of trouble? The fact that he rejects the criteria for proper basicality purveyed by the classical foundationalist? But why should *that* be thought to commit him to such tolerance of irrationality? ...

[C]riteria for proper basicality must be reached from below rather than above; they should not be presented as obiter dicta, but argued to and tested by a relevant set of examples. But there is no reason to assume, in advance, that everyone will agree on the examples. The Christian will of course suppose that belief in God is entirely proper and rational; if he doesn't accept this belief on the basis of other propositions, he will conclude that it is basic for him and quite properly so. Followers of Bertrand Russell and Madalyn Murray O'Hair may disagree; but how is that relevant? Must my criteria, or those of the Christian community, conform to their examples? Surely not. The Christian community is responsible to its set of examples, not to theirs.

Accordingly, the Reformed epistemologist can properly hold that belief in the Great Pumpkin is not properly basic, even though he holds that belief in God is properly basic and even if he has no full fledged criterion of proper basicality. Of course he is committed to supposing that there is a relevant *difference* between belief in God and belief in the Great Pumpkin, if he holds that the former but not the latter is properly basic. But this should be no great embarrassment; there are plenty of candidates. Thus the Reformed epistemologist may concur with Calvin in holding that God has implanted in us a natural tendency to see his hand in the world around us; the same cannot be said for the Great Pumpkin, there being no Great Pumpkin and no natural tendency to accept beliefs about the Great Pumpkin.

By way of conclusion then, the Reformed objection to natural theology, unformed and inchoate as it is, may best be seen as a rejection of classical foundationalism. As the Reformed thinker sees things, being self-evident, or incorrigible, or evident to the senses is not a necessary condition of proper basicality. He goes on to add that belief in God is properly basic. He is not thereby committed, even in the absence of a general criterion of proper basicality, to suppose that just any or nearly any belief—belief in the Great Pumpkin, for example—is properly basic. Like everyone should, he begins with examples; and he may take belief in the Great Pumpkin as a paradigm of irrational basic belief.

NOTES

1. *Institutes of the Christian Religion*, ed. J. T. McNeill and trans. Ford Lewis Battles (Philadelphia: Westminster Press, 1960), Book I, Chap. iii, sec. 1.
2. *Institutes*, I, iii, 3.
3. *Institutes*, V, v, 1.
4. *Institutes*, V, v, 2.
5. *Institutes*, I, vii, 4.
6. [although impossible.]

65 BELIEF WITHOUT ARGUMENT: A CRITIQUE

MICHAEL MARTIN

Michael Martin, whose work we read previously, does not find Plantinga's position persuasive. Martin points out that if theists can take belief in God as basic, atheists can take disbelief in God as basic. Furthermore, believers in the Great Pumpkin can take belief in the Great Pumpkin as basic. If Plantinga were correct, no reliable method would be available to assess any of these claims.

Belief in the existence of a spouse might be basic, because no plausible alternatives are workable. Belief in the existence of God, however, is only one possibility among others, many of which can be adopted without difficulty. Thus the justification for the two sorts of belief are not parallel.

What can one say about Plantinga's ingenious attempt to save theism from the charge of irrationality by making beliefs about God basic?

(1) Plantinga's claim that his proposal would not allow just any belief to become a basic belief is misleading. It is true that it would not allow just

From Michael Martin, *Atheism: A Philosophical Justification*, Temple University Press, 1990. Reprinted by permission of the publisher.

any belief to become a basic belief *from the point of view of Reformed epistemologists.* However it would seem to allow any belief at all to become basic from the point of view of *some* community. Although reformed epistemologists would not have to accept voodoo beliefs as rational, voodoo followers would be able to claim that insofar as they are basic in the voodoo community they are rational and, moreover, that reformed thought was irrational in this community. Indeed, Plantinga's proposal would generate many different communities that could *legitimately* claim that their basic beliefs are rational and that these beliefs conflict with basic beliefs of other communities. Among the communities generated might be devil worshipers, flat earthers, and believers in fairies just so long as belief in the devil, the flatness of the earth, and fairies was basic in the respective communities.

(2) On this view the rationality of any belief is absurdly easy to obtain. The cherished belief that is held without reason by *any* group could be considered properly basic by the group's members. There would be no way to make a critical evaluation of any beliefs so considered. The community's most cherished beliefs and the conditions that, according to the community, correctly trigger such beliefs would be accepted uncritically by the members of the community as just so many more examples of basic beliefs and justifying conditions. The more philosophical members of the community could go on to propose hypotheses as to the necessary and sufficient conditions for inclusion in this set. Perhaps, using this inductive procedure, a criterion could be formulated. However, what examples the hypotheses must account for would be decided by the community. As Plantinga says, each community would be responsible only to its own set of examples in formulating a criterion, and each would decide what is to be included in this set.

(3) Plantinga seems to suppose that there is a consensus in the Christian community about what beliefs are basic and what conditions justify these beliefs. But this is not so. Some Christians believe in God on the basis of the traditional arguments or on the basis of religious experiences; their belief in God is not basic. There would, then, certainly be no agreement in the Christian community over

whether belief in God is basic or nonbasic. More important, there would be no agreement on whether doctrinal beliefs concerning the authority of the pope, the makeup of the Trinity, the nature of Christ, the means of salvation, and so on were true, let alone basic. Some Christian sects would hold certain doctrinal beliefs to be basic and rational; others would hold the same beliefs to be irrational and, indeed, the gravest of heresies. Moreover, there would be no agreement over the conditions for basic belief. Some Christians might believe that a belief is properly basic when it is triggered by listening to the pope. Others would violently disagree. Even where there was agreement over the right conditions, these would seem to justify conflicting basic beliefs and, consequently, conflicting religious sects founded on them. For example, a woman named Jones, the founder of sect S_1, might read the Bible and be impressed that God is speaking to her and telling her that p. A man named Smith, the founder of sect S_2, might read the Bible and be impressed that God is speaking to him and telling him that ~p. So Jones's belief that p and Smith's belief that ~p would both be properly basic. One might wonder how this differs from the doctrinal disputes that have gone on for centuries among Christian sects and persist to this day. The difference is that on Plantinga's proposal each sect could *justifiably* claim that its belief, for which there might be no evidence or argument, was completely rational.

(4) So long as belief that there is no God was basic for them, atheists could also justify the claim that belief in God is irrational relative to their basic beliefs and the conditions that trigger them without critically evaluating any of the usual reasons for believing in God. Just as theistic belief might be triggered by viewing the starry heavens above and reading the Bible, so atheistic beliefs might be triggered by viewing the massacre of innocent children below and reading the writings of Robert Ingersoll. Theists may disagree, but is that relevant? To paraphrase Plantinga: Must atheists' criteria conform to the Christian communities' criteria? Surely not. The atheistic community is responsible to *its* set of examples, not to theirs.

(5) There may not at present be any clear criterion for what can be a basic belief, but belief

in God seems peculiarly inappropriate for inclusion in the class since there are clear disanalogies between it and the basic beliefs allowable by classical foundationalism. For example, in his critique of classical foundationalism, Plantinga has suggested that belief in other minds and the external world should be considered basic. There are many plausible alternatives to belief in an all-good, all-powerful, all-knowing God, but there are few, if any, plausible alternatives to belief in other minds and the external world. Moreover, even if one disagrees with these arguments that seem to provide evidence against the existence of God, surely one must attempt to meet them. Although there are many skeptical arguments against belief in other minds and the external world, there are in contrast no seriously accepted arguments purporting to show that there are no other minds or no external world. In this world, atheism and agnosticism are live options for many intelligent people; solipsism is an option only for the mentally ill.

(6) As we have seen, Plantinga, following Calvin, says that some conditions that trigger belief in God or particular beliefs about God also justify these beliefs and that, although these beliefs concerning God are basic; they are not groundless. Although Plantinga gave no general account of what these justifying conditions are, he presented some examples of what he meant and likened these justifying conditions to those of properly basic perceptual and memory statements. The problem here is the weakness of the analogy. As Plantinga points out, before we take a perceptual or memory belief as properly basic we must have evidence that our perception or memory is not faulty. Part of the justification for believing that our perception or memory is not faulty is that in general it agrees with the perception or memory of our epistemological peers—that is, our equals in intelligence, perspicacity, honesty, thoroughness, and other relevant epistemic virtues, as well as with our other experiences. For example, unless my perceptions generally agreed with other perceivers with normal eyesight in normal circumstances and with my nonvisual experience—for example, that I feel something solid when I reach out—there would be no justification for supposing that my belief that I see a rose-colored wall in front of me is properly basic. Plantinga admits that if I know my memory is unreliable, my belief that I had breakfast should not be taken as properly basic. However, one knows that one's memory is reliable by determining whether it coheres with the memory reports of other people whose memory is normal and with one's other experiences.

As we have already seen, lack of agreement is commonplace in religious contexts. Different beliefs are triggered in different people when they behold the starry heavens or when they read the Bible. Beholding the starry heavens can trigger a pantheistic belief or a purely aesthetic response without any religious component. Sometimes no particular response or belief at all is triggered. From what we know about the variations of religious belief, it is likely that people would not have theistic beliefs when they beheld the starry heavens if they had been raised in nontheistic environments. Similarly, a variety of beliefs and responses are triggered when the Bible is read. Some people are puzzled and confused by the contradictions, others become skeptical of the biblical stories, others believe that God is speaking to them and has appointed them as his spokesperson, others believe God is speaking to them but has appointed no one as His spokesperson. In short, there is no consensus in the Christian community, let alone among Bible readers generally. So unlike perception and memory, there are no grounds for claiming that a belief in God is properly basic since the conditions that trigger it yield widespread disagreement among epistemological peers.

C. BELIEF AS COMMITMENT

66 FAITH

RICHARD TAYLOR

Suppose you reach the conclusion that your religious belief is unreasonable. Should you abandon it?

Richard Taylor, whose work we read previously, accepts as obvious the contention that Christian belief is unreasonable. But rather than concluding that it ought to be abandoned, he urges that, if you wish, you may legitimately decide that reason should give way to faith. Such an approach has strong appeal to many religious adherents, and Taylor's defense of the appropriateness of their devotion is uncompromising and unapologetic.

"Our most holy religion," David Hume said, "is founded on *faith*, not on reason." (All quotations are from the last two paragraphs of Hume's essay "Of Miracles.") He did not then conclude that it ought, therefore, to be rejected by reasonable men. On the contrary, he suggests that rational evaluation has no proper place in this realm to begin with, that a religious man need not feel in the least compelled to put his religion "to such a trial as it is, by no means, fitted to endure," and he brands as "dangerous friends or disguised enemies" of religion those "who have undertaken to defend it by the principles of human reason."

I want to defend Hume's suggestion, and go a bit farther by eliciting some things that seem uniquely characteristic of *Christian* faith, in order to show what it has, and what it has not, in common with other things to which it is often compared. I limited myself to Christian faith, because I know rather little of any other, and faith is, with love and hope, supposed to be a uniquely Christian virtue.

FAITH AND REASON

Faith is not reason, else religion would be, along with logic and metaphysics, a part of philosophy, which it assuredly is not. Nor is faith belief resting on scientific or historical inquiry, else religion would be part of the corpus of human knowledge, which it clearly is not. More than that, it seems evident that by the normal, common-sense criteria of what is reasonable, the content of Christian faith is *un*reasonable. This, I believe, should be the starting point, the *datum*, of any discussion of faith and reason. It is, for instance, an essential content of the Christian faith that, at a certain quite recent time, God became man, dwelt among us in the person of a humble servant, and then, for a sacred purpose, died, to live again. Now, apologetics usually addresses itself to the *details* of this story, to show that they are not inherently incredible, but this is to miss the point. It is indeed *possible* to believe it, and in the strict sense the story is credible. Millions of people do most deeply and firmly believe it. But even the barest statement of the content of that belief makes it manifest that it does not and, I think, could not, ever result from rational inquiry. "Mere reason," Hume said, "is insufficient to convince us of its veracity." The Christian begins the recital of his faith with the words, "I believe," and it would be an utter distortion to construe this as anything like "I have

From Richard Taylor, "Faith," in Sidney Hook, ed., *Religious Experience and Truth*, New York University Press, 1961. Reprinted by permission of Ernest B. Hook.

inquired, and found it reasonable to conclude." If there were a man who could say that in honesty, as I think there is not, then he would, in a clear and ordinary sense, believe, but he would have no religious faith whatsoever, and his beliefs themselves would be robbed of what would make them religious.

Now if this essential and (it seems to me) obvious unreasonableness of Christian belief could be recognized at the outset of any discussion of religion, involving rationalists on the one hand and believers on the other, we would be spared the tiresome attack and apologetics upon which nothing ultimately turns, the believer would be spared what is, in fact, an uncalled-for task of reducing his faith to reason or science, which can, as Hume noted, result only in "exposing" it as neither, and the rationalist would be granted his main point, not as a conclusion triumphantly extracted, but as a datum too obvious to labor.

FAITH AND CERTAINTY

Why, then, does a devout Christian embrace these beliefs? Now this very question, on the lips of a philosopher, is wrongly expressed, for he invariably intends it as a request for reasons, as a means of putting the beliefs to that unfair "trial" of which Hume spoke. Yet there is a clear and definite answer to this question, which has the merit of being true and evident to anyone who has known intimately those who dwell in the atmosphere of faith. The reason the Christian believes that story around which his whole life turns is, simply, that he cannot help it. If he is trapped into eliciting grounds for it, they are grounds given after the fact of conviction.... One neither seeks nor needs grounds for the acceptance of what he cannot help believing. "Whoever is moved by *faith* to assent," Hume wrote, "is conscious of a continued miracle in his own person, which subverts all the principles of his understanding, and gives him a determination to believe...." It is this fact of faith which drives philosophers to such exasperation, in the face of which the believer is nonetheless so utterly unmoved.

The believer sees his life as a gift of God, the world as the creation of God, his own purposes, insofar as they are noble, as the purposes of God, and history as exhibiting a divine plan, made known to him through the Christian story. He sees things this way, just because they do seem so, and he cannot help it. This is why, for him, faith is so "easy," and secular arguments to the contrary so beside the point. No one seeks evidence for that of which he is entirely convinced, or regards as relevant what seems to others to cast doubt. The believer is like a child who recoils from danger, as exhibited, for instance, in what he for the first time sees as a fierce animal; the child has no difficulty *believing* he is in peril, just because he cannot help believing it, yet his belief results not at all from induction based on past experience with fierce animals, and no reassurances, garnered from *our* past experience, relieve his terror at all.

SOME CONFUSIONS

If this is what religious faith essentially is—if, as a believer might poetically but, I think, correctly describe it, faith is an involuntary conviction, often regarded as a "gift," on the part of one who has voluntarily opened his mind and heart to receive it—then certain common misunderstandings can be removed.

In the first place, faith should never be likened to an *assumption*, such as the scientist's assumption of the uniformity of nature, or what not. An assumption is an intellectual device for furthering inquiry. It need not be a conviction nor, indeed, even a belief. But a half-hearted faith is no religious faith. Faith thus has that much, at least, in common with knowledge, that it is a *conviction*, and its subjective state is *certainty*. One thus wholly distorts faith if he represents the believer as just "taking" certain things "on faith," and then reasons, like a philosopher, from these beginnings, as though what were thus "taken" could, like an assumption, be rejected at will.

Again, it is a misunderstanding to represent faith as "mere tenacity." Tenacity consists in stubbornly clinging to what one hopes, but of which one is not fully convinced. The child who is instantly convinced of danger in the presence of an animal is not being tenacious or stubborn, even in the face of verbal reassurances, and no more is the

Christian whose acts are moved by faith. The believer does not so much *shun* evidence as something that might *shake* his faith, but rather regards it as not to the point. In this he may appear to philosophers to be mistaken, but only if one supposes, as he need not, that one should hold only such beliefs as are rational.

Again, it is misleading to refer to any set of propositions, such as those embodied in a creed, as being this or that person's "faith." Concerning that content of belief in which one is convinced by faith, it is logically (though I think not otherwise) possible that one might be convinced by evidence, in which case it would have no more to do with faith or religion than do the statements in a newspaper. This observation has this practical importance, that it is quite possible—in fact, common—for the faith of different believers to be one and the same, despite creedal differences.

And finally, both "faith" (or "fideism") and "reason" (or "rationalism") can be, and often are, used as pejorative terms, and as terms of commendation. Which side one takes here is arbitrary, for there is no non-question-begging way of deciding. A rationalist can perhaps find reasons for being a rationalist, though this is doubtful; but in any case it would betray a basic misunderstanding to expect a fideist to do likewise. This is brought out quite clearly by the direction that discussions of religion usually take. A philosophical teacher will often, for instance, labor long to persuade his audience that the content of Christian faith is unreasonable, which is a shamefully easy task for him, unworthy of his learning. Then suddenly, the underlying assumption comes to light that Christian beliefs ought, therefore, to be abandoned by rational people! A religious hearer of this discourse might well reply that, religion being unreasonable but nonetheless manifestly worthy of belief, we should conclude with Hume that reason, in this realm at least, ought to be rejected. Now, one can decide *that* issue by any light that is granted him, but it is worth stressing that the believer's position on it is just exactly as good, and just as bad, as the rational sceptic's.

67   FAITH AND REASON

MICHAEL SCRIVEN

In the previous selection, Richard Taylor maintained that in deciding matters of religious belief, the appeal to faith is as appropriate as the use of reason. According to him, the choice between the two approaches is arbitrary.

Michael Scriven, a philosopher who teaches in the School of Behavioral and Organizational Sciences at Claremont Graduate University, argues that reason and faith are not on a par, because reason has passed tests of effectiveness that faith has not. Furthermore, while every religious believer relies on reason to assess the claims of ordinary experience, those who are not religious believers have no need to rely on religious faith in any aspect of their lives. If the criteria for religious truth are not connected with the criteria for everyday truth, then faith, unlike reason, should not be treated as a reliable guide.

From Michael Scriven, *Primary Philosophy*, McGraw-Hill, 1966. Reprinted by permission of the publisher.

We must now contend with the suggestion that reason is irrelevant to the commitment to theism because this territory is the domain of another faculty: the faculty of faith. It is sometimes even hinted that it is morally wrong and certainly foolish to suggest we should be reasoning about God. For this is the domain of faith or of the "venture of faith," of the "knowledge that passeth understanding," of religious experience and mystic insight.

Now the normal meaning of *faith* is simply "confidence"; we say that we have great faith in someone or in some claim or product, meaning that we believe and act as if they were very reliable. Of such faith we can properly say that it is well founded or not, depending on the evidence for whatever it is in which we have faith. So there is no incompatibility between this kind of faith and reason; the two are from different families and can make a very good marriage. Indeed if they do not join forces, then the resulting ill-based or inadequate confidence will probably lead to disaster. So faith, in this sense, means only a high degree of belief and may be reasonable or unreasonable.

But the term is sometimes used to mean an *alternative to reason* instead of something that should be founded on reason. Unfortunately, the mere use of the term in this way does not demonstrate that faith is a possible route to truth. It is like using the term "winning" as a synonym for "playing" instead of one possible outcome of playing. This is quaint, but it could hardly be called a satisfactory way of proving that we are winning; any time we "win" by changing the meaning of winning, the victory is merely illusory. And so it proves in this case. To use "faith" *as if* it were an alternative way to the truth cannot by-pass the crucial question whether such results really have any likelihood of being true. A rose by any other name will smell the same, and the inescapable facts about "faith" in the new sense are that it is still *applied to* a belief and is still supposed to imply *confidence in* that belief: the belief in the existence and goodness of God. So we can still ask the same old question about that belief: Is the confidence justified or misplaced? To say we "take it on faith" does not get it off parole.

Suppose someone replies that theism is a kind of belief that does not need justification by evidence. This means either that no one cares whether it is correct or not or that there is some other way of checking that it is correct besides looking at the evidence for it, i.e., giving reasons for believing it. But the first alternative is false since very many people care whether there is a God or not; and the second alternative is false because any method of showing that belief is likely to be true is, by definition, a justification of that belief, i.e., an appeal to reason. You certainly cannot show that a belief in God is likely to be true just by having confidence in it and by saying this is a case of knowledge "based on" faith, any more than you can win a game just by playing it and by calling that winning.

It is psychologically possible to have faith in something without any basis in fact, and once in a while you will turn out to be lucky and to have backed the right belief. This does not show you "really knew all along"; it only shows you cannot be unlucky all the time…. But, in general, beliefs without foundations lead to an early grave or to an accumulation of superstitions, which are usually troublesome and always false beliefs. It is hardly possible to defend this approach just by *saying* that you have decided that in this area confidence is its own justification.

Of course, you might try to *prove* that a feeling of great confidence about certain types of propositions is a reliable indication of their truth. If you succeeded, you would indeed have shown that the belief was justified; you would have done *this* by justifying it. To do this you would have to show what the real facts were and show that when someone had the kind of faith we are now talking about, it usually turned out that the facts were as he believed, just as we might justify the claims of a telepath. The catch in all this is simply that you have got to show what the real facts are in some way *other* than by appealing to faith, since that would simply be assuming what you are trying to prove. And if you can show what the facts are in this other way, you do not need faith in any new sense at all; you are already perfectly entitled to confidence in any belief that you have shown to be well supported.

How are you going to show what the real facts are? You show this by any method of investigation that has itself been tested, the testing being done by still another tested method, etc., through a series of tested connections that eventually terminates in our ordinary everyday reasoning and testing procedures of logic and observation.

Is it not prejudiced to require that the validation of beliefs always involve ultimate reference to our ordinary logic and everyday-plus-scientific knowledge? May not faith (religious experience, mystic insight) give us access to some new domain of truth? It is certainly possible that it does this. But, of course, it is also possible that it lies. One can hardly accept the reports of those with faith or, indeed, the apparent revelations of one's own religious experiences on the ground that they *might* be right. So *might* be a fervent materialist who saw his interpretation as a revelation. Possibility is not veracity. Is it not of the very greatest importance that we should try to find out whether we really can justify the use of the term "truth or knowledge" in describing the content of faith? If it is, then we must find something in that content that is known to be true in some other way, because to get off the ground we must first push off against the ground—we cannot lift ourselves by our shoelaces. If the new realm of knowledge is to be a realm of knowledge and not mythology, then it must tell us something which relates it to the kind of case that gives meaning to the term "truth." If you want to use the old word for the new events, you must show that it is applicable.

Could not the validating experience, which religious experience must have if it is to be called true, be the experience of others who also have or have had religious experiences? The religious community could, surely, provide a basis of agreement analogous to that which ultimately underlies scientific truth. Unfortunately, agreement is not the only requirement for avoiding error, for all may be in error. The difficulty for the religious community is to show that its agreement is not simply agreement about a shared mistake. If agreement were the only criterion of truth, there could never be a shared mistake; but clearly either the atheist group or the theist group shares a mistake. To decide which is wrong must involve appeal to something other than mere agreement. And, of course, it is clear that particular religious beliefs are mistaken, since religious groups do not all agree and they cannot all be right.

Might not some or all scientific beliefs be wrong, too? This is conceivable, but there are crucial differences between the two kinds of belief. In the first place, any commonly agreed religious beliefs concern only one or a few entities and their properties and histories. What for convenience we are here calling "scientific belief" is actually the sum total of all conventionally founded human knowledge, much of it not part of any science, and it embraces billions upon billions of facts, each of them perpetually or frequently subject to checking by independent means, each connected with a million others. The success of *this* system of knowledge shows up every day in everything that we do: we eat, and the food is not poison; we read, and the pages do not turn to dust; we slip, and gravity does not fail to pull us down. We are not just relying on the existence of agreement about the interpretation of a certain experience among a small part of the population. We are relying directly on our extremely reliable, nearly universal, and independently tested senses, and each of us is constantly obtaining independent confirmation for claims based on these, many of these confirmations being obtained for many claims, independently of each other. It is the wildest flight of fancy to suppose that there is a body of common religious beliefs which can be set out to exhibit this degree of repeated checking by religious experiences. In fact, there is not only gross disagreement on even the most fundamental claims in the creeds of different churches, each of which is supported by appeal to religious experience or faith, but where there is agreement by many people, it is all too easily open to the criticism that it arises from the common cultural exposure of the child or the adult convert and hence is not independent in the required way.

This claim that the agreement between judges is spurious in a particular case because it only reflects previous common indoctrination of those in agreement is a serious one. It must always be met by direct disproof whenever agreement is appealed to in science, and it is. The claim that the food is not poison cannot be explained away as a myth of some subculture, for anyone, even if told nothing about the eaters in advance, will judge that the people who ate it are still well. The whole methodology of testing is committed to the doctrine that any judges who could have learned what they are expected to say about the matter they are judging are completely valueless. Now anyone exposed to religious teaching, whether a believer or not, has long known the standard for such experiences, the usual symbols, the appropriate circumstances, and so on. These suggestions are usually very deeply implanted, so that they cannot be avoided by good intentions, and consequently members of our culture are rendered entirely incapable *of* being independent observers. Whenever observers are not free from previous contamination in this manner, the only way to support their claims is to examine independently testable *consequences* of the novel claims, such as predictions about the future. In the absence of these, the religious-experience gambit, whether involving literal or analogical claims, is wholly abortive.

A still more fundamental point counts against the idea that agreement among the religious can help support the idea of faith as an alternative path to truth. It is that every sane theist also believes in the claims of ordinary experience, while the reverse is not the case. Hence, the burden of proof is on the theist to show that the *further step* he wishes to take will not take him beyond the realm of truth. The two positions, of science and religion, are not symmetrical; the adherent of one of them suggests that we extend the range of allowable beliefs and yet is unable to produce the same degree of acceptance or "proving out" in the ordinary field of human activities that he insists on before believing in a new instrument or source of information. The atheist obviously cannot be shown his error in the way someone who thinks that there are no electrons can be shown his, *unless some of the arguments for the existence of God are sound....* If some of them work, the position of religious knowledge is secure; if they do not, nothing else will make it secure.

In sum, the idea of separating religious from scientific knowledge and making each an independent realm with its own basis in experience of quite different kinds is a counsel of despair and not a product of true sophistication, for one cannot break the connection between everyday experience and religious claims, for purposes of defending the latter, without eliminating the consequences of religion for everyday life. There is no way out of this inexorable contract: if you want to support your beliefs, you must produce some experience which can be shown to be a reliable indicator of truth, and that can be done only by showing a connection between the experience and what we know to be true in a previously established way.

So, if the criteria of religious truth are not connected with the criteria of everyday truth, then they are not criteria of truth at all and the beliefs they "establish" have no essential bearing on our lives, constitute no explanation of what we see around us, and provide no guidance for our course through time.

D. THE SIGNIFICANCE OF BELIEF

68 THEOLOGY AND FALSIFICATION

ANTONY FLEW, R. M. HARE, AND BASIL MITCHELL

The exchange that follows has probably given rise to more commentary than any other single work in twentieth-century philosophy of religion. The central issue is not whether God exists but whether the claim that God exists has meaning.

Antony Flew (1923–2010), who was a professor of philosophy at York University, argued that in order for a belief to be meaningful, it must be open to the possibility of disproof. For instance, my belief that my computer works well would be disproved by its going on and off uncontrollably. What evidence, however, would theists accept as a disproof of either God's existence or God's love for us? If no matter what evils may occur someone maintains that God is good, then against what evils does God's goodness offer protection? In other words, if God's goodness is compatible with all possible events, how does a world filled with God's goodness differ from one without it?

R. M. Hare (1919–2002), who was a professor of philosophy at the University of Oxford, responded to Flew's challenge by introducing the notion of a *blik*, an undefined term that appears akin to an unprovable assumption. (As a former student of mine, Dr. Victor Goldenberg, suggested, Hare may have derived the word from the German word *Blick* meaning "view.") In any case, Hare claimed that we all have *bliks* about the world and that Christian belief is one example. He grants that some *bliks* are sane and others insane but does not explain his basis for drawing this distinction.

Basil Mitchell (1917–2011), who was a professor of religion at the University of Oxford, claimed that evidence does count against Christian doctrines but that for a person of faith such evidence can never be allowed to be decisive. Does this reply, however, lead theism to suffer what Flew called "death by a thousand qualifications"? This question is but one of many provocative issues raised in the much-discussed selection that follows.

A

Antony Flew

Let us begin with a parable. It is a parable developed from a tale told by John Wisdom in his haunting and revelatory article "Gods."[1] Once upon a time two explorers came upon a clearing in the jungle. In the clearing were growing many flowers and many weeds. One explorer says, "Some gardener must tend this plot." The other disagrees, "There is no gardener." So they pitch their tents and set a watch. No gardener is ever seen. "But perhaps he is an invisible gardener." So they set up a barbed-wire fence. They electrify it. They patrol with bloodhounds. (For they remember how H. G. Wells's *The Invisible Man* could be

From Antony Flew and Alasdair MacIntyre, eds., *New Essays in Philosophical Theology*, SCM Press, 1955. Reprinted by permission of Scribner, an imprint of Simon & Schuster Adult Publishing Group.

both smelt and touched though he could not be seen.) But no shrieks ever suggest that some intruder has received a shock. No movements of the wire ever betray an invisible climber. The bloodhounds never give cry. Yet still the Believer is not convinced. "But there is a gardener, invisible, intangible, insensible to electric shocks, a gardener who has no scent and makes no sound, a gardener who comes secretly to look after the garden which he loves." At last the Sceptic despairs, "But what remains of your original assertion? Just how does what you call an invisible, intangible, eternally elusive gardener differ from an imaginary gardener or even from no gardener at all?"

In this parable we can see how what starts as an assertion, that something exists or that there is some analogy between certain complexes of phenomena, may be reduced step by step to an altogether different status, to an expression perhaps of a "picture preference."[2] The Sceptic says there is no gardener. The Believer says there is a gardener (but invisible, etc.). One man talks about sexual behaviour. Another man prefers to talk of Aphrodite (but knows that there is not really a superhuman person additional to, and somehow responsible for, all sexual phenomena). The process of qualification may be checked at any point before the original assertion is completely withdrawn and something of that first assertion will remain (Tautology). Mr. Wells's invisible man could not, admittedly, be seen, but in all other respects he was a man like the rest of us. But though the process of qualification may be, and of course usually is, checked in time, it is not always judiciously so halted. Someone may dissipate his assertion completely without noticing that he has done so. A fine brash hypothesis may thus be killed by inches, the death by a thousand qualifications.

And in this, it seems to me, lies the peculiar danger, the endemic evil, of theological utterance. Take such utterances as "God has a plan," "God created the world," "God loves us as a father loves his children." They look at first sight very much like assertions, vast cosmological assertions. Of course, this is no sure sign that they either are, or are intended to be, assertions. But let us confine ourselves to the cases where those who utter such sentences intend them to express assertions. (Merely remarking parenthetically that those who intend or interpret such utterances as crypto-commands, expressions of wishes, disguised ejaculations, concealed ethics, or as anything else but assertions, are unlikely to succeed in making them either properly orthodox or practically effective.)

Now to assert that such and such is the case is necessarily equivalent to denying that such and such is not the case. Suppose then that we are in doubt as to what someone who gives vent to an utterance is asserting, or suppose that, more radically, we are sceptical as to whether he is really asserting anything at all, one way of trying to understand (or perhaps it will be to expose) his utterance is to attempt to find what he would regard as counting against, or as being incompatible with, its truth. For if the utterance is indeed an assertion, it will necessarily be equivalent to a denial of the negation of that assertion. And anything which would count against the assertion, or which would induce the speaker to withdraw it and to admit that it had been mistaken, must be part of (or the whole of) the meaning of the negation of that assertion. And to know the meaning of the negation of an assertion, is as near as makes no matter, to know the meaning of that assertion. And if there is nothing which a putative assertion denies then there is nothing which it asserts either: and so it is not really an assertion. When the Sceptic in the parable asked the Believer, "Just how does what you call an invisible, intangible, eternally elusive gardener differ from an imaginary gardener or even from no gardener at all?" he was suggesting that the Believer's earlier statement had been so eroded by qualification that it was no longer an assertion at all.

Now it often seems to people who are not religious as if there was no conceivable event or series of events the occurrence of which would be admitted by sophisticated religious people to be a sufficient reason for conceding "There wasn't a God after all" or "God does not really love us then." Someone tells us that God loves us as a father loves his children. We are reassured. But then we see a child dying of inoperable cancer of the throat. His earthly father is driven frantic in his efforts to help, but his Heavenly Father reveals no obvious sign of concern. Some qualification is made—God's love is "not a merely human love" or it is "an inscrutable love," perhaps—and we realize that such sufferings are quite compatible with the truth of the assertion that "God loves us as a father (but, of course, …)." We are reassured again. But then perhaps we ask: what is this assurance of God's (appropriately qualified) love worth, what is this apparent guarantee really a guarantee against? Just what would have to happen not merely (morally and wrongly) to tempt but also (logically and rightly) to entitle us to say "God does not love us" or even "God does not exist"? I therefore put to the succeeding symposiasts the simple central questions, "What would have to occur or to have occurred to constitute for you a disproof of the love of, or of the existence of, God?"

B

R. M. Hare

I wish to make it clear that I shall not try to defend Christianity in particular, but religion in general—not because I do not believe in Christianity, but because you cannot understand what Christianity is, until you have understood what religion is.

I must begin by confessing that, on the ground marked out by Flew, he seems to me to be completely victorious. I therefore shift my ground by relating another parable. A certain lunatic is convinced that all dons want to murder him. His friends introduce him to all the mildest and most respectable dons that they can find, and after each of them has retired, they say, "You see, he doesn't really want to murder you; he spoke to you in a most cordial manner; surely you are convinced now?" But the lunatic replies "Yes, but that was only his diabolical cunning; he's really plotting against me the whole time, like the rest of them; I know it I tell you." However many kindly dons are produced, the reaction is still the same.

Now we say that such a person is deluded. But what is he deluded about? About the truth or falsity of an assertion? Let us apply Flew's test to him. There is no behaviour of dons that can be enacted which he will accept as counting against

his theory; and therefore his theory, on this test, asserts nothing. But it does not follow that there is no difference between what he thinks about dons and what most of us think about them—otherwise we should not call him a lunatic and ourselves sane, and dons would have no reason to feel uneasy about his presence in Oxford.

Let us call that in which we differ from this lunatic, our respective *bliks*. He has an insane *blik* about dons; we have a sane one. It is important to realize that we have a sane one, not no *blik* at all; for there must be two sides to any argument—if he has a wrong *blik*, then those who are right about dons must have a right one. Flew has shown that a *blik* does not consist in an assertion or system of them; but nevertheless it is very important to have the right *blik*.

Let us try to imagine what it would be like to have different *bliks* about other things than dons. When I am driving my car, it sometimes occurs to me to wonder whether my movements of the steering-wheel will always continue to be followed by corresponding alterations in the direction of the car. I have never had a steering failure, though I have had skids, which must be similar. Moreover, I know enough about how the steering of my car is made, to know the sort of thing that would have to go wrong for the steering to fail —steel joints would have to part, or steel rods break, or something—but how do I know that this won't happen? The truth is, I don't know; I just have a *blik* about steel and its properties, so that normally I trust the steering of my car; but I find it not at all difficult to imagine what it would be like to lose this *blik* and acquire the opposite one. People would say I was silly about steel; but there would be no mistaking the reality of the difference between our respective *bliks*—for example, I should never go in a motor-car. Yet I should hesitate to say that the difference between us was the difference between contradictory assertions. No amount of safe arrivals or bench-tests will remove my *blik* and restore the normal one; for my *blik* is compatible with any finite number of such tests.

It was Hume who taught us that our whole commerce with the world depends upon our *blik* about the world; and that differences between *bliks* about the world cannot be settled by observation of what happens in the world. That was why, having performed the interesting experiment of doubting the ordinary man's *blik* about the world, and showing that no proof could be given to make us adopt one *blik* rather than another, he turned to backgammon to take his mind off the problem. It seems, indeed, to be impossible even to formulate as an assertion the normal *blik* about the world which makes me put my confidence in the future reliability of steel joints, in the continued ability of the road to support my car, and not gape beneath it revealing nothing below; in the general non-homicidal tendencies of dons; in my own continued well-being (in some sense of that word that I may not now fully understand) if I continue to do what is right according to my lights; in the general likelihood of people like Hitler coming to a bad end. But perhaps a formulation less inadequate than most is to be found in the Psalms: "The earth is weak and all the inhabiters thereof: I bear up the pillars of it."

The mistake of the position which Flew selects for attack is to regard this kind of talk as some sort of *explanation*, as scientists are accustomed to use the word. As such, it would obviously be ludicrous. We no longer believe in God as an Atlas—*nous n'avons pas besoin de cette hypothèse.*[3] But it is nevertheless true to say that, as Hume saw, without a *blik* there can be no explanation; for it is by our *bliks* that we decide what is and what is not an explanation. Suppose we believed that everything that happened, happened by pure chance. This would not of course be an assertion; for it is compatible with anything happening or not happening, and so, incidentally, is its contradictory. But if we had this belief, we should not be able to explain or predict or plan anything. Thus, although we should not be *asserting* anything different from those of a more normal belief, there would be a great difference between us; and this is the sort of difference that there is between those who really believe in God and those who really disbelieve in him.

The word "really" is important, and may excite suspicion. I put it in, because when people have had a good Christian upbringing, as have most of those who now profess not to believe in

any sort of religion, it is very hard to discover what they really believe. The reason why they find it so easy to think that they are not religious, is that they have never got into the frame of mind of one who suffers from the doubts to which religion is the answer. Not for them the terrors of the primitive jungle. Having abandoned some of the more picturesque fringes of religion, they think that they have abandoned the whole thing—whereas in fact they still have got, and could not live without, a religion of a comfortably substantial, albeit highly sophisticated, kind, which differs from that of many "religious people" in little more than this, that "religious people" like to sing Psalms about theirs—a very natural and proper thing to do. But nevertheless there may be a big difference lying behind—the difference between two people who, though side by side, are walking in different directions. I do not know in what direction Flew is walking; perhaps he does not know either. But we have had some examples recently of various ways in which one can walk away from Christianity, and there are any number of possibilities. After all, man has not changed biologically since primitive times; it is his religion that has changed, and it can easily change again. And if you do not think that such changes make a difference, get acquainted with some Sikhs and some Mussulmans of the same Punjabi stock; you will find them quite different sorts of people.

There is an important difference between Flew's parable and my own which we have not yet noticed. The explorers do not *mind* about their garden; they discuss it with interest, but not with concern. But my lunatic, poor fellow, minds about dons; and I mind about the steering of my car; it often has people in it that I care for. It is because I mind very much about what goes on in the garden in which I find myself, that I am unable to share the explorers' detachment.

C

Basil Mitchell

Flew's article is searching and perceptive, but there is, I think, something odd about his conduct of the theologian's case. The theologian surely would not deny that the fact of pain counts against the assertion that God loves men. This very incompatibility generates the most intractable of theological problems—the problem of evil. So the theologian *does* recognize the fact of pain as counting against Christian doctrine. But it is true that he will not allow it—or anything—to count decisively against it; for he is committed by his faith to trust in God. His attitude is not that of the detached observer, but of the believer.

Perhaps this can be brought out by yet another parable. In time of war in an occupied country, a member of the resistance meets one night a stranger who deeply impresses him. They spend that night together in conversation. The Stranger tells the partisan that he himself is on the side of the resistance—indeed that he is in command of it, and urges the partisan to have faith in him no matter what happens. The partisan is utterly convinced at that meeting of the Stranger's sincerity and constancy and undertakes to trust him.

They never meet in conditions of intimacy again. But sometimes the Stranger is seen helping members of the resistance, and the partisan is grateful and says to his friends, "He is on our side."

Sometimes he is seen in the uniform of the police handing over patriots to the occupying power. On these occasions his friends murmur against him: but the partisan still says, "He is on our side." He still believes that, in spite of appearances, the Stranger did not deceive him. Sometimes he asks the Stranger for help and receives it. He is then thankful. Sometimes he asks and does not receive it. Then he says, "The Stranger knows best." Sometimes his friends, in exasperation, say "Well, what *would* he have to do for you to admit that you were wrong and that he is not on our side?" But the partisan refuses to answer. He will not consent to put the Stranger to the test. And sometimes his friends complain, "Well, if *that's* what you mean by his being on our side, the sooner he goes over to the other side the better."

The partisan of the parable does not allow anything to count decisively against the proposition "The Stranger is on our side." This is because he has committed himself to trust the Stranger. But he of course recognizes that the Stranger's

ambiguous behaviour *does* count against what he believes about him. It is precisely this situation which constitutes the trial of his faith.

When the partisan asks for help and doesn't get it, what can he do? He can (*a*) conclude that the stranger is not on our side or; (*b*) maintain that he is on our side, but that he has reasons for withholding help.

The first he will refuse to do. How long can he uphold the second position without its becoming just silly?

I don't think one can say in advance. It will depend on the nature of the impression created by the Stranger in the first place. It will depend, too, on the manner in which he takes the Stranger's behaviour. If he blandly dismisses it as of no consequence, as having no bearing upon his belief, it will be assumed that he is thoughtless or insane. And it quite obviously won't do for him to say easily, "Oh, when used of the Stranger the phrase 'is on our side' *means* ambiguous behaviour of this sort." In that case he would be like the religious man who says blandly of a terrible disaster "It is God's will." No, he will only be regarded as sane and reasonable in his belief, if he experiences in himself the full force of the conflict.

It is here that my parable differs from Hare's. The partisan admits that many things may and do count against his belief: whereas Hare's lunatic who has a *blik* about dons doesn't admit that anything counts against his *blik*. Nothing *can* count against *bliks*. Also the partisan has a reason for having in the first instance committed himself, viz. the character of the Stranger; whereas the lunatic has no reason for his *blik* about dons—because, of course, you can't have reasons for *bliks*.

This means that I agree with Flew that theological utterances must be assertions. The partisan is making an assertion when he says, "The Stranger is on our side."

Do I want to say that the partisan's belief about the Stranger is, in any sense, an explanation? I think I do. It explains and makes sense of the Stranger's behaviour: it helps to explain also the resistance movement in the context of which he appears. In each case it differs from the interpretation which the others put upon the same facts.

"God loves men" resembles "the Stranger is on our side" (and many other significant statements, e.g., historical ones) in not being conclusively falsifiable. They can both be treated in at least three different ways: (1) As provisional hypotheses to be discarded if experience tells against them; (2) As significant articles of faith; (3) As vacuous formulae (expressing, perhaps, a desire for reassurance) to which experience makes no difference and which make no difference to life.

The Christian, once he has committed himself, is precluded by his faith from taking up the first attitude: "Thou shalt not tempt the Lord thy God." He is in constant danger, as Flew has observed, of slipping into the third. But he need not; and, if he does, it is a failure in faith as well as in logic.

D

Antony Flew

It has been a good discussion: and I am glad to have helped to provoke it. But now—at least in *University*—it must come to an end: and the Editors of *University* have asked me to make some concluding remarks. Since it is impossible to deal with all the issues raised or to comment separately upon each contribution, I will concentrate on Mitchell and Hare, as representative of two very different kinds of response to the challenge made in "Theology and Falsification."

The challenge, it will be remembered, ran like this. Some theological utterances seem to, and are intended to, provide explanations or express assertions. Now an assertion, to be an assertion at all, must claim that things stand thus and thus; *and not otherwise*. Similarly an explanation, to be an explanation at all, must explain why this particular thing occurs; *and not something else*. Those last clauses are crucial. And yet sophisticated religious people—or so it seemed to me—are apt to overlook this, and tend to refuse to allow, not merely that anything actually does occur, but that anything conceivably could occur, which would count against their theological assertions and explanations. But in so far as they do this their supposed explanations are actually bogus, and their seeming assertions are really vacuous.

Mitchell's response to this challenge is admirably direct, straightforward, and understanding. He agrees "that theological utterances must be assertions." He agrees that if they are to be assertions, there must be something that would count against their truth. He agrees, too, that believers are in constant danger of transforming their would-be assertions into "vacuous formulae." But he takes me to task for an oddity in my "conduct of the theologian's case. The theologian surely would not deny that the fact of pain counts against the assertion that God loves men. This very incompatibility generates the most intractable of theological problems, the problem of evil." I think he is right. I should have made a distinction between two very different ways of dealing with what looks like evidence against the love of God: the way I stressed was the expedient of qualifying the original assertion; the way the theologian usually takes, at first, is to admit that it looks bad but to insist that there is—there must be—some explanation which will show that, in spite of appearances, there really is a God who loves us. His difficulty, it seems to me, is that he has given God attributes which rule out all possible saving explanations. In Mitchell's parable of the Stranger it is easy for the believer to find plausible excuses for ambiguous behaviour: for the Stranger is a man. But suppose the Stranger is God. We cannot say that he would like to help but cannot: God is omnipotent. We cannot say that he would help if he only knew: God is omniscient. We cannot say that he is not responsible for the wickedness of others: God creates those others. Indeed an omnipotent, omniscient God must be an accessory before (and during) the fact to every human misdeed; as well as being responsible for every nonmoral defect in the universe. So, though I entirely concede that Mitchell was absolutely right to insist against me that the theologian's first move is to look for an *explanation*, I still think that in the end, if relentlessly pursued, he will have to resort to the avoiding action of *qualification*. And there lies the danger of that death by a thousand qualifications, which would, I agree, constitute "a failure in faith as well as in logic."

Hare's approach is fresh and bold. He confesses that "on the ground marked out by Flew, he seems to me to be completely victorious." He therefore introduces the concept of *blik*. But while I think that there is room for some such concept in philosophy, and that philosophers should be grateful to Hare for his invention, I nevertheless want to insist that any attempt to analyse Christian religious utterances as expressions or affirmations of a *blik* rather than as (at least would-be) assertions about the cosmos is fundamentally misguided. *First*, because thus interpreted they would be entirely unorthodox. If Hare's religion really is a *blik*, involving no cosmological assertions about the nature and activities of a supposed personal creator, then surely he is not a Christian at all? *Second*, because thus interpreted, they could scarcely do the job they do. If they were not even intended as assertions then many religious activities would become fraudulent, or merely silly. If "You ought *because* it is God's will" asserts no more than "You ought," then the person who prefers the former phraseology is not really giving a reason, but a fraudulent substitute for one, a dialectical dud cheque. If "My soul must be immortal *because* God loves his children, etc." asserts no more than "My soul must be immortal," then the man who reassures himself with theological arguments for immortality is being as silly as the man who tries to clear his overdraft by writing his bank a cheque on the same account. (Of course neither of these utterances would be distinctively Christian: but this discussion never pretended to

be so confined.) Religious utterances may indeed express false or even bogus assertions: but I simply do not believe that they are not both intended and interpreted to be or at any rate to presuppose assertions, at least in the context of religious practice; whatever shifts may be demanded, in another context, by the exigencies of theological apologetic.

One final suggestion. The philosophers of religion might well draw upon George Orwell's last appalling nightmare *1984* for the concept of *doublethink*. "*Doublethink* means the power of holding two contradictory beliefs simultaneously, and accepting both of them. The party intellectual knows that he is playing tricks with reality, but by the exercise of *doublethink* he also satisfies himself that reality is not violated" (*1984*, p. 220). Perhaps religious intellectuals too are sometimes driven to doublethink in order to retain their faith in a loving God in face of the reality of a heartless and indifferent world. But of this more another time, perhaps.

NOTES

1. P. A. S., 1944–5, reprinted as Chap. X of *Logic and Language*, Vol. I (Blackwell, 1951), and in his *Philosophy and Psychoanalysis* (Blackwell, 1953).
2. Cf. J. Wisdom, "Other Minds," *Mind*, 1940; reprinted in his *Other Minds* (Blackwell, 1952).
3. [We have no need for that hypothesis.]

69   THE HIDDENNESS OF GOD

ROBERT McKIM

Is believing in God important? If so, why does God remain hidden to so many? Why does God not take steps to be revealed in a manner accessible to all?

From Robert McKim, *Religious Ambiguity and Religious Diversity*, Oxford University Press, 2001. Reprinted by permission of the publisher.

According to Robert McKim, Professor of Religious Studies and of Philosophy at the University of Illinois at Urbana-Champaign, the evidence suggests that whether we believe in God doesn't much matter, because if believing made an important difference, the evidence of God's existence would be more apparent.

THE HIDDEN EMPEROR

Once upon a time, in a faraway and geographically isolated land, there was a small community that had lived without contact with other communities for so long that the very memory that there were other peoples had been lost almost entirely. Only a few of the elders could recall from their childhood the stories that used to be told of visitors from afar, of distant peoples and communities, of powerful princes and lords, and of their vast empires. Some of the very oldest people with the best memories could recall that back in the old days there were some who said (or was it that they remembered hearing reports about its having been said?—it was so long ago and so hard to tell) that their territory was actually itself part of one of those great empires, and one that was ruled over by a great and good emperor. But these stories had not been told for so long that even the old people had difficulty remembering them, and the young were downright skeptical.

And then one day there arrived an outsider who claimed to be an emissary and who bore astonishing news. He declared that some of the old stories were true. He said that the small, isolated community was indeed part of a great empire, an empire that stretched farther than anyone could have imagined. And—more astonishing still—the ruler of all this, the emissary said, pointing to the familiar hillsides and fields, to the rude dwellings and away to the horizon in all directions, is a great and wise emperor who deserves loyalty and obedience from all his subjects. And that includes you, said the visitor. And—could it be yet more astonishing?—the emperor is generally known to his subjects throughout the rest of the empire as the "Hidden Emperor," for he never lets himself be seen clearly by any of his subjects. Not even his closest, most loyal, and most devoted servants are sure exactly what he looks like. But it is widely believed that he travels incognito throughout the empire, for he has various remarkable powers that make this possible, including the power to make himself invisible, the power to travel from place to place with great speed, and even the power to understand what people are thinking. Indeed, so great are his powers in these respects, said the visitor, that it is hardly an exaggeration to say that he is always present throughout the entire empire.

Never had anything quite like this been heard. Mouths were agape, eyes were wide in astonishment. What are we to do, what does the emperor want from us and what are we to expect from him? people asked. "He wants your loyalty, trust, and obedience, and he offers protection and help in time of trouble," replied the emissary.

At this point a man in the crowd, a tallish bearded man with a puzzled expression, and of the sort that is inclined to twiddle with his beard in an irritating way, replied as follows. "But why," he asked—and the emissary knew what was coming, for he had been through this many times and knew that in every community there is a trouble-maker or two and that beard twiddling and a puzzled expression are among the best indicators that trouble is brewing—"why does the emperor have to be hidden? Why can't we see the emperor for ourselves? I know that it is not my place to ask"—a familiar line to the seasoned emissary, who has heard it all before and can recognize false modesty at a glance—"but why couldn't the emperor's existence and presence be as clear as *your* presence and existence? And"—now for the coup de grâce, thought the emissary, the sign that we are contending here with a *serious* thinker—"if it is important for the emperor to be hidden, why are you here informing us about him?"

After the tall bearded man had spoken, there was silence for a few minutes. The fact was that no one quite knew what would happen next, or what it was proper to say to the emissary. Had the bearded man gone too far? Had he spoken improperly? Would he be reprimanded or punished?

Would they all be reprimanded or punished? Should he be silenced?

Then an old woman, known for her wisdom and insight, and of that generation among whom belief in the great emperor had not entirely been lost, spoke up. "I, for one, think that things are much better this way. As long as the emperor, and may he and his blessed relatives live for ever," she added, with a glance at the emissary, "as long as the emperor is hidden, we have a type of freedom that would otherwise be unavailable to us. We are free to decide whether or not to believe that there is an emperor. If the facts of the matter were clear to us, and it were just plain obvious that the emperor exists, belief would be forced on us. As long as the facts are unclear, we are in a position to exercise control over what we think. And even though our esteemed visitor has come to explain the situation to us, we are still in a position to decide whether or not to believe what he says."

At this the bearded man became downright exasperated, saying, "Listen here. What is so great about being able to make up your mind in conditions in which the facts are unclear? Surely if the facts are unclear, we ought simply to believe that the facts are unclear. It's absurd to suggest that there is something especially admirable or good about deciding that the emperor exists under circumstances in which it is unclear whether the emperor exists. Do you think that it would also be good for us to be able to choose whether or not to believe, say, that two plus two equals four in circumstances in which *that* is not clear, or for us to be able to choose what to believe about who our parents are in circumstances in which *that* is not clear?"

"This may seem absurd to you," interjected the woman, "since you are the sort of man who likes to strut around as if you had all the answers to life's questions even though nobody else has quite noticed, but what you have to understand is that this arrangement has the great advantage of permitting our willingness to acknowledge our status as subservient underlings in the emperor's realm to play a role in determining whether or not we believe that the emperor exists."

"And I will tell you," said the woman, warming to her theme and enjoying the attention of the crowd, and what she took to be the approving look of the visiting emissary, "I will tell you about another benefit of our current situation. The fact that we do not know what the emperor looks like permits him to come among us, looking like one of us. Long ago, when I was a little girl, it used to be said that when you entertain a stranger, you should remember that you might be entertaining the emperor. In fact people used to say, 'Every poor stranger is the emperor.' I don't suppose that they really meant it, but you can see what they had in mind. And there was another saying, too, now that I remember it. We used to say, when we wished to show respect for someone, that 'You are He.' Of course, if you knew that a visitor in your house really was the emperor, you would be quite dazed and overwhelmed, and even ashamed by how little you had to offer such a guest."

"Damn it all," said the man with the puzzled look, "this is all nonsense. If the emperor wanted us to believe in him, he would make his existence apparent to us. Don't listen to that old bag. It's as simple as this. If the emperor existed, he would want us to know him and to know about him. If so, he would make his presence apparent to us. He does not do so even though he could do so. The only sensible conclusion is that *there is no emperor. There is no emperor! There is no emperor!*"

After this intemperate outburst yet another voice was heard from the crowd, the voice of one who prides himself on taking a sober, comprehensive, and balanced view of things, and in the process takes himself much too seriously. "Maybe we *are* part of the empire," said this new interlocutor. "Certainly we have some evidence that this is so, not least of which is the fact that our honored visitor, who appears to me to have an open and trustworthy countenance, has come to tell us that this is so. The recollections of some of our senior members are also relevant here. Surely they give us some reason to believe there to be an emperor. But if there is an emperor —and I certainly do not rule out this possibility— it is hard to believe that it matters to him whether we believe that he exists. If it mattered very much to the emperor that we believe that he exists, then surely it would be clearer than it now is that there is an emperor. After all, where has the emperor been all this time? Furthermore, the beliefs that we hold about the emperor under current conditions, if we hold any, ought to reflect the fact that they are held under conditions of uncertainty. Any beliefs we hold in this area ought in fact to be held with tentativeness, and with an awareness that we may be wrong."

In the fullness of time, and after the emissary had gone his way, it came to pass that three schools of thought developed, each of which embraced one of the views that were expressed on that day. There were those who agreed with the old woman, and who were known by their opponents as the "Imperialists." Then there were the Skeptics. All of their bearded members had a strong inclination toward beard-twiddling. And there were the Tentative Believers. They were known to their detractors as "the half-baked believers." So who was right? ...

THE DISADVANTAGES OF GOD'S HIDDENNESS

If God exists but is hidden, this is a perplexing state of affairs. One reason that it is perplexing is internal to theism and arises from the fact that the theistic traditions place such importance on belief. Typically each theistic tradition asserts that to fail to hold theistic beliefs, and especially to fail to hold its theistic beliefs, or at least what it considers to be the most important among them, is to go wrong in a very serious way whereas to adopt theistic beliefs, and especially the set of theistic beliefs associated with it, is a worthwhile and important thing to do. These traditions say, too, that one ought to regret or even feel guilty about a failure to believe. Yet if God is hidden, belief is more difficult than it would be if God were not hidden. If God exists, and if the facts about God's existence and nature were clear, belief would be ever so much easier for us. The theistic traditions are inclined to hold human beings responsible and even to blame them if they are nonbelievers or if their belief is weak. But does this make any sense?

God's hiddenness creates uncertainty and contributes to profound disagreement about the existence and nature of God. Indeed, I would suggest that it contributes *more* to the occurrence of nonbelief than does the presence of evil in the world (or of *other* evil in the world, if the hiddenness of God is understood as a type of evil). This is not to deny that there are people who are nontheists because of evils that they either encounter or are familiar with; but it seems that the explanation in most cases of how it has come about that people do not believe that God exists (whether they are atheists or agnostics or members of nontheistic religions) is not that they consider God's existence to be incompatible with various evils. Rather, it is that they have nothing that they understand as an awareness of God. They do not understand themselves to be familiar with God. Consequently, they do not even reach a point where evil is perceived as a problem....

Another reason that the hiddenness of God is perplexing has to do with the sort of personal relationship with God that some theists advocate. This is also a reason that is internal to theism, or at least to theism of a certain sort, especially evangelical and fundamentalist Christianity. The personal relationship in question is understood to involve trust, respect, and, above all, ongoing intimate communication. Is it not reasonable to suppose that if God were less hidden, this sort of relationship would be more widespread?

The hiddenness of God, therefore, seems to be a particularly acute problem for strands of theism that emphasize the importance of fellowship and communication with God. But it is also a problem for the other major strands of theism because they all emphasize the importance and value of belief. And they declare that God cares about us; if God exists and if God cares about us, why does God leave human beings to such an extent in the dark about various religiously important facts? If God does not care about us, there is less to explain. Theism typically requires, too, that we put our trust and confidence in God: But why, then, are the facts about God not more clear? If God exists and the facts about God's existence and nature were more clear, people would be more likely to see that they ought to put their trust and confidence in God and would be more willing and more able to do so.

Another important, and related, disadvantage associated with divine hiddenness is this. If God exists, God is worthy of adoration and worship: given the good, wise, just (etc.) nature of God, and the relation between God and God's creatures, a worshipful response from human beings would be appropriate. For if God exists, God is our Creator and we owe all we have to God. But if many of us are in the dark about the existence and nature of God, then this appropriate human response is made more difficult than it otherwise would be. So part of the cost of divine hiddenness is its contribution to the large-scale failure of human beings to respond to God in ways that seem appropriate in the case of a good, just, and wise creator.

And there are further costs. The profound disagreements about God, and more broadly the profound disagreements that there are about numerous matters of religious importance, often play a role in promoting and exacerbating social conflict. If God exists and if the facts about God were as clear as they could be, there might not be as much room for disagreement, and hence such disagreements would not contribute to social conflict. The mystery surrounding God also provides opportunities for charlatans and frauds to pose as experts on the nature and activities of God, and for religious authorities in numerous traditions to acquire and exercise, and sometimes abuse, power and control over others.

To each of these apparent disadvantages, or costs, of God's hiddenness there corresponds an advantage or benefit that, it appears, would accrue if God were not hidden. Thus if God were not hidden, and the facts about God were clear for all to see, it appears that belief would be easier for us, a personal relationship with God would be facilitated, more people would worship God, religious disagreement would be less likely to exacerbate social tensions, and there would be fewer opportunities for people to pose as experts and to acquire power and influence over others....

There is, then, some reason to think that, if God exists, it must not matter greatly to God whether we believe. This applies to belief that God exists, to various standard theistic beliefs about God, such as beliefs about the activities and character of God, and to belief in God. At least that we should hold such beliefs ... here and now and under our current circumstances probably does not matter greatly. There is also considerable reason to believe that it is not important that everyone should accept any particular form of theism, such as Judaism or Islam. If it were very important that we should accept theism or any particular form of theism, our circumstances probably would be more conducive to it.

PART EIGHT

Beyond Death

A. HEAVEN AND HELL

70 TWO CHRISTIAN CONCEPTS OF HEAVEN

COLLEEN McDANNELL AND BERNHARD LANG

One feature of Christianity and Islam (as well as some branches of other religions) is the belief that life on earth is followed by an afterlife in which some persons abide forever in a place of joy while others endure everlasting suffering in a place of doom. Many people find these visions compelling and embrace a religion that emphasizes them. The concepts of heaven and hell, however, raise a variety of philosophical issues.

To begin with, what would heaven be like? In the next selection, Colleen McDannell, Professor of History and of Religious Studies at the University of Utah, and Bernhard Lang, Professor of Religion at the University of Paderborn in Germany, find that throughout the history of Christianity two different models of heaven have emerged. One centers on finding blessedness in eternal solitude with God; the other focuses on experiencing the joy of being in the presence of loved ones.

From Colleen McDannell and Bernhard Lang, *Heaven: A History*, Second Edition, Yale University Press, 1988. Reprinted by permission of the publisher.

How have Christians visualized life everlasting?... Two major images dominate theology, pious literature, art, and popular ideas. Some Christians expect to spend heavenly life in "eternal solitude with God alone." Others cannot conceive of blessedness without being reunited with friends, spouse, children, or relatives. Using convenient theological jargon we have termed these views theocentric – "centering in God," and anthropocentric – "focusing on the human."... These two concepts do not depend on the level of sophistication of those presenting the image (theologians versus lay people), or time frame (early versus contemporary), or theological preference (Protestant versus Catholic). Rather, we have found that throughout Christian history anthropocentric and theocentric models emerge, become prominent, and weaken....

The theocentric model presupposes a distinct view of the relationship between God and the human creature. The inequality of the two is emphasized, with God being absolutely superior. He claims complete surrender: emotional, intellectual, even physical. Unless guided by the divine will alone, human beings are lost. Once autonomy is surrendered, however, one can be assured of everlasting life. This attitude appeals to those who accord a lower priority to social commitments than to spiritual values. The theocentric heaven is preferred by people who, for various reasons, seek distance from "the world." Religious enthusiasts and charismatic leaders; philosophers inspired by some form of Platonism; members of celibate groups who want to lead the unmarried life of the angles even here on earth; reformers who discover the power of a demanding God and find themselves in an alien and often hostile world: these Christians find rest in an eternity filled with the divine. Conversely, the theocentric view has little appeal for others who prefer the settled, "normal" life of family, work, and business. The world, with all its compromises and lack of true religious

heroism, constantly threatens a full commitment to Christian ideals....

The anthropocentric view of heaven presupposes a value system fundamentally different from that of the theocentric model. In general, the world is looked upon more optimistically. Social life, marriage, sexuality, and work are divinely instituted and eternal. God permits them to be enjoyed by men and women in both worlds. Ideas of eternal life are modelled not on the enthusiastic worship of religious charismatics, but on an idealized life of leisure, service, and spiritual growth. The divine is no longer experienced solely in ecstasy, extraordinary events, and heroic commitment, but in the calm course of everyday life. Moreover, the loneliness of the ascetic world-renouncer is considered a deficient mode of existence, not a preparation for eternity. Since the natural world, personal relationships, and work itself are sacred, they must continue in some form in the next life. The anthropocentric system of values is related to a socially-established Christianity....

Although the two models often co-exist, one of them can generally be considered the dominant view for a given time and place. But the leading position, whether occupied by the theocentric or the anthropocentric view, cannot be firmly established in the long run. Whenever the theocentric model is given its full expression, a softening of its uncompromising quality is called for. Since human love and longing cannot be utterly suppressed, even the most rigorous theocentric theology retains a human element. The anthropocentric alternative receives a fair hearing. Likewise, when the human dimension threatens to weaken or supplant the divine, the pendulum again swings to the other side. Like human passion, the love of God can never be suppressed or forgotten. Even the most human-centered views of the afterlife endow heaven with divine presence. A basic tension occurs at the heart of the Christian mentality – a tension foreshadowed in its founder's injunction to love both God and neighbor.

71 SINNERS IN THE HANDS OF AN ANGRY GOD

JONATHAN EDWARDS

Hell is far easier to envision than heaven, for we are all familiar with the nature of misery. The vividness of damnation was famously portrayed by Jonathan Edwards (1703–1758), a leading Puritan minister and acute philosopher, when on July 8, 1741, in a meetinghouse in Enfield, Connecticut, he preached what has been called "America's most famous sermon."

He described sinners in the hand of God, ready at any moment to drop the evildoers into the fires of hell. According to a contemporary account of the audience's reaction, "the shrieks and cries were piercing and amazing." The wailing was so great that Edwards was unable to finish.

Here are some highlights from that sermon.

Almost every natural man that hears of hell, flatters himself that he shall escape it; he depends upon himself for his own security; he flatters himself in what he has done, in what he is now doing, or what he intends to do; every one lays out matters in his own mind how he shall avoid damnation, and flatters himself that he contrives well for himself, and that his schemes won't fail. They hear indeed that there are but few saved, and that the bigger part of men that have died heretofore are gone to hell; but each one imagines that he lays out matters better for his own escape than others have done: He don't intend to come to that place of torment; he says within himself, that he intends to take care that shall be effectual, and to order matters so for himself as not to fail.

But the foolish children of men miserably delude themselves in their own schemes, and in their confidence in their own strength and wisdom; they trust to nothing but a shadow. The bigger part of those that heretofore have lived under the same means of grace, and are now dead, are undoubtedly gone to hell: and it was not because they were not as wise as those that are now alive: it was not because they did not lay out matters as well for themselves to secure their own escape. If it were so, that we could come to speak with them, and could inquire of them, one by one, whether they expected when alive, and when they used to hear about hell, ever to be the subjects of that misery, we doubtless should hear one and another reply, "No, I never intended to come here; I had laid out matters otherwise in my mind; I thought I should contrive well for my self; I thought my scheme good; I intended to take effectual care; but it came upon me unexpected; I did not look for it at that time, and in that manner; it came as a thief; death outwitted me; God's wrath was too quick for me; Oh my cursed foolishness! I was flattering my self, and pleasing my self with vain dreams of what I would do hereafter, and when I was saying peace and safety, then sudden destruction came upon me."

So that, thus it is, that natural men are held in the hand of God over the pit of Hell; they have deserved the fiery pit, and are already sentenced to it; and God is dreadfully provoked, his anger is as great towards them as to those that are actually suffering the executions of the fierceness of his wrath in hell, and they have done nothing in the least to appease or abate that anger, neither is God in the least bound by any promise to hold them up one moment; the Devil is waiting for them, Hell is gaping for them, the flames gather and flash about

A sermon preached at Enfield, Connecticut, July 8, 1741.

them, and would fain lay hold on 'em, and swallow them up; the fire pent up in their own hearts is struggling to break out: and they have no interest in any Mediator, there are no means within reach that can be any security to them. In short, they have no refuge, nothing to take hold of, all that preserves them every moment is the mere arbitrary will, and uncovenanted unobliged forbearance of an incensed God.

APPLICATION

The use may be of awakening to unconverted persons in this congregation. This that you have heard is the case of every one of you that are out of Christ. That world of misery, that lake of burning brimstone is extended abroad under you. There is the dreadful pit of the glowing flames of the wrath of God; there is hell's wide gaping mouth open; and you have nothing to stand upon, nor any thing to take hold of, there is nothing between you and Hell but the air; 'tis only the power and mere pleasure of God that holds you up.

You probably are not sensible of this; you find you are kept out of Hell, but don't see the hand of God in it, but look at other things, as the good state of your bodily constitution, your care of your own life, and the means you use for your own preservation. But indeed these things are nothing; if God should withdraw his hand, they would avail no more to keep you from falling, than the thin air to hold up a person that is suspended in it....

However unconvinced you may now be of the truth of what you hear, by & by you will be fully convinced of it. Those that are gone from being in the like circumstances with you, see that it was so with them; for destruction came suddenly upon most of them, when they expected nothing of it, and while they were saying, peace and safety: now they see, that those things that they depended on for peace and safety, were nothing but thin air and empty shadows.

The God that holds you over the pit of Hell, much as one holds a spider, or some loathsome insect, over the fire, abhors you, and is dreadfully provoked; his wrath towards you burns like fire; he looks upon you as worthy of nothing else, but

to be cast into the fire; he is of purer eyes than to bear to have you in his sight; you are ten thousand times so abominable in his eyes as the most hateful venomous serpent is in ours. You have offended him infinitely more than ever a stubborn rebel did his prince: and yet 'tis nothing but his hand that holds you from falling into the fire every moment: 'Tis is to be ascribed to nothing else, that you did not go to Hell the last night; that you was suffer'd to awake again in this world, after you closed your eyes to sleep: and there is no other reason to be given why you have not dropped into Hell since you arose in the morning, but that God's hand has held you up: There is no other reason to be given why you han't gone to Hell since you have sat here in the house of God, provoking his pure eyes by your sinful wicked manner of attending his solemn worship. Yea, there is nothing else that is to be given as a reason why you don't this very moment drop down into Hell.

O sinner! Consider the fearful danger you are in: 'tis a great furrnace of wrath, a wide and bottomless pit, full of the fire of wrath, that you are held over in the hand of that God, whose wrath is provoked and incensed as much against you as against many of the damned in Hell. You hang by a slender thread, with the flames of divine wrath flashing about it, and ready every moment to singe it, and burn it asunder; and you have no interest in any Mediator, and nothing to lay hold of to save yourself, nothing to keep off the flames of wrath, nothing of your own, nothing that you ever have done, nothing that you can do, to induce God to spare you one moment....

How dreadful is the state of those that are daily and hourly in danger of this great wrath, and infinite misery! But this is the dismal case of every soul in this congregation, that has not been born again, however moral and strict, sober and religious, they may otherwise be. Oh that you would consider it, whether you be young or old. There is reason to think, that there are many in this congregation now hearing this discourse, that will actually be the subjects of this very misery to all eternity. We know not who they are, or in what seats they sit, or what thoughts they now have: it may be they are now at ease, and hear all these things without much disturbance, and are now flattering themselves that they are not the persons, promising themselves that they shall escape. If we knew that there was one person, and but one, in the whole congregation, that was to be the subject of this misery, what an awful thing would it be to think of! If we knew who it was, what an awful sight would it be to see such a person! How might all the rest of the congregation lift up a lamentable and bitter cry over him! But, alass! instead of one, how many is it likely will remember this discourse in Hell? And it would be a wonder if some that are now present, should not be in Hell in a very short time, before this year is out. And it would be no wonder if some person that now sits here in some seat of this meeting-house in health, and quiet & secure, should be there before tomorrow morning. Those of you that finally continue in a natural condition, that shall keep out of Hell longest, will be there in a little time! your damnation don't slumber; it will come swiftly, and, in all probability very suddenly upon many of you. You have reason to wonder, that you are not already in Hell. 'Tis doubtless the case of some that heretofore you have seen and known, that never deserved Hell more than you, and that heretofore appeared as likely to have been now alive as you: Their case is past all hope; they are crying in extreme misery and perfect despair; but here you are in the land of the living, and in the house of God, and have an opportunity to obtain salvation. What would not those poor damned, hopeless souls give for one day's such opportunity as you now enjoy!

And now you have an extraordinary opportunity, a day wherein Christ has flung the door of mercy wide open, and stands in the door calling and crying with a loud voice to poor sinners; a day wherein many are flocking to him, and pressing into the kingdom of God; many are daily coming from the East, West, North and South; many that were very lately in the same miserable condition that you are in, are now in an happy state, with their hearts filled with love to him that has loved them and washed them from their sins in his own blood, and rejoicing in hope of the glory of God. How awful is it to be left behind at such a day! To see so many others feasting, while you are pining and perishing! To see so many rejoycing and singing for joy of heart, while you have cause to mourn for sorrow of heart, and howl for vexation of spirit! How can you rest one moment in such a condition? Are not your souls as precious as the souls of the people at Suffield, where they are flocking from day to day to Christ?

Are there not many here that have lived long in the world, that are not to this day born again, and so are aliens from the commonwealth of Israel, and have done nothing ever since they have lived, but treasure up wrath against the day of wrath? Oh sirs, your case in an especial manner is extreamly dangerous; your guilt and hardness of heart is extreamly great. Don't you see how generally persons of your years are pass'd over and left, in the present remarkable & wonderful dispensation of God's mercy? You had need to consider your selves, and wake throughly out of sleep; you cannot bear the fierceness and wrath of the infinite God.

And you that are young men, and young women, will you neglect this precious season that you now enjoy, when so many others of your age are renouncing all youthful vanities, and flocking to CHRIST? You especially have now an extraordinary opportunity; but if you neglect it, it will soon be with you as it is with those persons that spent away all the precious days of youth in sin, and are now come to such a dreadful pass in blindness and hardness.

And you children that are unconverted, don't you know that you are going down to Hell, to bear the dreadful wrath of that God that is now angry with you every day, and every night? Will you be content to be the children of the Devil, when so many other children in the land are converted, and are become the holy and happy children of the King of Kings?

And let every one that is yet out of Christ, and hanging over the pit of Hell, whether they be old men and women, or middle aged, or young people, or little children, now hearken to the loud calls of God's word and providence. This acceptable year of the LORD, that is a day of such great favour to some, will doubtless be a day of as remarkable vengeance to others. Men's hearts harden, and their guilt increases apace at such a day as this, if they neglect their souls; and never was there so great danger of such persons being given up to hardness of heart, and blindness of mind. God seems now to be hastily gathering in his elect in all parts of the land; and probably the bigger part of adult persons that ever shall be saved, will be brought in now in a little time, and that it will be as it was on the great outpouring of the Spirit upon the Jews in the Apostles days, the election will obtain, and the rest will be blinded. If this should be the case with you, you will eternally curse this day, and will curse the day that ever you was born, to see such a season of the pouring out of God's spirit; and will wish that you had died and gone to Hell before you had seen it.

Now undoubtedly it is, as it was in the days of John the Baptist, the axe is in an extraordinary manner laid at the root of the trees, that every tree that brings not forth good fruit, may be hewen down, and cast into the fire.

Therefore let every one that is out of CHRIST, now awake and fly from the wrath to come. The wrath of Almighty God is now undoubtedly hanging over great part of this congregation: Let every one fly out of Sodom: *Haste and escape for your lives, look not behind you, escape to the mountain, least you be consumed.*

72 ISLAM AND THE LAST JUDGMENT

NINIAN SMART

Islam, founded in Arabia in the 7th century, is now a worldwide religion with more than one billion adherents. The term "Islam" is derived from the Semitic root "s-l-m," meaning primarily "peace" or secondarily "surrender," suggesting that peace comes to those who surrender to God. The scripture of Islam is the Quar'an (in English "Koran"), from an Arabic word *al-qur'an* meaning "a recitation."

The central claim of Islam is that "There is no god but God, and Muhammed is His Prophet." An adherent to Islam is known as a Muslim (in Arabic, one who submits), and Muslims submit to the will of God, praising God, praying five times daily, and seeking to act in accord with God's will. Those who act appropriately expect everlasting reward in heaven; those who act inappropriately anticipate everlasting punishment in hell.

More about the life of Muhammad, the Messenger of God, and about basic Islamic beliefs, including its visions of heaven and hell, is found in the next selection. Its author is Ninian Smart (1927–2001), a leading authority on the world's religions, who taught at the University of Lancaster and the University of California at Santa Barbara.

The few great urban cultures which existed in the Arabian peninsular had, by the sixth century A.D., fallen into decay…. The larger part of the Arabian population continued, or returned to, a nomadic existence—the life of the Bedouin in which still characterizes great areas of the Arab world. In the northwest part of the peninsula, the Hejaz, there were three towns of some importance—Taif, Mecca, and Medina. These, especially Mecca, formed commercial centers and staging

Ninian Smart, *The Religious Experience of Mankind*, Charles Scribner's Sons, 1969. Reprinted by permission of the publisher.

posts on the great caravan routes which straddled the desert. It was from Mecca that the Prophet of Islam, Muhammad, came.

Religious practices of this time were not altogether different from those of the Hebrews before Abraham. They combined polytheistic and animistic elements....

In addition to the religious influences of this polytheistic culture the Hejaz was exposed in some degree both to Christianity and Judaism. As early as the sixth century B.C. there had been Jewish settlements in the north. From the fourth century A.D. there was a large community in the Yemen, to the south. Perhaps half the population of Medina were Jewish, and much of the land, together with quite a lot of the craft work, was in the hands of the Jews. The Jews played a large part in the economic life of the country, and their prosperity contrasted with the relative poverty of the Arabs. Christians were active in Mecca, and both the Monophysite and Nestorian Churches had been moderately successful in proselytizing the people of the northern part of Arabia. The Monophysite Arabs, however, were frequently persecuted in the name of Christian orthodoxy. This was a factor in their later alienation from the Church and their acceptance of Islam....

It was against the milieu of this mixture of pagan religion and the teachings of both Judaism and Christianity that Muhammad began his mission. Born about A.D. 570, he belonged to the tribe of the Quraysh. His father died just before he was born, and he was brought up in the home of his grandfather. His father's name was Abdullah, meaning "slave of Allah." His grandfather's occupation—the giving of water from the sacred well of Zamzam created by command of Allah to gathering pilgrims—indicates that reverence for the high god of the polytheistic Arabs was part of his family tradition. The boy lived for two years in his grandfather's house, and when the grandfather died, he was transferred to the guardianship of his uncle. As a young man he was employed by a wealthy widow, Khadija, as superintendent of camels engaged in trade with Damascus. At the age of twenty-five he married Khadija, although she was fifteen years his senior. She had six children by him. Discounting the many legends that

grew up around his life, there is little else that we know about his early years, except the fact that he had contact with a certain Zayd, who remonstrated with him about his idolatry. Zayd may have been either a Christian or a Jewish convert, though Arabic sources report him as neither. In any case, he was an early influence on Muhammad's life and seems to have been the catalyst in turning him away from the polytheistic faith of most of his fellows.

Muhammad was of a specially religious disposition. It was his habit to go into the hills to practice prayer and meditation. At the age of forty, his dissatisfactions and his yearnings were resolved by a dramatic call which started him on his career as a prophet....

What was the nature of his message? First and foremost Muhammad preached the unity and majesty of the one God Allah. No longer was Allah to be regarded as a high god who lived in amity with other deities. He was unique. It was blasphemous to offer worship to any other being. He was, moreover, a righteous God who passed judgment on the sinner....

Yet for all the terrifying majesty of God as revealed to Muhammad in his prophetic experiences, Allah was also a merciful being. Though terrible to the unfaithful, and overwhelming in his glory to the pious, he was also loving and compassionate....

There is a strong analogy between the visions of the Old Testament prophets and those of Muhammad. The term *nabi*, which in the Hebrew scriptures is used as the word for prophet, was applied to Muhammad. Like his spiritual forebears in ancient Israel, Muhammad not only had some kind of direct acquaintance with the numinous power of God, which led him again and again to affirm Allah's uniqueness and majesty; he also spoke typically through a form of impassioned utterance which was framed in verse of religious power. Arabic poetry flowed from his lips during ecstasy, a phenomenon which was detected also among the Hebrew prophets. His strong insistence on righteousness and uprightness, and his condemnation of cheating and idolatry are reflections of the same ethical impulse which shaped the Jewish heritage. No doubt Muhammad was influenced by Christian and Jewish teaching, but his message was original and unique. This was why he preached a faith separate from, though sympathetic to Judaism and Christianity. It was a faith for Arabs, unfettered by the particularity of Jewish law. Christianity was suspect not merely because it seemed to compromise with idolatry and polytheism, but also because it was characterized by division and persecution....

The basic doctrines preached by Muhammad were simple and forceful. He said that there was but one God, Allah, and he, Muhammad, was his Prophet. He saw himself as the last in a line of prophets, and was the "seal of the prophets," for in him God's revelation reached finality. The line stretched from Moses down to Jesus. Belief in Muhammad's apostleship necessitated the recognition of the unerring nature of the Qur'an, which he claimed had originated in heaven. Below Allah there was a range of angelic beings who carried out his behests. But these angels were, as in Christian belief, creatures, and in no way were to be considered divine or supernatural in their own right. Among angels, one had fallen, Iblis (derived from the Greek word *Diabolos*). He and his agents often obstructed the work of the faithful. But this was within the limits laid down by Allah.

The omnipotence of Allah was so strongly stressed in the Qur'an that not only did Allah guide the faithful to the truth, but in some sense also he led the wicked astray. This theology was not fully worked out in the scripture itself. The Arabic term meaning "to lead astray" does not quite have the positive significance which the English translation suggests. It was rather a matter of letting people lose their way. Nevertheless, it was ultimately the will of Allah which controlled man's destiny. In an important sense it was Allah who destined men either to salvation or to damnation. This was in line with the most obvious emphasis throughout Muhammad's teachings on the oneness of God and on his majesty and power.

As in later Judaism and Christianity, there was belief in a Last Judgment, in which men's deeds would be weighed and assigned either to heaven or to hell. Both these regions were described in extremely vivid terms. The inmates of hell would be covered with fire, and would beseech those in paradise to pour cooling water on them. But the fire would be unsparing. Angels presiding over the torment would also be relentless. The sinners would eat the fruit of a strange tree which rose up from the bottom of hell, and it would boil up like oil in their bellies. On the other hand, the righteous would enter a region where there were gardens and fountains, and they would be clothed in beautiful raiment. Delicious food and wine would be served to them by celestial youths as they reclined at their ease on couches. And dark-eyed maidens too would wait on their commands —fresh and delightful mates. Thus the contrast between the two fates, when the dreaded last trumpet sounded, was violently drawn. This eschatology reinforced the insistence on serving Allah through righteous and just behavior. It was also an important factor in the faith and courage that animated the warriors of Islam. Death would be rewarded by something more splendid than plunder and power. Disloyalty would be punished by something worse than earthly torture and execution. Good and evil stood out in stark distinction. The judgment of Allah, though inscrutable, was foreshadowed in his acceptance and guidance of the faithful.

73 THE PROBLEM OF HELL

MARILYN McCORD ADAMS

Some may view the infinite rewards of heaven as undeserved by those who have performed only finite acts of goodness, but far more upsetting to most is that in hell finite wickedness receives infinite punishment. How can any finite evil, no matter how terrible, merit never-ending suffering? In the next selection, this question is addressed by Marilyn McCord Adams, whose work we read previously. Although herself an Episcopal priest, she finds the doctrine of hell to be unacceptable.

Since the 1950s, syllabi in analytic philosophy of religion have given the problem of evil pride of place. So-called atheologians have advanced as an argument against the existence of God the alleged logical incompossibility of the statements

I. God exists, and is essentially omnipotent, omniscient, and perfectly good

and

II. Evil exists.

The decision of Christian philosophers to reply from a posture of "defensive apologetics" and to let their (our) opponents define the value terms has carried both costs and benefits. For if it has limited the store of valuables available as defeaters of evil, it has also restricted the range of ills to be accounted for, to the ones secular philosophers believe in.

In my judgment, this bargain has proved bad, because it has been a distraction from the most important dimensions of the problem of evil. If what is fundamentally at stake—for David Hume and ... for Christian philosophers—is the consistency of *our* beliefs, then *our* value theory is the one that should come into play.... Moreover, the agreement to try to solve the problem by exclusive appeal to this world's (i.e., non-transcendent, created) goods has been curiously correlated with a reluctance to confront this world's worst evils (viz., horrors participation in which seems *prima*

facie to suffice to ruin individual lives). The best-of-all-possible-worlds and free-will approaches try to finesse the existence of the worst evils by operating at a vague and global level. Elsewhere I have urged Christian philosophers to renounce secular value parsimony, to reach under the lid of our theological treasure chest for the only good big enough to defeat horrendous evils—viz., God Himself![1] On the other hand, our refusal to trade with our own store of valuables has allowed us to avoid dealing publicly with our own dark side.[2] For even if, as I argue, this-worldly horrors can be given positive meaning through integration into an overall beatific relation of loving intimacy with God, what about the postmortem evil of hell, in which the omnipotent creator turns effectively and finally against a creature's good?

My own view is that hell poses the principal problem of evil for Christians. Its challenge is so deep and decisive, that to spill bottles of ink defending the logical compossibility of (I) with this-worldly evils while holding a closeted belief that

III. Some created persons will be consigned to hell forever

is at best incongruous and at worst disingenuous. My purpose here is to engage the problem of hell at two levels: a theoretical level, concerning the logical compossibility of (I) and (III); and a pragmatic level, concerning whether or not a God

From "The Problem of Hell: A Problem of Evil for Christians," in *Reasoned Faith: Essays in Philosophical Theology in Honor of Norman Kretzmann*, ed. Eleonore Stump, Cornell University Press, 1993. Reprinted by permission of the publisher.

who condemned some of His creatures to hell could be a logically appropriate object of standard Christian worship. My own verdict is no secret: statement (III) should be rejected in favor of a doctrine of universal salvation.

1. THE PROBLEM, FORMULATED

1.1. Theoretical Dimension

The argument for the logical incompossibility of (I) with (III), mimics that for (I) with (II):

1. If God existed and were omnipotent, He would be able to avoid (III).
2. If God existed and were omniscient, He would know how to avoid (III).
3. If God existed and were perfectly good, He would want to avoid (III).
4. Therefore, if (I), not (III).

Obviously, the soundness of this argument depends on the construals given to the attribute terms and to 'hell'. As just noted, there is an important disanalogy between this and the parallel argument for the general problem of evil: viz., that if 'evil' takes on varying extensions in different value theories, nevertheless, (II) gets its bite from the fact that most people agree on a wide range of actually extant evils. By contrast, (III) enjoys no straightforward empirical support but rests on and must be in the first instance interpreted by the authorities that tell us so. Tradition counts Scripture among the witnesses. For example, the Gospel according to Matthew speaks in vivid imagery of the disobedient and unfaithful being "cast into outer darkness" where there is "weeping and gnashing of teeth" (Matt. 13:42, 50; 22:13) or being thrown into the "unquenchable fire" "prepared for the devil and all his angels" (Matt. 13:42, 50; 18:8–9; 22:13; cf. 3:10). Cashing the metaphors, it says of Judas that it would have been better for him never to have been born (Matt. 26:24). Mainstream medieval theology took such pictures at face value. Duns Scotus is typical in understanding that the reprobate will be forever given over to their guilt[3] and the torment of their inordinate appetites, deprived of both natural and supernatural happiness, and

made to suffer perpetual fiery torture, which distracts their intellects so much that they can think of nothing else.[4]

Likewise, we can distinguish an *abstract* from a *concrete* version of the problem, depending on whether "some created persons" in statement (III) ranges over persons created in utopian antemortem environments and circumstances or only over persons in circumstances with combinations of obstacles and opportunities such as are found in the antemortem life experiences of persons in the actual world. Since the doctrine of hell is asserted by many Christians to be not merely logically possible but true, faith that embraces both (I) and (III) and seeks understanding will not complete its task unless it faces the concrete as well as the abstract version of the problem.

Premiss (1) is true because an omnipotent creator could altogether refrain from making any persons or could annihilate created persons any time He chose; either way, He could falsify (III). Again, many traditional theologians (e.g., Augustine, Duns Scotus, Ockham, Calvin) have understood divine sovereignty over creation—both nature and soteriology—to mean that nothing (certainly not creatures' rights) binds God as to what soteriological scheme (if any) He establishes. For example, God could have had a policy of not preserving human persons in existence after death, or He could have legislated temporary reform school followed by life in a utopian environment for all sinners. In these, and many other ways, God could avoid (III), and such was within His power.[5]

Likewise, (3) would be true if "perfectly good" is construed along the lines of person-relative goodness:

'God is good to a created person p' iff [if and only if] God guarantees to p a life that is a great good to p on the whole, and one in which p's participation in deep and horrendous evils (if any) is defeated within the context of p's life',

where

'Evil is horrendous' iff 'Participation in e by p (either as a victim or a perpetrator) gives everyone *prima facie* reason to believe that p's life cannot—given its inclusion of e—be a great good to p on the whole'.

The traditional hell is a paradigm horror, one which offers not merely prima facie but conclusive reason to believe that the life of the damned cannot be a great good to them on the whole. Any person who suffers eternal punishment in the traditional hell will, on the contrary, be one within whose life good is engulfed and/or defeated by evils.

For all we know, however, (3) may be false if divine goodness is evaluated in relation to God's role as producer of global goods. It is at least epistemically possible that (III) be true of a world that exhibits maximum variety with maximum unity or of a very good world that displays the best balance of moral good over moral evil which God could weakly actualize.[6] And in general, it is epistemically possible that the world have a maximally good overall order and still include the horrors of damnation for some created persons. Aquinas rationalizes this conclusion when he explains that since the purpose of creation is to show forth God's goodness, some must be damned to manifest his justice and others saved to advertise His mercy.[7]

1.2. Pragmatic Implications

The pragmatic consequences of reconciling (I) with (III) by restricting divine goodness to its global dimension are severe. First of all, this assumption makes human life a bad bet. Consider (adapting John Rawls's device) persons in a preoriginal position, surveying possible worlds containing managers of varying power, wisdom, and character, and subjects with diverse fates. The subjects are to answer, from behind a veil of ignorance as to which position they would occupy, the question whether they would willingly enter a given world as a human being. Reason would, I submit, render a negative verdict already for worlds whose omniscient and omnipotent manager permits antemortem horrors that remain undefeated within the context of the human participant's life and a fortiori for worlds some or most of whose human occupants suffer eternal torment.[8]

Second, it would make pragmatically inconsistent any worship behavior that presupposes that God is good to the worshipper or to created persons generally. For given the traditional assumption that the identity of the elect is secret, so much

so that there are no certain (or even very probabilifying) empirical signs by means of which humans can make an antemortem distinction between the saved and the damned, actual created persons are left to worry about whether this latter "fate-worse-than-death" is theirs. Nor would the knowledge that *we* were among the elect greatly relieve our pragmatic difficulty, given Christ's command to love our neighbors as ourselves.

If (III) were true, open-eyed worship would have to be of a God who mysteriously creates some persons for lives so horrendous on the whole and eternally, that it would have been better for them never to have been born, of a God who is at worst cruel (not that He had any obligation to be otherwise) and at best indifferent to our welfare. Christian Stoicism practices a species of such worship, one in which the believer (i) recognizes his or her insignificant place in the universe and (ii) by a series of spiritual exercises humbly accepts it (thereby submitting to God's inscrutable will), (iii) praises its Maker for His world-organizing activity, and (iv) finds dignity in this capacity for self-transcendence. Some even speak of divine love for them, in making them parts of His cosmic order and endowing them with the capacity for dignity, even when they are crushed by it. But the fact of such love carries no implication that God is *good to* them in the sense defined in section 1.1.[9] Notice, however, that Stoic worship that is honest (i.e., not based on denial and repression) is very difficult, indeed psychologically impossible for many, perhaps most, people. Avoiding pragmatic inconsistency requires vigilance against smuggling in the assumption to which none would be epistemically entitled, that after all God does care for me!

2. FREE WILL AND THE PROBLEM OF HELL

Many Christians find the Stoic bullet hard to bite but insist that it is unnecessary even if (III) is true. Mounting a kind of free-will defense, they claim that God has done a good thing in making incompatibilist free creatures. Like any good governor or parent, He has established a set of general conditional decrees, specifying sanctions and rewards for various sorts of free actions. His preference ("antecedent" or "perfect" will) is that everyone should be saved, but He has given us scope to work out our own destinies. Damnation would never happen but for the errant action of incompatibilist free creatures within the framework of divine regulations. It is not something God *does*, but rather allows; it is neither God's means, nor His end, but a middle-known but unintended side effect of the order He has created. Thus, (3) is true only regarding God's antecedent but not His all-things-considered preferences, and the incompossibility argument (in section 1.1) fails....

... I maintain that damnation is a horror that exceeds our conceptual powers. For even if we could experience for a finite period of time some aspect of hell's torments (e.g., the burning of the fire, deep depression, or consuming hatred) or heaven's bliss (e.g., St. Teresa's joyful glimpse of the Godhead), we are unavoidably unable to experience their cumulative effect in advance and so unable more than superficially to appreciate what is involved in either. It follows that human agents are unavoidably unable to exercise their free choice with fully open eyes....

Where soteriology is concerned, Christians have traditionally disagreed about human nature along two parameters. First, some hold that human nature was created in ideal condition and placed in a utopian environment: i.e., that *ab initio* humans had enough cognitive and emotional maturity to grasp and accurately apply relevant normative principles, while (on the occasion of their choice) their exercise of these abilities was unobstructed by unruly passions or external determinants of any kind. Others maintain, on the contrary, that humans are created immature and grow to adult competence through a messy developmental process. Second, where salvation is concerned, some take the human race collectively, while others consider humans individualistically. According to the Augustinian doctrine of the fall, Adam and Eve began as ideal agents in utopian Eden. The consequence of their sin is not only individual but collective: agency impaired by "ignorance" (clouded moral judgment) and "difficulty" (undisciplined emotions), which passes from the first parents to the whole family of their descendants. In his earlier works, Augus-

tine insists that despite such inherited handicaps, the reprobate still bring damnation on themselves, because God has offered help sufficient to win the difficult struggle through faith in Christ.[10] In later ... works, Augustine abandons the idea that God confers on each fallen human grace sufficient for salvation; he concedes that damnation is the consequence of such divine omissions and Adam's original free choice to sin. Nevertheless, the damned deserve no pity, because the family collectively brought it on themselves through Adam's free choice of will.[11]...

For my own part, I reject the notion of a historical fall and read Genesis 2–3 ... as about the childhood of the human race. I deny not only that we human beings do have, but also that we ever had, ideal agency. Therefore, I conclude, that reasoning about it is relevant at most to the abstract and not to the concrete problem of hell.

By contrast, a realistic picture of human agency should recognize the following: (a) We human beings start life ignorant, weak, and helpless, psychologically so lacking in a self-concept as to be incapable of choice. (b) We learn to "construct" a picture of the world, ourselves, and other people only with difficulty over a long period of time and under the extensive influence of other non-ideal choosers. (c) Human development is the interactive product of human nature and its environment, and from early on we humans are confronted with problems that we cannot adequately grasp or cope with, and in response to which we mount (without fully conscious calculation) inefficient adaptational strategies. (d) Yet, the human psyche forms habits in such a way that these reactive patterns, based as they are on a child's inaccurate view of the world and its strategic options, become entrenched in the individual's personality. (e) Typically, the habits are unconsciously "acted out" for years, causing much suffering to self and others before (if ever) they are recognized and undone through a difficult and painful process of therapy and/or spiritual formation. (f) Having thus begun *immature*, we arrive at adulthood in a state of *impaired freedom*, as our childhood adaptational strategies continue to distort our perceptions and behavior. (g) We adults with impaired freedom are responsible for our choices, actions, and even the character molded by our unconscious adaptational strategies, in the sense that we are the *agent causes* of them. (h) Our assessments of moral responsibility, praise, and blame cannot afford to take this impairment into account, because we are not as humans capable of organizing and regulating ourselves in that finetuned a way. And so, except for the most severe cases of impairment, we continue to hold ourselves *responsible to one another*.[12]

Taking these estimates of human nature to heart, I draw two conclusions: first, that such impaired adult human agency is no more competent to be entrusted with its (individual or collective) eternal destiny than two-year-old agency is to be allowed choices that could result in its death or serious physical impairment; and second, that the fact that the choices of such impaired agents come between the divine creator of the environment and their infernal outcome no more reduces divine responsibility for the damnation than two-year-old agency reduces the responsibility of the adult caretaker. Suppose, for example, that a parent introduces a two-year-old child into a room filled with gas that is safe to breathe but will explode if ignited. Assume further that the room contains a stove with brightly colored knobs, which if turned will light the burners and ignite the gas. If the parent warns the child not to turn the knobs and leaves, whereupon the child turns the knobs and blows itself up, surely the child is at most marginally to blame, even if it knew enough to obey the parent, while the parent is both primarily responsible and highly culpable. Or suppose a terrorist announces his intention to kill one hundred citizens if anyone in a certain village wears a red shirt on Tuesday. The village takes the threat seriously, and everyone is informed. If some adult citizen slips up and wears his favorite red shirt on Tuesday, he will be responsible and culpable, but the terrorist who set up the situation will be much more culpable.

Once again, my further conclusion is not that God would (like the parent and the terrorist) be culpable if He were to insert humans into a situation in which their eternal destiny depended on their exercise of impaired agency, for I deny that God has any obligations to creatures.... Rather, God (like

the parent or the terrorist) would bear primary responsibility for any tragic outcomes,[13] and God would be cruel to create human beings in a world with combinations of obstacles and opportunities such as are found in the actual world and govern us under a scheme according to which whether or not we go to the traditional hell depends on how we exercise our impaired adult agency in this life—cruel, by virtue of imposing horrendous consequences on our all-too-likely failures....

I take the Bible seriously; indeed, as an Episcopal priest, I am sworn to the claim that "the Holy Scriptures of the Old and New Testaments" are "the Word of God" and "contain all things necessary to salvation"[14] ... I feel bound to weigh the tradition behind (III). I, too, pay my respects by identifying some deep truths expressed by the doctrine of hell. The first ... is that created persons have *no rights* against God, because God has *no obligations* to creatures: in particular, God has no obligation to be good to us; no obligation not to ruin us whether by depriving our lives of positive meaning, by producing or allowing the deterioration or disintegration of our personalities, by destroying our bodies, or by annihilating us. Second, the horrendous ruin of a created person represented by eternal torment in hell constitutes a (negative and mirror image) measure—perhaps the most vivid we can understand—of how *bad* it is, how utterly indecent, not to respond to God appropriately; and for all that, because of the radical incommensuration between God and creatures, the measure is inadequate.

Nevertheless, I have insisted in print for more than twenty years that the doctrine is false on its traditional construal, because neither the ontological gap between God and creatures nor the radical impropriety of our comportment toward God is a good indication of God's intentions and policies toward us. God does not stand on rights and obligations, nor does He treat us according to such "deserts".

As I see it, both the defenders of hell and I are confronted with a theological balancing act. The *prima facie* logical incompossibility of (I) and (III) and the accompanying pragmatic difficulties force us into a position of weighing some items of tradition more than others. Because I do not regard

Scripture as infallible on any interpretation, I do not feel bound to translate into theological assertion some of the apocalyptic imagery and plot lines of the New Testament. Nevertheless, I do not regard my universalist theology as un-Scriptural, because I believe the theme of definitive divine triumph is central to the Bible, is exemplified in Christ Jesus, and is the very basis of our Christian hope.

Surprisingly many religiously serious people reject the doctrine of universal salvation, on the pragmatic ground that it leads to moral and religious laxity. Withdraw the threat, and they doubt whether others—perhaps even they themselves—would sustain the motivation for moral diligence and religious observance.

My pastoral experience suggests, on the contrary, that the disproportionate threat of hell ... produces despair that masquerades as skepticism, rebellion, and unbelief. If your father threatens to kill you if you disobey him, you may cower in terrorized submission, but you may also (reasonably) run away from home....

4. THE RELEVANCE OF FEELINGS

... I want to close with a ... methodological contention ... that feelings are highly relevant to the problem of evil and to the problem of hell, because they are one source of information about how bad something is for a person. To be sure, they are not an infallible source. Certainly they are not always an articulate source. But they are *a* source. Where questions of value are concerned, reason is not an infallible source either. That is why so-called value calculations in abstraction from feelings can strike us as "cold" or "callous". I do not believe we have any infallible faculties at all. But our best shot at valuations will come from the collaboration of feelings and reason, the latter articulating the former, the former giving data to the latter.

... I invite anyone who agrees ... that the saved can in good conscience let their happiness be unaffected by the plight of the damned because the destruction of the latter is self-willed ... spend a week visiting patients who are dying of emphysema or of the advanced effects of alcoholism, to listen with sympathetic presence, to enter into their point of view on their lives, to face their pain and despair. Then ask whether one could in good conscience dismiss their suffering with, "Oh well, they brought it on themselves!"[15]

I do not think this is sentimental. Other than experiencing such sufferings in our own persons, such sympathetic entering into the position of another is the best way we have to tell what it would be like to be that person and suffer as they do, the best data we can get on how bad it would be to suffer that way. Nor is my thesis especially new. It is but an extension of the old Augustinian-Platonist point, that where values are concerned, what and how well you see depends not simply on how well you think, but on what and how well you love ... I borrow a point from Charles Hartshorne[16] when I suggest that sensitivity, sympathetic interaction, is an aspect of such loving, one that rightfully affects our judgment in ways we should not ignore.

NOTES

1. Cf. my article "Problems of Evil: More Advice to Christian Philosophers", *Faith and Philosophy* 5 (1988): 121–43; esp. pp. 135–37; and "Theodicy without Blame", *Philosophical Topics* 16 (1988): 215–45; esp. pp. 234–37.
2. The ability thus afforded has actually been cited as a strategic advantage by some Christian philosophers.
3. Duns Scotus, *Opus Oxoniense* in *Opera Omnia* (Paris: Vives, 1891), IV, d. 46, q. 4. n. 6; Wadding-Vives 20, 459.
4. Duns Scotus, *Op. Ox.* IV, d. 46, q. 4, n. 5; Wadding-Vives 20, 457.
5. Cf. my *William Ockham* (Notre Dame: University of Notre Dame Press, 1987), chap. 30, 1257–97; and "The Structure of Ockham's Moral Theory", *Franciscan Studies* 46 (1986): 1–35.
6. Alvin Plantinga takes this line in numerous discussions, in the course of answering J. L. Mackie's objection to the free-will defense, that God could have made sinless free creatures. Plantinga insists that, given incompatibilist freedom in creatures, God cannot strongly actualize any world He wants. It is logically possible that a world with evils in the amounts and of the kinds found in this world is the best that He could do, Plantinga argues, given His aim of getting some moral goodness in the world. See section 2.2 below.
7. Thomas Aquinas, *Summa theologica* I, q. 23, a. 5, ad 3.

8. Cf. my "Horrendous Evils and the Goodness of God," *Proceedings of the Aristotelian Society*, Supplementary Volume 63 (1989): 297–310; esp. 303.

9. Cf. Diogenes Allen, "Natural Evil and the God of Love," *Religious Studies* 16 (1980): 439–56.

10. Augustine, *De libero arbitrio*. Corpus Scriptorum Ecclesiasticorum Latinorum, vol. 74. (Vindobonae: Hoelder-Pichler-Tempsky, 1956), passim.

11. This position is especially clear in Augustine, *De gratia et libero arbitrio* (A.D. 426), and Augustine, *De correptione et gratus* (A.D. 426 or 427).

12. Cf. my "Theodicy without Blame," *Philosophical Topics* 16 (1988): pp. 231–32.

13. Contrary to what William Craig maintains, "'No Other Name': A Middle Knowledge Perspective on the Exclusivity of Salvation through Christ," *Faith and Philosophy* 6 (1989): pp. 176–77.

14. "The Ordination of a Priest," *The Book of Common Prayer* (1979), p. 526.

15. Years ago Rogers Albritton persuaded me, at the theoretical level, that some suffering is too bad for the guilty. My introspective and pastoral experience since then tells in the same direction.

16. Charles Hartshorne, *The Divine Relativity* (New Haven: Yale University Press, 1948, 1964), chap. 3, 116–58.

74   WHOM DOES GOD CONSIGN TO HELL?

STEPHEN C. DAVIS

Stephen C. Davis, Professor of Philosophy at Claremont McKenna College, maintains that hell exists and that some are condemned to it for eternity. He admits, however, that he does not know how a person can experience joy in heaven while a loved one is in hell. Nor does Davis see how, assuming as he does that salvation is found only in accepting Jesus, people who lived before the time of Jesus could have been condemned to hell for not believing in someone who hadn't yet lived. Davis is sure that God's scheme for salvation is just, but suggests that some matters lie beyond our present understanding.

Christianity traditionally teaches that at least some people, after death, live eternally apart from God. Let us call those who believe this doctrine *separationists*, because they hold that these people are eternally separated both from God and from the people who are with God. Some Christians, on the other hand, espouse the quite different doctrine known as *universalism*.[1] Universalists believe that all human beings will ultimately live eternally with God, i.e., that no one will be eternally condemned....

Though I am sympathetic with the intentions of those who espouse universalism, I am not a universalist myself, and will argue against the doctrine in this paper. What I will do here is: (1) state the strongest doctrine of universalism...; (2) present the strongest arguments in favor of it...; (3) reply to these arguments from a separationist standpoint; and (4) make a case for separationism....

Let me now sketch what I take to be a strong doctrine of universalism: God does indeed hate sin and does indeed judge sinners. But God's judgment is always therapeutic; it is designed to bring people to repentance. Thus God's wrath is an

From Stephen C. Davis, "Universalism, Hell, and the Fate of the Ignorant," *Modern Theology* 6 (1990). Reprinted by permission of Blackwell Publishers.

integral part of God's loving strategy for reconciling people to God. Some are reconciled to God in this life; some die unreconciled. But God continues to love even those who die apart from God, and to work for their reconciliation. If there is a hell, it exists only for a time, i.e., until the last recalcitrant sinner decides to say yes to God. It is *possible* that hell will exist forever because it is possible some will deny God forever. But after death, God has unlimited time, arguments, and resources to convince people to repent. God will not force anyone into the kingdom; the freedom of God's creatures is always respected. But because of the winsomeness of God's love, we can be sure that God will emerge victorious and that all persons will eventually be reconciled to God. We are all sinners and deserve punishment, but God's love is so great and God's grace so attractive that eventually all persons will be reconciled to God. This, then, is what I take to be a strong version of universalism. Now, what about the arguments in favor? Let me mention five of them.

1. *The Bible implies that universalism is true.* Many universalists are quite prepared to admit that their doctrine is not taught in the Bible and indeed that separationism seems much more clearly taught. Nevertheless, they do typically argue that universalism is at least implied or suggested in various texts. First, it can be pointed out that many texts show that it is God's intention that everyone be reconciled to God. Second, it can be shown that the work of God's grace in Christ was designed for the salvation of everyone. Third, texts can be cited in which God's total victory is proclaimed and in which it is said that everything will ultimately be reconciled to God. Finally, there are texts which seem to the universalists explicitly to predict that all will eventually be reconciled to God.[2]...

2. *How can God's purposes be frustrated?* Universalists sometimes argue as follows: eternal sin and eternal punishment would obviously frustrate God's intention that no one be eternally lost. But if God is truly sovereign, how can any divine intention be frustrated? If separationism is true, some will eternally resist God and it follows that god is at least a partial failure. Surely if God is omnipotent nothing can eternally frustrate the di-

vine aims; if it is God's aim that all be rescued, all *will* be rescued.[3]

3. *How can a just God condemn people to eternal torment?* Universalists frequently argue that no one deserves *eternal* punishment. Perhaps terrible sinners deserve to suffer terribly for a terribly long time. But surely sin should be punished according to its gravity; why do they deserve to suffer for an *infinitely* long time? They certainly do not cause anyone else (or even God) *eternal* sorrow or pain. Suppose we decide that some tyrant, say Nero, deserved to suffer a year in hell for every person he ever killed, injured, treated unfairly, insulted, or even inconvenienced. Suppose further that on this criterion he deserved to suffer for 20,000 years. The problem, however, is that once he has served this sentence he will not have made even the slightest dent in eternity. According to separationism, he must suffer forever. Is this just? It does not seem so. (And this is not even to speak of more run-of-the-mill sinners who perhaps never cause anyone serious harm.)

4. *How can the Blessed experience joy in heaven if friends and loved ones are in hell?* Obviously (so universalists will argue), they can't. People can only know joy and happiness in heaven if everyone else is or eventually will be there too. If the Blessed are to experience joy in heaven, as Christian tradition says they are, universalism must be true.

5. *What about the fate of those who die in ignorance of Christ?* Christianity has traditionally taught that salvation is to be found only in Christ. Jesus is reported as having claimed this very thing: "I am the way, and the truth, and the life; No one comes to the Father but by me" (John 14:6). And this claim seems to dovetail well with standard Christian notions about sin and salvation: there is nothing we can do to save ourselves; all our efforts at self-improvement fail; all we can do is trust in God as revealed in Christ; those who do not know God as revealed in Christ are condemned. And surely—so universalists argue—the traditional notion is unfair. It is not right to condemn to hell those who die in ignorance of Christ.

Suppose there was a woman named Oohku who lived from 370—320 b.c. in the interior of Borneo. Obviously, she never heard of Jesus

Christ or the Judeo-Christian God; she was never baptized, nor did she ever make any institutional or psychological commitment to Christ or to the Christian church. She *couldn't* have done these things; she was simply born in the wrong place and at the wrong time. Is it right for God to condemn this woman to eternal hell just because she was never able to come to God through Christ? Of course not. The only way Oohku can be treated fairly by God is if universalism is true. God is just and loving; thus, universalism is true.

These are the best arguments for universalism that I can think of. We now need to see how separationists will handle them and defend their own doctrine.

Let us begin with the biblical argument of the universalist.... My reply ... is as follows. It is true that when read in a certain way, a few New Testament and especially Pauline texts might lead one toward universalism. But a careful look shows that not even those texts actually imply universalism. Furthermore, biblically oriented Christians believe that problematical passages on any topic are to be interpreted in the light of the testimony of the whole of scripture, and universalism ... is inconsistent with that testimony.

Let me confess that I would deeply like universalism to be true. Like all Christians, I would find it wonderfully comforting to believe that all people will be citizens of the kingdom of God, and certain thorny intellectual problems, especially the problem of evil, might be easier to solve if universalism were true.[4] But as a matter of theological method, we cannot affirm a doctrine just because we would like it to be true. The fact is that separationism is taught in the Bible and that the so-called "universalistic passages" do not imply universalism. That is enough for me; that is why I am a separationist. Philosophical and theological arguments over what God should do are outweighed by the teaching of Scripture. God has revealed to us a doctrine of eternal judgment; we had best accept it. That God has not also revealed to us how to reconcile this doctrine with our understanding of God's love creates a theological problem which we must do our best to solve.

I will now briefly sketch the separationist doctrine I believe in and am prepared to defend. It differs from some traditional theological accounts at two points: (1) For exegetical reasons I do not believe people in hell suffer horrible fiery agony; and (2) while I believe hell in some sense can be spoken of as punishment, I do not believe it is a place where God, so to speak, gets even with those who deny God. It is not primarily a place of retribution.

We know little about hell. Much of what the New Testament says is clearly metaphorical or symbolic. For example, the New Testament uses the metaphor of fire to convey the suffering of people in hell. But this need not mean that condemned people actually suffer the pain of burns. Mark 9:48 describes hell as a place where "the worm does not die" and "the fire is not quenched." Why take the second literally and not the first? I would say both are metaphors of the eternality of hell. The parable of the rich man and Lazarus in Luke 16:19–31 has been taken by some interpreters as a picture of the after-life, but this does not seem sensible. It is a parable, i.e., a made-up story designed to convey a certain religious message. Furthermore, it is difficult to imagine that heaven and hell could be separated by a "great chasm" which cannot be crossed but across which communication can take place. There are many biblical metaphors for hell, e.g., everlasting fire, bottomless pit, outer darkness, place of weeping and gnashing of teeth, place of no rest, place where the uttermost farthing must be paid.[5] None, I would argue, is a literal description.

Hell is a place of separation from God. Not a total separation, of course—that would mean hell would not exist. Furthermore, the biblical tradition denies that anything or anyone can ever be totally separated from God.... But hell is separation from God as the source of true love, joy, peace, and light. It is not a place of agony, torment, torture, and utter horror (here I am opposing the lurid and even sadistic pictures of hell envisioned by some Christian thinkers). But there is no deep or ultimate joy there and I believe its citizens are largely miserable. To be apart from the source of love, joy, peace, and light is to live miserably.

Why are the damned in hell? I have already ruled out retribution or any notion of God's "getting even" with them.[6] To put it radically, I believe they are in hell because they choose to be in hell; no one is sent to hell against his or her will.[7] Sadly, some people choose to live their lives apart from God, harden their hearts, and will continue to do so after death; some will doubtless do so forever. For such people, living in God's presence might well seem worse than living in God's absence. Allowing them to live forever in hell is simply God's continuing to grant them the freedom that they enjoyed in this life to say yes or no to God. I nevertheless suspect that people in hell are deeply remorseful. Can people both freely choose hell over heaven, knowing they would be unable to endure heaven, but still be full of remorse that they cannot happily choose heaven? I believe this is quite possible.

Is the existence of hell consistent with God's love and power? Yes, it is. Some Christians try to justify the existence of hell by speaking of it as the "natural consequence" of a life of sin.[8] I accept the notion that hell is the natural consequence of a life of sin (and it is in this sense that hell is a punishment). But this in itself does not justify God in sending people to hell, for it does not justify the divinely–ordained laws of natural necessity that make hell sin's natural consequence. I claim, then, that the people who are in hell are there because they freely choose it, i.e., freely choose not to live in God's presence. If so, then hell can be an expression not only of divine justice but of divine love.

I have been replying to the biblical argument of the universalist. Now I must comment on the others.

How can God's purposes be frustrated? I agree that God desires the salvation of everyone; thus separationism implies that at least one of God's desires is not satisfied: some people will be lost. How can this be, if God is sovereign? The answer is that God created us as free agents; God gave us the ability to say yes or no to God. One of the risks God ran in so doing was precisely that God's purposes *would* be frustrated, and this,

sadly, is exactly what has happened. God's will is flaunted whenever anyone sins. It is just not true that "God's will is always done." (Otherwise, why did Jesus teach his disciples to pray, "May your will be done on earth as it is in heaven"—as if God's will is not always done on earth?) Furthermore, it seems that sovereignty entails only *the power* to impose one's will, not the actual imposition of it.

How can a just God condemn someone to eternal torment? In the first place, as already noted, I believe the citizens of hell are there because they freely choose to be there; they have hardened their hearts and would be unable to endure heaven. Unless one bows to God and makes the divine will one's own, heaven is too much to bear and one chooses hell. Thus, as I noted, it is not only just but loving that God allows them to live forever in hell. Second, hell may have the effect on many of strengthening their resolve never to repent; sin may voluntarily continue; and if it is right for evil-doers to experience the consequences of the evil deeds they do here and now, this will be true of the evil deeds they do after death. Third, Christians believe their salvation is a matter of grace alone; we deserve to be condemned, but out of love rather than sheer justice God forgives us and reconciles us to God. The notion of grace, then, is at the heart of the Christian good news. God loves us though we are unlovable; God accepts us though we are unacceptable. But the thing to notice here is that if separationism is inconsistent with God's love, i.e., if a loving God cannot condemn anyone to hell, then our salvation (i.e., our rescue from hell) is no longer a matter of grace; it becomes a matter of our justly being freed from a penalty we don't really deserve. In the end, universalism overturns the Christian notion of grace.

How can the Blessed be joyous if friends and loved ones are in hell? I do not know an adequate answer to this question. I expect that if I knew enough about heaven I would know the answer, but I know little about heaven. The problem is perhaps less acute for me than for those separationists who believe hell is a place of permanent torture. If I am right, the Blessed need not worry that loved ones are in agony and are allowed to hope (see below) that God's love can even yet achieve a reconciliation. But there is still the question how, say, a wife can experience joy and happiness in heaven while her beloved husband is in hell. And that is the question I am unable to answer satisfactorily. It would seem to be unjust for God to allow the wrong choices of the damned—i.e., their rejection of God—to ruin the joy of the Blessed, who have chosen to love God. But how God brings it about that the Blessed experience the joy of the presence of God despite the absence of others, I do not know.

What about the fate of those who die in ignorance of Christ? The main point to note here is that the Bible does not speak in any connected or clear way on this question. Biblical Christians must take seriously those exclusivistic sayings of Jesus and the New Testament writers ... that create for us this problem. As an orthodox Christian, then, I do believe that salvation is to be found only in Christ. If any person at any time in this life or the next is ever reconciled to God, it is because of the saving work of Jesus Christ. His life, death, and resurrection made it possible. If I am somehow to be reconciled to God, if our imaginary friend Oohku is somehow to be reconciled to God, it is only through Christ that it happens.[9]

Some Christians have taken to heart the Bible's exclusivistic sayings and have concluded that people like Oohku must be lost, that their eternal destiny is hell. But this is to confuse the claim that the Bible is authoritative on matters of faith and practice with the claim that the Bible authoritatively tells us everything we might want to know about Christian faith and practice. It doesn't; I believe the Bible tells us enough so that we can read it, be convicted of sin, and learn how to come to God through Christ. But it does not answer all the questions we might want to ask it and it certainly does not say or imply that those who die in ignorance of Christ are lost. The Bible simply does not in any direct or thorough way address itself to the precise issue of the fate of people like Oohku. The Bible tells us what we *need* to know, not all that we might *want* to know.

What then must the separationist say about the fate of those who die in ignorance of Christ? Again, there is no clear or connected teaching in the Bible on this question; what we find are some vague and unformulated hints which can perhaps guide us but which cannot be used to justify a dogmatic position.... I am quite convinced that this much is true—God can indeed make us in any way God pleases and we have no authority over God to challenge this decision. But this by itself does not answer the question of the fate of those who die in ignorance of Christ.

I have also heard the following argument in favor of the claim that it is just for God to send the ignorant to hell: "We are *all* sinners and thus we *all* deserve hell. Thus *no one* is sent to hell who does not deserve hell. It is just that God has graciously allowed or elected some sinners to receive the unmerited gift of salvation. Like everyone else, Oohku deserves to go to hell, so she has no reason to complain when she is sent there." But the answer to this argument is that the described scheme is still radically unjust. Surely it is unfair to those who were not chosen to receive God's grace. Suppose I discover that my two sons are both equally guilty of some wrong—say they both trampled some of my wife's beloved roses in the back yard. And suppose I say to one of them: "You are guilty and your punishment is that you will be confined to your room." And suppose I say to the other one: "You are equally guilty, but as a gift of love, I'm going to let you go without punishment." Surely it is obvious on the face of it that I have been unfair....

Is there, then, any way for the problem of the ignorant to be solved in separationist terms? Here are three assumptions that underlie the position I will take: (1) the Bible does not tell us everything we might want to know about God and the divine will; (2) all people who are reconciled to God are reconciled to God through Christ; (3) it would be unfair for God to condemn the ignorant to hell because they do not believe in Christ. These assumptions push me in the direction of a theological conjecture: that there are ways those who are ignorant of Christ can be reconciled to God through Christ. In other words, if redemption is to be found only in Christ, and if the atoning work of Christ was intended for all people, and if God is loving and just, then it seems sensible to suppose that it must be causally possible for all people, wherever or whenever they live or however ignorant they are, to come to God through Christ. (I would like to stress that this is a conjecture, not a dogma or a teaching or even a firm belief.) …

As long as it is recognized that these are conjectures without systematic or clear biblical warrant, we might even suggest that Christ has the power to save human beings *wherever* they are, even in hell.[10] I recognize some will resist this suggestion. It is one thing—they will say—to suggest that the ignorant after death receive a chance (their first) to respond positively to the gospel. But it is quite another to suggest that those who have been condemned receive *other* chances to respond positively. But a question must be asked here: Is it possible that there are persons who would respond positively to God's love after death even though they have not responded positively to it before death? I believe this is possible. In fact, one reason for this latest conjecture is the observation that some who hear the gospel hear it in such a way that they are psychologically unable to respond positively. Perhaps they heard the gospel for the first and only time from a fool or a bigot or a scoundrel. Or perhaps they were caused to be prejudiced against Christianity by skeptical parents of teachers. Whatever the reason, I believe it would be unjust of God to condemn those who did indeed hear the good news but were unable to respond positively. This is why I suggest that even in hell, people can be rescued.[11]

Does this bring in universalism by the back door? Certainly not. I have little doubt some will say no to God eternally (the Bible predicts this, in fact), nor do I see any need for a "second chance" for those who have freely and knowingly chosen in this life to live apart from God. Perhaps God never gives up on people, but some folk seem to have hardened their heart to such a degree that they will never repent. For such people, hell as separation from God exists forever, just as it exists for them

now. But perhaps some who die in ignorance of Christ will hear the good news, repent, and be rescued. Perhaps even some citizens of hell will do so too. Again, the key word is *perhaps*. We have no ground to dogmatize here. I do not think we *know* the fate of those who die in ignorance of Christ. All I am sure of is that God's scheme for the salvation of human beings will turn out to have been just, perhaps in ways we cannot now understand.

NOTES

1. Among recent and contemporary Christians, Nicholas Berdyaev, William Temple, C. H. Dodd, Nels Ferre, William Barclay, J. A. T. Robinson, and John Hick have all defended some form of universalism. Karl Barth has been accused of espousing the doctrine.

2. First point: see Romans 11:32, I Timothy 2:4–6, II Peter 3:9. Second point: II Corinthians 5:14, 15; Titus 2:11; Hebrews 2:9; 1 John 2:2. Third point: see I Corinthians 15:22; cf. 23–28; II Corinthians 5:19; Colossians 1:19. Fourth point: see Romans 5:18; Philippians 2:9–11; John 1:29; 3:17; 12:32, 47.

3. See, for example, J. A. T. Robinson, *In the End, God* (London: James Clarke and Co., 1950), p. 107.

4. As, above all, John Hick has seen. See *Evil and the God of Love* (London: Macmillan and Co., 1966), pp. 98, 113–120, 183, 377–381.

5. Respectively: Matthew 25:41, Revelation 9:2, Matthew 8:12, Revelation 14:11, Matthew 5:26.

6. It must be admitted that there are New Testament texts that can be taken to imply that hell is an act of vengeance or retribution on sinners. See Matthew 5:22, 29; 8:12; 10:15; II Thessalonians 1:6–9; Hebrew 2:2–3; 10:28–31; II Peter 2:4–9, 12–13. Some even seem to suggest degrees of punishment corresponding to degrees of guilt. See Matthew 11:22–24; Luke 12:47–48; 20:47.

7. "To choose finally and for ever—unfathomable mystery of iniquity—to say 'No' to Jesus is to be held in a hell of one's own choosing and making. It is not God who makes hell, for hell is the contradiction of all that is God." T. F. Torrance, "Universalism or Election?" *Scottish Journal of Theology*, Vol. 2, No. 3 (September, 1949). p. 317.

8. See John Wenham, *The Goodness of God* (Down-er's Grove, Illinois: Inter-Varsity Press, 1974), p. 38fn, and P.T. Geach, *Providence and Evil* (Cambridge: Cambridge University Press, 1977), pp. 128, 138–140, 147.

9. As suggested by C. S. Lewis in *The Great Divorce* (New York: The Macmillan Company, 1957), pp. 120–124.

10. A suggestion also perhaps made (in literary form) by C. S. Lewis in *The Great Divorce.*

11. See Revelation 21:25, where the city of God is described as follows: "Its gates shall never be shut by day—and there shall be no night there."

75 DIVINE JUSTICE

GEORGE N. SCHLESINGER

Doesn't luck play a role in a person's chances for being welcomed into heaven or banished to hell? Do not uncontrollable features of a life, such as where or when one is born, offer some individuals advantages and place other people at a disadvantage? If so, isn't Divine justice unfair? George N. Schlesinger, Professor of Philosophy at the University of North Carolina at Chapel Hill, seeks to explain how God can equalize opportunities for salvation among those who have lived in unequal circumstances.

[I]t would be incompatible with Divine justice for any individual to suffer a loss due to his failure to conduct himself religiously, in case his lack of faith was not entirely a result of his freely willed choice but due to accidental, external circumstances. This implies that all human beings are entitled to be given the same opportunities and that access to convincing evidence for theism should be equally available to all, and not vary with an individual's accidental circumstances. Suppose I am a non-believer who has remained unconvinced by the various proofs for God's existence I have read or heard. There is, however, a new argument which would appeal to me so much that it would most likely convert me to theism. It so happens that I never get the chance to gain knowledge of the argument and thus persist in my ungodly ways. Is it not grossly unfair that, owing to circumstances beyond my control, I should be deprived of the sublime felicity I could have shared with the

righteous? Furthermore, should any of the truly convincing proofs be particularly ingenious and complex ... then it would require a high degree of intelligence to understand them. It is very hard to reconcile with an elementary sense of fairness ... that those capable of mastering elaborate logical arguments stand a much better chance of attaining spiritual salvation than their less fortunately endowed fellow beings. In addition, of course, concerning any novel proof that may have been lately constructed, we may well wonder about all the previous generations who were not lucky enough to survive and have the chance to be informed of such proofs which could have saved them.

[O]ur problem cannot be disposed of ... easily.... Let us consider, for instance, an individual who has grown up in a pagan society surrounded by people wholly devoted to the advancement of hedonistic objectives and to

From George N. Schlesinger, *New Perspectives on Old-Time Religion*, Oxford University Press, 1988. Reprinted by permission of the publisher.

whom transcendent spiritual values are entirely unknown. Such an individual may never have had the opportunity even to hear about the idea of monotheism and its demands for altruism, self-restraint, and the pursuit of piety. Can it be reasonable to condemn him as one who has freely chosen a Godless way of life, and to claim that his lack of belief is definitely the result of his wilfully averting his eyes from the evidence all around him that clearly points to theism? Any reasonably well-informed person would have to agree that this is an unjustifiable charge. After all, it is sensible to assume that basic human nature does not vary with geographic, climatic, or politico-economic circumstances, and that it has been fairly constant for the last couple of thousand years. Yet we find that in some societies—e.g. medieval Europe—nearly everyone takes theism for granted, while in others—e.g. in ancient Babylon—hardly a single individual subscribes to it. Surely, this is a strong enough indication that it is not solely a function of a person's goodwill whether he commits himself to religious belief; to a considerable extent also it is a function of the nature of the human environment into which he happens to be born. The climate of opinion prevailing during the formative years of a person's life is a crucial factor in determining what he will find rational, well supported by evidence, and credible.

The conclusion seems inescapable that an individual is not fully autonomous in the choice of beliefs he will adopt.... It will at least have to be conceded that there are extreme circumstances in which all the factors acting upon an individual conspire to make him unable to arrive at religious belief, and therefore, he can indeed not be charged with having willed himself into a state of disbelief. What then is going to be the ultimate fate of such an individual? It seems reasonable to suggest that Divine fairness requires that he should not be permitted to suffer the disadvantages normally entitled by Godless life; we should expect him to be granted the salvation usually set aside for the righteous.

It seems, however, that such a position is not compatible with perfect fairness either. For suppose I have grown up in a society fully permeated with religious ideas, surrounded by firmly believing pious people, in circumstances which preclude any acceptable excuse for not making use of the many opportunities to see the strong case for religion—and I actively repress all inclination to contemplate the desirability of embracing religious belief. As we have said earlier, I would be held responsible for wilfully closing my eyes to the truth and would consequently forfeit my right to salvation. Yet in another world, where all my characteristics and predilections are identical to those I possess in the actual world, except that I am born into ancient Babylonian society where I behave precisely as I do now, I will not have to suffer any loss for my ungodly behaviour my exclusive devotion to materialism, and my pursuit of sensual pleasures. Thus it would follow that the question of how I am going to fare, with respect to the most important good available to humans may depend on circumstances entirely outside my control, on the accident of my birth and on whether I happen to be living in this or that kind of society....

The correct answer, however, will become apparent once we realize two points, both of which are of fundamental importance to religious thought. The first point is that there are no circumstances under which an individual living upon this earth has absolute freedom to choose any complete set of beliefs; such beliefs are to a certain degree imposed upon him by the ideas prevailing in his environment and implanted into his mind by his upbringing. At the same time, there are virtually no conditions, either, under which he has no freedom whatever. No matter how strong and uniform the views held by the members of his society, a person will always have a certain amount of scope left for asserting his intellectual autonomy and for deviating to some degree from the ideology in which he happens to be immersed. The second important point is that the true amount of virtue embodied in a given individual is not determined by the absolute level of piety he has reached, but by the nature of the hostile circumstances he has had to contend with in order to raise himself to the level he has succeeded in attaining. It is common knowledge that even in a spiritually depraved society not every individual sinks to the same low level of turpitude; there do exist a number of nobler souls with some vestiges of spiritual aspirations who have a slight intimation of the possibilities for more elevated pursuits. Admittedly, even the finest members of such a society are likely to fail in their uphill struggle and will never acquire an articulate belief in theism; they may nevertheless be justifiably regarded as having covered a considerable distance in that direction by virtue of the unselfish acts they have occasionally performed, and by virtue of their heavenward gropings fuelled by their spiritual quest, however dimly perceived. Even in an environment that contains only factors that tend to eradicate religious sentiments from an individual's heart, it is by no means the case that a uniform level of crude hedonism prevails. There will be those who will not allow their inner voice to be completely drowned out by all the external noise and will lift themselves, so to speak, by their own spiritual boot straps to a level above the norm—that is, to a high altitude, relatively speaking. Now it makes good sense to assume that the measure of religious refinement is essentially the function of the magnitude of the struggle required in order to acquire the degree of piety one ultimately attains.... [T]he future bliss of the righteous varies with the measure to which the soul has been perfected to be attuned to receiving it. It follows therefore that those precious individuals who, in spite of all the impediments placed in their path, have risen to a relatively commendable level, will have earned a reward comparable to that secured by others placed in more favourable surroundings, who by the exertion of the same amount of free-willed determination have been capable of reaching a much higher degree of religiosity.

Now we should be able to see clearly the answer to the question of why it is not necessarily a violation of Divine fairness to permit some people to have access to certain proofs that are inaccessible to others, an answer which applies equally well in the context of any proof. The answer is based on the common supposition that different people have been created with different temperaments and what rationally appeals to one person does not necessarily do so to another. Some people are greatly impressed by arguments based on concrete tangible and visible evidence, even if the argument is not 100 per cent rigorous; others have a special predilection for abstract reasoning. Also

the amount of persuasion required very much depends on the general climate of opinion in which an individual may find himself. In a generation in which certain presuppositions made by all in earlier times are no longer taken for granted, a proof may be required for something which in the past required no proof. To put it briefly therefore: the different availability of proofs for theism need not be interpreted as a sign of discrimination, since it may be necessary to compensate for the initial differences that may exist in the mental and emotional facilities of different individuals and in the conditioning they have inevitably undergone in the society of which they are members.

Even more importantly, however, we should be able to realize now that it is quite possible for two individuals, who do not differ appreciably with respect to their physical make-up, innate dispositions, appetites, and potentials, to be placed by providence in very dissimilar environments. In such a case it is most likely that these two will end up holding fundamentally different sets of beliefs and will subscribe also to like principles of conduct. This, however, would be so only because one of them has had a variety of religious resources—in the form of argument, instruction, and personal example—at his disposal, which were unavailable to the other. In a situation like this ..., these two individuals will be judged by different criteria; full account will be taken of the nature of the different difficulties that were placed in the paths of the two individuals.

The idea that a worshipper's excellence at a given time is a function not solely of his positive religious achievements, but also of the amount of effort and toil required from him in order to reach the state of piety he has attained by that time, is an ancient idea. The first-century rabbi Ben Heh-Heh stated 'In accordance with the pain is the reward'; the refinement and ennoblement of an individual's soul is not to be gauged by the ultimate degree of his rectitude but by the amount of struggle and pain that went into reaching that degree. In spite of the fact that here upon earth a different criterion is usually applied by the judges appointed by society to assess people's guilt and innocence, there seems little doubt that Ben Heh-Heh's principle expresses a more refined sense of justice. This is, of course, an inevitable result of the limitation of mortal judges, who cannot as a rule be expected to be able to assess properly the magnitude of all the obstacles—both external and internal—an individual has had to contend with in order to do no worse than he has done. In general, therefore, at most what may be hoped for is that our human judges will succeed in making a more or less correct assessment of the palpable merit or demerit of an individual's act in an absolute sense, occasionally attempting to introduce some of the elements of a higher kind of justice, as when the court takes into account the extenuating circumstances of the accused. Of course, it is no more than a truism that human justice is imperfect and only Divine justice is perfect. Our point, however, is that the main factor responsible for this is not so much the moral frailty of earthly judges as it is

intellectual limitations and insufficient evidence. We humans have only a meagre capacity to discern what is relevant; we are able to take into account what lies in front of our eyes—not the many hidden influences that shape an individual's behaviour, influences stemming from his innate character and the environment in which he grew up. Naturally, however, in the ultimate context, the context which really matters, when it comes to determining an individual's ultimate fate, we expect nothing less than that a much fairer criterion is going to be employed, the criterion of relative achievement. In the 'celestial court' this must be the only appropriate criterion to employ; it is the criterion which an omniscient being is able to use, and a perfectly just being will want to use, to gauge our lives' true accomplishments.

76 RELIGIOUS LUCK

LINDA TRINKAUS ZAGZEBSKI

Linda Trinkaus Zagzebski, whose work we read previously, here explores what she terms "religious luck," the issue that George N. Schlesinger discussed in the previous selection. She finds his solution to the problem unsatisfactory and goes on to suggest that the matter is serious enough to cast doubt on the whole concept of hell.

I. INTRODUCTION

Moral luck occurs when a person's degree of moral responsibility for an act or a personal trait goes beyond the degree to which she controls it. If it exists, people are the proper objects of moral evaluation, including praise and blame, reward and punishment, because of something that is partly due to luck, Thomas Nagel has argued that this is not a mistake in our moral practices, but is a consequence of the right way of looking at morality. We cannot eliminate luck without destroying moral evaluation altogether. Nonetheless, most of us find moral luck repulsive—even,

perhaps, incoherent. Surely it must be the case that each of us has an equal chance at the one thing that matters most: our moral worth. While we must put up with elements of chance and fortune in the other aspects of our lives, how could this happen in morality? In fact, we could make a strong case for the view that a primary distinguishing feature of moral evaluation as opposed to other sorts of evaluation is that it is completely luck-free. And not only is it luck-free, it compensates for the prevalence of luck in the other areas of our lives. There is, then, a kind of ultimate cosmic justice. Nevertheless, Thomas Nagel, Bernard

From Linda Trinkaus Zagzebski, "Religious Luck," *Faith and Philosophy*, 11, 1994. Reprinted by permission of the publisher.

Williams, Joel Feinberg, and others have persuasively argued that morality is permeated with luck. If they are right, morality is threatened with inconsistency.

In this paper I will focus on the problems of moral luck identified by Nagel and Feinberg and will argue that they exist for Christian moral practice and Christian moral theories as well. In addition, the problem of luck for the Christian is worsened by several elements not found in secular morality, including the traditional doctrine of grace and the doctrine of an eternal heaven and hell. Historical disputes over these doctrines within Christianity do not go to the heart of the luck problem. At one time the dispute took the form of the controversy over predestination vs. free will. Nowadays it is more usual for the focus to be on the question of whether an eternal hell is consistent with divine justice, mercy, goodness, or love. The problem I am raising, however, is not a problem about free will or the coherence of the divine attributes, but is a problem internal to the concepts of moral responsibility, reward, and punishment as understood by the Christian. I will argue that while secular morality has no resources to handle moral luck, Christianity can do so either by eliminating it or by renduring it innocuous. I will consider five ways this might be done, none of which are options outside of Christian theology, but each of which raises problems of its own.

II. THE CASE FOR MORAL LUCK

In well-known papers by Bernard Williams and Thomas Nagel the existence of moral luck has been identified and illustrated with numerous examples.[1] Nagel argues that there are three main sources of moral luck: luck in consequences, luck in circumstances, and luck in constitution, the last of which might more properly be called luck in traits of character. Together they make luck so pervasive that it contaminates virtually every type of moral theory as well as common moral practice.

Consider first luck in consequences. The idea here is that the outcome of a person's act affects his degree of fault even though the way things turn out is to some extent beyond his control. To take one of Nagel's examples:

If someone has had too much to drink and his car swerves on to the sidewalk, he can count himself morally lucky if there are no pedestrians in his path. If there were, he would be to blame for their deaths, and would probably be prosecuted for manslaughter. But if he hurts no one, although his recklessness is exactly the same, he is guilty of a far less serious legal offense and will certainly reproach himself and be reproached by others much less severely.[2]

Although the example is a legal one, it is clear in the subsequent discussion that Nagel thinks that the degree of *moral* responsibility differs in the two cases even though the degree of control by the agent is the same.

Luck in consequences is the category given the most attention by both Williams and Nagel, but it is also the most vulnerable to objection.[3] I will therefore not make any of my claims in this paper depend upon there being luck of this type. Let us then consider the Kantian move of focusing moral assessment exclusively on the internal sphere of intentions or acts of will. What accrues to our discredit is not literally *what* we do, on this approach, but only those mental acts by which we do it.

Will this move eliminate the problem of moral luck? Unfortunately, it will not. For one thing, a person forms intentions only when the occasion arises, but the arising of the occasion is the result of circumstances largely beyond the agent's control. Again, to take one of Nagel's examples:

Ordinary citizens of Nazi Germany had an opportunity to behave heroically by opposing the regime. They also had an opportunity to behave badly, and most of them are culpable for having failed the test. But it is a test to which the citizens of other countries were not subjected, with the result that even if they, or some of them, would have behaved as badly as the Germans in like circumstances, they simply did not and therefore are not similarly culpable.[4]

In an earlier paper, Joel Feinberg made the same point that responsibility for one's inner states can in some circumstances be wholly a matter of luck.[5] He considers the case of Hotspur, the unfortunate slapper of Hemo, an equally unfortunate hemophiliac, who dies as the result of Hotspur's slap.

> Imagine that we have photographed the whole episode and are now able to project the film in such very slow motion that we can observe every stage of Hotspur's action and (constructively) even the "inner" anticipatory stages....
>
> At each of these cinematographic stages there is some state of affairs for which we might hold Hotspur responsible. We can also conceive of a third party, call him Witwood, who is in all relevant respects exactly like Hotspur but who, through luck, would have escaped responsibility at each stage, were he in Hotspur's shoes. We can imagine, for example, that had Witwood caused Hemo's mouth to hemorrhage, Hemo's life would have been saved by some new drug; or at an earlier stage, instead of becoming responsible for Hemo's cut mouth, Witwood lands only a glancing blow which does not cut; or again, instead of becoming responsible for the painful impact of hand on face. Witwood swings at a ducking Hemo and misses altogether. Though similar in his intentions and deeds to Hotspur, Witwood escapes responsibility through luck.
>
> The same good fortune is possible at earlier "internal" stages. For example, at the stage when Hotspur would begin to burn with rage, a speck of dust throws Witwood into a sneezing fit, preventing any rage from arising. He can no more be responsible for a feeling he did not have than for a death that did not happen. Similarly, at the point when Hotspur would be right on the verge of forming his intention, Witwood is distracted at just that instant by a loud noise. By the time the noise subsides. Witwood's blood has cooled, and he forms no intention to slap Hemo. Hotspur, then, is responsible—I suppose some would say "morally" responsible—for his intention, whereas Witwood, who but for an accidental intrusion on his attention would have formed the same intention, luckily escapes responsibility.[6]

Since the introduction of Witwood to the analysis of Hotspur is just a colorful way of talking about what Hotspur himself might have done if he had not been unlucky, the objection might be raised that the claim of moral luck in circumstances costs on the questionable view that there are true counterfactuals of freedom of the form: In

circumstances C Hotspur would have done X. But, in fact, the case rests on no such problematic counterfactuals. It is not necessary that the circumstances in which Hotspur would not have struck Hemo are precisely specifiable, even in principle. All that is required is that there are *some* counterfactual circumstances (perhaps with the proviso that these circumstances not be too far removed from the actual ones) in which Hotspur does not strike Hemo, and that it is beyond Hotspur's control that these circumstances do not obtain; and surely that much is true.

The natural response at this point of the story of Hotspur and Witwood is to go back even further, before the situation arose. As Feinberg describes the case, Hotspur and Witwood have the same character traits relevant to the type of situation described. They are equally irascible or sensitive about personal remarks, and so if we make the primary focus of moral judgment character traits themselves, Hotspur and Witwood are equally at fault and so Hotspur neither benefits nor suffers from moral luck arising from actual intentions or feelings. Feinberg does not pursue this line, but Nagel considers it briefly with examples of the traits of envy and conceit and claims that they also are not impervious to luck. As Nagel describes these cases, they are most naturally understood as qualities of temperament rather than vices, but considerations on the nature of virtues and vices show them to be heavily affected by luck as well, at least they are on a classical Aristotelian theory. To Aristotle traits of character are not inborn, but are habits acquired through imitation of others. The character of the persons to which one is exposed while young is clearly outside a person's control, yet it is the major factor in the acquisition of moral virtues and vices. So even if the primary moral responsibility of persons is for enduring traits of character rather than for intentions, acts, or their consequences, moral luck still exists....

III. THE LUCK OF THE CHRISTIAN

Christian ethics has some of the same problems of luck that face secular ethics. Perhaps Christian moral theorists are less inclined to hold a person responsible for consequences beyond those she can control, and to that extent Christian ethics does not face the most severe of the three types of moral luck identified by Nagel. Still, the range of objects of moral evaluation within Christian moral theories are all things that Nagel and Feinberg have demonstrated to my satisfaction to possess a degree of luck. To the extent that there is luck in one's moral responsibility for one's virtues and vices, the circumstances in which one forms one's intentions, and the resulting acts themselves, to that extent the Christian faces moral luck.[7] As the Christian understands morality, then, we are faced at least with luck in circumstances and in traits of character....

To make matters worse, traditional Christianity includes two doctrines which, on the face of it, magnify the problem of luck to infinity. These are the doctrines of grace and of an eternal heaven and hell.

Consider first the doctrine of grace. On all accounts grace is necessary for salvation and is an unearned gift of God. While accounts of grace within Christianity differ with respect to the question of how much our efforts can affect the reception of grace, no one suggests that it is wholly under our control. There is, then, religious luck....

Most serious of all, the reward or punishment to which a life of grace or the lack of it leads is an eternal heaven or hell. This element of Christian teaching multiplies the effects of moral luck and the luck of grace to infinity. I will not speculate here on the nature of eternity; eternal reward or punishment may not be infinite in duration. Nonetheless, it must be the case that an eternal reward is infinitely greater than an earthly reward and an eternal punishment is infinitely greater than an earthly punishment. A person controls her individual choices and acts and the series of choices and acts which make up her life only up to a point, yet her reward or punishment is infinite. This means that even in the best case, one in which we can assume that the cumulative luck in a person's life from natural qualities, circumstances, and consequences is fairly small, since an infinite reward or punishment is at stake, the effects of even a small degree of luck become infinite....

IV. WHAT MAKES LUCK A PROBLEM?

On the face of it the problem of luck in Christian moral theology is far greater, even infinitely greater than it is for secular moral practice and theory. But on the face of it Christian theology with its doctrines of an omniscient and provident God also has the resources to handle conceptual difficulties which would be impossible for a theory without such a deity. God can mend problems in moral evaluation that nothing can mend in ordinary moral practice. But before turning to the ways God can alleviate the problem of luck, let us look more closely at exactly what makes luck a problem for moral evaluation for ironically, the existence of an omniscient God worsens the problem of moral luck in one respect.

If there is an omniscient God it is not accurate to describe that which we do not control as pure luck—something that is nobody's fault. The luck described by Nagel and Feinberg occurs due to impersonal forces that have nothing against you (or *for* you) personally. So if Sarah had been born with a more naturally cheerful disposition, she would have found it much easier to acquire the virtues of benevolence. If Mark had arrived at the burning building a few moments earlier, he would have been the one to save the child instead of David. If the young gang member had not been born in poverty to a drug addicted mother and an absent father, he would not now be in court faced with a string of charges from car theft to murder. In each case there is nobody to blame for the bad luck. It just happened that way. But if there is an omniscient God, and especially if omniscience includes a degree of knowledge of what a person would do or would be likely to do in counterfactual circumstances, it does look as if God is picking on some people.

So moral luck for the Christian is faced with a dual problem. Not only is there the problem identified by Nagel and magnified by the doctrines of grace and eternal reward and punishment, but the element of luck for the Christian is not independent of the knowledge and will of God. God permits it to go on in full awareness of who will be morally lucky and who will be unlucky. There is not even the consolation of luck as impersonal chance....

V. FIVE WAYS TO DEAL WITH RELIGIOUS LUCK

Suppose that there are true counterfactuals of freedom and that God has Middle Knowledge. That is to say, for each person God knows what that person would freely choose to do in every possible situation. God would then be in a position to judge her, not just for her actual virtues and vices, the acts she in fact performs, and their actual consequences, but for the sum total of everything she would choose to do in every possible circumstance. Of course, some of those circumstances exhibit bad luck, but others exhibit good luck. It is reasonable to think, then, that luck is eliminated if her choices in the totality of possible circumstances are the basis for her moral assessment, Lovers of Middle Knowledge who are haters of moral luck may find this solution attractive. Such a procedure for moral assessment would no doubt have a levelling effect on the moral worth of human beings. After all, there is probably *some* possible circumstance in which almost anybody would do almost anything, whether it be good or bad. Whether this consequence is a good or a bad feature of this solution, I cannot say. A feature of it that many would find seriously defective, though, is that it makes the actual world meaningless as far as moral evaluation is concerned. In fact, there is really no reason to have an actual world at all for such purposes; God might just as well have created the beings he wanted and have gone straight on to their final judgment, skipping the in-between step of letting a particular world unfold. It must be admitted, then, that this approach is very far removed from our ordinary notions of moral evaluation. But, of course, the defender of this approach can always say that that is because our ordinary notions of moral evaluation are permeated with elements of luck, as Williams and Nagel have shown, and the proper response to this is to say so much the worse for our ordinary notions of moral evaluation. So while I do not

think this approach is absurd, it should be admitted that it is radical.

A second solution is to say that a person is morally evaluated for just that element of her character and her acts which she controls. Although Nagel does say that when we view ourselves from the outside that portion of the moral self that we control threatens to shrink into nothing, still, the argument that there is moral luck does not rest on such a position, and in this paper I have been leaving open the possibility that there is incompatibilist free will. If so, why couldn't our moral evaluation be determined by an omniscient God in proportion to our control?

The problem here is that it is not at all clear that there is any such thing as *the* proportion of our control. Recall Joel Feinberg's conclusion to the discussion of Hotspur and Witwood. There he claims that moral responsibility is indeterminate, not just relative to our epistemic situation, but in itself. The precise determinability of moral responsibility is an illusion, he says; moral responsibility is undecidable *in principle*. While Feinberg's argument may not be given with the care necessary to demonstrate such a dramatic conclusion, it does at least draw our attention to the range of questions that would have to have determinate answers if luck were to be eliminated by this move. Not only would there need to be a determinate degree of causal control a person has over a choice, but there would have to be a determinate degree of control that a person has over the fact that she is in certain actual circumstances rather than in any one of the infinite number of counterfactual circumstances. Further, there would have to be a determinate degree of her control over the fact that she has the virtues and vices that she has. It is highly doubtful that there is any such degree at all. And if not, even an omniscient judge could not base his evaluation on it.

A third solution is suggested by George Schlesinger in a discussion of divine justice.[8] The problem he addresses there is much more narrowly focused than the one I am raising here, but the solution might be applicable. Schlesinger is concerned about the fact that the religious beliefs requisite for salvation are much easier for some to acquire than others. As he puts it, different individuals have different opportunities to avail themselves of arguments and evidence for the existence of God:

> Suppose I am a non-believer who has remained unconvinced by the various proofs for God's existence I have read or hard. There is, however, a new argument which would appeal to me so much that it would most likely convert me to theism. It so happens that I never get the chance to gain knowledge of the argument and thus persist in my ungodly ways. Is it not grossly unfair that, owing to circumstances beyond my control, I should be deprived of the ultimate felicity I could have shared with the righteous?[9]

While Schlesinger puts the emphasis on the acceptance of theism based on argument, one need not be an evidentialist to agree that whatever it takes to believe in God is not something which everyone has an equal opportunity to obtain. Those who grow up in a happy religious home obviously have far greater opportunities for salvific Faith than those who grow up in deprived circumstances in which religion is either non-existent or, perhaps even worse, is associated in their experience with bigotry or hypocrisy. Schlesinger's answer is that "in accordance with the pain is the reward."[10] "The true amount of virtue embodied in a given individual is not determined by the absolute level of piety he has reached, but by the nature of the hostile circumstances he has had to contend with in order to raise himself to the level he has succeeded in attaining."[11] So the harder it is for a person to be saved, the greater his reward if he does his part in exhibiting a sincere good will; the easier it is for a person to be saved, the less the reward for making a lesser effort. So some people gamble for higher stakes with a lower chance of success, while others gamble for lower stakes with a higher chance of success.

I have two worries about this solution. In the first place it is not at all clear that the initial positions of the sincere person in a pagan society and the ordinary person in religiously ideal circumstances are really equal. After all, a real gambler has a choice between going for higher stakes with a lower chance of winning or going for lower stakes with a higher chance of winning. Much of

what makes the game fair is that the choice is his. But in the religious case as Schlesinger sees it, it is not up to us to choose the game we play. We do not get to decide initially how much of a risk we want to take. Secondly, this solution faces the same problem that infects the previous solution. Is it even possible in principle to determine a person's chance for salvation? Is there any such thing as the proportion of his success or failure that is due to efforts completely under his control? What Schlesinger does not mention is that luck in circumstances is only part of the problem. There is also luck in those traits of character which lead some people to make the greater efforts some need for salvation. What Schlesinger calls "a sincere good will" is itself partly a matter of luck.

The fourth solution is to embrace a doctrine of grace according to which grace not only does not aggravate luck, it eliminates it.[12] The idea here is that since God desires everyone to be saved, more grace is given to the morally unlucky. Everyone gets grace, but some get more of it to compensate for their bad moral luck. This does seem to be what a loving parent would do. A mother who loves all her children equally will not necessarily give each child equal attention and help. Those who need it more, get more. On this approach it would not be necessary for God to determine in advance a precise level of grace needed to neutralize the effects of moral luck since God can intervene at any time to provide more than enough grace when needed. The problem of the indeterminacy in moral responsibility or degree of control could therefore be circumvented on this approach.

This solution seems to me to be the best so far, but the problem is that it does not accord well with our experience. Of course it *might* be the case that truly corrupted criminals ... really did have more than enough chances to stay on the moral path and again later to reform themselves, but it certainly does not *seem* that way. What's more, an acceptance of this approach might lead to severe harshness in our moral assessment of others. That is, it suggests that the excuses people seem to have for their behavior are not really excuses after all since, unseen by us (and even themselves), they had even more opportunities for grace than most of us, but simply rejected it.

The fifth solution is that while God does not eliminate moral luck, he makes it innocuous through universal salvation. This solution involves severing the moral order from the order of salvation.

We have seen that Christian luck includes at least some of the kinds of luck discussed by Nagel and Feinberg, and that it is aggravated by several aspects of Christian doctrine. First, Christian luck is not blind, but is known in advance to an omniscient God. Second, there is some degree of inequality in the operation of grace. Third, and most serious of all, the doctrine of an eternal heaven and hell magnifies the extent of moral luck to infinity. What is most problematic in these doctrines is the way the concepts of grace, heaven, and hell are connected with the moral institution of rewards and punishments. Suppose, however, that there is no eternal hell. If so, we avoid the worst problem of an infinite degree of luck in punishment, and at the same time, an eternal heaven makes innocuous the effects of all the other sorts of moral and religious luck we have accumulated during our earthly existence, including inequality in the operation of grace. The fact that there is no blind luck and all of this is known to an omniscient God is an advantage rather than a disadvantage of this solution.

It might appear radical to sever the moral order from the order of salvation, but notice that the Christian is already committed to this in part since Christian theology dissociates what we get from what we deserve in the case of heaven. When the generosity of a reward-giver is extreme enough, it is inappropriate to call his gift a reward. Heaven is not a reward, and so it is not part of the moral order. Hell, however, *is* a punishment since all who go there deserve it. Such a view requires an awkward partial break between morality and ultimate destiny. The fifth solution to the problem of moral luck would make a clean break between the two.

In distinguishing the moral order from the order of salvation, it is not necessary to radically alter our moral intuitions and practices in order to deal with moral luck, the major defect of the first solution. The solution of universal salvation does not take away luck in the moral order; moral luck simply has no bearing on one's ultimate destiny. This means that we can accept morality as a finite institution with finite significance, as Nagel does. If morality requires finite punishments after death, there is nothing in this solution to prevent them from occurring. The point is that whatever the defects of the institution of morality as we know it, that is something we can live with as long as all is made well in eternity. A consequence of this solution is that morality is ultimately not as important as many of us think. In any case, it ought to be cut down to size, the only size it can realistically manage.

This solution will be attractive to those who already maintain for independent reasons that there is no eternal hell. The arguments I know of for this conclusion almost always rest on a consideration of the divine attributes, and the argument is that an eternal hell is inconsistent with either divine justice, mercy, goodness, or love. My argument here is concerned only with the problem of moral luck and the fact that the problem can be handled rather well if there is no eternal hell. Independent arguments for the nonexistence of hell might give this solution additional support. It should be admitted, though, that this approach does go against the dominant view in the Christian tradition. It is mostly dependent upon *a priori* philosophical reasoning, but, then, most of the other solutions are *a priori* as well. It is doubtful that the problem of moral luck as I have formulated it in this paper was even considered in the tradition, so it is no surprise that there is little in the tradition of direct relevance to the problem.[13]

VI. CONCLUSION

I have argued in this paper that moral luck really is a problem and its existence shows that common views on morality flirt with inconsistency. Some of the sources of moral luck identified by Thomas Nagel and Joel Feinberg are problems for Christian morality as well. Moreover, I have argued that there are several features of Christian doctrine that magnify the problem enormously. I have gone through five solutions to the problem. All of them in one degree or another modify traditional views about grace, heaven and hell, or the grounds for moral evaluation. The only way I know to maintain untouched the traditional doctrines I have referred to in this paper requires the denial that moral luck is a problem even when infinite rewards and punishments are at stake. I believe this view to be deeply counter to modern moral sensibilities, although I have not attempted to defend those sensibilities in this paper, only to call attention to them. Furthermore, all of the solutions have problems of their own. But in spite of this, it seems to me that if the problem of moral luck has a solution at all, it will have to be within a theological structure which goes beyond morality as normally discussed in the secular philosophical literature. Non-religious ethics simply does not have the resources to handle the problem. For the purposes of this paper, I have considered only those approaches which arise within the Christian tradition. Non-Christian religious solutions, such as reincarnation, would also be worth considering.

NOTES

1. Thomas Nagel, "Moral Luck," in Nagel, *Mortal Questions*, (Cambridge: Cambridge University Press, 1979); Bernard Williams, "Moral Luck," in Williams, *Moral Luck*. (Cambridge: Cambridge University Press, 1981). Earlier versions of both papers were published in *Proceedings of the Aristotelian Society*, Supplemental Vol. 50 (1976), pp. 115-35.
2. Nagel, p. 29.
3. Judith Jarvis Thomson, in "Morality and Bad Luck," *Meta-philosophy*, vol. 20, no. 3–4 (1989), pp. 203-21, claims that the argument that there is luck in consequences plays upon an ambiguity in the notion of blame. In the sense of blame which reflects discredit on a person, there is no luck in consequences. The two negligent drunk drivers are equally at fault. But there is also a sense

of blame in which we say a person is to blame *for* an undesirable state of affairs, such as a person's death. In this sense, the driver who actually kills someone is clearly to blame, while the one who does not is not.
4. Nagel, p. 34.
5. Joel Feinberg, "Problematic Responsibility in Law and Morals," in Feinberg, *Doing and Deserving*, (Princeton: Princeton University Press, 1970), pp. 25-37. Other papers in the collection are also relevant.
6. Feinberg, pp. 34-35.
7. Philip L. Quinn argues in "Tragic Dilemmas, Suffering Love, and the Christian Life," *Journal of Religious Ethics*, vol. 17, no. 1 (1989), pp. 151-83, that a different sort of moral luck exists for the Christian, and that is the moral dilemma. A person faces a moral dilemma when no matter what she chooses, she does the wrong thing. It is therefore a type of moral trap. Quinn argues that Shusaku Endo's novel *Silence* depicts a person faced with a situation in which the two great commandments—the command to love God with our whole heart and the command to love our neighbor as ourselves—command conflicting acts. If Quinn is right that the Jesuit missionary Sebastian Rodrigues faces a moral dilemma in Endo's novel, then that is another way in which moral luck arises for the Christian, but in this paper I will limit my discussion to the categories of moral luck identified by Nagel and Feinberg.
8. Schlesinger, *op, cit.*
9. Schlesinger, p. 184.
10. Schlesinger, p. 186.
11. Schlesinger, p. 188.
12. This solution was suggested to me by my colleague, Kenneth Rudnick, S. J.
13. A sixth solution was suggested to me by Stephen Davis. Suppose that God gives us the opportunity to make a luck-free choice in eternity and eternally rewards or punishes us on the basis of such a choice. Notice the similarity between Davis's suggestion and the Myth of Ur at the end of Plato's *Republic*.

B. RESURRECTION

77 RESURRECTION

JOHN H. HICK

The doctrine of the resurrection of the dead plays a central role in Christianity and Islam. But how is the concept of resurrection to be understood? Can it be explained so as to make it intelligible? In our next selection, answers to these questions are offered by John H. Hick (1922–2012), whose work we read previously.

Hick finds that resurrection is implicit in God's love for creatures made in God's image. How could God allow loved ones to pass out of existence? Furthermore, recall that in a previous selection Hick argues that life after death is required to justify all the world's pains and sorrows. In accord with that view, he asserts that God's purposes for us can only be realized in an existence beyond this life. Thus Hick concludes that God's plan for humanity would not be complete without resurrection.

What does "the resurrection of the dead" mean? Saint Paul's discussion provides the basic Christian answer to this question.[1] His conception of the general resurrection (distinguished from the unique resurrection of Jesus) has nothing to do with the resuscitation of corpses in a cemetery. It concerns God's re-creation or reconstitution of the human psychophysical individual, not as the organism that has died but as a *soma pneumatikon*, a "spiritual body," inhabiting a spiritual world as the physical body inhabits our present physical world.

A major problem confronting any such doctrine is that of providing criteria of personal identity to link the earthly life and the resurrection life. Paul does not specifically consider this question, but one may, perhaps, develop his thought along lines such as the following.

Suppose, first, that someone—John Smith—living in the USA were suddenly and inexplicably to disappear from before the eyes of his friends, and that at the same moment an exact replica of him were inexplicably to appear in India. The person who appears in India is exactly similar in both physical and mental characteristics to the person who disappeared in America. There is continuity of memory, complete similarity of bodily features including fingerprints, hair and eye coloration, and stomach contents, and also of beliefs, habits, emotions, and mental dispositions. Further, the "John Smith" replica thinks of himself as being the John Smith who disappeared in the USA. After all possible tests have been made and have proved positive, the factors leading his friends to accept "John Smith" as John Smith would surely prevail and would cause them to overlook even his mysterious transference from one continent to another, rather than treat "John Smith," with all John Smith's memories and other characteristics, as someone other than John Smith.

Suppose, second, that our John Smith, instead of inexplicably disappearing, dies, but that at the moment of his death a "John Smith" replica, again complete with memories and all other characteristics, appears in India. Even with the

---

From John H. Hick, *Philosophy of Religion*, Fourth Edition, Prentice-Hall, 1990. Reprinted by permission of Pearson Education, Inc.

corpse on our hands we would, I think, still have to accept this "John Smith" as the John Smith who died. We would have to say that he had been miraculously re-created in another place.

Now suppose, third, that on John Smith's death the "John Smith" replica appears, not in India, but as a resurrection replica in a different world altogether, a resurrection world inhabited only by resurrected persons. This world occupies its own space distinct from that with which we are now familiar. That is to say, an object in the resurrection world is not situated at any distance or in any direction from the objects in our present world, although each object in either world is spatially related to every other object in the same world.

This supposition provides a model by which one may conceive of the divine re-creation of the embodied human personality. In this model, the element of the strange and the mysterious has been reduced to a minimum by following the view of some of the early Church Fathers that the resurrection body has the same shape as the physical body,[2] and ignoring Paul's own hint that it may be as unlike the physical body as a full grain of wheat differs from the wheat seed.[3]

What is the basis for this Judaic-Christian belief in the divine re-creation or reconstitution of the human personality after death? There is, of course, an argument from authority, in that life after death is taught throughout the New Testament (although very rarely in the Old Testament). But, more basically, belief in the resurrection arises as a corollary of faith in the sovereign purpose of God, which is not restricted by death and which holds man in being beyond his natural mortality. In the words of Martin Luther, "Anyone with whom God speaks, whether in wrath or in mercy, the same is certainly immortal. The Person of God who speaks, and the Word, show that we are creatures with whom God wills to speak, right into eternity, and in an immortal manner." In a similar vein it is argued that if it be God's plan to create finite persons to exist in fellowship with himself, then it contradicts both his own intention and his love for the creatures made in his image if he allows men to pass out of existence when his purpose for them remains largely unfulfilled.

It is this promised fulfillment of God's purpose for man, in which the full possibilities of human nature will be realized, that constitutes the "heaven" symbolized in the New Testament as a joyous banquet in which all and sundry rejoice together.

NOTES

1. I Corinthians 15.
2. For example, Irenaeus, *Against Heresies*, Book II, Chap. 34, para. 1.
3. I Corinthians, 15:37.

78 LIFE AFTER DEATH

TERENCE PENELHUM

The doctrine of life after death often takes the form of either the resurrection of the body or the immortality of the soul. Both versions of postmortem survival, however, present two fundamental problems: (1) envisioning the kind of life survivors after death could lead, and (2) finding some means of determining whether the person who might survive death would be the same person who had lived.

From Terence Penelhum, *Religion and Rationality*, Random House, 1971. Reprinted by permission of the author.

In the next selection. Terence Penelhum, Professor Emeritus of Religious Studies at the University of Calgary, explores the ways these difficulties apply to each version of life after death. He concludes that the notion of postmortem disembodied existence—that is, the immortality of the soul—is unintelligible, and that the doctrine of bodily resurrection, while not absurd, cannot be shown to be true.

TWO CONCEPTS OF SURVIVAL

... There can be no doubt that the doctrine of the immortality of the soul, even though Greek in origin, has been held by many members of the Christian tradition, whether it belonged originally to that tradition or not. The doctrine of the resurrection of the body, certainly authentically a part of the Christian tradition (since some form of it is clearly held by St. Paul),[1] is part of the most widely used creed of the Christian Church. Let us leave aside their historical relationship and look at the logical possibilities they present. I shall begin with the doctrine of the immortality of the soul, or, as I prefer to word it, the doctrine of disembodied survival. Before doing so, however, I shall attempt to clear the ground a little by indicating the major sources of difficulty that philosophers have discovered in these doctrines.

These difficulties divide themselves naturally into two groups. There are, first of all, difficulties about envisaging the kind of life that survivors of death in either sense could be said to lead. It is not enough to say that the nature of this life is totally unknown, for if this is taken seriously to the extent of our being unable to say that these beings will possess personal characteristics as we now understand these, it seems to leave the belief that they will survive without any content. If one wishes to avoid this pitfall, one has to ascribe to the survivors some characteristics that persons as we know them possess. This does not seem impossible in the case of the doctrine of the resurrection of the body; though it can be made impossible if unlimited stress is placed on the claim that the body of the survivor is transformed. Radical transformation is to be expected as part of such a doctrine, but total transformation would rob the notion of survival of all clear meaning, for it is part of that notion that the *person* survives, and this seems to entail that the resulting being is a person also. But if the doctrine of the resurrection of the body is expressed in ways that avoid this danger, it is clearly possible for us to form a rough notion (which is all one can reasonably demand) of what such a future state would be like.

The difficulty seems much greater, however, when we consider the doctrine of disembodied survival. For it is not obviously intelligible to ascribe personal characteristics to a being that is denied to have any physical ones. The notion of human intelligence, for example, seems closely bound up with the things men can be seen to do and heard to say; the notion of human emotion seems closely bound up with the way men talk and behave; and the notion of human action seems closely bound up with that of physical movement. There is plenty of room for disagreement over the nature of these connections, but they cannot even exist in the case of an allegedly disembodied being. So can we understand what is meant by talk of disembodied intelligences, or disembodied sufferers of emotion, or disembodied agents? A natural answer to our present problem is: Disembodied survivors might have mental lives. They might, that is, think, imagine, dream, or have feelings. This looks coherent enough. On the other hand, for them to have anything to think *about* or have feelings *toward*, it might be necessary for them also to have that which supplies us with our objects of reflection or emotion, namely, perception. Some might also want to add the notion of agency (especially if they wish to use the doctrine of disembodied survival to offer explanations of the phenomena of psychical research). We must bear in mind, further, that disembodied persons could, of course, never perceive or meet each other, in any normal sense of these words. What we need to do, even at the risk of spinning fantasies, is to see how severely the belief in their disembodiment restricts the range of concepts that we can apply to them.

The second group of difficulties affects both doctrines, though in different ways. These are difficulties about the self-identity of the survivors. The belief that people survive is not merely the belief that after people's deaths there will be personal beings in existence. It is the belief that those beings will be the same ones that existed before death. One of the reasons for concern about the nature of the life a disembodied person might lead is that if this mode of life were *too* radically different from the sort of life we lead, those beings leading it could not be identified with us. This difficulty is critical, for even if we can readily understand what the future life that is spoken of would be like, its coming to pass would only be an interesting cosmic hypothesis, lacking any personal relevance, if the beings living that life were not ourselves. This requirement connects with another. We have to be able to form some concept of what it is for the future, post-mortem being to remain the same through time in the future life, quite apart from his also being identifiable with some previous person who existed in *this* life. If, for instance, our being able to identify a person whom we meet now as some person we knew previously depends on our being able to discern some feature that he still possesses; and if that feature is something that a being in the future life could not possess, then it needs to be shown that there could be post-mortem persons who persist through time at all. There would have to be some substitute, in the case of post-mortem persons, for the feature that establishes identity for pre-mortem persons. If we are not able to indicate what this would be, we have no adequately clear concept of what talk of post-mortem persons means.

These problems about identity arise in quite different ways for the two doctrines of disembodied survival and bodily resurrection. A proponent of the doctrine of disembodied survival has to face the problem of the continuing identity of the disembodied person through time, by showing that what makes that person identical through time could be some wholly *mental* feature and that the absence of a body does not render the notion of a body inapplicable. (He may or may not do this by claiming that we use mental rather than physical features to identify pre-mortem beings through time.) This task may not be hopeless, though it looks as though we depend on the physical continuity of people for our ability to reidentify them. He must also succeed in showing that some purely mental feature will serve to identify the post-mortem person with his pre-mortem predecessor.

In the case of the doctrine of the resurrection of the body, the problem of how the post-mortem, resurrected person can remain identical through time in the future state does not look very difficult, since the sort of life envisaged for this being is an embodied one, similar in enough respects (one may suppose) to our own. So even if we decided that the continuity of the body is a necessary condition of the continuance of a person through time, this condition could easily be said to be satisfied in the case of a resurrected person. Yet we still have a difficulty: Could a post-mortem person, even in this embodied state, be identified with any pre-mortem person? For if the doctrine of resurrection is presented in a form that entails the annihilation of a person at death, it could reasonably be argued that what is predicted as happening at the resurrection is not, after all, the reappearance of the original person but the (first) appearance of a *duplicate* person—no doubt resembling the former one but not numerically identical with him. If this can be argued and cannot be refuted, we are in the odd position of being unsure whether or not to say that the future persons are the former ones. Philosophers have often noted the extent to which problems of identity seem to involve not discoveries but decisions—decisions on what to *call* a particular situation. The literature of personal identity is full of actual and imagined stories introduced to help us discover, by deciding how to talk of them, what the conditions of application of our concepts are. The doctrine of the resurrection of the body seems to present us with just such a matter of decision—namely, would this admittedly conceivable future state properly be described as the reappearance of a former person or as the first appearance of a duplicate of him?

DISEMBODIED PERSONALITY

Let us now look at the first group of difficulties, those connected with the possibility of applying our normal concepts of personal life to post-mortem beings. These seem to arise, as we have seen already, only in connection with the belief that men survive without their bodies, and I shall therefore only discuss them in this connection....

Disembodied persons can conduct no physical performances. They cannot walk or talk (or, therefore, converse), open and close their eyes or peer (or, therefore, look), turn their heads and incline their ears (or, therefore, listen), raise their hands in anger or weep (or, therefore, give bodily expression to their emotions), or touch or feel physical objects. Hence they cannot perceive each other or be perceived by us. Can they, still, be said without absurdity to perceive physical things? Perhaps we could say so if we were prepared to allow that a being having a set of visual images corresponding to the actual disposition of some physical things was thereby *seeing* those things. We could say so if we were prepared to allow that a being having a sequence of auditory experiences that made him think correctly that a certain object was giving off a particular sound was thereby *hearing* that object. The notions of seeing and hearing would be attenuated, since they would not, if applied in such cases, entail that the person who saw was physically in front of the object he saw with his face turned toward it or that the person who heard was receiving sound waves from the object that was giving them off. On the other hand, many philosophers hold that such implications are at most informal ones that are not essential to the concepts in question. Perhaps we could also say even that disembodied percipients could *do* things to the objects (or persons) they see and hear. We might be able to say this if we imagined that sometimes these percipients had wishes that were immediately actualized in the world, without any natural explanation for the strange things that occurred; though obviously such fantasies would involve the ascription of occult powers to the spirits. We might prefer to avoid all talk of interaction between the world of the spirits and ours, however, by denying that a disembodied being can see or hear or act in our world at all. Perhaps their lives consist exclusively of internal processes—acts of imagination and reflection. Such a life would be life in a dream world; and each person would have his own private dream. It might include dream images "of" others, though the accuracy of any reflections they occasioned would be purely coincidental.

These informal suggestions indicate that it might be possible, given a good deal of conceptual elasticity, to accord to disembodied persons at least some of the forms of mental life with which we are familiar. It therefore seems overdoctrinaire to refuse to admit that such beings could be called persons. We must bear in mind, however, that they could hardly be said to have an *inter*personal existence. Not only would we be unable to perceive a disembodied person; but a disembodied person, being unable to perceive another disembodied person, could have no more reason than we have to believe that others besides himself existed. Only if he can perceive embodied persons would he be in a position to know from anything other than memory that they exist or that they act in particular ways. The logic of the concept of disembodied persons clearly rules out the possibility of there being a community of such persons, even though by exercising conceptual care and tolerance we do seem able to ascribe some sort of life to disembodied individuals. In response to this, a verificationist might demand that before we can understand the ascriptions we have considered we should be able to say how we would *know* that a disembodied individual was having some experience or performing some act. But since we are dealing with a possible use of predicates that we have already learned, this verificationist demand seems too stringent.

We have also had to put aside another question whose bearing cannot be disputed, since it casts doubt on our ability to think of disembodied individuals. In asking whether some of the notions of a personal mental life can be applied, we have had to assume that there is a continuing, nonphysical subject to whom they can be applied, who has the experience or who does the action. This notion is essential to our understanding of the suggestion that there is a plurality of distinct individuals (whether they form a community or not), that on some occasion an experience is had by one of them rather than another, and that on another occasion a second experience is had by the same individual (or, indeed, a different individual) as had the first. In daily life the distinction between individuals and the continuing identity of individuals through time seems to depend upon the fact that each individual person has a distinguishable and persisting body. In the absence of a body are we able to form any notion of what has the experience or does the actions, has certain other experiences or actions in its past, and will have others in its future? In what follows, in order to retain some degree of clarity and simplicity in a philosophical area where obscurity is especially easy, I shall concentrate on trying to provide some account of what it might be for a disembodied person to retain identity through time. The philosophical theories we shall look at are usually also intended to offer some answer to the problem of distinguishing between two or more contemporaries—the problem, that is, of individuation. It is in any case hard to see how that question could have an answer if the problem of identity through time does not. I shall now turn, then, to the second, and more fundamental, of our two problems in the logic of the concept of survival.

THE PROBLEM OF IDENTITY

The logical problems one has to contend with when examining the concept of survival are to a large extent extensions of those that have puzzled philosophers when they have tried to analyze the notion of personal identity. We all recognize one another; we are all familiar enough with the experience of wondering who someone is; and most of us know the embarrassment that follows when one makes a mistake about who someone is. Our day-to-day thinking about these matters suggests that we take it for granted that there are clearly understood factors that determine whether the man before us is Smith or not, or is who he says he is or not, even though we may be unable to decide sometimes, through lack of information, whether these factors obtain. Philosophers have

been puzzled, however, when they have tried to say what these factors are. Skeptical philosophers have even wondered whether any such factors can be isolated; and if they cannot be, they have suggested, our assumption that people do retain their identities from one period of time to the next may be an illusion....

MENTAL AND BODILY CRITERIA OF IDENTITY

One way of trying to avoid this confusion is to resort to ... the doctrine of spiritual substance. This is the doctrine that in spite of the changingness of our mental lives, there is some hidden core to it that persists unchanged throughout, thus providing a backdrop against which the changes occur. This backdrop need not be *unchanging*: It could be subject only to gradual change. The tacit assumption that it cannot change at all is only the result of assuming that identity and change are always inconsistent. But even if we allow that the spiritual substance to which the occurrences in our mental lives belong might itself be subject to gradual change, the doctrine is without value. For if the doctrine implies that we can find this relatively permanent core within by looking into ourselves, then it is false; for we cannot.... If on the other hand, it is admitted that the doctrine postulates something that is not accessible to observation, there is another difficulty: It can at best be a matter of happy accident that when we judge someone before us to be the same person as someone we knew before, we are right. For the only thing that would make this judgment reliable is the knowledge that the features possessed by the present and the past person belonged to the same substance. Yet when the substance is inaccessible even to the person himself, how could we ever know that an identity judgment was true? It is obvious that our basis for such judgments must be something other than what the doctrine requires it to be, for how, otherwise, could we learn to make such judgments in the first place?

We base our identity judgments, at least of others, upon the observation of their physical appearance. This fact, plus the mysteriousness of the doctrine of spiritual substance, has made it very tempting for philosophers to say that what makes a person the same from one period to the next is the continuance of his body throughout the two periods. The human body has the relative stability that we associate with a great many observable material objects and is not usually subject to the rapid changes that go on in the human mind. The plausibility of the claim that bodily continuity is a necessary and sufficient condition of personal identity derives also from the fact that our judgments about the identity of persons are in the vast majority of cases based on our having looked at them, talked to them, and recognized them. This may be why even philosophers who have tacitly identified the person with his mind have assumed that a person cannot consist only of thoughts, feelings, images, and other fleeting and changing phenomena, but must consist, beneath this, of something more stable. For they have, perhaps, been looking within the mind itself for something that has the relative stability of the body, even though they have officially abandoned any belief that the body provides persons with their continuing identity.

Suppose, however, that they were to abandon body surrogates like spiritual substance. Suppose they were not to assume that the identity of a person consists in the persistence of some relatively stable element such as his body, but were to concentrate their attention solely upon what they consider to be the contents of his mental life. If they were to do this, it would seem that their only hope of giving an account of the self-identity of persons would be to suggest the existence of some relationship among the fleeting elements of which human mental life is composed. An appropriate relationship does seem available. Some of the later experiences in a man's life history are, the story might go, memories of the earlier ones. And only the same person who had the earlier experiences could have a memory of one of them among his later experiences. So we have here the possibility of a purely mental standard of identity: that person A at time T_2 is the same as person B at some earlier time T_1 if and only if, among the experiences that person A has at T_2 there are memories of experiences that person B had at T_1. In the literature of the subject these two

criteria of identity (bodily continuity and memory) have contended for priority.

The claim that personal identity can be understood solely in terms of memory can be accepted by someone who does not believe that a person can be identified with his mind or that anyone ever survives physical death. A philosopher who does not believe these things might still believe that the embodied person before him can be identified with Smith, whom he used to know, only if the person before him has the appropriate memories. But it is clear that someone who does believe those things must reject the thesis that only bodily continuity can be a criterion of personal identity. For if it is a necessary condition of a person's continuing that his body should continue, no one could survive in a disembodied form. Someone who accepts the doctrine of disembodied survival, therefore, will naturally incline toward the view that memory is the one necessary and sufficient condition of personal identity, since he must reject the traditional alternative position.

There is an artificiality about speaking, as I have, about two competing positions here. For in daily life it looks as though we use both standards of identity, resorting to one or the other depending on circumstances. Sometimes we decide who someone is by ascertaining facts about their physical appearance, height, weight, and the rest. Sometimes we decide who someone is by trying to determine whether or not they can remember certain past events that the person they claim to be could not fail, we think, to recall. Indeed, the barrier between these two methods becomes less clear than it first seems, when we reflect that we might try to reach our decision by seeing what skills a person has retained or what performances he can carry out. But although both standards are used, one might still have priority over the other. This would be the case if the other would not be available to us if the one were not or if the description of the one required some reference to the other.

It might look as though the use of the bodily criterion of identity presupposes that of memory in some way. For we cannot know, without resorting to our own or someone else's memory of the person in question, whether the body before us is the same one that the person we think he is had in the past. This is true, but it does not show that the man's own memories determine who he is. It only shows that other people could not determine the necessary physical facts about him unless they could rely on their own memories to do it, and this is not the same thing.

There are two arguments that tend to show, I think, that the bodily criterion has priority over the memory criterion. The first one, which is the less fundamental, rests on the fact that people forget things. We cannot say that the man before us is the man who performed some past action if and only if he remembers doing that action, for people forget actions they have done. But one might object on two counts that this need not refute the claim that his having the memory of that action is what makes that action his rather than someone else's. For, first, all we mean by this is that he *could* remember doing it, not that he *does* remember doing it; and, second, all we need is that he be able to remember doing some action or having some experience that the person who did the original action also did, or had.

Let us take these objections in order. The first will not do, for what do we mean when we say that he could remember doing the action in question? If we mean that it is in practice possible to get him to recall doing it, for instance, by psychoanalysis, then the retort is that all practicable methods might fail without thereby showing that the action was not done by him. If, on the other hand, we merely mean that it is in theory possible, then this requires further elucidation: Something that is possible in theory but not in practice is possible in virtue of some condition that in practice cannot bring it about. And this condition can only be the very fact that we are trying to elucidate, namely, the fact that the action was done by him and not by someone else. The other objection does not hold either, for a similar sort of reason. If we say that although the man before us cannot remember doing the action in question, he did do it because he can remember having some experience that the past person who did that action had, this presupposes that we understand what makes the past person who had that experience the same past person who did the original action.

There must therefore be some standard of identity, actually satisfied, that we are appealing to in order to presuppose this. To say that this standard is itself that of memory is to raise our original question all over again.

The second and more fundamental argument rests on the fact that the notion of remembering is ambiguous. To say that someone remembers some action or event may mean merely that he believes he did it or witnessed it (without, at least consciously, basing this belief upon being told about it). It is possible, of course, for someone to remember something in this sense without what he remembers having happened at all and without its having happened to *him* even if it did occur. The more common use of the notion of remembering, however, concedes the truth of the man's belief, so that to say that the man remembers some action or event is to say that his claim to know about it is correct. Let us call these sense (i) and sense (ii) of "remember." Then we can say that to remember in sense (i) is to believe that one remembers in sense (ii).

It is apparent that memory in sense (1) cannot provide a criterion of personal identity. It is certainly not a sufficient condition of a man before us being the person that he claims to be that he remembers, in sense (i), doing or experiencing something done or experienced by the man he claims to be. For he could believe that he remembered doing something in this sense, even if nobody had done it. So we have to lean on sense (ii) of "remember." But this leads into a deeper problem. Let us simplify our discussion by concentrating solely upon a person's remembering doing an action or having an experience or witnessing an event and leave aside the complexities involved in someone's remembering some fact, such as that Cáesar was murdered. To say that someone, in sense (ii), remembers, is not merely to report that he believes something, but to accept his belief to be true. But an integral part of his belief is not only that some action was done, some experience had, or some event witnessed, but that it was done or had or witnessed *by him*. In other words, to say that he remembers in sense (ii) is not just to say that he now has some mental image or some conviction, even though it is likely to include this; it is to say that the past action, experience, or event that he refers to is part of his own past. But it now becomes clear that we cannot even state the memory criterion of identity without having some prior (and therefore independent) notion of the identity of the person. So the identity of the person must in the end rest upon some other condition, and the claim that it could rest solely upon memory must be false. The bodily criterion of identity is the natural one to refer to here. If, because of some commitment to dualism, one refuses to resort to it, it becomes wholly mysterious what the criterion of personal identity can be.

IDENTITY AND SURVIVAL

We can now return to the problem of survival. We were considering how far it is possible to make sense of the notion of the persistence of a disembodied person through time and of the claim that some particular future disembodied person will be identical with one of us in this world here and now. We can also ask how far the doctrine of the resurrection of the body frees us from the difficulties that the doctrine of disembodied survival encounters.

If bodily continuity is a necessary condition of the persistence of a person through time, then we cannot form any clear conception of the persistence of a person through time without a body nor of the identity of such a person with some previous embodied person. The previous reflections about the notion of personal identity leave us with two results: first, that to attempt to understand the self-identity of a person solely in terms of memory is impossible and, second, that when we are considering the case of flesh-and-blood persons there seems no alternative but to conclude that bodily continuity is a necessary condition of personal identity. These conclusions by themselves do not show that no substitute for bodily continuity could be invented when discussing the case of disembodied personality. But some substitute for it would have to be supplied by invention, and until it is, the notion of disembodied personal identity makes no sense.

The main line of argument is now plain, but for greater completeness it may be desirable to apply it to the doctrine of disembodied survival in a little more detail. An adherent of this doctrine, anxious to avoid admitting the necessity of the bodily criterion of personal identity, might perhaps claim that a survivor of death would intelligibly be said to be identical with someone who had died, because he remembered the actions and experiences of that person. And he might be said intelligibly to persist through time in his disembodied state because later and earlier experiences in the afterlife could be similarly connected by memories.

Let us take the latter suggestion first. It is that the disembodied person who has some experience at some future time FT_2 will be identical with the disembodied person who will have had some experience at an earlier future time FT_1 if, along with the experience at FT_2, there is a memory of the one he had at FT_1. The difficulty is to make sense not only of a phrase like "along with the experience there is a memory," but also, of what it means to speak of a memory here at all. For it will have to be a memory in sense (ii). And to say that the disembodied person has a memory at FT_2 in sense (ii) of some experience had at FT_1 is to assume that the two experiences will have been had by the same person; and this time, since we have no bodily criterion of identity to fall back on, we have no way of interpreting this claim.

If we turn now to the problem of identifying the disembodied person with some person who has died, we find the same difficulty. To say that he can be so identified because he remembers the deeds or experiences of that person is once again to use the notion of remembering in sense (ii). But to do this is to presuppose that we understand what it is for the remembering to be identical with the person who did those deeds or had those experiences. And we do not actually understand this. For although the person who did those deeds had a body, the rememberer, by hypothesis, does not have one and therefore cannot have the same body. It does not seem possible, therefore, to find any answer to the problem of self-identity for disembodied persons.

What about the doctrine of the resurrection of the body? Given that we are talking of the future existence of persons with bodies, the notion of their lasting through time in their future state does not seem to present any logical difficulties. But what of their identity with ourselves? If we assume some one-to-one correspondence between the inhabitants of the next world and of this (that is, assume at least that the inhabitants of the next world each resemble, claim to be, and claim to remember the doings of inhabitants of this one), it might seem foolish to deny that they will be identical with ourselves. But foolishness is not logical absurdity. It is conceivable that there might be a future existence in which there were large numbers of persons each resembling one of us and having uncanny knowledge of our pasts. And if that world does come to be in the future, we shall not be in it. What would make it a world with us in it, rather than a world with duplicates of us in it and not ourselves? Unless we can give a clear answer to this, it seems, very paradoxically, to be a matter of arbitrary choice whether to say these future people are us or not.

Surely, the answer might run, they will have the same bodies that we now have. But this is precisely what is not obvious. Apart from questions about whether the future bodies are like ours in youth, maturity, or old age, the dissolution of the earthly body means that the future body will be in some sense new. To say that it is the old one re-created is merely to say it is the same one without giving any reason for saying it is identical with the original body rather than one very much like it. To answer this way, then, seems merely to face the same puzzle again. To say

that the future beings will remember in sense (ii) our doings and feelings is to raise the same questions here as before. The only possible solution seems to be to insist that in spite of the time gap between the death of the old body and the appearance of the new one, something persists in between. But what? The person disembodied? If so, then the doctrine of the resurrection of the body does not avoid the difficulties that beset the doctrine of disembodied survival, for the simple reason that it falls back upon that very doctrine when its own implications are understood.

This argument does not show that the doctrine of the resurrection of the body is absurd in the way in which the doctrine of disembodied survival is. It shows rather that the doctrine of resurrection is merely one way, and a question-begging way, of describing a set of circumstances that can be described equally well in another fashion. Yet the difference between the two alternative descriptions is a vital one. For it comes to no less than the original question, namely, do we survive? It is a question that the doctrine provides an answer to but one that seems to have no conclusive grounds, even if the circumstances envisaged in the doctrine were admitted to be forthcoming.

The belief in survival, then, at least in this version, does not run into insuperable difficulties of logic. But it does not seem possible to describe a set of future circumstances that will unambiguously show it to be true.

NOTE

1. See I Corinthians, Chapter 15.

79   DO WE NEED IMMORTALITY?

GRACE M. JANTZEN

Without life after death, would Christianity be pointless? In the next selection, Grace M. Jantzen (1948–2006), who was Professor of Religion, Culture, and Gender at the University of Manchester, argues that a belief in immortality is not central to Christianity.

In a previous selection John H. Hick observed that if God loved human beings, God would not allow them to pass out of existence. Jantzen replies that most species of animals that lived on earth are now extinct. Did God not value them?

Jantzen interprets eternal life not as endless survival but as a quality of present existence that can be found here and now. She concludes that if we have only one life, then we cannot postpone seeking enjoyment and fulfillment both for ourselves and for those about whom we care.

The doctrine of life after death is often taken to be an essential ingredient in Christian theology. Baron Friedrich Von Hügel, when he said that "Religion, in its fullest development, essentially requires, not only this our little span of earthly years, but a life beyond,"[1] was only echoing the words of St Paul: "If in this life only we have hope in Christ, we are of all men most miserable."[2] And more recently, others, among them John Hick, have devoted much energy to a consideration of life after death. Hick writes that "Any religious understanding of human existence—not merely one's own existence but the life of humanity as a whole—positively requires some kind of immortality belief and would be radically incoherent without it."[3]

In this article I propose to look behind the arguments for and against the possibility of life after death, to investigate the various motives for wanting it, ranging from the frivolously irreligious to the profound. I shall argue that the belief in immortality is not so central to Christian thought and practice as is often believed, and indeed that a rich Christian faith does not require a doctrine of life after death in order to be profound and meaningful.

SELF-REGARDING MOTIVES

To begin with the obvious, our desire for immortality is not a desire for just any sort of continued existence: the less musical among us might prefer extinction to an eternity of playing harps and singing hymns, and given a choice, we would all prefer extinction to hell. H. H. Price has offered a picture of a life after death which is entirely the product of our desires—but which might turn out to be a highly undesirable state. In his description, the postmortem world is a world in which our wishes would immediately fulfil themselves, a world whose laws "would be more like the laws of Freudian psychology than the laws of physics."[4] As Price points out, this might be much less pleasant than we might have thought; because our desires, when we include all those we have repressed, are not in mutual harmony. They incorporate, for instance, desires for punishment and suffering for the wrongs we have done. He offers the following grim comments: "Each man's purgatory, would be just the automatic consequence of his own desires; if you like, he would punish himself by having just those images which his own good feelings demand. But, if there is any consolation in it, he

From Grace M. Jantzen, "Do We Need Immortality?" *Modern Theology*, 1 (1984). Reprinted by permission of Blackwell Publishing Ltd.

would have those unpleasant experiences because he wanted to have them; exceedingly unpleasant as they might be, there would still be something in him which was satisfied by them."[5] Price's point is that if all our repressed desires suddenly came true, this would be horrifying, and we would have to set about the difficult process of altering our characters so that when we get what we want, we want what we get.

The popular desire for immortality is very little like this. Life after death is often pictured, rather, as the fulfilment of longings for pleasure: it will be a paradise where there will be no more suffering and pain, where we will be happily reunited with those we love in perpetual feasting and gladness. It must be admitted that some religious pictures of heaven reinforce this frankly hedonistic conception. In the Koran we find that heaven is a beautiful garden filled with fruits and flowers. "There the Muslims drink the wine they have been denied on earth, wine that has no after-effects. It is brought to them by handsome youths, and dark-eyed houris wait on their every pleasure."[6] Similar descriptions of a hedonistic paradise of feasting and delight can be found in Christian writings, except that the dark-eyed houris are conspicuously absent, probably because of Christianity's long-standing suspicion of the sorts of delights the presence of these creatures would signal.

One of the appeals of such a description of paradise is that in this eternal delight there is no more separation from those we love; we are all eternally reunited. This, however, might prove a mixed blessing. Apart from the fact that with some of those we love, the relationship improves if there are periods of space between our togetherness, there is also the consideration that heaven would not be a private party—everyone is invited. Now, what might it be like to find oneself at the heavenly feast seated next to a Neanderthal man? Surely conversation would lag, and it is doubtful whether the silences could be filled by enjoyment of the same food. Christianity has sometimes avoided this social embarrassment by consigning the vast majority of mankind to hell, but that is not a possibility with which many of us could acquiesce and still enjoy the feast.

The point behind these frivolous comments is that it is not quite so easy to give a picture of unending delight as might be thought; it is against scenarios of this sort that Bernard Williams' comments on the tedium of immortality have some point.[7] A paradise of sensuous delights would become boring; it would in the long run be pointless and utterly unfulfilling. We can perhaps imagine ways of making a very long feast meaningful; we do, after all, cope with lengthy terrestrial social occasions by choosing interesting conversational partners, and making the dinner occasions not merely for food and drink but also for stimulating discussion and for giving and receiving friendship the value of which extends beyond the termination of the dinner. But if the feasting literally never came to an end, if there were no progress possible from the sensuous enjoyment of paradise to anything more meaningful, then we might well wish, like Elina Macropolis, to terminate the whole business and destroy the elixir of youth. It is important to notice, however, that on this view survival is tedious simply because there is no progress, no point to the continued existence except the satisfaction of hedonistic desires. But this picture is much too simple-minded. Christians (and Muslims too, of course) have long recognized this, and have taken the hedonistic descriptions of the Scriptures as symbolic of something more meaningful than eternal self-indulgence, as we shall see.

Death is sometimes seen as evil because it means the curtailment of projects; immortality would be required to give significance to life because it would allow those projects to be meaningfully continued. Of course, most of our projects would not require all eternity to complete. But even in this life, one enterprise leads to another, and provided endless progress were possible, we might pursue an endless series of challenging and absorbing tasks, each one developing into another, without any risk of boredom. This might also give more point to some of our earthly projects: the painstaking acquisition of languages and techniques would be worthwhile beyond the few years we have to employ them here. This way of thinking about survival is probably more attractive to an intellectual whose current projects could easily be extended into the future, than, say, to a labourer who considers the prospect of endless projects as enough to make him feel tired already. Still, given the opportunity, perhaps he too would develop interests which he would genuinely like to pursue.

The notion that life after death would provide an opportunity for the fulfilment of projects is not, of course, presented as an argument for the likelihood of survival but as an argument for its desirability. But does it succeed? There is considerable pull toward saying that it does, especially for those who have far more interests than they can possibly develop even assuming an average life-span. An after-life in which we could all pursue what we are really interested in without worrying about earning daily bread or having the notion that the project itself is fulfilling—so that a fulfilled person is one who completes fulfilling projects—but then we have gone round in a circle. Personal fulfilment involves something like actualizing our potential, completing projects which "do ourselves justice." But this then is problematical again: what is meant by "our potential"? If it means the whole variety of things that many of us would enjoy doing and could do well with suitable training, then this life is much too short for fulfilment, and immortality appears attractive.

But while this shows that immortality may be desirable (for some people, in some forms) it is possible to give an alternative account of fulfilment which does not require survival. If death is seen as the limit of life, then "death gains what significance it has, not by serving as a state characterizing things, but as a function which orders members of the limited series."[8] Thus if we take seriously the fact that our existence will terminate, this will affect our choice about life: if we will not live forever, then we must do while we can those things which are really important to do. On this view, a fulfilled person would be a person who picked such projects for his life that were genuinely worthwhile and suitable for his abilities and aptitudes, and was able to bring them to completion: Einstein, who lived to an old age and had accomplished significant projects, would be described as fulfilled, but a person who never had any projects at all, and lived in continuous aimless frustration, "In the evening saying 'Would it were morning' and in the morning saying 'Would it were evening'" would not be so describable. Neither would be the person who had projects but died before he could accomplish them. We do distinguish fulfilled and unfulfilled people in these ways, without reference to immortality. This does not of course mean that immortality is not desirable, especially for those who through no fault of their own are not able to complete their projects in their life-times. But it does mean that we do not have to postulate an after-life to make sense of the very concept of fulfilled and meaningful human life.

Also, if death is a limit, this gives a significance and urgency to our choices which they would not otherwise have. If we could go on pursuing an endless series of projects, it might not matter very much which ones we chose first: we could always do others later. Nor would it matter how vigorously we pursued them—for there would always be more time—nor how challenging they were or how well they developed us and brought out the best in us—for there would always be other opportunities. But if fulfilment is something which must be reached in this life if it is to be reached at all, we will be far less cavalier about the choices we make affecting our own fulfilment, and also, very importantly, in our relationships with others for whose fulfilment we are partly responsible. A great many of our projects, and arguably the most significant of them, have to do not merely with ourselves but with others: our fulfilment is not simply a matter of, say, satisfying our individual intellectual curiosities, but is bound up with the fulfilment of family, friends, students. If we really have only this life, then enjoyment and fulfilment cannot be postponed to another, either for ourselves or for those we care about.

MORAL MOTIVES

It is sometimes argued that immortality is required on moral grounds. Such an argument can take the Kantian form: immortality is necessary as a postulate of practical reason. Since the Summum Bonum involves happiness as well as virtue, and since in this life we often find a disparity between the two, it is necessary to postulate a life after death where the imbalance will be redressed. Otherwise the universe is ultimately unjust, out of joint.

I do not wish to linger long over this, but simply make three points, none of them original. First, maybe we should just admit that the universe is out of joint; it hardly seems obvious, even (or especially) from the point of view of Christian theology, that it is not. Second, even if it is, that does not rob morality—even on a Kantian system—of its point. An act of intrinsic worth is still worthwhile even if it will never receive any happiness in reward; furthermore, morality retains its meaning even if we are all going to perish. (It is not pointless for the dying to show kindness to one another.) Those who say that if there is no life after death then nothing— including morality— in this life is meaningful are implicitly admitting that there is nothing in this life which is worthwhile for its own sake, independent of eternal consequences; that everything, even love, is only a means to an end, and an end which this life cannot give. Kant himself could not have accepted such a view. Third, the Kantian view of reward has a peculiarity. What sort of happiness is it which is to be the reward of virtue? Suppose we think of it as some variant of the hedonistic paradise described earlier: then for reasons already given, the more moral one was— the more one valued that which was intrinsically good—the less happiness one would find in such ultimately pointless eternal self-indulgence. On the other hand, if Kant was speaking of the satisfactions of fulfilment rather than of a hedonistic utopia, then for the one who truly pursues virtue, becoming virtuous will itself be the fulfilment; virtue will be its own reward.

A more interesting argument for the requirement of immortality arises, not from the idea that virtue needs to be rewarded, but from the fact that none of us is sufficiently virtuous. If part of the point of life is moral development, and none of us develops fully in this life, would it not be desirable for this process to continue beyond the grave? There is considerable connection between this argument and the previous ones; except that here there is no request for happiness as a compensation for virtue, but rather for fulfilment of the very virtue that one has sought, albeit with only

moderate success. There are at least two aspects of this, which I shall consider separately.

The first is encapsulated by Dostoyevsky in *The Brothers Karamazov*. "Surely I haven't suffered simply that I, my crimes and my sufferings, may manure the soil of the future harmony for somebody else. I want to see with my own eyes the hind lie down with the lion and the victim rise up and embrace his murderer. I want to be there when everyone suddenly understands what it has all been for."[9] This is not a desire for happiness in any hedonistic sense, but a desire to see the point, the fruition of all one's efforts. It is a natural enough human desire, of course; yet I do not think that it can be used as an argument that morality requires immortality, for the assumption here surely is that all the toil and suffering does have a point, whether we are "there" to understand it in the end or not. Even if we are not present at the final denouement, this does not make working toward it less worthwhile, for once again, the value of doing that cannot depend on what we individually get out of it. Although Dostoyevsky here touches, as he so often does, a very deep nerve of desire, he surely cannot be interpreted to mean that if that desire remains forever unfulfilled, there was no meaning to the suffering in the first place.

The second aspect of the longing for immortality is the longing for perfection in virtue. This is part of what prompted the more positive conceptions of purgatory, where that was seen not as a place of retributive punishment until one had suffered proportionately to the sins one had committed on earth, but rather as a place of moral purification and advance, "Where human spirits purge themselves, and train/To leap up into joy celestial."[10] This, clearly, is not an unworthy motive for desiring life after death (though in more cynical moments one might wonder how universally it is shared—how many people desire immortality because they truly want to become better). Yet it too has some problems.

In the first place, it is not obvious that simple extension of life would result in moral improvement: more time can be opportunity for deterioration as well as for advance; the person who says, "I would be better, if only I had a little longer" is justifiably suspect. Still, although time does not automatically produce growth, it may be true that it is necessary for growth. But once again it is worth thinking about the concept of death as a limit. If immortality is denied, and if moral growth is valued, there is an urgency to moral improvement, both for oneself and for others, which might easily be ignored if it were thought that there was endless time available. And as we have already seen, it will not do to say that such moral improvement, with its struggle and frequent failure, would be worthless if all ends at death, for this would hold true only if moral improvement were a means to an end, rather than intrinsically valuable.

RELIGIOUS MOTIVES

Those who say that immortality will be the scene of moral progress do not, of course, usually have in mind nothing but temporal extension to bring this about: as Fichte once said, "By the mere getting oneself buried, one cannot arrive at blessedness."[11] Rather, they believe that in the life after death there will be some strong inducements to improvement. In Price's non-theistic purgatory the unpleasantness of getting what we want may lead us to revise our desires and characters, while according to some theistic conceptions of purgatory, the punishments for our sins will purge us—sometimes in Clockwork Orange fashion—of our innate sinfulness. The most interesting theory of inducement to moral perfection, and one that forms a bridge to specifically religious arguments for the need for immortality, is the idea that the lure of divine love, more obvious in the next life than in this one, will progressively wean us from our self-centeredness and purify us so that at last our response will be perfect love reciprocated. John Hick, in his discussion of universal salvation, argues that given the assumption that man has been created by God and is "basically oriented towards him, there is no final opposition between God's saving will and our human nature acting in freedom."[12] Thus God, extending his love ever again towards us, will not take "no" for an answer but will ultimately woo successfully, not by overriding our freedom, but by winning us over so that eventually we freely choose him and his perfection. Hick says, "if there

is continued life after death, and if God is ceaselessly at work for the salvation of his children, it follows that he will continue to be at work until the work is done; and I have been arguing that it is logically possible for him eventually to fulfil his saving purpose without at any point overriding our human freedom."[13]

But even granting Hick's basic assumptions of humanity's created bias toward God, God in loving pursuit of men and women, and endless time for "the unhurried chase," there are still problems with his conclusion. It is not clear that genuine freedom could be preserved while still guaranteeing the ultimate result: surely if there is freedom there is always the possibility of refusal. Hick's response, presumably, would be to agree that refusal is possible but that, given his assumptions, it becomes less and less likely as time goes on. Yet significantly to the extent that theists, Hick among them, wish to use the fact of human freedom as a (partial) resolution of the problem of evil, one aspect of their defence is that, though persons were created with a bias toward God, their freedom made it possible for them to choose rebellion, thus bringing moral evil in its train: evil is the price of freedom gone wrong. I do not see how one can have it both ways: if evil choices were made in the past even when there seemed no particular reason for them, how can Hick be confident that they will not be repeated endlessly in the future, especially since in the latter case they are made by characters already considerably warped by previous evil choices? The only way that I can see out of this for Hick is by increasing the emphasis on the divine pressure, but that runs the risk of undermining the very freedom which must here be preserved.

It is important to see the implications of human freedom for a Christian doctrine of redemption. One aspect of choice not sufficiently considered is its finality. Of course decisions can sometimes be reversed; we can often change our minds. And when we do so, when there is genuine repentance and conversion, Christianity teaches that God "makes all things new," brings creativity out of chaos, Easter out of Calvary. But the fact that we can sometimes freely change our minds is not the same as saying that in the end it makes no difference what our intermediate choices are because ultimately we will all (freely) be brought to the same goal. If it is true that whether I choose p or not-p, in the end I will get p, the idea of choice has been robbed of all significance—and that is so even if I can be persuaded that in the end it will really be p that I do want. So if I perpetually choose selfishness and distrust and dishonesty, and my character is formed by these choices, it seems perverse to say that eventually these choices will be reversed and I will attain the same moral perfection as I would have if I had all along chosen integrity and compassion. Part of what it means to be free is that our choices have consequences; it is playing much too lightly with the responsibility of freedom to suggest that these consequences, at least in their effects upon ourselves, are always reversible, even if only in the endless life to come. For that matter, if everyone is perfected, then even the consequences of our choices upon others will finally be overridden: all, in the end, will be as though no one had ever chosen evil at all. Morally revolting as is the thought of God committing people to eternal flames, one of the reasons why traditional theology has so long retained a doctrine of hell is surely to guard this aspect of freedom: there is no such thing as automatic salvation.

In spite of the strong reinforcement which the belief in immortality receives from Scripture and Christian tradition, a surprising amount can also be found which calls into question the idea that immortality is a religious requirement. In the first place, it is sometimes held that, of all the evils and sufferings in this world, death is the worst. On a traditional theistic view, evil must eventually be overcome, and all the wrongs made good; and this requires that death, "the last enemy," may not be proud. Death, too, shall die, when all who have ever lived will live again. This assumes, of course, that death is an evil; and if what I have said about death as a limit is correct, then that cannot be retained without some qualifications. Still, although death is not the worst evil, and not an unqualified evil, this does not amount to saying that it is not an evil at all; consequently in a world where evil was eradicated, death, too, would have no place.

But can this be used as an argument for a religious requirement of life after death? I am not sure that it can. If the perfect world dawns, death will perhaps not be found in it; but does this mean that death in this very imperfect world is followed by immortality? One might argue that only if it is, is God just: the sufferings of this present world can only be justified by the compensation of eternal life. But this, in the first place, is shocking theodicy: it is like saying that I may beat my dog at will provided that I later give him a dish of his favourite liver chowder. What happens after death—no matter how welcome—does not make present evil good.[14] But if life after death cannot be thought of as a compensation for otherwise unjustified present evils, surely death itself—permanent extinction—must be an evil from which a Christian may hope to escape? Well, on what grounds? We do not escape other evils and sufferings which a perfect world would not contain; why should we expect to escape this one? A Christian surely must recognize that there are many aspects of the problem of evil which he cannot explain; maybe he should just accept that death is another one. But would not death make the problem of evil not just more mysterious than it already is, but actually in principle unsolvable? Wouldn't we have to conclude that God is unjust? I don't know. If we can retain a belief in divine justice amid present evil and suffering, horrific as it is, I am not sure that relinquishing the prospect of life after death would necessarily alter the case. Of course it might tip the balance psychologically, making us "of all men, most miserable," but that is another matter. If the present evils can be relegated to the mysterious purposes of God, it seems presumptuous to assume that these purposes could not include our extinction.

A very persuasive argument for the requirement for immortality for Christian theology gathers up strands from several of these lines of thought, but places special emphasis on the personal love of God. If, as Christians maintain, God loves and values each of us individually, then we can trust him not to allow us to perish forever. We are worth more to him than that. Thus Helen Oppenheimer, in her discussion of problems of life after death, recognizes the great philosophical complexities regarding personal identity, resurrection, and the rest, but finally says that if we believe in God at all, we must also believe that if we keep on looking we will find the solution to these problems, because it is as unthinkable that a loving God would permit a relationship with one he loves to be severed by extinction of that loved one as it is to think that we would willingly allow our dearest friends to perish if it were in our power to provide them with a full and rich life.[15]

This approach has the merit, first of not pretending that the puzzles of identity and/or resurrection are easily solvable, second, of treating death seriously, and third, of placing the doctrine of immortality within the context of a doctrine of personal relationship with God. Death is not seen as a mild nuisance which can be quickly left behind never to be repeated; immortality is not automatic, and could not be expected at all were it not for the intervention of an omnipotent God. It is only because Christianity stakes itself on the unfailing love of God, following the man who dared to call God "Father" rather than "Judge," that life after death can even be considered.

But even though this seems to me a sounder starting place, given basic assumptions of Christian theology, than the belief that human beings are endowed with naturally immortal souls, I still have problems with it. It is comforting to be told that the love of God will not allow the termination of a relationship with him; it is also much more religiously satisfying to see this relationship as of central importance, and all the descriptions of the delights of paradise as mere symbolic gropings after the enjoyment of this divine fellowship. Nevertheless, Christian theology does hold that there are other things which are precious to God and which, in spite of that, perish forever. Christian theologians increasingly recognize that it is not the case that the whole earth, every primrose, every songbird, all the galaxies of all the heavens, exist for the benefit of humanity alone. Yet if it is true that God brought about the existence of all these things and takes delight in them, then it is also true that some of the things he delights in perish forever: a popular book of natural history estimates that 99 percent of all species of animals which have lived on earth are now extinct.[16]

We cannot have it both ways. "Are not three sparrows sold for a farthing?" Jesus asked. "Yet not one of them falls to the ground without your heavenly Father's knowledge."[17] These words of Jesus have often (and rightly) been taken as his teaching of the tender concern of the Father for all his creatures; what has not been noticed so often is that Jesus never denies that sparrows do fall. If the analogy which Jesus is drawing to God's care for persons (who, he says, "are of more value than many sparrows") is taken to its logical conclusion, the implication, surely, is not that we will not die but that our death will not go unnoticed. If a Christian admits that God allows some things which he values to perish, it will need further argument to show why this should not also be true of human beings: the primroses, presumably, are not loved less simply because they are temporary.

But perhaps they are temporary because they are loved less? Because they are not of such enduring worth to God (as human beings are) they are allowed to perish? This still leaves me uneasy. It is one thing to believe that we are individually valued by God, and valued perhaps in a way that other things are not; it is quite another to say that this value must result in our immortality. How can we be so sure? The analogy with persons we love whom we would not willingly allow to perish assumes that our relationship with God is in this respect just like our relationship with them. But even if we accept this analogy as the best we have for our relationship with God, we must still admit that there must be considerable disanalogies as well: how do we know that the case of endless preservation is not one of them? We may believe that God looks upon us with love and compassion, but that does not seem to me to be any guarantee that he wills our everlasting existence—that is a further (very large) step. We are taught, to be sure, that God wishes to bring us to eternal life; but it is a glaring confusion to equate eternal life with endless survival. As the notion of eternal life is used in the Johannine writings, for instance, it is spoken of as a present possession, a quality of life, not a limitless quantity; nor is it something that happens after death but in this present lifetime.

Furthermore, if there were no life after death, this in itself would not mean that religion would be pointless. Just as that which is morally valuable is valuable for its own sake and not for the reward it can bring, so also trust in God, if it is worthwhile at all, is worthwhile even if it cannot go on forever. A relationship with another human being does not become pointless just because at some time it will end with the death of one of the partners; why should it be thought that a relationship with God would be pointless if one day it too should end? Shneur Zalman, the Jewish founder of the Chabad, once exclaimed, "Master of the Universe! I desire neither Paradise nor Thy bliss in the world to come. I desire Thee and Thee alone."[18] And the hymn of Fenelon has become the common property of Christendom:

> My God I love Thee: not because I hope for heaven thereby,
> Nor yet because who love Thee not are lost eternally...
> Not for the sake of winning heaven, nor of escaping hell;
> Not from the hope of gaining aught, not seeking a reward;
> But as thyself hast loved me, O ever loving Lord...
> Solely because thou art my God and my most loving King.[19]

It is true, of course, that these words (and many more examples could be given) were written by men who did believe in immortality; the point, however, is that according to them, the value of the relationship with God, the vision of God, cannot be measured by measuring its temporal duration.

But perhaps it will still be objected that if God will one day allow me to perish, this shows that all the teaching about his love for me is a vast fraud—if he really loved me, he would preserve my life. I can only reply that for reasons already given, this does not seem obvious to me. I cannot forget the primroses. They perish. Must we conclude that they are not precious to God?

I am not arguing that there is no life beyond the grave or that it is irrational to hope for it or for Christians to commit their future to God in trust. But if what I have said is correct, then it would be presumptuous to be confident that life after death is a matter of course, guaranteed, whatever the problems, by the requirements of morality and religion. We should not neglect the significant change

of verb in the Nicene Creed: from affirmations "I believe in God," "I believe in Jesus Christ," and so on, we come to the rather more tentative "And I look for the resurrection of the dead and the life of the world to come." Christian faith and Christian commitment bases itself not first and foremost on a hope of survival of death, but on the intrinsic value of a relationship with God, without any reservations about what the future holds—here or hereafter.

NOTES

1. Baron F. Von Hügel, *Eternal Life*, 2nd edition (Edinburgh: T. & T. Clark, 1913), p. 396.
2. I Cor. 15: 19.
3. John Hick, *Death and Eternal Life* (London: Fontana, 1976), p. 11.
4. H. H. Price, "Survival and the Idea of 'Another World'," in J. Donnelly (ed.), *Language, Metaphysics and Death* (New York: Fordham University Press, 1978), p. 193.
5. Ibid., p. 192.
6. Alfred Guillaume, *Islam*, 2nd edition (Harmondsworth, Middlesex: Penguin, 1954), p. 198.
7. Bernard Williams, "The Macropolis Case: Reflections of the Tedium of Immortality," in his *Problems of the Self* (Cambridge: Cambridge University Press, 1973).
8. James Van Evra, "On Death as a Limit," in Donnelly, *Language, Metaphysics and Death*, p. 25.
9. F. Dostoyevsky, *The Brothers Karamazov*, II. V. 4.
10. Dante, *The Divine Comedy: Purgatory*, I. 5 & 6.
11. Fichte, *Sämmtliche Werke Vol. 5* (1845–6), p. 403, quoted in Von Hügel, *Eternal Life*, p. 176.
12. Hick, *Death and Eternal Life*, p. 254.
13. Ibid., p. 258. "Salvation" as Hick uses the term involves moral perfection.
14. And of course it may put a different complexion on things that were perceived as evil in our imperfect state of knowledge, so that we see that it was a necessary condition for good; but that is not at issue here.
15. Helen Oppenheimer in a University Sermon preached in St Mary's, Oxford, in 1979.
16. Richard E. Leakey, *The Making of Mankind* (London: Book Club Associates, 1981), p. 20.
17. Matt. 10:29.
18. Quoted in Isidore Epstein, *Judaism* (Harmondsworth, Middlesex: Penguin, 1959), p. 279.
19. Quoted from *Hymns Ancient and Modern*, 106.

C. REINCARNATION

80 HINDUISM AND THE SELF

JOEL KUPPERMAN

While Christians and Muslims typically hope for resurrection, most adherents of Indian thought accept some version of the doctrine of reincarnation. Different religions, however, offer differing views of the self, rebirth, and the highest spiritual state. Our next selection focuses on the Hindu outlook, as assessed by Joel Kupperman, Professor of Philosophy at the University of Connecticut.

The Upanishads written in India mainly in the eighth to sixth centuries BCE,... were—and remain—the core texts of Hinduism, which continues to be by far the dominant religion of India and to have adherents in some other countries of South Asia as well....

The ancient Hindu answer to the questions of life and death is tempered by the doctrine of reincarnation, which ... was shared with ancient Greece. After death one will enter a new life. The ancient Greeks spoke of the river Lethe (forgetfulness) from which one must drink before entering the new life, and the ancient inhabitants of India also tended to assume that in the new life one would remember very little or nothing of the old one. There was the possibility of reincarnation as an animal. The Law of Karma held that how favorable a reincarnation was (i.e., whether it was in a privileged social caste or in a low caste or as an animal) depended in a fairly automatic way on the degree of virtue contained in the old life. It was as if light souls rose and heavy souls sank....

But ... the endless round of reincarnation ... might seem a tedious prospect. The Upanishads promise that, in a spiritual state referred to as *moksha* (liberation or release), you can have permanent spiritual fulfillment after death. In order to have this, you must follow the path of joy rather than the path of pleasure....

We therefore will have to look closely at pleasure and at joy. First, though, we need to understand the metaphysics of the Upanishads, the picture of the world that underlies the ethical advice about how to prepare for life after death. The metaphysics centers on a single, deceptively simple claim: *atman* is Brahman.

"*ATMAN* IS BRAHMAN" AND THE PROBLEM OF SELF

Atman (pronounced "Aht-man") and Brahman are central to classical Hindu philosophy. Are they central to experience? Perhaps this is not true, at least explicitly, for most of us. But the ancient Indian argument is that it should become true. The right kind of experience is claimed to provide evidence for the identification of *atman* with Brahman.

Let us begin with Brahman.... [T]he ancient religion of India worshiped many gods and goddesses. Three gods were paramount: Brahma the creator, Vishnu the preserver, and Shiva the destroyer. If it seems strange that a god of destruction is one of the three main gods, reflect on what

From Joel Kupperman, *Classic Asian Philosophy: A Guide to the Essential Texts*, Second Edition, Oxford University Press, 2007. Reprinted by permission of the publisher.

it would be like in the world if nothing ever was destroyed or died. The world would become undesirably cluttered, and also stagnant. There also are major goddesses, the most important being the great goddess Devi …

One needs to be mindful of the difference between Brahma, who is merely one god, and Brahman, who is everything. With the idea of Brahman, Hinduism makes the transition to a religion of a single divine reality. This transition was accomplished in different ways by different cultures. The simplest way is to deny that the gods and goddesses your ancestors worshiped really exist. Zoroaster in ancient Persia came up with an ingenious twist. The many gods, *devas*, who had been worshiped did exist, but were evil rather than good; there is only one God. The Upanishads present a different way of fitting what had been popular religion into a sophisticated worldview. The gods and goddesses all are—if they are properly understood—aspects or personae of the single divine reality, Brahman. This is subtly accommodating to popular religion. The gods and goddesses can continue to be worshiped, but those in the know will be mindful that they are all aspects of Brahman.

Thus far I have been presenting the outlines of a worldview without giving the reasons for it. The reasons for identifying all gods and goddesses with Brahman will emerge when we look at the sources of the idea of *atman*. The link is that gods and goddesses, like human beings, have desires, aversions, and characteristic forms of behavior. In short they have personalities. The central argument underlying the metaphysics of the Upanishads is that personality has only a superficial kind of reality.

The best way of appreciating this view is to examine a persistent feature of human experience, sense of self. Most of us have a feeling, which is familiar but hard to analyze, that there is a "me" close to the surface of our normal experience. When we wake up in unfamiliar surroundings we may not know where we are, but there is the familiar "me." Usually we know who we are by name, but even in cases of amnesia there will be the "me" (although now it is more mysterious).

This "me" gives us a strong sense of ways in which actions and experience in a life—our life—are unified. It enables us to have immediate knowledge, not based on evidence, of connections….

Can such a self change? Intuitively it might seem that the answer is "Yes." You are the same person you were a few years ago, even though undoubtedly you have changed in some respects. Reflective examination, though, undermines this intuitive confidence. We could imagine someone who is more like you were a few years ago than you now are. What then? The usual response is that, all the same, you (now) are you (then). Given continuous surveillance, we could have tracked you during the intervening period; and this continuity strengthens our sense of identity, even if the changes in you were in fact very great.

This line of thought would leave us with an identity that looks tempered by matters of degree. The ancient Greek philosopher Heraclitus is famous for the cryptic utterance "You can't step in the same river twice." What he presumably meant is that the river is constantly changing (different water flows through, there can be tiny variations in the positions of the river banks, etc.) so that, strictly speaking, today's river is not (entirely) the same as yesterday's river. In much the same spirit he might have argued that you can't be the same person today that you were yesterday. But a possible response is that we have conventions of language that enable rivers and persons to keep their names, and to count as the same by being pretty much the same.

These conventions usually work pretty well. But there are imaginable cases in which they start to break down. Some of these involve great change. If the river became very like what we would normally call a lake, that would put our sense of being confronted with the "same" river under considerable pressure. We could imagine cases in which someone's brain were entirely taken over by a terrible virus that had its own personality (and perhaps even its own name), in which there would be great hesitation in judging that what we were confronting is the same person we had known….

There is one alternative ... if we want to do justice to our intuitive sense of an unchanging "me" throughout life. This is to look for a core of self that has no elements of individual natures that grow and change. This would be a core that underlies (and is separate from) personality, thought patterns, bodily nature, and so forth.

This is *atman*. In the view of the Upanishads, this is what, at the deepest level, you are.

What I am suggesting is that the Upanishads' view of *atman* makes good philosophical sense if it is seen as the conclusion of the following (largely implicit) argument.

> Each of us has a persistent "me."
> This "me" (as it intuitively seems) must be unchanging.
> But personality, thought patterns, and so on, do change.
> Therefore the persistent "me" cannot include such elements.

The further conclusion is that your persistent "me," lacking all elements of individuality, is the same as anyone else's persistent "me." Once individuality is subtracted, what is there to distinguish you (qualitatively) from anyone else? The Upanishads indeed assume something broader: that the inner nature of all things, and not merely of all conscious beings, will be the same. This yields an image of the universe as a field of inner realities that are all at bottom the same. The inner realities of gods and goddesses, once their individualities are discounted, are included in this. The name for this field of inner realities is Brahman. *Atman*, then, is Brahman in somewhat the way in which a drop of water is the ocean of which it is a part. Whether the identity of *atman* and Brahman should be viewed straightforwardly as a matter of the same thing in two different guises, or as an identity between part and whole, becomes a debatable subject in Hindu philosophy.

SOME IMPLICATIONS

The religious implication of this philosophy is that folk polytheism is not repudiated or scorned. But there is a higher interpretation in which what is worshiped is always in fact a single divine reality, which takes the diverse forms of the traditional gods and goddesses. We also are parts of that single divine reality, which in the drama of the universe plays the part of you (and indeed plays all the parts, as well as being the scenery). Someone who accepts the Upanishads can say "I am God," which in Christianity, Judaism, and Islam would be considered heretical and blasphemous, but in the intellectual forms of Hinduism would be taken for granted....

The philosophical implications of the claimed identity of *atman* and Brahman are complicated. They include a philosophical monism—the entire universe is one thing—which is what would remind some readers of Spinoza. But they include also an account of what we are that is more complex and qualified than one might at first think.

There is the sense, of course, in which (if the Upanishads are right) you never change: Brahman is always Brahman. But, on the other hand, there are obvious respects in which you *do* change, especially as you come to think of yourself as Brahman.

There also is the problem of the layers of individual personality that surround the *atman*. According to the Upanishads, they are not the real you or any part of the real you. But all the same they are there, and the Upanishads talk about the importance of seeing beneath them (and perhaps, to a degree, getting rid of them).

Are these individualistic elements of personality Brahman? If they are, then what is so special about *atman*? If they are not, then it cannot be true that the entire universe is Brahman.

These difficulties about the status of your individual personality are peculiarly philosophical, not least in the way in which one hardly knows what to say. We need to put them aside for a little while. We can become clearer about them if we first investigate what is supposed to happen after you begin to think you have, underneath the layers of individual personality, an *atman*.

THE SEARCH FOR *ATMAN*

Including your *atman* in your knowledge is not easy, but it is required both for enlightenment and for liberation. If philosophical Hinduism were like some forms of religion we might be familiar with, then all you would have to do is say sincerely "I've got an *atman* and it's Brahman" and (assuming that you are also a moral person) you would be saved. The Upanishads make it clear that this is not true. What *will* make a difference to the quality of your life ... is if you come thoroughly to think in terms of *atman* as Brahman. This requires, among other things, a clear experiential sense of your *atman*. Merely an abstract formulation will not do.

There is a huge difference between believing something, more or less, and thoroughly thinking in terms of it. Imagine this case. Bloggs sincerely believes (he could pass a lie detector test on this) that there is life after death, including the possibility of a heaven that is far more gratifying than life here on earth. He also believes that his chances for heaven are excellent, and indeed at present are as good as they are ever likely to be. Someone then says to him, "Good news, Bloggs. You are going to die in the next five minutes." Bloggs will be happy, right?

Well he may be. But it seems likely that many genuinely religious people would not be. What is relevant is the extent to which an idea, or a set of ideas, engrosses one's mind. The Upanishads clearly assume that the metaphysical claim "*atman* is Brahman" generates an ethical imperative. One should take steps to change one's moment-to-moment thinking so that it is entirely engrossed by the idea that *atman* is Brahman. This process is facilitated by prolonged experiential contact with the nature of one's *atman*.

Clearly yoga, which in ancient Sanskrit simply means "technique," is important in this search. Someone who wishes to encounter the core of her or his being, underneath layers of changing personality, needs to have a steady mind, one that does not wander. Physical techniques that steady and calm bodily impulses can make a difference. Quiet surroundings with few distractions can help.

The evidence suggests that the Upanishads gave rise to cultural practices in which some members of the upper castes (who were thought to be the only ones ready for enlightenment, at least in this lifetime) devoted themselves to meditative search for their *atmans*. Sometimes people would begin this in their youth, but there also was a pattern in which people led normal family lives to the point at which their children were grown, and then—at the stage at which in our society they might begin to think about retirement communities—they would withdraw from normal life and spend their lives in remote locations seeking spiritual enlightenment....

On one persistent interpretation in Hindu philosophy, the experience of *atman* would have to be nondual. That is, it would not be a matter of the meditator scrutinizing something psychic and saying "aha, this is *atman*." Rather there would be a state of experience in which there was no separation between the knower and the known, no polarization within the experience. Indeed, the experience would have to be oddly featureless, but very calm. More than one of the Upanishads insists that it would be totally unlike normal waking experience or dreaming, but rather more like dreamless sleep (although not entirely the same). Presumably, then, any identification of *atman* would be after the experience, and not within it.

It should be emphasized here that there is great variety in Hindu philosophy, and one should not assume more consensus than there is in Western philosophy. What I am presenting here is what seems to me a dominant and compelling interpretation of the Upanishads.

It cannot too strongly be emphasized also that what the Upanishads ask for is extremely difficult, making it very unlikely that more than a small number of people in any generation would be entirely successful. Experiential knowledge of *atman* and coming entirely to think in terms of its identity with Brahman would have to be a full-time job. It would require an extreme preoccupation with one's inner nature that accentuates the introspective turn so prominent in Indian culture....

Someone whose thinking is entirely engrossed by the view that *atman* is Brahman presumably would no longer draw any boundaries within the world, and would not know her or his own name. One irony is that, while such a person would have reached enlightenment, the notion that she or he had reached enlightenment would seem (to that person) entirely meaningless. Indeed, the very desire to attain enlightenment, which had to get the difficult process starting, would have faded away (along with all other desires) well before the final victory. The individual's enlightenment, in short, would seem real from the outside—from the point of view of those who still think of the world in terms of distinct individuals and are not enlightened—but not from the inside.

It is time to say more about the emotions of the path to enlightenment, and specifically of pleasure and joy. Why is pleasure considered a trap? Any answer must consider the variety of things that are labeled "pleasure," and what many of them have in common. A great many sensory gratifications count as pleasures, including the obvious examples of food, drink, and sex, along with less obvious examples of bodily relaxation and of relief from discomfort. Seeing good friends is a pleasure, as is the thought that one has nothing to reproach oneself with. For someone who enjoys mathematics, an elegant proof can provide pleasure.

It should be clear that pleasures are very diverse, but that they typically are keyed to something that produces them. The something can be an object, an experience, or a thought. A natural thought is that the value of a pleasure will depend on, among other things, what it is keyed to. The value of the pleasure afforded by an extremely subtle and exquisite experience might seem to exceed that afforded by a warm shower on a cold day. We might not know what to say about the pleasure of activities that we judge less than worthless. What value does the pleasure of the sadist, after a good day in the torture chamber, have?

One of the general characteristics of pleasures, despite the great diversity, is that they tend to be brief. This is part of the contrast with happiness. We do, it is true, speak of being happy about something, perhaps something that happens to us; and such feelings or moods, keyed as they are to an occasion, can be brief. But there is also a sense in which someone can be happy, period—without the happiness being about anything specific. Such "global" happiness can go on for weeks, months, or an entire life. Pleasure, keyed

as it is to things that come and go, cannot be indefinitely prolonged, and must be renewed. Another contrast between pleasure and global happiness is that, according to some psychologists, global happiness requires a high degree of self-acceptance. That is, you can't be happy (in this sense) unless you basically like yourself. Pleasure, on the other hand, seems to depend mainly on whatever it is, outside the self, that it is keyed to.

An obvious problem with pleasure, then, is that caring about it has an element of built-in vulnerability. The world outside of us may not provide what we want. There is a more subtle problem. It can be argued that pleasures often require periods of prior frustration if they are to seem at all intense or meaningful, and also that they are addictive. If we get the pleasure we want—the argument goes—it is just a matter of time before we want more (or perhaps some different pleasures). This after-pleasure interval is marked by an increasing sense of boredom. Hence, there is a cycle in which the pleasure is paid for in advance by frustration and is paid for again in boredom. And this is in the favorable case, the one in which we actually get the pleasure. Sometimes we pay in frustration and then get nothing.

A simple example of the frustration-pleasure link is this: you could come to get intense pleasure from a simple glass of water. It is easy: just don't have anything to drink for the next couple of days, and then you will be amazed at how pleasant the glass of water is. Perhaps some of the sensual pleasures that people most look forward to would seem less interesting—in the way that glasses of water do to us—in a parallel universe of instant gratification?

There has been considerable cross-cultural awareness of this downside of pleasures. Is it true for all pleasures? Perhaps the role of prior frustration is less marked in the cases of the pleasure of being with friends, or of enjoying the elegant proof in mathematics, than it is in the case of purely sensory pleasures? Something like this seems to have been the thought of the ancient Greek philosopher Epicurus, who (despite the misleading associations that the word "epicurean" has acquired) recommended a strategy in life that emphasized pleasures such as those of the companionship of friends and downplayed sensory pleasures. A deliberately simple life, he contended, would minimize pain.

Clearly, from the point of view of the Upanishads, pleasures of all sorts (but especially of the kinds eschewed by Epicurus) have multiple disadvantages. They are distracting. Once people get hooked on them, they think about them a great deal. They tend to be inherently outward-focusing, providing an emphasis on the possible sources of satisfaction. Pleasures lead to emotional waves of desire and frustration, with some mixture perhaps of recollected gratification, which must spoil the calm needed in the search for *atman*.

Joy is harder than pleasure to talk about. For one thing, it is a much less common part of life for most of us. Also, it is easier to talk about an emotional experience if you can refer to a common "objective correlative": that is, refer to the kind of thing in the presence of which the emotional experience often occurs. Good food, sex, meetings with greatly missed friends, and so forth, all provide ready ways of talking about pleasure. But joy seems much less predictable than pleasure is, and it is far harder to think of regular occasions of joy.

Joy is like happiness in one respect. We do speak sometimes of joy in relation to specific things and occurrences. Much as we are happy about this or that, we also say that such and such gives me joy. A young child or a personal achievement can give someone joy in this sense. Alongside this object-keyed sense, there is one in which joy simply comes; it is not about anything in particular. The poet, standing in a field of daffodils, can be surprised by joy. The joy scarcely is *in* the daffodils. They are the almost accidental setting for something that comes from inside. Besides "global" happiness we can speak of global (objectless) joy. This is the joy that is praised by the Upanishads.

It is easier to say this much about joy than it is to specify why and when it arises. Why is there so little joy in the daily lives of most of us? Is it that we have so many concerns? If we look for people who do seem from time to time to experience joy, the best examples are small children, and perhaps also adults living simple lives in difficult circumstances. Calcutta, a city of incredible poverty, has been termed a "city of joy," something that would be unlikely to be said of a prosperous center of business activity.

One thought is that our development after early childhood consists to a large degree of emotional cocooning, protecting ourselves from the sharp emotions (both negative and positive) of small children, and also insulating ourselves from the rawness of the world. Perhaps suffering, as in the case of the poet who was finally surprised by joy, rips away the cocoon?

If this were the whole story, then it would appear that (at least in some cases) joy is like pleasure in being a poor bargain: in itself it is valued, but the advance payment is proportionally steep. However, I do not think that this is what the Upanishads have in mind. The path to enlightenment that they recommend is difficult, in terms of the effort required and the disruption of ordinary life. But there is no suggestion that it is painful or that one suffers.

The crucial features of joy in their view might seem to be the following: (1) Joy comes from inside and in that sense is not dependent on occasions and circumstances. (2) Joy comes from a psychic life that is uncluttered and therefore relatively open. (3) In some cases joy is related to a sense of well-functioning in this psychic life. To be in tune with the world, so to speak, can be a source of joy.

This concept of joy makes it understandable that the Upanishads view the search for enlightenment as a path that, without requiring antecedent suffering, will lead to predictable joy. The quiet inner satisfaction of the mystic who is nearly there could be intense and very rewarding. The emotional trade-off is that you give up pleasure, with its distractions and risks, for something in the end that is much greater and more predictable.

THE WORLD OF SUPERFICIAL REALITY

We need to return to the question of what kind of reality individual personality has. The negative judgment on it by now should be apparent.

Your individual personality is not really you. The real you, which never changes, is *atman*, which is identical with Brahman (which also never changes).

Are the outer layers of individual personality, which surround your *atman*, then an illusion? They certainly are not a *delusion*: that is, they are not like introspective hallucinations that have no footing in the world as it really is. An illusion, as opposed to a delusion, is something that distorts a reality that is there (but in a different form from the one that you take it to have). In this sense, the Upanishads do hold that individual personality is an illusion.

Nevertheless, it is an illusion that has an experiential life of its own. One of the striking things about the progress to enlightenment, though, is that the experiential life of individual personality is more ample and noticeable at the beginning than it is toward the end. Ancient Hindu texts convey a sense that to be enlightened or nearly enlightened is to be highly impersonal in affect, manner, and self-presentation. It is as if the layers of individual personality, once seen through, also begin to fade away. When you have seen one enlightened person, you have seen them all.

It sometimes seems as if the Upanishads want to say two divergent things at the same time. One is that there is a sense in which to become enlightened, fully engrossed in the mode of thought that goes along with the claim that *atman* is Brahman, is to become Brahman. Certainly the person on the way to enlightenment becomes more Brahman-ish, losing personality characteristics that might look as if they distinguish a person from the rest of the universe. But the Upanishads clearly insist that such a person (like all of us) always was Brahman. Everything is Brahman.

Along this line there are clear statements that individual personality characteristics are parts of the reality that Brahman spins out of itself, creating the universe out of itself like a spider spinning a web. If our atman is Brahman, then these personality characteristics also are Brahman. Are they equally Brahman? A recurrent metaphor is that each of us is like a drop of water in the ocean that is Brahman. Perhaps the individual personality characteristics could be compared to froth surrounding the drops of water? …

[W]e can take the Upanishads to be presenting two different frameworks within which what is real can be understood and described. What is thought of as the deeper truth is provided by the framework that is informed by "*atman* is Brahman." In this framework there is only one reality, Brahman. Everything is Brahman, and nothing ever changes.

Let us call this framework Ultimate Reality. There is also a framework of Superficial Reality, which represents the view of anyone whose thinking has not been entirely engrossed by the idea that *atman* is Brahman. In this framework there are countless individuals, including humans, animals, plants, pieces of furniture, gods and goddesses. Each of these things has its own characteristics. There is change, including processes of creation, preservation, destruction, life and death, spiritual fulfillment, spiritual sloth, and outright sin.

It is important to the Upanishads that there are truths within the framework of Superficial Reality. The phrase "superficial reality" may sound belittling, but anyone who writes a book, for which it is expected there will be readers, is (from the point of view of the authors of the Upanishads) operating within a framework of superficial reality. People who are fully enlightened do not write books. It is highly doubtful that they even know who (as individuals) they are or that there are differences between them and other people.

CONCLUSION

The Upanishads begin, both theoretically and practically, with self. The true self of the reader is put in question: it cannot be the individual personality, because one wakes up every morning recognizing oneself as the same person, and it would be hard to account for the precision and certainty of that knowledge given the changeable nature of individual personality. Thus we can find the true nature of who we are only by meditating beneath the surface of everything individual. This leads us to *atman*. Encountering *atman* saves the theory that everyone has an unchanging self, but it also is a first step toward personal liberation.

The full world picture of the Upanishads has been argued to be really a split screen. The deepest truth is that, because *atman* is Brahman, everything is Brahman. The entire universe is a single divine reality, which never really changes. On the other side of the split screen, we can see a universe full of individual things and beings that are constantly changing. In the view of the Upanishads it is true that some humans have more immediate spiritual potential than others do. The former are urged to want to allow the vision of *atman* as Brahman to engross their thinking, which will lead them to joy and to a spiritual achievement that will preclude any further reincarnations. In the process of this achievement, they will care less and less about the goal. When the idea of being a liberated individual comes to seem entirely meaningless, they will have arrived.

81 THE BUDDHIST CONCEPT OF SELF

THOMAS P. KASULIS

The Buddhist outlook on the self, reincarnation, and the highest spiritual state diverges in crucial ways from the Hindu perspective. The similarities and differences between the two are explored in our next selection. Its author is Thomas P. Kasulis, Professor in the Departments of Comparative Studies and of East Asian Languages and Literatures at The Ohio State University.

Buddhism did not begin twenty-five centuries ago as a philosophical system. Yet, insofar as its founder Gautama Siddartha made claims about the nature of self and reality, the seeds of philosophical reflection, analysis, and argument were already planted. The Buddha himself may not have been a philosopher in the strictest sense of the term: the earliest texts give us less of a philosophical system than a set of practical sermons, intriguing metaphors, and provocative parables. At around the time of the Buddha, however, a tradition of Indian thought that can be loosely identified as "Hindu" was already well underway, as can be seen in sections of some later Vedas and especially the early Upaniṣads. As the Hindu philosophers sharpened their own skills and became more systematic in their rationales, the Buddha's followers found themselves in philosophical competition with not only a set of indigenous beliefs, but increasingly also with sophisticated analyses supporting those beliefs.

The issue of personhood and its nature turned out to be a key point of contention. No idea in Hinduism was more central and had more philosophical luster than *ātman*, which could mean simply "self" but in Hindu thought typically added the connotations of "true self" or "soul." In fact, some early Hindu texts identified the true self with the oneness of reality, *brahman*. Buddhism, on the other hand, explicitly took the position of denying the reality of such a self. The Buddha himself made *anātman*, the negation of *ātman*, an emblem of his break from the Hindu tradition around him....

From Thomas P. Kasulis, "The Buddhist concept of self," in Eliot Deutsch and Ron Bontekoe, eds., *A Companion to World Philosophies*, Blackwell Publishers, 1997. Reprinted by permission of the publisher.

In developing an understanding of Buddhist philosophical views in relation to personhood, it is useful to bear in mind two general principles behind Buddhist thought. First, Buddhist philosophy arises out of Buddhist praxis. Of course, one could claim that there is always a connection between theory and praxis on some level, but there are important distinctions in how the two may interrelate. For example, sometimes a theory of reality precedes the development of a certain praxis that is then used as a means of verification within the theory. In the case of controlled laboratory experimentation, for instance, the scientist's practical procedures developed out of a theory that events follow a specific kind of reproducible pattern ("causes") that can be observed and measured by strictly empirical means. It is not always true, however, that theory precedes praxis in this way. For example, the praxis of learning and using language preceded the subsequent development of linguistic theory about language acquisition. In such cases, the praxis (of acquiring and using speech) was not acquired to confirm or disconfirm a theory, but rather the theory of reality (including the linguistics and cognitive science of how the mind and body work) was a metapractical reflection on the praxis in order to explain how and why the praxis works. In an analogous fashion, as we shall see, Buddhist philosophies about the self tend to arise out of metapractical reflection rather than prior theoretical systematization.

This point about the priority of praxis has clear philosophical implications. For example, Buddhism generally shies away from speculative metaphysics and argumentation about cosmic realities. It is typically less interested in analyzing reality to increase our understanding of it and more interested in probing and eliminating our resistance to accepting realities that, at least on some level, we already recognize. For example, what we ordinarily experience is impermanent and not eternal. Buddhism's inclination is to examine our flight from accepting that apparent fact and our quest to try to access some other reality transcendent to our ordinary sensory experience. To put this in terms more familiar to the contemporary West, Buddhism is more interested in the psychological than in the metaphysical aspects of philosophical reflection.

Of course, no philosophical position can be totally devoid of all assumptions about reality. Any philosophical position ultimately makes some initial assumptions within which it then develops its case. There is one premise that Buddhism does take as an unprovable starting point – namely, that there is a real presence besides the workings of the mind, and that the presence does not disguise itself to our ordinary ways of knowing. Again, using a Western terminology that offers only a rough fit, we can say that Buddhism is foundationally *realist* rather than, say, idealist or even constructivist.

In discussing phenomenal appearance, it is important to add one further point about the general Indian context. In Buddhism, as in most other Indian philosophical systems, the "ordinary sensory experience" to which we have referred are products of six, not five, senses. Besides the five outwardly directed senses usually recognized in the West, Buddhism includes also the sense of inner awareness or introspection. From the Buddhist standpoint, that I feel hungry or embarrassed, for example, are as "empirical" and "objective" as that I see the color red or hear a thud. Introspection is not considered a different order of knowing from extrospection. The acceptance of the reality and objective accessibility of psychological states is important to Buddhist praxis as the foundation for its understanding of self.

According to tradition, the Buddha developed his distinctive forms of praxis in response to a pervasive sense of anguish, anxiety, or unsatisfactoriness (*duḥkha*). Through a series of meditations that allowed him to cease making conceptual constructions, he introspectively focused on the stream of immediately available psychophysical events. He concluded that what we directly experience is what actually is and that anguish arises from our refusal to accept what exists for what it is. Ordinarily, he claimed, we project onto the immediately accessible phenomena a desire for things to be otherwise: to be "mine" rather than simply "to be"; to be enduring instead of transient; to be substantial – to be independently existing entities – instead of interdependent processes. Through the meditative praxis, the Buddha was purportedly able to disengage those projections. In so doing, he was able to gain the insight that allowed him not to form the fixations or attachments that lead to our ordinary sense of ego, substantiality, permanence, and self-dependency. In other words, the fruits of the praxis carried over into his ordinary life by liberating him from the tendency to structure his experiences around those categories. Freed of their effects, he was said to be able to accept things for what they are. The anguish disappeared.

The story of the Buddha's awakening (*"buddha"* means "awakened one") is peppered with various accounts of his achieving supernormal or paranormal powers (the ability to remember previous lifetimes, for example). It is significant, however, that none of those powers were considered necessary for underpinning his account of reality and of the self. To duplicate the Buddha's insight, one need not add something to what one ordinarily experiences. On the contrary, the Buddhist praxis is aimed at disengaging the conditioned responses that lead one to think things are other than they are. The praxis is a therapy that eliminates delusional, anxiety-provoking behaviors or constructions of reality. In this context philosophical analysis, with its propensity to build systems around fixed categories, could be a liability rather than a positive tool. The early Buddhist texts relate the Buddha's own hesitation to enter into analyses not conducive to breaking the patterns leading to delusion. For better or worse, however, Buddhism developed in India at a time when Hindu philosophical reflection, speculation, and analysis were beginning to blossom. The Buddhists found themselves being asked philosophical questions that could not be avoided. To understand Indian Buddhist philosophy, especially its analysis of the self as *anātman*, we need to appreciate that larger intellectual context of the time.

In the Buddha's era there was already an Indian trend toward distrusting the ordinary senses. It is significant, therefore, that Buddhist praxis worked against that tendency. The Hindu texts

often referred to *māyā*, the idea that reality takes on an illusory mask that must be understood if its true nature is to be fathomed. According to this common Hindu view, reality does not appear to us the way it essentially is. What we see as multiplicity, evanescence, and distinctions may be, in fact, only the superficial appearance of a deeper, transcendent reality of oneness and changelessness (*brahman*). Therefore, with the proper knowledge, we may still see the illusion, but also see through it to the reality beyond. This allows a detached (sometimes even playful) engagement with the world analogous to how we might find ourselves caught up in the illusion of a magic show or cinema. While enjoying the show, we also *know* that the distinctions with which we are engaged are illusions.

Buddhism disagrees fundamentally with the Hindu viewpoint. In Buddhism, the issue to be addressed is not illusion, but delusion. According to Buddhism, we experience the unreal not because the real presents a false appearance, but because we project our own desires onto what is presented. In that projection we delude ourselves. The goal of Buddhism, therefore, is not to see through the appearances, but instead to accept them without the distortion of egocentric projections. The phenomenal world is not illusion (*māyā*), but "suchness" or "thusness" (*tathatā*). This difference had a fundamental impact on the *ātman/anātman* debate between Hindu and Buddhist philosophies of self.

The general position developed in many Hindu Upaniṣads was that behind the sensory functions, there must be a faculty or agency possessing the function. If there is seeing or hearing, for example, there must be that which sees or hears. Yet whatever the seer or hearer is, it itself must be unseen or unheard, or there would be an infinite regress: we could endlessly ask, if the seer is itself seen, then what sees that seer? Therefore, argued this group of Hindu philosophers, there must be something that is the subject, but never the object, of human sensory experience (including introspection). It is the unseen, unheard, untasted, untouched, unsmelled, and unintrospected self behind a person's various experiences. It itself is unchanging and inaccessible to ordinary sensory knowing, yet it defines what one is: it is the *ātman*, the "true self."

The gist of this Hindu argument already existed in the early Upaniṣads current at the time of the Buddha and the details were further developed by subsequent philosophical analysis in the ensuing few centuries. It is important to point out, however, that the acceptance of *ātman* was not just the result of abstract reasoning. There was an experiential or practical component to the belief as well.

For understanding the Hindu position, the central point is what we mean by "direct experiential knowledge." If we limit such knowledge to what is accessible to the six senses, then *ātman's* very definition excludes its verification. We need not limit "direct experiential knowledge" in that way, however. Yogic disciplines for controlling the mind and body were already highly developed in ancient India, and adepts were said to be capable of achieving a state of complete quiet in which sensory experience (including inner awareness) disappeared altogether. This "experience" (if that Western term can be stretched to apply to such an event) was said to have no subject–object distinction and to be simply a state of oneness. The "I" would be doing nothing other than being "I" – a state of pure *ātman* awareness without discrimination or distinctions.

One might question the possibility of such an event. For example, what continuity would there be between the trance state and the return to normal consciousness? With no distinctions, what or who would emerge from such a state and how would that be connected to the person who existed before the trance event? To such questions, a common reply was to refer to the everyday event of dreamless sleep. It lacks content, the subject–object distinction, and even inner awareness. Yet, when we awake every morning, we remember who we are and have been. To the proponents of the *ātman* theory this was further evidence that personal identity resides in a level of reality not accessible to ordinary sensory experience and which is beyond distinctions. This justified, in

their view, the identification of the true self (*ātman*) with monistic reality (*brahman*).

At least in general form, it is that type of theory of *ātman* that the Buddha rejected in his position of *anātman*. Even in its earliest texts, Buddhism rejected both parts of the Hindu theory of *ātman* – namely, (1) the logical argument that action requires an independently existing agent (for there to be seeing, there must be a seer that is not itself seen); and (2) the metapractical argument that the possibility of having events of sensory cessation implies there is a "true self" behind the experience. Let us consider Buddhism's critique of each of these issues.

As we have seen in our discussion of Buddhist praxis, the Buddha maintained that what we experience through the senses (and, therefore, what really is) is a nexus of interconnected processes, not unchanging things (such as *ātman*). Buddhism insists that a process does not require an agent that has or undergoes the change. Ordinary language can be misleading. We say "the river flows in its channel," but this does not mean that the river is something other than the continuing process of water's flowing in the channel. Similarly, nature does not "cause" or "undergo" the change of seasons; the changing of the seasons is one of the processes that constitutes "nature." The analogy to an idea of self is clear: "I" am not what "has" or "undergoes" the processes of psychophysical change. Rather, those processes themselves constitute what is called "I."

According to traditional Buddhist thought, there are five interrelated processes constituting the self: the physical bodily form, sensations or feelings, sense perceptions, habitual mental formations or volitional tendencies, and consciousness. The self is, therefore, the name for the continuities and interactions among those five processes and not something in addition to them. An implication of this theory is that the self is an activity, not a thing, and that its nature is to be the locus where the five processes intersect. Not only is there no "soul" or "true self" behind that locus of events, but there is also no tendency to identify the "real self" with consciousness alone. For

Buddhism, there are no sharp lines demarcating the boundaries of the self. In everyday circumstances it may often be convenient to think of a person's existence as strictly bounded, but that is no different from thinking of the boundaries of a river as clearly defined. If we try to be too precise, however, the sharp distinctions disappear. As the river is interdependent with its riverbank – splashing up against its sides, eroding chunks to settle into its own riverbed – so too is the self conditioned by surrounding factors separated from the self by fuzzy boundaries.

With this process image of the self, the various schools of Buddhist philosophy addressed in slightly different ways the issue of continuity. Common to all of them was the idea that the self is an ongoing interaction with other processes. Persons have an identity not because they contain some unchanging core, but precisely because they do change. The self is a pattern of the linked changes, each changing condition leading to reconfigurations that help set the conditions for the next phase. The continuity of the self is in the continuity of those patterned, conditioned changes.

This Buddhist critique undercuts the Hindu argument for *ātman* as the "true self" or the "unseen seer." If seeing, for example, is a psychophysical process, there does not have to be some self or seer behind the process. The interrelated psychophysical processes themselves are what we call "I." A Buddhist philosopher can be as sophisticated in the analysis of these constituent processes as a scientist might be in analyzing a river in terms of the geology of the riverbed and the water's erosion patterns, the rainfall cycles, the seepage of minerals or artificial toxins into the water, the biosystem of river life, and so forth. Yet, just as the scientist does not find, nor feel any need to look for, the "river" as something other than those processes,

so too does the Buddhist rest content with a characterization of the self as the name for a set of interrelated psychophysical processes.

With this logical critique behind us, let us turn to Buddhism's metapractical ground for rejecting the Hindu assertion of *ātman*: the reflection on the nature and meaning of the trance state of sensory cessation. Significantly, the Buddha did not deny the possibility of such an experience. In fact, a famous account of his death reports that while giving his last sermon to his assembled disciples, he interrupted his talk because of stomach pain to enter a trance. Reenergized, he then continued his lecture. The disagreement with Hinduism, then, is not whether such a state of sensory-cessation is possible, but the metapractical issue of the meaning of that state. For at least some Hindus, that state suggests what the true self may be. For Buddhists, on the other hand, it means only that under the right conditions the flow of sensory experience can be temporarily frozen. There is for them no reason to jump to the conclusion that such a frozen state is more fundamental or truer than other states. For the Buddhist, it is noteworthy that such trance states and dreamless sleep are temporary events. Those purported experiences of eternity are themselves transient and temporary. Even in dreamless sleep or trance states, there is a continuity of some processes defining the self – the physical processes of the body, for example.

In summation, by rejecting the contemporaneous notion of *ātman*, the early Indian Buddhist philosophers were not denying the existence of the self, but only insisting that there were logical, empirical, and metapractical reasons for denying the self as a substantial, permanent, transcendent entity. The Buddhists certainly maintain that the self exists, but only as a name, like "river" or "nature," for a set of interrelated processes.

82 THE JAIN PATH

JEFFERY D LONG

Jainism is an ancient nontheistic Indian religion still practiced today. Jains believe in the principle of karma, the idea of reincarnation, and the ultimate goal of Nirvāṇa.

The Jain tradition stresses nonviolence against any living being. Its adherents are vegetarians and do not serve as butchers or soldiers. Its monks and nuns wear a gauze mask over the mouth to prevent the unintentional inhalation of an innocent insect. They also sweep the ground in front of them as they walk, so as not to crush anything alive. The ascetic goal of neglecting every personal interest can in rare cases lead monks or nuns to starve themselves to death, thus ridding the soul of all passions and bringing an appropriate close to an ethical life.

Although accounting for less than 0.5 percent of India's population, Jains have had a significant impact on the country's religious, social, political, and economic life. Our next selection, written by Jeffery D Long, a Professor of Religious Studies at Elizabethtown College in Pennsylvania, assesses this influential religious tradition.

INTRODUCTION

Jainism is an ancient tradition of nonviolence and, according to many of its contemporary adherents, deep ecological wisdom. Originating in India and having many affinities with Hinduism and Buddhism, it is a tradition that is relatively unknown in the West.

Like Hindus and Buddhists, Jains affirm the reality of a universal moral principle of cause and effect called *karma*. Derived from a Sanskrit word meaning 'act', karma governs all action. It can be likened to Newton's Third Law of Motion: for every action there is an equal and opposite reaction. But traditional Indic worldviews do not make the sharp distinction, so typical of modern Western thought, between the realms of fact and value. Karma thus manifests not only in the form of physical laws, such as gravity, but also as a moral law governing action. If one engages in actions that are violent, or motivated by hatred, selfishness, or egotism, the universe will respond in kind, producing suffering in the one who has caused suffering to others. Similarly, if one engages in actions that are benevolent, pure, and kind, the universe will respond benevolently, and one will have pleasant experiences. There are Western expressions that convey a similar sensibility to that of the idea of karma: You reap what you sow. What goes around comes around.

Like Hindus and Buddhists, Jains deduce from the principle of karma the idea of rebirth, or reincarnation. All religions must address the issue of why bad things happen to good people and good things happen to bad people. Why, if there is universal justice – which is essentially what karma amounts to – does the world in which we live appear to be as unjust as it does? Indic religions explain this phenomenon in terms of past and future lives. Today's joy or suffering may be the fruit of karma from a previous life. And the actions one takes today will inevitably bear fruit, if not in this life, then in a future one.

Like Hindus and Buddhists, Jains see the ultimate good as escape from the cycle of rebirth – *mokṣa*, or liberation from karmic bondage, or *nirvāṇa*, as it is also called in all of these traditions, a state of absorption in unending bliss. But, as for most Hindus and Buddhists, this final

From Jeffery D Long, *Jainism: An Introduction*, I. B. Tauris, 2009. Reprinted by permission of the publisher.

goal is widely conceived as remote and difficult to attain, the more immediate goal of religious activity being merit-making: the acquisition of 'good karma'.

Like Buddhists, and unlike most Hindus, Jains do not affirm the idea of a God, at least as this idea is understood in the Abrahamic religions – a creator and moral arbiter of the universe. Karmic 'reward' and 'punishment' is a wholly impersonal process, and we are each responsible for our own joy and suffering. There is no divine judge. It is up to us to follow the path that leads to ultimate freedom, or not.

Unlike Hinduism, but like Buddhism and other world religions, Jainism does have a founding figure. But this figure is a 'founder' in only a limited sense; for, according to Jainism, he is not so much the 'founder' of a tradition as a rediscoverer and re-initiator of eternal truths and an eternal path that have been re-discovered and re-initiated again and again throughout beginningless time. Mahāvīra, the 'Great Hero', lived at about the same time and in the same region as the Buddha.... One could call Mahāvīra the founder of the Jain community as it exists today. But Jain tradition tells us that he is the 24th in a series of *Tīrthaṅkaras*, or 'fordmakers': beings who discover the way across the river of rebirth to the further shore of liberation and build a *tīrtha*, or ford, that others may use to make their way across as well. This *tīrtha* is the Jain community.

This metaphorical usage of *tīrtha* to refer to the Jain community has become so prominent over time that it has gradually eclipsed the original meaning of the word – a ford or crossing over a river – to the point that today it simply means 'religious community'. Among Jains today, Mahāvīra is said to have established four *tīrthas*: Jain monks, Jain nuns, Jain laymen, and Jain laywomen. These make up the fourfold Jain community....

For those Westerners who have heard of Jainism, it may bring to mind images of ascetics – of monks and nuns – wearing what appear to be surgical face-masks in order to protect insects and microorganisms from being inhaled, and sweeping the ground in front of them with a broom or whisk to protect tiny creatures from being stepped on – a practice of nonviolence so radical as to defy easy comprehension.

But though this picture is not an inaccurate one, it is one-sided. The commitment of the Jains to a radically ascetic practice of nonviolence should not be minimized; but it should also not be exaggerated. A tiny percentage of Jains are actually monks or nuns who practice the kind of nonviolent asceticism most Western representations of Jainism bring to mind – a life of constant mindfulness of what one could call one's environmental impact. Though such asceticism evokes great admiration and reverence from the typical, lay practitioner of Jainism, it is not uncommon to hear lay Jains admit, quite frankly, that such asceticism is beyond their own, current ability to practice. One also hears the hope expressed that the layperson may someday, perhaps later in life or in a future rebirth, feel the call of renunciation and take up the life of the Jain ascetic. The point is that although, as Jains, laypersons understand and admire what Jain ascetics do, they regard such ascetic practice much as many non-Jains do: as extraordinary and extremely difficult....

... Today, there are approximately 4.2 million Jains in the world. Although there are Jain communities in the UK, North America, and elsewhere – such as ... [a] community in central Pennsylvania – the vast majority of Jains continue to live in India, where they have existed for over two and a half millennia as a small but highly influential minority....

A common stereotype of the Jains, in both India and the West, is that they constitute a highly affluent merchant community. In fact, although many Jains do practice business professions – and many have been quite successful in these pursuits – there are also Jains who practice other professions, such as farming, and whose level of material wealth is relatively modest.

And then there are of course the Jain *sādhus* and *sādhvīs*, or monks and nuns, who have practically no material possessions to speak of, and who live a life of deliberate simplicity and nonviolence. Indeed, the strict commitment to *ahiṃsā*, or nonviolence, which the Jain monks and nuns embody, is the source of another stereotype of the Jains as a whole: that all Jains wear a face-mask to avoid accidentally ingesting insects, or that they carefully sweep the ground free of insects to avoid treading upon them as they walk. Only monks and nuns practice nonviolence to such a strict degree....

Though Jainism, like Buddhism, arose partly in reaction to the caste system of Hinduism, Jains, like many other minority communities in India, are organized into castes – hereditary communities that tend to practice a particular occupation and that determine whom one may marry....

Finally, the Jains are also divided into subsects. The two most ancient ones, the Digambaras and the Śvetāmbaras, differ mainly with regard to issues relating to monastic practice: specifically, with regard to whether a monk should wear clothing and whether a woman can practice monasticism to the extent available to a man. Indeed, the names of these two groups are indicative of the issues on which they differ. The word *Śvetāmbara* means 'white-clad', and Śvetāmbara monks and nuns wear very simple white robes. In addition to wearing these white robes, a Śvetāmbara monk or nun will also typically carry a begging bowl, from which he or she will eat food provided by the Jain lay community, and a small broom for the purpose of gently brushing aside small insects that may be in their pathway. The modest dress of Śvetāmbara ascetics is a symbol of their detachment and their status as ascetics in the Jain community. Śvetābaras make up, by far, the majority of Jains....

Digambara means 'sky-clad'. Digambara monks, figuratively speaking, 'wear' the sky: they wear no clothing at all. They do not carry a begging bowl, but eat only that much food as they can hold in their hands. Some carry the small broom that is also used by the Śvetāmbaras for the purpose of protecting small creatures from accidentally being stepped or sat upon; but this is not personal, but community property. In any event, the broom exists to protect other beings – unlike clothing, which protects one's own body.

From a Digambara perspective, the wearing of clothing suggests that one is overly attached to the body – that one wishes to protect it. It also suggests that one has a sense of shame that implies a lack of spiritual maturity, of awareness that it is the soul and not the body that is of ulti-

mate significance. A critic could of course ask, if the body is not what is important, why it matters whether one wears clothing or not. But for the Digambaras, practice is a necessary measure of spiritual attainment....

Women are barred from the practice of monastic nudity due to the fear that a nude female ascetic would be vulnerable to sexual assault. Rebirth as a woman is therefore an unfortunate state, since it prevents one from engaging in monastic practice to the degree necessary for attaining liberation – from the practice of monastic nudity....

The immediate salvific aspiration of these women, like that of any Jain layperson, is therefore a better rebirth – meaning, in their case, rebirth as a man. Liberation is a more distant goal, requiring the practice of monastic nudity – a practice available only to males.

From a Śvetāmbara point of view, it is the attitude of detachment, rather than the actual practice of nudity, that is of ultimate importance in one's pursuit of liberation from the rebirth cycle. Women are as capable as men of attaining *moksa*....

The debates between the Śvetāmbaras and the Digambaras over the necessity of actual monastic nudity versus an attitude of detachment, as well as debates regarding the related issue of the possibility of spiritual liberation for women, have been extensive. An entire literature has been produced as a result....

WHAT IS JAINISM?

But what makes a Jain a Jain? Mahatma Gandhi once famously said that there are in fact as many religions as there are people – that everyone, even members of the same tradition, will tend to interpret the beliefs and practices of their traditions differently, or pursue their practices in subtly different ways.

But allowing for the inevitability that Jains, like all other religious persons, will disagree amongst themselves on certain issues, what can be said by way of a reasonable generalization about the set of views and practices called *Jainism*?

Let us begin by discussing the views and practices shared between Jainism and other Indic traditions, and situating Jainism in its context. Then we can narrow down our examination to the variations on these common themes that are distinctively Jain.

In Jainism, as well as Hinduism and Buddhism, one encounters a universe without beginning or end. According to this cosmology, we have all been undergoing a process of birth, life, death, and rebirth since time without beginning. Though Buddhism adds a layer of complexity to this model, with its *anātman* or 'no self' doctrine, the basic idea is that the physical body is not our true self. The body, rather, is the vehicle of that which is even more fundamental to us – the *jīva*, or *jīvātman*, which corresponds roughly to what Western religious traditions call the soul.

Unlike the body, which is impermanent, the soul has no beginning and no end. In the Indic traditions, it is the soul, and not the body, with which we ought to be primarily concerned. What will happen to us after the body dies? And where were we – if the soul is what we really are – before this body was born? How is the nature of our rebirth, the type of body we inhabit, determined?...

Karma, the net effect of all of our previous choices, produces the experiences of the present moment, in which we are currently making the choices that will produce our future experiences. In effect, we are all creating and re-creating the universe at every moment with our collective choices. This includes the type of body we inhabit. At the time of the death of the body, the karma of the soul will determine what kind of body the soul will inhabit next, including the location of its birth, its social circumstances, etc. One is therefore, in effect, choosing the nature of one's next rebirth all of the time. Good karma will lead to a good rebirth, in circumstances conducive to spiritual advancement. Bad karma will lead to rebirth in painful circumstances. Of course most of us, having a mix of good and bad karma, are born into circumstances in which we feel pleasure and pain, freedom and limitation, in various measures.

All of this depends, again, on our karma, which is changing to some extent at every moment, as we make moral choices and engage in action based upon them. It is not only in the afterlife that karma has its effects. These can occur in this life as well.

According to such a worldview, what should one do? Clearly, one should engage in good activities – do good works – so the karmic effects that one experiences will be good ones, and a great deal of Hindu, Buddhist, and Jain religious activity is centered around the earning of merit, or good karma, through good actions.

But the philosophy of renunciation that all of these traditions share is based on the insight that the highest good does not consist of making an endless effort toward bettering and maintaining the karmic situation of one's soul. Is there no rest for the soul? Is there no higher aim to give life a purpose and a meaning? Is it not the case, given that we are limited beings, that even the most heroic good deeds will produce karmic effects that will eventually wear out, and that we will again have to continue doing good works in order to maintain our karmic state?

The Buddhist tradition expresses this idea with its First Noble Truth: that existing ... inevitably involves *dukkha*, or suffering. This is an idea shared by Hindus and Jains as well. *Dukkha* does not mean that we are always unhappy. But it means that the highest happiness available to us through the karmically conditioned experiences of this life is limited and impermanent....

According to ... the Vedānta philosophy of Hinduism as found in the *Upaniṣads*, true happiness, lasting happiness, consists of liberation from the otherwise endless cycle of engaging in action and experiencing its karmic results, a cycle which we experience as the cycle of birth, death, and rebirth, or *saṃsāra*.

But how, if karma is a universal law, is such liberation to be achieved? This is the central question on which the various Indic traditions diverge; for each conceives of the basic cosmological vision outlined above in subtly different ways....

THE JAIN VISION

In the realm of practice, the religious tradition that probably has the closest similarities to Jainism is Theravāda Buddhism, particularly with its organization of the community into a fourfold schema of male and female ascetic and lay practitioners in relations of mutual dependence.... Jainism and Theravāda Buddhism share a good deal of philosophical terminology as well, particularly with regard to the topic of karmic influx, and the cessation of this influx as a precondition for *nirvāṇa*.

But the distinctively Jain vision of karma, rebirth, and liberation ... [conceives] of the universe in a way that is radically dualistic: that is, as consisting of two completely different types of entity called *jīva* and *ajīva*, or spirit and matter.

Jīvas, according to Jain teaching, when in their pure, unobscured state, have the four characteristics of unlimited knowledge, perception, bliss, and energy or power – sometimes called the 'four infinitudes'. There are many *jīvas* – as many as there are living beings in the cosmos. The word *jīva* is derived from the Sanskrit verbal root *jīv*, which means 'live', suggesting that this concept is closely connected to the idea of a living being, as its essential 'life force'. But though there are many *jīvas*, each *jīva* is identical in terms of its four essential characteristics. They have the same nature, although they are numerically distinct....

This is the main *metaphysical* difference between Vedānta[1] – in which all souls are ultimately one – and Jainism.... The unity of souls, according to Jainism, is a unity of *nature* or *essence*. All souls are 'one' in the same sense in which all apples are 'one'. There is not one 'supreme apple' of which all actual apples are different manifestations or appendages. But all apples share certain characteristics that mark them off as apples. In the same way, all the *jīvas* have the same four essential characteristics. But their numerical distinctiveness is not illusory.

... Jainism is non-theistic. Jains, especially contemporary Jains, do use the word 'God' in their discourse. I have heard Jains say, very much like Hindus, that 'God dwells within you' or that 'God dwells within all beings', and I was once even told by a Jain monk, 'May God bless you'. Beyond the issue of heterodoxy, which does permit theistic language to creep into Jain discourse, there seems to be a concern in the Jain community to avoid the misunderstanding that because Jains are not theists in the conventional sense,

that they are also necessarily materialists (materialism and atheism generally going hand-in-hand in the contemporary world). Jain atheism, in other words, is not to be taken as a denial of spiritual values, or of karma or rebirth.

What Jains deny is that there is a *creator* God. When the term 'God' is used in a positive sense (as in the examples I have given), it refers to the *jīva*. It is the soul, in its pure state that is divine in Jainism. There is no need for a creator because the cosmos has always existed.

But why, if all souls have the same essential nature, are there different types of living being? Why are all our experiences different? Why are we not all omniscient, infinitely perceptive, infinitely blissful, and infinitely powerful? Why do we not experience our divinity? The answer, according to Jainism, is that our *jīvas* have all been associated, throughout their beginningless existence, with *ajīva* – non-soul or matter – of a particular kind, and it is the disassociation of *jīva* from *ajīva* that is the chief aim of Jain asceticism.

Ajīva, according to Jainism, is the negation of *jīva*. Everything that *jīva* is, *ajīva* is not. *Ajīva* is not conscious (and therefore not blissful) and has no inherent powers of its own (though, as we shall see in a moment, it does exhibit certain behaviors as a result of impetus from the *jīva*). The differences among living beings are due to *ajīva*.

The particular type of *ajīva* that adheres to each *jīva*, producing the various kinds of experience that living beings have, is called *karma*. This is the same 'karma' to which the other Indic traditions refer when they are speaking of the universal law of cause and effect that governs all action.

In other words, karma is understood in Jainism to be a material substance which *produces* the universal law of cause and effect, which produces experiences in our souls according to certain regular patterns – an understanding unique to the Jain tradition.

As we have seen, Jainism shares with ... other Indic traditions ... a belief in *karma*, *saṃsāra*, and *nirvāṇa* or *mokṣa*. So, like the Hindus and Buddhists, Jains believe that we wander from lifetime to lifetime (the literal meaning of *saṃsāra* being 'wandering about'), impelled by the law of cause and effect – *karma* – to be reborn until we attain liberation – *moksa* – from this process.

The particulars of this process differ, of course, in different traditions. In Advaita, or non-dualistic, Vedānta, we wander from life to life until we realize that what we really are – the *ātman*, or Self, is identical to Brahman. Not unlike the *jīva* of Jainism, which is pure bliss, perception, consciousness, and power, Brahman is described as infinite being, consciousness, and bliss.

The difference, again, is that Brahman is one. There is no numerical division in it…. But in Jainism the *jīvas*, though of one nature, are many, and this plurality is real, not illusory.

In theistic forms of Vedānta, in which the pre-eminent manifestation of Brahman is Īśvara – or God – the personal deity, it is by the grace of God that one becomes free from karmic bondage. In Buddhism, the term 'self' is avoided, but the process is arguably not fundamentally different from Advaita – the deconstruction of the empirical ego followed by the spontaneous arising of insight into the true nature of reality, leading to *nirvāṇa*, the state of freedom from suffering and further rebirth.

In Vedānta, however, karma is simply a universal law. 'For every action there is an equal and opposite reaction' – not only in the realm of physics, but in the realm of morality as well. In Buddhism, karma is more of a psychological reality. Instead of a self, it is karmic energy that is reborn, like a flame passing one candle to another. This energy must be resolved for *nirvāṇa* to occur, which is likened to flame being blown out.

But in Jainism, karma is actually a form of subtle matter, and the mechanism by which the bondage of the soul occurs, as well as the path to its eventual liberation, is the central concern of the tradition. According to Jainism, all *jīvas*, all souls, throughout their beginningless existence, have been bound to karmic matter.

How did this process begin? These traditions do not concern themselves with the question of the origins of the process. But one sometimes comes across the analogy of mud. When one encounters mud, one does not have to ask the question, 'How did dirt and water come together to form this mud?' to be able to sort out and separate the two. Similarly, one need not postulate an origin of how soul and matter (or on a Buddhist account, pure mind and false consciousness) came to be enmeshed with one another in order to discern a distinction between the two and initiate the process of their separation.

How does this process work? What is the path to the purification of the soul, of removing the 'dirt' of karmic matter from the 'water' of pure consciousness? According to the Jain account, karmic matter is attracted to the *jīva* by the arising of passions within the *jīva*….

A passion is a kind of deformation in the structure of the soul, which is otherwise, as mentioned above, inherently omniscient and blissful. The passions arise in response to stimuli: to experiences.

Experiences, in turn, are the effects of karmic matter previously embedded in the soul through the process of attraction by the passions.

In other words, karmic bondage is a vicious circle. At any given point in the journey of the soul through *saṃsāra* – its wandering process of birth, death, and rebirth in the material world – it contains karmic particles that it has attracted through its passionate responses to prior stimuli. As these particles produce their effects, in the form of various experiences, more passions are elicited, and more particles are attracted, which will lead to more experiences, and so on. Until the soul has purified itself of karmic matter, giving rise to pure knowledge and pure bliss, the process will continue.

Different types of passion attract different types of karmic matter. Different types of karmic matter, in turn, produce different types of experience, and a vast and elaborate literature exists which analyzes the types of karmic matter, their effects, and the passions that elicit them. A central concern of Jainism is cultivating control over the passions so the influx of karmic matter can be kept to a minimum.

It is not a deterministic system, however, because, like all systems that involve the notion of karma, there is an element of free will in the present moment in terms of how one is going to respond to one's current experience. In the terms we have been using, it is *not* the case that karma determines the type of passion that will arise in response to the experience that it produces. We are in control, ultimately, of how we respond to stimuli. It is this element of freedom that makes a path of liberation from karma possible; for this freedom opens up a space for human action that can shape the future of one's relationship to the karmic process. The literature on Jain karma theory exists precisely as a guide to the practitioner so that she may control her passions in such a way as to produce the most desirable karmic results, the most desirable ultimately being none at all. True freedom – *mokṣa* – is complete freedom from karmic determination.

Karmic particles are frequently referred to in Jain literature as 'seeds'. The analogy is a good one. Just as a seed falls into the soil, the karmic particle embeds itself within the soul. Just like a seed, the karmic particle eventually bears fruit, in the form of an experience. And, like a seed, the precise timing and manner in which karma bears fruit depends upon a variety of factors. Different kinds of karma come to fruition in different ways and at different times, just like different seeds. But just as seeds need the right kind of soil to grow and to bear fruit, as well as factors like water and sunlight, in the same way, the fruition of karma can be affected by the soul environment in which it finds itself. The function of much of Jain asceticism is to create an environment that is inhospitable to karmic fruition, but that can lead, rather, to the destruction of karma. The metaphor is often used, extending the seed analogy, of 'cooking' the seeds of our karma in the 'fires' of asceticism so that they cannot grow or bear fruit.

So one dimension of Jain asceticism involves the purification and purgation of the soul, freeing it from the karmic matter that is already embedded in it, and which deforms it, obscuring its true nature as infinite knowledge and bliss, and threatening to attract more such matter through the passions its fruition can evoke.

The other dimension of Jain asceticism involves the prevention of the influx of more karmic matter through the control of the passions. This is where Jain meditation comes in: the practice of *sāmāyika*, or equanimity in the face of both joy and sorrow…. [T]he Jain tradition holds that experiences faced with equanimity, and the actions arising therefrom, do not attract additional karmic matter to the soul. Ascetics and laypersons both practice *sāmāyika*. The Jain layperson is said to be

the most like an ascetic – to come closest to the ascetic state – while engaging in this practice. Through the practice of *sāmāyika*, one learns not to give in to the passions which attract karma to the soul. One practices *not* automatically reacting to joy with attraction and sorrow with aversion, but reacting to both with equanimity – or in other words, *not* reacting to them.

The *jīva*, in its ideal state, could be compared to a smooth body of water – like a lake on a windless day – clear and untroubled by turbulence or waves. But the *jīvas* of most beings, non-liberated beings, are not in their ideal state. They are like lakes whose waters are filled with waves and whirlpools, which correspond to emotional states called, in Jainism, the passions. These passions can be seen as deformations on the smooth surface of the soul. These deformations attract particles of karmic matter to the soul, further deforming it and making it 'sticky'. The passions' effect of drawing karma to the soul is sometimes compared to the way that wetting a cloth makes it attract dust.

The passions are essentially reactions to experiences, and are of three basic types: attraction, aversion, and neutrality. We either like an experience, wanting more of it; we dislike it, and so want to avoid it; or we are indifferent to it. Experiences are the result of karmic particles or 'seeds' coming to fruition. These experiences, in turn, produce passions, which attract more karmic seeds, which also come to fruition, producing more experiences, leading to more passions, and so on. Again, no beginning to this process is posited in the Jain tradition. There was no 'fall' from a higher, spiritual state, in which originally pure souls began to be contaminated by karmic matter. It is simply the way things have always been, throughout beginningless time.

Put most simply, the goal of Jainism as a spiritual practice is the removal of the karmic matter that obscures the true nature of the *jīva* and causes it to be bound to the cycle of rebirth in the material world and to prevent the further influx of such matter. The result of successful removal of karmic matter from the *jīva* and the prevention of further karmic influx is *mokṣa* – liberation from rebirth.

Because it is the passions that attract karma to the *jīva*, an essential component of the Jain path is to cultivate a disposition of detachment or calm equanimity in the face of all our experiences, both pleasant and unpleasant. For this reason, many Jains, like Buddhists and Hindus, practice a form of meditation, in order to cultivate the calm mental state most conducive to spiritual freedom....

But while meditation and equanimity – can help one to avoid accumulating additional karmic matter, there are still karmic particles that need to be removed from the *jīva* if one is to achieve liberation. This removal is achieved through difficult ascetic activities, such as fasting, meditating for long periods of time in difficult positions – such as, the distinctively Jain standing meditation posture – and the giving up of material comforts to which one has developed attachment.

In terms of karma, ascetic activities serve a double function. By helping the Jain practitioner to exert a greater control over the passions through self-discipline, they aid in reducing karmic influx. But because ascetic activities are inherently difficult, they also, in effect, substitute for the unpleasant experiences that one's bad karma would inevitably create anyway, given time. One essentially pays one's karmic debt in advance by taking on such difficult practices, and so accelerates one's progress toward liberation. Again, just as a seed, once cooked, cannot sprout, in the same way, a karmic seed has its effects negated by the voluntary suffering that is involved in the practice of asceticism. The seed is essentially brought to premature fruition, and so removed from the soul. Without the aid of ascetic practice, one would have to wait for one's karmas to come to fruition on their own, which could take many lifetimes.

THE IMPORTANCE OF *AHIṂSĀ*

The strict asceticism of Jain monks and nuns is closely connected with the ethical ideal of *ahiṃsā*, which is generally translated as nonviolence, but which is actually much more radical than the English word 'nonviolence' might suggest. It is not simply a matter of refraining from actual, physical harm. *Ahiṃsā* is the absence of even a desire to do harm to any living being, in thought, word, or deed.

The Jain ethos of *ahiṃsā* is a direct outcome of Jain karma theory. The passions that attract karma of the worst kind – karma whose fruition leads to the greatest suffering – are those associated with violence. To practice *ahiṃsā* is to wish to harm no living thing, either deliberately (which of course produces the worst karmic effects) or even through one's carelessness (which, though not as bad as intentional violence, is still regarded in Jainism as carrying a negative karmic effect).

As I have discussed previously, there is a frank recognition in the Jain tradition that not all human beings are prepared for the level of asceticism that is required in order to purge the *jīva* completely from karmic matter and thus end its cycle of suffering the vicissitudes of *saṃsāra*. Some souls are still sufficiently deluded that they continue to choose the time-bound pleasures of the material world over the infinite bliss of a purified and liberated soul, seeing the asceticism of the Jain monk or nun as a terrible burden, rather than a path to freedom. This, in fact, includes many Jains, who deeply revere those who have undertaken the ascetic path, knowing that they themselves, in this life at least, could never take on such a difficult practice.

In the Jain community, the recognition of different spiritual levels, with different duties appropriate to each, issues in the construction of a fourfold community of male and female lay and ascetic practitioners. For the ascetic, male or female, the chief task is the practice of absolute *ahiṃsā*. For a very small number of such ascetics, this culminates in ... the complete renunciation of material sustenance, in the recognition that even the digestive process involves violence to microscopic organisms.

But for the layperson, male or female, there is an understanding that such a total renunciation is both impossible and undesirable. As in Theravāda Buddhism, the laity is devoted not so much to *nirvāṇa* as to the avoidance of bad karma and the accumulation of good karma, in the hope that this will aid them in their spiritual path, leading to progressively better rebirths in which, eventually, they may feel the call of renunciation.

Nirvāṇa, though ultimately desirable, is a more distant goal than a meritorious rebirth.

This is an important way in which Jainism (and Hinduism and Buddhism) differs from most Western religions. In Western religions, there is typically one good that is to be achieved – salvation – and that good is an all-or-nothing prospect: one is either saved and goes to heaven or is damned for all eternity. And there is only one lifetime in which the matter can be decided. In the Indic traditions, however, there is a hierarchy of goods that are not mutually incompatible. One hopes for this-worldly benefits – happiness, long life, prosperity, and so on – and an extension of these benefits into one's next life – that is, a good rebirth. Both of these goods – this-worldly benefits in this life and a rebirth in which more such benefits are forthcoming – can be achieved through meritorious action. They are effects of … 'good karma'. And then there is the highest good, in which one gives up, or renounces, worldly goods in the pursuit of liberation. The idea of a hierarchy of goods is in fact formalized in the Hindu tradition, in which the … 'aims of man' are ranked as pleasure, prosperity, goodness, and, finally, liberation – the ultimate good. To be sure, the last of these is regarded as both intrinsically and infinitely more desirable than the first three. But it takes time to awaken to this realization, and there is no time limit imposed on the process of doing so.

The ethos of storing up merit leads to all manner of positive charitable activities, for which the Jain community is justifiably famous. But all such activities are ultimately in the service of spiritual liberation. To give, for a Jain layperson, is actually a mentally purifying act – a mini-renunciation – in preparation for the ultimate renunciation for which the layperson hopes eventually to be ready – if not in this life, then in a future rebirth.

Meritorious action is also a type of *ahiṃsā*. *Ahiṃsā* is not a negative ideal of only avoiding harm. It entails compassion for all living beings. Western writers on Jainism, especially Christian missionaries, have often sought to criticize the Jain ideal of *ahiṃsā* on the basis of the claim that this ideal involves no positive ethic of helping

suffering beings, but that it is only a matter of not hurting them – essentially, of doing nothing.

This, however, is a distortion of the Jain tradition, ignoring, as it does, the high level of Jain involvement in charity. Compassion is said to be essential to a right view of reality – both a condition for and a product of spiritual evolution.

The centrality of *ahiṃsā* to Jainism is difficult to exaggerate, though an exclusive focus on the ascetic *ahiṃsā* of the Jain monks and nuns can create a one-sided impression of the Jain community. *Ahiṃsā* is the central ethical principle of Jainism, embodied in the often-quoted statement *ahiṃsā paramo dharmaḥ* – *ahiṃsā* is the highest duty.

Why is *ahiṃsā* so central to Jainism? In terms of the Jain karma theory outlined above, a central Jain insight is that the worst passions, the ones that attract the heaviest, most obscuring karmic particles into the soul, are those that are involved in committing acts of violence. Acts of violence typically involve a high degree of intense passion, such as anger and hatred. Negative passions like these, which obscure our perception that all souls are essentially the same as our own, bind us even more tightly to *saṃsāra*. In order to ensure a better rebirth, one in which we are more likely to make spiritual progress – and certainly in order to purify the soul and reach liberation – it is essential that we avoid any thought, word, or deed that involves the desire to do harm.

According to a Jain understanding, however, it is very difficult to avoid doing any harm whatsoever to living beings. The universe is filled with microscopic organisms – a fact of which Mahāvīra, interestingly, was sharply aware in the fifth century BCE. The most basic of these are called *nigodas*. For human beings, the very act of being alive involves the destruction of such tiny life forms. Eating, digesting food, breathing, sitting, and moving about: all involve the destruction of *nigodas* on a massive scale.

Such activities are generally not carried out with the intention of doing harm. One could argue that the requisite intent to do harm – and so the passion with which this intent is normally associated – is absent from such activities, and that they must therefore be without karmic consequence. But this is not a traditional Jain understanding. Once one is aware of the existence of tiny life forms in the air one breathes, in the water one drinks, and on the surfaces on which one travels and rests one's body, one becomes responsible for the harm that one does. Also, unlike Buddhism, which sees motive as the chief determinant of the morality of an act – of whether it involves a good or a bad karmic result – Jainism teaches that the actual consequences of action are always a major factor.

Jain monks and nuns therefore spend a good deal of their time in the effort to have a minimal negative impact upon their environment. Jain asceticism consists primarily of curbing activities that might lead to the accidental destruction of life, and to cultivating mindfulness of the life forms with which one shares the physical universe. A well-known symbol of this ascetic ideal is the *muhpattī*, a cloth that some Jain monks and nuns wear over their mouths to avoid accidentally inhaling or ingesting small organisms.

Central though the ascetic ideal of *ahiṃsā* is to the Jain community and its view of itself, it would be an exaggeration to suggest that all, or even most, Jains are constantly preoccupied with avoiding harm to microorganisms. There is a frank recognition in the Jain community, as in Buddhism, that most people are not yet at the spiritual level where they would wish to renounce life as a layperson and the activities that go with day-to-day existence....

For the layperson, of course, avoidance of the destruction of life on a microscopic level may be simply impossible. One needs to eat, to drink, and to prepare food both for oneself and for one's children, as well as for wandering Jain ascetics (though ascetics are forbidden from taking food prepared explicitly for them). Where do Jains draw the line? For the layperson, it is a matter of intention. One knows that one's daily actions involve the destruction of life on a microscopic scale. But one does not willfully or deliberately take the life of any being. Even for laypersons, this is not simply a matter of behavior, but of cultivating an attitude of harmlessness toward all living things.

In practical terms, this means Jains overwhelmingly – if they are practicing and not merely nominal Jains – are vegetarian. Jains are not traditionally, as is sometimes thought, vegans, though in recent years a growing number of Jains have become vegan. A vegan does not consume any animal products at all. Jains in India do drink milk and use milk products, since cows are not harmed in the process. But they do not eat eggs.

Jains are also forbidden to engage in activities for their livelihood which involve the direct taking of life. One will not typically find a Jain butcher or Jain executioner, for example. Indeed, the injunction to avoid direct taking of life is the reason so many Jains go into business professions. Trading in goods made by others is less likely to force one into situations where one must directly take life oneself....

SALLEKHANĀ: THE FAST TO THE DEATH

The most controversial of Jain ascetic practices – though, it must be emphasized, a quite rare one – is the practice of self-starvation – known as *sallekhanā* or *santhāra* – occasionally undertaken by Jain monks and nuns, and the rare layperson...

This practice – as Jains emphasize quite strongly – is *not* a form of suicide. It is not undertaken out of passion or because of despair or anger. It can only be undertaken with the permission of one's spiritual preceptor, or *guru*. The guru's duty is to ensure that one's motives in undertaking this fast to the death are pure – that one is doing it out of a genuine sense of detachment from the body and out of compassion for all of the living beings that one will save by not continuing to eat, breathe, and consume resources. Such a holy death is seen as having great capacity to advance the soul on its path to liberation, and to be possible only for beings who have perfected their compassion and their wisdom to such a degree that they would rather die than cause pain or death for even the tiniest of creatures....

JAIN WORSHIP AND DEVOTION

Though having an absolutely central place in the Jain path, an excessive focus on ethics and ascetic practices – especially rare and radical practices like *sallekhanā* – is one of the factors that has led to the stereotype of Jainism as an austere tradition, with nothing to offer its followers but a strict set of moral rules.

It therefore often comes as a surprise ... that some of the most ornate and magnificent temples in India are Jain temples. Devotion, or *bhakti*, plays as important a role in the life of the Jain layperson as it does for the Hindu (or for that matter, the Muslim or the Christian)....

The rationale for Jain *bhakti* is different from that found in more conventionally theistic traditions, such as Hinduism. Hindu devotion is about the devotee's relationship with the deity, who is seen as interacting with the devotee. Jain devotion is seen, at least by ascetics, more as a form of meditation on the ideal that the deity – typically one of the Jinas – embodies.

NOTE

1. [A school of Hinduism.]

D. NIRVANA

83 WHAT THE BUDDHA TAUGHT

WALPOLA RAHULA

Walpola Rahula (1907–1997), a Buddhist monk, was a professor of history and literature of religions at Northwestern University. In our next selection, he seeks to explain the Buddhist goal of attaining *nirvana*, a term drawn from the Sanskrit word for "extinction." Nirvāṇa is the goal of life, a state of existence in which all that causes suffering is absent. It is attainable both in this life and beyond.

... [W]hat is Nirvāṇa? Volumes have been written in reply to this quite natural and simple question; they have, more and more, only confused the issue rather than clarified it. The only reasonable reply to give to the question is that it can never be answered completely and satisfactorily in words, because human language is too poor to express the real nature of the Absolute Truth or Ultimate Reality which is Nirvāṇa. Language is created and used by masses of human beings to express things and ideas experienced by their sense organs and their mind. A supramundane experience like that of the Absolute Truth is not of such a category. Therefore there cannot be words to express that experience, just as the fish had no words in his vocabulary to express the nature of the solid land. The tortoise told his friend the fish that he (the tortoise) just returned to the lake after a walk on the land. 'Of course' the fish said, 'You mean swimming.' The tortoise tried to explain that one couldn't swim on the land, that it was solid, and that one walked on it. But the fish insisted that there could be nothing like it, that it must be liquid like his lake, with waves, and that one must be able to dive and swim there.

Words are symbols representing things and ideas known to us; and these symbols do not and cannot convey the true nature of even ordinary things. Language is considered deceptive and misleading in the matter of understanding of the Truth. So the *Laṅkāvatāra-sūtra* says that ignorant people get stuck in words like an elephant in the mud.

Nevertheless we cannot do without language. But if Nirvāṇa is to be expressed and explained in positive terms, we are likely immediately to grasp an idea associated with those terms, which may be quite the contrary. Therefore it is generally expressed in negative terms—a less dangerous mode perhaps. So it is often referred to by such negative terms as 'Extinction of Thirst', 'Uncompound', 'Unconditioned', 'Absence of desire', 'Cessation', 'Blowing out' or 'Extinction'.

Let us consider a few definitions and descriptions of Nirvāṇa as found in the original Pali texts:

'It is the complete cessation of that very 'thirst', giving it up, renouncing it, emancipation from it, detachment from it.'

From Walpola Rahula, *What the Buddha Taught*, Grove Press, 1974. Reprinted by permission of the publisher.

'Calming of all conditioned things, giving up of all defilements, extinction of "thirst", detachment, cessation, Nibbāna.'[1]

'O bhikkhus,[2] what is the Absolute (Unconditioned)? It is, O bhikkhus, the extinction of desire the extinction of hatred), the extinction of illusion. This, O bhikkhus, is called the Absolute.'

'[T]he extinction of "thirst" is Nibbāna.'

'O bhikkhus, whatever there may be things conditioned or unconditioned, among them detachment is the highest. That is to say, freedom from conceit, destruction of thirst, the uprooting of attachment, the cutting off of continuity, the extinction of "thirst", detachment, cessation, Nibbāna.'

The reply of Sāriputta, the chief disciple of the Buddha, to a direct question. 'What is Nibbāna?' ... is identical with the definition ... given by the Buddha (above): 'The extinction of desire, the extinction of hatred, the extinction of illusion.'...

'The abandoning and destruction of desire and craving for these Five Aggregates of Attachment[3]: that is the cessation of *dukkha*.'

'The cessation of Continuity and becoming is Nibbāna.'

And further, referring to Nirvāṇa the Buddha says:

'O bhikkhus, there is the unborn, ungrown, and unconditioned. Were there not the unborn, ungrown, and unconditioned, there would be no escape for the born, grown, and conditioned. Since there is the unborn, ungrown, and unconditioned, so there is escape for the born, grown, and conditioned.'

'Here the four elements of solidity, fluidity, heat and motion have no place; the notions of length and breadth, the subtle and the gross, good and evil, name and form are altogether destroyed; neither this world nor the other, nor coming, going or standing, neither death nor birth, nor sense-objects are to be found.'

Because Nirvāṇa is thus expressed in negative terms, there are many who have got a wrong notion that it is negative, and expresses self-annihilation. Nirvāṇa is definitely no annihilation of self, because there is no self to annihilate. If at all, it is the annihilation of the illusion, of the false idea of self.

It is incorrect to say that Nirvāṇa is negative or positive. The ideas of 'negative' and 'positive' are relative, and are within the realm of duality. These terms cannot be applied to Nirvāṇa, Absolute Truth, which is beyond duality and relativity.

A negative word need not necessarily indicate a negative state. The Pali or Sanskrit word for health is *ārogya*, a negative term, which literally means 'absence of illness'. But *ārogya* (health) does not represent a negative state. The word 'Immortal' (or its Sanskrit equivalent *Amrta* or Pali *Amata*), which also is a synonym for Nirvāṇa, is negative, but it does not denote a negative state. The negation of negative values is not negative. One of the well-known synonyms for Nirvāṇa is 'Freedom' (Pali *Mutti*, Skt. *Mukti*). Nobody would say that freedom is negative. But even freedom has a negative side: freedom is always a liberation from something which is obstructive, which is evil, which is negative. But freedom is not negative. So Nirvāṇa, *Mutti* or *Vimutti*, the Absolute Freedom, is freedom from all evil, freedom from craving, hatred and ignorance, freedom from all terms of duality, relativity, time and space.

We may get some idea of Nirvāṇa as Absolute Truth from the *Dhātuvibhaṅga-sutta* (No. 140) of the *Majjhima-nikāya*. This extremely important discourse was delivered by the Buddha to Pukkusāti,[4] whom the Master found to be intelligent and earnest, in the quiet of the night in a potter's shed. The essence of the relevant portions of the sutta[5] is as follows:

A man is composed of six elements: solidity, fluidity, heat, motion, space and consciousness. He analyses them and finds that none of them is 'mine', or 'me'; or 'my self'. He understands how consciousness appears and disappears, how pleasant, unpleasant and neutral sensations appear and disappear. Through this knowledge his mind becomes detached. Then he finds within him a pure equanimity (*upekhā*), which he can direct towards the attainment of any high spiritual state, and he knows that thus this pure equanimity will last for a long period. But then he thinks:

'If I focus this purified and cleansed equanimity on the Sphere of Infinite Space and develop a mind conforming thereto, that is a mental creation. If I focus this purified and cleansed equanimity on the Sphere of Infinite Consciousness ... on the Sphere of Nothingness ... or on the Sphere of Neither-perception nor Non-perception and develop a mind conforming thereto, that is a mental creation. Then he neither mentally creates nor wills continuity and becoming ... or annihilation. As he does not construct or does not will continuity and becoming or annihilation, he does not cling to anything in the world; as he does not cling, he is not anxious; as he is not anxious, he is completely calmed within. And he knows: 'Finished is birth, lived is pure life, what should be done is done, nothing more is left to be done.'

Now, when he experiences a pleasant, unpleasant or neutral sensation, he knows that it is impermanent, that it does not bind him, that it is not experienced with passion. Whatever may be the sensation, he experiences it without being bound to it. He knows that all those sensations will be pacified with the dissolution of the body, just as the flame of a lamp goes out when oil and wick give out.

'Therefore, O bhikkhu, a person so endowed is endowed with the absolute wisdom, for the knowledge of the extinction of all *dukkha*[6] is the absolute noble wisdom.

'This his deliverance, founded on Truth, is unshakable. O bhikkhu, that which is unreality is false; that which is reality Nibbāna, is Truth. Therefore, O bhikkhu, a person so endowed is endowed with this Absolute Truth. For, the Absolute Noble Truth is Nibbāna, which is Reality.

Elsewhere the Buddha unequivocally uses the word Truth in place of Nibbāna: 'I will teach you the Truth and the Path leading to the Truth. Here Truth definitely means Nirvāna.

Now, what is Absolute Truth? According to Buddhism, the Absolute Truth is that there is nothing absolute in the world, that everything is relative, conditioned and impermanent, and that there is no unchanging, everlasting, absolute substance like Self, Soul or *Ātman* within or without. This is the Absolute Truth. Truth is never negative, though there is a popular expression as negative truth. The realization of this Truth, i.e., to see things as they are without illusion or ignorance, is the extinction of craving 'thirst', and the cessation of *dukkha*, which is Nirvāna. It is interesting and useful to remember here the Mahāyāna view of Nirvāna as not being different from *Samsāra*. The same thing is Samsāra or Nirvāna according to the way you look at it—subjectively or objectively. This Mahāyāna view was probably developed out of the ideas found in the original Theravāda Pali texts, to which we have just referred in our brief discussion.

It is incorrect to think that Nirvāna is the natural result of the extinction of craving. Nirvāna is not the result of anything. If it would be a result, then it would be an effect produced by a cause. It would be 'produced' and 'conditioned'. Nirvāna is neither cause nor effect. It is beyond cause and effect. Truth is not a result nor an effect. It is not produced like a mystic, spiritual, mental state.... TRUTH IS. NIRVĀNA IS. The only thing you can do is to see it, to realize it. There is a path leading to the realization of Nirvāna. But Nirvāna is not the result of this path. You may get to the mountain along a path, but the mountain is not the result, not an effect of the path. You may see a light, but the light is not the result of your eyesight.

People often ask: What is there after Nirvāna? This question cannot arise, because Nirvāna is the Ultimate Truth. If it is Ultimate, there can be nothing after it. If there is anything after Nirvāna, then that will be the Ultimate Truth and not Nirvāna. A monk named Rādha put this question to the Buddha in a different form: 'For what purpose (or end) is Nirvāna?' This question presupposes something after Nirvāna, when it postulates some purpose or end for it. So the Buddha answered: 'O Rādha, this question could not catch its limit (i.e., it is beside the point). One lives the holy life with Nirvāna as its final plunge (into the Absolute Truth), as its goal, as its ultimate end.'

Some popular inaccurately phrased expressions like 'The Buddha entered into Nirvāṇa or Parinirvāṇa[7] after his death' have given rise to many imaginary speculations about Nirvāṇa. The moment you hear the phrase that 'the Buddha entered into Nirvāṇa or Parinirvāṇa', you take Nirvāṇa to be a state, or a realm, or a position in which there is some sort of existence, and try to imagine it in terms of the senses of the word 'existence' as it is known to you. This popular expression 'entered into Nirvāṇa' has no equivalent in the original texts. There is no such thing as 'entering into Nirvāṇa after death'. There is a word parinibbuto used to denote the death of the Buddha or an Arahant[8] who has realized Nirvāṇa, but it does not mean 'entering into Nirvāṇa'. Parinibbuto simply means 'fully passed away', 'fully blown out' or 'fully extinct', because the Buddha or an Arahant has no re-existence after his death.

Now another question arises: What happens to the Buddha or an Arahant after his death, parinirvāṇa? This comes under the category of unanswered questions. Even when the Buddha spoke about this, he indicated that no words in our vocabulary could express what happens to an Arahant after his death. In reply to a Parivrājaka[9] named Vaccha, the Buddha said that terms like 'born' or 'not born' do not apply in the case of an Arahant, because those things—matter, sensation, perception, mental activities, consciousness—with which the terms like 'born' and 'not born' are associated, are completely destroyed and uprooted, never to rise again after his death.

An Arahant after his death is often compared to a fire gone out when the supply of wood is over, or to the flame of a lamp gone out when the wick and oil are finished. Here it should be clearly and distinctly understood, without any confusion, that what is compared to a flame or a fire gone out is *not* Nirvāṇa, but the 'being' composed of the Five Aggregates who realized Nirvāṇa. This point has to be emphasized because many people, even some great scholars, have misunderstood and misinterpreted this simile as referring to Nirvāṇa. Nirvāṇa is never compared to a fire or a lamp gone out.

There is another popular question: If there is no Self, no Ātman, who realizes Nirvāṇa? Before we go on to Nirvāṇa, let us ask the question: Who thinks now, if there is no Self? We have seen earlier that it is the thought that thinks, that there is no thinker behind the thought. In the same way, it is wisdom, realization, that realizes. There is no other self behind the realization. In the discussion of the origin of dukkha we saw that whatever it may be—whether being, or thing, or system—if it is of the nature of arising, it has within itself the nature, the germ, of its cessation, its destruction. Now dukkha, saṃsāra, the cycle of continuity, is of the nature of arising; it must also be of the nature of cessation. Dukkha arises because of 'thirst', and it ceases because of wisdom. 'Thirst' and wisdom are both within the Five Aggregates…

Thus, the germ of their arising as well as that of their cessation are both within the Five Aggregates. This is the real meaning of the Buddha's well-known statement: 'Within this fathom-long sentient body itself, I postulate the world, the arising of the world, the cessation of the world, and the path leading to the cessation of the world.' This means that all the Four Noble Truths are found within the Five Aggregates, i.e., within ourselves…. This also means that there is no external power that produces the arising and the cessation of dukkha.

When wisdom is developed and cultivated according to the Fourth Noble Truth[10], it sees the secret of life, the reality of things as they are. When the secret is discovered, when the Truth is seen, all the forces which feverishly produce the continuity of saṃsāra in illusion become calm and incapable of producing any more karma-formations, because there is no more illusion, no more 'thirst' for continuity. It is like a mental disease which is cured when the cause or the secret of the malady is discovered and seen by the patient.

In almost all religions the *summum bonum* can be attained only after death. But Nirvāṇa can be realized in this very life; it is not necessary to wait till you die to 'attain' it.

He who has realized the Truth, Nirvāna, is the happiest being in the world. He is free from all 'complexes' and obsessions, the worries and troubles that torment others. His mental health is perfect. He does not repent the past, nor does he brood over the future. He lives fully in the present. Therefore he appreciates and enjoys things in the purest sense without self-projections. He is joyful, exultant, enjoying the pure life, his faculties pleased, free from anxiety, serene and peaceful. As he is free from selfish desire, hatred, ignorance, conceit, pride, and all such 'defilements', he is pure and gentle, full of universal love, compassion, kindness, sympathy, understanding and tolerance. His service to others is of the purest, for he has no thought of self. He gains nothing, accumulates nothing, not even anything spiritual, because he is free from the illusion of Self, and the 'thirst' for becoming.

Nirvāna is beyond all terms of duality and relativity. It is therefore beyond our conceptions of good and evil, right and wrong, existence and non-existence. Even the word 'happiness' which is used to describe Nirvāna has an entirely different sense here. Sāriputta once said: 'O friend, Nirvāna is happiness! Nirvāna is happiness!' Then Udāyi asked: 'But, friend Sāriputta, what happiness can it be if there is no sensation?' Sāriputta's reply was highly philosophical and beyond ordinary comprehension: 'That there is no sensation itself is happiness'.

Nirvāna is beyond logic and reasoning. However much we may engage, often as a vain intellectual pastime, in highly speculative discussions regarding Nirvāna or Ultimate Truth or Reality, we shall never understand it that way. A child in the kindergarten should not quarrel about the theory of relativity. Instead, if he follows his studies patiently and diligently, one day he may understand it. Nirvāna is 'to be realized by the wise within themselves'. If we follow the Path patiently and with diligence, train and purify ourselves earnestly, and attain the necessary spiritual development, we may one day realize it within ourselves—without taxing ourselves with puzzling and high-sounding words.

NOTES

1. [In Sanskrit, "Nirvana."]
2. [Buddhist monk.]
3. [Matter, Sensations, Perceptions, Mental Formations, Consciousness.]
4. [A student of the Buddha.]
5. [Sermon.]
6. [Suffering.]
7. [The final passing away of one who is free from rebirth.]
8. [One who is free from rebirth.]
9. [A wandering religious mendicant.]
10. [The Noble Eightfold Path leading to the cessation of suffering: Right Understanding, Right Thought, Right Speech, Right Action, Right Livelihood, Right Effort, Right Mindfulness, Right Concentration.]

84 THE CESSATION OF SUFFERING

CHRISTOPHER W. GOWANS

In the next selection, Christopher W. Gowans, whose work we read previously, considers philosophical perplexities that arise in seeking to explain the Buddhist concept of Nirvana-after-death. Does the notion cohere with the Buddhist not-self doctrine? Furthermore, in the absence of consciousness, which is supposed to be extinguished after death, how is happiness possible?

In an important respect, stream-observers[1] are in a better position to evaluate the life of an *arahant*[2] who is still alive than they are to assess the state of an *arahant* who has died. We could observe a living *arahant* and judge whether he has a truly good life. However, we cannot directly observe the state of an *arahant* after death. From the Buddha's perspective, an unenlightened person cannot fully comprehend the worth of an *arahant*'s life before or after death. But he thought stream-observers could comprehend enough to conclude that it would be worthwhile to undertake the Eightfold Path.[3] We now need to consider whether or not the state of an *arahant* beyond this life is sufficiently coherent to make this preliminary assessment. There are several philosophical perplexities on the horizon.

The most important problem concerns what it means to say a person has attained *Nibbāna*-after-death.[4] Since *Nibbāna* as ultimate reality is beyond change and conditioning, the fact that a person attains *Nibbāna* cannot result in a change to *Nibbāna* itself: it does not change. Hence, a person's attainment of *Nibbāna*-after-death must involve a transformation within the person. But the Buddha regularly speaks as if a person in this life is nothing more than the aggregates,[5] and he says a person who attains *Nibbāna*-after-death abandons all the aggregates (in my terminology, the person is not a substance-self, and the process-self is completely dissolved with the attainment of

Nibbāna-after-death). The consequence is that there does not seem to be anything left of a person who attains *Nibbāna*-after-death. However, there must be something left or attainment of *Nibbāna*-after-death would be annihilation – and this the Buddha denies.

There are four main responses to this problem. First, it may be contended that, despite what the Buddha says, *Nibbāna*-after-death really is annihilation of the person. Even if what he claims about *Nibbāna* as ultimate reality is correct, his overall position entails that attainment of *Nibbāna*-after-death could be nothing else but the complete cessation of the person. Second, it may be argued that, in spite of the Buddha's not-self doctrine, there surely is a self *in some sense* that permanently exists through this life and attains *Nibbāna*-after-death. If this attainment is not annihilation, then there must be a self that attains *Nibbāna*. Both of these interpretations attribute an unintended inconsistency to the Buddha's teaching. The remaining interpretations take a different approach. The third says the rational irresolvability of this problem is part of the Buddha's teaching. Though it is true from a rational standpoint that this is a problem, the Buddha acknowledges that his teaching concerning *Nibbāna* is 'unattainable by mere reasoning.' For one who is enlightened all will be clear, but for others nothing more can be said than this. The difficulty with this interpretation is that it

From Christopher W. Gowans, *Philosophy of the Buddha*, Routledge, 2003. Reprinted by permission of Taylor & Francis Group.

seems to deprive stream-observers of a solid rationale for undertaking the Eightfold Path. It requires them to have considerable faith in the Buddha as a prelude to achieving enlightenment for themselves.

The fourth interpretation maintains that there is an aspect of the person that, like *Nibbāna* as ultimate reality, is beyond space and time, change and conditioning, and so on. Though any label misleads, it will be convenient to call this aspect of the person its *liberated dimension*. This dimension cannot be identified with the aggregates and it cannot be described as any kind of self: both the process-self and the substance-self presuppose categories that the liberated dimension is beyond. On this interpretation, it is the liberated dimension that persists in *Nibbāna*-after-death. If this were the case, the Buddha could consistently maintain both the not-self doctrine and the view that attainment of *Nibbāna* is not complete annihilation. But if both *Nibbāna* and the liberated dimension are beyond change and conditioning, what would it mean for a person to attain *Nibbāna*? Attainment involves change, and both *Nibbāna* and the liberated dimension do not change. What would have to be said is that *Nibbāna* and the liberated dimension have always been united in the appropriate way (however union might be understood). This does not change. To attain *Nibbāna* means that the person dissolves all sense of selfhood as an illusion and thereby discovers the previously hidden fact that the liberated dimension and *Nibbāna* have always been united. Here an analogy may help. Suppose your living room window overlooks a beautiful mountain valley, but nothing can be seen because the window is too dirty. Cleaning the window enables you to see the valley. But this does not create the fact that your living room overlooks the valley. It merely reveals what was already the case. Similarly, on this interpretation, enlightenment creates no new reality, but by cleansing the person of the illusion of selfhood it reveals the fact that the liberated dimension has always been united with *Nibbāna* – and this ends suffering and brings the greatest bliss.

In support of this interpretation is the fact that a fundamental premise of the Buddha's teaching is that the person, though not a self, is capable of attaining the highest happiness of *Nibbāna*-after-death. This suggests that the Buddha was committed to this view or something close to it. On the other hand, he did not directly formulate the problem about the meaning of the attainment of *Nibbāna*, and he did not explicitly articulate this understanding of the person as a resolution of that problem (nor for any other reason). His primary instinct was to say little about *Nibbāna* and to focus on the means to its attainment. This interpretation could be defended only on the ground that it makes the best overall sense of the Buddha's teaching in comparison with the other three.

Two related perplexities should also be mentioned. They both are rooted in the fact that an *arahant* who attains *Nibbāna*-after-death has abandoned all the aggregates. First, one of the aggregates is consciousness. Hence, it seems that an *arahant* who attains *Nibbāna*-after-death is not conscious. But what could it mean to attain *Nibbāna* without being conscious? Would this be any different than annihilation? It might be said that consciousness, as one of the aggregates, is inescapably tied up with the illusion of selfhood. For this reason, one who attains *Nibbāna* cannot be conscious in this sense. However, there might be another form of consciousness that involves no notion of selfhood and is present in one who attains *Nibbāna*…. Of course, we might wonder whether consciousness-without-selfhood is really possible. Perhaps animals have such consciousness. But it seems unlikely that our liberated dimension is akin to animal consciousness: animals are below humans in the Buddha's cosmology. In the end, the Buddha might respond in this way: the distinction between what is and is not conscious applies to the conditioned world of our experience, and since *Nibbāna* is beyond this world, in this respect nothing meaningful can be said about the *arahant* after death.

Second, another of the aggregates is feelings or sensations. Attaining *Nibbāna* is said to be the highest happiness, but how is happiness possible in the absence of feelings? The Buddha has something to say in response to this question. The happiness of *Nibbāna*-after-death is not a matter of pleasant feelings, and it is immeasurably higher than any form of happiness available to the unenlightened in the cycle of rebirth. For example, we hear of a happiness that comes with 'the ending of perception and feeling' and a 'delight apart from sensual pleasures'. Most people would probably acknowledge that happiness is not merely pleasant feelings (and the absence of painful ones). Much that is ordinarily associated with happiness, such as a fulfilling family life or a satisfying job, cannot plausibly be understood simply in terms of pleasant feelings. But it is another matter whether we can envision a form of happiness in the absence of *any* of the aggregates. The issue here is closely related to the last: it is hard to imagine a state we would consider the highest happiness without some form of consciousness. As before, the Buddha was less inclined to explain this than to encourage us to experience it for ourselves by following the Eightfold Path.

NOTES

1. [See reading 46, note 1.]
2. [See reading 46, note 5.]
3. [See reading 83, note 10.]
4. [See reading 46, section 4.]
5. [See reading 83, note 3.]

PART NINE

Religious Pluralism

85 THE CHALLENGE OF RELIGIOUS DIVERSITY

PHILIP L. QUINN AND KEVIN MEEKER

Does the existence of numerous religious traditions undermine the reasonableness of commitment to one? The problem is presented in the following selection by Philip L. Quinn (1940–2004), who was a professor of philosophy at the University of Notre Dame, and Kevin Meeker, a professor of philosophy at the University of South Alabama.

Imagine that you were raised in a small, mostly evangelical Christian farming community in South Dakota. As far back as you can remember, you have believed in a personal God. While growing up, you were taught various Christian doctrines in Sunday School. Almost all the adults you knew accepted these doctrines, and so you took most of them for granted. You tried your best to live a good Christian life.

But now you are at the university. You elect to take a course in religious studies on Hinduism. In it you learn that advaita Hindus do not believe in a personal God; instead, for them, ultimate re-ality is the nonpersonal Brahman. As it happens, a classmate who also resides on your dormitory floor is a practicing advaita Hindu. The material from the class and discussions with this classmate inspire you to study the issue of what reasons there are for being a Christian.

You discover that arguments for the existence of a personal God come in many varieties: ontological, cosmological, teleological, and so on. But you also learn that scholars disagree on whether such arguments are any good. By the same token, you find out that there are arguments for the existence of Brahman and learn that they too are

From Philip L. Quinn and Kevin Meeker, *The Philosophical Challenge of Religious Diversity*, Oxford University Press, 2000. Reprinted by permission of the publisher.

disputed. You read about Christians who report experiences of God. Indeed, when you reflect on the matter, you recall a couple of experiences of your own that could well be taken to be experiences of God guiding you. But you also read reports by advaita Hindus about their experiential contact with Brahman. You read reports about how the Christian system of belief and practice has helped many people become good and holy, but you also find out that there are reports of a lot of good and holy people among the advaita Hindus. You quickly realize that it is unlikely that you will discover undisputed arguments or reasons that will establish the superiority of your own evangelical Christianity to advaita Hinduism or vice versa. And, of course, you recognize that you probably would have reached similar conclusions if you had been investigating Buddhism or Islam or Judaism or Taoism instead of advaita Hinduism.

So what should you do? Should you stick with the Christian system of belief and practice in which you were raised? Should you try to switch to one of its competitors? Or should you become a skeptic about all the religious systems of belief and take a stand outside all the religious practices? Once you have become genuinely puzzled by questions like these, you have felt the challenge of religious diversity. Of course, you need not doubt your own religion to feel the force of this challenge; simply wondering what justifies you in remaining in a tradition as opposed to switching to some other perspective poses similar questions. Or you might wonder how rationally to convince someone from another tradition that yours is true. In all such situations, the challenge of religious diversity looms large.

Needless to say, the awareness of religious diversity is not new. But many scholars argue that this awareness has recently acquired new significance…. Among the factors involved in this change is the better acquaintance people have with religions other than their own. After all, modern technologies of travel and communication facilitate contacts between adherents of different religions. Along the same lines, modern scholarship has produced fine translations of texts from a variety of religious traditions, and cultural anthropologists have provided fascinating thick descriptions of the practices of such traditions. Moreover, those who live in religiously pluralistic democracies have ample opportunities to develop first-hand familiarity with religions other than their own without leaving home. Finally, twenty-four hour a day news broadcasts have confronted us with graphic illustrations of what can transpire when diverging religions clash in such places as Belfast, Beirut, and Bosnia. Brief reflection on these factors should make it easy to see why the issue of religious diversity has become increasingly significant….

It is also worth noting that the issue of religious diversity in general has not been on the radar screen of *academic* philosophy in the twentieth century as much as one might expect. For philosophy of religion in the middle part of the century was almost exclusively preoccupied with abstract questions about the meaningfulness of religious language. Now that the range of topics discussed has widened considerably, the issue of religious diversity is again receiving critical attention. And this is a healthy sign. For religious diversity is a practical problem for many people. As we noted earlier, modern technology and demographics have made the problem more acute and pressing. Unlike many very abstract philosophical problems, then, this one has the potential to engage nonphilosophers in a down-to-earth issue, and the philosophical discussion of it promises to aid nonphilosophers in further reflecting about what is at stake.

86   REJECTING RELIGIONS

ELIZABETH SECORD ANDERSON

Elizabeth Secord Anderson is Professor of Philosophy and of Women's Studies at the University of Michigan. She finds that the evidence offered for all religions is equal and that, therefore, none of it is credible. Thus she rejects every religion.

Every year in my town, Ann Arbor, Michigan, there is a summer art fair. Not just artists, but political and religious groups, set up booths to promote their wares, be these artworks or ideas. Along one street one finds booths of Catholics, Baptists, Calvinists, Christian Orthodox, other denominational and nondenominational Christians of all sorts, Muslims, Hindus, Buddhists, Baha'i, Mormons, Christian Scientists, Jehovah's Witnesses, Jews for Jesus, Wiccans, Scientologists, New Age believers–representatives of nearly every religion that has a significant presence in the United States. The believers in each booth offer evidence of exactly the same kind to advance their religion. Every faith points to its own holy texts and oral traditions, its spiritual experiences, miracles and prophets, its testimonies of wayward lives turned around by conversion, rebirth of faith, or return to the church. Each religion takes these experiences and reports them as conclusive evidence for *its* peculiar set of beliefs. Here we have purported sources of evidence for higher, unseen spirits or divinity, which systematically point to *contradictory* beliefs. Is there one God, or many? Was Jesus God, the son of God, God's prophet, or just a man? Was the last prophet Jesus, Muhammad, Joseph Smith, or the Rev. Sun Myung Moon?

Consider how this scene looks to someone like me, who was raised outside of any faith. My father is nominally Lutheran, in practice religiously indifferent. My mother is culturally Jewish but not practicing. Having been rejected by both the local Lutheran minister and the local rabbi (in both cases, for being in a mixed marriage), but thinking that some kind of religious education would be good for their children, my parents helped found the local Unitarian church in the town where I grew up. Unitarianism is a church without a creed; there are no doctrinal requirements of membership. (Although Bertrand Russell once quipped that Unitarianism stands for the proposition that there is *at most* one God, these days pagans are as welcome as all others.) It was a pretty good fit for us, until New Age spiritualists started to take over the church. That was too loopy for my father's rationalistic outlook, so we left. Thus, religious doctrines never had a chance to insinuate themselves into my head as a child. So I have none by default or habit.

Surveying the religious booths every year at the Ann Arbor art fair, I am always struck by the fact that they are staffed by people who are convinced of their own revelations and miracles, while most so readily disparage the revelations and miracles of other faiths. To a mainstream Christian, Jew, or Muslim, nothing is more obvious than that founders and prophets of other religions, such as Joseph Smith, the Rev. Moon, Mary Baker Eddy, and L. Ron Hubbard, are either frauds or delusional, their purported miracles or cures tricks played upon a credulous audience (or worse, exercises of black magic), their prophecies false, their metaphysics absurd. To me, nothing is more obvious than that the evidence cited on behalf of Christianity, Judaism, and Islam is of exactly the same type and quality as that cited on behalf of

From Elizabeth Secord Anderson, "If God Is Dead, Is Everything Permitted?" in Louise M. Antony, ed., *Philosophers Without Gods: Meditations on Atheism and the Secular Life*, Oxford University Press, 2007. Reprinted by permission of the publisher.

such despised religions. Indeed, it is on a par with the evidence for Zeus, Baal, Thor, and other long-abandoned gods, who are now considered ridiculous by nearly everyone.

The perfect symmetry of evidence for all faiths persuades me that the *types* of extraordinary evidence to which they appeal are not credible. The sources of evidence for theism—revelations, miracles, religious experiences, and prophecies, nearly all known only by testimony transmitted through uncertain chains of long-lost original sources—systematically generate contradictory beliefs, many of which are known to be morally abhorrent or otherwise false. Of course, ordinary sources of evidence, such as eyewitness testimony of ordinary events, also often lead to conflicting beliefs. But in the latter case, we have independent ways to test the credibility of the evidence—for instance, by looking for corroborating physical evidence. In the former cases, the tests advanced by believers tend to be circular: don't believe that other religion's testimonies of miracles or revelations, since they come from those who teach a false religion (Deut. 13:1–5). It is equally useless to appeal to

the certainty in one's heart of some experience of divine presence. For exactly the same certainty has been felt by those who think they've seen ghosts, been kidnapped by aliens, or been possessed by Dionysus or Apollo. Furthermore, where independent tests exist, they either disconfirm or fail to confirm the extraordinary evidence. There is no geological evidence of a worldwide flood, no archaeological evidence that Pharaoh's army drowned in the Red Sea after Moses parted it to enable the Israelites to escape. Jesus' central prophecy, that oppressive regimes would be destroyed in an apocalypse, and the Kingdom of God established *on Earth, within the lifetime of those witnessing his preaching* (Mark 8:38–9:1, 13:24–27, 30), did not come to pass. If any instance of these extraordinary sources of evidence is what it purports to be, it is like the proverbial needle in the haystack—except that there is no way to tell the difference between it and the hay. I conclude that none of the evidence for theism—that is, for the God of Scripture—is credible. Since exactly the same types of evidence are the basis for belief in pagan Gods, I reject pagan religions too.

87 RELIGIOUS PLURALISM AND SALVATION

JOHN H. HICK

John H. Hick (1922–2012), whose work we read previously, believes that despite the differences among religions, in at least one crucial respect all are fundamentally similar. Each can be viewed as offering a path to salvation, a way of shifting believers from self-centeredness to concentration on a divine reality. In light of this consideration, Hick urges all religious adherents to reject the view that their own religions are superior to all others.

In particular, Hick maintains that Christians should recognize the "arbitrary and contrived notion" that the salvation of all persons depends on their believing in the Trinity and resurrection. Whether such a doctrinal transformation would undermine or enhance Christianity is a crucial question.

From John H. Hick, "Religious Pluralism and Salvation," *Faith and Philosophy* 5 (1988). Reprinted by permission of the journal.

I

The fact that there is a plurality of religious traditions, each with its own distinctive beliefs, spiritual practices, ethical outlook, art forms, and cultural ethos, creates an obvious problem for those of us who see them, not simply as human phenomena, but as responses to the Divine. For each presents itself implicitly or explicitly, as in some important sense absolute and unsurpassable and as rightly claiming a total allegiance. The problem of the relationship between these different streams of religious life has often been posed in terms of their divergent belief-systems. For whilst there are various overlaps between their teachings there are also radical differences: is the divine reality (let us refer to it as the Real) personal or non-personal; if personal, is it unitary or triune; is the universe created, or emanated, or itself eternal; do we live only once on this earth or are we repeatedly reborn? and so on and so on. When the problem of understanding religious plurality is approached through these rival truth-claims it appears particularly intractable.

I want to suggest, however, that it may more profitably be approached from a different direction, in terms of the claims of the various traditions to provide, or to be effective contexts of, salvation. "Salvation" is primarily a Christian term, though I shall use it here to include its functional analogues in the other major world traditions. In this broader sense we can say that both Christianity and these other faiths are paths of salvation. For whereas preaxial religion was (and is) centrally concerned to keep life going on an even keel, the post-axial traditions, originating or rooted in the "axial age" of the first millennium B.C.E.—principally Hinduism, Judaism, Buddhism, Christianity, Islam—are centrally concerned with a radical transformation of the human situation.

It is of course possible, in an alternative approach, to define salvation in such a way that it becomes a necessary truth that only one particular tradition can provide it. If, for example, from within Christianity we define salvation as being forgiven by God because of Jesus' atoning death, and so becoming part of God's redeemed community, the church, then salvation is by definition Christian salvation. If on the other hand, from within Mahayana Buddhism, we define it as the attainment of *satori* or awakening, and so becoming an ego-free manifestation of the eternal Dharmakaya, then salvation is by definition Buddhist liberation. And so on. But if we stand back from these different conceptions to compare them, we can, I think, very naturally and properly see them as different forms of the more fundamental conception of a radical change from a profoundly unsatisfactory state to one that is limitlessly better because rightly related to the Real. Each tradition conceptualizes in its own way the wrongness of ordinary human existence—as a state of fallenness from paradisal virtue and happiness, or as a condition of moral weakness and alienation from God, or as the fragmentation of the infinite One into false individualities, or as a self-centeredness which pervasively poisons our involvement in the world process, making it to us an experience of anxious, unhappy unfulfillment. But each at the same time proclaims a limitlessly better possibility, again conceptualized in different ways—as the joy of conforming one's life to God's law; as giving oneself to God in Christ, so that "it is no longer I who live, but Christ who lives in me" (Galatians 2:20), leading to eternal life in God's presence; as a complete surrender (*islam*) to God, and hence peace with God, leading to the bliss of paradise; as transcending the ego and realizing oneness with the limitless being-consciousness-bliss (*satchitananda*) of Brahman; as overcoming the ego point of view and entering into the serene selflessness of nirvana. I suggest that these different conceptions of salvation are specifications of what, in a generic formula, is the transformation of human existence from self-centeredness to a new orientation, centered in the divine Reality. And in each case the good news that is proclaimed is that this limitlessly better possibility is actually available and can be entered upon, or begin to be entered upon, here and now. Each tradition sets forth the way to attain this great good: faithfulness to the Torah, discipleship to Jesus, obedient living out of the Qur'anic way of life, the Eightfold Path of the Buddhist dharma, or the three great Hindu *margas* of mystical insight, activity in the world, and self-giving devotion to God.

II

The great world religions, then, are ways of salvation. Each claims to constitute an effective context within which the transformation of human existence can and does take place from self-centeredness to Reality-centeredness. How are we to judge such claims? We cannot directly observe the inner spiritual quality of a human relationship to the Real; but we can observe how that relationship, as one's deepest and most pervasive orientation, affects the moral and spiritual quality of a human personality and of a man's or woman's relationship to others. It would seem, then, that we can only assess these salvation-projects insofar as we are able to observe their fruits in human life. The inquiry has to be, in a broad sense, empirical. For the issue is one of fact, even though hard to define and difficult to measure fact, rather than being settleable by a priori stipulation.

The word "spiritual" which occurs above is notoriously vague; but I am using it to refer to a quality or, better, an orientation which we can discern in those individuals whom we call saints —a Christian term which I use here to cover such analogues as arahat, bodhisattva, jivanmukti, mahatma. In these cases the human self is variously described as becoming part of the life of God, being "to the Eternal Goodness what his own hand is to a man"; or being permeated from within by the infinite reality of Brahman; or becoming one with the eternal Buddha nature. There is a change in their deepest orientation from centeredness in the ego to a new centering in the Real as manifested in their own tradition. One is conscious in the presence of such a person that he or she is, to a startling extent, open to the transcendent, so as to be largely free from self-centered concerns and anxieties and empowered to live as an instrument of God/Truth/Reality.

It is to be noted that there are two main patterns of such a transformation. There are saints who withdraw from the world into prayer or meditation and saints who seek to change the world— in the medieval period a contemplative Julian of Norwich and a political Joan of Arc, or in our own century a mystical Sri Aurobindo and a political Mahatma Gandhi. In our present age of sociological consciousness, when we are aware that our inherited political and economic structures can be analyzed and purposefully changed, saintliness is more likely than in earlier times to take social and political forms. But, of whichever type, the saints are not a different species from the rest of us; they are simply much more advanced in the salvific transformation.

The ethical aspect of this salvific transformation consists in observable modes of behavior. But how do we identify the kind of behavior which, to the degree that it characterizes a life, reflects a corresponding degree of reorientation to the divine Reality? Should we use Christian ethical criteria, or Buddhist, or Muslim ... ? The answer, I suggest, is that at the level of their most basic moral insights the great traditions use a common criterion. For they agree in giving a central and normative role to the unselfish regard for others that we call love or compassion. This is commonly expressed in the principle of valuing others as we value ourselves, and treating them accordingly. Thus in the ancient Hindu *Mahabharata* we read that "One should never do to another that which one would regard as injurious to oneself. This, in brief, is the rule of Righteousness" (*Anushana parva*, 113:7). Again, "He who ... benefits persons of all orders, who is always devoted to the good of all beings, who does not feel aversion to anybody ... succeeds in ascending to Heaven" (*Anushana parva*, 145:24). In the Buddhist *Sutta Nipata* we read, "As a mother cares for her son, all her days, so towards all living things a man's mind should be all-embracing" (149). In the Jain scriptures we are told that one should go about "treating all creatures in the world as he himself would be treated" (*Kitanga Sutra*, I.ii.33). Confucius, expounding humaneness (*jen*), said, "Do not do to others what you would not like yourself" (*Analects*, xxi, 2). In a Taoist scripture we read that the good man will "regard [others'] gains as if they were his own, and their losses in the same way" (*Thai Shang*, 3). The Zoroastrian scriptures declare, "That nature only is good when it shall not do unto another whatever is not good for its own self" (*Dadistan-i-dinik*, 94:5). We are all familiar with Jesus' teaching, "As ye would that men should do to you, do ye also to them likewise" (Luke 6:31). In the Jewish Talmud we read "What is hateful to yourself do not do to your fellow man. That is the whole of the Torah" (*Babylonian Talmud*, Shabbath 31a). And in the Hadith of Islam we read Muhammad's words, "No man is a true believer unless he desires for his brother that which he desires for himself" (*Ibn Madja*, Intro. 9). Clearly, if everyone acted on this basic principle, taught by all the major faiths, there would be no injustice, no avoidable suffering, and the human family would everywhere live in peace.

When we turn from this general principle of love/compassion to the actual behavior of people within the different traditions, wondering to what extent they live in this way, we realize how little research has been done on so important a question. We do not have, much more to go on than general impressions, supplemented by travellers' tales and anecdotal reports. We observe among our neighbors within our own community a great deal of practical loving-kindness; and we are told, for example, that a remarkable degree of self-giving love is to be found among the Hindu fishing families in the mud huts along the Madras shore; and we hear various other similar accounts from other lands. We read biographies, social histories, and novels of Muslim village life in Africa, Buddhist life in Thailand, Hindu life in India, Jewish life in New York, as well as Christian life around the world, both in the past and today, and we get the impression that the personal virtues (as well as vices) are basically much the same within these very different religion-cultural settings and that in all of them unselfish concern for others occurs and is highly valued. And, needless to say, as well as love and compassion we also see all-too-abundantly, and apparently spread more or less equally in every society, cruelty, greed, hatred, selfishness, and malice.

All this constitutes a haphazard and impressionistic body of data. Indeed I want to stress, not how easy it is, but on the contrary how difficult it is, to make responsible judgments in this area. For not only do we lack full information, but the fragmentary information that we have has to be interpreted in the light of the varying natural conditions of human life in different periods of history and in different economic and political circumstances. And I suggest that all that we can presently arrive at is the cautious and negative conclusion that we have no good reason to believe that any one of the great religious traditions has proved itself to be more productive of love/compassion than another.

The same is true when we turn to the large-scale social outworkings of the different salvation projects. Here the units are not individual human lives, spanning a period of decades, but religious cultures spanning many centuries. For we can no more judge a civilization than a human life by confining our attention to a single temporal cross-section. Each of the great streams of religious life has had its times of flourishing and its times of deterioration. Each has produced its own distinctive kinds of good and its own distinctive kinds of evil. But to assess either the goods or the evils cross-culturally is difficult to say the least. How do we weigh, for example, the lack of economic progress, and consequent widespread poverty, in traditional Hindu and Buddhist cultures against the endemic violence and racism of Christian civilization, culminating in the twentieth century Holocaust? How do we weigh what the west regards as the hollowness of arranged marriages against what the east regards as the hollowness of a marriage system that leads to such a high proportion of divorces and broken families? From within each culture one can see clearly enough the defects of the others. But an objective ethical comparison of such vast and complex totalities is at present an unattainable ideal. And the result is that we are not in a position to claim an over-all moral superiority for any one of the great living religious traditions.

Let us now see where we have arrived. I have suggested that if we identity the central claim of each of the great religious traditions as the claim to provide, or to be an effective context of, salvation; and if we see salvation as an actual change in human beings from self-centeredness to a new orientation centered in the ultimate divine Reality; and if this new orientation has both a more elusive "spiritual" character and a more readily observable moral aspect—then we arrive at the modest and largely negative conclusion that, so far as we can tell, no one of the great world religions is salvifically superior to the rest.

III

If this is so, what are we to make of the often contradictory doctrines of the different traditions? In order to make progress at this point, we must distinguish various kinds and levels of doctrinal conflict.

There are, first, conceptions of the ultimate as Jahweh, or the Holy Trinity, or Allah, or Shiva, or Vishnu, or as Brahman, or the Dharmakaya, the Tao, and so on.

If salvation is taking place, and taking place to about the same extent, within the religious systems presided over by these various deities and absolutes, this suggests that they are different manifestations to humanity of a yet more ultimate ground of all salvific transformation. Let us then consider the possibility that an infinite transcendent divine reality is being differently conceived, and therefore differently experienced, and therefore differently responded to from within our different religio-cultural ways of being human. This hypothesis makes sense of the fact that the salvific transformation seems to have been occurring in all the great traditions. Such a conception is, further, readily open to philosophical support. For we are familiar today with the ways in which human experience is partly formed by the conceptual and linguistic frameworks within which it occurs. The basically Kantian insight that the mind is active in perception, and that we are always aware of our environment as it appears to a consciousness operating with our particular conceptual resources and habits, has been amply confirmed by work in cognitive psychology and the sociology of knowledge and can now be extended with some confidence to the analysis of religious awareness. If, then, we proceed inductively from the phenomenon of religious experience around the world, adopting a religious as distinguished from a naturalistic interpretation of it, we are likely to find ourselves making two moves. The first is to postulate an ultimate transcendent divine reality (which I have been referring to as the Real) which, being beyond the scope of our human concepts, cannot be directly experienced by us as it is in itself but only as it appears through our various human thought-forms. And the second is to identify the thought-and-experienced deities and absolutes as different manifestations of the Real within different historical forms of human consciousness. In Kantian terms, the divine noumenon, the Real *an sich*, is experienced through different human receptivities as a range of divine phenomena, in the formation of which religious concepts have played an essential part.

These different "receptivities" consist of conceptual schemas within which various personal, communal, and historical factors have produced yet further variations. The most basic concepts in terms of which the Real is humanly thought-and-experienced are those of (personal) deity and of the (non-personal) absolute. But the Real is not actually experienced either as deity in general or as the absolute in general. Each basic concept becomes (in Kantian terminology) schematized in more concrete form. It is at this point that individual and cultural factors enter the process. The religious tradition of which we are a part, with its history and ethos and its great exemplars, its scriptures feeding our thoughts and emotions, and perhaps above all its devotional or meditative practices, constitutes an uniquely shaped and coloured "lens" through which we are concretely aware of the Real specifically as the personal Adonai, or as the Heavenly Father, or as Allah, or Vishnu, or Shiva ... or again as the non-personal Brahman, or Dharmakaya, or the Void or the Ground.... Thus, one who uses the forms of Christian prayer and sacrament is thereby led to experience the Real as the divine Thou, whereas one who practices advaitic yoga or Buddhist zazen is thereby brought to experience the Real as the infinite being-consciousness-bliss of Brahman, or as the limitless emptiness of *sunyata* which is at the same time the infinite fullness of immediate reality as "wondrous being."

Three explanatory comments at this point before turning to the next level of doctrinal disagreement. First, to suppose that the experienced deities and absolutes which are the intentional objects of worship or content of religious meditation, are appearances or manifestations of the Real, rather than each being itself the Real *an sich*, is not to suppose that they are illusions—any more than the varying ways in which a mountain may appear to a plurality of differently placed observers are illusory. That the same reality may be variously experienced and described is true even of physical objects. But in the case of the infinite, transcendent divine reality there may well be much greater scope for the use of varying human conceptual schemas producing varying modes of phenomenal experience. Whereas the concepts in terms of which we are aware of mountains and rivers and houses are largely (though by no means entirely) standard throughout the human race, the religious concepts in terms of which we become aware of the Real have developed in widely different ways within the different cultures of the earth.

As a second comment, to say that the Real is beyond the range of our human concepts is not intended to mean that it is beyond the scope of purely formal, logically generated concepts—such as the concept of being beyond the range of (other than purely formal) concepts. We would not be able to refer at all to that which cannot be conceptualized in any way, not even by the concept of being unconceptualizable! But the other than purely formal concepts by which our experience is structured must be presumed not to apply to its noumenal ground. The characteristics mapped in thought and language are those that are constitutive of human experience. We have no warrant to apply them to the noumenal ground of the phenomenal, i.e., experienced, realm. We should therefore not think of the Real *an sich* as singular or plural, substance or process, personal or non-personal, good or bad, purposive or non-purposive. This has long been a basic theme of religious thought. For example, within Christianity, Gregory of Nyssa declared that:

> The simplicity of the True Faith assumes God to be that which He is, namely, incapable of being grasped by any term, or any idea, or any other device of our apprehension, remaining beyond the reach not only of the human but of the angelic and all supramundane intelligence, unthinkable, unutterable, above all expression in words, having but one name that can represent His proper nature, the single name being "Above Every Name" (*Against Eunomius*, I, 42).

Augustine, continuing this tradition, said that "God transcends even the mind" (*True Religion*, 36:67), and Aquinas that "by its immensity, the divine substance surpasses every form that our intellect reaches" (*Contra Gentiles*, I, 14, 3). In Islam the Qur'an affirms that God is "beyond what they describe" (6:101). The Upanishads declare of Brahman, "There the eye goes not, speech goes not, nor the mind" (*Kena Up*, 1, 3), and Shankara wrote that Brahman is that "before which words recoil, and to which no understanding has ever attained" (Otto, *Mysticism East and West*, E. T. 1932, p. 28).

But, third, we might well ask, why postulate an ineffable and unobservable divine-reality-in-itself? If we can say virtually nothing about it, why affirm its existence? The answer is that the reality or non-reality of the postulated noumenal ground of the experienced religious phenomena constitutes the difference between a religious and a naturalistic interpretation of religion. If there is no such transcendent ground, the various forms of religious experience have to be categorized as purely human projections. If on the other hand there is such a transcendent ground, then these phenomena may be joint products of the universal presence of the Real and of the varying sets of concepts and images that have crystallized within the religious traditions of the earth. To affirm the transcendent is thus to affirm that religious experience is not solely a construction of the human imagination but is a response—though always culturally conditioned—to the Real.

Those doctrinal conflicts, then, that embody different conceptions of the ultimate arise, according to the hypothesis I am presenting, from the variations between different sets of human conceptual schema and spiritual practice. And it seems that each of these varying ways of thinking-and-experiencing the Real has been able to mediate its transforming presence to human life. For the different major concepts of the ultimate do not seem—so far as we can tell—to result in one religious totality being soteriologically more effective than another.

IV

The second level of doctrinal difference consists of metaphysical beliefs which cohere with although they are not exclusively linked to a particular conception of the ultimate. These are beliefs about the relation of the material universe to the Real: creation ex nihilo, emanation, an eternal universe, an unknown form of dependency...? And about human destiny: reincarnation or a single life, eternal identity or transcendence of the self...? Again, there are questions about the existence of heavens and hells and purgatories and angels and devils and many other subsidiary states and entities. Out of this mass of disputed religious issues let me pick two major examples: is the universe created ex nihilo, and do human beings reincarnate?

I suggest that we would do well to apply to such questions a principle that was taught by the Buddha two and a half millennia ago. He listed a series of "undetermined questions" (*avyakata*)—whether the universe is eternal, whether it is spatially infinite, whether (putting it in modern terms) mind and brain are identical, and what the state is of a completed project of human existence (a Tathagata) after bodily death. He refused to answer these questions, saying that we do not need to have knowledge of these things in order to attain liberation or awakening (nirvana); and indeed that to regard such information as soteriologically essential would only divert us from the single-minded quest for liberation. I think that we can at this point profitably learn from the Buddha, even extending his conception of the undetermined questions further than he did—for together with almost everyone else in his own culture he regarded one of our examples, reincarnation, as a matter of assured knowledge. Let us, then, accept that we do not *know* whether, e.g., the universe was created ex nihilo, nor whether human beings are reincarnated; and, further, that it is not necessary for salvation to hold a correct opinion on either matter.

I am not suggesting that such issues are unimportant. On their own level they are extremely important, being both of great interest to us and also having widely ramifying implications within our belief systems and hence for our lives. The thought of being created out of nothing can nourish a salutary sense of absolute dependence. (But other conceptions can also nurture that sense.)

The idea of reincarnation can offer the hope of future spiritual progress; though, combined with the principle of karma, it can also serve to validate the present inequalities of human circumstances. (But other eschatologies also have their problems, both theoretical and practical). Thus these—and other—disputed issues do have a genuine importance. Further, it is possible that some of them may one day be settled by empirical evidence. It might become established, for example, that the "big bang" of some fifteen billion years ago was an absolute beginning, thus ruling out the possibility that the universe is eternal. And again, it might become established, by an accumulation of evidence, that reincarnation does indeed occur in either some or all cases. On the other hand it is possible that we shall never achieve agreed knowledge in these areas. Certainly, at the present time, whilst we have theories, preferences, hunches, inherited convictions, we cannot honestly claim to have secure knowledge. And the same is true, I suggest, of the entire range of metaphysical issues about which the religions dispute. They are of intense interest, properly the subject of continuing research and discussion, but are not matters concerning which absolute dogmas are appropriate. Still less is it appropriate to maintain that salvation depends upon accepting some one particular opinion or dogma. We have seen that the transformation of human existence from self-centeredness to Reality-centeredness seems to be taking place within each of the great traditions despite their very different answers to these debated questions. It follows that a correct opinion concerning them is not required for salvation.

V

The third level of doctrinal disagreement concerns historical questions. Each of the great traditions includes a larger or smaller body of historical beliefs. In the case of Judaism these include at least the main features of the history described in the Hebrew scriptures; in the case of Christianity, these plus the main features of the life, death, and resurrection of Jesus as described in the New Testament; in the case of Islam, the main features of the history described in the Qur'an;

in the case of Vaishnavite Hinduism, the historicity of Krishna; in the case of Buddhism, the historicity of Guatama and his enlightenment at Bodh Gaya; and so on. But although each tradition thus has its own records of the past, there are rather few instances of direct disagreement between these. For the strands of history that are cherished in these different historical memories do not generally overlap; and where they do overlap they do not generally involve significant differences. The overlaps are mainly within the thread of ancient Near Eastern history that is common to the Jewish, Christian, and Muslim scriptures; and within this I can only locate two points of direct disagreement—the Torah's statement that Abraham nearly sacrificed his son Isaac at Mount Moriah (Genesis 22) versus the Muslim interpretation of the Qur'anic version (in Sura 37) that it was his other son Ishmael; and the New Testament witness that Jesus died on the cross versus the Qur'anic teaching that "they did not slay him, neither crucified him, only a likeness of that was shown them" (Sura 4:156). (This latter however would seem to be a conflict between an historical report, in the New Testament, and a theological inference—that God would not allow so great a prophet to be killed—in the Qur'an.)

All that one can say in general about such disagreements, whether between two traditions or between any one of them and the secular historians, is that they could only properly be settled by the weight of historical evidence. However, the events in question are usually so remote in time, and the evidence so slight or so uncertain, that the question cannot be definitively settled. We have to be content with different communal memories, enriched as they are by the mythic halo that surrounds all long-lived human memories of events of transcendent significance. Once again, then, I suggest that differences of historical judgment, although having their own proper importance, do not prevent the different traditions from being effective, and so far as we can tell equally effective, contexts of salvation. It is evidently not necessary for salvation to have correct historical information. (It is likewise not necessary for salvation, we may add, to correct scientific information.)

VI

Putting all this together, the picture that I am suggesting can be outlined as follows: our human religious experience, variously shaped as it is by our sets of religious concepts, is a cognitive response to the universal presence of the ultimate divine Reality that, in itself, exceeds human conceptuality. This Reality is however manifested to us in ways formed by a variety of human concepts, as the range of divine personae and metaphysical impersonae witnessed to in the history of religions. Each major tradition, built around its own distinctive way of thinking-and-experiencing the Real, has developed its own answers to the perennial questions of our origin and destiny, constituting more or less comprehensive and coherent cosmologies and eschatologies. These are human creations which have, by their association with living streams of religious experience, become invested with a sacred authority. However they cannot all be wholly true; quite possibly none is wholly true; perhaps all are partly true. But since the salvific process has been going on through the centuries despite this unknown distribution of truth and falsity in our cosmologies and eschatologies, it follows that it is not necessary for salvation to adopt any one of them. We would therefore do well to learn to tolerate unresolved, and at present unresolvable, differences concerning these ultimate mysteries.

One element, however, to be found in the belief-systems of most of the traditions raises a special problem, namely that which asserts the sole salvific efficacy of that tradition. I shall discuss this problem in terms of Christianity because it is particularly acute for those of us who are Christians. We are all familiar with such New Testament texts as "There is salvation in no one else [than Jesus Christ], for there is no other name under heaven given among men by which we must be saved" (Acts 4:12), and with the Catholic dogma *Extra ecclesiam nulla salus* (No salvation outside the church) and its Protestant equivalent—never formulated as an official dogma but nevertheless implicit within the eighteenth and nineteenth century Protestant missionary expansion—no salvation outside Christianity. Such a dogma differs from other elements of Christian belief in that it is not only a statement about the potential relationship of Christians to God but at the same time about the actual relationship of non-Christians to God. It says that the latter, in virtue of being non-Christians, lack salvation. Clearly such a dogma is incompatible with the insight that the salvific transformation of human existence is going on, and so far as we can tell going on to a more or less equal extent, within all the great traditions. Insofar, then, as we accept that salvation is not confined to Christianity we must reject the old exclusivist dogma.

This has in fact now been done by most thinking Christians, though exceptions remain, mostly within the extreme Protestant fundamentalist constituencies. The *Extra ecclesiam* dogma, although not explicitly repealed, has been outflanked by the work of such influential Catholic theologians as Karl Rahner, whose new approach was in effect endorsed by Vatican II. Rahner expressed his more inclusivist outlook by suggesting that devout people of other faiths are "anonymous Christians," within the invisible church even without knowing it, and thus within the sphere of salvation. The Pope [John Paul II] in his Encyclical *Redemptor Hominis* (1979), expressed this thought even more comprehensively by saying that "every man without exception has been redeemed by Christ" and "with every man without any exception whatever Christ is in a way united, even when man is unaware of it" (para. 14). And a number of Protestant theologians have advocated a comparable position.

The feature that particularly commends this kind of inclusivism to many Christians today is that it recognizes the spiritual values of other religions, and the occurrence of salvation within them, and yet at the same time preserves their conviction of the ultimate superiority of their own religion over all others. For it maintains that salvation, wherever it occurs, is Christian salvation; and Christians are accordingly those who alone know and preach the source of salvation, namely in the atoning death of Christ.

This again, like the old exclusivism, is a statement not only about the ground of salvation for Christians but also for Jews, Muslims, Hindus,

Buddhists, and everyone else. But we have seen that it has to be acknowledged that the immediate ground of their transformation is the particular spiritual path along which they move. It is by living in accordance with the Torah or with the Qur'anic revelation that Jews and Muslims find a transforming peace with God; it is by one or other of their great *margas* that Hindus attain to *moksha;* it is by the Eightfold Path that Theravada Buddhists come to *nirvana;* it is by *zazen* that Zen Buddhists attain to *satori;* and so on. The Christian inclusivist is, then, by implication, declaring that these various spiritual paths are efficacious, and constitute authentic contexts of salvation, because Jesus died on the cross; and, by further implication, that if he had not died on the cross they would not be efficacious.

This is a novel and somewhat astonishing doctrine. How are we to make sense of the idea that the salvific power of the dharma taught five hundred years earlier by the Buddha is a consequence of the death of Jesus in approximately 30 C.E.? Such an apparently bizarre conception should only be affirmed for some very good reason. It was certainly not taught by Jesus or his apostles. It has emerged only in the thought of twentieth century Christians who have come to recognize that Jews are being salvifically transformed through the spirituality of Judaism, Muslims through that of Islam, Hindus and Buddhists through the paths mapped out by their respective traditions, and so on, but who nevertheless wish to retain their inherited sense of the unique superiority of Christianity. The only outlet left for this sense, when one has acknowledged the salvific efficacy of the various great spiritual ways, is the arbitrary and contrived notion of their metaphysical dependency upon the death of Christ. But the theologian who undertakes to spell out this invisible causality is not to be envied. The problem is not one of logical possibility—it only requires logical agility to cope with that—but one of religious or spiritual plausibility. It would be a better use of theological time and energy, in my opinion, to develop forms of trinitarian, christological, and soteriological doctrine which are compatible with our awareness of the independent salvific authenticity of the other great world faiths. Such forms are already available in principle in conceptions of the

Trinity, not as ontologically three but as three ways in which the one God is humanly thought and experienced; conceptions of Christ as a man so fully open to and inspired by God as to be, in the ancient Hebrew metaphor, a "son of God"; and conceptions of salvation as an actual human transformation which has been powerfully elicited and shaped, among his disciples, by the influence of Jesus.

There may indeed well be a variety of ways in which Christian thought can develop in response to our acute late twentieth century awareness of the other world religions, as there were of responding to the nineteenth century awareness of the evolution of the forms of life and the historical character of the holy scriptures. And likewise there will no doubt be a variety of ways in which each of the other great traditions can rethink its inherited assumption of its own unique superiority. But it is not for us to tell people of other traditions how to do their own business. Rather, we should attend to our own.

88 A DEFENSE OF RELIGIOUS EXCLUSIVISM

ALVIN PLANTINGA

In response to those like John Hick who urge religious adherents to reject the superiority of their own religions, Alvin Plantinga, whose work we read previously, maintains that his belief in Christianity is true, whereas beliefs incompatible with Christianity are false. Is he, therefore, intellectually mistaken or morally arrogant? In the next selection he argues against such charges.

... I find myself with religious beliefs ... that I realize aren't shared by nearly everyone else. For example, I believe both

1. The world was created by God, an almighty, all-knowing, and perfectly good personal being (one that holds beliefs; has aims, plans, and intentions; and can act to accomplish these aims).
2. Human beings require salvation, and God has provided a unique way of salvation through the incarnation, life, sacrificial death, and resurrection of his divine son.

Now there are many who do not believe these things. First, there are those who agree with me on (1) but not (2): They are non-Christian theistic religions. Second, there are those who don't accept either (1) or (2) but nonetheless do believe that there is something beyond the natural world, a something such that human well-being and salvation depend upon standing in a right relation to it. Third, in the West and since the Enlightenment, anyway, there are people—*naturalists*, we may call them—who don't believe any of these three things. And my problem is this: When I become really aware of these other ways of looking at the world, these other ways of responding religiously to the world, what must or should I do? What is the right sort of attitude to take? What sort of impact should this awareness have on the

From Alvin Plantinga, "A Defense of Religious Exclusivism," in Louis Pojman and Michael Rea, eds., *Philosophy of Religion: An Anthology*, Sixth Edition, Wadsworth Cengage Learning, 2012. Reprinted by permission of the publisher.

beliefs I hold and the strength with which I hold them? My question is this: How should I think about the great religious diversity the world in fact displays? Can I sensibly remain an adherent of just one of these religions, rejecting the others? And here I am thinking specifically of *beliefs.* Of course, there is a great deal more to any religion or religious practice than just belief, and I don't for a moment mean to deny it. But belief is a crucially important part of most religions; it is a crucially important part of *my* religion; and the question I mean to ask here is, What does the awareness of religious diversity mean or should mean for my religious beliefs?...

Now there are several possible reactions to awareness of religious diversity. One is to continue to believe—what you have all along believed; you learn about this diversity but continue to believe that is, take to be true—such propositions as (1) and (2) above, consequently taking to be false any beliefs, religious or otherwise, that are incompatible with (1) and (2). Following current practice, I will call this *exclusivism;* the exclusivist holds that the tenets or some of the tenets of *one* religion—Christianity, let's say—are in fact true; he adds, naturally enough, that any propositions, including other religious beliefs, that are incompatible with those tenets are false. And there is a fairly widespread apprehension that... exclusivism as such is or involves a vice of some sort: It is wrong or deplorable. It is this claim I want to examine. I propose to argue that exclusivism need not involve either epistemic or moral failure and that, furthermore, something like it is wholly unavoidable, given our human condition.

These objections, of course, are not to the *truth* of (1) or (2) or any other proposition someone might accept in this exclusivist way (although objections of that sort are also put forward); they are instead directed to the *propriety or rightness* of exclusivism. There are initially two different kinds of indictments of exclusivism: broadly moral, or ethical, indictments and other broadly intellectual, or epistemic, indictments. These overlap in interesting ways as we will see below. But initially, anyway, we can take some of the complaints about exclusivism as *intellectual* criticisms: It is *irrational* or *unjustified* to think in an exclusivistic way.

The other large body of complaint is moral: There is something *morally* suspect about exclusivism—it is arbitrary, or intellectually arrogant, or imperialistic.... I want to consider both kinds of claims or criticisms; I propose to argue that the exclusivist as such is not necessarily guilty of any of these charges.

I turn to the moral complaints: that the exclusivist is intellectually arrogant, or egotistical or self-servingly arbitrary, or dishonest, or imperialistic, or oppressive. But first, I provide three qualifications. An exclusivist, like anyone else, will probably be guilty of some or of all of these things to at least some degree, perhaps particularly the first two. The question, however, is whether she is guilty of these things just by virtue of being an exclusivist. Second, I will use the term *exclusivism* in such a way that you don't count as an exclusivist unless you are rather fully aware of other faiths, have had their existence and their claims called to your attention with some force and perhaps fairly frequently, and have to some degree reflected on the problem of pluralism, asking yourself such questions as whether it is or could be really true that the Lord has revealed Himself and His programs to us Christians, say, in a way in which He hasn't revealed Himself to those of other faiths. Thus, my grandmother, for example, would not have counted as an exclusivist. She had, of course, *heard* of the heathen, as she called them, but the idea that perhaps Christians could learn from them, and learn from them with respect to religious matters, had not so much as entered her head; and the fact that it *hadn't* entered her head, I take it, was not a matter of moral dereliction on her part. This same would go for a Buddhist or Hindu peasant. These people are not, I think, properly charged with arrogance or other moral flaws in believing as they do.

Third, ... an exclusivist, as I use the term, not only believes something like (1) or (2) and thinks false any proposition incompatible with it; she also meets a further condition C that... includes (a) being rather fully aware of other religions, (b) knowing that there is much that at the least looks like genuine piety and devoutness in them, and (c) believing that you know of no arguments that would necessarily convince all or most honest and intelligent dissenters.

Given these qualifications then, why should we think that an exclusivist is properly charged with these moral faults? I will deal first and most briefly with charges of oppression and imperialism: I think we must say that they are on the face of it wholly implausible. I daresay there are some among you who reject some of the things I believe; I do not believe that you are thereby oppressing me, even if you do not believe you have an argument that would convince me. It is conceivable that exclusivism might in some way *contribute* to oppression, but it isn't in itself oppressive.

The more important moral charge is that there is a sort of self-serving arbitrariness, an arrogance or egotism, in accepting such propositions as (1) or (2) under condition C; exclusivism is guilty of some serious moral fault or flaw. According to Wilfred Cantwell Smith,"... except at the cost of insensitivity or delinquency, it is morally not possible actually to go out into the world and say to devout, intelligent, fellow human beings: '... we believe that we know God and we are right; you believe that you know God, and you are totally wrong.'"[1]

So what can the exclusivist have to say for himself: Well, it must be conceded immediately that if he believes (1) or (2), then he must also believe that those who believe something incompatible with them are mistaken and believe what is false. That's no more than simple logic. Furthermore, he must also believe that those who do not believe as he does—those who believe neither (1) nor (2), whether or not they believe their negations—*fail* to believe something that is deep and important and that he *does* believe. He must therefore see himself as *privileged* with respect to those others—those others of both kinds. There is something of great value, he must think, that *he* has and *they* lack. They are ignorant of something—something of great importance—of which he has knowledge. But does this make him properly subject to the above censure?

I think the answer must be no. Or if the answer is yes, then I think we have here a genuine moral dilemma; for in our earthly life here below, as my Sunday School teacher used to say, there is

no real alternative; there is no reflective attitude that is not open to the same strictures. These charges of arrogance are a philosophical tar baby. Get close enough to them to use them against the exclusivist and you are likely to find them stuck fast to yourself. How so? Well, as an exclusivist, I realize that I can't convince others that they should believe as I do, but I nonetheless continue to believe as I do. The charge is that I am, as a result, arrogant or egotistical, arbitrarily preferring my way of doing things to other ways.[2] But what are my alternatives with respect to a proposition like (1)? There seem to be three choices. I can continue to hold it; I can withhold it,... believing neither it nor its denial, and I can accept its denial. Consider the third way, a way taken by those pluralists who, like John Hick, hold that such propositions as (1) and (2) and their colleagues from other faiths are literally false, although in some way still valid responses to the Real. This seems to me to be no advance at all with respect to the arrogance or egotism problem; this is not a way out. For if I do this, I will then be in the very same condition as I am now: I will believe many propositions others don't believe and will be in condition C with respect to those propositions. For I will then believe the denials of (1) and (2) (as well as the denials of many other propositions explicitly accepted by those of other faiths). Many others, of course, do not believe the denials of (1) and (2) and in fact believe (1) and (2). Further, I will not know of any arguments that can be counted on to persuade those who do believe (1) or (2) (or propositions accepted by the adherents of other religions). I am therefore in the condition of believing propositions that many others do not believe and furthermore am in condition C. If, in the case of those who believe (1) and (2), that is sufficient for intellectual arrogance or egotism, the same goes for those who believe their denials.

So consider the second option: I can instead *withhold* the proposition in question. I can say to myself: "The right course here, given that I can't or couldn't convince these others of what I believe, is to believe neither these propositions nor their denials." The pluralist objector to exclusivism can say that the right course, under condition

C, is to abstain from believing the offending proposition and also abstain from believing its denial; call him, therefore, "the abstemious pluralist." But does he thus really avoid the condition that, on the part of the exclusivist, leads to the charges of egotism and arrogance in this way? Think, for a moment, about disagreement. Disagreement, fundamentally, is a matter of adopting conflicting propositional attitudes with respect to a given proposition. In the simplest and most familiar case, I disagree with you if there is some proposition p such that I believe p and you believe $-p$. But that's just the simplest case; there are also others. The one that is presently of interest is this: I believe p and you withhold it, fail to believe it. Call the first kind of disagreement "contradicting"; call the second "dissenting."

My claim is that if contradicting others (under the condition C spelled out above) is arrogant and egotistical, so is dissenting (under that same condition). Suppose you believe some proposition p but I don't; perhaps you believe that it is wrong to discriminate against people simply on the grounds of race, but I, recognizing that there are many people who disagree with you, do not believe this proposition. I don't disbelieve it either, of course, but in the circumstances I think the right thing to do is to abstain from belief. Then am I not implicitly condemning your attitude, your *believing* the proposition, as somehow improper—naive, perhaps, or unjustified, or in some other way less than optimal? I am implicitly saying that my attitude is the superior one; I think my course of action here is the right one and yours somehow wrong, inadequate, improper, in the circumstances at best second-rate. Of course, I realize that there is no question, here, of *showing* you that your attitude is wrong or improper or naive; so am I not guilty of intellectual arrogance? Of a sort of egotism, thinking I know better than you, arrogating to myself a privileged status with respect to you? The problem for the exclusivist was that she was obliged to think she possessed a truth missed by many others; the problem for the abstemious pluralist is that he is obliged to think that he possesses a virtue others don't or acts rightly where others don't. If, in condition C, one is arrogant by way of believing a proposition others don't, isn't one equally, under those reflective conditions, arrogant by way of withholding a proposition others don't?...

So the abstemious pluralist is hoist with his own petard; but even apart from this dialectical argument (which in any event some will think unduly cute), aren't the charges unconvincing and implausible? I must concede that there are a variety of ways in which I can be and have been intellectually arrogant and egotistic; I have certainly fallen into this vice in the past and no doubt am not free of it now. But am I really arrogant and egotistic just by virtue of believing what I know others don't believe, where I can't show them that I am right? Suppose I think the matter over, consider the objections as carefully as I can, realize that I am finite and furthermore a sinner, certainly no better than those with whom I disagree; but suppose it still seems clear to me that the proposition in question is true. Can I really be behaving immorally in continuing to believe it? I am dead sure that it is wrong to try to advance my career by telling lies about my colleagues; I realize there are those who disagree; I also realize that in all likelihood there is no way I can find to show them that they are wrong; nonetheless I think they are wrong. If I think this after careful reflection, if I consider the claims of those who disagree as sympathetically as I can, if I try my level best to ascertain the truth here, and it *still* seems to me sleazy, wrong, and despicable to lie about my colleagues to advance my career, could I really be doing what is immoral by continuing to believe as before? I can't see how. If, after careful reflection and thought, you find yourself convinced that the right propositional attitude to take to (1) and (2) in the face of the facts of religious pluralism is abstention from belief, how could you properly be taxed with egotism, either for so believing or for so abstaining? Even if you knew others did not agree with you?...

Return to the case of moral belief. King David took Bathsheba, made her pregnant, and then, after the failure of various stratagems to get her husband Uriah to think the baby was his, arranged for him to be killed. The prophet Nathan came to David and told him a story about a rich man and a poor man. The rich man had many flocks and herds; the poor man had only a single ewe lamb, which grew up with his children, "ate at his table, drank from his cup, lay in his bosom, and was like a daughter to him." The rich man had unexpected guests. Rather than slaughter one of his own sheep, he took the poor man's single ewe lamb, slaughtered it, and served it to his guests. David exploded in anger: "The man who did this deserves to die!" Then, in one of the most riveting passages in all the Bible, Nathan turns to David and declares, "You are that man!" And then David sees what he has done.

My interest here is in David's reaction to the story. I agree with David: Such injustice is utterly and despicably wrong; there are really no words for it. I believe that such an action is wrong, and I believe that the proposition that it *isn't* wrong— either because really *nothing* is wrong, or because even if some things are wrong, *this* isn't—is false. As a matter of fact, there isn't a lot I believe more strongly. I recognize, however, that there are those who disagree with me; and once more, I doubt that I could find an argument to show them that I am right and they wrong. Further, for all I know, their conflicting beliefs have for them the same internally available epistemic markers, the same phenomenology, as mine have for me. Am I then being arbitrary, treating similar cases differently in continuing to hold, as I do, that in fact that kind of behavior *is* dreadfully wrong? I don't think so. Am I wrong in thinking racial bigotry despicable, even though I know that there are others who disagree, and even if I think they have the same internal markers for their beliefs as I have for mine? I don't think so. I believe in serious actualism, the view that no objects have properties in worlds in which they do not exist, not even nonexistence. Others do not believe this, and perhaps the internal markers of their dissenting views have for them the same quality as my views have for me. Am I being arbitrary in continuing to think as I do? I can't see how.

And the reason here is this: in each of these cases, the believer in question doesn't really think the beliefs in question *are* on a relevant epistemic par. She may agree that she and those who dissent are equally convinced of the truth of their belief and even that they are internally on a par, that the internally available markers are similar, or relevantly similar. But she must still think that there is an important epistemic difference, she thinks that somehow the other person has *made a mistake*, or *has a blind spot*, or hasn't been wholly attentive, or hasn't received some grace she has, or is in some way epistemically less fortunate. And, of course, the pluralist critic is in no better case. He thinks the thing to do when there is internal epistemic parity is to withhold judgment; he knows that there are others who don't think so, and for all he knows that belief has internal parity with his; if he continues in that belief, therefore, he will be in the same condition as the exclusivist; and if he doesn't continue in this belief, he no longer has an objection to the exclusivist.

But couldn't I be wrong? Of course I could! But I don't avoid that risk by withholding all religious (or philosophical or moral) beliefs; I can go wrong that way as well as any other, treating all religions, or all philosophical thoughts, or all moral views as on a par. Again, there is no safe haven here, no way to avoid risk. In particular, you won't reach a safe haven by trying to take the same attitude toward all the historically available patterns of belief and withholding; for in so doing, you adopt a particular pattern of belief and withholding, one incompatible with some adopted by others. "You pays your money and you takes your choice," realizing that you, like anyone else, can be desperately wrong. But what else can you do? You don't really have an alternative. And how can you do better than believe and withhold according to what, after serious and responsible consideration, seems to you to be the right pattern of belief and withholding?

NOTES

1. Wilfred Cantwell Smith, *Religious Diversity* (New York: Harper & Row, 1976), p. 14.
2. John Hick, "...the only reason for treating one's tradition differently from others is the very human but not very cogent reason that it is one's own!" *An Interpretation of Religion* (New Haven, Conn.: Yale Univ. Press, 1989), p. 2.

89   THE PROBLEM OF RELIGIOUS DIVERSITY

LINDA TRINKAUS ZAGZEBSKI

Faced with an array of religious traditions, a person might, like Elizabeth Secord Anderson, reject them all, or like John H. Hick, embrace them all, or, like Alvin Plantinga, choose one (likely the most familiar) and reject the others. In our next selection, Linda Trinkaus Zagzebski, whose work we read previously, considers different responses to the issue of religious diversity and explores the situation in which one trusts one's own beliefs yet admires those with conflicting beliefs.

EXCLUSIVISM AND INCLUSIVISM

The most common position on religious diversity among Christians until approximately the middle of the twentieth century was exclusivism: There is only one true religion – mine – and nobody who practices any other religion can be saved. This view is *exclusivist* in two senses. First, it is exclusivist about truth, since it maintains that the doctrines of only one religion are true. Of course, this view needs to be qualified because the teachings of every religion evolve over time even if the central teachings remain the same, so even from a perspective internal to a given religion, various prohibitions can change, such as eating meat on Friday among Catholics, and the teaching of a religion about other religions can also change, just to take some obvious examples. So exclusivism about truth needs to be clarified by reference to central doctrines, and the way to do that can be fairly complicated. How would we determine the set of central Christian doctrines? Does it include only the content of one of the creeds of the early Church? If so, which one? Does it include all the Hebrew and Christian Scriptures? Does it include documents of Church councils? Does it include the writings of prominent theologians? The answer to the last question is undoubtedly no, but the question is not silly and it shows the complexity of the position. Of course, exclusivism about truth does not commit a person to denying that other religions teach many truths. It is only when the teachings of other religions conflict with the teachings of one's own that exclusivism is relevant. Notice finally that exclusivism is the position that only one religion teaches the truth in its central doctrines, but exclusivists always add that that religion is their own. I've never heard of anyone who maintained that only one religion teaches the truth, but it is somebody else's religion that does so.

The position above is exclusivist in a second sense as well. It is exclusivist about salvation. Salvation or something comparable can be attained only in the way a certain religion says it can be attained. For religions that require belief, an individual has to believe in the doctrines of a particular religion in order to be saved. In the Christian form of salvation exclusivism, this means that only Christians can go to heaven. There are also forms of salvation in other religions and views that are exclusivist about the form of salvation they teach. For example, Buddhists teach that nirvana can only be reached by following certain practices. Exclusivism about salvation is obviously quite severe, and it is the first form of exclusivism to be rejected by many Christians.

From Linda Trinkaus Zagzebski, *Philosophy of Religion: An Historical Introduction.* Blackwell Publishing, 2007. Reprinted by permission of the publisher.

Exclusivism about truth, and perhaps also about salvation, has sometimes been defended by an account that explains why the believers in a particular religion are epistemically privileged. Alvin Plantinga defends exclusivism about truth in Christianity by arguing that it is part of Christian doctrine that the Holy Spirit has given the gift of Faith in God to some people and not others. And surely Plantinga is right that, if there is a God, God could give a special gift to some people. If so, it would follow that the reason for diversity among religions is that some people are epistemically privileged in their religious beliefs and some are not....

There is a third kind of exclusivism, exclusivism about rationality. This kind of exclusivism is much stronger than exclusivism about truth. The exclusivist about rationality maintains that the teachings of only one religion are rational. It is irrational to believe the teachings of any other religion in so far as they conflict with the teachings of the one that is rational. In my experience, religious people who have thought about religious diversity and who try to be as fair-minded as possible typically deny this form of exclusivism even when they accept exclusivism about truth. So they combine exclusivism about truth with inclusivism about rationality. They say, "Our beliefs are true and the beliefs of other religions are false in so far as they are incompatible with ours, but the beliefs of many other religions are still rational. The people who practice those religions are justified in believing what they believe, given their circumstances. If we had been born in their circumstances and had their experiences, we would probably believe what they believe."

It is hard to fault this position since it seems to go as far as possible in the direction of being understanding and non-judgmental, while not compromising one's commitment to one's own beliefs. But there is a problem in combining exclusivism about truth with inclusivism about rationality. One of the main reasons we want to have rational beliefs is that we think there is a close connection between rationality and truth. What makes it a good thing for humans to be rational is that it puts us in as good a position to get truth as we can get. There is a close correspondence

between rationality and truth. But suppose there are nine religions, each of which has a different and incompatible teaching on the origin of the universe. At most one of these theories can be true. But are they all rational? Presumably we would want to say yes, assuming that there are no significant differences in intelligence, sensitivity to religious experience, and intellectual and moral virtue among the adherents of the different religions. But if we say that all nine of these beliefs about the origin of the universe are rational, then clearly rationality in this case does not make it likely that a person gets the truth—less than one chance in nine, and so we cannot maintain that what makes rationality a good thing is that it makes it likely that we are going to get the truth. It appears, then, that combining exclusivism about truth with inclusivism about rationality forces us to conclude either that rationality is not really such a good thing, or if it is a good thing, its goodness cannot come from its close connection to truth. I call this the problem of the gap.

Notice also that it does not help to opt for none of the nine, but to adopt some scientific theory on the origin of the universe that conflicts with all nine ... Even if such a theory satisfies the same conditions for rationality satisfied by the nine religions, its rationality does not put it in a better position to be true as long as there are many competitors, each of which is rational.

Of course, we should not exaggerate the extent of the problem of the gap. There *are* classes of belief for which we think there is a close connection between rationality and truth, but those beliefs do not help solve the problem of religious diversity because they are beliefs in which we can realistically expect agreement. And there are probably some religious beliefs in this category. For example, the belief that compassion is good is an almost universal belief, ... And if we move to a sufficiently high level of generality, we can find agreement about some of the most fundamental religious beliefs—e.g., there is something wrong with the human condition, and when we are in contact with ultimate reality there is the possibility for both profound moral improvement and a higher level of consciousness. But belief at the level necessary for agreement is very thin, and unless we are content to ignore all but such thin beliefs, the fact that particular religious beliefs conflict with the beliefs of others remains a problem.

So religious diversity poses a problem for both religious believers and non-believers. No matter what we believe, we face a problem in our understanding of rationality. If we retain our beliefs because we judge that they are rational, and also judge that the conflicting beliefs of the atheist and of other religions are rational, we cannot maintain that the rationality of each such belief makes it likely to be true. It appears that we have no reason to think that one rational belief is preferable to a conflicting rational belief on the grounds that it is rational. The most we can say is that the rationality of a belief makes it preferable to an irrational alternative. Rationality may be more truth-conducive than irrationality, but one rational belief may not be preferable to another with respect to truth-conduciveness. On the other hand, if we give up our beliefs on the grounds that their rationality is not closely connected to getting the truth, we are forced to say that both atheists and believers in all of the world's major religions should give up their beliefs. That seems to force us into agnosticism, but if we take that option, we are forced to admit that we have given up any chance of getting the truth about a very important matter, an issue that directly impacts the desirability of our lives.

As far as I know, the problem of the gap has never been fully resolved. But in the next two sections I will propose two ways to resolve or avoid it.

THE PLURALISM OF JOHN HICK

An influential perspective on religious diversity is the theory of John Hick, who for some time has promoted a position about the comparative value of the major world religions he calls pluralism. Hick maintains that all the major religions are salvific in that they all offer a path to radically transform human persons from self-centeredness to reality-centeredness, a life centered in ultimate reality. Each religion has something analogous to Christian saints, who are the models for this trans-

formation. The fruit of transformation is a life of love and compassion, and Hick proposes that, since we have evidence that all the great religions are productive of a life of love and compassion, we should conclude that they all offer genuine paths to salvation. Hick thinks that the metaphysical conclusion we ought to draw from this is that the salvific ground in ultimate reality is the same in all religions. Hick then uses Immanuel Kant's distinction between the noumenal and phenomenal worlds to explain how so many religions can all be in touch with the same ultimate reality.

Kant argued that it makes no sense to think that we can know the noumenal world, or the world as it is "in itself," independent of our capacity to experience it. What we can know is the world of possible experience, the phenomenal world. That world is necessarily connected to the ways in which it presents itself to our experience, through intuitions of space and time, and through the concepts that permit us to make judgments about it, such as the concepts of cause and of substance. Similarly, Hick argues that we cannot experience God/ultimate reality as he/it is in itself directly any more than we can experience the world of things-in-themselves according to Kant. All we can do is to experience ultimate reality through the experiential and conceptual forms that each culture has developed. Each religion is a different phenomenal manifestation of the one ultimate reality. And like Kant, Hick maintains that phenomenal reality is as real as it's going to get for us; it is not an illusion. It is the only way we humans can experience the world. So the Hindu world, the Christian world, the Muslim world, and the Buddhist world are distinct phenomenal worlds that are related to the world of reality-in-itself in the same way the world of ordinary human experience is related to the world of things-in-themselves.

There is an important difference between Hick and Kant. What Kant means by the phenomenal world is the world as it has to be in order to be experienced by human beings, and so there is only one such world. It is the world of trees, animals, chairs, and all the other objects of our experience that have spatial and temporal relations to each other and are potentially affected by our actions. But Hick cannot make the parallel claim about religious phenomenal worlds, since he maintains that there are as many of them as there are religious traditions. But he *can* say that ultimate reality cannot be experienced except through cultural forms, so each religion is a different lens through which ultimate reality is experienced. We are not equipped with a particular religious lens by nature the way we are equipped with Kant's conceptual categories, but we have to have one lens or another. The Muslim world, the Hindu world, the Buddhist world, and the Christian world are all phenomenally real worlds on a par with the reality of trees, houses, and animals in Kantian metaphysics.

Notice that Hick's pluralism solves the problem of the gap. All the great world religions are true in the sense that they all put human beings in contact with religious phenomenal reality. Of course, if you insist that a belief is not true unless it puts a person in contact with noumenal reality, the world of things-in-themselves, then all the world religions are false. But according to Hick, there is no more reason to complain about the lack of contact with noumenal reality in the religious realm than there is to complain about the lack of contact with things-in-themselves in Kant's metaphysics. The problem of the gap is solved, then, because all the great world religions are both rational and true in the sense just explained.

Hick does not think that every doctrine of every religion can be explained in this way, however. There are two types of religious teachings that do not fit the Kantian model. The doctrine of creation *ex nihilo* and the doctrine of reincarnation are examples of what Hick calls transhistorical truth claims. If one religion teaches that the supreme being created the entire material world out of nothing and another religion teaches that the material world is eternal, they cannot both be right and their differences cannot be explained by reference to different religious phenomenal worlds. If one religion teaches that after death you are reincarnated, and another religion teaches that your body will some day be resurrected and rejoined with your soul, and a third religion teaches that you will be annihilated as an individual person but assimilated into something else, one of these religions may be right and the others wrong, or maybe one is more right than another, but something is going to happen to you after death. It cannot be all three.

Some religions also make historical claims that cannot be explained on the Kantian model. Either Jesus raised Lazarus from the dead or he didn't. Either there was an empty tomb on Easter morning or there wasn't. Hick says that the grounds for these beliefs ought to be the same as the grounds for any historical belief if they are taken literally. Some of these beliefs are false and disputes about them cannot be resolved by reference to the pluralism of phenomenal worlds. But even if they are not literally true, they may be true as myths. A true myth evokes the response of transforming a person into one who is reality-centered, whereas a false myth does not. Hick thinks that the Incarnation is an example of a true myth.

Hick's position on religious diversity has many defenders and many detractors. I want to mention just three problems with it. First, if Hick truly means that each phenomenal world is a real one, then … he is a polytheist. Perhaps the charge of polytheism is not quite fair because Hick is a phenomenal polytheist and a noumenal mono-something (not "theist" because he is not willing to call the ultimate reality "God"). But on the noumenal level Hick is committed to the most negative of negative theologies: We cannot say that the ultimate reality is personal or impersonal, one or many, temporal or timeless, God or being itself. So Hick's position appears to be a combination of polytheism and negative theology. Neither of these positions may be very appealing, although … there is a strong strain of negative theology among the mystics who say that we cannot hope to know what God is really like, only what he is not.

A second problem involves the kind of belief that is justified if one accepts Hick's pluralism. Pluralism seems to threaten religious commitment. Christians who become convinced that Christianity is no more true than Hinduism are bound to interpret that as weakening the connection they thought obtained between Christian doctrine and the truth, and the same point applies to the convictions of Hindus, Muslims, Buddhists, and others. To wholeheartedly embrace a particular religion is to think of that religion as giving one a superior understanding of the nature of the universe and one's relationship to that universe than one would have had without it. This is particularly important for those who think that the universe had a personal creator who providentially guides the temporal world, hears prayers, and responds to them. To be told that the idea that I have a relationship with a personal God is no more true than the idea that there is an impersonal force of unknown qualities which may or may not relate to me at all is to be told that my faith is groundless, or at least, such a reaction is eminently understandable.

Third, Hick's separation of salvific beliefs that are phenomenal manifestations of ultimate reality from historical beliefs and transhistorical beliefs about the origin of the universe and the afterlife is not compatible with the central teachings of some religions. In Christianity, for example, beliefs about ultimate reality include historical beliefs about the Incarnation, the Redemption, and the Resurrection. These historical beliefs cannot be separated from the theological beliefs that on Hick's account are about phenomenal reality. Hick's pluralism, then, extends only to a limited subset of the beliefs of major religions and, as Hick is aware, some religions would not accept the way in which he distinguishes those beliefs that are religiously important from those that are not.

SELF-TRUST AND RELIGIOUS BELIEF

The problem of the gap between rationality and truth arises from a perspective external to the self. We look at our beliefs the same way we look at the beliefs of others and we think that from that perspective nobody has a privileged epistemic position. That follows if we assume that the external viewpoint is committed to intellectual egalitarianism. If one religion is rational, so are they all, barring special reason to think some of them are untrustworthy. But then there are no grounds for choice among them.

But how do we know what we would see from an external perspective? Maybe we would see that one religion does have a privileged connection to truth. When we say that from an external perspective all religions are roughly equal in rationality and one is no more likely to be true than another, aren't we really just admitting that we cannot figure out how to adopt the external perspective on religion? We *do* have some idea how this perspective works in physics and mathematics. We also have an idea how it works in the law and in ethics—it is the principle of impartiality. But what principle would the external observer of religion use to adjudicate among the different viewpoints on religion? Since we don't know, we assume there isn't one.

This problem is not limited to beliefs about religion. The vast majority of our important beliefs about morality and politics also suffer from this problem, as well as a host of beliefs about matters of personal interest—e.g., whether one movie is better than another, whether my alma mater is one of the most distinguished universities in the country, whether my spouse is looking good today, and so on. If we insist on adopting the external viewpoint on all our beliefs, we jeopardize many of the beliefs most important to us, including those we use in governing our lives.

We might think the problem does not arise when the belief is about an unimportant matter, but that is not the case. Suppose that I recall reading somewhere that coffee is very high in anti-oxidants and I encounter another person who believes that coffee has no such benefit. Suppose also that there is no reason to think one of us is an expert in this area and no reason to think one of us did a more careful reading of the news reports and any relevant follow-ups. If I evaluate my beliefs from an external viewpoint, I will withhold belief in whether coffee is high in anti-oxidants, and I might be willing to do that because it is not likely to have a significant impact on my life. But is it obvious that I should automatically trust another as much as myself? If I do, even though many of the beliefs I would have to give up are unimportant, the *quantity* of beliefs I would have to give up is very important. The conclusion is that if we evaluate our own beliefs the same way we evaluate the beliefs of other people, we are bound to end up with skepticism about all but a very few beliefs – not enough to base a worthwhile life upon.

Many philosophers these days are attempting to put the challenge of skepticism aside and get on with the business of living a life, which includes accepting with confidence the beliefs needed to live a life with energy and purpose. Doing that requires a substantial degree of trust in oneself and the forces that have shaped one into the person one is.... [A]ny normal, non-skeptical life will have to include a significant degree of self-trust in our intellectual faculties, procedures, and opinions. The reason is that any defense of our most fundamental faculties, procedures, and opinions will make use of those same faculties and opinions. For example, we test a memory by perception, we test one perception by another perception, we test much of what we believe by consulting other people, so we use beliefs about them to test other beliefs, and so on. We cannot get outside of the circle of our faculties and opinions to test the reliability of the faculties and opinions taken as a whole; we have to trust them.

An important element of self-trust is trust in our emotions. Emotion dispositions can be reliable or unreliable, and particular emotions may fit or not fit their objects. But we cannot tell whether our emotion dispositions are reliable without using those same dispositions in conjunction with our other faculties. How can we tell whether our disposition to pity is reliably directed at the pitiful, whether our disposition to disgust is reliably directed towards the disgusting, whether we reliably fear the fearsome, or admire the admirable without appealing to further emotions? We trust what we think we see when we take a hard look in good environmental conditions, and if others agree, we take that as confirmation. Similarly, we trust what we feel upon reflection when we feel admiration or pity or revulsion and we take the agreement of others as confirmation. We trust the emotion we have as an adult more than an emotion we had in the same circumstances as a child, just as we trust a belief we have as an adult more than our childish belief. So the grounds for

trusting our emotions are similar to the grounds for trusting our perceptions and beliefs.

Furthermore, trust in the beliefs that lead to action requires emotional self-trust. My belief that I ought to escape a situation is often grounded in fear. The belief that I ought to help another person is typically grounded in compassion for her. The belief that I may not treat people in certain ways is grounded in respect for them. If I trust the belief, I must trust the emotion. So epistemic self-trust requires emotional self-trust. Both emotional and epistemic self-trust are compatible with revising what we trust, but it takes self-trust to trust that the process of revision is trustworthy.

One of the emotions I need to trust is admiration. Admiration is a basic emotion, one that does not have other emotions as parts, and I do not think we can explain what a basic emotion feels like. But I assume that all normal people have experienced the emotion of admiration, and so they know what it is in the same way they know what fear or love or anger is. I would describe the admirable as something like the imitably attractive. We feel a positive emotion towards the person we admire that would lead to imitating the person given the right practical conditions. To trust the emotion of admiration means to have confidence that it is appropriate to feel the kind of attraction and desire to imitate that is intrinsic to admiration. We trust our emotion of admiration for the same reason we trust our other emotions: we have no choice.

Trusting my emotion of admiration may lead me to trusting some of the beliefs of another person more than my own. That can happen when I notice that another person has the traits I admire in myself to a greater degree than I have myself, or she may form her belief in a more admirable way in the particular case than I have myself. Another possibility is that she is very much like my present self, only she has more experience, so she is related to me now the way I am related to my younger self. In such cases I can easily trust another person more than myself, either because I admire the other person more than myself and I trust my admiration, or because the other person has other elements I trust in myself in a greater degree than I have myself, e.g., she has more experience.

For the same reason, I will trust some people more than other people. I do that because of the way I trust myself. It follows that intellectual egalitarianism should be rejected.

Now let us return to conflict in beliefs. Suppose that I trust my emotion of admiration in some case more than I trust a given belief I have. And suppose that the person I admire has a belief that conflicts with mine, and there is no other person I admire just as much whose belief agrees with mine. Self-trust would lead me to trust the admired person's belief more than my own. If I am able to imitate the admired person by adopting her belief without changing anything else about myself that I trust even more than I trust the person I admire, then self-trust should lead me to change my belief. That is because admiration includes imitation, given the right circumstances.

But let's consider a harder case. Suppose a person I admire and therefore trust has a belief that conflicts with one of the beliefs I have that I trust. I am then faced with a conflict within self-trust. It is because of self-trust that I trust my belief, and it is because of self-trust that I trust the emotion of admiration that grounds my trust in the other person. But even if I trust my admiration more than the belief, it still does not follow that I should change it. Admiration is an emotion that leads me to imitate the admirable person in suitable circumstances, but often the circumstances are not suitable. I can easily admire Olympic gold medal winners without having the slightest inclination to imitate them, and I can admire the belief system of a Hindu without the inclination to adopt that system for myself. The reason why I would not is the same in both cases: I can't do it. It is not compatible with the self that I am. But the more interesting question is whether I should try. Some religious beliefs are not central to our sense of self, but many of them are. Whether I should change an important religious belief is not simply determined by how much I trust the belief itself, but how much I trust the other aspects of myself that I would have to change if I changed the belief. Given the social construction of belief, trusting a belief commits me to trusting both the individual persons from whom I learned the belief, and the traditions and historical institutions upon which I depend to interpret the belief. Religious beliefs are usually connected to a network of other beliefs, emotions, experiences, institutional loyalties, and connections with many other admirable people, all of which I trust. So I can admire a Hindu for being a great Hindu and an Olympic swimmer for being a great swimmer without any inclination to imitate them. And I think that an intellectually conscientious person will often respond that way.

In the typical case, then, a person's trust in those aspects of himself that he would have to change if he converted to another religion will be greater than his trust in the way an admirable person of another religion believes in her religion. But sometimes trust in the latter can be greater, and so conversion can be compatible with intellectual conscientiousness. I think this is an important consequence of our analysis of self-trust. We should be suspicious of any account of conscientious belief that has the consequence that radical conversion is never a conscientious thing to do, and we also should be suspicious of any account of conscientious belief that requires us to give up the beliefs we have that conflict with the beliefs of others on the grounds that conscientiousness demands an external perspective on the self.

In a situation in which a choice whether to convert is made, some element of self-trust becomes the bottom line – that to which we refer in adjudicating between those elements of ourselves that pull us one way and those that pull in another direction....

If I trust my admiration of others with beliefs that conflict with mine more than I trust the aspects of myself from which I gain my beliefs and the traditions that support them, then it is right for me to doubt my beliefs, and perhaps change them. But there is no standpoint outside of self-trust from which I can determine which is more trustworthy – myself or others – so it can easily happen that I have full confidence in my beliefs, emotions, and their sources in family, tradition, and the historical circumstances that shape me.

Admiration may not require me to change my beliefs, but it adds something important to the dialogue between people with conflicting religious beliefs that did not exist in the pre-modern era.

What it adds is the feeling that I *would* imitate them if I had grown up with a different social construction of the self. That prevents me from taking the line "We're right, so they're wrong, and that's the end of that." Of course, we think we're right, but there's more to be said. Tolerance comes not from thinking that everybody is right, but trusting that we *are* right in the admiration we have for many people who have very different beliefs, and that logically requires us to think of them as like the self I could have been if I had been raised in a different way.

90   ON RELIGIOUS DIVERSITY

ROBERT McKIM

Maintaining that religious beliefs exhibit ambiguity and that we can learn from people of integrity who hold different views than ours, Robert McKim, whose work we read previously, proposes what he terms "the global approach," according to which we should take seriously the outlooks of others, seeking with humility to understand their doctrines and practices. He maintains that this global approach is consistent with belonging to, and finding comfort in, a particular religious tradition.

THE EXTRAORDINARY DIVERSITY OF RELIGIONS

Before we start, a word on the extraordinary diversity of the phenomena of religion. Nobody who has reflected about these matters could fail to be aware of this diversity. There are similarities among the traditions, to be sure, but there is little, if anything, they all have in common. Here I state the obvious. There are the well-known global traditions, each of which is itself a set of different sects and strands. There are also numerous other traditions, such as the religion of the Parsees, Zoroastrianism, the Druidic religion of the Celts, numerous indigenous traditions, polytheisms of various sorts such as those of Greece or Rome or Scandinavia, and different types of animism. It seems that there never has been a culture without its own religion. There have been, and are, irreligious groups within cultures, but there does not seem to have survived for long a whole culture that was without a religion....

It is hard to exaggerate the extent of the differences among the traditions. Consider just one area of disagreement, namely, the question of what a human being consists in, and compare Hinduism and Christianity on this matter. According to Hinduism—and here I simplify greatly—there is reincarnation for all living things, including human beings. We become free of the cycle of rebirths only when we realize that the soul within each of us, the *Atman*, is in fact *Brahman*, the world-soul, so that the notion that we are distinct individuals is, at the deepest level, an illusion. To recognize that the *Atman* is *Brahman* is to achieve enlightenment, which is the goal for each human being, and there are various techniques (yogas) for achieving this state.

According to Christianity, on the other hand—again, simplifying greatly—there is no reincarnation.

From Robert McKim, *On Religious Diversity*, Oxford University Press, 2012. Reprinted by permission of the publisher.

Each person is created by God and starts to exist somewhere between conception and birth. Salvation, which is a matter of reconciliation with God, is by grace, whether bestowed directly by God on each individual or through the church and its sacraments, and it is made possible by the death and resurrection of Jesus. Needless to say, this is just an example of the profound differences among the traditions.

In spite of this great diversity, we find that among those who hold the various views associated with the major traditions are many people of integrity. These are people who, at least in the ideal case, know a great deal, avoid exaggeration, admit ignorance when it seems appropriate to them to do so, have an interest in the truth, and are intelligent, serious, sincere, insightful, decent, sensible, and reflective. When I talk of "people of integrity" in what follows, these are the people I have in mind. It is not as if all of the people of integrity belong to one particular religion (or to none). You could sensibly believe that all (or most, or more) people of integrity are to be found in your own tradition only if you lacked contact with people of other religious traditions or managed to distance yourself mentally from them—perhaps by seeing them as less than fully human, as primitive, as cognitively defective, or as corrupt. Each tradition needs to acknowledge, as an operating assumption, that no single tradition may reasonably be distinguished from the others by virtue of the integrity of its adherents. It is especially implausible to impute a lack of integrity to others as an explanation of why they accept worldviews that are different from ours. Many devoutly religious people, in particular, find it especially difficult to concede this in the case of others who know little, and care less, about matters that are most precious to them.

Here is another equally important point to keep in mind. If you are a serious member of a religious tradition, your own tradition *feels* right. When you follow its path, you feel that you are on the right path. You have a sense of inner conviction. Your life experience—both in terms of the character of your everyday mundane experience and in terms of any manifestly religious experience you may enjoy—seems to be consistent with and even expressive of your religious perspective. The

beliefs, practices, celebrations, and much more besides that are associated with your tradition feel right and appropriate, whereas those of other traditions typically feel strange and alien, assuming you even give them a moment's thought. But now consider what it must be like to be an observant Orthodox Jew or a devout Shiite Muslim, Presbyterian, or Buddhist, assuming that you do not answer to any of these descriptions. Is the sense of being on the right path any less developed, the sense of inner conviction less intense, the sense that one's life experience meshes with one's religious perspective less deep for those others? Of course not. And if we are not familiar with others and their views, with what it feels like to be one of them and with what it is like to see the world from their point of view, we should consider this as a deficiency in us and not in them.

THE CASE FOR OPENNESS

… An arrangement in which we are open to learning from others and they are open to learning from us may appeal to some in some traditions for the following reason. We may feel that if there is fair and open competition in this regard, with everyone having access to central aspects of other religious traditions, and in particular if others have access to what we regard as the highly attractive aspects of our tradition, our tradition will come out ahead and be vindicated in the face of the competition, emerging as the tradition that is most worthwhile, most worthy of loyalty, and so on, and be recognized as such by all comers.…[1]

More important, though, is a line of thought that has to do with the caliber of those who hold views that we do not hold. In particular, the beliefs from which we might learn something are held by people who are intelligent, honest, and insightful; by people who reason with as much care as they can; and so forth—in short, by people of integrity. The fact that views that differ from, or are even opposed to, ours have had a central place in enduring cultures whose members include many people of integrity strongly suggests that there may be something valuable or worthwhile about those views. We ought to respect the rationality and seriousness of people of this caliber. The respect for others in question is a matter of respecting them as people who probably have been responsible in the ways in which they have acquired and maintained whatever beliefs they hold that are relevant to religion. Of course, there is no suggestion here that we should willy-nilly endorse the views of others, either in part or as a whole. The point is rather that a way to give expression to the respect that such people are owed is to be open to learning something from them. What we have here is a line of reasoning that speaks in favor of openness to others having true beliefs of their own and to learning from them.

A closely related point is that among the processes and strategies we use in acquiring and testing our beliefs is the strategy of relying on the views of those who seem to be reliable. In almost every area of our lives, we have no choice but to rely on the testimony of others. Broadly speaking, people of integrity deserve to be included in the category of those who seem to be reliable. If so, it seems reasonable to think that those who can best lay claim to being reliable are to be found among religious thinkers of many major enduring religious communities. But if so, the relevant people to whom we should listen are deeply divided, and there are many points of view to which we should pay attention and from which we should be open to learning. It is easy to see how unsatisfactory it would be in other fields of enquiry in which there are different positions on central issues, were one group to refuse to see what they could learn from others. This applies in medicine, literary criticism, psychology, physics, and philosophy, for example. The expectation in the area of religion is not that each group would treat others as being on a par with it. Rather, the claim is that there is something wrong with treating other religions as so far below par that we think we have nothing to learn from them....

ON RELIGIOUS AMBIGUITY

John Hick has made the following interesting observations about what he characterizes as the religious ambiguity of the universe:

> The universe is religiously ambiguous in that it is possible to interpret it, intellectually and experien-

tially, both religiously and naturalistically. The theistic and anti-theistic arguments are all inconclusive, for the special evidences to which they appeal are also capable of being understood in terms of the contrary world view. Further, the opposing set of evidences cannot be given objectively quantifiable values. (*An Interpretation of Religion: Human Responses to the Transcendent*, 12)

... Hick understands the ambiguity of the universe to include both intellectual and experiential elements. He means, first, that a sober and careful intellectual assessment of the available evidence would yield the result that the universe is ambiguous. And he means, second, that the universe is open to being experienced in a variety of ways. The idea is in part that a Buddhist, a Hindu, a Confucianist, a Christian, a Muslim, and so forth may each interpret everything he encounters, including his own feelings and all aspects of his experience, in accordance with his religious perspective....

I consider this experiential ambiguity (if we want a name for it) to include the following additional elements. Many people in many different religious traditions experience the world around them, their own lives, and indeed everything in their experience on which their religious outlook has any bearing through the perspective provided by their tradition. This includes important events in their lives that the religions purport to interpret, such as birth, death, bereavement, coming of age, and the inner struggles that are part of almost every human life. When the religions provide their adherents with a way to understand such phenomena, it does not seem to those adherents that what they experience is discordant with their interpretation of it. On the contrary, they generally feel that what they experience can be comprehended through their religious perspective and its concepts and categories. So their experience normally fits with their expectations in a more or less hand-in-glove fashion, despite whatever anomalies that cause perplexity or elicit reflection there may be. Each of the many competing alternative readings of those phenomena that the religions purport to describe meshes with the experience of a particular religious community, generally providing those who adopt it with a way to interpret what they experience that feels right and that feels natural. Often, their interpretation of their experience feels so right and so natural that they cannot imagine an alternative. Presumably, a religion that did not have a capacity to mesh with the experience of its followers would be discarded. Hence there is a certain inevitability involved in the capacity of religions to fit with the experience of their adherents....

Broadly speaking, I believe that Hick is correct in his contention that our circumstances are religiously ambiguous. One can imagine there having been but one plausible interpretation of those phenomena that the religions propose to interpret, such as human nature, death, suffering, and the origins of the universe. It might have been that there was not a lot of room for different interpretations and that someone who doubted the tenets of, say, the one obviously correct religion would be as foolish as someone who doubted the existence of other people or of the external world. But things are not at all like that....

THE GLOBAL APPROACH

... The global approach requires that each of us sets out to see the point of view of others on matters of religious significance. It involves an open, exploratory, curious approach to others and an attempt to learn about them and their traditions, history, ideas, perspectives, insights, customs, experiences, sacred texts, and more. It asks why anyone should settle for the comparatively meager diet that is to be found within any single religious tradition—given the global abundance of religious ideas, religious texts, religious experience, and so on. Rather than thinking that *my* sacred texts, *my* coreligionists, *my* experiences, and *my* history are the ones that count, the global approach calls for the cultivation of arrangements in which we are open to learning from and about others and they, in turn, are open to learning from and about us. This approach involves taking each other seriously as possible sources of insight and even as possible sources of knowledge. All of human religious experience, including that of the members of other traditions, is viewed as a resource, as part of the relevant data, as something to be curious about, as the proper province of each, when one is thinking about religion.[2] So a vast expanse of religious resources opens up before each of us when we take this approach. For example, to get some remote grasp of the religious experience of others is an immensely difficult task. And there are so many others, and there is so much to learn about each of them. The global approach looks on the major religious traditions as *our* traditions, as part of a common human heritage, and as valuable repositories of forms of life, each of which has its own dignity.

If this approach were put into practice, each tradition could expect and would be guaranteed an audience from the others. Each would become an object of reflection and study, an object of respectful curiosity to the others. This approach also requires each of us to consider that if there are perspectives whose appeal is not apparent to us and that seem alien, so that it is difficult for us to have a sense of what matters to those who have adopted them, difficult for us to understand what it is like to be one of them or what it is like to worship or practice as they do, for example—or that even seem foolish or unintelligible to us—the relevant deficiency, if there is one, may lie with us and not with the tradition in question.

The difficulty of adopting the global approach might be formulated as an objection: the point would be just that the global approach represents a hopeless aspiration given, say, the variety of forms of religious experience that need to be understood and taken account of. In addition, human beings seem to have an extremely limited capacity to grasp and to ponder points of view other than their own, and even to have the vaguest grasp of how things look to people from other traditions. So while a vast expanse of religious resources is opened up before each of us, because of ambiguity, each of us cannot take account of more than a limited portion thereof. But the obvious rejoinder to these objections is that the impossibility of taking the global approach in a full and comprehensive way provides no reason to doubt that we should do the best we can in this regard.

On account of the curiosity toward others that it involves, we might refer to the global approach as the "curious approach." Curiosity involves wanting to know about others and being interested in others. But here are two very different types of curiosity. There is, first, a sort of curiosity that involves keeping others at arm's length. This is the curiosity of the detached external observer. You are open to learning *about* them but not *from* them. You can have this sort of curiosity about others while your attitude to them is that they are odd, outlandish, or exotic, for example. You still want to know about them—about, say, their history, beliefs, interests, or conceptual framework—for whatever reason. Maybe this is just the way you are. Some people just catch your interest. Distinct from this is a sort of curiosity that involves a willingness to learn from others, an openness to the possibility that they may know or reasonably believe something that we are unaware of, and an attendant intellectual humility. This is the sort of curiosity that is part of the global approach. When deployed while dealing with religious others, this sort of curiosity is creative, admirable, and inspiring. It does not involve dilettantism, voyeurism, or nosiness. It is instead a courteous and kindly inquisitiveness, a wanting to know you on your terms, not on mine.

On account of the intellectual humility it involves, we could also refer to the global approach as the "humble approach." Among the central components of this humility are a willingness to engage in critical scrutiny of one's own views, a willingness to accept that one's views may be mistaken, and a willingness to revise one's views. One recognizes that one's tradition is one among many and probably has much to learn from the others. This intellectual humility is valuable in many ways. For example, its possession may help people avoid false beliefs. It may help people become more knowledgeable or more likely to be justified in their beliefs. It may promote the disciplined study of a variety of religious perspectives. It may promote good relations among different groups. It may also be good or even excellent in itself, quite

apart from its beneficial consequences. Situations that have the following two features call for intellectual humility. First, such situations concern important issues in the sense that it matters greatly what people think about them, making a lot of difference to how they think and act. Second, in these situations, people of integrity have come to different conclusions. So we have a path from the character of religious diversity to intellectual humility, quite apart from the case for the global approach, and hence for the intellectual humility that it involves, that is derivative from the fact of ambiguity.

There is much to be said about implementing the global approach. If it were to be implemented within existing religious traditions, we might have forms of Christianity that encourage, say, reading the Sufis or the Upanishads and much more besides. We might have forms of Islam that encourage reading the Gospels, Thomas Merton, the teachings of the Buddha, and more besides. And so on for each of the other traditions. Taking this approach could involve, for example, open-ended conversation between partners from different traditions, with no advance idea about where it might lead. Perhaps it would require new institutions. In the absence of such institutions, however, people have no choice but to go it alone within the existing institutions if they take the global approach. Indeed, in our current circumstances in which we lack institutions that would sustain the global approach, each of us has, in fact, to some extent an obligation to go it alone in this respect, with the extent to which any particular individual has this obligation being a function of her abilities, opportunities, interests, relevant knowledge, and so forth.

The possible results of taking the global approach provide another interesting area of inquiry. Perhaps there will emerge from an acquaintance with other worldviews some awareness that the traditions represent a number of honest attempts to grapple with difficult and obscure matters. One's own religion may be seen as somewhat more optional. Views may be toned down in a situation in which a variety of alternatives confront people, perhaps because they find that even without being fully aware of it, they are entering into an inner dialogue with those alternatives. The global approach may foster or encourage new forms of religiousness. Who can say what would emerge if the major traditions were to take this approach?[3] And who can say what would be the forms of religious practice and observance and the forms of celebration that would emerge?

My earlier case for an openness to learning from others included the familiar point that each religion may understand itself to have something to gain from arrangements in which the members of each tradition are in a position to learn about other traditions. My case also included an appeal to the caliber of those who disagree with us—in particular to the fact that they are people of integrity. In part, the argument was that we ought to respect the rationality and seriousness of such people, where this includes respecting them as people who probably have been responsible in the ways in which they have acquired and maintained whatever beliefs they hold that are relevant to religion. Another part of the argument was that among the processes and strategies we normally and properly use in acquiring and testing our beliefs is the strategy of relying on the views of those who seem to be reliable. Broadly speaking, people of integrity deserve to be included in this category. And such people seem to be found in many traditions. One justification for not being open to learning about other traditions would be that you considered their members to be inferior or careless in their beliefs, for example. But this line of thought is not sustainable once the integrity of members of other groups is recognized.

An appeal to ambiguity serves to buttress this case. In part, the appeal is to the plethora of considerations that sustain the point of view of others. This includes whatever distinctive religious experience others may enjoy. If we believe our situation to be religiously ambiguous, then, even if we know little about what sustains the views of others, such as their distinctive religious experiences, we should at least be aware that there *is* much that sustains their views, even if we do not

know what it is. The appeal to ambiguity and the appeal to the integrity of many outsiders mutually reinforce each other. For one thing, the fact of ambiguity provides a way to account for why we disagree with others that does not involve thinking less of them than we think of ourselves or of our own group. Thus a recognition of ambiguity can help to liberate us from the feeling that there is something wrong with those who do not see things as we see them.

The idea of being open to learning from others, which is central to the global approach, admits of a large spectrum of possibilities along the following lines.... At one end of this spectrum is a slight openness to the possibility that some others have a different perspective on what we both see or to the possibility that others see some things that we do not see, combined with, in either case, some modest degree of willingness to learn something relatively unimportant from such others. At the other end is an enthusiastic, curious, vigorous exploration of other traditions in the search for deeply important truths, an investigation conducted in a spirit of discovery and accompanied even by a willingness to revise what we have antecedently believed. We take others very seriously indeed if we see them as likely possible sources of new beliefs on anything like this scale. So there is a spectrum of possibilities, from the modest to the robust. I take the case that I have offered to support a position that is toward the robust end of the spectrum.

While taking the global approach involves in effect belonging to a larger community of inquirers, it will normally be as a member of a particular tradition that one so belongs. The benefits of belonging to a particular community, including the particular sort of comfort and stability and the shared sense of meaning that issue from belonging, need not be thought of as abandoned by virtue of assuming the larger perspective. One can still identify with one's religious tradition and be deeply attracted to it. One can feel its religious sentiments, hear its call, and feel its appeal, even while concurrently feeling the appeal of the global approach.

Moreover, even if you accept that an area of religious significance exhibits ambiguity, you can nevertheless, without inconsistency, see things from a particular religious point of view. It is natural to pay especially close attention to, and give priority to, the body of data that is most familiar to you, where this includes your own experience. Your own experience has a special immediacy, a special intimacy, and a special accessibility. It probably is experience that is available within the tradition with which you are most familiar, to which you are most loyal, and with which you identify yourself. Normally, the experiences of others are likely to be poorly understood and mediated through testimony, if there is any acquaintance with them at all.

In addition, a recognition that there is ambiguity is consistent with believing that if all of the evidence were somehow accessible to us, it may turn out that the tradition whose claims are best supported by the evidence as a whole is *your* tradition, whether that be Orthodox Judaism, Sunni Islam, Zen Buddhism, or Wesleyan Methodism. There is no reason to deny that there is a way that things are, religiously speaking. Nor is there reason to deny that if somehow we had access to all of the evidence, *some* account of those phenomena that religions purport to interpret would present itself to us as manifestly correct. More important, a recognition that there is ambiguity concerning religious matters may reasonably be combined with confidence or hope or faith on the part of people in various traditions that if somehow all of the relevant evidence were to be taken into account, some of the central tenets of their tradition would be preserved relatively intact. Perhaps those tenets would emerge in modified form. Or perhaps those tenets, or some of them, would be found to have some special relevance or to exhibit some special insight. This, too, might occur in ways that we cannot now anticipate.

There probably are forms of religiousness, and perhaps even entire religious traditions, that will discourage, reject, or even prohibit an acknowledgment of ambiguity. However, if a persuasive non-tradition-specific case can be made for ambi-

guity, as I believe to be the case, then it has application even in the case of traditions that are not receptive to it. We should reject the idea that traditions are to be evaluated solely in the terms in which they wish to be evaluated. There is also the question whether a tradition might be modified from the inside to better reflect this ambiguity. The extent to which this might be done and the extent to which one can be an insider in good standing while seeking to make such modifications are worthwhile areas for further inquiry. In spite of any official prohibition, a member of such a tradition might also operate privately with his own sense of what it is to belong, or he might make it a project to reconcile disparate components of his thinking, for example. Last, the ambiguity under discussion calls for more fellow feeling, empathy, and recognition of kindred spirits and fellow travelers across the major traditions.

The global approach calls for exploration of a certain frontier. There are already heroes on this frontier, and John Hick is one of them, regardless of whether we find his particular conclusions convincing. Early explorers provide maps of faraway places that others later improve upon. How much more impressive it is to take it upon oneself to travel far and to provide such a map, as Hick has done, than it is to dig in one's heels and refuse to budge from the home turf or—worse—even to deny that there is anything about faraway places that it is worthy of exploration, as if the shadow of the parish pump could embrace the whole world.

NOTES

1. Of course, people may miscalculate in this regard. Quite the reverse may occur in the wake of extensive mutual exposure, and members of our group may be drawn to one or more other traditions. What seems to be a fairly widespread unwillingness to experiment in this area probably bespeaks an inchoate awareness of the risks.

2. Wilfred Cantwell Smith remarks that "young people today not only are, but are beginning to see and to feel themselves as, heirs to the whole religious history of humankind (*Towards a New Theology: Faith and the Comparative History of Religion* [Philadelphia: Westminster, 1981], 18). He also makes the

bold—indeed, remarkable, assertion that "the new way that we are beginning to be able to see the global history of humankind is presumably the way that God has seen it all along" (18).

3. David Bohm writes as follows about the outcome of a sort of dialogue that he advocates: A new kind of mind thus begins to come into being which is based on the development of a common meaning that is constantly transforming in the process of the dialogue" (*Unfolding Meaning* [London: Routledge, 1987], 175, quoted by Lee Nichol, "Editor's Foreword" to David Bohm; *Dialogue*, x).

PART TEN

Non-Supernatural Religion

91 RELIGION RECONSIDERED

STEVEN M. CAHN

In the next selection I seek to explain why neither the theory nor the practice of religion requires a commitment to supernaturalism. In other words, ritual, prayer, metaphysical beliefs, and moral commitments can all be interpreted within a framework that does not violate the methods or results of scientific inquiry.

Most of us suppose that all religions are akin to the one we happen to know best. But this assumption can be misleading. For example, many Christians believe that all religions place heavy emphasis on an afterlife, although the central concern of Judaism is life in this world, not the next. Similarly, many Christians and Jews are convinced that a person who is religious must affirm the existence of a supernatural God. They are surprised to learn that religions such as Jainism, Theravada Buddhism, and Mimamsa Hinduism deny the existence of a Supreme Creator of the world.

To numerous theists as well as atheists, the concept of a nontheistic religion appears contradictory. I propose to show, however, that nothing in the theory or practice of religion—not ritual,

not prayer, not metaphysical belief, not moral commitment—necessitates a commitment to traditional theism. In other words, one may be religious while rejecting supernaturalism.

Let us begin with the concept of ritual. A ritual is a prescribed symbolic action. In the case of religion, the ritual is prescribed by the religious organization, and the act symbolizes some aspect of religious belief. If the religion is supernaturalistic (that is, if it believes in a supernatural God), then those who reject such theology may consider any ritual irrational. Yet although particular rituals may be based on irrational beliefs, nothing about the practice of ritual is inherently irrational.

Consider the act of two people shaking hands when meeting. This act is a ritual, prescribed by our

From Steven M. Cahn, *Puzzles & Perplexities: Collected Essays*, Second Edition, Lexington Books, 2007. Edited by the author and reprinted with his permission.

society and symbolic of the individuals' mutual respect. The act is in no way irrational. If people shook hands in order to ward off evil demons, then shaking hands would indeed be irrational. But that is not the reason why people shake hands. The ritual has no connection with God or demons but indicates the attitude one person has toward another.

Does the ritual of handshaking escape irrationality only because the ritual is not prescribed by any specific organization and is not part of an elaborate ceremony? Consider commencement at a college. The graduates and faculty members all wear peculiar hats and robes, and the participants stand and sit at appropriate times. The activities, however, are not at all irrational. Indeed, the rites of graduation day, far from being irrational, are symbolic of commitment to the process of education and the life of reason.

At first glance, rituals may seem a comparatively insignificant feature of life, yet they are a pervasive and treasured aspect of human experience. Who would want to eliminate the festivities associated with holidays such as Independence Day or Thanksgiving? What would college football be without songs, cheers, flags, and the innumerable other symbolic features surrounding the game? Those who disdain popular rituals typically proceed to establish their own distinctive ones, ranging from characteristic habits of dress to the use of drugs, symbolizing a rejection of traditional mores.

Religious persons, like all others, search for an appropriate means of emphasizing their commitment to a group or its values. Rituals provide such a means. Granted, supernaturalistic religion has often infused its rituals with superstition, but non-religious rituals can be equally superstitious. For instance, most Americans view the Fourth of July as an occasion on which they can express pride in their country's heritage. With this purpose in mind, the holiday is one of great significance. However, if the singing of the fourth verse of "The Star-Spangled Banner" four times on the Fourth of July were thought to protect our country against future disasters, then the original meaning of the holiday would soon be lost in a maze of superstition.

A naturalistic (i.e., nonsupernaturalistic) religion need not utilize ritual in a superstitious manner, because such a religion does not employ rituals to please a benevolent deity or appease an angry one. Rather, naturalistic religion views rituals, as one of its exponents has put it, as "the enhancement of life through the dramatization of great ideals."[1] If a group places great stress on justice or freedom, why should it not utilize ritual in order to emphasize these goals? Such a use of ritual serves to solidify the group and strengthen its devotion to its expressed purposes. These are buttressed if the ritual in question has the force of tradition, having been performed by many generations who have belonged to the same group and struggled to achieve the same goals. Ritual so conceived is not a form of superstition; rather, it is a reasonable means of strengthening religious commitment, as useful to naturalistic as to supernaturalistic religion.

Let us next turn to the concept of prayer. Some might suppose that naturalistic religion could have no use for prayer, because prayer is supposedly addressed to a supernatural being, and proponents of naturalistic religion do not believe in the existence of such a being. This objection, however, oversimplifies the concept of prayer, focusing attention on one type while neglecting an equally important but different sort.

Supernaturalistic religion makes extensive use of petitionary prayer, prayer that petitions a supernatural being for various favors. These may range all the way from the personal happiness of the petitioner to the general welfare of all society. Because petitionary prayer rests on the assumption that a supernatural being exists, such prayer clearly has no place in a naturalistic religion.

Not all prayers, however, are prayers of petition. Some prayers are prayers of meditation. These are not directed to any supernatural being and are not requests for granting favors. Rather, these prayers provide the opportunity for persons to rethink their ultimate commitments and rededicate themselves to their ideals. Such prayers may take the form of silent devotion or oral repetition of certain central texts. Just as Americans repeat the Pledge of Allegiance and reread the Gettysburg Address, so adherents of naturalistic religion repeat the statements of their ideals and reread the documents that embody their traditional beliefs.

Granted, supernaturalistic religions, to the extent that they utilize prayers of meditation, tend to treat these prayers irrationally, by supposing that if the prayers are not uttered a precise number of times under certain specified conditions, then the prayers lose all value. Yet prayer need not be viewed in this way. Rather, as the biologist Julian Huxley wrote, prayer "permits the bringing before the mind of a world of thought which in most people must inevitably be absent during the occupations of ordinary life.... [I]t is the means by which the mind may fix itself upon this or that noble or beautiful or awe-inspiring idea, and so grow to it and come to realize it more fully."[2]

Such a use of prayer may be enhanced by song, instrumental music, and various types of symbolism. These elements, fused together, provide the means for adherents of naturalistic religion to engage in religious services akin to those engaged in by adherents of supernaturalistic religion. The difference between the two services is that those who participate in the latter come to relate themselves to God, while those who attend the former come to relate themselves to their fellow human beings and the world in which we live.

Thus far we have discussed how ritual and prayer can be utilized in naturalistic religion, but to adopt a religious perspective also involves metaphysical beliefs and moral commitments. Can these be maintained without recourse to supernaturalism?

If we use the term *metaphysics* in its usual sense, referring to the systematic study of the most basic features of existence, then a metaphysical system may be either supernaturalistic or naturalistic. Representative of a supernaturalistic theory are the views of Descartes and Leibniz. Representative of a naturalistic theory are the views of Spinoza and Dewey.

Spinoza's *Ethics*, for example, one of the greatest of all metaphysical works, explicitly rejects the view that any being exists apart from Nature itself. Spinoza identifies God with Nature as a whole and urges that the good life consists in coming to understand Nature. In his words, "our salvation, or blessedness, or freedom consists in a constant and eternal love toward God."[3] Spinoza's concept of God, however, is explicitly not the supernaturalistic concept of God, and Spinoza's metaphysical system thus exemplifies not only a naturalistic metaphysics but also the possibility of reinterpreting the concept of God within a naturalistic framework.

Can those who do not believe in a supernaturalistic God commit themselves to moral principles, or is the acceptance of moral principles dependent on the acceptance of supernaturalism? Some have assumed that those who reject a supernatural God are necessarily immoral, for their denial of the existence of such a God leaves them free to act without fear of divine punishment. This assumption, however, is seriously mistaken.

To act morally is not to be motivated by threat of retribution from a powerful being but by the desire to act as one ought to act. An action is not right because it is commanded by God; rather, it is commanded by God because it is right. Thus morality does not rest on supernaturalism. Religious skeptics can be moral persons (as well as immoral ones), just as religious believers can be immoral persons (as well as moral ones).

In sum, naturalistic religion is a genuine possibility. Reasonable people may perform rituals, utter prayers, accept metaphysical beliefs, and commit themselves to moral principles without believing in supernaturalism. Indeed, even a religion such as Christianity or Judaism may be reinterpreted to eliminate any commitment to supernaturalism. Consider, for example, those Christians who accept the "Death of God"[4] or those Jews who belong to the influential Reconstructionist movement in Judaism.[5]

Such options are philosophically respectable. Whether to choose any of them is for each person to decide.

NOTES

1. Jack Cohen, *The Case for Religious Naturalism* (New York: Reconstructionist Press, 1958), p. 150.
2. Julian Huxley, *Religion Without Revelation* (New York: New American Library, 1957), p. 141.
3. Spinoza, *Ethics*, ed. James Gutmann (New York: Hafner, 1957), pt 5, prop. 36, note.
4. See John H. T. Robinson, *Honest to God* (Philadelphia: Westminster, 1963).
5. See Mordecai M. Kaplan, *Judaism as a Civilization* (New York: Schocken, 1967).

92 CONFUCIUS: THE SECULAR AS SACRED

HERBERT FINGARETTE

Confucius (c. 551–c. 479 B.C.E.), whose original name was K'ung Ch'ui, or Master K'ung, was a Chinese sage who urged the adoption of an ethical system that stressed benevolence and personal integrity, thereby seeking to preserve peace and stable government. His sayings are found in the *Analects*, a work probably arranged by his disciples. For more than two millennia his thought has permeated the Chinese religious outlook.

While his ideas about God and the afterlife remain unclear, he stressed the importance of virtuous action in this life and close attention to *li*, a Chinese term referring to ceremony performed with care and conviction. This key concept is explored in our next selection, which was written by Herbert Fingarette, Professor Emeritus of Philosophy at the University of California, Santa Barbara. He stresses that for Confucius the proper object of attention is action in this world, not speculation about a transcendent realm.

Confucius saw, and tried to call to our attention, that the truly, distinctively human powers have, characteristically, a magical quality. His task, therefore, required, in effect, that he reveal what is already so familiar and universal as to be unnoticed. What is necessary in such cases is that one come upon this "obvious" dimension of our existence in a new way, in the right way. Where can one find such a new path to this familiar area, one which provides a new and revealing perspective? Confucius found the path: we go by way of the notion of *li*.

One has to labor long and hard to learn *li*. The word in its root meaning is close to "holy ritual," "sacred ceremony." Characteristic of Confucius's teaching is the use of the language and imagery of *li* as a medium within which to talk about the entire body of the *mores*, or more precisely, of the authentic tradition and reasonable conventions of society. Confucius taught that the ability to act according to *li* and the will to submit to *li* are essential to that perfect and peculiarly human virtue or power which can be man's. Confucius thus does two things here: he calls our

attention to the entire body of tradition and convention, and he calls upon us to see all this by means of a metaphor, through the imagery of sacred ceremony, holy rite.

The (spiritually) noble man is one who has labored at the alchemy of fusing social forms (*li*) and raw personal existence in such a way that they transmuted into a way of being which realizes *te*, the distinctively human virtue or power.

Te is realized in concrete acts of human intercourse, the acts being of a pattern. These patterns have certain general features, features common to all such patterns of *li*: they are all expressive of "man-to-man-ness," of reciprocal loyalty and respect. But the patterns are also specific: they differentiate and they define in detail the ritual performance-repertoires which constitute civilized, i.e., truly human patterns of mourning, marrying and fighting, of being a prince, a father, a son and so on. However, men are by no means conceived as being mere standardized units mechanically carrying out prescribed routines in the service of some cosmic or social law. Nor are they self-sufficient, individual souls who happen to

---

consent to a social contract. Men become truly human as their raw impulse is shaped by *li*. And *li* is the fulfillment of human impulse, the civilized expression of it—not a formalistic dehumanization. *Li* is the specifically humanizing form of the dynamic relation of man-to-man.

The novel and creative insight of Confucius was to see this aspect of human existence, its form as learned tradition and convention, in terms of a particular revelatory image: *li*, i.e, "holy rite," "sacred ceremony," in the usual meaning of the term prior to Confucius.

In well-learned ceremony, each person does what he is supposed to do according to a pattern. My gestures are coordinated harmoniously with yours—though neither of us has to force, push, demand, compel or otherwise "make" this happen. Our gestures are in turn smoothly followed by those of the other participants, all effortlessly. If all are "self-disciplined, ever turning to *li*," then all that is needed—quite literally—is an initial ritual gesture in the proper ceremonial context; from there onward everything "happens." What action did Shun (the Sage-ruler) take? "He merely placed himself gravely and reverently with his face due south; that was all." (15:4) Let us consider in at least a little detail the distinctive features of action emphasized by this revelatory image of Holy Rite.

It is important that we do not think of this effortlessness as "mechanical" or "automatic." If it is so, then, as Confucius repeatedly indicates, the ceremony is dead, sterile, empty: there is no *spirit* in it. The truly ceremonial "takes place"; there is a kind of spontaneity. It happens "of itself." There is life in it because the individuals involved do it with seriousness and sincerity. For ceremony to be authentic one must "participate in the sacrifice"; otherwise it is as if one "did not sacrifice at all." (3:12) To put it another way, there are two contrasting kinds of failure in carrying out *li:* the ceremony may be awkwardly performed for lack of learning and skill; or the ceremony may have a surface slickness but yet be dull, mechanical for lack of serious purpose and commitment. Beautiful and effective ceremony requires the personal "presence" to be fused with learned ceremonial skill. This ideal fusion is true *li* as sacred rite.

Confucius characteristically and sharply contrasts the ruler who uses *li* with the ruler who seeks to attain his ends by means of commands, threats, regulations, punishments and force. (2:3) The force of coercion is manifest and tangible, whereas the vast (and sacred) forces at work in *li* are invisible and intangible. *Li* works through spontaneous coordination rooted in reverent dignity. The perfection in Holy Rite is esthetic as well as spiritual.

Having considered holy ceremony in itself, we are now prepared to turn to more everyday aspects of life. This is in effect what Confucius invites us to do; it is the foundation for his perspective on man.

I see you on the street; I smile, walk toward you, put out my hand to shake yours. And behold—without any command, stratagem, force, special tricks or tools, without any effort on my part to make you do so, you spontaneously turn toward me, return my smile, raise your hand toward mine. We shake hands—not by my pulling your hand up and down or your pulling mine but by spontaneous and perfect cooperative action. Normally we do not notice the subtlety and amazing complexity of this coordinated "ritual" act. This subtlety and complexity become very evident, however, if one has had to learn the ceremony only from a book of instructions, or if one is a foreigner from a nonhandshaking culture.

Nor normally do we notice that the "ritual" has "life" in it, that we are "present" to each other, at least to some minimal extent. As Confucius said, there are always the general and fundamental requirements of reciprocal good faith and respect. This mutual respect is not the same as a conscious feeling of mutual respect; when I am *aware* of a respect for you, I am much more likely to be piously fatuous or perhaps self-consciously embarrassed; and no doubt our little "ceremony" will reveal this in certain awkwardnesses. (I put out my hand too soon and am left with it hanging in midair.) No, the authenticity of the mutual respect does not require that I consciously feel respect or focus my attention on my respect for you; it is fully expressed in the correct "live" and spontaneous performance of the *act.* Just as an aerial acrobat must, at least for the purpose at hand, possess (but not think about his) complete trust in his partner if the trick is to come off, so we who shake hands, though the stakes are less, must have (but not think about) respect and trust. Otherwise we find ourselves fumbling awkwardly or performing in a lifeless fashion, which easily conveys its meaninglessness to the other.

Clearly it is not necessary that our reciprocal respect and good faith go very far in order for us to accomplish a reasonably successful handshake and greeting. Yet even here, the sensitive person can often plumb the depths of another's attitude from a handshake. This depth of human relationship expressible in a "ceremonial" gesture is in good part possible because of the remarkable specificity of the ceremony. For example, if I am your former teacher, you will spontaneously be rather obvious in walking toward me rather than waiting for me to walk toward you. You will allow a certain subtle reserve in your handshake, even though it will be warm. You will not slap me on the back, though conceivably I might grasp you by the shoulder with my free hand. There are indescribably many subtleties in the distinctions, nuances and minute but meaningful variations in gesture. If we do try to describe these subtle variations and their rules, we immediately sound like Book 10 of the *Analects*, whose ceremonial recipes initially seem to the modern American reader to be the quintessence of quaint and extreme traditionalism. It is in just such ways that social activity is coordinated in civilized society, without effort or planning, but simply by spontaneously initiating the appropriate ritual gesture in an appropriate setting. This power of *li*, Confucius says, depends upon prior learning. It is not inborn.

The effortless power of *li* can also be used to accomplish physical ends, though we usually do not think of it this way. Let us suppose I wish to bring a book from my office to my classroom. If I have no magic powers, I must literally take steps—walk to my office, push the door open, lift the book with my own muscles, physically carry it back. But there is also magic—the proper ritual expression of my wish which will accomplish my wish with no such effort on my part. I turn politely, i.e., ceremonially, to one of my students in class and merely express in an appropriate and polite (ritual) formula my wish that he bring me

the book. This proper ceremonial expression of my wish is all; I do not need to force him, threaten him, trick him. I do not need to do anything more myself. In almost no time the book is in my hands, as I wished! This is a uniquely human way of getting things done.

The examples of handshaking and of making a request are humble; the moral is profound. These complex but familiar gestures are characteristic of human relationships at their most human: we are least like anything else in the world when we do not treat each other as physical objects, as animals or even as subhuman creatures to be driven, threatened, forced, maneuvered. Looking at these "ceremonies" through the image of *li*, we realize that explicitly sacred rite can be seen as an emphatic, intensified and sharply elaborated extension of everyday *civilized* intercourse.

The notion that we can use speech only to talk *about* action or indirectly to *evoke* action has dominated modern Western thought. Yet contemporary "linguistic" analysis in philosophy has revealed increasingly how much the ritual word is itself the critical act rather than a report of, or stimulus to, action…. Professor J. L. Austin was one of those who brought the reality and pervasiveness of this phenomenon to a focus in his analyses of what he called the "performative utterance."[1] These are the innumerable statements we make which function somewhat like the "operative" clause in a legal instrument. They are statements, but they are not statements *about* some act or inviting some action; instead they are the very execution of the act itself.

"I give and bequeath my watch to my brother," duly said or written is not a report of what I have already done but is the very act of bequeathal itself. In a marriage ceremony, the "I do" is not a report of an inner mental act of acceptance; it is itself the act which seals my part of the bargain. "I promise…" is not a report of what I have done a moment before inside my head, nor is it indeed a report of anything at all; the uttering of the words is itself the act of promising. It is by words, and by the ceremony of which the words form a part, that I bind myself in a way which, for a man "ever turning to *li*," is more powerful, more inescapable than strategies or force. Confucius truly tells us that the man who uses the power of *li* can influence those above him—but not the man who has only physical force at his command.

There is no power of *li* if there is no learned and accepted convention, or if we utter the words and invoke the power of the convention in an inappropriate setting, or if the ceremony is not fully carried out, or if the persons carrying out the ceremonial roles are not those properly authorized ("authorization"—again a ceremony). In short, the peculiarly moral yet binding power of ceremonial gesture and word cannot be abstracted from or used in isolation from ceremony. It is not a distinct power we happen to use in ceremony; it is the power *of* ceremony. I cannot effectively go through the ceremony of bequeathing my servant to someone if, in our society, there is no accepted convention of slavery; I cannot bet two dollars if no one completes the bet by accepting; I cannot legally plead "Guilty" to a crime while eating dinner at home. Thus the power of *li* cannot be used except as the *li* is fully respected....

For present purposes it is enough to note how many are the obvious performative formulas in our own language and ceremony,[2] and also to note that there may be less obvious but no less important performative formulas, for example, those formulas in which one expresses one's own wish or preference or choice. "I choose this one" excludes the objection, made after one receives it, that one was not speaking truly. For to say it in the proper circumstances is not to report something already done but is to take the "operative" step in making the choice.

The upshot of this approach to language and its "ceremonial" context was, in the reasoning of Professor Austin, paradoxical. He came to feel forced toward the conclusion that ultimately *all* utterances are in some essential way performative. This remains an open question, but it suffices for us to recall that it is now a commonplace of contemporary analytical philosophy (as it was a basic thesis of pragmatist philosophies) that we use words to *do* things, profoundly important and amazingly varied things.

Indeed, the central lesson of these new philosophical insights is not so much a lesson about language as it is about ceremony. What we have come to see, in our own way, is how vast is the area of human existence in which the substance of that existence *is* the ceremony. Promises, commitments, excuses, pleas, compliments, pacts—these and so much more are ceremonies or they are nothing. It is thus in the medium of ceremony that the peculiarly human part of our life is lived. The ceremonial act is the primary, irreducible event; language cannot be understood in isolation from the conventional practice in which it is rooted; conventional practice cannot be understood in isolation from the language that defines and is part of it. No purely physical motion is a promise; no word alone, independent of ceremonial context, circumstances and roles can be a promise. Word and motion are only abstractions from the concrete ceremonial act.

From this standpoint, it is easy to see that not only motor skills must be learned but also correct use of language. For correct use of language is *constitutive* of effective action as gesture is. Correct language is not merely a useful adjunct; it is of the essence of executing the ceremony....

Of course we must be leery of reading our own contemporary philosophical doctrines into an ancient teaching. Yet I think that the text of the *Analects*, in letter and spirit, supports and enriches our own quite recently emerging vision of man as a ceremonial being.

In general, what Confucius brings out in connection with the workings of ceremony is not only its distinctively human character, its linguistic and magical character, but also its moral and religious character. Here, finally, we must recall and place at the focus of our analysis the fact that for Confucius it is the imagery of Holy Ceremony that unifies and infuses all these dimensions of human existence....

Rite brings out forcefully not only the harmony and beauty of social forms, the inherent and ultimate dignity of human intercourse; it brings out also the moral perfection implicit in achieving one's ends by dealing with others as beings of equal dignity, as free coparticipants in *li*. Furthermore, to act by ceremony is to be completely open to the other; for ceremony is public, shared, transparent; to act otherwise is to be secret, obscure and devious, or merely tyranni- cally coercive. It is in this beautiful and dignified, shared and open participation with others who are ultimately like oneself (12:2) that man realizes himself. Thus perfect community of men—the Confucian analogue to Christian brotherhood— becomes an inextricable part, the chief aspect, of Divine worship—again an analogy with the central Law taught by Jesus.

Confucius wanted to teach us, as a corollary, that sacred ceremony in its narrower, root mean- ing is not a totally mysterious appeasement of spir- its external to human and earthly life. Spirit is no longer an external being influenced by the cere- mony; it is that that is expressed and comes most alive *in* the ceremony. Instead of being diversion of attention from the human realm to another transcendent realm, the overtly holy ceremony is to be seen as the central symbol, both expressive of and participating in the holy as a dimension of all truly human existence.

NOTES

1. J. L. Austin, "Performative Utterances," in *Philo- sophical Papers* (London: Oxford University Press, 1961), pp. 220–239; *How to Do Things with Words* (London: Oxford University Press, 1962); "Performatif-Constatif," in *La Philosophie Analy- tique*, Cahiers de Royaumont, Phil. No. V (Edi- tions de Mincit, Paris, 1962), 271–305.

I have offered a systematic analysis of the concept of the performative, which I believe concords with and amplifies the points I am here making in con- nection with Confucius, though my analysis of performativeness was intended to be entirely gen- eral. See Herbert Fingarette, "Performatives," *American Philosophical Quarterly*, Vol. 4 (1967).

2. Though the list could go on interminably, I men- tion here just a few more terms which commonly enter into formulas having an obvious performa- tive function: "I christen you," "I appoint you," "I pick this (or him)," "I congratulate you," "I welcome you," "I authorize you," "I challenge you," "I order you," "I request you."

93   A DISCUSSION OF HEAVEN

XUNZI

Xunzi (pronounced shun-see), or Master Xun, was a Confucian scholar of the third century B.C.E. His philosophical system rested on the view that human nature is selfish but open to improvement through study and moral education. He considered any belief in supernatural- ism to be pointless, because whatever Heaven may be, it is not concerned with human action, has no mind or will, and provides no rewards or punishments. Rites are not appeals to other- worldly forces but human inventions that ornament social life and serve as expressions of emotion. In his view, "You pray for rain and it rains. Why? For no particular reason, I say. It is just as though you had not prayed for rain and it rained anyway." Xunzi's rationalism strongly influenced the later development of Confucianism.

Heaven's ways are constant. It does not prevail because of a sage like Yao; it does not cease to prevail because of a tyrant like Jie. Respond to it with good government, and good fortune will re- sult; respond to it with disorder, and misfortune will result. If you encourage agriculture and are

From *Xunzi: Basic Writings*, trans. Burton Watson, Columbia University Press, 2003. Reprinted by permission of the publisher.

frugal in expenditures, then Heaven cannot make you poor. If you provide the people with the goods they need and demand their labor only at the proper time, then Heaven cannot afflict you with illness. If you practice the Way and are not of two minds, then Heaven cannot bring you misfortune. Flood or drought cannot make your people starve, extremes of heat or cold cannot make them fall ill, and strange and uncanny occurrences cannot cause them harm. But if you neglect agriculture and spend lavishly, then Heaven cannot make you rich. If you are careless in your provisions and slow to act, then Heaven cannot make you whole. If you turn your back upon the Way and act rashly, then Heaven cannot give you good fortune. Your people will starve even when there are no floods or droughts; they will fall ill even before heat or cold come to oppress them; they will suffer harm even when no strange or uncanny happenings occur. The seasons will visit you as they do a well-ordered age, but you will suffer misfortunes that a well-ordered age does not know. Yet you must not curse Heaven, for it is merely the natural result of your own actions. Therefore, he who can distinguish between the activities of Heaven and those of mankind is worthy to be called the highest type of man.

To bring to completion without acting, to obtain without seeking—this is the work of Heaven. Thus, although the sage has deep understanding, he does not attempt to exercise it upon the work of Heaven; though he has great talent, he does not attempt to apply it to the work of Heaven; though he has keen perception, he does not attempt to use it on the work of Heaven. Hence it is said that he does not compete with Heaven's work. Heaven has its seasons; earth has its riches; man has his government. Hence man may form a triad with the other two. But if he sets aside that which allows him to form a triad with the other two and longs for what they have, then he is deluded. The ranks of stars move in progression, the sun and moon shine in turn, the four seasons succeed each other in good order, the yin and yang go through their great transformations, and the wind and rain pass over the whole land. All things obtain what is congenial to them and come to life, receive what is nourish-

ing to them and grow to completion. One does not see the process taking place, but sees only the results. Thus it is called godlike. All men understand that the process has reached completion, but none understands the formless forces that bring it about. Hence it is called the accomplishment of Heaven. Only the sage does not seek to understand Heaven.

When the work of Heaven has been established and its accomplishments brought to completion, when the form of man is whole and his spirit is born, then love and hate, delight and anger, sorrow and joy find lodging in him. These are called his heavenly emotions. Ears, eyes, nose, mouth, and body all have that which they perceive, but they cannot substitute for one another. They are called the heavenly faculties. The heart dwells in the center and governs the five faculties, and hence it is called the heavenly lord. Food and provisions are not of the same species as man, and yet they serve to nourish him and are called heavenly nourishment. He who accords with what is proper to his species will be blessed; he who turns against it will suffer misfortune. These are called the heavenly dictates. To darken the heavenly lord, disorder the heavenly faculties, reject the heavenly nourishment, defy the heavenly dictates, turn against the heavenly emotions, and thereby destroy the heavenly accomplishment is called dire disaster. The sage purifies his heavenly lord, rectifies his heavenly faculties, cherishes the heavenly nourishment, obeys the heavenly dictates, nourishes the heavenly emotions, and thereby preserves the heavenly accomplishment. In this way he understands what is to be done and what is not to be done. Hence Heaven and earth too perform their functions and all things serve him. His actions are completely ordered; his nourishment of the people is completely appropriate; his life is without injury. This is what it means to truly understand Heaven. Hence the really skilled man has things which he does not do; the really wise man has things that he does not ponder.

When he turns his thoughts to Heaven, he seeks to understand only those phenomena which can be regularly expected. When he turns his thoughts to earth, he seeks to understand only those aspects that can be taken advantage of. When he turns his thoughts to the four seasons, he seeks to understand only the changes that will affect his undertakings. When he turns his thoughts to the yin and yang, he seeks to understand only the modulations which call for some action on his part. The experts may study Heaven; the ruler himself should concentrate on the Way.

Are order and disorder due to the heavens? I reply, the sun and moon, the stars and constellations revolved in the same way in the time of Yu as in the time of Jie. Yu achieved order; Jie brought disorder. Hence order and disorder are not due to the heavens.

Are they then a matter of the seasons? I reply, the crops sprout and grow in spring and summer, and are harvested and stored away in autumn and winter. It was the same under both Yu and Jie. Yu achieved order; Jie brought disorder. Hence; order and disorder are not a matter of the seasons.

Are they due to the land? I reply, he who acquires land may live; he who loses it will die. It was the same in the time of Yu as in the time of Jie. Yu achieved order; Jie brought disorder. Hence order and disorder are not due to the land....

Heaven does not suspend the winter because men dislike cold; earth does not cease being wide because men dislike great distances; the gentleman does not stop acting because petty men carp and clamor. Heaven has its constant way; earth has its constant dimensions; the gentleman has his constant demeanor. The gentleman follows what is constant; the petty man reckons up his achievements. This is what the *Odes* means when it says:

> If you have no faults of conduct,
> Why be distressed at what others say?

The king of Chu has a retinue of a thousand chariots, but not because he is wise. The gentleman must eat boiled greens and drink water, but not because he is stupid. These are accidents of circumstance. To be refined in purpose, rich in virtuous action, and clear in understanding; to live in the present and remember the past—these are things which are within your own power. Therefore the

gentleman cherishes what is within his power and does not long for what is within the power of Heaven alone. The petty man, however, puts aside what is within his power and longs for what is within the power of Heaven. Because the gentleman cherishes what is within his power and does not long for what is within Heaven's power, he goes forward day by day. Because the petty man sets aside what is within his power and longs for what is within Heaven's power, he goes backward day by day. The same cause impels the gentleman forward day by day, and the petty man backward. What separates the two originates in this one point alone.

When stars fall or trees make strange sounds, all the people in the country are terrified and go about asking, "Why has this happened?" For no special reason, I reply. It is simply that, with the changes of Heaven and earth and the mutations of the yin and yang, such things once in a while occur. You may wonder at them, but you must not fear them. The sun and moon are subject to eclipses, wind and rain do not always come at the proper season, and strange stars occasionally appear. There has never been an age that was without such occurrences. If the ruler is enlightened and his government just, then there is no harm done even if they all occur at the same time. But if the ruler is benighted and his government ill-run, then it will be no benefit to him even if they never occur at all. Stars that fall, trees that give out strange sounds—such things occur once in a while with the changes of Heaven and earth and the mutations of the yin and yang. You may wonder at them, but do not fear them.

Among all such strange occurrences, the ones really to be feared are human portents. When the plowing is poorly done and the crops suffer, when the weeding is badly done and the harvest fails; when the government is evil and loses the support of the people; when the fields are neglected and the crops badly tended; when grain must be imported from abroad and sold at a high price, and the people are starving and die by the roadside— these are what I mean by human portents. When government commands are unenlightened, public works are undertaken at the wrong season, and agriculture is not properly attended to, these too are human portents....

[W]hen ritual principles are not obeyed, family affairs and outside affairs are not properly separated, and men and women mingle wantonly, so that fathers and sons begin to doubt each other, superior and inferior become estranged, and bands of invaders enter the state—these too are human portents. Portents such as these are born from disorder, and if all three types occur at once, there will be no safety for the state. The reasons for their occurrence may be found very close at hand; the suffering they cause is great indeed. You should not only wonder at them, but fear them as well....

You pray for rain and it rains. Why? For no particular reason, I say. It is just as though you had not prayed for rain and it rained anyway. The sun and moon undergo an eclipse and you try to save them; a drought occurs and you pray for rain; you consult the arts of divination before making a decision on some important matter. But it is not as though you could hope to accomplish anything by such ceremonies. They are done merely for ornament. Hence the gentleman regards them as ornaments, but the common people regard them as supernatural. He who considers them ornaments is fortunate; he who considers them supernatural is unfortunate.

94 REASON IN RELIGION

GEORGE SANTAYANA

George Santayana (1863–1952), born in Spain, was a graduate from Harvard University, where he became a professor of philosophy. He then returned to Europe, where he wrote extensively, including in his output not only philosophy but also poetry and a novel, *The Last Puritan*. Eventually he retired to a convent in Italy.

Reason in Religion was one of the five volumes in Santayana's *The Life of Reason*, which also includes *Reason in Common Sense*, *Reason in Society*, *Reason in Art*, and *Reason in Science*. The work sought to show how the main branches of human thought and activity can be viewed within a naturalistic framework.

Santayana saw religion as offering not literal truth but imaginative visions, akin to poetry but dealing with higher and more practical themes. Which religion one practices, like which language one speaks, is a historical accident. Yet religions can open vistas that enrich experience and deepen insight.

Experience has repeatedly confirmed that well-known maxim of Bacon's, that "a little philosophy inclineth man's mind to atheism, but depth in philosophy bringeth men's minds about to religion." In every age the most comprehensive thinkers have found in the religion of their time and country something they could accept, interpreting and illustrating that religion so as to give it depth and universal application. Even the heretics and atheists, if they have had profundity, turn

From George Santayana, *Reason in Religion*, Collier Books, 1962. Reprinted by permission of Simon & Schuster, Inc.

out after a while to be forerunners of some new orthodoxy. What they rebel against is a religion alien to their nature; they are atheists only by accident, and relatively to a convention which inwardly offends them, but they yearn mightily in their own souls after the religious acceptance of a world interpreted in their own fashion. So it appears in the end their atheism and loud protestation were in fact the hastier part of their thought, since what emboldened them to deny the poor world's faith was that they were too impatient to understand it. Indeed, the enlightenment common to young wits and worm-eaten old satirists, who plume themselves on detecting the scientific ineptitude of religion—something which the blindest half see—is not nearly enlightened enough: it points to notorious facts incompatible with religious tenets literally taken, but it leaves unexplored the habits of thought from which those tenets sprang, their original meaning, and their true function. Such studies would bring the sceptic face to face with the mystery and pathos of mortal existence. They would make him understand why religion is so profoundly moving and in a sense so profoundly just. There must needs be something humane and necessary in an influence that has become the most general sanction of virtue, the chief occasion for art and philosophy, and the source, perhaps, of the best human happiness. If nothing, as Hooker said, is "so malapert as a splenetic religion," a sour irreligion is almost as perverse.

At the same time, when Bacon penned the sage epigram we have quoted he forgot to add that the God to whom depth in philosophy brings back men's minds is far from being the same from whom a little philosophy estranges them. It would be pitiful indeed if mature reflection bred no better conceptions than those which have drifted down the muddy stream of time, where tradition and passion have jumbled everything together. Traditional conceptions, when they are felicitous, may be adopted by the poet, but they must be purified by the moralist and disintegrated by the philosopher. Each religion, so dear to those whose life it sanctifies, and

fulfilling so necessary a function in the society that has adopted it, necessarily contradicts every other religion, and probably contradicts itself. What religion a man shall have is a historical accident, quite as much as what language he shall speak. In the rare circumstances where a choice is possible, he may, with some difficulty, make an exchange; but even then he is only adopting a new convention which may be more agreeable to his personal temper but which is essentially as arbitrary as the old.

The attempt to speak without speaking any particular language is not more hopeless than the attempt to have a religion that shall be no religion in particular. A courier's or a dragoman's speech may indeed be often unusual and drawn from disparate sources, not without some mixture of personal originality; but that private jargon will have a meaning only because of its analogy to one or more conventional languages and its obvious derivation from them. So travellers from one religion to another, people who have lost their spiritual nationality, may often retain a neutral and confused residuum of belief, which they may egregiously regard as the essence of all religion, so little may they remember the graciousness and naturalness of that ancestral accent which a perfect religion should have. Yet a moment's probing of the conceptions surviving in such minds will show them to be nothing but vestiges of old beliefs, creases which thought, even if emptied of all dogmatic tenets, has not been able to smooth away at its first unfolding. Later generations, if they have any religion at all, will be found either to revert to ancient authority, or to attach themselves spontaneously to something wholly novel and immensely positive, to some faith promulgated by a fresh genius and passionately embraced by a converted people. Thus every living and healthy religion has a marked idiosyncrasy. Its power consists in its special and surprising message and in the bias which that revelation gives to life. The vistas it opens and the mysteries it propounds are another world to live in; and another world to live in—whether we expect ever to pass wholly into it or no—is what we mean by having a religion....

Religion pursues rationality through the imagination. When it explains events or assigns causes, it is an imaginative substitute for science. When it gives precepts, insinuates ideals, or remoulds aspiration, it is an imaginative substitute for wisdom—I mean for the deliberate and impartial pursuit of all good. The conditions and the aims of life are both represented in religion poetically, but this poetry tends to arrogate to itself literal truth and moral authority, neither of which it possesses. Hence the depth and importance of religion become intelligible no less than its contradictions and practical disasters. Its object is the same as that of reason, but its method is to proceed by intuition and by unchecked poetical conceits. These are repeated and vulgarised in proportion to their original fineness and significance, till they pass for reports of objective truth and come to constitute a world of faith, superposed upon the world of experience and regarded as materially enveloping it, if not in space at least in time and in existence. The only truth of religion comes from its interpretation of life, from its symbolic rendering of that moral experience which it springs out of and which it seeks to elucidate. Its falsehood comes from the insidious misunderstanding which clings to it, to the effect that these poetic conceptions are not merely representations of experience as it is or should be, but are rather information about experience or reality elsewhere —an experience and reality which, strangely enough, supply just the defects betrayed by reality and experience here.

Thus religion has the same original relation to life that poetry has; only poetry, which never pretends to literal validity, adds a pure value to existence, the value of a liberal imaginative exercise. The poetic value of religion would initially be greater than that of poetry itself, because religion deals with higher and more practical themes, with sides of life which are in greater need of some imaginative touch and ideal interpretation than are those pleasant or pompous things which ordinary poetry dwells upon. But this initial advantage is neutralised in part by the abuse to which religion is subject, whenever its symbolic rightness is taken for scientific truth. Like poetry, it improves the world only by imagining it improved, but not content with making this addition to the mind's furniture—an addition which might be useful and ennobling—it thinks to confer a more radical benefit by persuading mankind that, in spite of appearances, the world is really such as that rather arbitrary idealisation has painted it. This spurious satisfaction is naturally the prelude to many a disappointment, and the soul has infinite trouble to emerge again from the artificial problems and sentiments into which it is thus plunged. The value of religion becomes equivocal. Religion remains an imaginative achievement, a symbolic representation of moral reality which may have a most important function in vitalising the mind and in transmitting, by way of parables, the lessons of experience. But it becomes at the same time a continuous incidental deception; and this deception, in proportion as it is strenuously denied to be such, can work indefinite harm in the world and in the conscience.

On the whole, however, religion should not be conceived as having taken the place of anything better, but rather as having come to relieve situations which, but for its presence, would have been infinitely worse. In the thick of active life, or in the monotony of practical slavery, there is more need to stimulate fancy than to control it. Natural instinct is not much disturbed in the human brain by what may happen in that thin superstratum of ideas which commonly overlays it. We must not blame religion for preventing the development of a moral and natural science which at any rate would seldom have appeared; we must rather thank it for the sensibility, the reverence, the speculative insight which it has introduced into the world.

95 JUDAISM WITHOUT SUPERNATURALISM

MORDECAI M. KAPLAN

Mordecai M. Kaplan (1881–1983), born in Lithuania, became a leading American rabbi. In 1922 he founded the Reconstructionist movement, which along with Orthodox, Conservative, and Reform, is now one of the four braches of Judaism. In his magnum opus *Judaism as a Civilization*, Kaplan developed the view that Judaism is not just a religion but a religious civilization. Moreover, he argued that God should not be understood as a supernatural being but as a force within nature that impels human beings to strive for a worthwhile life.

Reconstructionism has been a leader in achieving religious equality for women. Also, while the movement's congregations hold services that are rich in ritual, prayer books have been rewritten to remove elements at odds with reason. For example, the traditional prayer, "Trust in the Lord with all thy heart and lean not upon thine own understanding," is a part of the liturgy Kaplan explicitly refused to recite.

At no point in the contest between the traditionalist and the modernist approach to Judaism is their mutually irreconcilable character so pronounced as at the issue whether the Jewish religion is an immutable way of life or is subject to change. The traditionalists assume that the Jewish religion is a complete, finished and perfect system of beliefs and practices, inherently relevant to all conditions of human life. The modernists regard the Jewish religion as an evolving, growing pattern of beliefs and practices. It accordingly gives rise to new ideas about God, man and the world and to new ways of life, in response to changing circumstances and new challenges....

Existentially, Judaism is the religious civilization of the Jewish People. As an existential living reality, Judaism has had to undergo change, with every marked change in the situation of the Jewish People. The one element in the situation which would most affect the character of Judaism would naturally be the climate of thought, including ideas about God, the world, and the nature and destiny of man....

We are still in the throes of the crisis created by the spirit of modernism, with its negation of supernaturalism. "Supernaturalism" is here used in the specific sense of the suspension of natural law to make possible the occurrence of events which God himself brings about, to reward or punish, to help or hinder, human beings in their particular strivings, according as these are in keeping with, or contrary to, His will....

Modernism is rendering the foregoing supernaturalist world outlook obsolete for an increasing number of human beings. Too much has been learned about various religious traditions, with their myths, legends and wonder tales, to permit the average thoughtful person, who is accustomed to integrate his knowledge into a coherent pattern, to place any more credence in the miracles recorded in the Jewish tradition than in those of any other. So far, no reliable record has been found of any event in which there is definite proof that it was made possible through the suspension of natural law....

Religion does not always manage to free itself from the shackles of magic with its superstitious fears and fawning flatteries, but when it does, it opens up to man vistas of high attainment and achievement. In the long run, this is increasingly

---

From Mordecai M. Kaplan, *Religion Without Supernaturalism*, The Reconstructionist Press, 1958. Reprinted by permission of the publisher.

coming to be the function of religion, while its function as magic is constantly shrinking.

From the adoption of the frame of human values, which derive their significance from man's striving for salvation, perfection or self-transcendence, it is but one logical step to the belief in God as the Power that impels man to pursue that course and that enables him at least to come within sight of its destination. We experience the reality of God in whatever gives us a sense of life's worthwhileness, despite the evils that mar life, and in whatever drives us to follow our sense of moral responsibility, regardless of consequences.

We must learn to redefine the term "religion" in such a way as not to be put in a position of having to declare as irreligious or anti-religious, not only the intellectual elite, but virtually most healthy-minded persons. How essential this is may be inferred from an interesting experiment conducted by an outstanding psychologist with a mixed group of highly educated and healthy-minded men and women. "So far as religion is concerned," writes A. H. Maslow, "none of my subjects are orthodoxly religious, but, on the other hand, I know only of one who describes himself as an atheist. All the others from whom I have information hesitate to call themselves atheists. They say that they believe in God, but describe this God more as a metaphysical concept than as a personal figure. *Whether or not they could be called religious people as a group must then depend entirely on the conception or definition of religion that we choose to use.* (Emphasis mine.) If religion is defined only in social-behavioral terms, then these are all 'religious' people, the atheists included. But if, more conservatively, we use the term 'religion' so as to include and stress the supernatural element (certainly the more common usage) then our answer must be quite different, for then almost none of them is religious."[1]

The only alternative to the traditional and supernaturalist conception of God's self-manifestation that can make a difference in people's lives is not the metaphysical approach but the social-behavioral one. It may well be that the human mind is forever and intrinsically incapable of grappling *existentially* with ultimates, and is permanently and inherently limited to theorizing about them *conceptually* or by means of ideas—which are abstractions from reality. That God, as ultimate reality, is unknowable is a commonplace of all thinking other than that which is entirely naive. Theologians constantly remind us that all our affirmations concerning God have to be translated into negatives, if they are to approximate the truth. Consequently, religion which aims to improve human nature and the conditions of human living cannot be based on the ultimate nature of God. Its field of operations must be the nature of man. It has to focus its attention on that aspect of man's nature which is in need of being fully humanized, on what the human being ought to become, if he is to reflect the image of God. *It is the business of religion not to give a metaphysical conception of God, but to make clear what we mean by the belief in God, from the standpoint of the difference that belief makes in human conduct and striving.*

The point of contact between man and God, or as it is fashionable to state it nowadays, the encounter between man and God, is man's sense of freedom and responsibility. It is at that point that religion has to function, so that man can utilize his freedom and responsibility intelligently, righteously and creatively. This is where the attributes of wisdom, justice and love, in the conception of God, have to be stressed.

There is nothing in this function of religion that requires resorting to supernaturalism. The freedom and responsibility of which human nature is capable are the natural manifestations, on a self-conscious level, of the cosmic principle of polarity. Freedom expresses the pole of selfhood, and responsibility the pole of otherhood, or cooperation. Is the human polarity of freedom and responsibility, with its promise of human metamorphosis into a higher type of being, futile dreaming and self-delusion, or is it as existentially real as the world of sense and sound we inhabit? If the latter is the case, then the self-conscious will to salvation is the immanent aspect of that cosmic reality for which no term can be more appropriate than "God." Whatever else human beings may have sought to express by the term "God," it has always had the connotation of man's responsibility for what he does and his freedom to choose between right and wrong, good and evil.

There is nothing in this conception of man's encounter with God that in any way calls for the suspension of nature's laws as evidence of God's existence and power....

Nor does naturalist religion commit us to the choice of either submitting to the authority of the past or treating the past as nothing more than a far-off milepost, left behind in our progress toward the future. In this respect, too, the synthesis of naturalism with religion points to a third alternative: We should accept the past as no more authoritative than the present. It should have the right to a vote, but not the right to veto, in the determination of what we have to do to achieve salvation.

NOTE

1. *The Self*, "Self-actualizing People: A Study of Psychological Health," pp. 183-184.

96 HONEST TO GOD

JOHN A. T. ROBINSON

John A. T. Robinson (1919–1963), born in England, served as Dean of Clare College at the University of Cambridge and then became Bishop of Woolwich. He argued that the concept of a God needed to be recast, giving up the notion of a being "up there" or "out there." Instead, Christians should conceive of ultimate reality as identical to love.

Robinson's work played a central role in the mid-twentieth century movement popularly known as "the Death of God." No one claimed, however, that God had died; rather, a concept of God had been thought by some, including Robinson, to have become untenable. In its place he proposed that God be understood as not separate from the world but inherent in its structure.

UP THERE OR OUT THERE?

THE Bible speaks of a God 'up there'. No doubt its picture of a three-decker universe, of 'the heaven above, the earth beneath and the waters under the earth', was once taken quite literally. No doubt also its more sophisticated writers, if pressed, would have been the first to regard this as symbolic language to represent and convey spiritual realities. Yet clearly they were not pressed. Or at any rate they were not oppressed by it. Even such an educated man of the world as St Luke can express the conviction of Christ's ascension—the conviction that he is not merely alive but reigns in the might and right of God—in the crudest terms of being 'lifted up' into heaven, there to sit down at the right hand of the Most High.[1] He feels no need to offer any apology for this language, even though he of all New Testament writers was commending Christianity to what Schleiermacher called its 'cultured despisers'. This is the more remarkable because, in contrast, he leaves his readers in no doubt that what we might regard as the scarcely more primitive notions of God entertained by the Athenians,[2] that the deity lives in temples made by man and needs to be served by human hands, were utterly superseded by Christianity.

Moreover, it is the two most mature theologians of the New Testament, St John and the later Paul, who write most uninhibitedly of this 'going

From John A. T. Robinson, *Honest to God*, The Westminster Press, 1963. Reprinted by permission of the publisher.

up' and 'coming down'. No one has ascended into heaven but he who descended from heaven, the Son of man.[3]

Do you take offence at this? Then what if you were to see the Son of man ascending where he was before?[4]

In saying, 'He ascended', what does it mean but that he had also descended into the lower parts of the earth? He who descended is he who also ascended far above all the heavens, that he might fill all things.[5]

They are able to use this language without any sense of constraint because it had not become an embarrassment to them. Everybody accepted what it meant to speak of a God up there, even though the groundlings might understand it more grossly than the gnostics. For St Paul, no doubt, to be 'caught up to the third heaven'[6] was as much a metaphor as it is to us (though for him a considerably more precise metaphor). But he could use it to the spiritually sophisticated at Corinth with no consciousness that he must 'demythologize' if he were to make it acceptable.

For the New Testament writers the idea of a God 'up there' created no embarrassment—because it had not yet become a difficulty. For us too it creates little embarrassment—because, for the most part, it has ceased to be a difficulty. We are scarcely even conscious that the majority of the words for what we value most are still in terms of height, though as Edwyn Bevan observed in his Gifford Lectures,[7] 'The proposition: Moral and spiritual worth is greater or less in ratio to the distance outwards from the earth's surface, would certainly seem to be, if stated nakedly like that, an odd proposition.' Yet it is one that we have long ago found it unnecessary to explain away. We may indeed continue to have to tell our children that heaven is not in fact over their heads nor God literally 'above the bright blue sky'. Moreover, whatever we may accept with the top of our minds, most of us still retain deep down the mental image of 'an old man in the sky'. Nevertheless, for most of us most of the time the traditional language of a three-storeyed universe is not a serious obstacle. It does not worry us intellectually, it is not an 'offence' to faith, because we have long since made a remarkable transposition, of which

we are hardly aware. In fact, we do not realize how crudely spatial much of the Biblical terminology is, for we have ceased to perceive it that way. It is as though when reading a musical score what we actually saw was not the notes printed but the notes of the key into which mentally we were transposing it. There are some notes, as it were, in the Biblical score which still strike us in the old way (the Ascension story, for instance) and which we have to make a conscious effort to transpose, but in general we assimilate the language without trouble.

For in place of a God who is literally or physically 'up there' we have accepted, as part of our mental furniture, a God who is spiritually or metaphysically 'out there'. There are, of course, those for whom he is almost literally 'out there'. They may have accepted the Copernican revolution in science, but until recently at any rate they have still been able to think of God as in some way 'beyond' outer space. In fact the number of people who instinctively seem to feel that it is no longer possible to believe in God in the space-age shows how crudely physical much of this thinking about a God 'out there' has been. Until the last recesses of the cosmos had been explored or were capable of being explored (by radio-telescope if not by rocketry), it was still possible to locate God mentally in some *terra incognita*. But now it seems there is no room for him, not merely in the inn, but in the entire universe: for there are no vacant places left. In reality, of course, our new view of the universe has made not the slightest difference. Indeed, the limit set to 'space' by the speed of light (so that beyond a certain point—not all that much further than our present range—everything recedes over the horizon of visibility) is even more severe. And there is nothing to stop us, if we wish to, locating God 'beyond' it. And there he would be quite invulnerable—in a 'gap' science could never fill. But in fact the coming of the space-age has destroyed this crude projection of God—and for that we should be grateful. For if God is 'beyond', he is not *literally* beyond anything.

But the idea of a God spiritually or metaphysically 'out there' dies very much harder. Indeed, most people would be seriously disturbed by the thought that it should need to die at all. For it *is* their God, and they have nothing to put in its place. And for the words 'they' and 'their' it would be more honest to substitute 'we' and 'our'. For it is the God of our own upbringing and conversation, the God of our fathers and of our religion, who is under attack. Every one of us lives with some mental picture of a God 'out there', a God who 'exists' above and beyond the world he made, a God 'to' whom we pray and to whom we 'go' when we die. In traditional Christian theology, the doctrine of the Trinity witnesses to the self-subsistence of this divine Being outside us and apart from us. The doctrine of creation asserts that at a moment of time this God called 'the world' into existence over against himself. The Biblical record describes how he proceeds to enter into contact with those whom he has made, how he establishes a 'covenant' with them, how he 'sends' to them his prophets, and how in the fullness of time he 'visits' them in the person of his Son, who must one day 'come again' to gather the faithful to himself.

This picture of a God 'out there' coming to earth like some visitor from outer space underlies every popular presentation of the Christian drama of salvation, whether from the pulpit or the presses. Indeed, it is noticeable that those who have been most successful in communicating it in our day—Dorothy Sayers, C. S. Lewis, J. B. Phillips—have hesitated least in being boldly anthropomorphic in the use of this language. They have not, of course, taken it literally, any more than the New Testament writers take literally the God 'up there', but they have not apparently felt it any embarrassment to the setting forth of the Gospel. This is sufficient testimony to the fact that there is a readymade public for whom this whole frame of reference still presents no difficulties, and their very achievement should make us hesitate to pull it down or call it in question.

Indeed, the last thing I want to do is to appear to criticize from a superior position. I should like to think that it were possible to use this mythological language of the God 'out there' and make the same utterly natural and unself-conscious transposition as I have suggested we already do with the language of the God 'up there'. Indeed, unless we become used to doing this and are able

to take this theological notation, as it were, in our stride, we shall cut ourselves off from the classics of the Christian faith, just as we should be unable to read the Bible were we to stumble at *its* way of describing God. I believe, however, that we may have to pass through a century or more of reappraisal before this becomes possible and before this language ceases to be an offence to faith for a great many people. No one wants to live in such a period, and one could heartily wish it were not necessary. But the signs are that we are reaching the point at which the whole conception of a God 'out there', which has served us so well since the collapse of the three-decker universe, is itself becoming more of a hindrance than a help.

In a previous age there came a moment when the three-decker likewise proved an embarrassment, even as a piece of mental furniture. But in this case there was a considerable interval between the time when it ceased to be taken literally as a model of the universe and the time when it ceased to perform a useful function as a metaphor. An illustration of this is to be seen in the doctrine of hell. In the old scheme, hell was 'down there'. By Shakespeare's time no one thought of it as literally under the earth, but still in *Hamlet* it is lively and credible enough as a metaphor. But a localized hell gradually lost more and more of its purchase over the imagination, and revivalist attempts to stoke its flames did not succeed in restoring its power. The tragedy in this instance is that no effective translation into terms of the God 'out there' was found for the Devil and his angels, the pit and the lake of fire. This element therefore tended to drop out of popular Christianity altogether—much to the detriment of the depth of the Gospel.

But the point I wish to make here is that the supersession of the old scheme was a gradual one. After it had been discredited scientifically, it continued to serve theologically as an acceptable frame of reference. The image of a God 'up there' survived its validity as a literal description of reality by many centuries. But today I believe we may be confronted by a double crisis. The final psychological, if not logical, blow delivered by modern science and technology to the idea that there might *literally* be a God 'out there' has *coincided* with an awareness that the *mental* picture of such a God may be more of a stumbling-block than an aid to belief in the Gospel. There is a double pressure to discard this entire construction, and with it any belief in God at all.

Moreover, it is not merely a question of the speed of adjustment required. The abandonment of a God 'out there' represents a much more radical break than the transition to this concept from that of a God 'up there'. For this earlier transposition was largely a matter of verbal notation, of a change in spatial metaphor, important as this undoubtedly was in liberating Christianity from a flat-earth cosmology. But to be asked to give up any idea of a Being 'out there' at all will appear to be an outright denial of God. For, to the ordinary way of thinking, to believe in God means to be convinced of the existence of such a supreme and separate Being. 'Theists' are those who believe that such a Being exists, 'atheists' those who deny that he does.

But suppose such a super-Being 'out there' is really only a sophisticated version of the Old Man in the sky? Suppose belief in God does not, indeed cannot, mean being persuaded of the 'existence' of some entity, even a supreme entity, which might or might not be there, like life on Mars? Suppose the atheists are right—but that this is no more the end or denial of Christianity than the discrediting of the God 'up there', which must in its time have seemed the contradiction of all that the Bible said? Suppose that all such atheism does is to destroy an idol, and that we can and must get on without a God 'out there' at all? Have we...

CHRISTMAS AND TRUTH

THE doctrine of the Incarnation and Divinity of Christ is on any count central to the entire Christian message and crucial therefore for any reinterpretation of it. It is also the point where resistance to reinterpretation is likely to be at its maximum and where orthodoxy has its heaviest investment in traditional categories. This is true both at the level of technical theology ... and at the popular level, where one will quickly be accused of destroying the Christmas story. But if it is necessary in our thinking about God to move to a position 'beyond naturalism and supranaturalism', this is no less important in our thinking about Christ. Otherwise we shall be shut up, as we have been hitherto, to an increasingly sterile choice between the two.

Traditional Christology has worked with a frankly supranaturalist scheme. Popular religion has expressed this mythologically, professional theology metaphysically. For this way of thinking, the Incarnation means that God the Son came down to earth, and was born, lived and died within this world as a man. From 'out there' there graciously entered into the human scene one who was not 'of it' and yet who lived genuinely and completely within it. As the God-man, he united in his person the supernatural and the natural: and the problem of Christology so stated is how Jesus can be fully God and fully man, and yet genuinely one person....

But suppose the whole notion of 'a God' who 'visits' the earth in the person of 'his Son' is ... mythical? Suppose there is no realm 'out there' from which the 'Man from heaven' arrives? Suppose the Christmas myth (the invasion of 'this side' by 'the other side')—as opposed to the Christmas history (the birth of the man Jesus of Nazareth)—has to go? Are we prepared for that? Or are we to cling here to this last vestige of the mythological or metaphysical world-view as the only garb in which to clothe story with power to touch the imagination? Cannot perhaps the supranaturalist scheme survive at least as part of the 'magic' of Christmas?

Yes, indeed, it can survive—as myth. For myth has its perfectly legitimate, and indeed profoundly important, place. The myth is there to indicate the significance of the events, the divine depth of the history. And we shall be grievously impoverished if our ears cannot tune to the angels' song or our eyes are blind to the wise men's star. But we must be able to read the nativity story without assuming that its truth depends on there being a literal interruption of the natural by the supernatural, that Jesus can only be Emmanuel— God with us—if, as it were, he came through from another world. For, as supranaturalism becomes less and less credible, to tie the action of God to such a way of thinking is to banish it for increasing numbers into the preserve of the pagan myths and thereby to sever it from any real connection with history. As Christmas becomes a pretty story, naturalism—the attempt to explain Christ, like everything else, on humanistic presuppositions—is left in possession of the field as the only alternative with any claim to the allegiance of intelligent men.

Naturalism has on the whole been remarkably favourable to Christianity in the realm of Christology. Once the 'dogma' of his deity has been put out of the way, the humanist picture of Jesus is noticeably sympathetic, especially when compared with the sharpness of its 'antitheism'. Indeed, the non-Christian secularist view of Jesus shades imperceptibly into the estimate of his person in Liberal Christianity. To do it justice, let us then take the naturalistic interpretation of Christ at its highest and most positive.

This has even been ready to use the epithet 'divine' of Jesus—in the sense that he was the most God-like man that ever lived, that what he said and did was so beautiful and so true that he must have been a revelation, indeed, the supreme revelation, of God. According to this view, the divine is simply the human raised to the power of '*x*'. As Kierkegaard put it in a devastating parody more than a hundred years ago, 'If the thing is well said, the man is a genius—and if it is unusually well said, then God said it'. And by this Jesus is put 'on the same level as all those who have no authority, on the same level as geniuses, poets and the thinkers'.[8] He is one of them, albeit the highest of them.

Unfortunately this is clearly not what the New Testament is saying of Jesus.... To say that Jesus had a unique experience of God, that he displayed all the qualities of God, that he was like God or that God was like him—this can never add up to saying that he was 'of one substance' with the Father....

Yet the Liberals were entirely justified in the courage with which they were prepared to abandon the supranaturalistic scaffolding by which hitherto the whole structure had been supported. That house had to collapse, and they had the faith to see that Christianity need not collapse with it. Moreover, however inadequate the Liberal theology may now appear to us, it undoubtedly helped many to hold on to their faith at a time when otherwise they might have thrown it up completely. As the supranaturalistic scheme of

things became incredible, a naturalistic theology was all that stood between an entire generation and abandoning the spirit and power of Jesus altogether. And the spirit and power was able in many cases to prove itself greater than the theology. Yet equally the theology has not sufficed to commend the spirit and power. Modern humanistic naturalism has found less and less need to speak of Jesus as in any sense 'divine'. The belief that we are at this point and in this person in touch with *God* has increasingly been left to the religious minority that can still accept the old mythology as physically or metaphysically true. This is a dangerous situation for the Christian faith....

THE CLAIM OF THE NEW TESTAMENT

But ... we should stop and pose the prior question of what it is we have to reinterpret, of what in fact the New Testament is saying. For I believe that the supranaturalist, like the naturalist, estimate of Christ, whatever its intention, tends to be a distortion of the Biblical truth. I do not say it necessarily is, since the mythological-metaphysical framework can obviously provide the setting, as it has in the past, for an entirely orthodox Christology. But in practice popular preaching and teaching presents a supranaturalistic view of Christ which cannot be substantiated from the New Testament. It says simply that Jesus *was* God, in such a way that the terms 'Christ' and 'God' are interchangeable. But nowhere in Biblical usage is this so. The New Testament says that Jesus was the Word of God, it says that God was in Christ, it says that Jesus is the Son of God; but it does not say that Jesus was God, simply like that.[9]

What it does say is defined as succinctly and accurately as it can be in the opening verse of St John's Gospel. But we have to be equally careful about the translation. The Greek runs: *kai theos en ho logos*. The so-called Authorized Version has: 'And the Word was God.' This would indeed suggest the view that 'Jesus' and 'God' were identical and interchangeable. But in Greek this would most naturally be represented by 'God' with the article, not *theos* but *ho theos*. But, equally, St John is not saying that Jesus is a 'divine' man, in the sense with which the ancient world was familiar or in the sense in which the Liberals spoke of him. That would be *theios*. The Greek expression steers carefully between the two. It is impossible to represent it in a single English word, but the New English Bible, I believe, gets the sense pretty exactly with its rendering, 'And what God was, the Word was'. In other words, if one looked at Jesus, one saw God—for 'he who has seen me, has seen the Father'.[10] He was the complete expression, the Word, of God. Through him, as through no one else, God spoke and God acted: when one met him one was met—and saved and judged—by God. And it was to this conviction that the Apostles bore their witness. In this man, in his life, death and resurrection they had experienced God at work; and in the language of their day they confessed, like the centurion at the Cross, 'Truly this man was the Son of God'.[11] Here was more than just a man: here was a window into God at work. For 'God was in Christ reconciling the world to himself'.[12]

The essential difference comes out in the matter of Jesus' claims. We are often asked to accept Christ as divine because he claimed to be so—and the familiar argument is pressed: 'A man who goes around claiming to be God must either be God—or else he is a madman or a charlatan.... And, of course, it is not easy to read the Gospel story and to dismiss Jesus as either mad or bad. Therefore, the conclusion runs, he must be God.

But I am not happy about this argument. None of the disciples in the Gospels acknowledged Jesus because he claimed to be God, and the Apostles never went out saying, 'This man claimed to be God, therefore you must believe in him'. In fact, Jesus himself said in so many words, 'If I claim anything for myself, do not believe me'. It is, indeed, an open question whether Jesus ever claimed to be the Son of God, let alone God.[13] He may have acknowledged it from the lips of others—but on his own he preferred 'the Son of Man'. In Mark 14.61 f., he is reported to reply to the question at his trial, 'Are you the Christ, the Son of the Blessed?', with the simple words, 'I am'. But in the parallel passage in Matthew[14] he gives an equivocal answer: 'The words are yours' (as he does in all the Gospels

when questioned by Pilate)—and what conceivable interest would Matthew have in watering down Jesus' claim?[15] We cannot be sure what titles Jesus claimed, and we should be wise, like the Apostles, not to rest our faith on them. Their message was rather that 'God has made him both Lord and Christ, this Jesus whom you crucified'.[16] That is to say, through the Resurrection God vindicated and set his seal upon this man as the one through whom he spoke and acted in final and decisive fashion. He vested himself utterly and completely in the man Christ Jesus; in him all his fullness dwelt.[17] What God was, the Word was.

There is a paradox running through all the Gospels that Jesus makes no claims for himself in his own right and at the same time makes the most tremendous claims about what God is doing through him and uniquely through him. Men's response to him *is* men's response to God: men's rejection of him *is* men's rejection of God. And the fourth Gospel merely highlights this paradox (it does not, as is usually said, present quite a different picture of the claims of Jesus) when it combines the saying that 'the Son can do nothing of his own accord, but only what he sees the Father doing'[18] with the uncompromising assertion, 'No one comes to the Father, but by me'.[19] Jesus never claims to be God, personally: yet he always claims to bring God, completely.

This paradox[20] is the point from which our reinterpretation of Christology must start. As the summary of his ministry in the fourth Gospel, Jesus cries out and says, 'He who believes in me, believes not in me but in him who sent me. And he who sees me sees him who sent me'.[21] Jesus, that is to say, reveals God by being utterly transparent to him, precisely as he is nothing 'in himself'....

And thus it comes about that it is only on the Cross that Jesus can be the bearer of the final revelation and the embodiment of God's decisive act: it is 'Christ crucified' who is 'the power of God and the wisdom of God'.[22] For it is in this ultimate surrender of self, in love 'to the uttermost',[23] that Jesus is so completely united to the Ground of his being that he can say, 'I and the Father are one.... The Father is in me and I am in the Father'.[24]

It is in Jesus, and Jesus alone, that there is nothing of self to be seen, but solely the ultimate, unconditional love of God. It is as he emptied himself utterly of himself that he became the carrier of 'the name which is above every name',[25] the revealer of the Father's glory[26]—for that name and that glory is simply Love. The 'kenotic' theory of Christology, based on this conception of self-emptying, is, I am persuaded, the only one that offers much hope of relating at all satisfactorily the divine and the human in Christ.[27] Yet the fatal weakness of this theory as it is stated in supranaturalist terms is that it represents Christ as stripping himself precisely of those attributes of transcendence which make him the revelation of God.[28] The underlying assumption is that it is his omnipotence, his omniscience, and all that makes him 'superhuman', that must be shed in order for him to become truly man. On the contrary, it is as he empties himself not of his Godhead but of himself, of any desire to focus attention on himself, of any craving to be 'on an equality with God',[29] that he reveals God. For it is in making himself nothing, in his utter self-surrender to others in love, that he discloses and lays bare the Ground of man's being as Love.

… For the humanist, to believe in a 'religion of love' is to affirm the conviction that love *ought to be* the last word about life, and to dedicate oneself to seeing that it everywhere prevails. Thus Professor R. B. Braithwaite maintains that to assert that God is love (*agape*) is to declare one's 'intention to follow an *agapeistic* way of life'.[30] Belief is the avowal of a policy, the declaration that love is the supremely valuable quality. And such belief, of course, requires no revelation.

But the Christian affirmation is not simply that love *ought to be* the last word about life, but that, despite all appearances, it *is*. It is the conviction, again, that 'there is nothing … in the world as it is or the world as it shall be … that can separate us from the love of God in Christ Jesus our Lord'. And that takes an almost impossible amount of believing. It is frankly incredible *unless* the love revealed in Jesus is indeed the nature of ultimate reality, unless he is a window through the surface of things into *God*. Christianity stands or falls by revelation, by Christ as the disclosure of the final truth not merely about human nature (that we might accept relatively easily) but about

all nature and all reality. The Christian's faith cannot rest in the capacities of man…. No, the Christian's faith is in Christ as the revelation, the laying bare, of the very heart and being of ultimate reality. And that is why, in the categories of traditional theology, it was so necessary to insist that he was *homousios*, of one substance, with the Father. For unless the *ousia*, the being, of things deep down *is* Love, of the quality disclosed in the life, death and resurrection of Jesus Christ, then the Christian could have little confidence in affirming the ultimate personal character of reality. And this—not his religiosity, nor his belief in the existence of a Person in heaven—is what finally distinguishes him from the humanist and the atheist.

NOTES

1. Acts 1.9-11.
2. Acts 17.22-31.
3. John 3.13.
4. John 6.61 f.
5. Eph. 4.9 f.
6. II Cor. 12.2.
7. *Symbolism and Belief* (1938), p. 30. Chs. II and III on 'Height' are a *locus classicus* for the conception of God 'up there.'
8. 'Of the Difference between a Genius and an Apostle' (1847) in *The Present Age* (Eng. tr., 1940), pp. 146 f.
9. Or, rather, not in any passage that certainly require to be interpreted in this way. Passages that *may* be so interpreted are Rom. 9.5 and Heb. 1.8. But see in each case the alternative translations in the Revised Standard Version or the New English Bible.
10. John 14.9.
11. Mark 15.39.
12. II Cor. 5.19.
13. Indeed, by implication he *denied* being God: 'Why do you call me good? No one is good but God alone' (Mark 10.18).
14. Matt. 26.63 f.
15. I believe that the original text in Mark was probably 'You have said that I am,' and that Matthew has shortened this to 'You have said,' while the answer in Mark has subsequently been abbreviated (and heightened) to 'I am." See my book, *Jesus and His Coming* (1957), pp. 43–51.
16. Acts 2.36.
17. Col. 1.19.
18. John 5.19.

19. John 14.6.
20. Fastened on also by D. M. Baillie, *God Was in Christ* (1948), pp. 125–32.
21. John 12.44 f.
22. I Cor. 1.23 f.
23. John 13.1.
24. John 10.30, 38.
25. Phil. 2.5-11.
26. John 17.4 f.
27. Cf. in particular its superb elaboration in P. T. Forsyth, *The Person and Place of Jesus Christ* (1909), pp. 313–16.
28. See the damaging criticisms of D. M. Baillie, *op. cit.*, pp. 94–8, and A. M. Ramsey, *From Gore to Temple* (1960), pp. 30–43.
29. Phil. 2.6.
30. *An Empiricist's View of the Nature of Religious Belief* (1955), p. 18.

97 RELIGION—WITHIN REASON

CHARLES FRANKEL

Charles Frankel (1917–1979) was Professor of Philosophy at Columbia University, Assistant Secretary of State for Educational and Cultural Affairs in Lyndon Johnson's administration, and President and Director of the National Humanities Center. Our final selection is the Ware Lecture he delivered to the American Unitarian Association in 1957.

He spoke not as an adherent of any religion nor an opponent of all. Rather, he recognized that throughout history religions have been a force for both good and evil. They have given rise to sublime ideals and saintly acts, but also to ignoble sentiments and horrendous practices. His conclusion is that, shorn of irrationality, religion can make a distinctive contribution to our lives, providing deliverance from vanity, triumph over meanness, and endurance in the face of tragedy.

Religion is a primordial phenomenon on the human scene, and it has always been a troublesome one. It is not a habit of men to be reasonable about the things they care for most, and it has not been their habit to be reasonable about religion. No balanced estimate of religion's role in human history can overlook the fact that it has been a principal repository of sanctimonious foolishness and of beliefs and practices that do no credit to anything in man but his credulity and ferocity. Religions have imposed impossible demands on human flesh; they have encouraged hypocrisy and fanaticism in the human mind, they have perpetuated ideas and moral codes that have nothing to be said for them except that they rest on a revelation that lies beyond human logic and human moral sensibilities.

But religion has also been the principal teacher and comforter of mankind. It is through their religions that men have built for themselves worlds with which their hearts could make some contact—worlds in which their sense of what ultimately counts has become vivid and immediate and has found some satisfaction. Men have received from their religions an organized picture of the forces that play around human life and through it; they have received a moral estimate of these forces; they have learned about the saints

From Charles Frankel, *The Love of Anxiety and Other Essays*, Dell Publishing Co., Inc., 1967. Reprinted by permission of The Unitarian Register.

and heaven and hell; they have had their minds fixed on the moral geography of this world and on the distant possibilities that lie beyond it....

Religion has not been the only vehicle by which men have sought for all that could beyond all worlds be thought. In its own different way, mathematics, for example, has had the same object. But for most of its history, religion has been the principal vehicle of organized imagination available to ordinary men. It has been the shelter of the arts, the home of music, the stimulus which has lifted men's minds from seen things in front of them to unseen things beyond. When men have taken their religions seriously, and when they have also been blessed with a native irony and good sense, they have been chastened, strengthened, and released. And most of all, they have been consoled.

It is equally true to say of religion, then, that it has made this world supportable and that it has made it insupportable. And so it is natural to ask whether a line can be drawn between these two sides of religion—between the ennobling and the degrading in religion, the rational and the irrational. Is it possible to have a religion tame enough not to encourage us in our follies, but yet not so tame that it leaves us unmoved? Can religion be brought under the governance of reason and still retain its afflatus and charm?

The question is a recurrent one. In asking it, men have wished, in the first place, to find religious beliefs that squared with the best warranted knowledge available and with the standards of responsible inquiry in other domains. And they have wished, in the second place, to keep religion within decent moral and social bounds. For whatever may be its place in the politics of eternity, religion is also a human institution that must take its place among the going affairs of men and be measured at least in part by its effects on other human activities.

Religion is hard to define, and not least because there is really no such thing as religion. There are only religions—and they do not always see eye to eye on what their main business is. Nevertheless, if we look with an anthropologist's eye at what are normally called religions, they will be seen, I believe, to have at least four aspects; and if we look at our ordinary language, we can also note at least four ways in which we normally use the words "religion" and "religious." "Religion" stands for a certain kind of psychological experience; for a creed—a set of beliefs about what are thought to be the most important facts in the universe and about the values and commitments that men should adopt in view of these facts; for a social institution in which ritual plays a large and crucial part; and, finally, for a kind of ethic, a "way of life" that seems to go beyond the conventions and necessities of practical life. Each of these elements of religion may occur in the absence of the others. But by and large, and for the mass of humanity, they come together. The health or illness of a religion usually depends on the degree to which these four aspects of its activities constitute an integrated whole.

Each of these aspects of religion is now challenged in fundamental ways in which it has not been challenged before. And it would be well to begin an examination of these challenges by looking at religion as a psychological phenomenon. For religion as a personal experience is frequently a very persuasive affair. It leads men to hold convictions on which they are prepared to do battle with the world, convictions which they regard as immune to criticism from any external source. It provides, therefore, a dramatic arena for studying the interplay of religion and reason.

Since the time of William James there has been more or less agreement about the major traits of religion considered as a psychological phenomenon. Religious experience, in its intense forms, seems to be a vivid sense of a truth come alive, a feeling that things come together in a pattern that has meaning and purpose. In religious experience men have the intuition that the disparate parts of their lives, the scattered fragments of their world, are somehow parts of a larger order....

A religious experience, accordingly, is felt as a moment of illumination and reorientation, a way of seeing things as they have not been seen before. Our ordinary habits are arrested, our conventional world is shaken up, the pieces of the puzzle finally come together. Having had this experience, we have the feeling that the world exists on two levels, one really real, the other not so real. We have the feeling that we can see *through* things—through the dross and vanity of our ordinary affairs—to what they invisibly but really mean. With this feeling there goes the sense of having a new power that is not quite one's own and of being actively committed to something more enduring and important than one's own personal interests and ambitions. The religious man is lifted out of himself. He may be lifted out of himself to such an extent that he feels not merely bound to what is outside him but wholly at one with it. He has found his proper element; and as he bathes in it, the old distinction between subject and object disappears.

Clearly, the experience is an impressive one for those who have had it. It is impressive enough from any point of view to suggest two questions. The first is a question of fact: What is the state of religious feeling today, and where do we find it?

The answer cannot be encouraging, I suspect, to anyone concerned about the future of organized religion—or, at any rate. concerned about more than its external forms. To find examples in the past of the kind of experience I have descried one would go to the classic literature of the saints and mystics—Saint Paul, Saint Augustine, Pascal, Jakob Boehme. To find examples of this sort of experience today one goes to the literature of secular politics. Some fresh and touching examples of religious feeling can, of course, be found on the contemporary scene within the traditional setting of our inherited religions. But for the most part the religious feeling that seems to be making the difference and moving the world is the feeling that has been aroused by the abstractions and symbols of an era of ideologies. A release from the dark night of the soul, a sense of comradeship in the service of a higher cause, an answer to the desire to find a coherence and pattern in the world—these air what our ideologies offer.

Much current discussion of the decline of religious feeling and the modern world seems to me beside the point. For the present century is a period of religious feeling which is perhaps as widespread, and at least as intense, as can be found in any of the so-called "Ages of Belief." Similarly, the rise, real or alleged, in church attendance seems to

me equally irrelevant in judging the present state of our inherited religions, or in guessing their future. For it is the language of secular ideologies that one hears in most churches. In short, whether inside the churches or outside the churches, the challenge to inherited religion is the same: it is that religious emotions have shifted from their traditional objects.

But there is still a second question to ask. It is a question of principle. What place should religious experience have, what credit should we give it, in forming our ultimate beliefs? Are the conclusions to which a religious experience may lead us subject to the same tests that any other beliefs must meet? Or do they stand in a world of their own, immune to criticism from the outside?

There is a puzzling feature of what we have called religious experience, and it has led at least some to think twice about what is meant by "reason." Religious feeling is an externalized feeling, a feeling directed outward from the self. And yet, curiously enough, it does not seem to have a clear and definite object. Money, an ikon, a Beatrice, the memory of Christ crucified—in one sense, all these are objects of religious emotion. But to the extent that they are objects of *religious* emotion their enchantment does not in the end seem to be their own. Religious feelings move toward them and then through them toward what they symbolize—and what they symbolize cannot apparently be seen in any ordinary sense or described in any ordinary way. The ultimate object of religious worship cannot be easily located in time or space; the more we pursue it the more it eludes our grasp; in the ordinary sense, it is not really an object at all. Attempt to state clearly and definitely what it is that you feel religious about, and it is likely to seem trite, or foolish, or sentimental. Even more likely, you will fail in being more than vague. We usually describe God, it should be noticed, by announcing what He is not. The natural language of religion seems to be parable and paradox.

Thus it is that discussions of the relation of religion to reason can be so unsatisfactory. The partisans of reason and the partisans of religion pass each other like ships in the night. The partisan of reason would like to know what it is that the religious believer asserts as the result of having had a religious experience; and he would like to take that assertion and determine whether it is true or false, probable or improbable, in accordance with the standards he employs for criticizing other beliefs. On the other hand, the man who has had a religious experience, and who has been moved to hold certain conclusions as a result, is convinced that any attempt to pin down religious assertions by such rules is to miss their very essence. Religious belief, he is convinced, has a status of its own. To hold a religious belief is not like holding any other kind of belief. Therefore it cannot be examined in the way we examine other kinds of belief, or be judged by the same standards.

This position can be stated in the language of current philosophy. It has been said by some recent philosophers that to seek to judge religious beliefs in the light of their truth, and to mean by truth the same thing that we mean in other domains, is to commit a peculiarly awful kind of mistake—what is called a "category mistake." Consider, for example, the case of a man who says of a lady, "She wears her grief like a new spring dress." Imagine his plight if he heard this statement rejected as false by some unimaginative listener, and on the ground that no one can wear grief because it has no sleeves or other physical properties. Yet the partisan of reason, it is asserted, is just as unimaginative as this with regard to religion. He fails to see that religious language arises in response to the unusual sort of experience that religion represents. It has the task of conveying what cannot quite be conveyed in words, of talking about events and objects that are not like ordinary events and objects. So religion has to use words in a stretched and unusual way; it has its own inner logic; and it is a radical mistake, as well as evidence of a lack of imagination, to judge it by any logic but its own.

This position, as you will recognize, is not a wholly new one. But it has recently come forward again dressed (I use the word in its religious or stretched sense) in the costume of current and highly creditable styles in philosophy. In this form it has found favor among an increasing number of contemporary philosophers and theologians. I must confess, however, that I remain unpersuaded. In explaining why I am unpersuaded, I come to the question of religion as a creed. Can the claim be sustained that religion provides a special avenue to truth? Does it give us valid insights into the nature of the universe and of man's place and purpose within it which we could not acquire in any other way, and which we cannot criticize from any external point of view?

The assertion that religious beliefs occupy a world that is wholly their own seems to me indefensible on a number of grounds. For one thing, it does not help us to choose among religions—which, after all, have a number of quite different things to say about the world. For another, it isolates religion from everything else—which is the last thing that anyone would think that a lover of religion would wish to do. But I shall dwell on two other considerations—namely, that this position is overly enthusiastic in its estimate of how unusual religious experience is and that it is artificial in its characterization of religious belief.

Let me ask, first, how unusual religious experience is. I do not mean whether religious experiences are frequent. I mean whether, when they do occur, they exhibit characteristics so special that it is legitimate to develop a brand-new department of logic to take care of them. This does not seem to me to be the case. For it is not only so-called religious experiences that leave us with the belief that words can never wholly capture what is sensed or felt. Take any object or event that is not wholly novel, or that is not so routine that you do not pay genuine attention to it: it comes soaked in associations and meanings. If we should try to track down and state all these associations, we should never succeed. It should be no surprise that words are not substitutes for concrete experiences, or that something of what we feel or sense will always pass through the net of language. This is as true in every other domain as in religion. And it should neither be deplored nor converted into an argument for the supreme truth of the unutterable. For it is precisely because language is not identical with that which it expresses or describes that we can use it to formulate true statements about selected features of our experience.

To use it in this way, however, we have to use it in accordance with certain rules: among other things, we have to delimit the area of our attention, to assign stable meanings to our words, to use them with precision and consistency. If religious language cannot be used in this way, it can only be because those who use it do not wish to do so—and this means that they are not using language in the way it has to be used if beliefs capable of being called true or false are to be formulated.

There is no reason, of course, why language must always be used in this way, and many reasons why it should not. Language has other purposes, including the expression of religious emotions, which are as important as inquiry after truth. But when language is not used in a way that is appropriate for inquiry after truth, then we should not claim the value of truth for what it says. We cannot have our cake and eat it too. We cannot say that religious beliefs deal with the unutterable and then claim that they are true.

But the argument that "religious truth" is a special kind of truth seems to me to be questionable on much simpler grounds. It seems to me to falsify the actual way in which most people hold their religious beliefs. It is true that there is an aura of ineffable mystery about many—perhaps most—traditional religious beliefs. But at least some of these doctrines assert the occurrence of specific historical events, or the existence of certain facts or laws. When the believer says that these doctrines are true, he means, unless I am gravely mistaken, that they are true in a quite ordinary sense of the word. He may accept the story of the Exodus from Egypt, for example, and care about it, and take it to his heart, because of all that it represents—the age-old sufferings of his people, the strength their faith has given them, the transcendent significance of freedom. But if he believes that it is true, he believes also that it actually happened—that if he had been present at the right time and place he would have seen quite real individuals fleeing from slavery in Egypt.

If this is not the case, it would be difficult to explain why so many who have held religious beliefs have been disturbed when they have come across historical or other findings that seem to challenge what they believe. Philosophical or theological arguments which inform them that they ought not to be disturbed—that, indeed, they are committing a "category mistake" when they are disturbed—seem to be saving religious belief at the price of discarding what most people mean when they say they believe in one or another of the traditional religions.

The point, elementary though it may be, is worth emphasizing because much has recently been said about the "poetic" or "symbolic" truth of religion. The great religions, it need hardly be said, are storehouses of stories and traditions that are symbols and archetypes of recurrent human experiences. One can read out of these stories generalizations about the human scene that are plainly true—though it should be added that not all of them are. But if we accept a religion on these grounds, we accept it on the same grounds on which we might accept, say, Goethe's *Faust* as true. So we give up precisely the claim which, in most people's minds, distinguishes the stories of religion from other stories—namely, that they are not merely "symbolically" true, but true without a qualifying adjective.

I should add that it seems to me not impossible that a religion could draw the genuine and passionate adherence of its members while it claimed nothing more than to be a poetry in which men might participate and from which they might draw strength and light. The special power of religious stories, their difference from Goethe's *Faust*, lies in the fact that men through the ages have participated in them, that they have no individual author but come to us as collective products, drenched in the sufferings and hopes of our ancestors. I suspect that it is this symbolic and imaginative power of religion that has in fact drawn many of its adherents in the past. And a rational religion, claiming no special revelation and no absolute validity for all men, and admitting that its stories were legends and its gods simply personifications of human ideals, would not necessarily be less moving than the traditional religions of the past. It would only be less demanding of intellectual sacrifices. But to proceed on this path such a religion would have to say what few religions, past and present, have been willing to say—that religion can make no claim to a special insight into truth. It can claim only to speak the truth in a peculiarly arresting and beautiful way—and this only sometimes.

Could such a religion succeed? I believe that it could—provided only that it spoke always with the tongues of angels.

This brings me to religion as ritual. The religious emotion is different from other emotions of illumination and reorientation because it is usually the result of a specific performance. The poetry of religion is different from other poetry because it is a poetry in which men act together. Religion, in short, is a social ritual. It turns around certain regular, disciplined performances, which are repeated on specified occasions. They are practiced by men together; and they normally serve to give men a sense of closer community with each other. For the power of a ritual derives from the fact that it symbolizes things beyond itself, things of peculiar and inescapable importance.

Voltaire once remarked that religion would never die because there would always be people who liked to sing and drink on Saturday evening and wished to continue on Sunday morning. Unless one has an unreasoning prejudice against singing and drinking, the remark does not so much deflate religion as explain it. Over the long pull men have not gone to church only, or even mainly, out of a sense of duty, or as the result of having been nagged into it, or even because they thought it helped them remain, or seem, respectable. They have gone because churches were beautiful, because their friends were there, because music and dancing and bread and wine are naturally delightful—and doubly so when they stand for those things on which a man believes that his whole fate turns. The dangers of ritual are notorious—its hypnotic effects, its support of outworn traditions and used-up ideals, its suppression of spontaneity, its tendency to degenerate into an empty form. But these dangers are not inevitable to ritual.

When a ritual is attached to beliefs that we think are true, and when the ideals it portrays have an appeal of their own, it is the social instrument by which ordinary things become extraordinary, and the everyday currency of our lives takes on ideal meanings.

The decline of an effective ritual in contemporary religions seems to me no less important in estimating their future than their decline in intellectual substance. In part, the appeal of religious ritual has declined because men can find their entertainment elsewhere. In part it has declined because it has become increasingly abstract. Historically, the church in most communities was the home of a wide variety of activities. It was the center for charity, for education, for news, for gossip, for organizing collective action and exerting political pressure. Rituals practiced under such conditions came suffused with the memories and emotions of a common life. Religious rituals today, unhappily, have less to lean on and less of an immediate and pressing nature to do.

But there is also another reason, I suspect, for the decline of an effective religious ritual. It emerges in part when we reflect on the obvious fact that the rituals of the religions we inherit generally symbolize the experience of agrarian peoples while we are living in a mainly urban and suburban civilization. This obvious fact has a deeper implication. The rituals of the major religions have characteristically symbolized the great inescapable facts of human destiny, and facts immediately present to everyone's view—birth, sex, the cycle of the seasons, death. But while these remain inescapable facts of our destiny, they are for us less and less everyday facts with which we live. They are rumors and reports, things we seal off in hospital rooms or have to learn about initially by hearsay. I hope that I shall not be misunderstood: I am not proposing that we return to dying in the streets because it will have educational effects on our children. I mean only that those of us who grow up or live out our lives in the modern city and suburb see few things that have not been made by man. And so, for all our abstract knowledge of the ways of the world, it is hard to take home to our hearts the truth that the rituals of the great religions celebrate—that, in the end, man does not live in a world he has made for himself.

I come in this way to my final theme—religion considered as a distinctive ethic, and religion in its relation to ethics. I want to make a modest case for a point that I think is unduly neglected; and I may introduce it best, I think, by a brief observation about the currently popular dictum that the world's ills would be cured if only we lived up to our religions. This dictum seems to me to propose a policy that is not only impossible but would be the cause of considerable trouble if it were possible. It is the believer in Sean O'Casey's *The Plough and the Stars* who replies indignantly to the blasphemies of an unbeliever: "There's no reason to bring religion into it. I think we ought to have as great a regard for religion as we can, so as to keep it out of as many things as possible."

It is easy to forget that the religions of the world have not always come to make the world more comfortable, but at least sometimes, if their leading apostles can be believed, to make it more uncomfortable. For it must simply be faced that religions have a habit of making extreme claims on their adherents. A man seriously committed to a religious faith has much more than what now passes in many quarters for religion—that is, a bland sense of good-fellowship together with a pleasant conviction that he belongs to the same club the universe belongs to. A man who is serious about his religion is likely to feel that his life depends upon it. If he believes that his religion deals with the things of another world, he may view everything in this world as a contamination and a curse—in which case he is likely to quarantine himself. If he believes that his religion has come to make the world over, he may feel that it is involved everywhere—in which case he will find it difficult to make any compromises. Both these attitudes may be admirable, but neither makes for decent living conditions.

It is the barest truism to say that in our ordinary affairs we employ moral standards, and must employ moral standards, that are not wholly compatible with what our religions, taken uncompromisingly, demand of us. Few things could be more

attractive, for example, than the vision of Saint Francis' comradeship with the beasts of the field. But few things would be more inconvenient than the conversion of Saint Francis' example into a general social policy. Some may take this as a proof of original sin. I confess that I accept it with a measure of relief.

Nor is it only the secular-minded who are anxious that we keep our religious propensities within bounds. Most of those who have been responsible for the practical administration of religious groups also have made it plain that while there is a religious morality proper to saints, there is also a compromise more appropriate for ordinary men. "The unmarried man," wrote Saint Paul, "is anxious about the Lord's affairs, how best to satisfy the Lord; the married man is anxious about worldly affairs, how best to satisfy his wife—so he is torn in two directions." But Saint Paul accepted the necessity of compromise in most cases: "There is so much immorality that every man had better have a wife of his own and every woman a husband of her own.... But what I have just said is by way of concession, not command."[1]

But the limitations of transcendental religion—of religion as the worship of perfections, however conceived—also suggests something of what religion has done, and might still do. It is usual in current discussions of the relation of religion to morals to focus on the relations of religion to practical morality, to the morality of concrete achievement. It does not seem to me that religion is either necessary or sufficient to a moral life in this secular and worldly sense—although, despite what I have said about the dangers of religious fanaticism and otherworldliness, religion need not be incompatible with, and can obviously sometimes help, the secular moral life. But all this leaves out what may well be the distinctive contribution that an emancipated religion might make to morality.

Religion has frequently meant a morality with a special flavor, a special angle of vision on any morality. It might still mean, as it has sometimes meant in the past, this morality of transcendence: the attitude that comes from looking beyond even human ideals and the human effort to realize them—the willing commitment to what lies beyond human powers to change.

No unusual or occult vision is needed to produce this attitude, and the conclusions to which it leads need neither offend our common sense nor cause us to withdraw from the ordinary concerns of men. At the conclusion of the *Iliad* there is an experience which produces such an attitude, and it comes, in the midst of a foolish and brutal war, to Priam, a king and patriot, and to Achilles, the sulky, impulsive, and bullying warrior. Priam, the father of the slain Hector, comes to Achilles to beg for the return of his son's body:

> "Think of your father [says Priam], who is such even as I am, on the sad threshold of old age.... Think on your own father and have compassion upon me, who am the more pitiable, for I have steeled myself as no man has ever yet steeled himself before me, and have raised to my lips the hand of him who slew my son."
>
> Thus spoke Priam, and the heart of Achilles yearned as he be-thought him of his father. He took the old man's hand and moved him gently away. The two wept bitterly—Priam ... weeping for Hector, and Achilles, now for his father and now for Patroclus, till the house was filled with their lamentation. But when Achilles was now sated with grief and had unburdened the bitterness of his sorrow, he left his seat and raised the old man by the hand.... Then he said: "Unhappy man, you have indeed been greatly daring.... Sit now upon this seat, and for all our grief we will hide our sorrows in our hearts, for weeping will not avail us. The immortals know no care, yet the lot they spin for man is full of sorrow.... Even so did it befall Peleus; the gods endowed him with all good things from his birth upwards.... But even on him, too, did heaven send misfortune, for there is no race of royal children born to him in his house, save one son who is doomed to die all untimely; nor may I take care of him now that he is growing old, for I must stay here at Troy to be the bane of you and your children.
>
> "And you too, O Priam, I have heard that you were aforetime happy.... But from the day when the dwellers in heaven sent this evil upon you, war and slaughter have been about your city continually. Bear up against it, and let there be some intervals in your sorrow. Mourn as you may for

your brave son, you will take nothing by it. You cannot raise him from the dead; ere you do so yet another sorrow shall befall you."

Then Achilles has Hector's body washed and anointed, and places it upon a bier to be returned to Priam.

> "Sir," he said, "your son is now laid upon his bier and is ransomed according to your desire. You shall look upon him when you take him away at daybreak; for the present let us prepare our supper."[2]

It is proper that the *Iliad* ends here, with this recognition by its principal actors of their common sorrow and helplessness. For while the war will go on, it cannot have the same meaning for either side afterwards.

Such an experience has neither magic nor mystery about it. But it is not different from what, in religious language, is called "transfiguration." Those who have it are illuminated and reoriented. They are, at least for the moment, taken out of themselves and brought before larger and more enduring things, things they cannot change. And yet these men themselves are changed—and changed, singularly enough, from passive sufferers to active agents. They regain the initiative. Even though they may be in the grip of an inexorable fate, they are not overwhelmed by events. They do what they have to do; and they do it out of an active decision that it must be done. "Let us prepare our supper," says Achilles. "You can weep for your dear son hereafter." "Come, get up and let us go," says Jesus. "Here is my betrayer close at hand."

Such an attitude—the attitude that comes from looking occasionally at the unchanging and unmoved sky—is not an easy one. But it seems to me a main source from which we might draw resolution, powers of endurance, and charity. We might draw from it, too, something else about which much is said these days—a tragic sense of life—and something else intimately connected with it—a sense of proportion, a sense of humor. For neither tragedy nor comedy can exist except as we recognize the gap between our high images of our destiny and what in fact we are. There is humility in such an attitude, but there is a triumph over meanness in it, too. It is the only sure triumph over our condition that we mortal beings can have.

Those who truly love God, said Spinoza, cannot expect that God will love them in return. Most religions in the past, and most today, have not encouraged such an attitude, but rather its reverse. They have fed us on sweets. But I cannot help but think that in their best moments it has been this message of deliverance from our vanity and from the vanity of things, of willing commitment to the necessities that are not of our making, that has been at their heart.

NOTES

1. I Corinthians.
2. Samuel Butler translation.

INDEX